The
AMERICAN HERITAGE®
Student Science *dic•tion•ar•y*

TABLE OF CONTENTS

ENTRIES WITH NOTES

Did You Know?

acceleration
acid rain
adaptation
aerodynamics
alchemy
allergy
amber
antibody
artificial intelligence
aspirin
atmospheric pressure
baking soda
bat
battery
benzene
big bang
biomass
bird
black hole
blood type
brain
Burgess Shale
cactus
cancer
capillary action
carbon
cathode-ray tube
Celsius
centripetal force
charge
circadian rhythm
compound eye
conduction
current
cyclone
desert
DNA
Doppler effect
dwarf star
earthquake
eclipse
electromagnetic radiation
endorphin
evolution
enzyme
fat
fault
fiber optics
fluorescence
force
fungus
gene
glass
Gondwanaland
gravity
graywater
heavy water
hologram
hormone
infrared
Internet
iridium
keratin
laser
lightning
magnetism
mimicry
mirror
moon
neutrino
nuclear reactor
oxidation
ozone
pixel
plate tectonics
pollination
program
pulsar
quasar
radioactivity
radiocarbon dating
rain forest
red blood cell
sickle cell anemia
sleep
solar cell
solar system
solution
sound[1]
space-time
subatomic particle
sublimation
symbiosis
tail
thermodynamics
transpiration
turbojet
ultrasound
vaccine
vitamin
wetland
whale
worm
zero

Usage

bacterium
berry
bug
byte
centigrade
data
deduction
disk
electronic
endemic
fruit
germ
heritable
hypothesis
infectious
light-year
megabyte
metal
meteor
mitosis
nuclear
ocean
refraction
revolution
stalagmite
temperature
thorn
tidal wave
vapor
velocity
weight

Word History

algebra
amphibian
brontosaurus
calculus
chlorophyll
element
entomology
gastropod
helium
humor
hydrophobia
influenza
mercury
noble gas
oxygen
pahoehoe
planet
rhinoceros
Rigel

Biography

Archimedes
Bohr, Neils
Carver, George Washington
Copernicus, Nicolaus
Darwin, Charles
Einstein, Albert
Franklin, Benjamin
Galileo Galilei
Harvey, William
Herschel, William and Caroline
Hutton, James
Jenner, Edward
Lavoisier, Antoine
Leeuwenhoek, Anton van
Mendel, Gregor
Newton, Isaac
Pasteur, Louis
Pauling, Linus
Priestly, Joseph
Tesla, Nikola
Vesalius, Andreas

Understanding basic science means understanding its vocabulary. Each field of science is distinguished by a group of important concepts and categories that scientists use to construct ways of looking at and explaining what happens in the natural world. This Dictionary is designed to help you understand these concepts and categories through an understanding of the language that describes them. The Dictionary explains the meanings of scientific terms in ways that even beginning students can follow, but at the same time encourages the reader to learn more in building a more complex vocabulary.

Even basic science raises large questions that defy simple explanations. For this reason many of the entries in this book go beyond the usual one-sentence definition to include additional information of various kinds. For example, the entry for **glacier** tells you not only what a glacier is but also how it forms and how it moves. Other entries, such as **eclipse**, include extended definitions for related terms—in this case, **solar eclipse** and **lunar eclipse**. And entries for more than a hundred of the most interesting and important scientific terms, such as **big bang, DNA**, and **plate tectonics**, feature *Did You Know?* notes with lively, in-depth explanations of the scientific phenomena that make our world such a fascinating place.

This Dictionary includes other kinds of explanatory notes as well. We often use scientific terms loosely in our everyday language, unaware of the exactness that scientists like to observe. For many of these words the Dictionary includes *Usage* notes that discuss these differences. For example, would you call a tomato a *berry*? Do you think of a cucumber as a *fruit*? The notes at **berry** and **fruit** explain why botanists would answer "yes" to these questions, even though most other people would say "no." And the note at **infectious** tells you the distinction that scientists make between this word and the very similar words *contagious* and *communicable*.

Word History notes discuss the origins and often surprising history of scientific terms. Thus the note at **calculus** tells you how a simple Latin word meaning "pebble" came to be used for a sophisticated form of mathematics. And because the history of science is full of inspiring stories of people struggling to solve difficult problems, this book includes more than 300 entries for the men and women from around the world who have developed the scientific knowledge we have today. Some of their most important discoveries, and some of their failures too, are described in the *Biography* notes at such entries as **Archimedes, Darwin,** and **Pasteur**.

Because we learn not just from words but from images too, this Dictionary includes more than 425 full-color photographs and drawings to complement its definitions. Together with their captions, these images bring complicated ideas and structures to life in a way that a definition alone sometimes can't. The book also includes a number of full-page graphic features (what we call *A Closer Look*), as well as a number of Tables and Charts. See the Table of Contents for a list of these features.

Making this book has charged its editors and production staff with wonder and excitement at the explanations of phenomena, the patterns of order, and the intellectual achievements that make science the powerful tool it is. We hope that this book conveys this wonder and excitement, rendering it both infectious and contagious.

Joseph P. Pickett
Vice President, Executive Editor

Compare cross-reference
use this to learn other words that make important distinctions in a subject area

guideword

art caption
provides additional explanation

entry word

pronunciation
see key on page viii

***See also* cross-reference**
use this to find related entries in a particular area

biographical entry

boiling point

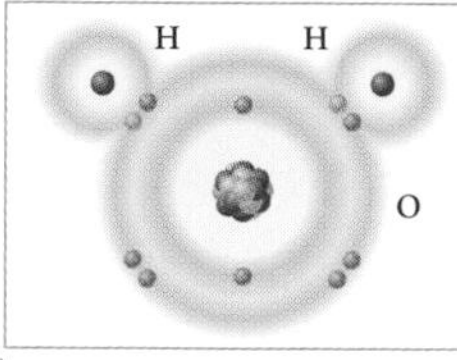

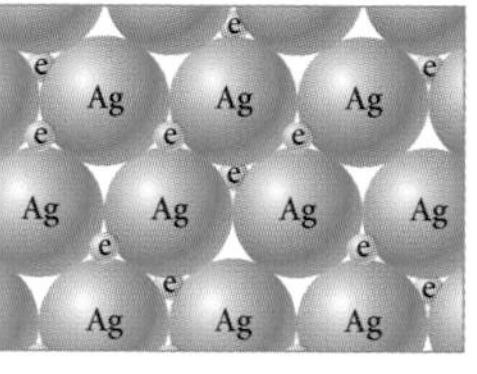

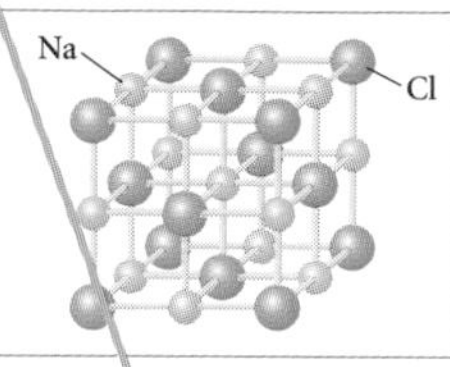

■ **bond**

In a water molecule (left), *each hydrogen atom (H) shares an electron (yellow) with the oxygen atom (O), forming covalent bonds. In silver* (center), *a metal, the negatively charged electrons (e) "float" around positively charged silver atoms (Ag), illustrating metallic bonding. In sodium chloride or salt* (right), *the sodium atom (Na) donates an electron to the chlorine atom (Cl), forming an ionic bond.*

boil•ing point (boi′lĭng) The temperature at which a liquid changes to a vapor or gas. As the temperature of a liquid rises, the pressure of escaping vapor also rises, and at the boiling point the pressure of the escaping vapor is equal to that exerted on the liquid by the surrounding air, causing bubbles to form. Typically boiling points are measured at sea level. At higher altitudes, where atmospheric pressure is lower, boiling points are lower.

bond (bŏnd) A force of attraction that holds atoms or ions together in a molecule or crystal. Bonds are usually created by a transfer or sharing of one or more electrons. There are single, double, and triple bonds. *See also* **covalent bond, ionic bond, metallic bond.**

bone (bōn) **1.** The hard, dense, calcified tissue that forms the skeleton of most vertebrates. Bone serves as a framework for the attachment of muscles and protects vital organs, such as the brain. It also contains large amounts of calcium, a mineral that is essential for proper cell function. Blood cells and platelets are produced in the marrow, the central cavity of bone. *See more at* **osteoblast, osteocyte. 2.** Any of the bones in a skeleton, such as the femur of a mammal.

bone marrow The spongy, red tissue that fills the bone cavities of mammals. Bone marrow is the source of red blood cells, platelets, and most white blood cells.

Bon•net (bô-nĕ′), **Charles** 1720–1793. Swiss naturalist who discovered parthenogenesis, by demonstrating that aphid eggs could develop without fertilization. Bonnet was also one of the first scientists to study photosynthesis.

bon•y fish (bō′nē) A fish having a bony rather than cartilaginous skeleton. Most living species of fish are bony fish. *Compare* **cartilaginous fish, jawless fish.**

book lung (bo͝ok) The breathing organ of scorpions, spiders, and some other arachnids. It consists of membranes arranged in several parallel folds like the pages of a book.

Boole (bo͞ol), **George** 1815–1864. British mathematician who wrote important works on many different areas of mathematics. He developed a method to describe reasoning using algebra that is now known as Boolean algebra.

Bool•e•an algebra (bo͞o′lē-ən) A mathematical system dealing with the relationship between sets, used to solve problems in logic and engineering. Variables consist of 0 and 1 and operations are expressed as *and*, *or*, and *not*. Boolean algebra has been important in the development of modern computers and computer programs.

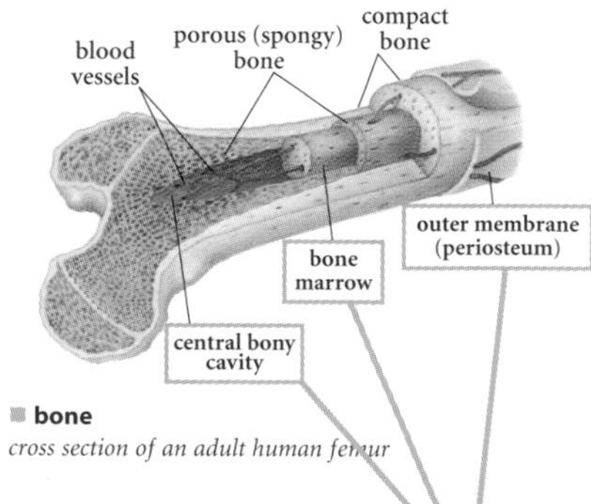

■ **bone**
cross section of an adult human femur

46

***See more* cross-reference**
use this to find additional information at other entries

art labels
identify key terms

Did You Know? note

Other notes include Usage, Biography, and Word History See list of notes on p. iv

scientific field label

irregular plural

nested entry

defines a closely related term that is derived from the entry word

run-on with part of speech

chemical formula

Did You Know?
Burgess Shale

Early animals on the Earth included many oddities. These animals had bizarre combinations of legs, spines, segments, and heads found in no animals since, as if Nature were trying out different models to see what might work best. Many of these animals became extinct and left no descendants. Others may have evolved into groups that are well known today. We know a lot about these bizarre life forms thanks to the *Burgess Shale,* a 540-million-year-old formation of black shale in the Rocky Mountains of British Columbia. Unlike most rocks in which fossils are preserved, the Burgess Shale preserved the soft parts of organisms that normally would have rotted away (by reacting with oxygen) before the animals became fossils. This happened because the animals were killed instantly by a mudslide deep in the ocean, where there is very little oxygen. After the mud buried the animals, it hardened into shale. Thanks to this, we know a lot about the period of early animal evolution known as the Cambrian Explosion.

buoy•an•cy (boi′ən-sē) The upward force that a fluid exerts on an object that is less dense than itself. Buoyancy allows a boat to float on water.

bu•rette (byo͞o-rĕt′) A glass tube with fine gradations and with a tapered bottom that has a valve. It is used especially in laboratories to pour a measured amount of liquid into another container.

Bur•gess Shale (bûr′jĭs) A rock formation in the western Canadian Rockies that contains numerous fossilized invertebrates from the early Cambrian Period.

burl (bûrl) A large, rounded outgrowth on the trunk or branch of a tree.

burn (bûrn) *Verb.* **1.** To be on fire; undergo combustion. A substance burns if it is heated up enough to react chemically with oxygen. *See Note*

burl
a burl on a western red cedar

at **oxidation.** —*Noun.* **2.** *Medicine* An injury produced by fire, heat, radiation, electricity, or a caustic chemical agent. Burns are classified according to the degree of damage done to the tissues.

bur•sa (bûr′sə) *Plural* **bursae** (bûr′sē) *or* **bursas.** A flattened sac containing a lubricating fluid that reduces friction between a muscle or tendon and a bone. ❖ Inflammation of a bursa is called **bursitis** (bər-sī′tĭs).

bu•tane (byo͞o′tān′) An organic compound, C_4H_{10}, found in natural gas and produced from petroleum. Butane is used as a fuel, refrigerant, and propellant in aerosol cans. —*Adjective* **butyl** (byo͞o′təl)

butte (byo͞ot) A steep-sided hill with a flat top, often standing alone in an otherwise flat area. A butte is smaller than a mesa.

but•ter•fly (bŭt′ər-flī′) Any of various insects having slender bodies, knobbed antennae, and four broad wings that are usually brightly colored. Unlike moths, butterflies tend to hold their wings upright and together when at rest. *Compare* **moth.**

bu•tyr•ic acid (byo͞o-tîr′ĭk) A colorless fatty acid found in butter and certain plant oils. It has an unpleasant odor and is used in disinfectants and drugs.

by•pass (bī′păs′) An alternative pathway for the flow of blood or other body fluid, created by a surgeon as a detour around a blocked or diseased organ.

by-prod•uct (bī′prŏd′əkt) Something produced in the process of making something else. For

51

PRONUNCIATION

This Dictionary provides pronunciations using standard pronunciation symbols as explained in the key below. The pronunciations appear in parentheses following boldface entry words. If an entry word has a variant spelling and the two words have the same pronunciation, the pronunciation follows the variant spelling. If the variant does not have the same pronunciation, pronunciations follow the forms to which they apply. If a word has multiple common pronunciations, the first pronunciation is generally more common than the other; however, they are often equally common.

Stress

Stress, the relative degree of emphasis with which a word's syllables are spoken, is indicated in three ways. An unmarked syllable has the weakest stress in the word. A bold mark (**′**) indicates the strongest stress. A lighter mark (′) indicates a secondary level of stress. Words of one syllable show no stress mark, since there is no other stress level to which the syllable is compared.

Pronunciation Key

A list of the pronunciation symbols used in this Dictionary is given here in the column headed Symbol. The column headed Examples contains words chosen to illustrate how the symbols are pronounced. The letters that correspond in sound to the symbols are shown in boldface.

The nonalphabetical symbol (ə) is called *schwa*. It is used to represent a reduced vowel (a vowel that receives the weakest level of stress within a word). The schwa sound varies, sometimes according to the vowel it is representing and often according to the sounds surrounding it:

ab•a•cus	(ăb**′**ə-kəs)
ab•do•men	(ăb**′**də-mən)
ac•ti•nide	(ăk**′**tə-nīd′)
cu•mu•lus	(kyo͞om**′**yə-ləs)

Pronunciation Key

Symbol	Examples	Symbol	Examples	Symbol	Examples	Symbol	Examples
ă	pat	ĭ	pit	o͝o	took	v	valve
ā	pay	ī	pie, by	o͞o	boot	w	with
âr	care	îr	deer, pier	ou	out	y	yes
ä	father	j	judge	p	pop	z	zebra, xylem
b	bib	k	kick, cat, pique	r	roar	zh	vision,
ch	church	l	lid, needle	s	sauce		pleasure,
d	deed, milled	m	mum	sh	ship, dish		garage
ĕ	pet	n	no, sudden	t	tight, stopped	ə	about, item,
ē	bee	ng	thing	th	thin		edible,
f	fife, phase,	ŏ	pot	*th*	this		gallop,
	rough	ō	toe	ŭ	cut		circus
g	gag	ô	caught,	ûr	urge, term,	ər	butter
h	hat		paw, for		firm, word,		
hw	which	oi	noise		heard		

A Abbreviation of **area.**

a– A prefix meaning "without" or "not" when forming an adjective (such as *amorphous,* without form, or *atypical,* not typical), and "absence of" when forming a noun (such as *arrhythmia,* absence of rhythm). Before a vowel or *h* it becomes *an–* (as in *anhydrous, anoxia*).

a•a (ä′ä) A type of lava having a rough, jagged surface. It is relatively slow moving in its molten state, advancing in the form of massive blocks. *See Note at* **pahoehoe.**

aard•vark (ärd′värk′) A burrowing mammal of southern Africa, having a stocky body, large ears, and a long tubular snout with a snake-like tongue that it uses for feeding on ants and termites.

ab•a•cus (ăb′ə-kəs) *Plural* **abacuses** *or* **abaci** (ăb′ə-sī′) A computing device consisting of a frame holding parallel rods with sliding beads.

ab•a•lo•ne (ăb′ə-lō′nē) Any of various edible mollusks that have a large, ear-shaped shell. The shell has a row of holes along the outer edge, and the interior is lined with mother-of-pearl.

ab•do•men (ăb′də-mən) **1.** In humans and other mammals, the portion of the body that lies between the chest and the pelvis. The abdomen contains the stomach, intestines, liver, spleen, and pancreas. **2.** A region similar to the abdomen in other vertebrates, such as a snake. **3.** In insects, arachnids, and other arthropods, the last, most posterior segment of the body. —*Adjective* **abdominal** (ăb-dŏm′ə-nəl).

abacus

On a Chinese abacus, the columns of beads go from right to left and represent ones, tens, hundreds, thousands, and so on. The beads above the crossbar have a value of five; the beads below the crossbar have a value of one. The beads are totaled when moved down or up toward the crossbar.

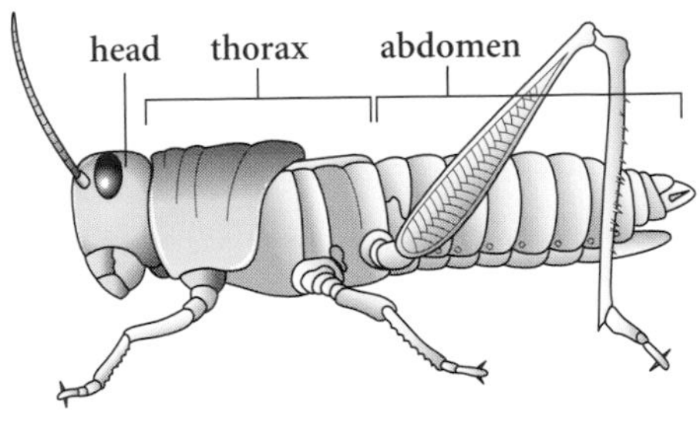

abdomen

a grasshopper, with wings not drawn in order to show the whole abdomen

ab•er•ra•tion (ăb′ə-rā′shən) **1.** A deviation in the normal structure or number of chromosomes in an organism. **2.** The failure of a lens, mirror, or telescope to bring rays of light coming from a source, such as a star, to a single focus, causing a distorted or blurred image.

ab•la•tion (ă-blā′shən) **1.** The wearing away or destruction of the outer or forward surface of an object, such as a meteorite or a spacecraft, as it moves very rapidly through the atmosphere. The friction of the air striking the object heats and often melts or burns its outer layers. **2.** The process by which snow and ice are removed from a glacier or other mass of ice. Ablation typically occurs through melting, sublimation, or wind erosion.

ab•o•ma•sum (ăb′ō-mā′səm) The fourth division of the stomach in ruminant animals, and the only one having glands that secrete acids and enzymes for digestion. It corresponds anatomically to the stomachs of other mammals. *See more at* **ruminant.**

ab•ra•sion (ə-brā′zhən) **1.** The process of wearing away or rubbing down by means of friction. **2.** A scraped area on the skin.

ab•scess (ăb′sĕs′) A collection of pus that forms at one place in the body and is surrounded by inflamed tissue.

ab•scis•sa (ăb-sĭs′ə) The distance of a point from the y-axis on a graph in the Cartesian coordinate system. It is measured parallel to the x-axis. For example, a point having coordinates (2,3) has 2 as its abscissa. *Compare* **ordinate.**

ab•so•lute humidity (ăb′sə-lo͞ot′) The amount of water vapor present in a unit volume of air, usually expressed in kilograms per cubic meter. *Compare* **relative humidity.**

absolute scale A temperature scale having absolute zero as the lowest temperature. The Kelvin scale is an absolute scale.

absolute temperature Temperature measured or calculated on an absolute scale.

absolute value The value of a number without regard to its sign. For example, the absolute value of +3 (written |+3|) and the absolute value of -3 (written |-3|) are both 3.

absolute zero The lowest possible temperature of matter, at which all molecules stop moving. Absolute zero is equal to –459.67°F or –273.15°C.

ab•sorp•tion (əb-sôrp′shən) **1.** *Biology.* The movement of a substance, such as a liquid or solute, across a cell membrane by means of diffusion or osmosis. **2.** *Chemistry.* The process of drawing a gas or liquid into a solid through the minute spaces between its parts. *Compare* **adsorption. 3.** *Physics.* The taking up and storing of energy, such as radiation, light, or sound, without it being reflected or transmitted.

absorption spectrum The pattern of dark lines and colors made when light passes through an absorbing medium, such as a gas or liquid. The dark lines represent the colors that are absorbed. Because each type of atom absorbs a unique range of colors, the absorption spectrum can be used to identify the composition of distant substances, such as the gaseous outer layers of stars.

Ac The symbol for **actinium.**

AC Abbreviation of **alternating current.**

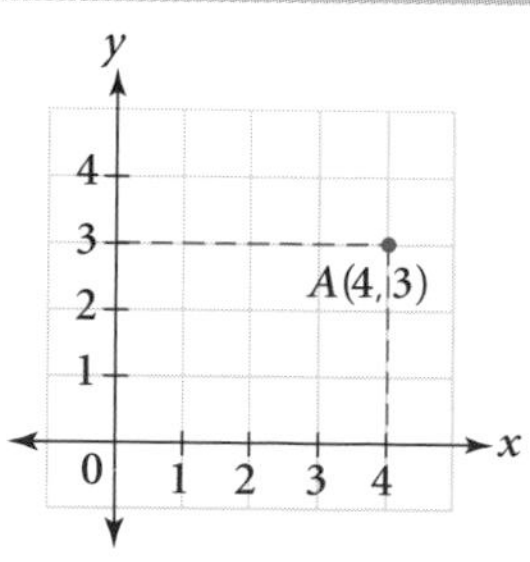

abscissa
The coordinates for A are (4,3); the abscissa is 4.

Did You Know?
acceleration

Most people know that an object has weight because of the pull of gravity, but did you know that weight is actually an indication that an object is being accelerated? When you're in an elevator, for example, as the elevator accelerates upward or downward you feel as if your weight is changing—you feel heavier when the elevator is accelerating upward, and lighter as it accelerates downward. Stand on a bathroom scale in the elevator, and you'll see that the effect is real: the readout on the scale does indeed change as the elevator accelerates. When it accelerates upward and you feel heavier, the readout increases; when it accelerates downward and you feel lighter, the readout decreases. Exactly what *is* changing as you move upward and downward in the elevator? It isn't your mass—the amount of matter in your body. That remains the same. Actually, it's your acceleration that is changing. Your speed and direction are changing, as the elevator moves faster or slower and goes up or down. So the changes in your weight shown on the scale actually are a measure of changes in your acceleration.

ac•cel•er•a•tion (ăk-sĕl′ə-rā′shən) The rate of change of the speed or direction of a moving body with respect to time. *See more at* **gravity, relativity.**

acceleration of gravity The acceleration of a body falling freely under the influence of the Earth's gravity. It is equal to approximately 32 feet (9.8 meters) per second per second.

ac•com•mo•da•tion (ə-kŏm′ə-dā′shən) The adjustment in the focal length of the lens of the eye. Accommodation permits images at different distances to be focused on the retina.

a•cel•lu•lar (ā-sĕl′yə-lər) Not made up of cells or not containing cells. The hyphae of some fungi are acellular.

Did You Know?

acid rain

We normally think of rain as something pure and natural, but in many parts of the world it is polluted with harmful acids from the moment it forms in the sky. How does this happen? When coal, gasoline, and oil are burned as fuels, they give off the gases sulfur dioxide and nitrogen oxide. In the atmosphere, these compounds combine with water vapor to form highly corrosive sulfuric and nitric acids. Prevailing winds carry these acids away from the industrial areas where they originate, and they fall to earth as *acid rain.* Acid rain is a serious environmental problem in parts of the world where there are many factories, power plants, and automobiles close together, as in parts of the United States, Canada, Europe, and Asia. It harms forests and soils and pollutes lakes and rivers, killing fish and other aquatic life. It can also damage buildings and monuments by eating away the stone and metal that they are made of.

–aceous A suffix used to form adjectives meaning "made of" or "resembling" a particular substance or material, such as *silicaceous,* containing silicon.

ac•et•al•de•hyde (ăs′ĭ-tăl′də-hīd′) A colorless, flammable liquid, C_2H_4O, used to make acetic acid, perfumes, and drugs.

ac•e•tate (ăs′ĭ-tāt′) **1.** A salt or ester of acetic acid. **2.** Cellulose acetate or a product made from it, especially fibers or film. *See more at* **cellulose.**

a•ce•tic acid (ə-sē′tĭk) A clear, pungent acid, $C_2H_4O_2$, occurring naturally in vinegar and also produced commercially. It is used as a solvent and in making rubber, cellulose acetate plastics, paints, and dyes.

ac•e•tone (ăs′ĭ-tōn′) A colorless, extremely flammable liquid, C_3H_6O, that is widely used as a solvent, for example in nail-polish remover.

a•cet•y•lene (ə-sĕt′l-ēn′) A colorless, highly flammable and explosive gas, C_2H_2. It is used in gas lighting and in cutting and welding metal.

a•ce•tyl•sal•i•cyl•ic acid (ə-sēt′l-săl′ĭ-sĭl′ĭk) The chemical name for aspirin.

A•chil•les tendon (ə-kĭl′ēz) A large tendon at the back of the leg connecting the calf muscles with the heel bone. The Achilles tendon is the strongest tendon in the body.

ac•id (ăs′ĭd) Any of a class of compounds that form hydrogen ions when dissolved in water. They also react, in solution, with bases and certain metals to form salts. Acids turn blue litmus paper red, have a sour taste, and have a pH of less than 7. *Compare* **base.** —*Adjective* **acidic.**

acid rain Rain, snow, or other precipitation containing a high amount of acidity.

ac•ne (ăk′nē) A skin disease in which the oil glands become clogged and infected, often causing pimples to form, especially on the face. It is commonest during adolescence.

a•cous•tics (ə-ko͞o′stĭks) **1.** *Used with a singular verb.* The scientific study of sound and its trans-

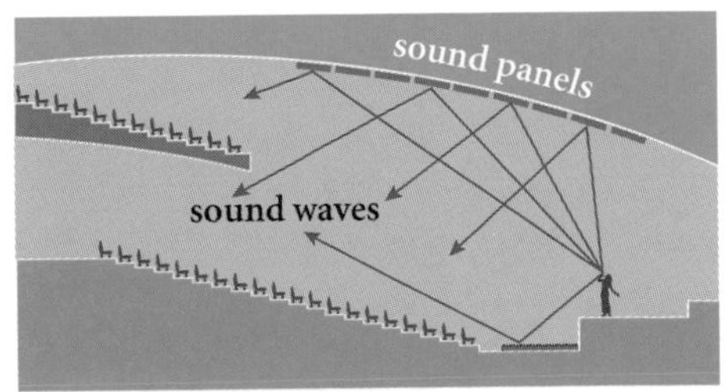

acoustics

Sound waves from a stage are deflected by sound panels and distributed throughout an auditorium.

mission. **2.** *Used with a plural verb.* The total effect of sound, especially as produced in an enclosed space: *a concert hall with excellent acoustics.*

ac•quired immune deficiency syndrome (ə-kwīrd′) *See* **AIDS.**

a•cryl•ic acid (ə-krĭl′ĭk) A colorless, corrosive liquid, $C_3H_4O_2$, that readily forms polymers. It is used to make plastics, paints, synthetic rubbers, and textiles.

ACTH (ā′sē′tē-āch′) Short for *adrenocorticotropic hormone.* A hormone secreted by a lobe of the pituitary gland. It stimulates the adrenal glands to produce cortisone and related hormones.

ac•ti•nide (ăk′tə-nīd′) Any of a series of chemically similar metallic elements with atomic numbers ranging from 89 (actinium) to 103 (lawrencium). All of these elements are radioactive, and two of the elements, uranium and plutonium, are used to generate nuclear energy. *See* **Periodic Table,** pages 262–263.

ac•tin•i•um (ăk-tĭn′ē-əm) A silvery-white, highly radioactive metallic element of the actinide series that is found in uranium ores. It is about 150 times more radioactive than radium and is used as a source of alpha rays. Its most stable isotope has a half-life of about 22 years. *Symbol* **Ac.** *Atomic number* 89. *See* **Periodic Table,** pages 262–263.

ac•ti•no•mor•phic (ăk′tə-nō-môr′fĭk) Relating to a flower that can be divided into equal halves along any diameter; radially symmetrical. The flowers of the rose and tulip, for example, are actinomorphic.

ac•ti•va•tion energy (ăk′tə-vā′shən) The least amount of energy needed for a chemical reaction to occur. For example, striking a match on the side of a matchbox provides the activation energy, in the form of heat, necessary for the chemicals in the match to catch fire.

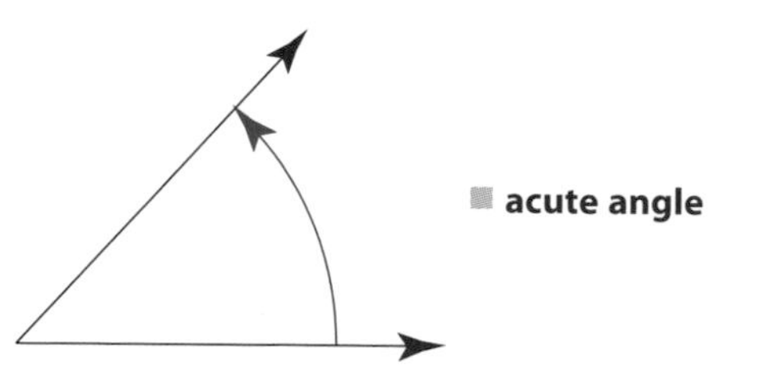

acute angle

ac•tive site (ăk′tĭv) The part of an enzyme where the substance that the enzyme acts upon (called the substrate) is catalyzed. *See more at* **enzyme.**

active transport The movement of ions or molecules across a cell membrane in the direction opposite that of diffusion, that is, from an area of lower concentration to one of higher concentration. The energy needed for active transport is supplied by ATP.

ac•u•punc•ture (ăk′yo͝o-pŭngk′chər) The practice of inserting thin needles into the body at specific points to relieve pain, treat a disease, or anesthetize a body part during surgery. Acupuncture has its origin in traditional Chinese medicine and has been in use for more than 5,000 years.

a•cute angle (ə-kyo͞ot′) An angle whose measure is between 0° and 90°. *Compare* **obtuse angle.**

Ad•ams (ăd′əmz), **Walter Sydney** 1876–1956. American astronomer who in 1915 discovered the first white dwarf star. He demonstrated that the essential brightness of a star could be calculated by studying its spectrum and introduced a method for estimating the distance of stars based on their brightness.

ad•ap•ta•tion (ăd′ăp-tā′shən) A change or adjustment in an animal or plant that increases its chance of survival in a specific environment. Adaptation can involve changes in a body part or in behavior: *Wings are an adaptation of the forelimbs of a bird for flight.*

ADD Abbreviation of **attention deficit disorder.**

ad•dend (ăd′ĕnd′) A number that is added to another number.

ad•dic•tion (ə-dĭk′shən) **1.** A physical or psychological need for a habit-forming substance, such as drugs or alcohol. **2.** A habitual or compulsive involvement in an activity, such as gambling.

ad•di•tion (ə-dĭsh′ən) The act, process, or operation of adding two or more numbers to compute their sum.

ad•di•tive (ăd′ĭ-tĭv) *Noun.* **1.** A substance that is added in small amounts to something in order to improve its performance or quality, preserve its usefulness, or make it more effective. —*Adjective.* **2.** Being any of the primary colors

Did You Know?

adaptation

The gazelle is extremely fast, and the cheetah is even faster. These traits are *adaptations*—characteristics or behaviors that give an organism an edge in the struggle for survival. Darwinian theory holds that adaptations are the result of a two-stage process: random variation and natural selection. Random variation results from slight genetic differences. For example, one cheetah in a group may be slightly faster than the others and thus have a better chance of catching a gazelle. The faster cheetah therefore has a better chance of being well-fed and living long enough to produce offspring. Since the cheetah's young have the same genes that made this parent fast, they are more likely to be fast than the young of slower cheetahs. The process is repeated in each generation, and thereby great speed becomes an adaptation common to cheetahs. This same process of natural selection also favors the fastest gazelles.

red, green, or blue, whose wavelengths may be mixed with one another to produce all other colors. *See more at* **color. 3.** *Mathematics.* Marked by or involving addition.

ad•e•nine (ăd′n-ēn′) A base that is a component of DNA and RNA, forming a base pair with thymine in DNA and a base pair with uracil in RNA during transcription.

ad•e•noids (ăd′n-oidz′) Tonsils at the back of the throat that are swollen due to infection. Adenoids can block breathing through the nose.

a•den•o•sine (ə-dĕn′ə-sēn′) A compound, $C_{10}H_{13}N_5O_4$, that is found in living cells and is one of the nucleotides in DNA and is also a component of ADP, AMP, and ATP.

adenosine di•phos•phate (dī-fŏs′fāt′) *See* **ADP.**

adenosine mon•o•phos•phate (mŏn′ō-fŏs′-fāt′) *See* **AMP.**

adenosine tri•phos•phate (trī-fŏs′fāt′) *See* **ATP.**

ADHD Abbreviation of **attention deficit hyperactivity disorder.**

ad•i•a•bat•ic (ăd′ē-ə-băt′ĭk) Occurring without gain or loss of heat. The passage of sound through air is generally adiabatic.

ad•i•pose (ăd′ə-pōs′) Relating to or consisting of animal fat; fatty.

ad•ja•cent angle (ə-jā′sənt) Either of two angles having a common side and a common vertex.

ADP (ā′dē′pē′) Short for *adenosine diphosphate.* An organic compound, $C_{10}H_{15}N_5O_{10}P_2$, that is composed of adenosine and two phosphate groups. It is converted to ATP for the storage of energy during cell metabolism.

ad•re•nal gland (ə-drē′nəl) Either of two endocrine glands, one located above each kidney, that produce several important hormones. ❖ The outer part of the adrenal gland, called the **adrenal cortex,** produces steroid hormones. ❖ The inner part of the adrenal gland, called the **adrenal medulla,** produces epinephrine.

a•dren•a•line (ə-drĕn′ə-lĭn) *See* **epinephrine.**

ad•sorp•tion (ăd-sôrp′shən) The process by which molecules of a substance, such as a gas or a liquid, collect on the surface of another substance, such as a solid. The molecules are attracted to the surface but do not enter the solid's minute spaces, as in absorption. Some drinking

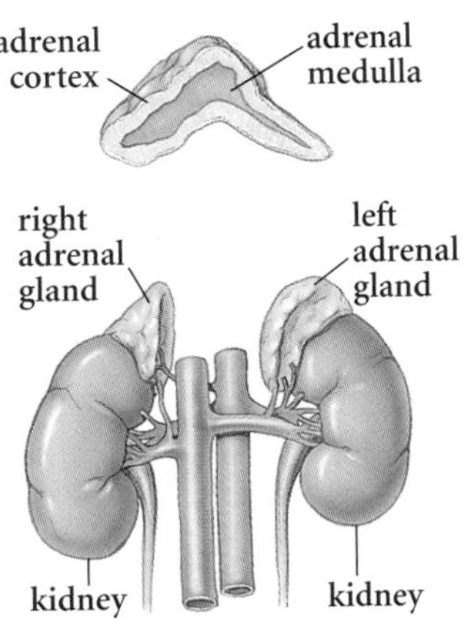

adrenal gland
top: *cross section of an adrenal gland*
bottom: *position of adrenal glands relative to kidneys*

water filters consist of carbon cartridges that adsorb contaminants. *Compare* **absorption** (sense 2).

a•dult (ə-dŭlt′, ăd′ŭlt) An animal or a plant that is fully grown and developed.

aer•ate (âr′āt) **1.** *Chemistry.* To add a gas, such as carbon dioxide, to a liquid. **2.** *Biology.* To supply with oxygen: *The lungs aerate the blood.*

aer•o•bic (â-rō′bĭk) Needing or using oxygen to live: *aerobic organisms.* ❖ Exercise that increases the activity of the heart and lungs improves the body's ability to use oxygen and is called **aerobic exercise.** *Compare* **anaerobic.**

aer•o•dy•nam•ic (âr′ō-dī-năm′ĭk) **1.** Relating to objects, such as the wings of airplanes, that are designed to reduce wind drag. **2.** Relating to aerodynamics.

aer•o•dy•nam•ics (âr′ō-dī-năm′ĭks) The study of the movement of air and other gases and of the forces involved in their movements. It is also the study of the way objects, such as cars and airplanes, interact with air when they are moving through it.

aer•o•nau•tics (âr′ə-nô′tĭks) **1.** The design and construction of aircraft. **2.** The study of the piloting and navigation of aircraft.

aer•o•sol (âr′ə-sôl′) **1.** A substance consisting of very fine particles of a liquid or solid suspended in a gas. Mist, which consists of very fine droplets of water in air, is an aerosol. *Compare* **emulsion, foam. 2.** A substance, such as paint, an insecticide, or a hair spray, packaged under pressure for use in this form.

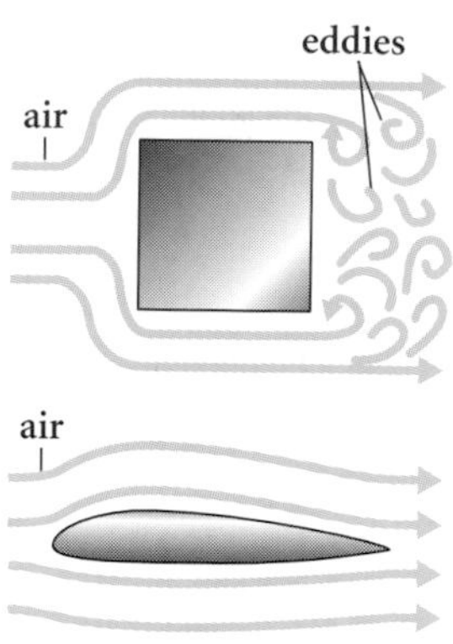

aerodynamic
top: *high wind drag on a less aerodynamic shape*
bottom: *low wind drag on a more aerodynamic shape*

aer•o•space (âr′ō-spās′) **1.** Relating to the Earth's atmosphere and the space beyond. **2.** Relating to the science and technology of flight.

aes•ti•va•tion (ĕs′tə-vā′shən) *Another spelling of* **estivation.**

af•fer•ent (ăf′ər-ənt) Relating to a nerve that carries sensory information toward the central nervous system. *Compare* **efferent.**

af•ter•shock (ăf′tər-shŏk′) A less powerful earthquake that follows a more forceful one. Aftershocks usually originate in the same place as the main earthquakes they follow.

Did You Know?

aerodynamics

The two primary forces in *aerodynamics* are lift and drag. *Lift* refers to forces perpendicular to the surface of an object (such as an airplane wing) that is traveling through the air. For example, airplane wings are designed so that when they move through the air, an area of low pressure is created above the wing; the low pressure produces a lift force that pulls the wing upward (in a direction perpendicular to the wing's broad surface), and the wing pulls the airplane up with it. *Drag* forces, which are parallel to the object's surface, are usually caused by friction. Drag makes it more difficult for airplane wings to slice through the air, and so drag forces push against the forward motion of the craft. Large wings usually generate a lot of lift, but they also produce a lot of drag. In designing airplane wings, engineers need to take into account such factors as the speed and altitude at which the plane will fly, so that they can find a wing shape that balances lift and drag as well as possible.

Louis Agassiz

Ag The symbol for **silver.**

a•gar (ā′gär′, ä′gär′) A jelly-like material obtained from marine algae, especially seaweed. It is used as a medium for growing bacterial cultures in the laboratory and as a thickener and stabilizer in food products.

Ag•as•siz (ăg′ə-sē), **(Jean) Louis (Rodolphe)** 1807–1873. Swiss-born American geologist and zoologist who in 1840 introduced the idea of the ice age. Agassiz carried out extensive fieldwork in Europe and the United States which led him to theorize that most of the Northern Hemisphere had once been covered by a vast sheet of ice. Earlier in his career, Agassiz published a groundbreaking study of fossil fish and was known as the greatest ichthyologist of his day.

ag•ate (ăg′ĭt) A type of very fine-grained quartz found in various colors that are arranged in bands or in cloudy patterns. The bands form when water rich with silica enters empty spaces in rock, after which the silica comes out of solution and forms crystals, gradually filling the spaces from the outside inward. The different colors are the result of various impurities in the water.

a•gent (ā′jənt) A substance that can cause a chemical reaction or a biological effect. *Compare* **reagent.**

Ag•ne•si (än-yā′zē), **Maria Gaetana** 1718–1799. Italian mathematician and philosopher whose major work, *Analytical Institutions* (1748), was the first comprehensive summary of the state of mathematical analysis. It brought together the work of authors writing in various languages, formulated new mathematical methods, and was widely used as a textbook for many years.

ag•o•nist (ăg′ə-nĭst) A muscle that actively contracts to produce a desired movement. *Compare* **antagonist.**

AIDS (ādz) Short for *acquired immune deficiency syndrome.* A severe disease caused by HIV, in which the immune system is attacked and weakened, making the body susceptible to other infections. The virus is transmitted through bodily fluids such as semen and blood.

ai•le•ron (ā′lə-rŏn′) A small section of the back edge of an airplane wing that can be moved up or down to control the plane's rolling and tilting movements.

air (âr) The colorless, odorless, tasteless mixture of gases that surrounds the Earth. Air contains about 78 percent nitrogen and 21 percent oxygen, with the remaining part being made up of argon, carbon dioxide, neon, helium, and other gases.

air bladder 1. An air-filled sac in many fish that helps maintain buoyancy or, in some species, helps in respiration, sound production, or hearing. Also called *swim bladder.* **2.** *See* **float.**

air•foil (âr′foil′) A part, such as an aircraft wing, designed to provide lift as air flows around its surface. Air passes over the airfoil faster than it passes beneath it, resulting in greater pressure below than above. Propellers are airfoils that are spun rapidly to provide propulsion.

air•plane (âr′plān′) Any of various vehicles that are capable of flight, are held up by the force of air flowing around their wings, and are driven by jet engines or propellers.

air sac 1. An air-filled space in the body of a bird that forms a connection between the lungs and

Maria Agnesi

bone cavities. **2.** *See* **alveolus. 3.** A sac-like enlargement in the trachea of an insect. **4.** A bag-like piece of skin or tissue below the jaw of certain animals, such as the bullfrog and orangutan, that can be inflated to increase sound production.

air vesicle *See* **float.**

air•waves (âr′wāvz′) Radio waves used to transmit radio and television signals.

Al The symbol for **aluminum.**

al•a•nine (ăl′ə-nēn′) A nonessential amino acid. *See more at* **amino acid.**

al•bi•no (ăl-bī′nō) A person or animal born without normal coloring as a result of an inherited inability to produce melanin. Mammals that are albinos have white hair, pale skin, and usually pinkish eyes.

al•bu•men (ăl-byo͞o′mən) The white of the egg of certain animals, especially birds and reptiles, consisting mostly of the protein albumin. The albumen supplies water to the growing embryo and also cushions it.

al•bu•min (ăl-byo͞o′mĭn) A class of proteins found in egg white, milk, blood, and various other plant and animal tissues. Albumins dissolve in water and form solid or semisolid masses when heated.

al•che•my (ăl′kə-mē) A medieval philosophy and early form of chemistry whose aims were the changing of common metals into gold, the discovery of a cure for all diseases, and the preparation of a potion that gives eternal youth. The imagined substance capable of turning other metals into gold was called the philosopher's stone.

al•co•hol (ăl′kə-hôl′) **1.** Any of a large number of colorless, flammable organic compounds that contain the hydroxyl group (OH). Names of alcohols usually end in *–ol.* **2.** Ethanol.

al•co•hol•ism (ăl′kə-hô-lĭz′əm) The excessive drinking of and dependence on alcoholic beverages.

Al•deb•a•ran (ăl-dĕb′ər-ən) A very bright binary star in the constellation Taurus. *See Note at* **Rigel.**

al•de•hyde (ăl′də-hīd′) Any of a class of highly reactive organic chemical compounds containing the group CHO. Aldehydes are used in resins, dyes, and organic acids.

Al•ex•an•der•son (ăl′ĭg-zăn′dər-sən), **Ernst Frederick Werner** 1878–1975. Swedish-born American electrical engineer and inventor who developed the first practical television system (1930) and color television (1955).

Did You Know?
alchemy

Because their goals were so unrealistic, and because they had so little success in achieving them, the practitioners of *alchemy* in the Middle Ages got a reputation as fakers and con artists. But this reputation is not fully deserved. While they never succeeded in turning lead into gold (one of their main goals), they did make discoveries that helped to shape modern chemistry. Alchemists discovered and purified a number of chemical elements, including mercury, sulfur, and arsenic. They invented early forms of some of the laboratory equipment used today, including beakers, crucibles, filters, and stirring rods. And they developed methods to separate mixtures and purify compounds by distillation and extraction that are still important.

al•ga (ăl′gə) *Plural* **algae** (ăl′jē) Any of various green, red, or brown organisms that grow mostly in water, ranging in size from single cells to large spreading seaweeds. Like plants, algae manufacture their own food through photosynthesis. They form a major component of marine plankton and are often visible as pond scum. Although they were once classified as plants, they do not have roots, stems, or leaves, and are now viewed as protists.

al•ge•bra (ăl′jə-brə) A branch of mathematics dealing with the relations and properties of quantities. It uses letters and other symbols to represent numbers, especially in equations to solve problems or to express general mathematical relationships.

al•go•rithm (ăl′gə-rĭth′əm) A step-by-step procedure for solving a problem, especially a mathematical rule or procedure used to compute a desired result.

Al•haz•en (ăl-hăz′ən) See **Ibn al-Haytham.**

a•li•en (ā′lē-ən) *Ecology.* Introduced to a region deliberately or accidentally by humans. Starlings, horses, and dandelions are species that are alien to North America but that have become widely naturalized throughout the continent. *Compare* **endemic, indigenous.**

al•i•men•ta•ry canal (ăl′ə-mĕn′tə-rē) *See* **digestive tract.**

al•i•phat•ic (ăl′ə-făt′ĭk) Relating to organic compounds that do not contain a benzene ring; not aromatic. Alkanes are aliphatic compounds. *Compare* **aromatic.**

al•ka•li (ăl′kə-lī′) *Plural* **alkalis** *or* **alkalies.** A chemical that acts like a base and reacts strongly with acids, especially a hydroxide or carbonate of an alkali metal.

alkali metal Any of a group of soft metals that form alkali solutions when they combine with water. They include lithium, sodium, potassium, rubidium, cesium, and francium. Except for cesium, which has a gold sheen, alkali metals are white. The alkali metals have one electron in their outer shell, and therefore react easily with other elements and are found in nature only in compounds. *See* **Periodic Table,** pages 262–263.

WORD HISTORY

algebra

For much of the Middle Ages, the center of scientific learning was not Europe, but the Islamic world of the Arabs. The Arabs studied the Greek classics of Plato and Aristotle while Europe nearly forgot about them. The Arabs were particularly interested in medicine and astronomy, and because astronomy requires making careful measurements and calculations, they became expert mathematicians. In the 800s, an Arabic mathematician named Muhammad al-Khwarizmi wrote a book called *The Book of Restoring and Balancing,* which explained the principles of algebra. Algebra had been developed earlier by mathematicians in Greece and India, but al-Khwarizmi's book, as the first comprehensive treatment of it, became a medieval bestseller. The Arabic word for "the restoring" in the book's title is *al-jabr,* which is the source of our word *algebra.* Al-Khwarizmi's own name is the source of another mathematical term in English, *algorithm.*

al•ka•line (ăl′kə-lĭn, ăl′kə-līn′) **1.** Capable of neutralizing an acid; basic. **2.** Relating to or containing an alkali. —*Noun* **alkalinity.**

alkaline-earth metal Any of a group of metallic elements that includes beryllium, magnesium, calcium, strontium, barium, and radium. Because the alkaline-earth metals have two electrons in their outer shell, they react easily with other elements and are found in nature only in compounds. *See* **Periodic Table,** pages 262–263.

al•ka•loid (ăl′kə-loid′) Any of a large class of complex organic compounds that contain nitrogen and mostly occur in plants. Alkaloids have a wide range of physiological effects and many uses in medicine, but they can also be toxic. Morphine, quinine, and nicotine are all alkaloids.

al•kane (ăl′kān′) Any of a group of hydrocarbons whose carbon atoms form chains linked by single bonds. Alkanes have the general formula C_nH_{2n+2} and include propane and butane.

al•kene (ăl′kēn′) Any of a group of hydrocarbons whose carbon atoms form chains linked by one or more double bonds. Alkenes have the general formula C_nH_{2n} and include ethylene. Also called *olefin.*

al•kyne (ăl′kīn′) Any of a group of hydrocarbons whose carbon atoms form chains linked by one or more triple bonds. Alkynes have the general formula C_nH_{2n-2} and include acetylene.

al•lan•to•is (ə-lăn′tō-ĭs) A membranous sac that grows out of the lower end of the alimentary canal in embryos of reptiles, birds, and mammals. In mammals, the blood vessels of the

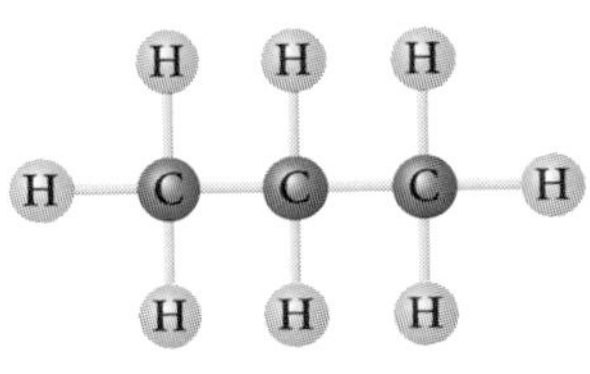

aliphatic
the straight chain of carbon atoms of a propane molecule

allantois develop into the blood vessels of the umbilical cord.

al•lele (ə-lēl′) Any of the possible forms in which a gene for a specific trait can occur. In almost all animal cells, two alleles for each trait are inherited, one from each parent. Alleles on each of a pair of chromosomes are called homozygous if they are similar to each other and heterozygous if they are different.

al•ler•gen (ăl′ər-jən) A substance, such as pollen, that causes an allergy.

al•ler•gy (ăl′ər-jē) A condition in which exposure to a particular substance or environmental influence, such as pollen, certain foods, or sunlight, causes an abnormal physiological reaction. The reaction may include difficulty in breathing, sneezing, skin rashes, and in severe cases, shock or death.

Did You Know?

allergies and allergens

Feeling miserable because of an allergic reaction? Perhaps you can find some comfort in the knowledge that the misery is an unhappy side effect of your immune system trying to protect you. The immune system recognizes that a particular substance, called an *allergen* (for example, dust, mold, or pollen), might be dangerous. Antibodies, special molecules whose job is to round up the invaders, charge into action. The immune system, however, can overreact, causing some people to be so sensitive to these outside substances that they develop unpleasant symptoms, such as rashes, runny noses, or even serious illness. People with severe symptoms can get a series of allergy shots that prevent or lessen the allergic reaction by training the immune system to accept the allergen. Oddly enough, many people develop allergies after repeated exposures to an allergen. The difference is that controlled, small exposures through shots prompt the immune system to grow accustomed to the allergen, while accidental, large exposures provoke the allergic reaction.

al•li•ga•tor (ăl′ĭ-gā′tər) A large, meat-eating, aquatic reptile having sharp teeth and powerful jaws. Alligators have a broader, shorter snout than crocodiles, and their teeth do not show when the jaws are closed. There are two species of alligators: one living in the southeast United States and one living in China.

al•lo•trope (ăl′ə-trōp′) Any of several crystalline forms of a chemical element. Charcoal, graphite, and diamond are all allotropes of carbon.

al•loy (ăl′oi′) A metallic substance made by mixing and fusing two or more metals, or a metal and a nonmetal, to obtain desirable qualities such as hardness, lightness, and strength. Brass, bronze, and steel are all alloys.

al•lu•vi•al fan (ə-lo͞o′vē-əl) A fan-shaped mass of sediment, especially silt, sand, gravel, and boulders, deposited by a river when its flow is suddenly slowed. Alluvial fans typically form where a river pours out from a steep valley through mountains onto a flat plain. Unlike deltas, they are not deposited into a body of standing water.

al•lu•vi•um (ə-lo͞o′vē-əm) Sand, silt, mud, or other matter deposited by flowing water, as in a riverbed, floodplain, or delta.

Al•pha Cen•tau•ri (ăl′fə sĕn-tôr′ē) A multiple star consisting of three stars in the constellation Centaurus. It is the star nearest Earth, at a distance of 4.4 light-years, and it is the third brightest star in the night sky. ❖ **Prox•i•ma Centauri** (prŏk′sə-mə) is the individual star in this system that is closest to Earth, but it is very faint and far from the system's center of mass.

alpha particle A positively charged particle that consists of two protons and two neutrons bound together. It is emitted by the nucleus of some elements undergoing radioactive decay and is identical to the nucleus of a helium atom. Alpha particles are the slowest and least penetrating forms of nuclear radiation. ❖ The process by which a radioactive element emits an alpha particle is called **alpha decay.** Alpha decay results in the atomic number of the atom being decreased by two and the mass number being decreased by four. *See more at* **radiation, radioactive decay.**

alpha ray A stream of alpha particles.

alluvial fan
Death Valley National Park

Al•tair (ăl-tīr′, ăl-târ′) A very bright star in the constellation Aquila. It is a variable binary star. *See Note at* **Rigel.**

al•ter•nate angles (ôl′tər-nĭt) Two angles formed on opposite sides of a line that crosses two other lines. The angles are both exterior or both interior, but not adjacent.

al•ter•nat•ing current (ôl′tər-nā′tĭng) An electric current that reverses its direction of flow at regular intervals. Because the voltage of alternating current can be easily controlled with transformers, this is the type of electricity generated by power stations. The transformers raise the voltage to make it easier to transmit over long distances, then lower the voltage for safer use in homes and buildings. *Compare* **direct current.** *See Notes at* **current, Tesla.**

al•ter•na•tive medicine (ôl-tûr′nə-tĭv) A health care practice that does not follow generally accepted medical methods and may not have a scientific explanation for its effectiveness. Examples of alternative medicines are homeopathy and herbal medicine.

al•ter•na•tor (ôl′tər-nā′tər) An electric generator that produces alternating current. The current reverses direction, back and forth, because the generator's coiled wire rotates rapidly within the magnetic field created by its two magnets, causing the charge of the wire to change from positive to negative, depending on which magnetic pole it is closest to.

al•tim•e•ter (ăl-tĭm′ĭ-tər) An instrument that measures and indicates the height above sea level at which an object, such as an airplane, is located.

al•ti•pla•no (äl′tĭ-plä′nō) A high mountain plateau, as in certain parts of the Andes Mountains.

al•ti•tude (ăl′tĭ-to͞od′) **1.** The height of a thing above a reference level, usually above sea level or the Earth's surface. **2.** *Astronomy.* The vertical angle between a celestial object and the horizon, as seen by the observer. Altitude and azimuth are the coordinates used to navigate with respect to the stars. **3.** *Mathematics.* The perpendicular distance from the base of a geometric figure, such as a triangle, to the opposite vertex, side, or surface.

al•to•cu•mu•lus (ăl′tō-kyo͞o′myə-ləs) A fleecy white or gray cloud formation, usually occurring in wide patches or bands. Altocumulus clouds form at middle levels of the atmosphere.

al•to•strat•us (ăl′tō-străt′əs) A cloud formation that extends in flat, smooth sheets or layers of varying thickness. Altostratus clouds form at middle levels of the atmosphere.

al•um (ăl′əm) Any of various crystalline salts in which a metal such as aluminum or chromium is combined with another metal such as potassium or sodium, especially aluminum potassium sulfate. Alum is widely used in industry as a hardener and purifier, and in medicine to induce vomiting and stop bleeding.

a•lu•mi•num (ə-lo͞o′mə-nəm) A lightweight, silvery-white metallic element that is easily shaped and a good conductor of electricity. It is the most abundant metal in the Earth's crust and is used to make a wide variety of products from soda cans to airplane components. *Symbol* **Al.** *Atomic number* 13. *See* **Periodic Table,** pages 262–263.

Al•va•rez (ăl′və-rĕz′), **Luis Walter** 1911–1988. American physicist who studied subatomic particles. Alvarez built a device called a hydrogen bubble chamber that made it possible to analyze the reactions occurring between atomic nuclei inside

Luis Walter Alvarez

it. His observations led to the theory that protons, neutrons, and electrons are made of quarks. With his son, geologist **Walter Alvarez** (born 1940), he developed a theory that the extinction of dinosaurs was caused by climate changes resulting from a giant asteroid striking the Earth. *See Note at* **iridium.**

al•ve•o•lus (ăl-vē′ə-ləs) *Plural* **alveoli** (ăl-vē′ə-lī′) Any of the tiny air-filled sacs arranged in clusters in the lungs that allow oxygen to diffuse into the bloodstream and carbon dioxide to diffuse out of it. Also called *air sac.*

Alz•heim•er's disease (äls′hī-mərz) A disease that causes degeneration of parts of the brain. Symptoms include the gradual loss of memory and other mental abilities. Alzheimer's disease most commonly affects the elderly.

Am The symbol for **americium.**

AM Abbreviation of **amplitude modulation.**

a•mal•gam (ə-măl′gəm) An alloy of mercury and another metal, especially silver, commonly used in dental fillings.

am•ber (ăm′bər) A hard, translucent, brownish-yellow substance that is the fossilized resin of ancient trees. It often contains fossil insects.

am•ber•gris (ăm′bər-grĭs′, ăm′bər-grēs′) A grayish, waxy material formed in the intestines of sperm whales, often found floating at sea or washed ashore. It is used to make perfumes.

a•me•ba (ə-mē′bə) *Another spelling of* **amoeba.**

am•er•i•ci•um (ăm′ə-rĭsh′ē-əm) A synthetic, silvery-white, radioactive metallic element of the actinide series that is produced artificially by bombarding plutonium with neutrons. Americium is used as a source of alpha particles for smoke detectors and gamma rays for industrial gauges. Its most stable isotope has a half-life of 7,950 years. *Symbol* **Am.** *Atomic number* 95. *See* **Periodic Table,** pages 262–263.

am•e•thyst (ăm′ə-thĭst) A purple or violet, transparent form of quartz used as a gemstone. The color is caused by the presence of iron compounds in the crystal structure.

am•ide (ăm′īd′) A compound containing the radical $CONH_2$.

a•mi•no acid (ə-mē′nō) Any of a large number of compounds that are found in living cells, contain carbon, oxygen, hydrogen, and nitrogen, and join together to form proteins. ❖ About 20 amino acids are needed by animal cells to produce proteins, but only about half, called **nonessential amino acids,** can be produced by animal cells. The remaining half, called **essential amino acids,** must be obtained from food.

Did You Know?

amber

The plot of the movie *Jurassic Park* turns on the extraordinary ability of *amber* to preserve ancient life as miniature fossils. In the movie, scientists extract dinosaur DNA from blood in the stomach of a mosquito that was trapped in amber during the Mesozoic Era. The scientists then use the DNA to create clones of the dinosaurs that end up terrorizing the park and the movie audience. What is amber, and how does it preserve such delicate tissues for millions of years? Certain trees, especially conifers, produce a sticky substance called *resin* to protect themselves against insects. Normally, it decays in oxygen through the action of bacteria. However, if the resin happens to fall into wet mud or sand containing little oxygen, it can harden and eventually fossilize, becoming the yellowish, translucent substance known as amber. If any insects or other organisms are trapped in the resin before it hardens, they can be preserved, often in amazing detail. While amber may sometimes preserve fragments of the DNA of the enclosed organisms, fossil mosquitoes would not contain enough dinosaur DNA to actually create clones, and the sight of dinosaurs again roaming the Earth, even in an island park, remains part of science fiction rather than real science.

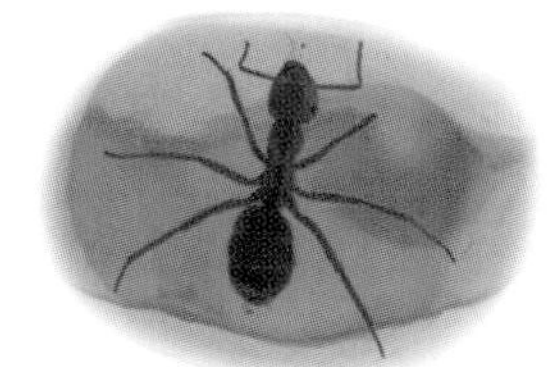

fossilized ant

am•me•ter (ăm′mē′tər) An instrument that measures an electric current and indicates its strength in amperes.

am•mo•nia (ə-mōn′yə) A colorless alkaline gas, NH_3, that is lighter than air and has a strongly pungent odor. It is used as a fertilizer and refrigerant, in medicine, and in making dyes, textiles, plastics, and explosives.

am•mo•nite (ăm′ə-nīt′) Any of the coiled fossil shells of a group of extinct mollusks related to the nautilus. Ammonites were especially abundant during the Mesozoic Era.

am•mo•ni•um (ə-mō′nē-əm) A positively charged ion, NH_4^+, derived from ammonia and found in a wide variety of organic and inorganic compounds.

am•ne•sia (ăm-nē′zhə) A partial or total loss of memory, usually caused by shock or brain injury.

am•ni•on (ăm′nē-ən) A sac of thin, tough membrane containing a watery liquid in which the embryo of a reptile, bird, or mammal is suspended. ❖ The watery fluid in the amnion is called **amniotic fluid.**

a•moe•ba (ə-mē′bə) *Plural* **amoebas** *or* **amoebae** (ə-mē′bē) A one-celled microscopic organism that constantly changes shape by forming pseudopods, temporary projections that are used for movement and for the ingestion of food. Amoebas are members of the group of organisms called protozoans.

a•mor•phous (ə-môr′fəs) **1.** Not made of crystals. Glass is an amorphous substance. **2.** Lacking definite form or shape.

AMP (ā′ĕm-pē′) Short for *adenosine monophosphate.* An organic compound, $C_{10}H_{14}N_5O_7P$, that is composed of adenosine and one phosphate group. It is formed by the breakdown of ATP during cell metabolism.

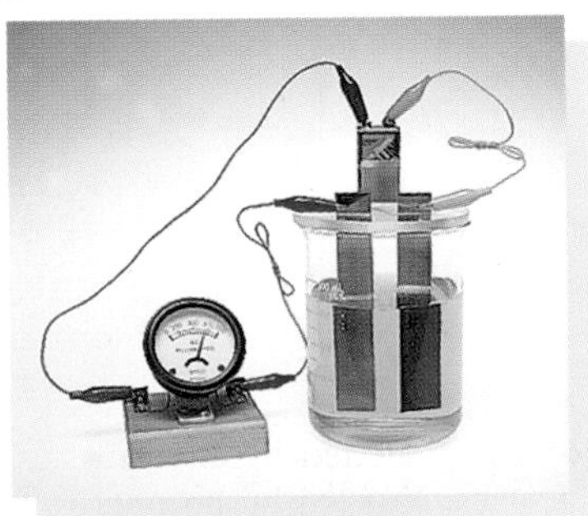

ammeter

The needle on the ammeter shows that a current is flowing through the circuit.

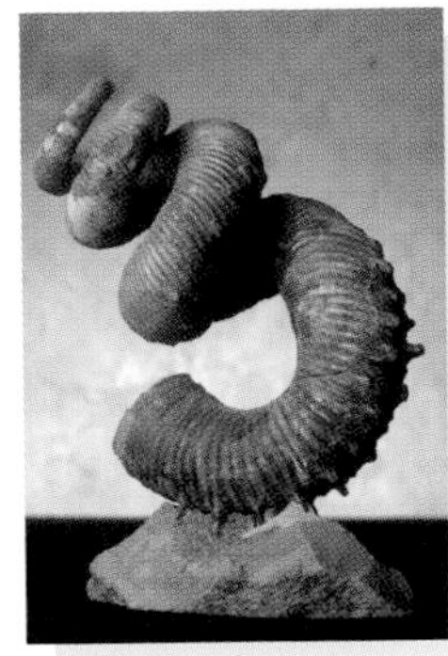

ammonite

two Cretaceous ammonites

am•pere (ăm′pîr′) A unit used to measure electric current. Electric current is measured by how great a charge passes a given point in a second. One ampere is equal to a flow of one coulomb per second.

Am•père (ăm′pîr′, äm-pĕr′), **André Marie** 1775–1836. French mathematician and physicist. He is best known for his analysis of the relationship between magnetic force and electric current, including the formulation of Ampère's law, a mathematical description of the strength of the magnetic field produced by the flow of energy through a conductor. The ampere unit of electric current is named for him.

am•phet•a•mine (ăm-fĕt′ə-mēn′) Any of a group of drugs that stimulate the nervous system, causing heightened alertness and a faster heartbeat and metabolism. Amphetamines are highly addictive.

am•phib•i•an (ăm-fĭb′ē-ən) A cold-blooded vertebrate animal having moist skin without scales. Most amphibians lay eggs in water, and their young breathe with gills but develop lungs

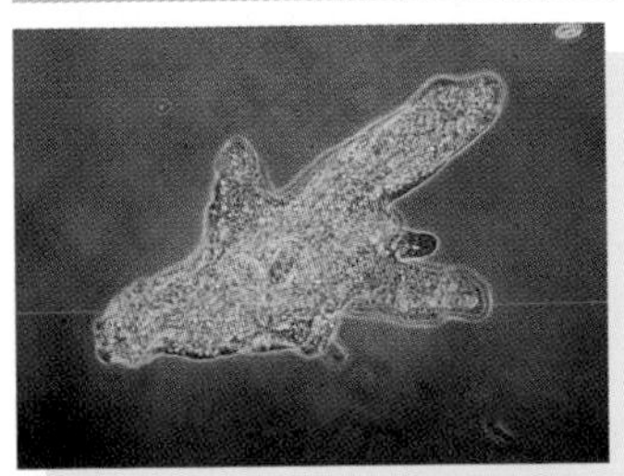

amoeba

WORD HISTORY

amphibian

Amphibians are not quite fish and not quite reptiles. Like fish, they spend part of their lives living in water and breathing with gills; like reptiles, they usually spend another part of their lives breathing air with lungs and able to live on land. This double life is also at the root of their name, *amphibian,* which, like many scientific words, comes from Greek. It is made up of the Greek prefix *amphi–,* meaning "both" or "double," and the Greek word *bios,* meaning "life." Both these elements are widely used in other scientific words in English: *bios,* for example, is also seen in words like *biology, antibiotic,* and *symbiotic.*

and breathe air as adults. Amphibians include frogs, toads, and salamanders.

am•phi•bole (ăm′fə-bōl′) Any of a large group of minerals composed of a silicate joined to various metals, such as calcium, magnesium, iron, or sodium. Hornblende is a mineral of the amphibole group.

am•phi•ox•us (ăm′fē-ŏk′səs) *See* **lancelet.**

am•pho•ter•ic (ăm′fə-tĕr′ĭk) Capable of reacting chemically as either an acid or a base. Water, ammonia, and the hydroxides of certain metals are amphoteric.

am•pli•fi•ca•tion (ăm′plə-fĭ-kā′shən) An increase in the magnitude or strength of an electric current, a force, or another physical quantity, such as a radio signal.

am•pli•tude (ăm′plĭ-to͞od′) One half the full extent of a vibration, oscillation, or wave. The amplitude of an ocean wave, for example, is the maximum height of the wave crest above the level of calm water, or the maximum depth of the wave trough below the level of calm water. The amplitude of a pendulum swinging through an angle of 90° is 45°. *See more at* **wave.**

amplitude modulation A method of radio broadcasting in which the amplitude of the wave that carries the sound signal changes to reflect the various sounds that are to be reproduced, while the frequency of the wave remains the same. *Compare* **frequency modulation.**

am•yl alcohol (ăm′əl, ā′məl) Any of various alcohols having the formula $C_5H_{11}OH$. Amyl alcohols are used to make solvents and esters.

am•y•lase (ăm′ə-lās′) Any of various enzymes that break down starches into their component sugars, such as glucose. Amylase is present in fluid secreted by the pancreas, in saliva in some mammals, and in plants.

a•nab•o•lism (ə-năb′ə-lĭz′əm) The phase of metabolism in which complex molecules, such as the proteins and fats that make up body tissue, are formed from simpler ones. *Compare* **catabolism.** —*Adjective* **anabolic.**

an•a•con•da (ăn′ə-kŏn′də) A very large, mostly aquatic snake of tropical South America. It suffocates its prey by coiling or drowning and is the largest snake known.

a•nad•ro•mous (ə-năd′rə-məs) Relating to fish that migrate up rivers from the sea to breed in fresh water. Salmon and shad are anadromous.

amphibian
top: *green frog*
bottom: *white axolotl, a type of salamander*

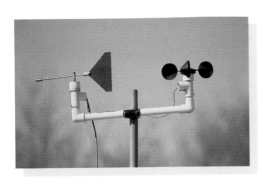

■ **anemometer**
a three-cup anemometer mounted with a weathervane

an•aer•o•bic (ăn′ə-rō**′**bĭk) Occurring or living in the absence of oxygen: *anaerobic bacteria. Compare* **aerobic.**

an•al•ge•sic (ăn′əl-jē**′**zĭk) A drug that deadens the sense of pain; a painkiller.

an•a•log (ăn**′**ə-lôg′) Relating to a device that uses continuously changing physical quantities to represent data. For example, the position of the hands of a clock is an analog representation of time.

a•nal•o•gous (ə-năl**′**ə-gəs) Similar in function but having different evolutionary origins, as the wings of a butterfly and the wings of a bird. *Compare* **homologous.**

a•nal•y•sis (ə-năl**′**ĭ-sĭs) *Plural* **analyses** (ə-năl**′**ĭ-sēz′) The separation of a substance into its parts, usually by chemical means, for the study and identification of each component. ❖ **Qualitative analysis** determines what substances are present in a compound. ❖ **Quantitative analysis** determines how much of each substance is present in a compound.

an•a•lyt•ic geometry (ăn′ə-lĭt**′**ĭk) The use of algebra to solve problems in geometry. In analytic geometry, geometric figures are represented by algebraic equations and plotted using coordinates.

an•a•phase (ăn**′**ə-fāz′) The stage of cell division in which the doubled set of chromosomes separates into two identical groups that move to opposite ends of the cell. In mitosis, anaphase is preceded by metaphase and followed by telophase. *See more at* **meiosis, mitosis.**

a•nat•o•my (ə-năt**′**ə-mē) **1.** The structure of an animal or a plant or any of its parts. **2.** The scientific study of the shape and structure of living things. —*Adjective* **anatomical** (ăn′ə-tŏm**′**ĭ-kəl).

An•ax•ag•o•ras (ăn′ăk-săg**′**ər-əs) 500?–428 B.C. Greek philosopher and astronomer who was the first to explain eclipses correctly. He also stated that the sun and stars were glowing stones and that the moon took its light from the sun.

an•dro•gen (ăn**′**drə-jən) Any of several steroid hormones, such as testosterone, that control the development and maintenance of physical characteristics in males.

An•drom•e•da (ăn-drŏm**′**ĭ-də) A constellation in the Northern Hemisphere near Perseus and Pegasus. It contains a spiral-shaped galaxy visible to the unaided eye.

–ane A suffix used to form the names of saturated hydrocarbons (hydrocarbons having only single bonds), such as *ethane. Compare* **–ene.**

a•ne•mi•a (ə-nē**′**mē-ə) A condition in which the concentration of red blood cells or the amount of hemoglobin is too low to supply enough oxygen to the tissues of the body. *See also* **sickle cell anemia.** —*Adjective* **anemic.**

an•e•mom•e•ter (ăn′ə-mŏm**′**ĭ-tər) An instrument that measures the speed and force of the wind. The most basic type of anemometer consists of a series of cups mounted at the end of arms that rotate in the wind. The speed with which the cups rotate indicates the wind speed.

a•nem•o•ne (ə-nĕm**′**ə-nē) *See* **sea anemone.**

an•er•oid barometer (ăn**′**ə-roid′) A barometer made up of a vacuum chamber covered by a thin elastic disk. High atmospheric pressure pushes against the disk and causes it to bulge inward,

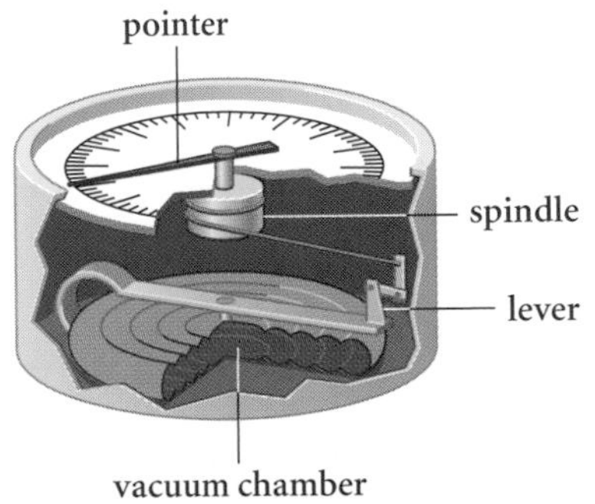

■ **aneroid barometer**
Expansion or contraction of the vacuum chamber, caused by a change in air pressure, forces the pointer to move.

while low pressure does not push as hard, allowing the disk to bulge outward.

an•es•the•sia (ăn′ĭs-thē′zhə) Loss of sensation to touch or pain, usually produced by nerve injury or by the administration of drugs, especially before surgery.

an•eu•rysm (ăn′yə-rĭz′əm) A swelling in the wall of an artery or vein caused by disease or injury.

an•gi•o•sperm (ăn′jē-ə-spûrm′) Any of a large group of plants that have flowers and produce seeds enclosed in an ovary or a fruit; a flowering plant. Most living plants are angiosperms. *Compare* **gymnosperm.**

an•gle (ăng′gəl) **1.** A geometric figure formed by two lines that begin at a common point or by two planes that begin at a common line. **2.** The space between such lines or planes, measured in degrees. *See also* **acute angle, obtuse angle, right angle.**

angle of incidence The angle formed by a ray or wave, as of light or sound, striking a surface and a line perpendicular to the surface at the point of impact. *See more at* **wave.**

angle of reflection The angle formed by a ray or wave reflected from a surface and a line perpendicular to the surface at the point of reflection. *See more at* **wave.**

angle of refraction The angle formed by the path of refracted light or other radiation and a line drawn perpendicular to the refracting surface at the point where the refraction occurred. *See more at* **wave.**

ang•strom (ăng′strəm) A unit of length equal to one hundred-millionth (10^{-8}) of a centimeter. It is used mainly to measure wavelengths of light and shorter electromagnetic radiation.

Ång•ström (ăng′strəm), **Anders Jonas** 1814–1874. Swedish physicist and astronomer who pioneered the use of the spectroscope in the analysis of radiation. By studying the spectrum of visible light given off by the sun, Ångström discovered that there is hydrogen in the sun's atmosphere. The angstrom unit of measurement is named for him.

an•gu•lar momentum (ăng′gyə-lər) A property of a body (or a group of bodies) rotating or traveling along a curved path. Angular momentum depends on the body's mass, its speed of motion, and the distance of its mass from the center of the rotation or curve. Angular momentum remains constant unless some outside force adds energy to or removes energy from the moving body. When an ice skater spinning with arms extended draws his arms in, he spins faster because his angular momentum must remain the same.

angular velocity The rate at which an object moving in a circular path changes its position, measured in revolutions per minute.

an•hy•dride (ăn-hī′drīd′) A chemical compound formed from another, especially an acid, by the removal of water.

an•hy•drous (ăn-hī′drəs) Not containing water.

an•i•mal (ăn′ə-məl) Any of a wide variety of multicellular organisms, most of which have a digestive tract, a nervous system, the ability to move voluntarily, and specialized sensory organs for recognizing and responding to their environment. Animals cannot manufacture their own food and must feed on plants, other animals, or other organic matter. Animals are grouped as a separate kingdom in taxonomy.

animal kingdom The category of living organisms that includes all animals. The scientific name of this kingdom is Animalia. *See Table at* **taxonomy.**

an•i•on (ăn′ī′ən) An ion that has a negative charge. Hydroxide and chloride ions are anions. *Compare* **cation.**

an•ky•lo•sau•rus (ăng′kə-lō-sôr′əs) *or* **an•ky•lo•saur** (ăng′kə-lō-sôr′) A large, plant-eating dinosaur of the Cretaceous Period having a squat, heavily armored body and a clubbed tail.

an•ne•lid (ăn′ə-lĭd) Any of various worms or worm-like animals having soft, elongated bodies that are divided into ring-like segments. The earthworm and leech are annelids.

an•nu•al (ăn′yo͞o-əl) *Botany. Adjective.* **1.** Completing a life cycle in one growing season. —*Noun.* **2.** An annual plant. Tomatoes and sunflowers are examples of annuals.

annual ring *See under* **growth ring.**

an•nu•lar (ăn′yə-lər) Forming or shaped like a ring.

an•ode (ăn′ōd′) **1.** The positive electrode in an electrolytic cell, toward which negatively charged particles are attracted. The anode has a positive charge because it is connected to the positively charged end of an external power supply. **2.** A part that attracts negatively charged particles in an electrical device, such as a battery or vacuum tube. *Compare* **cathode.**

a•nom•a•ly (ə-nŏm′ə-lē) Something that is unusual, irregular, or abnormal: *Flooding is an anomaly in desert regions of Africa. —Adjective* **anomalous.**

a•noph•e•les (ə-nŏf′ə-lēz′) Any of various mosquitoes that can transmit malaria to humans.

an•o•rex•i•a ner•vo•sa (ăn′ə-rĕk′sē-ə nûr-vō′sə) A disorder characterized by an abnormal fear of becoming obese and by persistent efforts to lose weight, leading to severe weight loss and malnourishment. It most commonly affects young women, who often stop menstruating, develop brittle bones, and experience other physical changes as a result.

ant (ănt) Any of various insects that live in large colonies composed of workers, soldiers, and a queen. Ants often tunnel in the ground or in wood. Only the males and the queen have wings. *See also* **queen, soldier, worker.**

an•tag•o•nist (ăn-tăg′ə-nĭst) A muscle that resists or counteracts another muscle, as by relaxing while the opposite one contracts. *Compare* **agonist.**

Ant•arc•tic Circle (ănt-ärk′tĭk) The parallel of latitude approximately 66°33' south. It forms the boundary between the South Temperate Zone and South Frigid Zone.

An•tar•es (ăn-târ′ēz) A reddish, very bright binary star in the constellation Scorpio. It is a supergiant.

an•ten•na (ăn-tĕn′ə) *Plural* **antennae** (ăn-tĕn′ē) **1.** One of a pair of long, slender, segmented structures on the head of insects, centipedes, millipedes, and crustaceans. Most antennae are organs of touch, but some are sensitive to odors and other stimuli. **2.** A metallic device for sending or receiving electromagnetic waves, such as radio waves or microwaves.

an•ther (ăn′thər) The pollen-bearing part at the upper end of the stamen of a flower. *See more at* **flower.**

an•thra•cite (ăn′thrə-sīt′) A hard, shiny coal that has a high carbon content. It is valued as a fuel because it burns with a clean flame and without smoke or odor, but it is much less abundant than bituminous coal. *Compare* **bituminous coal, lignite.**

antenna
left: *elderberry longhorn beetle*
right: *close-up of a cecropia moth*

an•thrax (ăn′thrăks′) An infectious, usually fatal disease of mammals, especially cattle and sheep, caused by a bacterium. It can spread to people, causing symptoms ranging from blistering of the skin to potentially fatal infection of the lungs.

an•thro•pol•o•gy (ăn′thrə-pŏl′ə-jē) The scientific study of humans, especially of their origin, their behavior, and their physical, social, and cultural development.

anti– A prefix whose basic meaning is "against." It is used to form adjectives that mean "counteracting" (such as *antiseptic,* preventing infection). It is also used to form nouns referring to substances that counteract other substances (such as *antihistamine,* a substance counteracting histamine), and nouns meaning "something that displays opposite, reverse, or inverse characteristics of something else" (such as *anticyclone,* a storm that circulates in the opposite direction from a cyclone). Before a vowel it becomes *ant–,* as in *antacid.*

an•ti•bi•ot•ic (ăn′tĭ-bī-ŏt′ĭk) A substance, such as penicillin, that is capable of destroying or weakening certain microorganisms, especially disease-causing bacteria or fungi. Antibiotics are obtained from other microorganisms, especially molds.

an•ti•bod•y (ăn′tĭ-bŏd′ē) A protein produced in the blood or tissues in response to the presence of a specific foreign antigen. Antibodies provide immunity against certain microorganisms and

Did You Know?

antibodies

Antibodies are complex, Y-shaped protein molecules that guard our bodies against diseases. The immune system's B lymphocytes, or B cells, develop into plasma cells, which can produce a huge variety of antibodies, each one capable of grabbing an invading molecule at the top ends of the Y. The molecules that antibodies recognize can be quite specific—they might exist only on a particular bacterium or virus. When that bacterium or virus enters the body, the antibodies quickly recognize its molecules, as if a sentry recognized an enemy soldier from his uniform. Once the invader is caught, the antibodies may make it inactive or lead it to cells that can destroy it. High numbers of a particular antibody may persist for months after an invasion. The numbers may then get quite small, but the experienced B cells can quickly make more of that specific antibody if necessary. Vaccines work by training B cells to do just that.

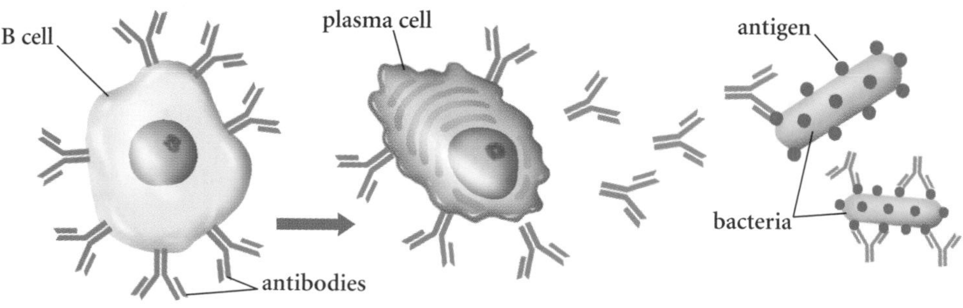

toxins by binding with them and often by deactivating them. Also called *immunoglobulin.*

an•ti•cline (ăn′tĭ-klīn′) A fold of rock layers that slope downward on both sides of a common crest. Anticlines form when rocks are compressed by plate-tectonic forces. They can be as small as a hill or as large as a mountain range. *Compare* **syncline.**

an•ti•cy•clone (ăn′tē-sī′klōn′) A system of winds that spiral outward around a region of high atmospheric pressure, circling clockwise in the Northern Hemisphere and counterclockwise in the Southern Hemisphere. *Compare* **cyclone.**

an•ti•dote (ăn′tĭ-dōt′) **1.** A substance that counteracts the effects of poison. **2.** Something that relieves or counteracts something: *Baking soda is often used as an antidote to indigestion.*

an•ti•gen (ăn′tĭ-jən) A substance that stimulates the production of an antibody when introduced into the body. Antigens include toxins, bacteria, viruses, and other foreign substances. *See Note at* **blood type.**

an•ti•his•ta•mine (ăn′tē-hĭs′tə-mēn′) Any of various drugs that relieve cold or allergy symptoms by blocking the action of histamine in the body.

an•ti•log•a•rithm (ăn′tē-lô′gə-rĭth′əm, ăn′tī-lô′gə-rĭth′əm) The number whose logarithm is a given number. For example, the logarithm of 1,000 (or 10^3) is 3, so the antilogarithm of 3 is

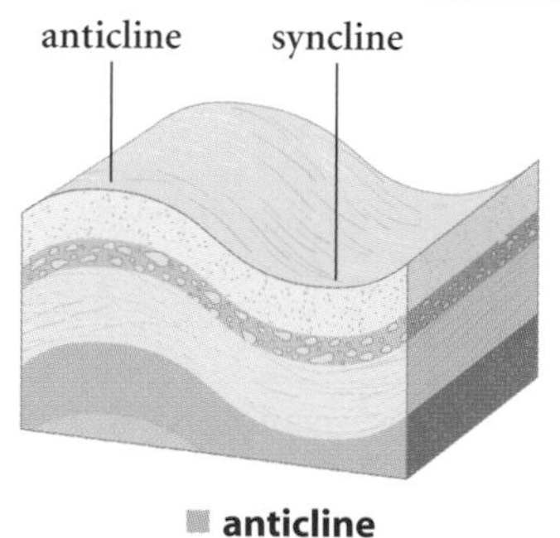

anticline

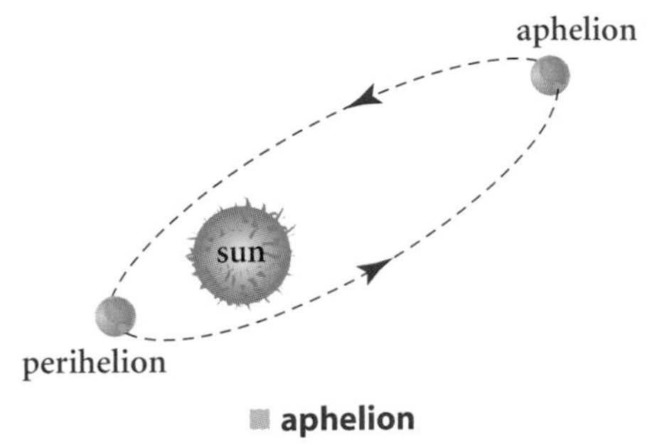

aphelion

1,000. In algebraic notation, if log $x = y$, then antilog $y = x$.

an•ti•mat•ter (ăn′tĭ-măt′ər) Matter that is made up of antiparticles corresponding to the particles that make up ordinary matter.

an•ti•mo•ny (ăn′tə-mō′nē) A metallic element having many forms, the most common of which is a hard, brittle, shiny, blue-white crystal. It is used in a variety of alloys, especially with lead in car batteries, and in making flameproofing compounds. *Symbol* **Sb.** *Atomic number* 51. *See* **Periodic Table,** pages 262–263.

an•ti•node (ăn′tĭ-nōd′) In a standing wave, the region or point of maximum amplitude between two adjacent nodes. *Compare* **node** (sense 3).

an•ti•ox•i•dant (ăn′tē-ŏk′sĭ-dənt, ăn′tī-ŏk′sĭ-dənt) A chemical compound or substance that inhibits oxidation. Certain vitamins, such as vitamin E, are antioxidants and may protect body cells from damage due to oxidation.

an•ti•par•ti•cle (ăn′tē-pär′tĭ-kəl, ăn′tī-pär′tĭ-kəl) A subatomic particle that corresponds to another subatomic particle but has certain characteristics, such as electric charge, with opposite values. The positron is the antiparticle of the electron.

an•tip•o•des (ăn-tĭp′ə-dēz′) Two places on directly opposite sides of the Earth, such as the North Pole and the South Pole.

an•ti•sep•tic (ăn′tĭ-sĕp′tĭk) A substance that prevents infection or rot by preventing the growth of microorganisms.

ant•ler (ănt′lər) A horny growth on the head of a deer, moose, elk, or other related animal, usually having one or more branches. Antlers typically grow only on males and are shed and grown again each year.

a•nus (ā′nəs) The opening at the lower end of the alimentary canal through which solid waste is excreted. —*Adjective* **anal.**

a•or•ta (ā-ôr′tə) The main artery of the circulatory system in mammals. It carries blood with high levels of oxygen from the left ventricle of the heart to all the arteries of the body except those of the lungs.

ap•a•tite (ăp′ə-tīt′) A usually green, transparent mineral consisting mainly of calcium phosphate. Apatite occurs as hexagonal crystals in igneous, metamorphic, and sedimentary rocks, and is used as a source of phosphate for making fertilizers. It is the mineral used to represent a hardness of 5 on the Mohs scale.

a•pat•o•sau•rus (ə-păt′ə-sôr′əs) *or* **a•pat•o•saur** (ə-păt′ə-sôr′) A very large sauropod dinosaur of the late Jurassic Period, having a long neck and tail and a relatively small head. *See Note at* **brontosaurus.**

ape (āp) Any of various large, tailless primates having long arms and broad chests. Apes include the chimpanzee, gorilla, and orangutan. They live in the wild only in the Eastern Hemisphere. *Compare* **monkey.**

a•pex (ā′pĕks) The highest point, especially the vertex of a triangle, cone, or pyramid.

a•phe•li•on (ə-fē′lē-ən) The point farthest from the sun in the orbit of a body, such as a planet or a comet, that travels around the sun.

a•phid (ā′fĭd, ăf′ĭd) Any of various small, soft-bodied insects that feed by sucking sap from plants. Aphids can be very destructive and can transmit plant diseases.

ap•o•gee (ăp′ə-jē) **1.** The point farthest from the Earth's center in the orbit of the moon or an artificial satellite. **2.** The point in the orbit of a body, such as a satellite, where it is farthest from the body around which it revolves, such as a planet. *Compare* **perigee.**

ap•pen•dix (ə-pĕn′dĭks) *Plural* **appendixes** *or* **appendices** (ə-pĕn′-dĭ-sēz′) A tubular projection attached to the cecum of the large intestine in humans and some other mammals. ❖ Inflammation of the appendix is called **appendicitis** (ə-pĕn′dĭ-sī′tĭs). ❖ Surgical removal of the appendix is called an **appendectomy** (ăp′ən-dĕk′tə-mē).

a•quar•i•um (ə-kwâr′ē-əm) A tank, bowl, or other container filled with water for keeping and displaying fish or other aquatic animals and plants.

BIOGRAPHY

Archimedes

Archimedes would still be famous today even without the legend that he ran through the streets of his home in Sicily naked. One of his most important discoveries was that of buoyancy: an object placed in water displaces a volume of water equal to its own volume. The story goes that the king of Archimedes's hometown of Syracuse wanted Archimedes to test a golden crown to make sure it was made of pure gold (and not gold mixed with silver). According to the story, Archimedes puzzled over the problem until one day when he was taking a bath he saw how his body made the water overflow, and in a flash of insight discovered the principle of displacement. He dashed through the neighborhood yelling *"Eureka!"* (Greek for "I've found it!"), forgetting to dress first. He knew that gold was heavier than silver and now realized that a given weight of gold would have less volume—and therefore displace less water—than an equal weight of silver. He determined the volume of the crown from the volume of water it displaced, weighed the crown, and found that indeed it was too light to be made of pure gold.

A•quar•i•us (ə-kwâr′ē-əs) A constellation in the Southern Hemisphere near Pisces and Aquila.

a•quat•ic (ə-kwăt′ĭk) Relating to, living in, or growing in water.

a•que•ous (ā′kwē-əs) Relating to or dissolved in water.

aqueous humor The clear, watery fluid that fills the chamber of the eye between the cornea and the lens.

aq•ui•fer (ăk′wə-fər) An underground layer of sand, gravel, or porous rock that collects water and holds it like a sponge. Much of the water we use is obtained by drilling wells into aquifers.

Aq•ui•la (ăk′wə-lə) A constellation in the Northern Hemisphere near Aquarius and Hercules.

Ar The symbol for **argon.**

Ar•a•bic numeral (ăr′ə-bĭk) One of the numerical symbols 1, 2, 3, 4, 5, 6, 7, 8, 9, or 0. They are called Arabic numerals because they were introduced into western Europe from sources of Arabic scholarship.

a•rach•nid (ə-răk′nĭd) Any of a group of arthropods having eight segmented legs, no wings or antennae, and a body divided into two parts. One part consists of the head and thorax joined together, and the other part is the abdomen. Spiders, mites, scorpions, and ticks are arachnids.

arc (ärk) A segment of a circle.

ar•chae•bac•te•ri•um (är′kē-băk-tîr′ē-əm) *See* **archaeon.**

ar•chae•ol•o•gy *or* **ar•che•ol•o•gy** (är′kē-ŏl′ə-jē) The scientific study of past human life and culture by the examination of physical remains, such as graves, tools, and pottery.

ar•chae•on (är′kē-ŏn′) *Plural* **archaea.** Any of a group of microorganisms that resemble bacteria but are different from them in certain aspects of their chemical structure, such as the composition of their cell walls. Archaea usually live in extreme environments, such as very hot or salty ones. The archaea are considered a separate kingdom in some classification systems, but a division of the prokaryotes in others. Also called *archaebacterium.*

ar•chae•op•ter•yx (är′kē-ŏp′tər-ĭks) An extinct primitive bird of the Jurassic Period, having characteristics of both birds and dinosaurs. Like dinosaurs, it had a long, bony tail, claws at the end of its fingers, and teeth. Like birds it had wings and feathers. Many scientists regard it as evidence that birds evolved from small meat-eating dinosaurs. *See Note at* **bird.**

Ar•che•an (är-kē′ən) The earlier of the two divisions of the Precambrian Eon, from about 3.8 to 2.5 billion years ago. During this time, the Earth had an atmosphere with little free oxygen, and the first single-celled life appeared. *See Chart at* **geologic time,** pages 148–149.

Ar•chi•me•des (är′kə-mē′dēz) 287?–212 B.C. Greek mathematician, engineer, and inventor. He made numerous mathematical discoveries, including the ratio of the radius of a circle to its circumference as well as formulas for the areas and volumes of various geometric figures. Archimedes created the science of mechanics, devising the first general theory of levers and finding methods for determining the center of gravity of a variety of bodies.

ar•cho•saur (är′kə-sôr′) Any of a mostly extinct group of reptiles which includes the dinosaurs, pterosaurs, and the modern crocodiles and other crocodilians.

Arc•tic Circle (ärk′tĭk) The parallel of latitude approximately 66°33' north. It forms the boundary between the North Temperate Zone and the North Frigid Zone.

Arc•tu•rus (ärk-to͝or′əs) The brightest star in the Northern Hemisphere. It is in the constellation Boötes.

ar•e•a (âr′ē-ə) The extent of a surface or plane figure as measured in square units.

ar•gi•nine (är′jə-nēn′) An essential amino acid. *See more at* **amino acid.**

ar•gon (är′gŏn′) A colorless, odorless element that is a noble gas and makes up about one percent of the atmosphere. It is used in electric light bulbs, fluorescent tubes, and radio vacuum tubes. *Symbol* **Ar.** *Atomic number* 18. *See* **Periodic Table,** pages 262–263.

ar•id (ăr′ĭd) Very dry, especially having less rainfall than is needed to support most trees or woody plants: *an arid climate; an arid region.*

Ar•ies (âr′ēz) A constellation in the Northern Hemisphere near Taurus and Pisces.

Ar•is•tot•le (ăr′ĭ-stŏt′l) 384–322 B.C. Greek philosopher and scientist who profoundly influenced Western thought. Aristotle wrote about virtually every area of knowledge, including most of the sciences. Throughout his life he made careful observations, collected specimens, and summarized all the existing knowledge of the natural world. He pioneered the study of zoology, developing a classification system for all animals and making extensive taxonomic studies. His systematic approach later evolved into the basic scientific method in the Western world.

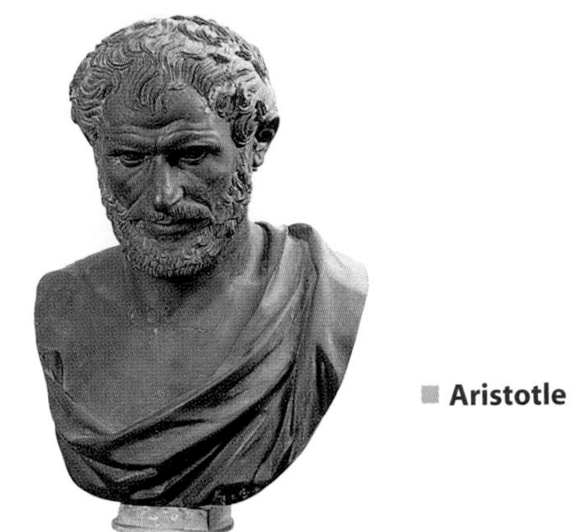

Aristotle

a•rith•me•tic (ə-rĭth′mĭ-tĭk) **1.** The mathematical study of numbers and their properties under the operations of addition, subtraction, multiplication, and division. **2.** Calculation using these operations.

ar•ith•met•ic mean (ăr′ĭth-mĕt′ĭk) The value obtained by dividing the sum of a set of quantities by the number of quantities in the set. For example, if there are three test scores 70, 83, and 90, the arithmetic mean of the scores is their sum (243) divided by the number of scores (3), or 81. *See more at* **mean.** *Compare* **average, median, mode.**

ar•ith•met•ic progression (ăr′ĭth-mĕt′ĭk) A sequence of numbers such as 1, 3, 5, 7, 9 . . ., in which each term after the first is formed by adding a constant to the preceding number (in this case, 2). *Compare* **geometric progression.**

ar•ma•dil•lo (är′mə-dĭl′ō) Any of several toothless, burrowing mammals of South America and southern North America. Armadillos have an armor-like covering of jointed bony plates and roll up into a ball when attacked.

ar•ma•ture (är′mə-chər) **1.** A rotating part of an electric motor or generator, consisting of wire wound around an iron core. The armature carries the electric current. **2.** A piece of soft iron connecting the poles of a magnet. **3.** The part of an electromagnetic device, such as a relay or loudspeaker, that moves or vibrates.

ar•o•mat•ic (ăr′ə-măt′ĭk) Relating to an organic compound containing at least one benzene ring or similar ring-shaped component. Naphthalene and TNT are aromatic compounds. *Compare* **aliphatic.**

ar•ray (ə-rā′) *Mathematics.* **1.** A rectangular arrangement of quantities in rows and columns. **2.** Numerical data ordered in a linear fashion, by magnitude.

Ar•rhe•ni•us (ə-rē′nē-əs), **Svante August** 1859–1927. Swedish physicist and chemist who first explained the process by which ions are formed or separated. He also investigated osmosis, toxins, and antitoxins.

ar•rhyth•mi•a (ə-rĭ*th*′mē-ə) An abnormal rhythm of the heart.

ar•se•nate (är′sə-nĭt, är′sə-nāt′) A chemical compound containing the group AsO_4.

ar•se•nic (är′sə-nĭk) A nonmetallic element most commonly occurring as a gray crystal, but also found as a yellow crystal and in other forms. Arsenic and its compounds are highly poisonous and are used to make insecticides, weed killers, and various alloys. *Symbol* **As.** *Atomic number* 33. *See* **Periodic Table,** pages 262–263.

ar•te•ri•ole (är-tîr′ē-ōl′) Any of the smaller branches of an artery, especially one that ends in the capillaries.

ar•te•ri•o•scle•ro•sis (är-tîr′ē-ō-sklə-rō′sĭs) A thickening and hardening of the walls of the arteries that interferes with the circulation of the blood. It can be caused by disease and is also associated with high blood pressure and diets that are rich in cholesterol and saturated fats. *See also* **atherosclerosis.**

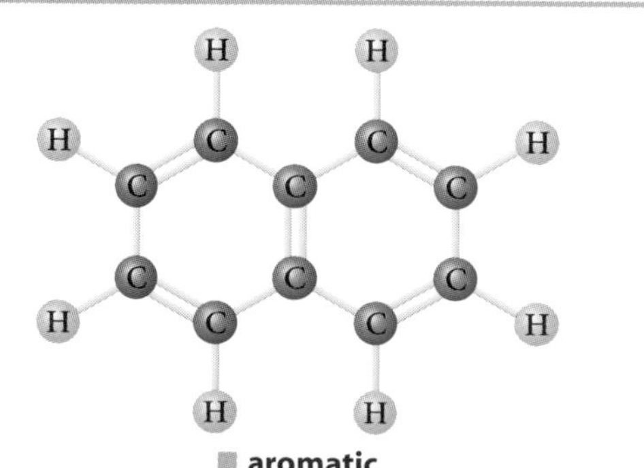

aromatic
The organic compound naphthalene is composed of two benzene rings.

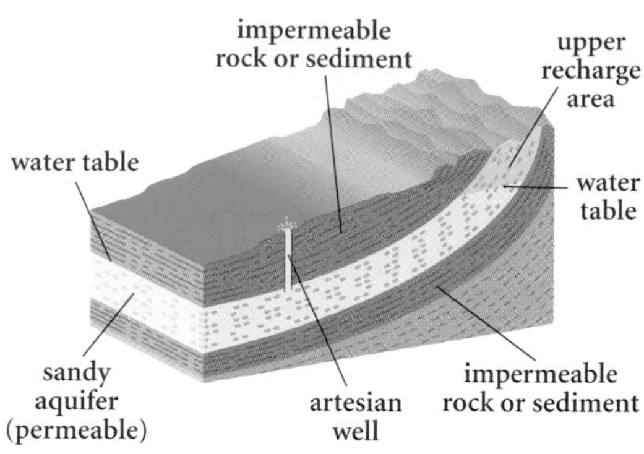

artesian well
If the water table in the recharge area is higher than the surface of a well, then the water will flow from the well without being pumped.

ar•ter•y (är′tə-rē) Any of the blood vessels that carry blood away from the heart. Arteries have muscular walls that expand and contract to help pump blood with high levels of oxygen to the tissues of the body. —*Adjective* **arterial** (är-tîr′ē-əl).

ar•te•sian well (är-tē′zhən) A deep well that passes through hard, nonporous rock or sediment and reaches an aquifer in which the water is under enough pressure to rise to a height above the water table. ❖ In a **flowing artesian well** the water is under enough pressure to rise to the surface without being pumped.

ar•thri•tis (är-thrī′tĭs) Inflammation and stiffness of a joint or joints. *See also* **osteoarthritis, rheumatoid arthritis.**

ar•thro•pod (är′thrə-pŏd′) Any of numerous invertebrate animals having a segmented body, segmented appendages, and an external skeleton. Crustaceans, insects, and arachnids are all arthropods. Arthropods make up the largest phylum in the animal kingdom.

ar•ti•fi•cial (är′tə-fĭsh′əl) Made by humans rather than occurring naturally: *artificial sweeteners; an artificial heart.*

artificial intelligence The ability of a computer or other machine to perform actions thought to require intelligence. Among these actions are log-

Did You Know?

artificial intelligence

One laboratory devoted to research on *artificial intelligence* explains what they do: "Our goal is to understand the nature of intelligence and to engineer systems that exhibit intelligence." You may think of a computer as smart, but it is actually just following directions very fast. A truly intelligent device would be more flexible and would engage in the kind of "thinking" that people really do. An example is vision. A network of sensors combined with systems for interpreting the data may produce the kind of pattern recognition that we take for granted as seeing and understanding what we see. In fact, developing software that can recognize subtle differences in objects (such as those we perceive in the faces of two people) is very difficult. Differences that we can perceive without deliberate effort require massive amounts of data and careful guidelines for a system of artificial intelligence to recognize. Computers are necessary to artificial intelligence because they allow researchers to manage all the data needed to try to imitate true intelligence. The attempt to create artificial intelligence should lead to a better understanding of the human brain. After all, you can't copy it if you don't know how it works.

ical deduction and inference, creativity, the ability to make decisions based on past experience or insufficient or conflicting information, and the ability to understand spoken language.

ar•ti•o•dac•tyl (är′tē-ō-dăk**′**təl) Any of various hoofed mammals having an even number of toes on each foot. Artiodactyls include the pig, sheep, ox, deer, giraffe, and hippopotamus. Also called *even-toed ungulate.*

As The symbol for **arsenic.**

as•bes•tos (ăs-bĕs**′**təs) Any of several fibrous mineral forms of magnesium silicate. Asbestos is resistant to heat, flames, and chemical action. Some forms have been shown to cause lung diseases. For this reason, asbestos is no longer used to make insulation, fireproofing material, and brake linings.

ASCII (ăs**′**kē) *Computer Science.* A code that assigns numbers to the letters of the alphabet, the digits 0 through 9, and punctuation marks. For example, the capital letter A is coded as 65. (In the binary number system used by computers, 65 is written 1000001.) By standardizing the code used in representing written text, ASCII enables computers to exchange information.

a•scor•bic acid (ə-skôr**′**bĭk) *See* **vitamin C.**

–ase A suffix used to form the names of enzymes. It is often added to the name of the compound that the enzyme breaks down, as in *lactase,* which breaks down lactose.

a•sep•tic (ə-sĕp**′**tĭk) Free of microorganisms that cause disease: *boiled the surgical instruments to make them aseptic.*

a•sex•u•al reproduction (ā-sĕk**′**sho͞o-əl) *See under* **reproduction.**

as•par•a•gine (ə-spăr**′**ə-jēn′) A nonessential amino acid. *See more at* **amino acid.**

as•par•tic acid (ə-spär**′**tĭk) A nonessential amino acid. *See more at* **amino acid.**

as•phalt (ăs**′**fôlt′) A thick, sticky, dark-brown mixture of petroleum tars used in paving, roofing, and waterproofing. Asphalt is produced as a by-product in refining petroleum or is found in natural beds.

as•phyx•i•a (ăs-fĭk**′**sē-ə) Suffocation resulting from a severe drop in the level of oxygen in the body, leading to loss of consciousness and sometimes death.

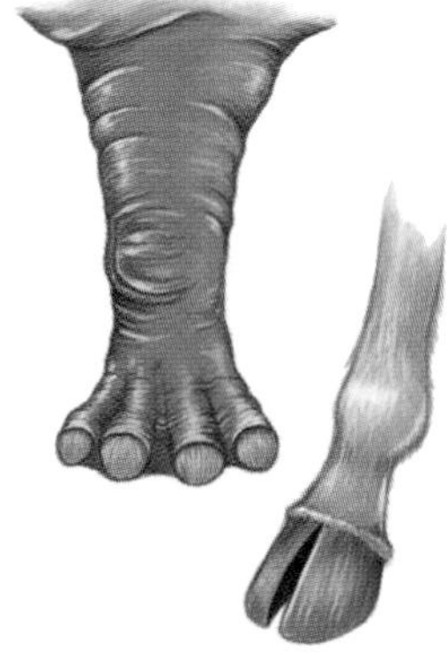

artiodactyl
left: *hippopotamus foot*
right: *giraffe foot*

Did You Know?

aspirin

The forest may not look like a drugstore. Nevertheless, plants have always provided humans with powerful medicine. For example, we no longer eat the bark of willow trees when we have headaches, but for thousands of years, people did just that. About 100 years ago, scientists studying willow bark figured out how it could be used to make acetylsalicylic acid, better known as *aspirin.* Aspirin and willow bark get broken down in the stomach to supply us with the same powerful painkiller. Quinine, which people use to control the fevers of the disease malaria, originally came from the cinchona tree. Recently, researchers developed a new cancer drug, taxol, from the needles of yew trees. In fact, about 45 percent of all cancer drugs are either natural products or slightly altered natural chemicals that scientists tinkered with to make more potent. Researchers still study traditional plant remedies hoping to find more medicines from nature.

as•pi•rate (ăs′pə-rāt′) To remove a liquid or gas from a body cavity by suction: *aspirate the lungs.*

as•pi•rin (ăs′pər-ĭn, ăs′prĭn) A white crystalline compound derived from salicylic acid and used as a drug to relieve fever and pain. Also called *acetylsalicylic acid.*

as•so•ci•a•tive property (ə-sō′shə-tĭv) A property distinguishing some mathematical operations, such as addition and multiplication, when they are applied more than once. Operations with the associative property give the same result regardless of the order in which the operations are performed. For example, 3 + (4 + 5) is equal to (3 + 4) + 5. *See also* **commutative property, distributive property.**

as•ta•tine (ăs′tə-tēn′) A highly unstable, radioactive element that is the heaviest of the halogen elements. The most stable of its many isotopes has a half-life of only about eight hours. *Symbol* **At.** *Atomic number* 85. *See* **Periodic Table,** pages 262–263.

as•ter•oid (ăs′tə-roid′) Any of numerous small, often irregularly shaped bodies that orbit the sun. Asteroids range from several hundred miles in diameter to the size of a speck of dust. ❖ Most are found in the region between the orbits of Mars and Jupiter known as the **asteroid belt.** *See Note at* **solar system.**

as•then•o•sphere (ăs-thĕn′ə-sfîr′) The upper part of the Earth's mantle. The asthenosphere lies beneath the lithosphere and consists of several hundred miles of partially molten rock. Because it is partially molten, seismic waves passing through this layer have slow velocities. *Compare* **atmosphere, hydrosphere, lithosphere.**

asth•ma (ăz′mə) A chronic disease characterized by a narrowing of the airways that is often caused by an allergy. It results in attacks of wheezing, coughing, difficulty in breathing, and tightness of the chest.

a•stig•ma•tism (ə-stĭg′mə-tĭz′əm) A defect of the eye in which the curvature of the cornea or lens is uneven. This prevents rays of light from being focused at a single point on the retina, resulting in indistinct or imperfect images.

as•tral (ăs′trəl) Relating to or coming from the stars; stellar: *astral distances.*

as•trin•gent (ə-strĭn′jənt) A substance, such as alum, that checks the flow of bodily secretions by causing tissue contraction.

astro– A prefix that means "star" (as in *astrophysics*), "celestial body" (as in *astronomy*), or "outer space" (as in *astronaut*).

as•trom•e•try (ə-strŏm′ĭ-trē) The scientific measurement of the positions and motions of celestial bodies.

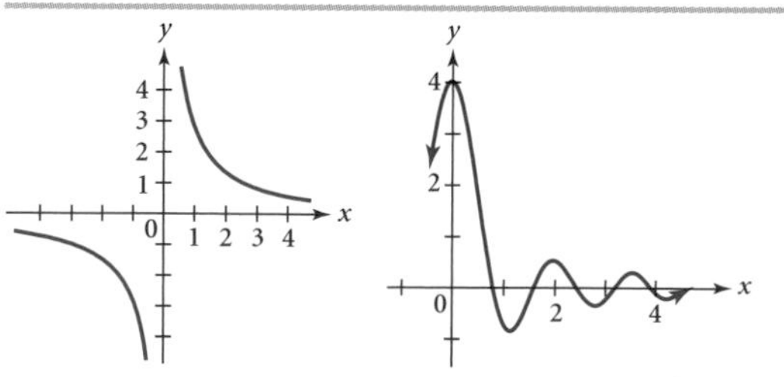

asymptote

left: *The x- and y-axes are both asymptotes of the curve (a hyperbola).*
right: *The x-axis is the asymptote of the wave.*

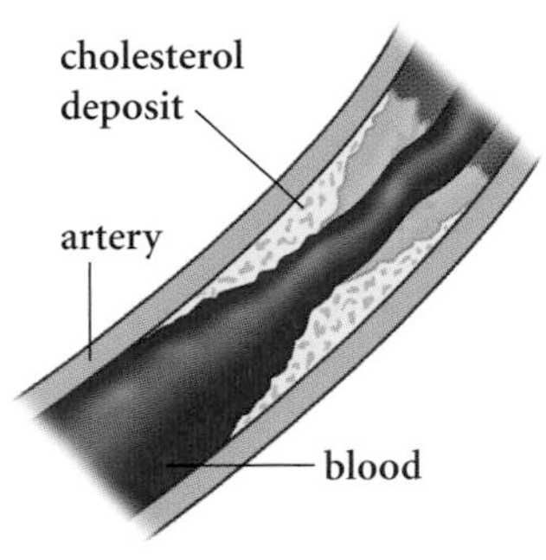

atherosclerosis
an artery narrowed by the buildup of cholesterol

as•tro•nom•i•cal unit (ăs′trə-nŏm′ĭ-kəl) A unit of length equal to the average distance from Earth to the sun, approximately 93 million miles (150 million kilometers). It is used to measure distances within the solar system.

as•tron•o•my (ə-strŏn′ə-mē) The scientific study of the universe and the objects in it, including stars, planets, and nebulae. Astronomy deals with the position, size, motion, composition, energy, and evolution of celestial objects. Astronomers analyze not only visible light but also radio waves, x-rays, and other ranges of radiation that come from sources outside the Earth's atmosphere.

as•tro•phys•ics (ăs′trō-fĭz′ĭks) The branch of astronomy that deals with the physical processes that occur in stars, galaxies, and interstellar space.

a•sym•me•try (ā-sĭm′ĭ-trē) Lack of symmetry or balance.

as•ymp•tote (ăs′ĭm-tōt′) A line whose distance to a given curve tends to zero. An asymptote may or may not intersect its associated curve.

At The symbol for **astatine.**

at•a•vis•tic (ăt′ə-vĭs′tĭk) Reappearing after being absent from a strain of organism for several generations. Used of an inherited trait. —*Noun* **atavism.**

a•tax•i•a (ə-tăk′sē-ə) Loss of muscular coordination as a result of damage to the central nervous system.

–ate A suffix used to form the name of a salt or an ester of an acid whose name ends in *–ic,* such as *acetate,* a salt or ester of acetic acid. Such salts or esters have one oxygen atom more than corresponding salts or esters with names ending in *–ite.* For example, a *sulfate* is a salt of sulfuric acid and contains the group SO_4, while a sulfite contains SO_3. *Compare* **–ite** (sense 2).

ath•er•o•scle•ro•sis (ăth′ə-rō-sklə-rō′sĭs) Narrowing of the walls of the arteries caused by deposits of fatty substances (called plaques), especially cholesterol. It is the most common form of arteriosclerosis.

ath•lete's foot (ăth′lēts) A contagious infection of the feet that usually affects the skin between the toes, causing it to itch, blister, and crack. It is caused by fungus.

at•mos•phere (ăt′mə-sfîr′) **1.** The mixture of gases that surrounds the Earth or some other celestial body. It is held by the force of gravity and forms various layers at different heights, including the troposphere, stratosphere, mesosphere, thermosphere, and exosphere. The Earth's atmosphere, called air, is rich in nitrogen and oxygen; that of Venus is mainly carbon dioxide.

atmosphere
The Earth's atmosphere is divided into layers primarily according to differences in temperature. In the troposphere and mesosphere, air temperature drops with altitude, while in the stratosphere and thermosphere it rises. The exosphere extends indefinitely into space.

Did You Know?

atmospheric pressure

The atmosphere that blankets the Earth gently presses down on us, and the subtle variations in this *atmospheric pressure* greatly affect the weather. For example, forecasters often talk of low pressure bringing rain. In areas of low air pressure, the air is less dense and relatively warm, which causes it to rise. The expanding and rising air naturally cools and the water vapor in the air condenses, forming clouds and the drops that fall as rain. In high pressure regions, on the other hand, the air is dense and relatively cool, which causes it to sink. The water vapor in the sinking air does not condense, leaving the skies sunny and clear. So if you're trying to hit a home run, would you prefer a beautiful, sunny day or one in which it looks like rain? On the overcast day, the ball has less air to push aside on its way out of the ballpark, making it easier to hit a homer.

Compare **asthenosphere, hydrosphere, lithosphere. 2.** A unit of pressure equal to the pressure of the air at sea level, about 14.7 pounds per square inch or 1,013 millibars.

at•mos•pher•ic pressure (ăt′mə-sfîr′ĭk) Pressure caused by the weight of the air. At sea level it has an average value of one atmosphere and gradually decreases as the altitude increases.

a•toll (ăt′ôl′, ā′tôl′) A coral island forming a ring that nearly or entirely encloses a shallow lagoon.

at•om (ăt′əm) The smallest unit of an element, consisting of protons and neutrons in a dense central nucleus orbited by a number of electrons. In electrically neutral atoms, the number of protons equals the number of electrons. Atoms remain intact in chemical reactions except for the removal, transfer, or exchange of certain electrons. *See Note at* **subatomic particle.**

a•tom•ic (ə-tŏm′ĭk) **1.** Relating to an atom or atoms. **2.** Employing nuclear energy: *atomic weapons. See Note at* **nuclear.**

atomic bomb A very destructive bomb that derives its explosive power from the fission of atomic nuclei, usually plutonium or uranium 235 (an isotope of uranium). Also called *atom bomb.*

atomic clock An extremely precise clock whose rate is controlled by the vibration of particular atoms or molecules whose frequency does not change. The standard kind of atomic clock, which is based on the vibrations of cesium atoms, gains or loses less than one second in three million years. Atomic clocks are used to help track satellites, run navigation systems, and study movements of the Earth's crust.

atomic energy *See* **nuclear energy.**

atomic mass The mass of a given atom or molecule, expressed in atomic mass units. *Compare* **atomic weight.**

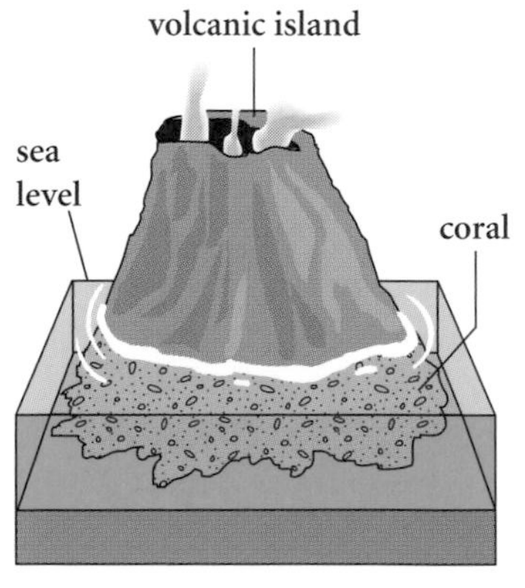

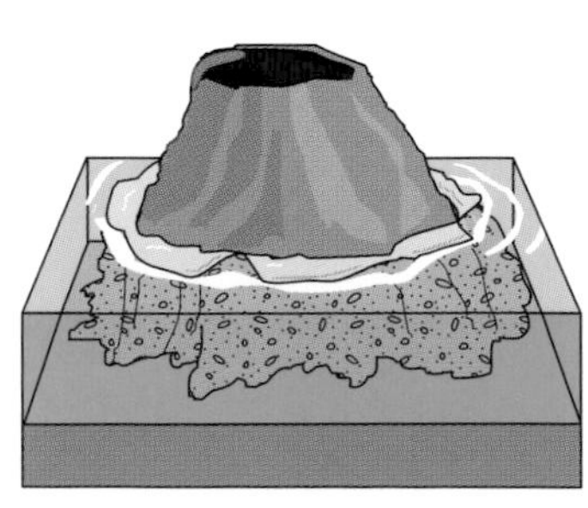

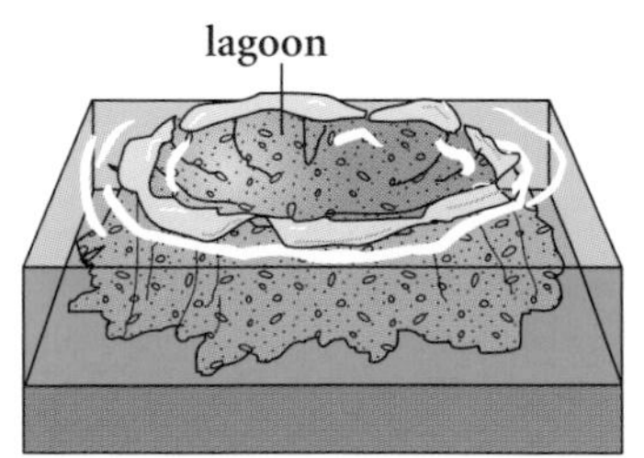

atoll

An atoll develops (from left to right) *when a volcanic island erodes and a ring of coral grows up around it. The depression left by the crater of an eroding volcano fills with water, forming a lagoon.*

Atom

Except for hydrogen, all atoms consist of a nucleus containing protons and neutrons, surrounded by fast-moving electrons. The electrons move at different energy levels, in what are known as shells. Hydrogen, the lightest element, consists of one proton and one electron only. The proton is located in the nucleus, and the electron orbits about it, in an electron shell (shown in red).

Hydrogen

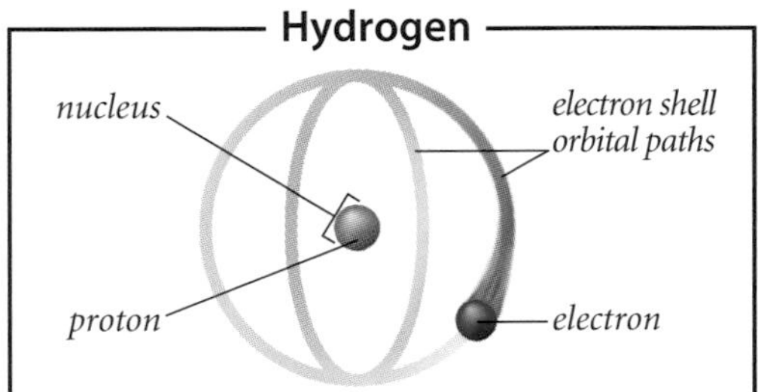

The next lightest element, helium, has two protons and two neutrons in its nucleus, and two electrons orbiting about it in the electron shell.

Helium

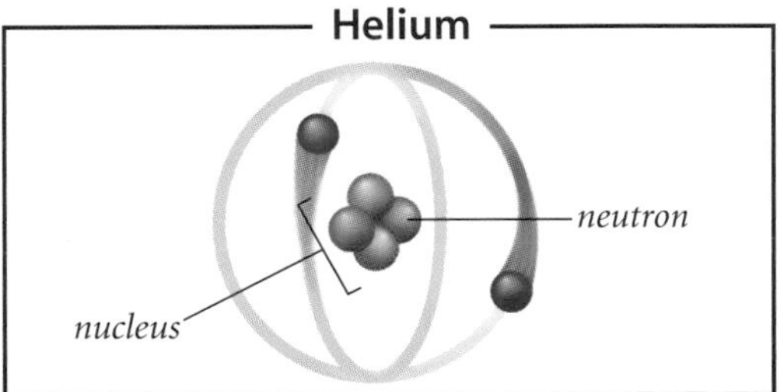

Lithium, the next lightest element, has three protons, three neutrons, and three electrons. Because the first electron shell can only hold two electrons, lithium's third electron is in a second electron shell (shown in green). This second shell can hold up to eight electrons.

Lithium

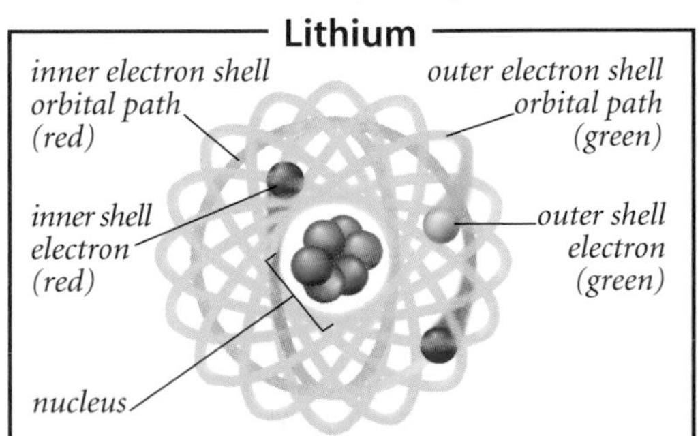

Larger atoms have as many as seven electron shells, each one successively larger than the one beneath it. The number of electrons orbiting in the outer shell determines how easily an element will react with other elements to form compounds. Elements whose outer shell is full are considered inert, and don't readily combine with other elements. Elements whose outermost shell has only one or two electrons will try to react with other elements to capture some of their electrons and fill their shell.

Oxygen

An oxygen atom, for example, has eight protons and eight neutrons in its nucleus, and eight electrons distributed throughout its two shells (shown in red and green). There are two electrons in the inner shell and six electrons in the outer shell. But because this outer shell has room for two more electrons, oxygen often reacts with other elements to gain two more electrons.

Water, one of the most common compounds on Earth, forms in this way. An oxygen atom combines with two hydrogen atoms, thus filling its outermost shell by sharing one electron each with two atoms of hydrogen.

Water (H_2O)

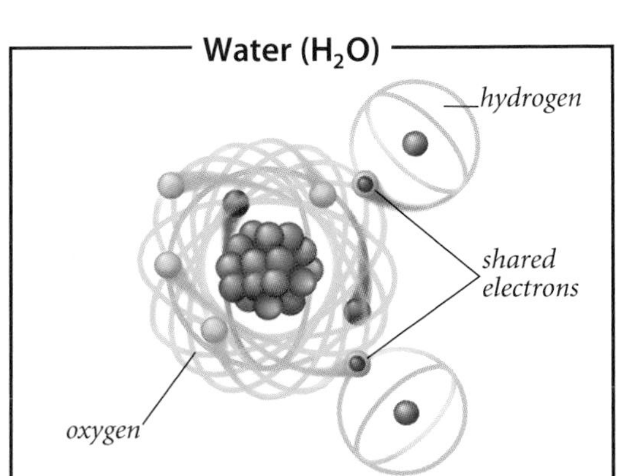

■ **aurora borealis**
photographed in Denali National Park, Alaska

atomic mass unit A unit of mass equal to $\frac{1}{12}$ the mass of an atom of the most common isotope of carbon (carbon 12), which is assigned a mass of 12. A hydrogen atom has a mass of 1 atomic mass unit since its mass is $\frac{1}{12}$ the mass of carbon 12.

atomic number The number of protons in the nucleus of an atom. In electrically neutral atoms, this number is also equal to the number of electrons orbiting about the atom's nucleus. The atomic number of an element determines its position in the Periodic Table.

atomic weight The average mass of a chemical element, expressed in atomic mass units. The atomic weight of an element having more than one principal isotope is calculated both from the atomic masses of the isotopes and from the relative abundance of each isotope in nature. For example, the atomic weight of the element chlorine is 35.453, determined by averaging the atomic masses and relative abundances of its two main naturally occurring isotopes, which have atomic masses of about 35 and 37. *Compare* **atomic mass.**

ATP (ā′tē′pē′) Short for *adenosine triphosphate.* An organic compound, $C_{10}H_{16}N_5O_{13}P_3$, that is composed of adenosine and three phosphate groups. It serves as a source of energy for many metabolic processes. ATP releases energy when it is broken down into ADP by hydrolysis during cell metabolism.

a•tri•o•ven•tric•u•lar (ā′trē-ō-vĕn-trĭk′yə-lər) Connecting or involving the atria and the ventricles of the heart.

a•tri•um (ā′trē-əm) *Plural* **atria.** A chamber of the heart that receives blood from the veins and pumps it into a ventricle. Mammals, birds, reptiles, and amphibians have two atria; fish have one. —*Adjective* **atrial.**

at•ro•phy (ăt′rə-fē) The wasting away of a body part, most commonly caused by disease or nerve damage.

at•ten•tion deficit disorder (ə-tĕn′shən) A condition whose symptoms include impulsiveness and a short attention span. It is usually diagnosed in childhood and can interfere with one's performance at school, in the workplace, and in social situations. ❖ Attention deficit disorder in which hyperactivity is present is called **attention deficit hyperactivity disorder.**

Au The symbol for **gold.**

AU Abbreviation of **astronomical unit.**

au•di•to•ry (ô′dĭ-tôr′ē) Relating to hearing or the organs of hearing: *the auditory canal of the ear.*

auditory nerve The nerve that carries sensory information for sound and balance from the ear to the brain. The auditory nerve is a cranial nerve.

Au•du•bon (ô′də-bŏn′), **John James** 1785–1851. American ornithologist and artist. His effort to catalog every species of bird in America resulted in the publication of *The Birds of America* (1827–1838), a collection of 1,065 life-size engravings of birds found in eastern North America. It is considered a classic work in ornithology and in American art.

au•ri•cle (ôr′ĭ-kəl) **1.** The visible part of the outer ear. **2.** An atrium of the heart.

Au•ri•ga (ô-rī′gə) A constellation in the Northern Hemisphere near Gemini and Perseus. It contains the bright star Capella.

au•ro•ra (ə-rôr′ə) *Plural* **auroras** *or* **aurorae** (ə-rôr′ē) A brilliant display of bands of light in the sky at night, especially in polar regions. The light is caused by charged particles from the sun that are drawn into the atmosphere by the Earth's magnetic field.

aurora aus•tra•lis (ô-strā′lĭs) An aurora that occurs in southern regions of the Earth. Also called *southern lights.*

aurora bo•re•al•is (bôr′ē-ăl′ĭs) An aurora that occurs in northern regions of the Earth. Also called *northern lights.*

aus•tra•lo•pith•e•cine (ô-strā′lō-pĭth′ĭ-sēn′) Any of several early hominids of eastern and southern Africa, known from fossils dating from about four million to about one million years ago. The most complete australopithecine skeleton found so far, named Lucy by its discoverers, is estimated to be just over three million years old. While many scientists believe that australopithecines are ancestors of modern humans, not enough fossils have yet been found to establish any direct descent.

au•tism (ô′tĭz′əm) A disorder of development in which a person's ability to interact with others is severely limited. People with autism often have abnormal behavior patterns, such as the repetition of specific movements or a tendency to focus on certain objects. —*Adjective* **autistic.**

auto– A prefix meaning "oneself," as in *autoimmune,* producing antibodies or immunity against oneself. It also means "by itself, automatic," as in *autonomic,* governing by itself.

au•to•im•mune (ô′tō-ĭ-myo͞on′) Relating to a reaction of the immune system in which antibodies are produced that attack the body's own cells and tissues, often causing illness.

au•to•nom•ic nervous system (ô′tə-nŏm′ĭk) The part of the nervous system of a vertebrate animal that regulates involuntary action, as of the intestines, heart, or glands. It is divided into two parts, the sympathetic nervous system and the parasympathetic nervous system.

au•top•sy (ô′tŏp′sē) A medical examination of a dead body to determine the cause of death.

au•to•troph•ic (ô′tə-trŏf′ĭk) Relating to an organism that manufactures its own food from inorganic substances, such as carbon dioxide and nitrogen, using light or ATP for energy. All green plants and algae, and some bacteria and protists, are autotrophs. ❖ An organism capable of producing food from inorganic substances is called an **autotroph** (ô′tə-trŏf′). *Compare* **heterotrophic.**

au•tumn (ô′təm) The season of the year occurring between summer and winter. In the Northern Hemisphere, it extends from the autumnal equinox to the winter solstice.

au•tum•nal equinox (ô-tŭm′nəl) The moment of the year when the sun crosses the celestial equator while moving from north to south. It occurs on September 22 or 23, marking the beginning of autumn in the Northern Hemisphere. *Compare* **vernal equinox.**

aux•in (ôk′sĭn) Any of various hormones or similar substances that promote and regulate the growth and development of plants. Auxins are produced in areas (called the meristem) in which new plant cells are formed. Auxins are also produced artificially in laboratories for purposes such as speeding growth and regulating how fast a fruit will ripen.

av•a•lanche (ăv′ə-lănch′) The fall or slide of a large mass, as of snow or rock, down the side of a mountain.

av•er•age (ăv′ər-ĭj) A number, especially the arithmetic mean, that is derived from and considered typical or representative of a set of numbers. *Compare* **arithmetic mean, median, mode.**

A•ver•y (ā′və-rē), **Oswald Theodore** 1877–1955. Canadian-born American bacteriologist who determined that DNA was the material that caused genetic changes in bacteria. His work was vital to scientists who later established that DNA is the carrier of genetic information in all living organisms.

a•vi•an (ā′vē-ən) Relating to birds.

a•vi•ar•y (ā′vē-ĕr′ē) A large cage or enclosure for birds, as in a zoo.

Av•i•cen•na (ăv′ĭ-sĕn′ə) *See* **Ibn Sina, Hakim.**

A•vo•ga•dro (ä′və-gä′drō), **Amedeo** 1776–1856. Italian chemist and physicist who formulated the hypothesis known as Avogadro's law, which states that equal volumes of gases, under equal conditions of temperature and pressure, contain equal numbers of molecules.

Avogadro's number The number of atoms or molecules in a mole of a substance, approximately 6.0225×10^{23}. *See more at* **mole**[3].

av•oir•du•pois weight (ăv′ər-də-poiz′) A system of weights based on a pound of 16 ounces, used in the United States to weigh everything except gems, precious metals, and drugs.

ax•il (ăk′sĭl) The angle between the upper side of a leaf or stem and the stem or branch that supports it. A bud is usually found in the axil.

ax•i•om (ăk′sē-əm) A principle that is accepted as true without proof; a postulate.

ax•is (ăk′sĭs) *Plural* **axes** (ăk′sēz′) **1.** An imaginary line around which an object rotates. In a rotating sphere, such as the Earth and other planets, the two ends of the axis are called poles. **2.** *Mathematics.* **a.** A line, ray, or line segment with respect to which a figure or object is symmetrical. **b.** In the Cartesian coordinate system, one of the reference lines from which or along which distances or angles are measured: *the x-axis.* **3.** *Anatomy.* The second cervical vertebra on which the head turns. **4.** *Botany.* The main stem or central part of a plant, about which plant parts, such as branches, are arranged. —*Adjective* **axial.**

ax•on (ăk′sŏn′) The long portion of a nerve cell that carries impulses away from the body of the cell. Also called *nerve fiber.*

az•i•muth (ăz′ə-məth) The horizontal angle measured clockwise between a celestial object and the northern point of the horizon as seen by the observer. Azimuth and altitude are the coordinates used to navigate with respect to the stars.

az•ur•ite (ăzh′ə-rīt′) A dark-blue copper carbonate mineral having a glassy luster and occurring in various forms. It is often found together with malachite. Azurite is used as a source of copper, as a gemstone, and as a dye.

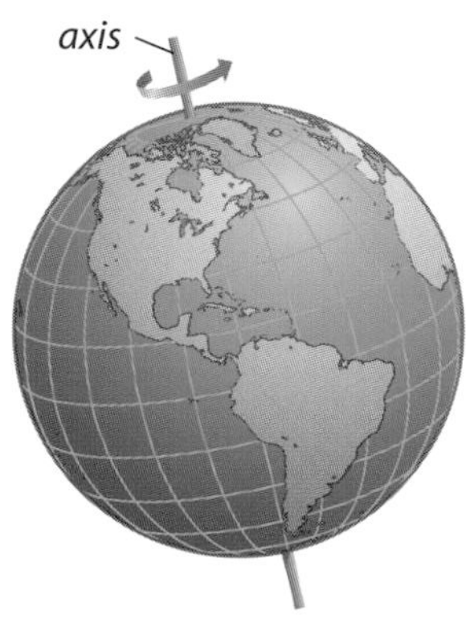

axis

B

B The symbol for **boron.**

Ba The symbol for **barium.**

Bab•bage (băb′ĭj), **Charles** 1792–1871. British mathematician, inventor, and pioneer of machine computing. In 1820 Babbage built a model of a mechanical device, called a difference engine, which was used to make repetitive calculations. Later he designed a much larger machine, called an analytical engine, which could be programmed with punched cards. Although the analytical engine was never finished, it is recognized as the forerunner of the modern computer.

Charles Babbage

ba•boon (bă-bo͞on′) Any of several large terrestrial monkeys of Africa and Asia. Baboons have a dog-like muzzle, a short tail, and bare calluses on the buttocks.

ba•cil•lus (bə-sĭl′əs) *Plural* **bacilli** (bə-sĭl′ī′) Any of various bacteria that are shaped like a rod.

back•bone (băk′bōn′) *See* **vertebral column.**

Ba•con (bā′kən), **Roger** 1214?–1292. English scientist and philosopher who is noted for the wide range of his knowledge and writing on scientific topics. Bacon asserted that mathematics is fundamental to science and that experimentation is essential to test scientific theories, ideas that were very advanced for his time. He did important work in the field of optics, explaining the principles of reflection and refraction and describing spectacles before they came into use. Bacon is also credited with predicting the invention of the airplane, the microscope, and the telescope.

bac•te•ri•ol•o•gy (băk-tîr′ē-ŏl′ə-jē) The scientific study of bacteria, especially in relation to disease.

bac•te•ri•um (băk-tîr′ē-əm) *Plural* **bacteria.** Any of a large group of one-celled organisms that lack a cell nucleus, reproduce by fission or by forming spores, and in some cases cause disease. They are found in all living things and in all of the Earth's environments, and usually live off

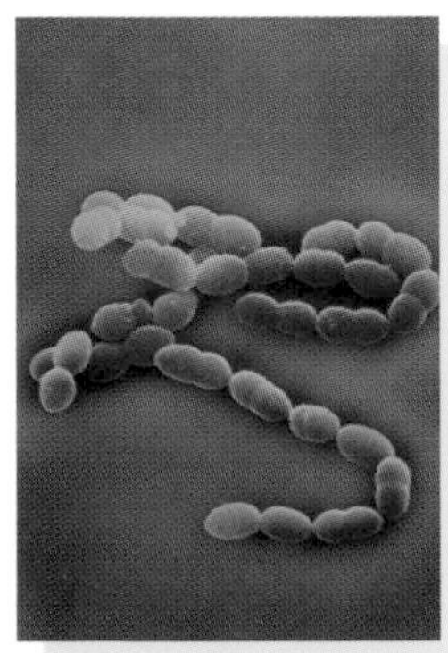

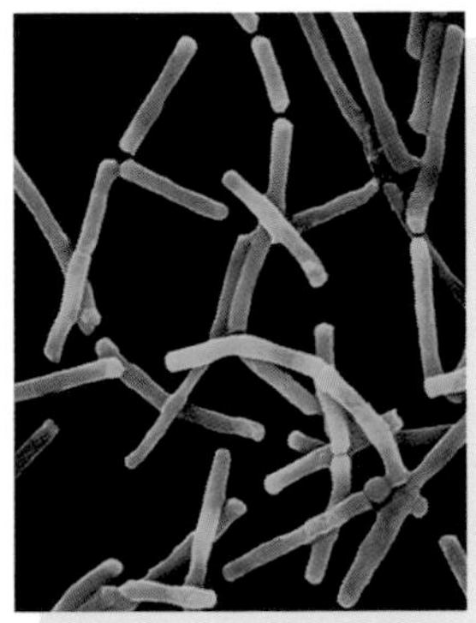

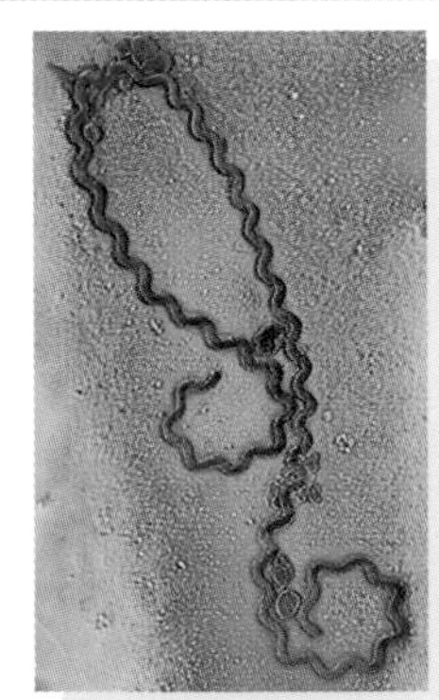

bacterium

left to right: *the three main types of bacteria—cocci (sphere-shaped), bacilli (rod-shaped), and spirilla (spiral-shaped)*

USAGE

bacterium/bacteria

It is important to remember that *bacteria* is the plural of *bacterium,* and that saying *a bacteria* is incorrect. It is correct to say *The soil sample contains millions of bacteria,* and *Tetanus is caused by a bacterium.*

other organisms. Bacteria make up most of the kingdom of prokaryotes. —*Adjective* **bacterial.**

bad•lands (băd′lăndz′) An area of heavily eroded land with numerous gullies or streambeds between ridges of variously colored sand, silt, and clay. Badlands usually form in dry regions where sudden, heavy rains wash away soil and keep most vegetation from becoming established.

Baeke•land (bāk′lănd′), **Leo Hendrik** 1863–1944. Belgian-born American chemist who developed Bakelite, the first plastic to harden permanently after heating (1907). His invention was a versatile and inexpensive material for manufacturing products such as telephones, cameras, and furniture.

bak•ing soda (bā′kĭng) A white crystalline compound, $NaHCO_3$, chemically known as sodium bicarbonate. It is used especially in beverages and as a leavening agent to make baked goods rise. Also called *bicarbonate of soda.*

bal•ance (băl′əns) To adjust a chemical equation so that the number of each type of atom, and the total charge, on the reactant (left-hand) side of the equation matches the number and charge on the product (right-hand) side of the equation.

badlands
Badlands National Park, South Dakota

ba•leen (bə-lēn′) A flexible horny substance hanging in plates from the upper jaw of certain whales. It is used by the whales to strain plankton from seawater when feeding. Also called *whalebone.*

bal•lis•tics (bə-lĭs′tĭks) The scientific study of the characteristics of projectiles, such as bullets or missiles, and the way they move in flight.

Bal•ti•more (bôl′tə-môr′), **David** Born 1938. American microbiologist who discovered the enzyme known as reverse transcriptase, which is capable of passing information from RNA to DNA. Prior to this discovery, it was assumed that

Did You Know?

baking soda

Baking soda is probably in your kitchen or refrigerator right now. A white, chalky powder, *baking soda* is the common name for the chemical sodium bicarbonate, $NaHCO_3$. Baking soda is a base and reacts with acids in what is called *neutralization,* because both the acid and the base are converted into more neutral substances on the pH scale. Neutralization with baking soda usually produces carbon dioxide gas, which you can observe bubbling forth if you mix vinegar (an acid) and baking soda. Such reactions are used in cooking to take advantage of the gas, as in getting a cake to rise. A small amount of baking soda, about a half teaspoon, can even be mixed with water and swallowed to neutralize the acid that may cause indigestion. That neutralization reaction produces carbon dioxide gas in your stomach, which you expel—as a burp. Baking soda also has the unique ability to neutralize substances that are more basic than it is. This ability to neutralize both acids and many bases is why baking soda is so effective at reducing odors, such as those unwanted ones in your refrigerator.

Joseph Banks

information could flow only from DNA to RNA. Baltimore's work led to increased understanding of viruses that cause AIDS and certain forms of cancer.

bam•boo (băm-bōō′) Any of various tall grasses having jointed, woody, and often hollow stems. Some species of bamboo can reach heights of 100 feet (30.5 meters) or more. The young shoots of some types of bamboo are used as food.

band (bănd) A specific range of electromagnetic wavelengths or frequencies, as those used in radio broadcasting.

Banks (băngks), Sir **Joseph** 1743–1820. British botanist who took part in Captain James Cook's voyage around the world (1768–1771), during which he discovered and cataloged many species of plant and animal life.

Ban•ne•ker (băn′ĭ-kər), **Benjamin** 1731–1806. American mathematician and astronomer. He correctly predicted a solar eclipse in 1789. Banneker published an almanac from 1791 to 1802 that contained tide tables, future eclipses, and medicinal information.

Ban•ting (băn′tĭng), Sir **Frederick Grant** 1891–1941. Canadian physiologist who isolated the hormone insulin, used in the treatment of diabetes. Banting conducted research into the secretions of the pancreas, including insulin. With Charles Best, he experimented with diabetic dogs, demonstrating that insulin lowered their blood sugar. Insulin was tested and proven effective on humans within months of the first experiments with dogs.

ba•o•bab (bā′ō-băb′) An African tree having a large trunk, bulbous branches, and hard-shelled fruit with an edible pulp. The baobab has spongy wood that holds large amounts of water, and the bark can be used to make rope, mats, paper, and other items. Baobabs can live up to 3,000 years.

bar (bär) A unit used to measure atmospheric pressure. It is equal to a force of 100,000 newtons per square meter of surface area, or 0.987 atmosphere.

barb (bärb) **1.** A sharp point projecting backward, as on the stinger of a bee. **2.** One of the hair-like branches on the shaft of a feather.

bar•bel (bär′bəl) A slender, whisker-like feeler extending from the head of certain fish, such as the catfish. It is used for touch and taste.

bar•bi•tu•rate (bär-bĭch′ər-ĭt) Any of a group of drugs that reduce the activity of the nervous system and are used as sedatives. Barbiturates are highly addictive.

bar•bule (bär′byōōl) A small barb or pointed projection, especially one that fringes the edges of the barbs of feathers.

Bar•deen (bär-dēn′), **John** 1908–1991. American physicist who was one of the inventors of the transistor (1947) and later helped to develop the theory of superconductivity. Bardeen's research explained why the electrical resistance of certain materials disappears at temperatures close to absolute zero, thereby allowing a current to flow through them.

bar•ite (bâr′īt) A usually white or clear mineral consisting of barium sulfate and occurring as flattened blades. Barite also occurs in a circular pattern of crystals that looks like a flower and, when colored red by iron stains, is called a desert rose. Barite is used as a source of barium.

bar•i•um (bâr′ē-əm) A soft, silvery-white metallic element that only occurs combined with other

Benjamin Banneker

barnacle
a colony of acorn barnacles

elements, especially in barite. Barium compounds are used in x-raying the stomach and intestines and in making fireworks and white pigments. *Symbol* **Ba.** *Atomic number* 56. *See* **Periodic Table,** pages 262–263.

barium sulfate A fine, white powder, $BaSO_4$. It is used in making textiles, rubber, and plastic and in taking x-rays of the digestive tract.

bark (bärk) The protective outer covering of the trunk, branches, and roots of trees and other woody plants. Bark is usually divided into inner bark, consisting of phloem (tissue that distributes a watery mixture of sugars and growth hormones made in the leaves and buds), and outer bark, consisting of layers of dead cells from the inner bark. The outer bark protects the tree from heat, cold, insects, and other dangers.

bar•na•cle (bär′nə-kəl) Any of various small, hard-shelled crustaceans that live in the ocean and attach themselves to underwater objects, such as rocks and the bottoms of ships.

Bar•nard (bär′nərd), **Christiaan Neethling** 1923–2001. South African surgeon who performed the first successful human heart transplant, in 1967.

ba•rom•e•ter (bə-rŏm′ĭ-tər) An instrument for measuring atmospheric pressure. Barometers are used to determine height above sea level and in weather forecasting. —*Adjective* **barometric** (băr′ə-mĕt′rĭk).

bar•ri•er island (băr′ē-ər) A long, narrow sand island that is parallel to the mainland and serves to protect the coast from erosion.

barrier reef A long, narrow ridge of coral deposits parallel to the mainland and separated from it by a deep lagoon.

ba•salt (bə-sôlt′, bā′sôlt′) A dark, fine-grained, igneous rock consisting mostly of feldspar, iron, and magnesium. Basalt makes up most of the ocean floor. It commonly forms when volcanic lava becomes solid. *See Table at* **rock.**

base (bās) **1.** *Chemistry.* Any of a class of compounds that contain hydroxyl ions (OH) and are capable of neutralizing acids in solution. They react with acids and certain metals to form water and salts. Bases turn red litmus paper blue, have a bitter taste, and have a pH of greater than 7. *Compare* **acid. 2.** *Mathematics.* **a.** The side or face of a geometric figure to which an altitude is or is thought to be drawn. The base can be, but is not always, the bottom part of the figure. **b.** The number that is raised to various powers to generate the principal counting units of a number system. The base of the decimal system, for example, is 10. **c.** The number that is raised to a particular power in a given mathematical expression. In the expression a^n, *a* is the base. **3.** *Biology.* One of the purines (adenine or guanine) or pyrimidines (cytosine, thymine, or uracil) found in DNA or RNA.

base pair The pair of nitrogen-containing bases, consisting of a purine linked by hydrogen bonds to a pyrimidine, that connects the complementary strands of a DNA molecule or of hybrid molecules joining DNA and RNA. The base pairs are adenine-thymine and guanine-cytosine in DNA, and adenine-uracil and guanine-cytosine in molecules joining DNA and RNA.

Did You Know?
bat

The well-known phrase "blind as a bat" is somewhat misleading. In fact, some bats have excellent eyesight, and bats on the whole are quite skilled in moving about and hunting prey in total darkness. Using a form of natural radar called *echolocation,* the bat emits a series of very high-pitched squeaks, inaudible to human ears, which reflect off objects in the bat's path. Relying on the pattern of echoes it hears, the bat can then avoid obstacles or home in on a specific target.

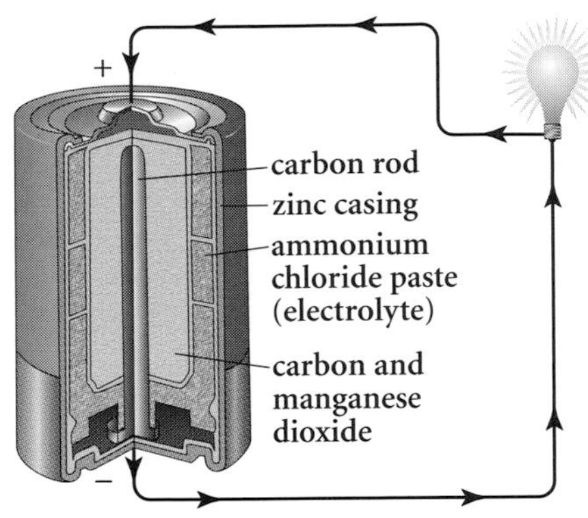

battery

Electrons flow from the zinc casing through the light bulb to the carbon rod, making the bulb glow. The zinc casing acts as a negative electrode, and the carbon rod acts as a positive electrode.

ba•sic (bā′sĭk) Having the chemical characteristics of a base; alkaline.

ba•sin (bā′sĭn) **1.** An enclosed area filled with water. **2.** A region drained by a river and the streams that flow into it. **3.** A low-lying area on the Earth's surface in which thick layers of sediment have accumulated. Some basins are bowl-shaped, and others are shaped like long valleys that have been filled in. Basins are important because they are often a source of valuable oil.

bat (băt) Any of various flying mammals that have thin wings consisting of skin that extends from the forelimbs to the hind limbs or tail. Bats are usually active at night and use echolocation to navigate.

bath•y•scaphe (băth′ĭ-skăf′, băth′ĭ-skāf′) A free-diving vessel used to explore the ocean at great depths. Bathyscaphes have a large floating hull attached to a round observation capsule that can hold one or more people.

bath•y•sphere (băth′ĭ-sfîr′) A spherical diving chamber in which people are lowered on a cable to explore the ocean depths.

bat•ter•y (băt′ə-rē) A device containing an electric cell or a series of electric cells that supplies a direct current by converting chemical, thermal, nuclear, or solar energy into electric energy. Common household batteries, such as those used in a flashlight, are usually made of dry cells (the chemicals producing the current are made into a paste). In other batteries, such as car batteries, these chemicals are in liquid form.

Did You Know?

battery

Where do *batteries* get the power to make things work? From chemical reactions that go on inside them. The substances inside a battery are arranged in such a way that when they react with each other they pull electrons away from the battery's positive terminal and push them toward the negative terminal. If the battery is not connected to anything, the reaction doesn't go on very long; the electrons gathered at the negative terminal repel any additional ones that further reactions would carry there. But if you connect the two terminals with a wire, electrons will flow along the wire from negative to positive. On the way, they give up some of their energy to power whatever device you've connected—a light bulb or CD player, for instance. Eventually, the chemical reactions inside the battery change the nature of the positive and negative terminals and of the chemicals between them, making them unable to generate power. In rechargeable batteries, you can restore the power-generating capacity of the terminals and the chemicals by running electrical current through the battery backwards.

baux•ite (bôk′sīt′) A soft, whitish to reddish-brown rock composed mainly of hydrous aluminum oxides. Bauxite forms from the breakdown of clays and is a major source of aluminum.

bay (bā) A body of water partially enclosed by land but having a wide outlet to the sea. A bay is usually smaller than a gulf.

bay•ou (bī′o͞o) A sluggish, marshy stream connected with a river, lake, or gulf. Bayous are common in the southern United States.

B cell Any of the lymphocytes that develop into plasma cells in the presence of a specific antigen, such as a bacterium or virus. The plasma cells then produce antibodies that attack or neutralize the antigen. B cells mature in the bone marrow before being released into the blood. *See Note at* **antibody.**

B complex *See* **vitamin B complex.**

Be The symbol for **beryllium.**

beach (bēch) The area of accumulated sand, stone, or gravel deposited along a shore by the action of waves and tides. Beaches usually slope gently toward the body of water they border and have a concave shape when viewed in cross section.

beak (bēk) **1.** The bill of a bird. **2.** A similar, often horny part forming the mouth of other animals, such as turtles and octopuses.

beak•er (bē′kər) A wide, cylindrical glass container with a pouring lip, used especially in laboratories.

bear (bâr) **1.** Any of various large mammals having a shaggy coat, a rounded head, and a short tail. Bears eat plants and other animals, especially insects and small rodents. Bears walk with the entire lower surface of their foot touching the ground. **2.** Any of various other animals, such as the koala, that resemble a true bear.

Beau•fort scale (bō′fərt) A scale for classifying the force of the wind, ranging from 0 (calm) to 12 (hurricane). The scale was devised in 1805 as a means of describing the effect of different wind velocities on ships at sea.

bea•ver (bē′vər) A large aquatic rodent having thick brown fur, webbed hind feet, and a broad flat tail. Beavers feed on bark and twigs. They have sharp front teeth adapted for gnawing and cutting down trees, which they use in constructing dams and lodges with underwater exits.

bec•que•rel (bĕ-krĕl′, bĕk′ə-rĕl′) A unit used to measure the rate of radioactive decay. Radioactive decay is measured by the rate at which the atoms making up a radioactive substance are transformed into different atoms. One becquerel is equal to one of these atomic transformations per second.

Bec•que•rel (bĕ-krĕl′, bĕk′ə-rĕl′) Family of French physicists, including **Antoine César** (1788–1878), one of the first investigators of electrochemistry; his son **Alexandre Edmond** (1820–1891), noted for his research on phosphorescence; and his grandson **Antoine Henri** (1852–1908), who discovered spontaneous radioactivity in uranium.

bed (bĕd) **1.** A layer of sediments or rock that extends under a large area and has other layers below and sometimes above it: *a bed of coal.* **2.** The bottom of a body of water.

bed•rock (bĕd′rŏk′) The solid rock that lies beneath the soil and other loose material on the Earth's surface.

bee (bē) Any of several winged, often stinging insects that have a hairy body and gather pollen and nectar from flowers. Most bees are solitary, but some bees, such as the honeybee, live in colonies with an organized social structure, consisting of workers, drones, and a queen. Bees are important pollinators of flowering plants. *See also* **drone, queen, worker.**

bee•tle (bēt′l) Any of numerous insects having biting mouthparts and hard forewings that cover the hind wings straight down the back when at rest. Beetles vary in size from nearly microscopic to several inches in length. *See Note at* **biomass.**

be•hav•ior (bĭ-hāv′yər) **1.** The actions displayed by an organism in response to its environment. **2.** One of these actions. Feeding and mating are examples of animal behaviors. **3.** The manner in which a physical system, such as a gas, a subatomic particle, or a wave, acts under specific conditions.

Bell (bĕl), **Alexander Graham** 1847–1922. Scottish-born American scientist and inventor. Bell's lifelong interest in the education of deaf people led him to conceive the idea of transmitting speech by electric waves. In 1876 his experiments with a telegraph resulted in his invention of the telephone. He later produced the first successful sound recorder, called a graphophone. Bell also invented the photophone, which trans-

Alexander Graham Bell

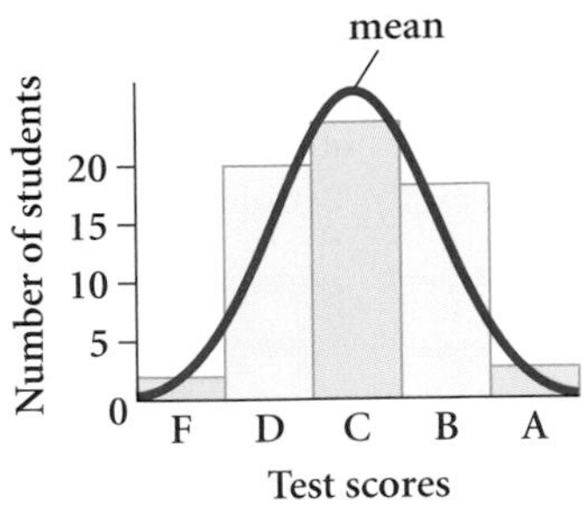

■ **bell curve**
graph showing the distribution of a set of test scores where the average grade was a C

mitted speech by light rays; the audiometer, an early hearing aid; and many other devices.

bel•la•don•na (bĕl′ə-dŏn′ə) Any of several alkaloids produced by the herb known as deadly nightshade. The alkaloids are poisonous but are also used in medicine, for example to increase the heart rate and treat Parkinson's disease.

Bell Bur•nell (bĕl′ bûr′nĕl′), **Susan Jocelyn** Born 1943. British astronomer. In 1967, working with astronomer Antony Hewish, she discovered the first pulsar.

bell curve A symmetrical bell-shaped curve that represents the typical distribution and frequency of the values of a set of random data. It slopes downward from a point in the middle corresponding to the mean.

be•nign (bĭ-nīn′) Not likely to spread or get worse; not malignant: *a benign tumor.*

ben•thos (bĕn′thŏs′) **1.** The bottom of a sea or lake. **2.** The organisms living on sea or lake bottoms.

ben•zene (bĕn′zēn′) A clear, colorless, flammable liquid, C_6H_6. It is derived from petroleum and used to make detergents, insecticides, motor fuels, and many other chemical products. ❖ The six carbon atoms of benzene are arranged in a ring, called a **benzene ring,** in which each atom bonds to its neighbors to form a hexagon. This ring is the basis of many organic compounds. —*Adjective* **benzyl.**

ben•zo•ic acid (bĕn-zō′ĭk) An aromatic, white, crystalline acid, $C_7H_6O_2$, used in preserving food, as a cosmetic, and in medicine.

ber•i•ber•i (bĕr′ē-bĕr′ē) A disease caused by a lack of thiamine in the diet. It causes nerve damage and circulatory problems.

ber•ke•li•um (bər-kē′lē-əm, bûrk′lē-əm) A synthetic, radioactive metallic element of the actinide series that is produced from americium, curium, or plutonium. Its most stable isotope has a half-life of about 1,400 years. *Symbol* **Bk.** *Atomic number* 97. *See* **Periodic Table,** pages 262–263.

Ber•noul•li (bər-nōō′lē) Family of Swiss mathematicians. **Jacques** (or **Jakob**) (1654–1705) was

Did You Know?
benzene ring

One of the key insights in the history of chemistry came in a dream. In 1865 chemists knew that a *benzene* molecule consisted of six carbon atoms and six hydrogen atoms. They also knew that carbon atoms have four bonds by which they can join with other atoms. But none of the chain-like structures that chemists knew about then worked with these numbers of atoms and bonds. The German chemist Friedrich August Kekulé had thought about this problem for a long time. One night he fell asleep and dreamed of snakes. One snake bit its own tail, forming a circle. Awakened by the image, Kekulé realized that the six carbon atoms in benzene formed a ring. Each carbon atom is bonded to a carbon atom on either side, forming a hexagon, and to a hydrogen atom extending out from the hexagon. Modern chemistry owes much of its power to the understanding of ringed carbon compounds that started with Kekulé's dream.

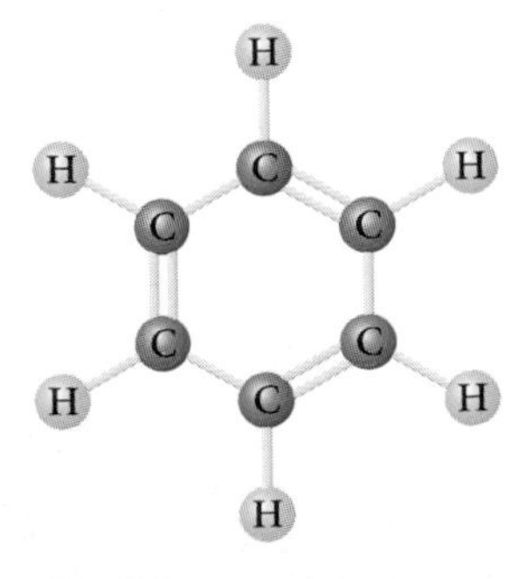

a major developer of calculus and made an important contribution to probability theory. His brother **Jean** (or **Johann**) (1667–1748) also developed calculus and contributed to the study of complex numbers and trigonometry. Jean's son **Daniel** (1700–1782) was one of the first scientists to understand the concept of conservation of energy.

ber•ry (bĕr′ē) **1a.** A fruit that develops from a single ovary and has many seeds in fleshy pulp. Grapes, bananas, tomatoes, and blueberries are true berries. **b.** Any small, juicy, fleshy fruit, such as a raspberry or strawberry, regardless of its botanical structure. **2.** A seed or dried kernel of certain kinds of grain or other plants such as wheat, barley, or coffee.

ber•yl (bĕr′əl) A usually green or bluish-green mineral that is a silicate of beryllium and aluminum. Beryl occurs as transparent to translucent prisms in igneous and metamorphic rocks. Transparent varieties, such as emeralds, are valued as gems. Beryl is the main source of the element beryllium.

be•ryl•li•um (bə-rĭl′ē-əm) A hard, lightweight, steel-gray metallic element that is an alkaline-earth metal and is found in various minerals, especially beryl. It has a high melting point and resists corrosion. Beryllium is used to make sturdy, lightweight alloys and to control the speed of neutrons inside the core of nuclear reactors. *Symbol* **Be.** *Atomic number* 4. *See* **Periodic Table,** pages 262–263.

Ber•ze•li•us (bər-zē′lē-əs), Baron **Jöns Jakob** 1779–1848. Swedish chemist who is regarded as one of the founders of modern chemistry. Berzelius developed the concepts of the ion and of ionic compounds and made extensive determinations of atomic weights. In 1811 he introduced the classical system of chemical symbols, in which the names of elements are identified by one or two letters.

Bes•se•mer process (bĕs′ə-mər) A method for making steel by forcing compressed air through molten iron to burn out carbon and other impurities.

Best (bĕst), **Charles Herbert** 1899–1978. American-born Canadian physiologist noted for his work with Frederick Banting on the isolation and use of insulin. Later in his career, Best discovered the vitamin choline and the enzyme histaminase, which breaks down histamine.

USAGE

berry

Most people think of a berry as a small, round fruit that grows on bushes and is eaten at breakfast or for dessert. If you ask them if they want berries with their cereal, they wouldn't expect you to put in a cucumber or tomato. But to a botanist, cucumbers and tomatoes are in fact berries, while strawberries and raspberries are not. How can this be? Scientists have to be careful about the names they use for things, and sometimes the precise meaning that they give to a word is different from the general meaning that ordinary people understand. That is the case with the word *berry.* To a botanist, a berry is a fleshy fruit consisting of a single ovary that has multiple seeds. Other true berries besides cucumbers and tomatoes are bananas, oranges, grapes, and blueberries. However, many fruits that are popularly called berries have a different structure and thus are not true berries. For example, strawberries and raspberries are aggregate fruits, developed from multiple ovaries of a single flower. The mulberry is not a true berry, either. It is a multiple fruit, like the pineapple, and is made up of the ovaries of several individual flowers.

be•ta carotene (bā′tə) A form of carotene widely found in plants and animals. Beta carotene is most efficiently converted to vitamin A in the liver.

beta particle A high-speed electron emitted by an atomic nucleus undergoing radioactive decay. A beta particle is created when a neutron becomes a proton. Beta particles have greater speed and penetrating power than alpha particles. ❖ The process by which a neutron becomes a proton and emits an electron is called **beta decay.** Beta decay results in the atomic number of an element being increased by one and its mass number staying the same. *See more at* **radiation, radioactive decay.**

beta ray A stream of beta particles.

Be•tel•geuse (bēt′l-jo͞oz′) A reddish, very bright variable star in the constellation Orion. It is a supergiant. *See Note at* **Rigel.**

Be•the (bā′tə), **Hans Albrecht** 1906–2005. German-born American physicist who was instrumental in the development of quantum physics. Bethe discovered that the sun and other stars derive their energy from a series of nuclear reactions, which came to be known as the carbon cycle, or Bethe cycle. Bethe also played an important role in the development of the atomic bomb, later working to educate the public about the threat of nuclear weapons.

Bh The symbol for **bohrium.**

Bhas•ka•ra (bäs′kə-rə) 1114–1185? Indian mathematician who wrote the first work containing a systematic use of the decimal system.

Bi The symbol for **bismuth.**

bi– A prefix meaning "two." It is often used to form adjectives meaning "having two of" or "having double" something, such as in *bilateral,* having two sides.

bi•car•bon•ate (bī-kär′bə-nāt′) The group HCO_3 or a compound containing it, such as sodium bicarbonate.

bicarbonate of soda *See* **baking soda.**

bi•ceps (bī′sĕps′) The muscle at the front of the upper arm that bends the elbow. The biceps has two points of attachment to bone at one end.

bi•cus•pid (bī-kŭs′pĭd) A tooth having two points or cusps, especially a premolar.

bi•en•ni•al (bī-ĕn′ē-əl) *Adjective.* **1.** Completing a life cycle normally in two growing seasons. —*Noun.* **2.** A biennial plant. Carrots, parsnips, and sugar beets are some examples of biennials.

big bang (bĭg) The violent explosion of an extremely small, hot, and dense body of matter between 12 and 18 billion years ago. It is viewed as the earliest event in a widely held model of the origin of the universe. *Compare* **steady state universe.**

Big Dipper A group of seven stars in the constellation Ursa Major. Four stars form the bowl and three form the handle in the outline of a dipper.

bi•lat•er•al symmetry (bī-lăt′ər-əl) Symmetrical arrangement of an organism or part of an organism along a central axis. A bilaterally symmetrical organism or part is divided into two equal halves. *Compare* **radial symmetry.**

Did You Know?

big bang

It's a chilling thought: In the 1920s, astronomers found that wherever they looked in space, distant galaxies were rapidly moving away from Earth. In other words, the universe was getting larger and larger. By calculating the speed of several galaxies and working back from there, astronomers learned that this expansion began between 12 and 18 billion years ago, when the entire universe was smaller than a dime and almost infinitely dense. According to the widely accepted theory of the *big bang*, a massive explosion kicked off the expansion and was the origin of space and time. Now scientists must figure out how much mass the universe contains in order to see what lies ahead. If there is enough mass, the gravity attracting all the pieces to each other will eventually stop the expansion and pull all the pieces of the universe back together in a "big crunch." The universe would then be a closed universe. However, there may not be enough mass to support a universe that is closed. If that is the case, then an open universe would expand forever, and all the galaxies and stars would drift away from each other and become dark and cold.

bile (bīl) A bitter, alkaline, greenish fluid produced by the liver and discharged into the small intestine, where it helps to digest fats and neutralize acids. A portion of the bile secreted by the liver is stored in the gallbladder.

bill (bĭl) The horny, projecting mouthparts of a bird. Bills have different sizes and shapes depending on how birds feed and what they eat.

bi•na•ry (bī′nə-rē) *Adjective.* **1.** Having two parts. **2.** *Mathematics.* Based on the number 2 or the binary number system. —*Noun.* **3.** *Astronomy.* A binary star.

binary digit Either of the digits 0 or 1, used in the binary number system.

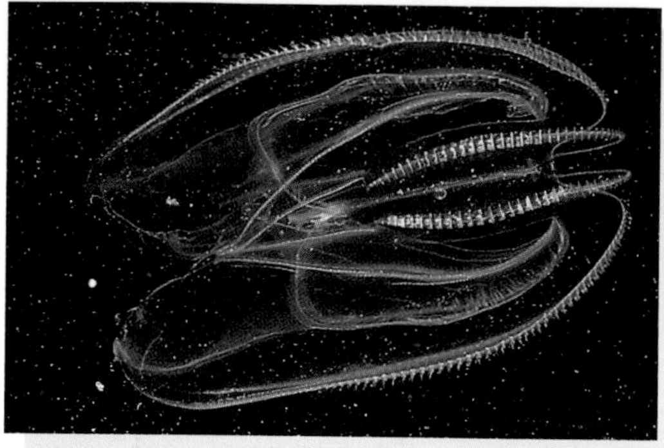

■ **bioluminescence**
Special cells give off light in the sea walnut, a kind of comb jelly.

binary fission *See* **fission** (sense 2).

binary number system A method of representing numbers that has 2 as its base and uses only the digits 0 and 1. Each successive digit represents a power of 2. For example, 10011 represents $(1 \times 2^4) + (0 \times 2^3) + (0 \times 2^2) + (1 \times 2^1) + (1 \times 2^0)$, or $16 + 0 + 0 + 2 + 1$, or 19.

binary star A system of two stars that orbit a common center of mass. The pair often appears as a single star to the unaided eye.

bin•oc•u•lar (bə-nŏk′yə-lər) *Adjective.* **1.** Relating to or involving both eyes at once: *binocular vision.* —*Noun.* **2.** An optical device, such as a pair of field glasses, designed for use by both eyes at once and consisting of two small telescopes. Often used in the plural as *binoculars.*

bi•no•mi•al (bī-nō′mē-əl) A mathematical expression having two terms, such as $3a + 2b$.

binomial nomenclature The system used in science to name an organism, consisting of two terms, the first being the genus and the second the species. *Passer domesticus,* the scientific name of the common house sparrow, is an example of binomial nomenclature.

bi•o•chem•is•try (bī′ō-kĕm′ĭ-strē) The scientific study of the chemical composition of living matter and of the chemical processes that go on in living organisms.

bi•o•de•grad•a•ble (bī′ō-dĭ-grā′də-bəl) Capable of being decomposed by the action of biological agents, especially bacteria: *a biodegradable detergent.*

bi•o•di•ver•si•ty (bī′ō-dĭ-vûr′sĭ-tē) The number and variety of different organisms found within a specified geographic region.

bi•o•eth•ics (bī′ō-ĕth′ĭks) The study of the ethics surrounding medical research and health-care practices.

bi•o•gen•e•sis (bī′ō-jĕn′ĭ-sĭs) Generation of living organisms from other living organisms.

bi•o•ge•og•ra•phy (bī′ō-jē-ŏg′rə-fē) The scientific study of the geographic distribution of plant and animal life.

bi•o•log•i•cal clock (bī′ə-lŏj′ĭ-kəl) An internal system of organisms that controls the cycle of various functions, such as sleep cycles in mammals and photosynthesis in plants. *See Note at* **circadian rhythm.**

bi•ol•o•gy (bī-ŏl′ə-jē) The scientific study of life and of living organisms. Botany, zoology, and ecology are all branches of biology.

Did You Know?
biomass

The matter that makes up the Earth's living organisms is called *biomass.* Insects alone make up an amazing amount of biomass. The biologist J.B.S. Haldane was once asked if the study of life on the Earth gave him any insights into God. Haldane replied jokingly that his research revealed that God must have "an inordinate fondness for beetles." Haldane made his comment because there are more beetle species—almost 400,000 now known—than species of any other animal. And beetles are only one kind of insect, of which there are almost one million species that are known and perhaps many millions more yet to be discovered. The number of individual insects is mind-boggling, about 10 quintillion (that's 10,000,000,000,000,000,000). So all those little critters add up. Insects together probably have more biomass than any other type of land animal. And if we added up all the weights of all the people in the world, the biomass of all the insects would be 300 times as great.

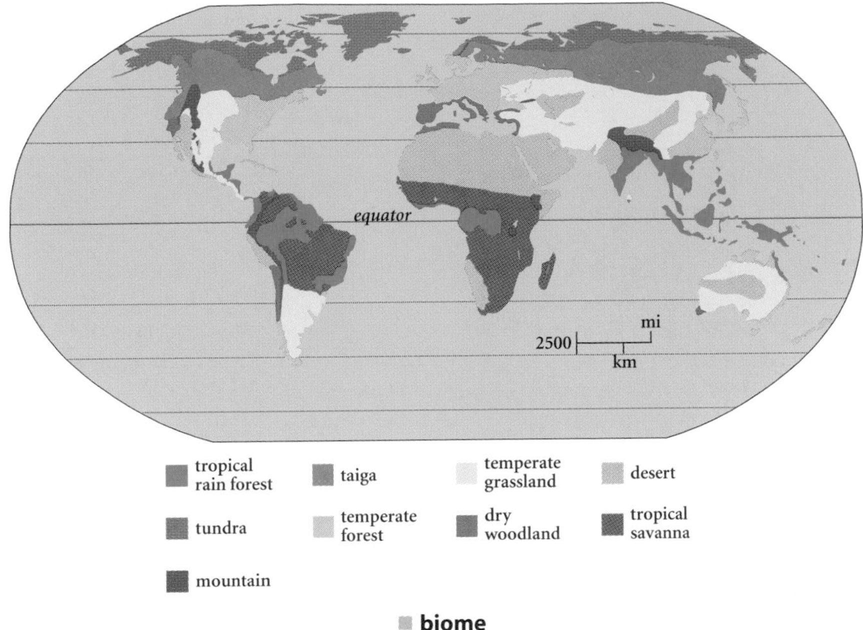

biome

bi•o•lu•mi•nes•cence (bī′ō-lo͞o′mə-nĕs′əns) Emission of light by living organisms, such as fireflies, glowworms, and certain fish, jellyfish, plankton, fungi, and bacteria. It occurs when chemical compounds react and give off light.

bi•o•mass (bī′ō-măs′) **1.** The total amount of living material in a given habitat. **2.** Organic materials, such as plant matter and manure, that have not become fossilized and are used as a fuel or energy source. Biomass fuels produce less carbon dioxide than some fossil fuels, such as petroleum.

bi•ome (bī′ōm′) A large community of plants and animals that occupies a distinct region defined by its climate and dominant vegetation. Grassland, tundra, desert, tropical rain forest, and deciduous and coniferous forests are all examples of biomes.

bi•o•me•chan•ics (bī′ō-mĭ-kăn′ĭks) The scientific study of the mechanics of motion in humans and other animals. Biomechanics is sometimes used by athletes to help analyze and improve their performance.

bi•on•ics (bī-ŏn′ĭks) The use of a system or design found in nature, such as the ability of plants to store solar energy, as a model for designing artificial systems, such as machines. —*Adjective* **bionic.**

bi•o•phys•ics (bī′ō-fĭz′ĭks) The science of using the laws of physics to understand biological processes. Biophysics involves the study of specific characteristics of living things, such as the ability of bats to navigate using echolocation.

bi•op•sy (bī′ŏp′sē) A sample of tissue removed by a surgeon from a living body for examination and diagnosis.

bi•o•rhythm (bī′ō-rĭ*th*′əm) A recurring biological process, such as sleep, that is controlled by the circadian rhythms of an organism.

bi•o•sphere (bī′ə-sfîr′) The parts of the land, sea, and atmosphere in which organisms live.

bi•o•tech•nol•o•gy (bī′ō-tĕk-nŏl′ə-jē) **1.** The use of a living organism to solve an engineering problem or perform an industrial task. Using bacteria that feed on hydrocarbons to clean up an oil spill is one example of biotechnology. **2.** The use of biological substances to engineer or manufacture a product or substance, as when cells that produce antibodies are cloned in order to study their effects on cancer cells. *See more at* **genetic engineering.**

bi•ot•ic (bī-ŏt′ĭk) Made up of living organisms; living: *the study of the effects of pollution on the biotic community of a marsh.*

bi•o•tin (bī′ə-tĭn) A vitamin belonging to the vitamin B complex that is important in the metabolism of carbohydrates and fats. It is found in liver, egg yolks, milk, yeast, and some vegetables.

bi•o•tite (bī′ə-tīt′) A dark-brown to black mica found in igneous and metamorphic rocks.

bi•ped (bī′pĕd′) An animal having two feet, such as a bird or human.

bi•ped•al (bī-pĕd′l) Standing or walking on two feet. ❖ The use of two feet for standing and walking is known as **bipedal locomotion.** The evolution of bipedal locomotion in humans was aided by the development of an upright head and backbone and of an arched foot.

bi•pin•nate (bī-pĭn′āt′) Relating to compound leaves that grow opposite each other on a larger stem; twice pinnate. Bipinnate leaves have a feathery appearance. The honey locust often has bipinnate leaves.

bird (bûrd) Any of numerous warm-blooded, egg-laying vertebrate animals that have wings for forelimbs, a body covered with feathers, a hard bill covering the jaw, and a four-chambered heart.

bis•muth (bĭz′məth) A brittle, pinkish-white, crystalline metallic element that occurs in nature as a free metal and in various ores. Bismuth has the greatest resistance to being magnetized of all metals and has the highest atomic number of all stable elements. It is used to make low-melting alloys for fire-safety devices. *Symbol* **Bi.** *Atomic number* 83. *See* **Periodic Table,** pages 262–263.

bit (bĭt) The smallest unit of computer memory. A bit holds one of two possible values, either of the binary digits 0 or 1. *See Note at* **byte.**

bit•map (bĭt′măp′) *Computer Science.* A set of bits that represents a graphic image, with each bit or group of bits corresponding to a pixel in the image.

bi•tu•men (bĭ-to͞o′mən) Any of various flammable mixtures of hydrocarbons and other substances found in asphalt and tar. Bitumens occur naturally or are produced from petroleum and coal.

bi•tu•mi•nous coal (bĭ-to͞o′mə-nəs) A soft type of coal that burns with a smoky, yellow flame. Bituminous coal is the most abundant form of coal, but because of its high sulfur content its use can contribute to air pollution and acid rain. *Compare* **anthracite, lignite.**

Did You Know?

birds: modern-day dinosaurs?

Did birds evolve from dinosaurs? Most scientists who research the origin of birds think so, and they have lots of evidence to support this view. Small meat-eating dinosaurs and primitive birds share about 20 characteristics that neither group shares with other kinds of animals. Just a few of these include hollow bones, the position of the pelvis, the structure of their eggs, the shape of the shoulder blade, and a collarbone shaped into a wishbone. Dinosaurs had scales, and birds have modified scales—their feathers—and scaly feet. And it may be that at least some dinosaurs had feathers. Recently discovered fossils of a small dinosaur show that it had a feather-like covering. In fact, some primitive fossil birds and small meat-eating dinosaurs are so alike that it is difficult to tell them apart based on their skeletons alone.

bi•va•lent (bī-vā′lənt) *Chemistry.* Having a valence of 2.

bi•valve (bī′vălv′) A mollusk, such as a clam or oyster, whose shell consists of two halves hinged together. *Compare* **univalve.**

Bk The symbol for **berkelium.**

Black (blăk), **Joseph** 1728–1799. Scottish chemist. In 1756 he discovered carbon dioxide, which he called "fixed air." In addition to further studies of carbon dioxide, Black formulated the concepts of latent heat and specific heat.

Black Death A widespread epidemic of bubonic plague that occurred in several outbreaks between 1347 and 1400. It originated in Asia and then swept through Europe, where it killed about a third of the population.

black dwarf The celestial object that remains after a white dwarf has used up all of its energy and no longer gives off detectable radiation. *See Note at* **dwarf star.**

black hole An extremely dense celestial object that has a gravitational field so strong that nothing can escape, not even light. A black hole is formed by the collapse of a massive star's core in a supernova. *See more at* **star.**

black lung A lung disease of coal miners that is caused by the long-term inhalation of coal dust.

black•wa•ter (blăk′wô′tər) Wastewater from flushed toilets. *See Note at* **graywater.**

Black•well (blăck′wĕl′), **Elizabeth** 1821–1910. British-born American physician who was the first woman to be awarded a medical doctorate in modern times (1849). She founded an infirmary for women and children in New York City that her sister **Emily Blackwell** (1826–1910), also a physician, directed. Emily Blackwell was the first woman doctor to perform major surgeries on a regular basis.

Elizabeth Blackwell

black widow A very poisonous spider, the female of which has a black body, typically with a red, hourglass-shaped mark on the underside. The female often eats the male after mating.

Did You Know?

black hole

One of the strangest objects in the universe is the burnt-out remnant of a large star, known as a *black hole.* The name comes from the fact that the star collapses into itself, becoming so dense that its gravitational pull keeps even light from escaping. And if light can't get out, then nothing that ever enters the black hole would ever escape. Rockets to the moon or Mars need to achieve what is called *escape velocity,* the speed necessary to overcome the Earth's gravity. But since nothing can ever go faster than the speed of light, nothing could ever go fast enough to reach the escape velocity necessary to pull out of a black hole. Here's how dense a black hole is: the sun has a diameter of about 864,000 miles (1,390,000 kilometers); for it to be as dense as a black hole, its entire mass would have to be squeezed down to a ball less than two miles across.

blad•der (blăd′ər) **1.** A sac-shaped organ that stores the urine secreted by the kidneys, found in all vertebrates except birds and a few species of mammals known as monotremes. In mammals, the bladder is connected to each kidney by a ureter. **2.** An air bladder.

blade (blād) **1.** The expanded part of a leaf or petal. *See more at* **leaf. 2.** The leaf of grasses and similar plants.

blas•tu•la (blăs′chə-lə) *Plural* **blastulas** *or* **blastulae** (blăs′chə-lē′) An embryo at the stage immediately following the division of the fertilized egg cell, consisting of a ball-shaped layer of cells around a fluid-filled cavity. *Compare* **gastrula.**

blight (blīt) **1.** Any of numerous plant diseases that cause leaves, stems, fruits, and tissues to wither and die. Rust, mildew, and smut are blights. **2.** The bacterium, fungus, or virus that causes such a disease.

blind spot (blīnd) A point on the retina that is not sensitive to light. The optic nerve attaches to the retina at this point.

block and tackle (blŏk) A device consisting of a fixed pulley and a movable one, in which the rope attached to the load is passed over the fixed pulley, around the movable pulley, then back around the fixed one. Each pulley can have multiple grooves or wheels for the rope to pass over additional times. The more times the rope is passed around the two pulleys, the less effort is needed to raise a load.

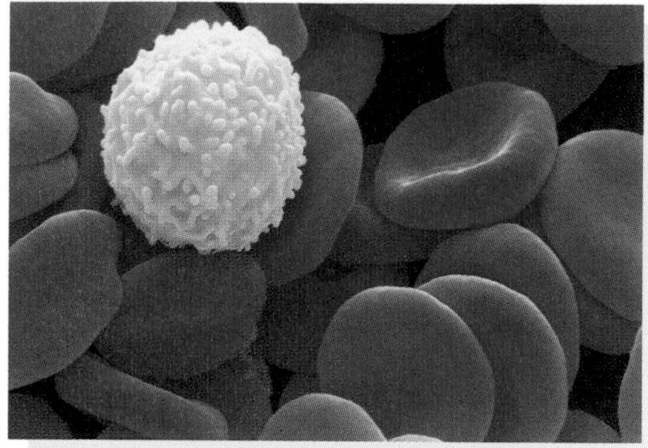

■ **blood cell**
white blood cell surrounded by red blood cells

blood (blŭd) **1.** The fluid that circulates through the body of a mammal or other vertebrate animal by the action of the heart, carrying oxygen and nutrients to the body's cells and removing waste products from them. In humans and other vertebrates, blood consists of plasma containing red blood cells, white blood cells, and platelets. **2.** A fluid that is similar in function in many invertebrate animals.

blood cell Any of the cells contained in blood; a red blood cell or white blood cell.

blood clot A group of blood cells and platelets that clump together to form a clot, usually in a blood vessel. Blood clots can interfere with the circulation of blood.

blood gas Any of the dissolved gases in blood plasma, especially oxygen and carbon dioxide.

blood group *See* **blood type.**

blood plasma The clear, liquid part of the blood, composed mainly of water and proteins, in which the blood cells are suspended. The blood plasma of mammals also contains platelets.

blood pressure The pressure of the blood in the vessels, especially the arteries, as it circulates through the body. Blood pressure varies with the strength of the heartbeat, the amount of blood being pumped, and the health of the blood vessels. *See more at* **high blood pressure.**

blood serum Blood plasma, especially blood plasma from which factors that cause clotting of the blood have been removed.

blood type Any of the four main types into which human blood is divided: A, B, AB, and O. Blood types are based on the presence or absence of certain substances, called antigens, on red blood cells. Also called *blood group.*

Did You Know?
blood types

Blood transfusions used to be a doctor's treatment of last resort, since they often caused people to get sick and die. But in the 1890s, a scientist named Karl Landsteiner began to solve the transfusion puzzle. He found that all human red blood cells belonged to one of four groups, or *blood types,* which he named A, B, AB, and O. The types refer to substances, called *antigens,* found on the surface of these cells. Antibodies circulating in a person's blood normally recognize the antigens in that same person's blood cells and don't react with them. However, if a person with one blood type is given blood of another type, the antibodies bind to the foreign antigens, causing clumping of the blood and other serious reactions. Thus the key to the transfusion puzzle is to give a person blood that has matching antigens. Today, hospitals always test a blood sample before a transfusion to make sure there is a good match.

blood vessel An elastic tube or passage in the body through which blood circulates; an artery, a vein, or a capillary.

blow•hole (blō′hōl′) **1.** A hole or one of a pair of holes used for breathing and located on top of the head of whales, porpoises, and dolphins. **2.** A hole in ice to which aquatic mammals come to breathe.

blub•ber (blŭb′ər) The thick layer of fat between the skin and the muscle layers of whales and other marine mammals. It insulates the animal from heat loss and serves as a food reserve.

blue-green alga (blo͞o′grēn′) *See* **cyanobacterium.**

blue shift A decrease in the wavelength of radiation emitted by an approaching celestial body as a result of the Doppler effect. Objects appear

■ **blowhole**
close-up of a beluga whale's blowhole

bluish because the shorter wavelengths of light are at the blue end of the visible spectrum. *Compare* **red shift.**

bog (bôg) An area of wet, spongy ground consisting mainly of decayed or decaying moss and other vegetation. Bogs form as the dead vegetation sinks to the bottom of a lake or pond, where it decays to form peat.

Bohr (bôr), **Niels Henrik David** 1885–1962. Danish physicist who investigated atomic structure and radiation. Bohr discovered that electrons orbit the nucleus of an atom at set distances, changing levels only when energy is lost or gained, and emitting or absorbing radiation in the process. His concepts were fundamental to the later development of quantum theory.

bohr•i•um (bôr′ē-əm) A synthetic, radioactive element that is produced by bombarding bismuth with chromium ions. Its most stable isotope has a half-life of 0.44 second. *Symbol* **Bh.** *Atomic number* 107. *See* **Periodic Table,** pages 262–263.

boil (boil) *Verb.* **1.** To change from a liquid to a gaseous state by heating or being heated to the boiling point. —*Noun.* **2.** The act or condition of boiling: *brought the water to a boil.*

boil•ing point (boi′lĭng) The temperature at which a liquid changes to a vapor or gas. As the temperature of a liquid rises, the pressure of escaping vapor also rises, and at the boiling point the pressure of the escaping vapor is equal to that exerted on the liquid by the surrounding air, causing bubbles to form. Typically boiling points are measured at sea level. At higher altitudes, where atmospheric pressure is lower, boiling

BIOGRAPHY

Niels Bohr

Before 1911 scientists thought that atoms were organized a bit like a plum pudding, with a mixture of electrons, protons, and neutrons loosely stuck together. Then Ernest Rutherford discovered the atomic nucleus and developed a model of the atom that was similar to the solar system, with negatively charged electrons orbiting a central nucleus the way planets revolve around the sun. Niels Bohr became interested in Rutherford's model, but it puzzled him because according to the laws of physics it should be very unstable. In trying to explain why it was not, Bohr proposed that the electrons could travel only in specific, successively larger orbits around the nucleus. Any increase or decrease in an electron's energy meant that the electron changed place, jumping to a higher or lower orbit. Bohr assumed that when an electron jumps from an outer orbit to an inner one, it emits light. His theory explained the way light is given off by hydrogen, the simplest atom, when its electron drops from a higher orbit to a lower one. Other scientists later expanded Bohr's theory into quantum theory.

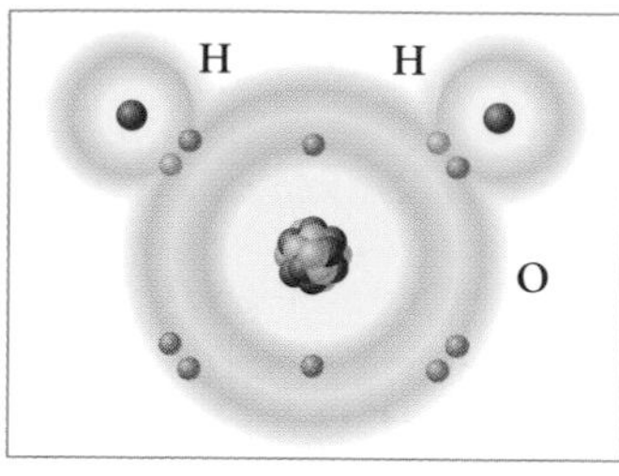

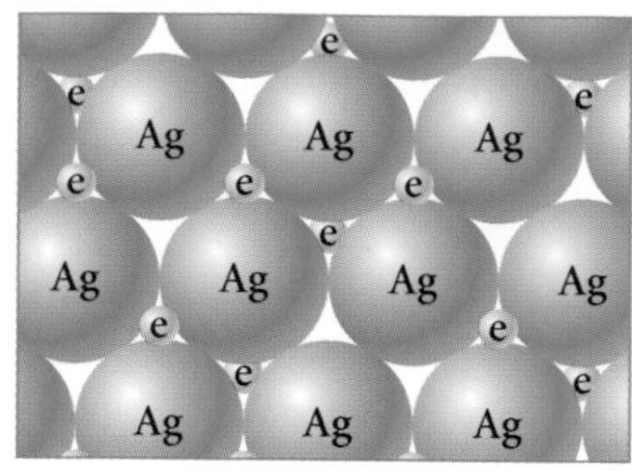

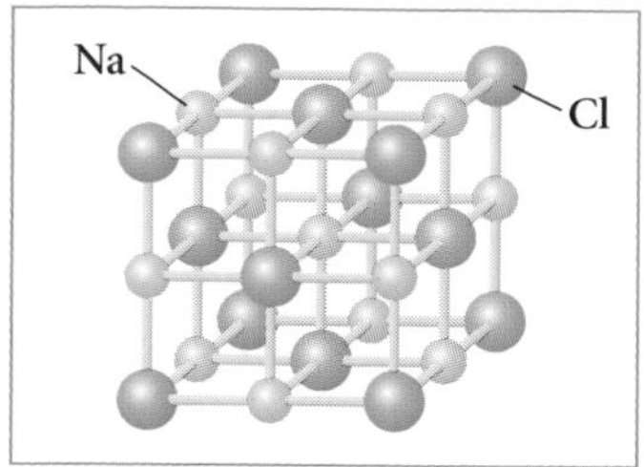

bond

In a water molecule (left), *each hydrogen atom (H) shares an electron (yellow) with the oxygen atom (O), forming covalent bonds. In silver* (center), *a metal, the negatively charged electrons (e) "float" around positively charged silver atoms (Ag), illustrating metallic bonding. In sodium chloride or salt* (right), *the sodium atom (Na) donates an electron to the chlorine atom (Cl), forming an ionic bond.*

points are lower. The boiling point of water at sea level is 212°F (100°C); that of mercury is 673.84°F (356.58°C).

Boltz•mann (bôlts′män′), **Ludwig** 1844–1906. Austrian physicist who developed statistical mechanics, the branch of physics that explains how the properties of atoms (such as mass and structure) determine the visible properties of matter (such as viscosity and heat conduction). Through his investigations of thermodynamics, Boltzmann developed numerous theories about the laws governing atomic motion and energy.

bond (bŏnd) A force of attraction that holds atoms or ions together in a molecule or crystal. Bonds are usually created by a transfer or sharing of one or more electrons. There are single, double, and triple bonds. *See also* **covalent bond, ionic bond, metallic bond.**

bone (bōn) **1.** The hard, dense, calcified tissue that forms the skeleton of most vertebrates. Bone serves as a framework for the attachment of muscles and protects vital organs, such as the brain. It also contains large amounts of calcium, a mineral that is essential for proper cell function. Blood cells and platelets are produced in the marrow, the central cavity of bone. *See more at* **osteoblast, osteocyte. 2.** Any of the bones in a skeleton, such as the femur in the leg of a mammal.

bone marrow The spongy, red tissue that fills the bone cavities of mammals. Bone marrow is the source of red blood cells, platelets, and most white blood cells.

Bon•net (bô-nĕ′), **Charles** 1720–1793. Swiss naturalist who discovered parthenogenesis, by demonstrating that aphid eggs could develop without fertilization. Bonnet was also one of the first scientists to study photosynthesis.

bon•y fish (bō′nē) A fish having a bony rather than cartilaginous skeleton. Most living species of fish are bony fish. *Compare* **cartilaginous fish, jawless fish.**

book lung (bo͝ok) The breathing organ of scorpions, spiders, and some other arachnids. It consists of membranes arranged in several parallel folds like the pages of a book.

Boole (bo͞ol), **George** 1815–1864. British mathematician who wrote important works on many different areas of mathematics. He developed a method to describe reasoning using algebra that is now known as Boolean algebra.

Bool·e·an algebra (bo͞o′lē-ən) A mathematical system dealing with the relationship between sets, used to solve problems in logic and engineering. Variables consist of 0 and 1 and operations are expressed as AND, OR, and NOT. Boolean algebra has been important in the development and programming of modern computers.

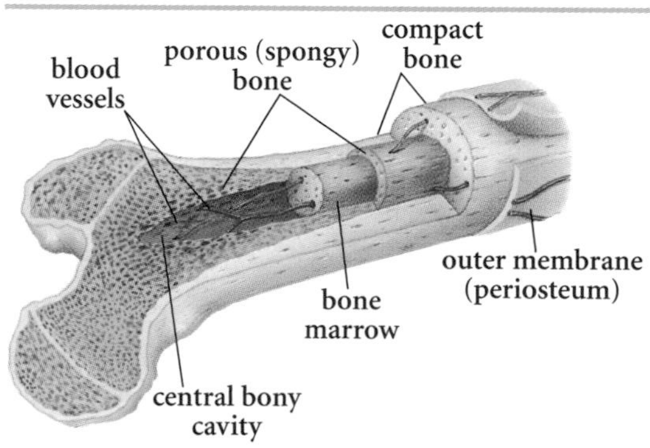

bone

cross section of an adult human femur

Bo•ö•tes (bō-ō′tēz) A constellation in the Northern Hemisphere near Virgo and Corona Borealis. It contains the bright star Arcturus.

bo•rate (bôr′āt′) A chemical compound containing the group BO_3.

bo•rax (bôr′ăks′) A white, crystalline powder and mineral used as an antiseptic, as a cleansing agent, and in fusing metals and making heat-resistant glass. The mineral is an ore of boron.

bo•ric acid (bôr′ĭk) A white or colorless crystalline compound, H_3BO_3, either naturally occurring or made from borax. It is used as an antiseptic and preservative, and in cements, enamels, and cosmetics.

bo•ron (bôr′ŏn′) A shiny, brittle, black nonmetallic element extracted chiefly from borax. It conducts electricity well at high temperatures but poorly at low temperatures. Boron is necessary for the growth of land plants and is used to make soaps, abrasives, and hard alloys. *Symbol* **B.** *Atomic number* 5. *See* **Periodic Table,** pages 262–263.

Bose (bōs), **Satyendra Nath** 1894–1974. Indian physicist known for his work in quantum theory, especially the development of a method used to describe the behavior of subatomic particles.

bot•a•ny (bŏt′n-ē) **1.** The scientific study of plants, including their growth, structure, and diseases. **2.** The plant life of a particular area: *the botany of the American southwest.*

bot•u•lism (bŏch′ə-lĭz′əm) A severe, sometimes fatal food poisoning caused by eating food infected with a bacterium that produces a powerful nerve toxin. The bacterium grows in food that has been improperly preserved. ❖ The nerve toxin produced by this bacterium is called **botulin** (bŏch′ə-lĭn).

bo•vine (bō′vīn′) *Adjective.* **1.** Relating to a cow or cattle. —*Noun.* **2.** An animal belonging to the genus *(Bos)* of ruminant mammals that includes the cow, wild ox, and yak.

bovine spon•gi•form en•ceph•a•lop•a•thy (spŭn′jĭ-fôrm′ ĕn-sĕf′ə-lŏp′ə-thē) *See* **mad cow disease.**

bow•el (bou′əl) The intestine, especially of a human. Often used in the plural as *bowels.*

Boyle (boil), **Robert** 1627–1691. English physicist and chemist whose book, *The Sceptical Chemist* (1661), marked the beginning of modern chemistry. Boyle rejected the traditional theory that all matter was composed of four elements and defined an element as a substance that cannot be reduced to other, simpler substances or produced by combining simpler substances. Boyle also conducted important physics experiments with Robert Hooke that led to the development of Boyle's law.

Boyle's law The principle that the volume of a given mass of gas will increase as its pressure decreases, and will decrease as its pressure increases, as long as its temperature remains constant. *Compare* **Charles's law.**

Br The symbol for **bromine.**

bra•chi•al (brā′kē-əl) Relating to or resembling the arm or a similar part.

bra•chi•o•pod (brā′kē-ə-pŏd′) Any of various invertebrate animals that live in the ocean and resemble clams but are sedentary. Brachiopods have paired upper and lower shells attached to a stalk, and hollow tentacles covered with cilia that sweep food particles into the mouth.

bra•chi•o•sau•rus (brā′kē-ə-sôr′əs) *or* **bra•chi•o•saur** (brā′kē-ə-sôr′) *Plural* **brachiosauri** *or* **brachiosaurs.** A massive sauropod dinosaur of the Jurassic and Cretaceous Periods. It had forelegs that were longer than its hind legs, and nostrils on top of its head.

brack•ish (brăk′ĭsh) Containing a mixture of seawater and fresh water; somewhat salty.

bract (brăkt) A small, leaf-like plant part growing just below a flower or flower stalk. Most bracts are thin and inconspicuous, but some are brightly colored.

Bragg (brăg), Sir **William Henry** 1862–1942. British physicist who invented a device used to measure x-ray wavelengths. With his son, the physicist Sir **William Lawrence Bragg** (1890–1971), he developed the technique of x-ray crystallography, used to determine the atomic structure of crystals.

Brahe (brä, brä′hē), **Tycho** 1546–1601. Danish astronomer who made the most accurate and extensive observations of the planets and stars in the age before the telescope. Brahe determined the position of 777 stars, demonstrated that comets follow regular paths, and observed the supernova of 1572, which became known as Tycho's star.

brain (brān) **1.** The part of the nervous system in vertebrates that is enclosed within the skull, is connected with the spinal cord, and is composed of gray matter and white matter. It receives and interprets impulses from sense organs, and it coordinates and controls body functions and activities, such as walking and talking. The brain is also the center of memory, thought, and feeling. **2.** A bundle of nerves in many invertebrate animals that is similar to the vertebrate brain in function and position.

brain•stem (brān′stĕm′) The part of the vertebrate brain located at the base of the brain and important in the control of many voluntary and involuntary body functions. In humans and other mammals, the brainstem is composed of the pons, medulla, and midbrain.

brass (brăs) A yellowish alloy of copper and zinc, usually 67 percent copper and 33 percent zinc. It sometimes includes small amounts of other metals. Brass is characterized by being strong and ductile, and by being resistant to many forms of corrosion.

breast (brĕst) An organ of female primates that contains milk-producing glands and usually occurs in pairs. It is present but undeveloped in the male.

breast•bone (brĕst′bōn′) *See* **sternum.**

breed (brēd) *Verb.* **1.** To produce or reproduce by giving birth or hatching: *Mosquitoes breed in water.* **2.** To raise animals or plants, often to produce new or improved types: *breed a new type of corn.* —*Noun.* **3.** A group of organisms having common ancestors and sharing certain traits that are not shared with other members of the same species. Breeds are usually produced by mating selected parents.

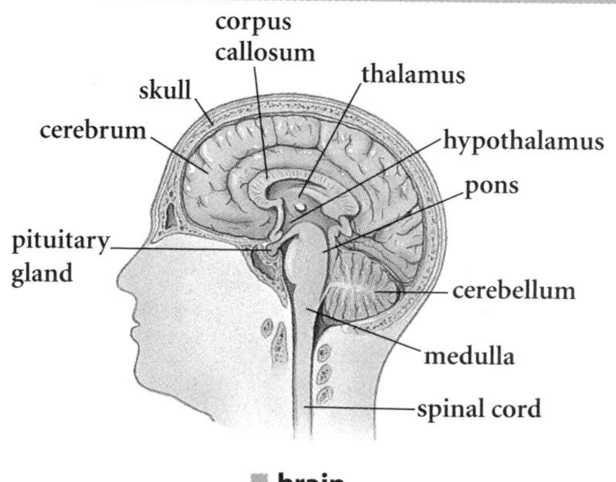

■ **brain**

Did You Know?
brain

At this very moment, these words are being scanned and interpreted by perhaps the most complex object in the world: the human brain. The bulbous organ that sits right behind your forehead is a collection of different parts that work together. For example, the two sides of the brain, called *hemispheres,* perform different tasks. The right hemisphere is responsible for musical and artistic ability and the ability to recognize faces. The left is where mathematical and logical analysis takes place, as well as most speech and language processing. Furthermore, each hemisphere is divided into four separate regions called *lobes,* which have their own jobs. Here's how specific the responsibilities of a particular brain area can be: in 2001 researchers discovered that there's a definite part of the brain (the medial ventral prefrontal cortex) where you make the connection that we call "getting" a joke. Got it?

brine (brīn) **1.** Water saturated with or containing large amounts of a salt, especially sodium chloride. **2.** The water of a sea or an ocean.

Brit•ish thermal unit (brĭt′ĭsh) The amount of heat that is needed to raise the temperature of one pound of water by one degree Fahrenheit. This unit is used mainly to measure heat, but it can be applied to other forms of energy.

brit•tle (brĭt′l) Likely to break, snap, or crack. *Compare* **ductile.**

broad-leaved (brôd′lēvd′) *also* **broad-leafed** (brôd′lēft′) Having broad leaves rather than needle-like or scale-like leaves. Azaleas, rhododendrons, and hollies are broad-leaved evergreens.

Bro•glie (brô-glē′), **Louis Victor De** 1892–1987. French physicist who was the first to theorize that subatomic particles can behave as waves. Influenced by Albert Einstein's concept that waves can behave as particles, De Broglie proposed that the opposite was also true: that electrons, for example, can behave as waves. De Broglie's work developed the study of wave mechanics, which was important in the development of quantum physics.

bro•mate (brō′māt′) A chemical compound containing the group BrO_3.

bro•me•li•ad (brō-mē′lē-ăd′) Any of various tropical and subtropical plants found mainly in the Americas, usually having long, stiff leaves and colorful flowers. Many species of bromeliad grow on trees as epiphytes. The pineapple and Spanish moss are bromeliads.

bro•mide (brō′mīd′) A compound, such as potassium bromide, containing bromine and another element or radical.

bro•mine (brō′mēn) A reddish-brown halogen element that can be found in combined form in ocean water. The pure form is a nonmetallic liquid that gives off a highly irritating vapor. It is used to make dyes, sedatives, and photographic film. *Symbol* **Br.** *Atomic number* 35. *See* **Periodic Table,** pages 262–263.

bron•chi•al tube (brŏng′kē-əl) A bronchus or any of the tubes branching from a bronchus. The bronchial tubes decrease in size as they descend into the lungs.

bron•chi•ole (brŏng′kē-ōl′) Any of the small, thin-walled tubes that branch from a bronchus and end in the alveolar sacs of the lung.

bron•chi•tis (brŏng-kī′tĭs) Inflammation of the bronchial tubes, often resulting from infection with a virus.

bron•chus (brŏng′kəs) *Plural* **bronchi** (brŏng′kī′, brŏng′kē′) Either of the two main tubular structures branching from the trachea and leading to the lungs, where they divide into smaller branches.

bron•to•sau•rus (brŏn′tə-sôr′əs) *or* **bron•to•saur** (brŏn′tə-sôr′) *An earlier name for* **apatosaurus.**

bronze (brŏnz) **1.** An alloy of copper and tin, sometimes with small amounts of other metals. Bronze is harder than brass and is used both in industry and in art. **2.** An alloy of copper and certain metals other than tin, such as aluminum.

brown dwarf (broun) A celestial body that is similar to a star but does not emit light because it does not have enough mass to ignite internal nuclear fusion. *See Note at* **dwarf star.**

WORD HISTORY

brontosaurus

Take a little deception, add a little excitement, stir them with a century-long mistake, and you have the mystery of the brontosaurus. Specifically, you have the mystery of its name. For 100 years this 70-foot-long, 30-ton vegetarian giant had two names. This case of double identity began in 1877, when bones of a large dinosaur were discovered. The creature was dubbed *apatosaurus,* a name that meant "deceptive lizard" or "unreal lizard." Two years later, bones of a larger dinosaur were found, and in all the excitement, scientists named it *brontosaurus* or "thunder lizard." This name stuck until scientists decided it was all a mistake—the two sets of bones actually belonged to the same type of dinosaur. Since it is a rule in taxonomy that the first name given to a newly discovered organism is the one that must be used, scientists have had to use the term *apatosaurus.* But "thunder lizard" had found a lot of popular appeal, and many people still prefer to call the beast *brontosaurus.*

Brown•i•an motion (brou′nē-ən) The random movement of microscopic particles suspended in a liquid or gas, caused by collisions between these particles and the molecules of the liquid or gas.

bry•o•phyte (brī′ə-fīt′) A member of a large group of seedless green plants that live on land and lack tissues (known as vascular tissues) that circulate water and dissolved nutrients. Bryophytes include the mosses and liverworts.

bry•o•zo•an (brī′ə-zō′ən) Any of various small aquatic animals that reproduce by budding and form moss-like or branching colonies attached to stones or seaweed.

Btu Abbreviation of **British thermal unit.**

bub•ble chamber (bŭb′əl) A device used to observe the movements of charged atomic particles, such as ions. A bubble chamber consists of a container filled with a very hot fluid. The paths of the charged particles are visible as trails of bubbles in the fluid. Bubble chambers are con-

USAGE

bug

The word *bug* is often used to refer to tiny creatures that crawl along, such as insects and even small animals that are not insects, such as spiders and millipedes. But for scientists, the word has a much narrower meaning. In strictest terms, the bugs are those insects that have mouthparts adapted for piercing and sucking. The mouthparts of these bugs are contained in a beak-shaped structure. Thus scientists would classify a louse, but not a beetle or a cockroach, as a bug. In fact, scientists often call lice and their relatives *true bugs,* to distinguish them better from what everyone else calls "bugs."

sidered more useful than cloud chambers, because the bubbles remain visible longer than the condensation clouds of cloud chambers do. *Compare* **cloud chamber.**

bu•bo (bo͞o′bō) A swelling of a lymph node, especially of the armpit or groin. Buboes are characteristic of bubonic plague.

bu•bon•ic plague (bo͞o-bŏn′ĭk) The most common form of plague, with symptoms including fever, vomiting, diarrhea, and inflamed lymph nodes (called buboes). It is transmitted by fleas from infected rats or other rodents. The Black Death was an epidemic of bubonic plague. *See more at* **plague.**

buck•min•ster•ful•ler•ene (bŭk′mĭn-stər-fo͝ol′ə-rēn′) An extremely stable, ball-shaped carbon molecule, C_{60}, whose structure looks like a geodesic dome. It is believed to occur naturally in soot. Also called *buckyball. See Note at* **carbon.**

buck•y•ball (bŭk′ē-bôl′) *See* **buckminsterfullerene.**

bud (bŭd) *Noun.* **1.** A small swelling on a branch or stem, containing an undeveloped flower, shoot, or leaf. **2.** A partly opened flower or leaf. **3.** A small outgrowth on a simple organism, such as a yeast or hydra, that grows into a complete new organism of the same species. **4.** A tiny part or organ, such as a taste bud, that is shaped like a bud. —*Verb.* **5.** To form or produce a bud or buds.

buff•er (bŭf′ər) **1.** *Chemistry.* A substance that prevents change in the acidity of a solution when an acid or base is added to the solution. **2.** *Computer Science.* A device or an area of a computer that temporarily stores data that is being transferred between two machines that process data at different rates, such as a computer and a printer.

Buf•fon (bo͞o-fôN′), Comte **Georges Louis Leclerc de** 1707–1788. French naturalist who spent his life compiling the *Histoire naturelle,* in which he attempted to discuss all of the facts about the natural world known at that time. It eventually reached 44 volumes and laid the foundation for later studies in biology, zoology, and anatomy.

bug (bŭg) An insect, spider, or similar small organism. In strict scientific usage, a bug is an insect belonging to the order of the true bugs. *See* **true bug.**

bulb (bŭlb) **1.** A round part of a stem that develops underground and contains the shoot of a new plant. A bulb is surrounded by leaf-like scales that provide nourishment to the new plant. Tulips, lilies, and onions grow from bulbs. *Compare* **corm, rhizome, runner, tuber. 2.** The part of an incandescent or fluorescent lamp that gives off light. The bulb of an incandescent lamp contains a filament inside a usually rounded piece of glass. The bulb of a fluorescent lamp is a glass tube or chamber containing a mixture of gases without a filament.

bu•li•mi•a (bo͞o-lē′mē-ə) An eating disorder in which episodes of binge eating are followed by fasting, self-induced vomiting, or other meas-

burette

Did You Know?
Burgess Shale

Early animals on the Earth included many oddities. These animals had bizarre combinations of legs, spines, segments, and heads found in no animals since, as if Nature were trying out different models to see what might work best. Many of these animals became extinct and left no descendants. Others may have evolved into groups that are well known today. We know a lot about these bizarre life forms thanks to the *Burgess Shale,* a 540-million-year-old formation of black shale in the Rocky Mountains of British Columbia. Unlike most rocks in which fossils are preserved, the Burgess Shale preserved the soft parts of organisms that normally would have rotted away (by reacting with oxygen) before the animals became fossils. This happened because the animals were killed instantly by a mudslide deep in the ocean, where there is very little oxygen. After the mud buried the animals, it hardened into shale. Thanks to this, we know a lot about the period of early animal evolution known as the Cambrian Explosion.

ures to prevent weight gain. It is most common among young women of normal or nearly normal weight.

Bun•sen (bŭn′sən), **Robert Wilhelm** 1811–1899. German chemist who with Gustav Kirchhoff discovered the elements cesium and rubidium. Bunsen also explained the action of geysers and invented various kinds of laboratory equipment, including the Bunsen burner.

Bunsen burner A small gas burner used in laboratories. It consists of a vertical metal tube connected to a gas fuel source, with adjustable holes at its base. These holes allow air to enter the tube and mix with the gas in order to make a very hot flame.

buoy•an•cy (boi′ən-sē) The upward force that a fluid exerts on an object that is less dense than itself. Buoyancy allows a boat to float on water.

bu•rette (byo͝o-rĕt′) A glass tube with fine gradations and with a tapered bottom that has a valve. It is used especially in laboratories to pour a measured amount of liquid from one container into another.

Bur•gess Shale (bûr′jĭs) A rock formation in the western Canadian Rockies that contains numerous fossilized invertebrates from the early Cambrian Period.

burl (bûrl) A large, rounded outgrowth on the trunk or branch of a tree.

burn (bûrn) *Verb.* **1.** To be on fire; undergo combustion. A substance burns if it is heated up enough to react chemically with oxygen. *See Note at* **oxidation.** —*Noun.* **2.** *Medicine.* An injury produced by fire, heat, radiation, electricity, or a caustic chemical agent. Burns are classified according to the degree of damage done to the tissues.

bur•sa (bûr′sə) *Plural* **bursae** (bûr′sē) *or* **bursas.** A flattened sac containing a lubricating fluid that reduces friction between a muscle or tendon and a bone. ❖ Inflammation of a bursa is called **bursitis** (bər-sī′tĭs).

bu•tane (byo͞o′tān′) An organic compound, C_4H_{10}, found in natural gas and produced from petroleum. Butane is used as a fuel, refrigerant, and propellant in aerosol cans. —*Adjective* **butyl** (byo͞o′təl).

butte (byo͞ot) A steep-sided hill with a flat top, often standing alone in an otherwise flat area. A butte is smaller than a mesa.

but•ter•fly (bŭt′ər-flī′) Any of various insects having slender bodies, knobbed antennae, and

burl
a burl on a western red cedar

WORD HISTORY

byte/bit

The word *bit* is short for *bi*nary digi*t*. A bit consists of one of two values, usually 0 or 1. Computers use bits because their system of counting is based on two options: switches on a microchip that are either *on* or *off*. Thus, a computer counts to seven in bits as follows: 0, 1, 10 [2], 11 [3], 100 [4], 101 [5], 110 [6], 111 [7]. Notice that the higher you count, the more adjacent bits you need to represent the number. For example, it requires two adjacent bits to count from 0 to 3, and it takes three adjacent bits to count from 0 to 7. A sequence of bits can represent not just numbers, but other kinds of data, such as the letters and symbols on a keyboard. The sequence of 0s and 1s that make up data are usually counted in groups of 8, and these groups of 8 bits are called *bytes*. The word *byte* is short for *b*inar*y* digi*t* *e*ight. To transmit one keystroke on a typical keyboard requires one byte of information (or 8 bits). To transmit the three-letter word *the* requires three bytes of information (or 24 bits).

four broad wings that are usually brightly colored. Unlike moths, butterflies tend to hold their wings upright and together when at rest. *Compare* **moth.**

bu•tyr•ic acid (byo͞o-tîr′ĭk) A colorless fatty acid found in butter and certain plant oils. It has an unpleasant odor and is used in disinfectants and drugs.

by•pass (bī′păs′) An alternative pathway for the flow of blood or other body fluid, created by a surgeon as a detour around a blocked or diseased organ.

by-prod•uct (bī′prŏd′əkt) Something produced in the process of making something else. For example, when plants produce carbohydrates by photosynthesis, oxygen is released as a by-product: *Asphalt and paraffin are by-products of the process of refining crude oil into gasoline.*

Byrd (bûrd), **Richard Evelyn** 1888–1957. American naval officer and explorer who established a base for scientific discovery in Antarctica.

By•ron (bī′rən), **Augusta Ada.** Countess of Lovelace. 1815–1852. British mathematician who collaborated with Charles Babbage on the design of the Analytical Engine, an early computer. She compiled detailed notations about how the machine could be programmed.

byte (bīt) A sequence of adjacent bits operated on as a unit by a computer. A byte usually consists of eight bits. Amounts of computer memory are often expressed in terms of megabytes (1,048,576 bytes) or gigabytes (1,073,741,824 bytes).

Augusta Ada Byron

C

c The symbol for the speed of light in a vacuum.

C 1. The symbol for **carbon. 2.** Abbreviation of **Celsius.**

Ca The symbol for **calcium.**

cac•tus (kăk′təs) *Plural* **cacti** (kăk′tī′) *or* **cactus-es.** Any of various plants that have thick, leafless, often spiny stems and grow in hot, dry places, chiefly in North and South America. Photosynthesis takes place in the stems of cacti, as the leaves have evolved into narrow spines to prevent water loss. Some kinds of cacti have brightly colored flowers and edible fruit.

cad•mi•um (kăd′mē-əm) A rare, bluish-white metallic element that occurs mainly in small amounts in zinc ores. It is soft and easily cut with a knife. Cadmium is plated onto other metals and alloys to prevent corrosion, and it is used to make rechargeable batteries and nuclear reactors. *Symbol* **Cd.** *Atomic number* 48. *See* **Periodic Table,** pages 262–263.

caf•feine (kă-fēn′) A bitter white alkaloid found in tea, coffee, and various plants. It is a mild stimulant.

cal•car•e•ous (kăl-kâr′ē-əs) Composed of or containing calcium or calcium carbonate. Many carbonate rocks are calcareous.

cal•ci•fi•ca•tion (kăl′sə-fĭ-kā′shən) **1.** *Medicine.* The accumulation of calcium or calcium salts in a body tissue. Calcification normally occurs in the formation of bone. **2.** *Geology.* **a.** The replacement of organic material, especially original hard material such as bone, with calcium carbonate during the process of fossilization. **b.** The accumulation of calcium in certain soils, especially soils of cool temperate regions where leaching takes place very slowly.

cal•cine (kăl-sīn′) To heat a substance to a high temperature without melting it, in order to turn it into a powder, oxidize it, or cause it to change in some other way.

cal•cite (kăl′sīt′) A usually white, clear, or pale-yellow mineral consisting of calcium carbonate. It occurs in many different forms and is the main component of chalk, limestone, and marble. Calcite is the mineral used to represent a hardness of 3 on the Mohs scale.

Did You Know?
cactus

The 2,000 species of cacti are known for living in extremely dry climates, such as the American Southwest. Cacti are excellent at conserving water. Their leaves are sharp spines, which have been known to cause great pain to animals interested in eating them. The spines also help the plant gather scarce water. Water vapor in the air condenses on the spines and then drips to the ground, where it is taken up by the roots. The roots are shallow and widely spread out to take advantage of this condensation and the rare desert rain showers. A cactus can be between 80 and 90 percent water, and its thick walls keep its water from evaporating. In fact, a cactus can be a thousand times better at conserving water than a different kind of plant of the same weight.

cal•ci•um (kăl′sē-əm) A silvery-white, moderately hard metallic element that is an alkaline-earth metal and occurs in limestone and gypsum. It is a basic component of leaves, bones, teeth, and shells, and is essential for the normal growth and development of most animals and plants. Calcium is used to make plaster, cement, and alloys. *Symbol* **Ca.** *Atomic number* 20. *See* **Periodic Table,** pages 262–263.

calcium carbonate A white or colorless crystalline compound, $CaCO_3$, occurring naturally in chalk, limestone, and marble. It is used to make toothpaste, white paint, and cleaning powder.

calcium chloride A white crystalline salt, $CaCl_2$. It attracts water very strongly, is used in refrigeration, and is spread on roads to melt ice and control dust.

WORD HISTORY

calculus

The branch of mathematics called calculus deals with problems that simple arithmetic or algebra cannot deal with, such as finding areas and volumes of unusual shapes and solids, and measuring rates of change. The word *calculus* comes from the Latin word that means "little stone, pebble." How did a word meaning "little stone" come to refer to this branch of mathematics? The answer comes from the counting practices of the ancient Romans over 2,000 years ago. They would add things up by using little pebbles or stones that represented particular numbers, as on an abacus. Later, the word *calculus* came to mean not just the pebble used in counting, but a counting system itself. Much more recently, it came to refer to the modern branch of mathematics, which was invented in the 17th century. The word *calculus,* incidentally, is also the source of the Latin word *calculare,* "to add up," which gives us our word *calculate.*

cal•cu•lus (kăl′kyə-ləs) The branch of mathematics that finds the maximum or minimum values of functions by means of differentiation and integration. Calculus can be used to calculate such things as rates of change, the area bounded by curves, and the volume bounded by surfaces. *See more at* **differentiation, integration.**

cal•i•brate (kăl′ə-brāt′) **1.** To check, adjust, or standardize a measuring instrument, usually by comparing it with an accepted model: *calibrate an oven thermometer.* **2.** To measure the diameter of the inside of a tube.

cal•i•for•ni•um (kăl′ə-fôr′nē-əm) A synthetic, radioactive metallic element of the actinide series that is produced from curium or berkelium. Californium emits a large number of neutrons and is used in the analysis of chemical components of substances. Its most stable isotope has a half-life of 800 years. *Symbol* **Cf.** *Atomic number* 98. *See* **Periodic Table,** pages 262–263.

cal•i•per (kăl′ə-pər) An instrument consisting of two curved, hinged legs, used to measure thickness and distance. Often used in the plural as *calipers.*

cal•lus (kăl′əs) An area of the skin that has become hardened and thick, usually because of prolonged pressure or rubbing.

cal•o•rie (kăl′ə-rē) **1.** A unit of heat equal to the amount of heat needed to raise the temperature of one gram of water by one degree Celsius. Also called *small calorie.* **2a.** A unit of heat equal to the amount of heat needed to raise the temperature of 1,000 grams of water by one degree Celsius. Also called *kilocalorie, large calorie.* **b.** This unit used as a measure of the amount of heat energy released by food as it is digested by the body.

ca•lyx (kā′lĭks, kăl′ĭks) The sepals of a flower considered as a group.

cam•bi•um (kăm′bē-əm) A tissue in the stems and roots of many seed-bearing plants, consisting of cells that divide rapidly to form new layers of tissue. The cambium is most active in woody plants, where it lies between the bark and wood of the stem. It is usually missing from monocotyledons, such as the grasses. ❖ The **vascular cambium** forms tissues that carry water and nutrients throughout the plant. On its outer surface the vascular cambium forms new layers of phloem, and on its inner surface, new layers of xylem. The growth of these new tissues causes the diameter of the stem to increase. ❖ The **cork cambium** creates cells that eventually become bark on the outside and cells that add to the cortex on the inside.

Cam•bri•an (kăm′brē-ən, kām′brē-ən) The first period of the Paleozoic Era, from about 540 to 505 million years ago, characterized by warm seas and desert land areas. During the Cambrian Period, animal life diversified rapidly and almost all modern animal phyla arose. *See Chart at* **geologic time,** pages 148–149.

Cambrian Explosion The rapid diversification of multicellular animal life that took place around the beginning of the Cambrian Period. It resulted in the appearance of almost all modern animal phyla. *See Note at* **Burgess Shale.**

cam•ou•flage (kăm′ə-fläzh′) Protective coloring or other appearance that conceals an animal and enables it to blend into its surroundings.

cam•phor (kăm′fər) A white, gum-like, crystalline compound, $C_{10}H_{16}O$, having a strong odor and evaporating easily. It is used as an insect repellent and in making plastics and explosives.

camouflage
stonefish camouflaged among rocks

can•cer (kăn′sər) **1.** A disease in which cells of a body part become abnormal and multiply without limit. Without treatment, the cells of some cancers may spread to and damage other tissues of the body. **2.** A tumor, especially a malignant one.

Did You Know?

cancer

The word *cancer* refers to any of a number of illnesses caused by abnormal cells that multiply out of control. In some people, exposure to certain viruses, toxic chemicals, or abnormal amounts of radiation can cause changes in the parts of a cell's DNA that normally control and limit cell growth. These portions of DNA, called *oncogenes,* direct cells to multiply abnormally. Large concentrations of cancer cells may produce lumps of cancerous tissue, called *tumors,* in a particular area of the body. Sometimes cancer cells break free from one area and travel through the bloodstream or lymph to other parts of the body, causing cancerous cells to grow there. Cancer treatments such as chemotherapy and radiation are designed to kill cancer cells, shrink tumors, and prevent the spread of the disease. With advances in the understanding of how genes work, scientists have begun using gene therapy to correct the faulty DNA that causes cancer cells to grow.

Cancer A constellation in the Northern Hemisphere near Leo and Gemini.

can•del•a (kăn-dĕl′ə) A unit used to measure the brightness of a source of light. *See Table at* **measurement.**

ca•nine (kā′nīn) *Adjective.* **1.** Relating to a family of meat-eating mammals that includes the dogs, wolves, foxes, and coyotes. **2.** Relating to any of the four pointed teeth located behind the incisors in most mammals. In carnivores, the canine teeth are adapted for cutting and tearing meat. —*Noun.* **3.** An animal belonging to the canine family of mammals. **4.** A canine tooth.

Ca•nis Major (kā′nĭs) A constellation in the Southern Hemisphere near Orion. It contains Sirius, the brightest star in the night sky.

Canis Minor A constellation in the Northern Hemisphere near Hydra and the celestial equator. It contains the bright star Procyon.

can•yon (kăn′yən) A long, deep, narrow valley with steep walls, cut into the earth by running water and often having a stream at the bottom.

ca•pac•i•tor (kə-păs′ĭ-tər) A device used to store electric charge. Capacitors consist of two charged metal plates separated by an electrical insulator. The charge is supplied by connecting the plates to a source of electricity. The positive charge is

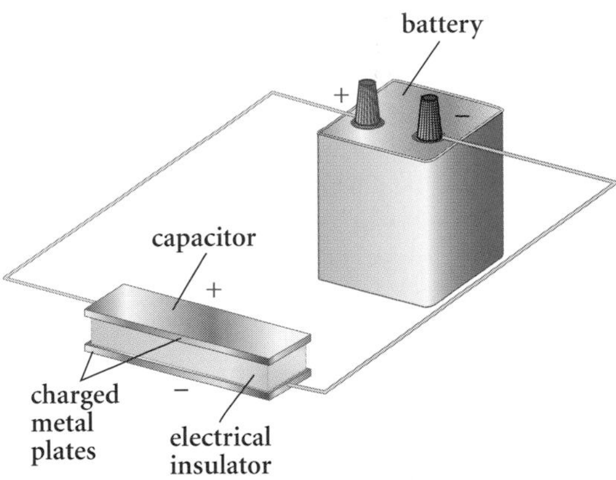

capacitor
A capacitor is charged when electrons from a power source, such as a battery, flow to one of the two plates. Because the electrons cannot pass through the insulating layer, they build up on the first plate, giving it a negative charge. Electrons on the other plate are attracted to the positive terminal of the battery, causing that plate to become positively charged.

Did You Know?
capillary action

The paper towel industry owes its existence to *capillary action.* Towels easily draw up water, much as a drop of blood to be taken for a test will defy gravity and travel up a small tube. In both cases, the force of gravity is still in effect, but it is being overwhelmed by the stickiness of liquids. The molecules of liquid stick to the sides of a narrow tube or the tiny channels in a towel, and other molecules stick to the first molecules, so the liquid crawls upwards. Some people think that this capillary action is responsible for moving water from the roots to the highest leaves of a tree, but it can only push water up so high. The remaining trip is powered by *transpiration pull.* As water evaporates from leaves, it sets up a suction that turns the entire tree into a straw through which the water on the bottom is pulled up.

stored on one of the plates, and the negative charge is stored on the other. Capacitors are used to regulate the flow of charge in electric circuits. ❖ The ability of a capacitor to store charge is called its **capacitance** (kə-păs′ĭ-təns). The capacitance depends on the size of the plates, the type of insulator, and the amount of space between the plates.

cape (kāp) A point of land projecting into a body of water.

Ca•pel•la (kə-pĕl′ə) A binary star in the constellation Auriga. It is one of the brightest stars in the night sky.

cap•il•lar•y (kăp′ə-lĕr′ē) Any of the tiny blood vessels that connect the smallest arteries to the smallest veins and form a network throughout the tissues of the body. The exchange of oxygen, nutrients, metabolic waste products, and carbon dioxide between the tissues and the blood all takes place in the capillaries.

capillary action The movement of a liquid along the surface of a solid caused by the greater attraction of the liquid's molecules to the surface of the solid than to each other. The liquid's molecules adhere to the solid surface and also to each other, so that each molecule pulls the next one along. Water moves through the roots of trees or into the pores of a sponge or towel by capillary action.

Cap•ri•corn (kăp′rĭ-kôrn′) *or* **Cap•ri•cor•nus** (kăp′rĭ-kôr′nəs) A constellation in the Southern Hemisphere near Aquarius and Sagittarius.

car•a•pace (kăr′ə-pās′) A hard outer covering or shell made of bone or chitin on the back of animals such as turtles, armadillos, and lobsters.

car•bide (kär′bīd′) A chemical compound consisting of carbon and a metal, such as calcium or tungsten. Many carbides are very hard and are used to make cutting tools and abrasives.

Did You Know?
carbon

Proteins, sugars, fats, and even DNA all contain many carbon atoms. The element *carbon* is also important, however, outside the chemistry of living things. The two most familiar forms of carbon—diamond and graphite—differ greatly because of the arrangement of their atoms. In diamond, each carbon atom bonds to four others in a dense network that makes the material the hardest substance known. But in graphite, each carbon atom bonds only to three others in a much looser arrangement of layers, each of which is weakly bonded to neighboring layers. Because individual layers of carbon in graphite are so loosely connected, they are easily scraped away, which is why it is used as pencil "lead" for writing. In 1985 an entirely new form of carbon was discovered in which carbon atoms join to make a sphere called a *buckminsterfullerene* or *buckyball,* after Buckminster Fuller, who created buildings with a similar appearance. Scientists are currently looking for uses for buckyballs and tubes made from them.

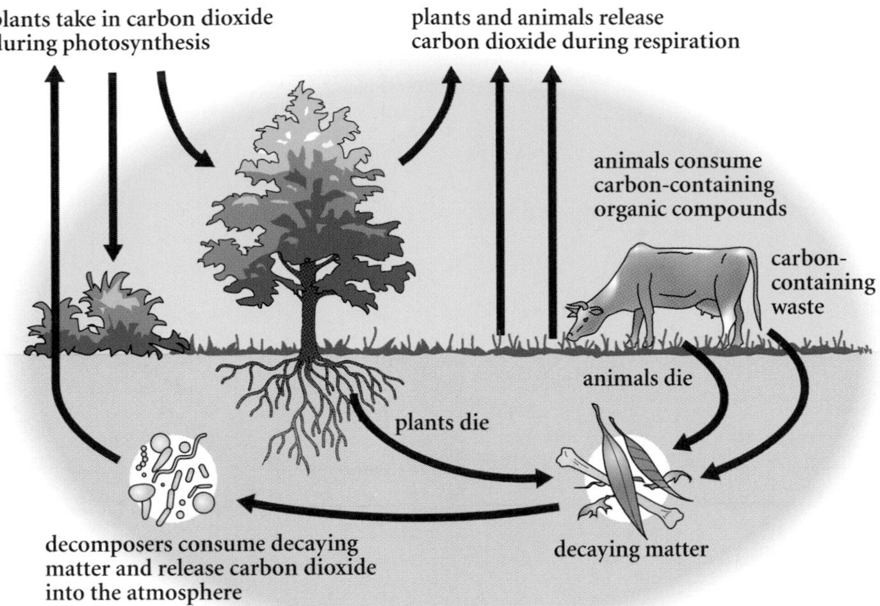
plants take in carbon dioxide during photosynthesis
plants and animals release carbon dioxide during respiration
animals consume carbon-containing organic compounds
carbon-containing waste
animals die
plants die
decomposers consume decaying matter and release carbon dioxide into the atmosphere
decaying matter

carbon cycle

car•bo•hy•drate (kär′bō-hī′drāt′) Any of a large class of organic compounds consisting of carbon, hydrogen, and oxygen, usually with twice as many hydrogen atoms as carbon or oxygen atoms. Carbohydrates are produced in green plants by photosynthesis and serve as a major energy source in animal diets. Sugars, starches, and cellulose are all carbohydrates.

car•bol•ic acid (kär-bŏl′ĭk) *See* **phenol.**

car•bon (kär′bən) A naturally abundant, nonmetallic element that occurs in all organic compounds and can be found in all plants and animals. Diamonds and graphite are pure forms, and carbon is a major part of coal, petroleum, and natural gas. Carbon can bond to itself and forms an enormous number of important molecules, many of which are essential for life. *Symbol* **C.** *Atomic number* 6. *See* **Periodic Table,** pages 262–263.

carbon 14 A naturally occurring radioactive isotope of carbon that is important in dating archaeological and biological remains by the technique known as radiocarbon dating. *See more at* **radiocarbon dating.**

car•bon•ate (kär′bə-nāt′) *Noun.* **1.** A compound containing the group CO_3. Carbonates include minerals such as calcite and rocks such as limestone. —*Verb.* **2.** To add carbon dioxide to a substance, such as a beverage.

carbon cycle The continuous process by which carbon is exchanged between organisms and the environment. Carbon dioxide is absorbed from the atmosphere by plants and algae and converted to carbohydrates by photosynthesis. Carbon is then passed into the food chain and returned to the atmosphere by the respiration and decay of animals, plants, and other organisms. The burning of fossil fuels also releases carbon dioxide into the atmosphere.

carbon dating *See* **radiocarbon dating.**

carbon dioxide A colorless, odorless gas, CO_2, that is present in the atmosphere and is formed when any fuel containing carbon is burned. It is breathed out of an animal's lungs during respiration, produced by the decay of organic matter, and used by plants in photosynthesis. Carbon dioxide is also used in refrigeration, fire extinguishers, and carbonated drinks.

carbon fixation The process by which carbon from the atmosphere is converted into carbon compounds, such as carbohydrates, in plants and algae, usually by photosynthesis.

Car•bon•if•er•ous (kär′bə-nĭf′ər-əs) The geologic time comprising the Mississippian (or Lower Carboniferous) and Pennsylvanian (or Upper Carboniferous) Periods of the Paleozoic Era, from about 360 to 286 million years ago. During the Carboniferous, widespread swamps formed in which plant remains accumulated and later hardened into coal. *See Chart at* **geologic time,** pages 148–149.

carbon monoxide A colorless, odorless gas, CO, formed when a compound containing carbon burns incompletely because there is not enough oxygen. It is present in the exhaust gases of automobile engines and is very poisonous.

car•cin•o•gen (kär-sĭn′ə-jən) A substance or agent that can cause cancer. Asbestos and tobacco products are examples of carcinogens.

car•ci•no•ma (kär′sə-nō′mə) A cancerous growth on the surface of the skin, blood vessels, or other organ or structure.

car•di•ac (kär′dē-ăk′) Relating to the heart: *a cardiac disorder.*

car•di•nal number (kär′dn-əl) A number, such as 3, 11, or 412, used in counting to indicate quantity but not order. *Compare* **ordinal number.**

cardinal point One of the four principal directions on a compass; north, south, east, or west.

car•di•ol•o•gy (kär′dē-ŏl′ə-jē) The branch of medicine that deals with the heart, its diseases, and their treatment.

car•di•o•pul•mo•nar•y resuscitation (kär′dē-ō-po͝ol′mə-nĕr′ē) *See* **CPR.**

car•di•o•vas•cu•lar (kär′dē-ō-văs′kyə-lər) Relating to the heart and blood vessels: *cardiovascular fitness.*

car•ni•vore (kär′nə-vôr′) **1a.** An animal that feeds chiefly on the flesh of other animals. Carnivores include predators such as lions and alligators, and scavengers such as hyenas and vultures. *Compare* **herbivore. b.** Any of a taxonomic order of mammals of this kind, generally having large, sharp canine teeth. Dogs, cats, bears, and weasels all belong to this order. **2.** A plant that eats insects, such as a Venus flytrap. —*Adjective* **carnivorous.**

Car•not (kär-nō′), **Nicolas Léonard Sadi** 1796–1832. French physicist and engineer who founded the science of thermodynamics. He was the first to analyze the working cycle and efficiency of the steam engine according to scientific principles. Through his experiments Carnot developed what would become the second law of thermodynamics and laid the foundation for work by Kelvin, Joule, and others.

Rachel Carson

car•o•tene (kăr′ə-tēn′) An organic compound that occurs as an orange-yellow to red pigment in many plants and in animal tissue. In animals, it is converted to vitamin A by the liver. Carotenes give plants such as carrots, pumpkins, and dandelions their characteristic color.

Ca•roth•ers (kə-rŭ*th*′ərz), **Wallace Hume** 1896–1937. American chemist who developed the synthetic material nylon, patented in 1937.

ca•rot•id artery (kə-rŏt′ĭd) Either of the two large arteries in the neck that carry blood to the head.

car•pal (kär′pəl) Any of the eight bones of the wrist lying between the forearm bones and the metacarpals. *See more at* **skeleton.**

carpal tunnel syndrome Pain, numbness, or tingling in the hand, caused by compression of a nerve in the wrist. The syndrome is usually caused by excessive repetition of specific motions of the wrist and fingers, such as typing at a computer keyboard.

car•pel (kär′pəl) The part of a pistil of a flowering plant that encloses an ovary. A pistil may consist of a single carpel or of several carpels joined together. A carpel is a modified leaf. *See more at* **flower.**

car•ri•er (kăr′ē-ər) **1.** A person or animal that serves as a host for a disease-causing organism and can transmit it to others, but does not have symptoms of the disease. Mosquitoes are carriers of malaria, for example. **2.** An organism that carries a gene for a trait but does not show the trait itself. Carriers can produce offspring that express the trait by mating with another carrier of the same gene.

Car•son (kär′sən), **Rachel Louise** 1907–1964. American marine biologist and writer whose best-known book, *Silent Spring* (1962), was an influential study of the dangerous effects of synthetic pesticides. Public reaction to the book resulted in stricter controls on pesticide use and shaped the ideas of the modern environmental movement.

Car•te•sian coordinate system (kär-tē′zhən) A system in which the location of a point is given by coordinates that represent its distances from perpendicular lines that intersect at a point called the origin. A Cartesian coordinate system in a plane has two perpendicular lines (the x-axis and y-axis); in three-dimensional space, it has three (the x-axis, y-axis, and z-axis).

car•ti•lage (kär′tl-ĭj) A strong, flexible connective tissue that is found in various parts of the body, including the joints, the outer ear, and the larynx. In the early development of most vertebrates, the skeleton forms as cartilage before most of it hardens into bone. —*Adjective* **cartilaginous.**

car•ti•lag•i•nous fish (kär′tl-ăj′ə-nəs) A fish whose skeleton is made mainly of cartilage. Sharks, rays, and skates are cartilaginous fishes. *Compare* **bony fish, jawless fish.**

Car•ver (kär′vər), **George Washington** 1864?–1943. American botanist, agricultural chemist, and educator whose work was instrumental in improving the agricultural efficiency of the United States. Carver taught Southern farmers the importance of techniques to improve the soil, including the variation of crops from season to season. To encourage them to do so he developed hundreds of uses for the peanut, soybean, and sweet potato, making them important cash crops.

Cas•si•o•pe•ia (kăs′ē-ə-pē′ə) A W-shaped constellation in the Northern Hemisphere near Andromeda and Cepheus.

caste (kăst) A group of social insects carrying out a specific function within a colony. In an ant colony, members of the caste of workers forage for food outside the colony or tend eggs and larvae, while members of the caste of soldiers defend the colony from attack.

BIOGRAPHY

George Washington Carver

After the Civil War, Southern farmers had a big problem: their cotton crops grew smaller year after year. George Washington Carver discovered and developed a way to restore the vitality of the soil by replenishing its organic materials. He introduced two new crops—peanuts and sweet potatoes—that would produce well in Alabama soil. To make them economically beneficial to farmers, he created 325 products made from peanuts, including plastics, synthetic rubber, shaving cream, and paper. He developed hundreds of other products from sweet potatoes and dozens of other native plants. Carver also introduced movable schools that brought practical agricultural knowledge directly to farmers.

Cas•tor (kăs′tər) A bright multiple star in the constellation Gemini.

cat (kăt) **1.** Any of various meat-eating mammals including the lion, tiger, jaguar, lynx, and cheetah. Most cats are solitary animals. All species except the cheetah have fully retractable claws. **2.** The house cat, domesticated since ancient times and widely kept as a pet or a killer of rodents.

ca•tab•o•lism (kə-tăb′ə-lĭz′əm) The phase of metabolism in which energy in the form of ATP is produced by the breakdown of complex molecules, such as proteins and fats, into simpler ones. *Compare* **anabolism.** —*Adjective* **catabolic.**

cat•a•lyst (kăt′l-ĭst) A substance that starts or speeds up a chemical reaction while undergoing no permanent change itself. All enzymes are catalysts. The enzymes in saliva, for example, are catalysts in digestion. —*Verb* **catalyze.**

cat•a•ract (kăt′ə-răkt′) **1.** A cloudiness in the lens of an eye or the membrane that covers it, causing partial or total blindness. **2.** A large, steep waterfall.

cat•er•pil•lar (kăt′ər-pĭl′ər) The worm-like larva of a butterfly or moth, often having fine hairs or brightly colored patterns. Caterpillars feed on plants.

cat•fish (kăt′fĭsh′) Any of numerous scaleless, usually freshwater fish having whisker-like feelers on the upper jaw.

cath•e•ter (kăth′ĭ-tər) A thin, flexible tube inserted into a duct of the body to remove a blockage or to drain fluid.

cath•ode (kăth′ōd′) **1.** The negative electrode in an electrolytic cell, toward which positively charged particles are attracted. The cathode has a negative charge because it is connected to the negatively charged end of an external power supply. **2.** A part that releases and emits electrons in an electrical device. Cathodes in vacuum tubes are usually made of a metal plate that is heated to release the electrons. *Compare* **anode.**

cathode ray A beam of electrons emitted from the negatively charged cathode of a vacuum tube. The electrons are usually absorbed by a positively charged anode. High-energy cathode rays can produce x-rays when they strike the anode.

cathode-ray tube A kind of vacuum tube designed to produce cathode rays, especially to form images on television or computer screens.

cat•i•on (kăt′ī′ən) An ion that has a positive charge. Hydrogen and ammonium ions are cations. *Compare* **anion.**

cat•kin (kăt′kĭn) A long, thin cluster of tiny, petalless flowers growing on willows, birches, oaks, poplars, and certain other trees. The flowers on a catkin are either all male or all female. *See more at* **flower.**

CAT scan (kăt) Short for *computerized axial tomography scan.* A cross-sectional view of an internal body part made by a computer that assembles a series of x-rays taken at different angles into a three-dimensional image. CAT scans are used in medicine to help diagnose a disease or disorder.

Did You Know?
cathode-ray tube

Cathode-ray tubes (also called CRTs) are the visual display units in such items as conventional television sets, computer monitors, hospital heart-monitoring devices, and laboratory oscilloscopes. They are generally made up of sealed glass tubes that have had the air drawn out of them. At one end of the tube is a phosphor-coated screen, and at the other end is an electron "gun." The gun is a cathode (in this case a negative electrode). It directs a beam of electrons, also called a *cathode ray,* toward the screen. Coils outside the tube create magnetic fields that steer the beam on its way toward the screen. When the beam strikes the screen, it causes the phosphors to glow, producing an image.

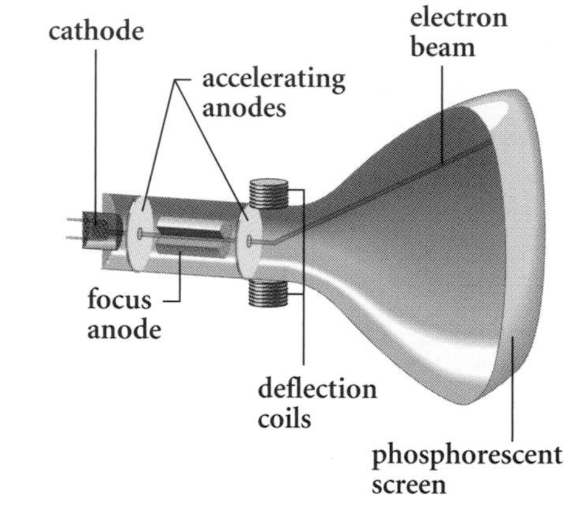

cau•dal (kôd′l) Of or near the tail or hind parts of an animal: *a fish's caudal fin.*

cave (kāv) A hollow or natural passage under the earth or in the side of a hill or mountain with an opening to the surface. Caves can form in many ways, but especially from the dissolving of limestone.

Cav•en•dish (kăv′ən-dĭsh), **Henry** 1731–1810. British chemist and physicist who discovered hydrogen. He also showed that it was the lightest of all the gases and established that water is a compound of hydrogen and oxygen.

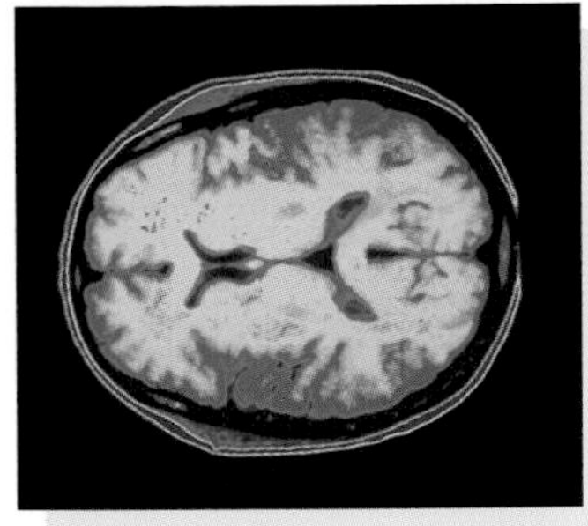

■ **CAT scan** *CAT scan of a healthy human brain*

cav•i•ta•tion (kăv′ĭ-tā′shən) The sudden formation and bursting of bubbles in a liquid caused by mechanical forces, such as the moving blades of a ship's propeller.

cc Abbreviation of cubic centimeter.

Cd The symbol for **cadmium.**

CD-ROM (sē′dē′rŏm′) A compact disk containing permanently stored data that cannot be altered.

Ce The symbol for **cerium.**

ce•cum (sē′kəm) A large pouch forming the beginning of the large intestine. The cecum attaches to the ileum.

ce•les•tial (sə-lĕs′chəl) Relating to the sky or the heavens. Stars and planets are celestial bodies.

celestial equator A great circle on the celestial sphere in the same plane as the Earth's equator.

celestial pole Either of the points at which the extensions of the Earth's axis intersect the celestial sphere.

celestial sphere An imaginary sphere with Earth at its center. The stars, planets, sun, moon, and other heavenly bodies appear to be located on this sphere.

cell (sĕl) **1.** The basic unit of living matter in all organisms, consisting of protoplasm enclosed within a cell membrane. All cells except bacterial cells have a distinct nucleus that contains the cell's DNA as well as other structures like mitochondria and the endoplasmic reticulum. The main source of energy for all of the biological processes that take place within a cell is ATP. *See more at* **eukaryote, prokaryote. 2.** Any of various devices or units within such devices that are capable of converting some form of energy into electricity. Solar cells convert sunlight into electricity, and car batteries contain cells that convert chemical energy into electricity. —*Adjective* **cellular.** *See A Closer Look, next page.*

cell division The process by which a cell divides into two or more cells. Cell division is the means of reproduction in organisms that reproduce asexually, as by fission or spore formation. In organisms that reproduce sexually, cell division is the source of all tissue growth and repair. The two main types of cell division are mitosis and meiosis.

cell membrane The thin membrane that forms the outer surface of the protoplasm of a cell and regulates the passage of materials in and out of the cell. It is made up of proteins and lipids.

cel•lu•lar respiration (sĕl′yə-lər) The process of metabolism in which cells obtain energy in the form of ATP by causing glucose and other food molecules to react with oxygen.

cellular slime mold *See under* **slime mold.**

cel•lu•lite (sĕl′yə-līt′) A deposit of fat, especially around the thighs, that causes dimpling of the skin lying over it.

cel•lu•lose (sĕl′yə-lōs′) A carbohydrate that is the main component of the cell walls of plants. It is insoluble in water and is used to make paper, cellophane, textiles, explosives, and other products. ❖ An important compound derived from cellulose is **cellulose acetate,** forming a durable material that is used in making movie film, magnetic tape, plastic film for wrapping and packaging, and textile fibers. It is often called *cellulose* or *acetate* for short.

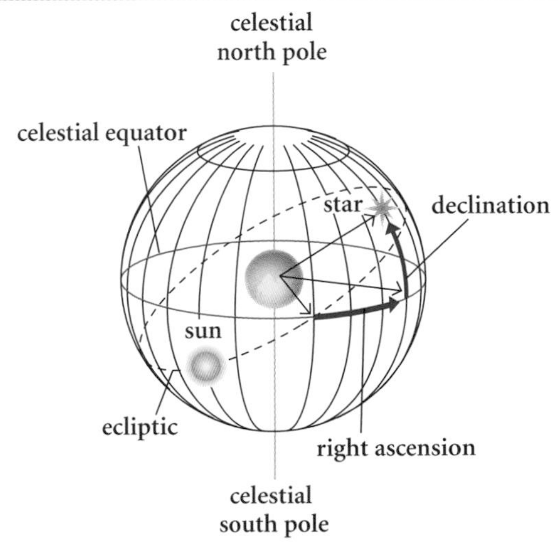

■ **celestial sphere**

A CLOSER LOOK

Cell

The cell is the basic structural unit of all organisms. From the simplest single-celled animals to the most complex multicellular ones, cells perform all of the chemical processes needed to sustain life. The cells of eukaryotes—which include most organisms except bacteria—are made up of the same basic elements: a protective cell membrane, cytoplasm, a distinct nucleus that carries much of the organism's DNA, and small bodies called organelles. Cells vary in shape and form depending on the tasks they perform.

Typical Animal Cell

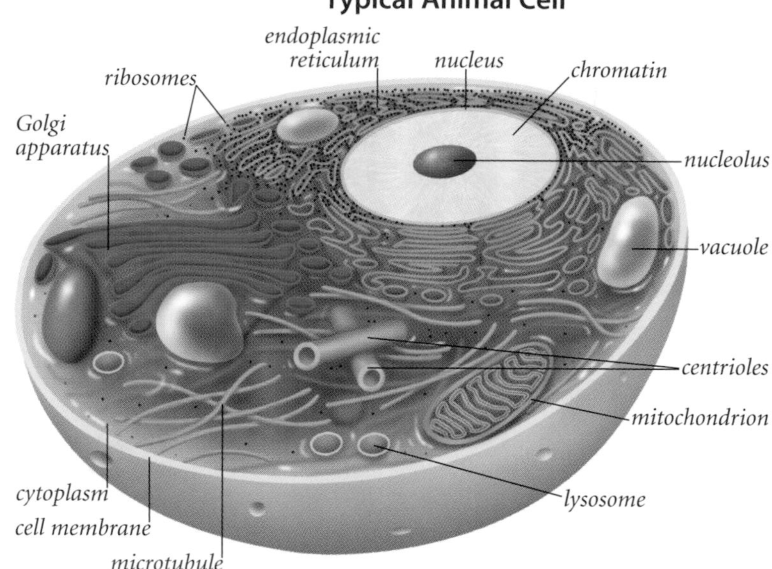

Typical Plant Cell

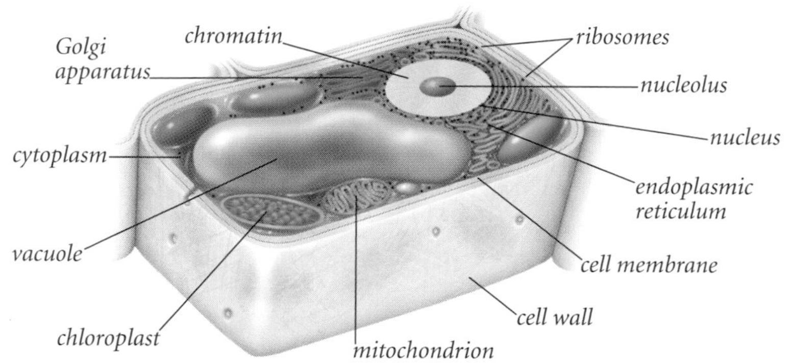

Specialized Cells

Nerve cell (neuron)

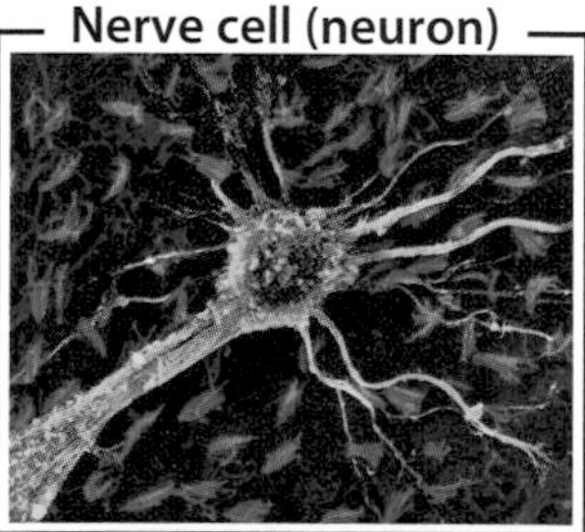

Nerve cells transmit electrical impulses within the nervous system.

Red blood cell

Red blood cells transport oxygen to and pick up carbon dioxide from the tissues of the body. They get their color from an iron-containing compound called hemoglobin.

Guard cell

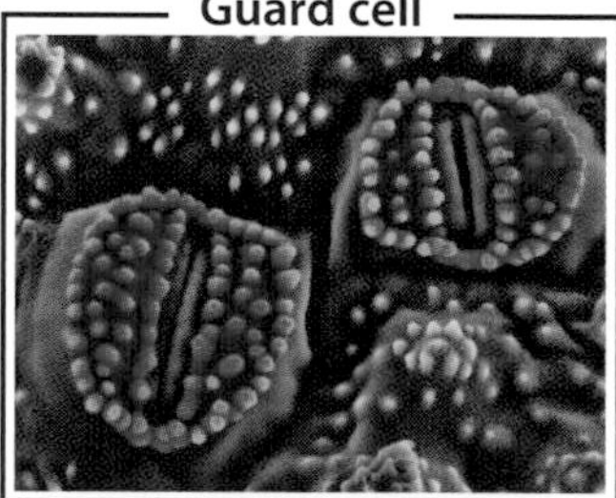

Guard cells open and close pores (called stomata) in leaves, letting air in and water vapor out.

Did You Know?

Celsius, Fahrenheit, and Kelvin scales

In the United States, a forecast of 37° might get you to wear a coat. In Canada, however, 37° would call for shorts and sandals. Do Canadians simply enjoy the cold more? Well, possibly, but the true difference is that the two countries use different temperature scales. The United States favors the *Fahrenheit* scale, in which 37° is wintry. Canadians, and most of the world, use the *Celsius* scale, in which 37° is equivalent to 98.6° Fahrenheit—body temperature! Scientists usually use Celsius, in which 0 is water's freezing point (32°F) and 100 is its boiling point (212°F). (To convert between scales, see the table of measurements at the entry for measurement.) Scientists also use the *Kelvin* scale, where 0 is as cold as anything could ever get, which is about –273° Celsius. (One Kelvin degree, or one kelvin, equals one Celsius degree.) If it's going to be 37 kelvins, you'd better wear all the clothes you have, because your molecules will barely be moving at all.

cell wall The outermost layer of cells in plants, bacteria, fungi, and many algae that gives shape to the cell and protects it from infection. In plants, it is made up mostly of cellulose. Most animal cells have a cell membrane rather than a cell wall.

Cel•si•us (sĕl′sē-əs) Relating to a temperature scale on which the freezing point of water is 0° and the boiling point of water is 100° under normal atmospheric pressure. *See Note at* **centigrade.**

Celsius, Anders 1701–1744. Swedish astronomer who devised the Celsius scale in 1742.

Cen•o•zo•ic (sĕn′ə-zō′ĭk) The most recent era of geologic time, from about 65 million years ago to the present. The Cenozoic Era is characterized by the formation of modern continents and the diversification of mammals and plants. *See Chart at* **geologic time,** pages 148–149.

USAGE

centigrade

Because of confusion over the prefix *centi–*, which originally meant 100 but developed the meaning $\frac{1}{100}$, scientists agreed to stop using the term *centigrade* in 1948. They use the term *Celsius* instead.

Cen•tau•rus (sĕn-tôr′əs) A constellation in the Southern Hemisphere near the Southern Cross and Libra. It contains Alpha Centauri, the star nearest Earth.

cen•ter of gravity (sĕn′tər) The point in a body through which the Earth's gravitational force acts and around which the body's weight is evenly balanced.

center of mass The point in a body that moves as though its entire mass were concentrated in it. It is usually in the same place as the center of gravity.

centi– A prefix meaning "a hundredth," as in *centigram,* a hundredth of a gram.

cen•ti•grade (sĕn′tĭ-grād′) *See* **Celsius.**

cen•ti•gram (sĕn′tĭ-grăm′) A unit of weight in the metric system equal to 0.01 gram. *See Table at* **measurement.**

cen•ti•li•ter (sĕn′tə-lē′tər) A unit of volume in the metric system equal to 0.01 liter. *See Table at* **measurement.**

cen•ti•me•ter (sĕn′tə-mē′tər) A unit of length in the metric system equal to 0.01 meter. *See Table at* **measurement.**

cen•ti•pede (sĕn′tə-pēd′) Any of various wormlike arthropods whose bodies are divided into many segments, each with a pair of legs. The front legs have venom glands and are used as pincers to catch prey. *Compare* **millipede.**

cen•tral angle (sĕn′trəl) An angle formed by two rays from the center of a circle, with the center forming the vertex.

central nervous system In vertebrate animals, the part of the nervous system that consists of the brain and spinal cord. *Compare* **peripheral nervous system.**

central processing unit The part of a computer that interprets and carries out instructions. It also transfers information to and from other components, such as a disk drive or the keyboard.

cen•trif•u•gal force (sĕn-trĭf′yə-gəl) The apparent force that seems to cause a body turning around a center to move away from the center. Centrifugal force is not a true force but is actually an example of inertia. *See Note at* **centripetal force.**

cen•tri•fuge (sĕn′trə-fyo͞oj′) A machine that separates substances of different densities by rotating them at very high speed. The denser substances are thrown farther outward than the less dense ones. A centrifuge can be used to separate cream from milk, or bacteria from a fluid.

cen•tri•ole (sĕn′trē-ōl′) Either of a pair of cylinder-shaped bodies found in the centrosome of an animal cell. During mitosis, the centrioles move apart to help form the spindle, which then distributes the chromosomes in the dividing cell. *See more at* **cell, meiosis, mitosis.**

cen•trip•e•tal force (sĕn-trĭp′ĭ-tl) The force that pulls an object moving in a circle toward the center of the circle and causes the object to follow a curving path. Earth's gravity acts as a centripetal force on the moon.

cen•tro•mere (sĕn′trə-mîr′) The region of the chromosome to which the spindle fiber is attached during mitosis. The centromere is where the chromatids join together in pairs before separating into individual chromosomes. *See more at* **meiosis, mitosis.**

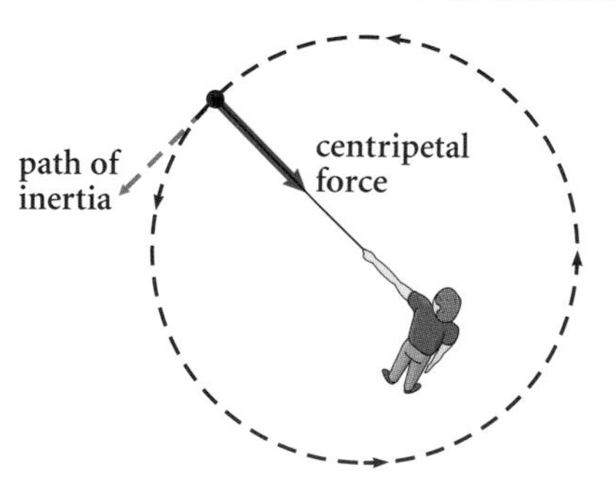

centripetal force

Centripetal force causes the ball being whirled at the end of a string to move in a circle about the person. If the string were to break, the ball would continue in a straight line along the path of inertia.

Did You Know?

centripetal force

In one popular carnival ride, people stand with their backs against the wall of a cylindrical chamber. The chamber spins rapidly and then the floor drops out, but the riders remain pressed against the wall and don't fall down. Why? Most people would say that the reason people "stick" to the wall is because a *centrifugal,* or outward, force is pushing them against it. In actuality, there is no outward force, no matter how strongly the people on the ride may think they feel one. In fact, it's just the opposite: the riders are really subject to an inward, or *centripetal,* force. As the ride spins, it forces the riders to travel in a circle. Objects (including people) in motion tend to travel in a straight line at constant speed unless they're acted on by some external force. To make an object travel along a curved path, you have to keep forcing it toward the "inside" of the curve. The walls of the ride do just that, pushing the riders toward the center; the friction between the riders and the wall holds them up, so they seem to defy gravity.

cen•tro•some (sĕn′trə-sōm′) A specialized region of the cytoplasm located next to the nucleus of a cell that in animal cells contains the centrioles.

ce•phal•ic (sə-făl′ĭk) Located on or near the head.

ceph•a•lo•chor•date (sĕf′ə-lə-kôr′dāt′) Any of various primitive chordate animals that lack a true vertebral column, having a notochord instead. The lancelets are cephalochordates.

ceph•a•lo•pod (sĕf′ə-lə-pŏd′) Any of various ocean mollusks, such as the octopus, squid, and nautilus, having long tentacles around the mouth, a large head, a pair of large eyes, and a sharp beak. If attacked, cephalopods squirt a cloud of dark inky liquid to confuse predators and make their escape.

ceph•a•lo•tho•rax (sĕf′ə-lə-thôr′ăks′) The combined head and thorax of arachnids, such as spiders, and of many crustaceans, such as crabs.

Ce•pheus (sē′fyo͞os′, sē′fē-əs) A constellation in the Northern Hemisphere near Cassiopeia and Draco.

cer•a•top•si•an (sĕr′ə-tŏp′sē-ən) Any of various medium-sized to large, plant-eating dinosaurs of the late Jurassic and Cretaceous Periods. Ceratopsians walked on four legs and had a broad bony plate covering the neck, a beaked mouth, and one or more horns on the head. Triceratops is an example of a ceratopsian.

ce•re•al (sîr′ē-əl) A grass, such as corn or wheat, whose starchy grains are used as food.

cer•e•bel•lum (sĕr′ə-bĕl′əm) The part of the vertebrate brain that is located below the cerebrum at the rear of the skull and coordinates balance and muscle activity. In humans and other mammals, the cerebellum is made up of two connecting parts, called hemispheres, consisting of a core of white matter surrounded by gray matter.

cer•e•bral (sĕr′ə-brəl, sə-rē′brəl) Relating to the brain or cerebrum.

cerebral cortex The outer layer of gray matter that covers the cerebral hemispheres in the brain of many vertebrate animals and is composed of folds of nerve cells and fibers. The cerebral cortex is responsible for higher functions of the nervous system, including voluntary activity and the senses of hearing, vision, and touch. In humans, it is the center of learning, language, and memory.

cerebral hemisphere Either of the two symmetrical halves of the cerebrum. *See Note at* **brain.**

cerebral palsy A disorder caused by brain injury usually at or before birth, having symptoms that include poor muscle control and that often involve paralysis or abnormal stiffness of the muscles. Other forms of disability, such as mental retardation, may also be present.

cer•e•bro•spi•nal fluid (sĕr′ə-brō-spī′nəl, sə-rē′brō-spī′nəl) The clear fluid that fills the cavities of the brain and spinal cord, serving to lubricate the tissues and to absorb shock.

cer•e•brum (sĕr′ə-brəm, sə-rē′brəm) The largest part of the vertebrate brain, filling most of the skull and consisting of two cerebral hemispheres divided by a deep groove and joined by a mass of nerve fibers. The cerebrum processes complex sensory information and controls voluntary muscle activity. In humans it is the center of thought, learning, and memory.

Ce•res (sîr′ēz) A dwarf planet that orbits the sun between Mars and Jupiter. Ceres was formerly classified as an asteroid and is located in the asteroid belt. It has a diameter of 580 miles (934 kilometers).

ce•ri•um (sîr′ē-əm) A shiny, gray metallic element of the lanthanide series. It is easily shaped and in pure form will ignite if scratched with a knife. It is used in glass polishing and as a catalyst in self-cleaning ovens. *Symbol* **Ce.** *Atomic number* 58. *See* **Periodic Table,** pages 262–263.

cer•vi•cal (sûr′vĭ-kəl) **1.** Relating to the cervix of the uterus. **2.** Located at or near the part of the spine that forms the neck.

cer•vix (sûr′vĭks) The narrowed, lower end of the uterus, extending into the vagina.

ce•si•um (sē′zē-əm) A soft, easily shaped, silvery-white element that is an alkali metal. It is liquid at room temperature and is the most reactive of all metals. Cesium is used to make photoelectric cells, electron tubes, and atomic clocks. *Symbol* **Cs.** *Atomic number* 55. *See* **Periodic Table,** pages 262–263.

ce•ta•cean (sĭ-tā′shən) Any of various, often very large marine mammals having an almost hairless body that resembles that of a fish. Cetaceans have a flat, horizontal tail and forelimbs modified into broad flippers. Whales, dolphins, and porpoises are cetaceans.

Cf The symbol for **californium.**

CFC Abbreviation of **chlorofluorocarbon.** *See under* **fluorocarbon.**

Chad•wick (chăd′wĭk), Sir **James** 1891–1974. British physicist who discovered the neutron in 1932.

Chain (chān), Sir **Ernst Boris** 1906–1979. German-born British biochemist who developed and purified penicillin with Howard Florey. Chain also helped to develop a way to manufacture the drug in large quantities and was involved in the first tests of its effects on humans.

chain reaction 1. *Physics.* A continuous series of nuclear fissions in which neutrons released from the splitting of one atomic nucleus collide with nearby nuclei, which in turn split and release

chalk
chalk cliffs, East Sussex, England

more neutrons to collide with other nuclei, thus keeping the reaction going. *See more at* **fission.** *See Note at* **nuclear reactor. 2.** *Chemistry.* A reaction in which a change in one molecule causes changes in many other molecules until a stable compound is formed.

chal•ced•o•ny (kăl-sĕd′n-ē) A type of quartz that has a waxy luster and varies from transparent to translucent. It is used as a gemstone. Agate and onyx are forms of chalcedony.

chal•co•py•rite (kăl′kə-pī′rīt′) A yellow metallic mineral consisting of iron, copper, and sulfur. Chalcopyrite usually occurs as shapeless masses of grains and is an important ore of copper. Because of its shiny look and often yellow color, it is sometimes mistaken for gold, and for this reason it is also called *fool's gold.*

chalk (chôk) A soft, white, gray, or yellow limestone formed primarily from fossil seashells and consisting mainly of calcium carbonate. Chalk is used in making lime, cement, and fertilizers, and as a whitening pigment in ceramics, paints, and cosmetics. The chalk used in classrooms, however, is usually artificial and not natural.

cha•me•leon (kə-mēl′yən) **1.** Any of various small lizards of the Eastern Hemisphere, having the ability to change color rapidly to blend in with their surroundings and large eyes that move independently of each other. **2.** Any of various small lizards of the Western Hemisphere that can also change their color.

cha•os (kā′ŏs′) *Mathematics.* A system, such as the weather, that develops from a set of often simple initial conditions but behaves very differently if the initial conditions are changed even slightly. Chaotic systems often appear random and unpredictable, but in fact have regular patterns that are repeated at any scale of observation. *See more at* **fractal.**

char•ac•ter•is•tic (kăr′ək-tə-rĭs′tĭk) *Mathematics.* The part of a logarithm to the base ten that is to the left of the decimal point. For example, if 2.749 is a logarithm, 2 is the characteristic. *Compare* **mantissa.**

char•coal (chär′kōl′) A black porous form of carbon produced by heating wood or bone in little or no air. Charcoal is used as a fuel, for drawing, and in air and water filters.

charge (chärj) **1.** A property of all particles of matter that determines whether they are attracted to or repulsed by other particles. Charge is usually designated as positive or negative. If an atom has more protons than electrons, it has a positive charge; if it has more electrons than protons, it has a negative charge. Particles with like charges repel each other; particles with different or opposite charges attract each other. **2.** The amount of electrical energy contained in an object, particle, or region of space.

Did You Know?
charge

Electric *charge* is a basic property of elementary particles of matter. The protons in an atom have a positive charge, while its electrons have a negative charge. In an ordinary atom, the number of protons equals the number of electrons, so the atom is electrically neutral. If an atom gains some electrons, it becomes negatively charged. If it loses some electrons, it becomes positively charged. Atoms that become charged are called *ions.* Every charged particle is surrounded by an *electric field,* the region of space in which the charge exerts a force. Because of their electric fields, particles with unlike charges attract one another, and those with like charges repel one another. *Static electricity* consists of charged particles at rest. Electric *current* consists of moving charged particles, especially electrons or ions.

Charles (chärlz), **Jacques Alexandre César** 1746–1823. French physicist and inventor who formulated Charles's law in 1787. In 1783 he became the first person to use hydrogen in balloons for flight.

Charles's law (chärl′zĭz) The principle that the volume of a given mass of gas will increase as its temperature increases, and will decrease as its temperature decreases, as long as its pressure remains constant. *Compare* **Boyle's law.**

chee•tah (chē′tə) A long-legged, swift-running wild cat of Africa and southwest Asia, having spotted, light-brown fur and claws that do not fully retract. Cheetahs are the fastest land animals, able to sprint at up to 70 miles (113 kilometers) per hour.

che•lo•ni•an (kĭ-lō′nē-ən) A turtle or tortoise.

chem•i•cal (kĕm′ĭ-kəl) *Adjective.* **1.** Relating to or produced by means of chemistry: *a chemical discovery; a chemical change.* —*Noun.* **2.** A substance obtained by or used in a chemical process; a chemical compound.

chemical engineering The branch of engineering that specializes in the development and manufacture of products involving chemicals.

chemical name The name of a chemical compound that shows the names of each of its elements or subcompounds. For example, the chemical name of baking soda is sodium bicarbonate.

chem•is•try (kĕm′ĭ-strē) **1.** The scientific study of the structure, properties, and reactions of the chemical elements and the compounds they form. **2.** The composition, structure, properties, and reactions of a substance.

che•mo•syn•the•sis (kē′mō-sĭn′thĭ-sĭs) The formation of organic compounds using the energy released from chemical reactions instead of the energy of sunlight. Bacteria living in deep, dark areas of the ocean are able to survive by chemosynthesis. They use energy derived from the oxidation of inorganic chemicals, such as sulfur from deep volcanic vents, to make their food. *Compare* **photosynthesis.**

che•mo•ther•a•py (kē′mō-thĕr′ə-pē) The treatment of disease, especially cancer, with chemicals that have a specific poisonous effect on the cancerous or disease-causing cells.

chert (chûrt) A hard, brittle, reddish-brown to green sedimentary rock consisting of very small crystals of quartz.

chick•en•pox (chĭk′ən-pŏks′) A highly contagious infection, usually of young children, that is caused by a virus. Symptoms include an itchy skin rash and fever. Also called *varicella.*

chim•pan•zee (chĭm′păn-zē′) A dark-haired African ape that is somewhat smaller than a gorilla, lives mostly in trees, and has a high degree of intelligence. Chimpanzees, the closest living relatives of humans, live in close-knit groups and have elaborate social interactions.

chip (chĭp) *See* **integrated circuit.**

chi•ro•prac•tic (kī′rə-prăk′tĭk) A system for treating disorders of the body, especially disorders of the bones, muscles, and joints, by manipulating the spine and other structures.

chi•tin (kīt′n) A tough, semitransparent substance that is the main component of the exoskeletons of arthropods, such as the shells of crustaceans and the outer coverings of insects. Chitin is a carbohydrate and is also found in the cell walls of certain fungi and algae.

chlo•rate (klôr′āt′) A chemical compound containing the group ClO_3.

chlo•ride (klôr′īd′) A compound, such as ammonium chloride, containing chlorine and another element or radical.

chlo•ri•nate (klôr′ə-nāt′) To add chlorine or one of its compounds to a substance. Water and sewage are chlorinated to be disinfected, and paper pulp is chlorinated to be bleached.

chlo•rine (klôr′ēn′) A greenish-yellow, gaseous halogen element that can combine with most other elements and is found chiefly in combination with sodium as common salt. Chlorine is very poisonous, being highly irritating to the nose, throat, and lungs, and causing suffocation. It is used in purifying water, as a disinfectant and bleach, and in making many important compounds such as chloroform. *Symbol* **Cl.** *Atomic number* 17. *See* **Periodic Table,** pages 262–263. *See Note at* **chlorophyll.**

chlo•ro•fluor•o•car•bon (klôr′ō-flo͝or′ō-kär′-bən) *See under* **fluorocarbon.**

chlo•ro•form (klôr′ə-fôrm′) A colorless, toxic, sweet-tasting liquid, $CHCl_3$, used chiefly as a solvent. It was also once used as an anesthetic.

chlo•ro•phyll (klôr′ə-fĭl) Any of several green pigments found in photosynthetic organisms, such as green plants. Chlorophyll is composed of carbon, hydrogen, magnesium, nitrogen, and oxygen. *See more at* **photosynthesis.**

chlo•ro•plast (klôr′ə-plăst′) A tiny structure in the cells of green algae and green plants that contains chlorophyll and creates glucose through photosynthesis. *See more at* **cell, photosynthesis.**

chol•er•a (kŏl′ər-ə) An infectious, sometimes fatal disease of the small intestine caused by a bacterium. It is contracted from contaminated water and food and causes severe diarrhea, vomiting, and dehydration.

cho•les•ter•ol (kə-lĕs′tə-rôl′) A fatty substance found in animals and plants that is a main component of cell membranes and is important in metabolism and hormone production. In vertebrate animals, cholesterol is a major component of the blood. Higher than normal amounts of cholesterol in the blood, which can occur from eating too many fatty foods, may lead to diseases of the arteries such as atherosclerosis.

WORD HISTORY

chlorophyll

From its name, we might think that chlorophyll has chlorine in it, but it doesn't. The *chloro–* of *chlorophyll* means "green"; chlorophyll in fact is the chemical compound that gives green plants their characteristic color. The name of the chemical element *chlorine* comes from the same root as the prefix *chloro–*, and is so called because it is a greenish-colored gas.

chor•date (kôr′dāt′) Any of a large group of animals having at some stage of development a nerve cord and flexible spinal column (called a notochord) running along the back, and gill slits. Chordates include the vertebrates, lancelets, and tunicates.

cho•ri•on (kôr′ē-ŏn′) The outer membrane that encloses the embryo of a reptile, bird, or mammal. In mammals, the chorion contributes to the development of the placenta.

chro•mate (krō′māt′) A chemical compound containing the group CrO_4.

chro•mat•ic (krō-măt′ĭk) Relating to color or colors.

chro•ma•tid (krō′mə-tĭd) Either of the two strands formed when a chromosome duplicates itself during cell division. The chromatids are joined together by a single centromere and later separate to become individual chromosomes. *See more at* **meiosis, mitosis.**

chro•ma•tin (krō′mə-tĭn) The substance distributed in the nucleus of a cell that condenses to form chromosomes during mitosis. It consists mainly of DNA and proteins called histones.

chro•ma•tog•ra•phy (krō′mə-tŏg′rə-fē) A technique used to separate the components of a chemical mixture by moving the mixture along a stationary material, such as gelatin. Different components of the mixture are caught by the material at different rates and form isolated bands that can then be analyzed.

chro•mi•um (krō′mē-əm) A hard, shiny, steel-gray metallic element that does not rust or become dull easily. It is used to plate other metals, to harden steel, and to make stainless steel and other alloys. *Symbol* **Cr.** *Atomic number* 24. *See* **Periodic Table,** pages 262–263.

chro•mo•some (krō′mə-sōm′) A structure in all living cells that carries the genes that determine heredity. In all cells except bacterial cells, the chromosomes are thread-like strands of DNA and protein that are contained in the nucleus. They occur in pairs in all of the cells of eukaryotes except the reproductive cells. In bacterial cells, which have no nucleus, the chromosome is a circular strand of DNA located in the cytoplasm.

chro•mo•sphere (krō′mə-sfîr′) A glowing, transparent layer of gas surrounding the photosphere of a star, especially the sun. The sun's chromosphere is several thousand miles thick and is composed mainly of hydrogen.

chro•nom•e•ter (krə-nŏm′ĭ-tər) An extremely accurate clock or other timepiece. Chronometers are used in scientific experiments, navigation, and astronomical observations.

chrys•a•lis (krĭs′ə-lĭs) **1.** The pupa of certain kinds of insects, especially of moths and butterflies, that is inactive and enclosed in a firm case or cocoon from which the adult eventually emerges. **2.** The case or cocoon of a chrysalis.

ci•ca•da (sĭ-kā′də) Any of various insects having a broad head and transparent wings. Male cicadas have a pair of sound-producing organs on the abdomen that produce a high-pitched buzz. Cicadas spend two or more years living underground as nymphs before emerging to live for short periods in trees as adults.

–cide A suffix that means "a killer of." It is used to form the names of chemicals that kill a specified organism, such as *pesticide,* a chemical that kills pests.

chrysalis

chrysalis of a small tortoiseshell butterfly

Did You Know?

circadian rhythm

Why do you sometimes wake up on time even if your alarm clock doesn't ring? How do nocturnal animals know when it is time to wake up? It's because you—and most other animals—have a kind of internal clock that controls the cycle of the day's biological activities, such as sleeping and waking. These daily biological activities are known as *circadian rhythms* because they are influenced by the regular intervals of light and dark in each 24-hour day. While the process underlying circadian rhythm is not completely understood, it is mainly controlled by the release of hormones. The brain regulates the amount of hormone released in response to the information it gets from light-sensitive cells in the eye, called *photoreceptors.* Circadian rhythms can be disrupted by changes in this daily schedule. For example, biologists have observed that birds exposed to artificial light for a long time sometimes build nests in the fall instead of the spring. In humans who travel long distances by air, the local time of day no longer matches the body's internal clock, causing a condition known as *jet lag.*

cil•i•um (sĭl′ē-əm) *Plural* **cilia.** A hair-like projection capable of a whipping motion and found in certain vertebrate cells and microscopic organisms, especially protozoans. Some microorganisms, such as paramecia, use cilia for movement. Cilia lining the human respiratory tract act to remove foreign matter from air before it reaches the lungs.

cin•cho•na (sĭng-kō′nə, sĭn-chō′nə) Any of several evergreen trees and shrubs of South America whose bark is the source of quinine and certain other drugs used to treat malaria.

cir•ca•di•an rhythm (sər-kā′dē-ən) A daily cycle of biological activity based on a 24-hour period and influenced by regular variations in the environment, such as the alternation of night and day.

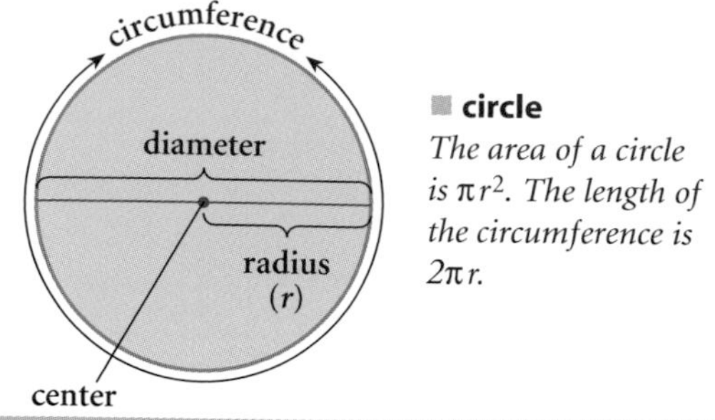

circle *The area of a circle is* πr^2. *The length of the circumference is* $2\pi r$.

cir•cle (sûr′kəl) A closed curve whose points are all on the same plane and at the same distance from a fixed point (the center).

cir•cuit (sûr′kĭt) **1.** A closed path through which an electric current flows or may flow. ❖ Circuits in which a power source is connected to two or more components (such as light bulbs), one after the other, are called **series circuits.** If the circuit is broken, none of the components receives a current. Circuits in which a power source is directly connected to two or more components are called **parallel circuits.** If a break occurs in the circuit, only the component along whose path the break occurs stops receiving a current. **2.** A system of electrically connected parts or devices: *a microchip containing all the circuits of a computer.*

circuit board In a computer, an insulated board on which interconnected circuits and components such as microchips are mounted or etched.

circuit breaker A switch that automatically interrupts the flow of an electric current if the current becomes too strong.

cir•cu•la•tion (sûr′kyə-lā′shən) The flow of blood as it is pumped by the heart to all the tissues of the body and then back to the heart. Blood that is rich in oxygen is carried away from the heart by the arteries, and blood that is low in oxygen is returned to the heart by the veins. Nutrients and waste products are exchanged between the blood and the tissues of the body through the circulation.

cir•cu•la•to•ry system (sûr′kyə-lə-tôr′ē) The system that circulates blood through the body, consisting of the heart and blood vessels. In all vertebrates and certain invertebrates, the circulatory system is completely contained within a network of vessels. In vertebrates, the lymphatic system is also considered part of the circulatory system.

circum– A prefix meaning "around," as in *circumscribe,* to draw a figure around another figure.

cir•cum•fer•ence (sər-kŭm′fər-əns) **1a.** The boundary line of a circle. **b.** The boundary line of a figure, area, or object. **2.** The length of such a boundary.

cir•cum•scribe (sûr′kəm-skrīb′) *Geometry.* To draw a figure around another figure so as to touch as many points as possible. A circle that is circumscribed around a triangle touches it at each of the triangle's three vertices.

cir•rho•sis (sĭ-rō′sĭs) A liver disease in which normal liver cells are gradually replaced by scar tissue, causing the organ to shrink, harden, and lose its function. Cirrhosis is most commonly caused by chronic alcohol abuse.

cir•ro•cu•mu•lus (sîr′ō-kyo͞om′yə-ləs) A grainy or rippled cloud formation, usually occurring in sheets or bands. Cirrocumulus clouds form at upper levels of the atmosphere.

cir•ro•strat•us (sîr′ō-străt′əs) A thin, hazy cloud formation made up of ice crystals, often covering the sky in sheets and producing a halo effect around the sun. Cirrostratus clouds form at upper levels of the atmosphere.

cir•rus (sîr′əs) A cloud formation made up of feathery white patches, bands, or streamers of ice crystals. Cirrus clouds form at upper levels of the atmosphere.

cit•rate (sĭt′rāt′) A salt or ester of citric acid, containing the group $C_6H_5O_7$.

circuit

Bulbs in a series circuit (left) *give off dim light since they each consume a portion of the power coming through a single circuit connected to the battery. In a parallel circuit* (right) *bulbs shine brightly since each is directly connected in its own circuit to the power source.*

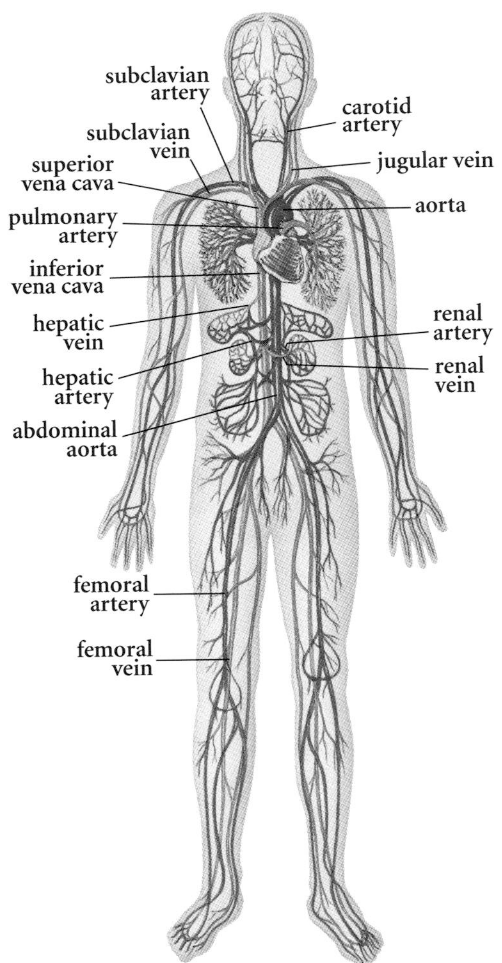

circulatory system

In the diagram above, the blood vessels of the circulatory system are colored according to whether they carry blood that is high in oxygen (red) or low in oxygen (blue). Most arteries, which carry blood away from the heart, are colored red; most veins, which carry blood back toward the heart, are colored blue.

cit•ric acid (sĭt′rĭk) A white, odorless acid, $C_6H_8O_7$, having a sour taste and occurring widely in plants, especially in citrus fruit. It is used in medicine and as a flavoring.

citric acid cycle *See* **Krebs cycle.**

cit•ro•nel•la (sĭt′rə-nĕl′ə) The pale-yellow, lemon-scented oil obtained from the leaves of a tropical Asian grass, used in insect repellents and perfumes.

cit•rus (sĭt′rəs) **1.** Any of various evergreen trees or shrubs bearing fruit with juicy flesh and a thick rind. Citrus trees are native to southern and southeast Asia but are grown in warm climates around the world. Many species have spines. The orange, lemon, lime, and grapefruit are citrus trees. **2.** The usually edible fruit of one of these trees or shrubs.

civ•il engineering (sĭv′əl) The branch of engineering that specializes in the design and construction of projects such as bridges, roads, and dams.

Cl The symbol for **chlorine.**

clam (klăm) Any of various bivalve mollusks having equal shells and a burrowing foot, some of which are edible. Clams include both marine and freshwater species.

class (klăs) A group of organisms ranking above an order and below a phylum or division. *See Table at* **taxonomy.**

clas•si•cal physics (klăs′ĭ-kəl) Physics that is based on Newton's laws of motion and does not make use of quantum mechanics and the theory of relativity. ❖ **Classical mechanics** refers to Newton's laws of motion and other principles of mechanics based on them. Classical mechanics does not work when dealing with bodies (such as electrons) moving at speeds close to that of light, or when making measurements of atoms and subatomic particles. These phenomena can only be described by quantum mechanics and the theory of relativity.

clas•si•fi•ca•tion (klăs′ə-fĭ-kā′shən) In biology, the systematic grouping of organisms according to the evolutionary or structural relationships between them. The traditional system of classification is called the Linnaean system. *See Table at* **taxonomy.**

clav•i•cle (klăv′ĭ-kəl) Either of two slender bones in humans and other primates that extend from the upper part of the sternum to the shoulder. Also called *collarbone. See more at* **skeleton.**

claw (klô) **1.** A sharp, curved nail at the end of a toe of a mammal, reptile, or bird. **2.** A pincer, as of a lobster or crab, used for grasping.

clay (klā) A stiff, sticky, earthy material that is soft and flexible when wet and consists mainly of various silicates of aluminum. It is widely used to make bricks, pottery, and tiles.

cleav•age (klē′vĭj) **1.** *Geology.* The breaking of certain minerals along specific planes, making smooth surfaces. These surfaces are parallel to the faces of the molecular crystals that make up the minerals. A mineral that exhibits cleavage breaks into smooth pieces with the same pattern of parallel surfaces regardless of how many times it is broken. Some minerals, like quartz, do not have a cleavage and break into uneven pieces with rough surfaces. **2.** *Biology.* In an embryo, the series of cell divisions by which a single fertilized egg cell becomes a many-celled blastula.

cleft palate (klĕft) Incomplete closure of the palate during development of an embryo, resulting in a split along part or all of the roof of the mouth. ❖ A vertical split or cleft in the upper lip that can occur with or without a cleft palate is called a **cleft lip**.

cli•mate (klī′mĭt) The general or average weather conditions of a certain region, including temperature, rainfall, and wind: *Caribbean islands have a year-round climate of warm breezes and sunshine.*

cli•ma•tol•o•gy (klī′mə-tŏl′ə-jē) The scientific study of climates, including the causes and long-term effects of variation in regional and global climates.

cli•max community (klī′măks′) An ecological community in which populations of plants or animals remain stable and exist in balance with each other and their environment. A climax community is the final stage of succession, remaining relatively unchanged until destroyed by an event such as fire or human interference. *See more at* **succession.**

clit•o•ris (klĭt′ər-ĭs, klĭ-tôr′ĭs) A sensitive external organ of the reproductive system in female mammals and some other animals that is capable of becoming erect. It is located above or in front of the urethra.

clo•a•ca (klō-ā′kə) The body cavity into which the intestinal, urinary, and genital canals empty in birds, reptiles, amphibians, most fish, and the primitive mammals known as monotremes. The cloaca has an opening for expelling its contents from the body.

clone (klōn) *Noun.* **1.** A cell, group of cells, or organism that is produced asexually from a single ancestor. The cells of an individual plant or animal are clones because they all descend from a single fertilized cell. A clone may be produced by fission, in the case of single-celled organisms, or by budding, as in the hydra. Some plants can produce clones from horizontal stems, such as runners. Clones of cells and some plants and animals can also be produced in a laboratory. **2.** A copy of a sequence of DNA, as from a gene, that is produced by genetic engineering. The clone is then transplanted into the nucleus of a cell from which genetic material has been removed. —*Verb.* **3.** To produce or grow a cell, group of cells, or organism from a single original cell. **4.** To make identical copies of a DNA sequence. *See more at* **genetic engineering.**

closed (klōzd) **1.** Relating to a curve, such as a circle, having no endpoints. **2.** Being a set with the property that the results produced by an operation (such as addition) on members of the set are also members of the set. The set of whole numbers is closed under addition (because whole numbers are the result of adding whole numbers), but not under division (because fractions may result from dividing one number by another).

closed circuit **1.** An electric circuit through which current can flow in an uninterrupted path. **2.** A television system in which the signal is usually sent by cable to a limited number of receivers.

closed universe A model of the universe in which there is enough matter, and therefore enough gravitational force, to stop the expansion started by the big bang. *See Note at* **big bang.**

clot (klŏt) A thickened or solid mass formed from a liquid: *a blood clot.*

cloud (kloud) **1.** A visible mass of condensed water droplets or ice particles floating in the atmosphere. Clouds take various shapes depending on the conditions under which they form and their height in the atmosphere, ranging from ground or sea level to several miles above the Earth. **2.** A distinguishable mass of particles or gas, such as the collection of gases and dust in a nebula.

cloud chamber A device used to observe the movements of charged atomic particles and subatomic particles, such as ions and electrons. Cloud chambers consist of a closed container connected to a piston and filled with a gas. When the piston is suddenly moved outwards, the vapor expands and cools, forming a visible cloud of tiny droplets on any charged particles present. *Compare* **bubble chamber.**

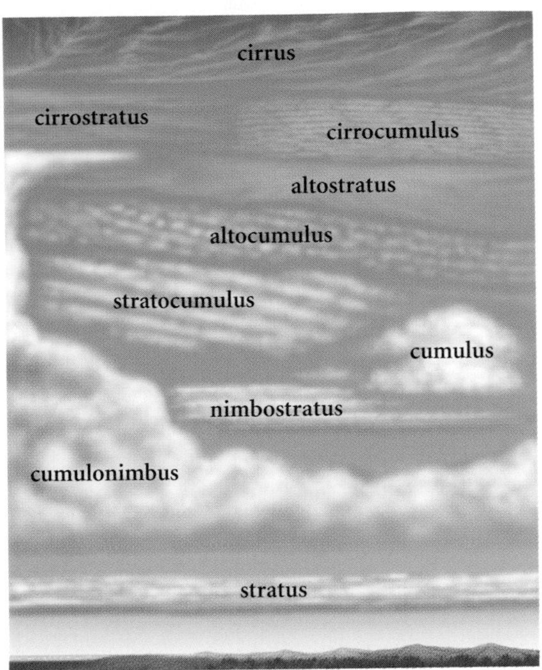

■ **cloud**

cloud seeding A method of making a cloud give up its moisture as rain, especially by releasing particles of dry ice or silver iodide into the cloud.

club moss (klŭb) Any of various primitive plants that resemble mosses and reproduce by spores, but have tissues (known as vascular tissues) that conduct fluids. Club mosses live in moist environments, have evergreen needle-like leaves, and often resemble miniature conifers. They live in tropical and temperate regions, with many tropical species growing in trees as epiphytes.

cm Abbreviation of **centimeter.**

Cm The symbol for **curium.**

cni•dar•i•an (nī-dâr′ē-ən) Any of various invertebrate animals that have a body with radial symmetry, tentacles, and a sac-like internal cavity. They have a single opening for ingesting food and eliminating wastes. Cnidarians include the jellyfishes, hydras, sea anemones, and corals. Also called *coelenterate.*

Co The symbol for **cobalt.**

co•ag•u•late (kō-ăg′yə-lāt′) To change a liquid into a solid or nearly solid mass: *Exposure to air coagulates the blood.*

coal (kōl) A dark-brown to black, natural solid substance formed from fossilized plants under conditions of great pressure, high humidity, and lack of air. Coal consists mainly of carbon and is widely used as a fuel and raw material. *See more at* **anthracite, bituminous coal, lignite.**

coal tar A thick, sticky, black liquid obtained by heating coal in the absence of air. It is used as a raw material for many dyes, drugs, and paints.

co•bal•a•min (kō-băl′ə-mĭn) *See under* **vitamin B complex.**

co•balt (kō′bôlt′) A silvery-white, hard, brittle metallic element that occurs widely in ores containing other metals. It is used to make magnetic alloys, heat-resistant alloys, and blue pigment for ceramics and glass. *Symbol* **Co.** *Atomic number* 27. *See* **Periodic Table,** pages 262–263.

co•bra (kō′brə) Any of several poisonous Asian or African snakes capable of spreading out the skin of the neck to form a flattened hood when excited.

coc•cus (kŏk′əs) *Plural* **cocci** (kŏk′sī, kŏk′ī) Any of various bacteria that are shaped like a sphere and are usually linked together to form chains.

coc•cyx (kŏk′sĭks) A small triangular bone at the base of the spine in humans and tailless apes. It is composed of several fused vertebrae. Also called *tailbone. See more at* **skeleton.**

coch•le•a (kŏk′lē-ə) A spiral tube of the inner ear that looks like a snail shell and contains the nerve endings necessary for hearing.

Cock•croft (kŏk′krôft′), Sir **John Douglas** 1897–1967. British physicist. With the physicist Ernest Walton, he developed the particle accelerator. Their experiments with it led to the first successful splitting of an atom in 1932.

cock•le (kŏk′əl) Any of various bivalve mollusks having rounded or heart-shaped shells with radiating ridges.

cock•roach (kŏk′rōch′) Any of numerous brownish or black insects having a flat body and usually long antennae. Certain species are common household pests.

co•coon (kə-ko͞on′) **1.** A case or covering of silky strands spun by an insect larva and inhabited for protection during its pupal stage. **2.** A similar protective structure, such as the egg cases made by spiders or earthworms.

co•ef•fi•cient (kō′ə-fĭsh′ənt) A number or symbol multiplied with a variable or an unknown quantity in an algebraic term. For example, 4 is the coefficient in the term $4x$, and x is the coefficient in $x(a + b)$.

coe•la•canth (sē′lə-kănth′) Any of various fish having lobed, fleshy fins. They are the only living varieties of an ancient order of lobe-finned fish. Coelacanths were thought to be extinct until a living species was discovered in 1938.

coe•len•ter•ate (sĭ-lĕn′tə-rĭt) *See* **cnidarian.**

co•ev•o•lu•tion (kō′ĕv-ə-lo͞o′shən) The evolution of two or more species that are dependent on one another, with each species adapting to changes in the other. The development of flowering plants and insects such as bees and butterflies that pollinate them is an example of coevolution.

co•he•sion (kō-hē′zhən) The force of attraction that holds molecules of a given substance together. It is strongest in solids, less strong in liquids, and least strong in gases. Cohesion allows the formation of drops in liquids, and clouds in the atmosphere.

cold-blood•ed (kōld′blŭd′ĭd) Having a body temperature that changes according to the temperature of the surroundings. Fish, amphibians, and reptiles are cold-blooded.

cold front (kōld) The forward edge of an advancing mass of cold air that pushes under a mass of warm air. A cold front is often accompanied by heavy showers or thunderstorms. *See more at* **front.**

col•la•gen (kŏl′ə-jən) The tough, fibrous protein found in bone, cartilage, skin, and other connective tissue. Collagen provides these body structures with the ability to withstand forces that stretch or lengthen them.

col•lar•bone (kŏl′ər-bōn′) *See* **clavicle.**

col•lin•e•ar (kə-lĭn′ē-ər) *Mathematics.* **1.** Sharing a common line, such as two intersecting planes. **2.** Lying on the same line, such as a set of points.

coelacanth

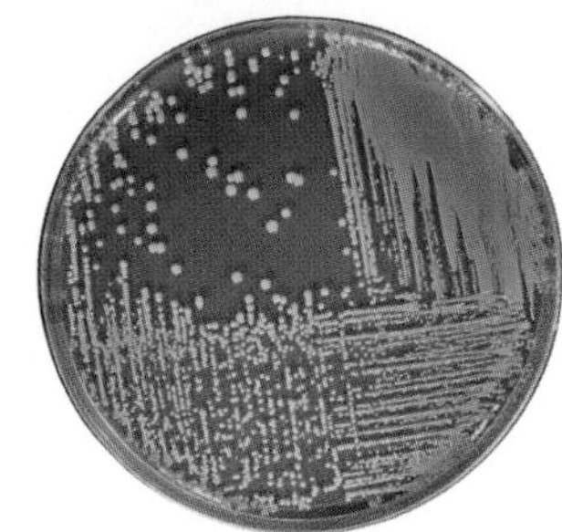

colony
colony of staphylococcus bacteria in a petri dish

col•li•sion zone (kə-lĭzh′ən) *See* **convergent plate boundary.**

col•loid (kŏl′oid′) A mixture in which very small particles of one substance are distributed evenly throughout another substance. The particles are generally larger than those in a solution, and smaller than those in a suspension. Paints, milk, and fog are examples of colloids. *Compare* **solution, suspension.**

co•lon (kō′lən) The longest part of the large intestine, extending from the cecum to the rectum. Food waste received from the small intestine is solidified and prepared for elimination from the body in the colon.

col•o•ni•za•tion (kŏl′ə-nĭ-zā′shən) *Ecology.* The spreading of a species into a new habitat.

col•o•ny (kŏl′ə-nē) A group of the same kind of animals, plants, or one-celled organisms living or growing together: *a colony of ants; a colony of bacteria.*

col•or (kŭl′ər) The sensation produced by the effect of light waves striking the retina of the eye. The color of something depends mainly on which wavelengths of light it emits, reflects, or transmits.

comet
Comet Hale-Bopp

A CLOSER LOOK

Color

When beams of colored light are mixed, or added, their wavelengths combine to form other colors. All colors can be formed by mixing wavelengths corresponding to the additive primaries red, green, and blue. When two of the additive primaries are mixed in equal proportion, they form the complement of the third. Thus cyan (a mixture of green and blue) is the complement of red; magenta (a mixture of blue and red) is the complement of green; and yellow (a mixture of red and green) is the complement of blue. Mixing the three additive primaries in equal proportions produces white light.

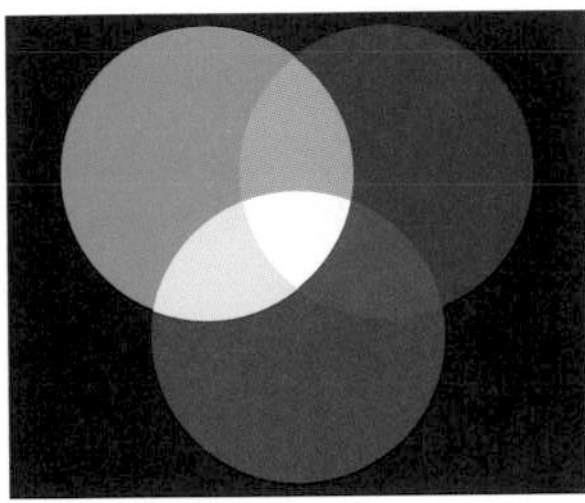

Additive Primaries

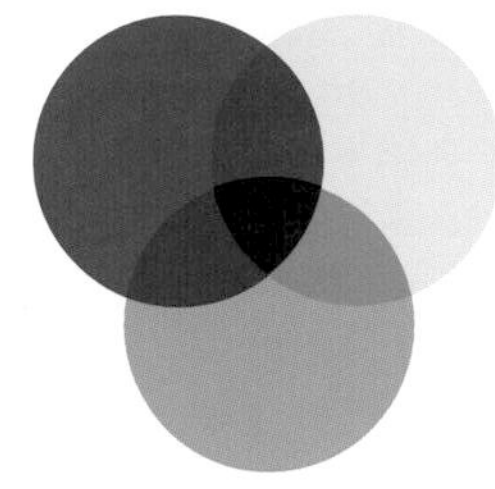

Subtractive Primaries

When light passes through a color filter, certain wavelengths are absorbed, or subtracted, while others are transmitted. The subtractive primaries cyan, magenta, and yellow can be combined using overlapping filters to form all other colors. Thus overlapping filters of cyan (blue and green) and magenta (blue and red) filter out all wavelengths except blue; magenta (blue and red) and yellow (red and green) filter out all except red; and yellow (red and green) and cyan (blue and green) filter out all except green. Combining all three subtractive primaries in equal proportions filters out all wavelengths, producing black.

We often describe different shades of color as being dark, light, bright, or pale. A particular color can be described scientifically in terms of its hue (red, green, blue, and so forth), its value (how light or dark it is), and its saturation (how intense or vivid it is). The diagram below organizes these aspects of color into three dimensions: a central disk or ring displaying the range of hues, a vertical axis representing the values from light to dark, and a horizontal axis representing the degree of saturation from pale to intense.

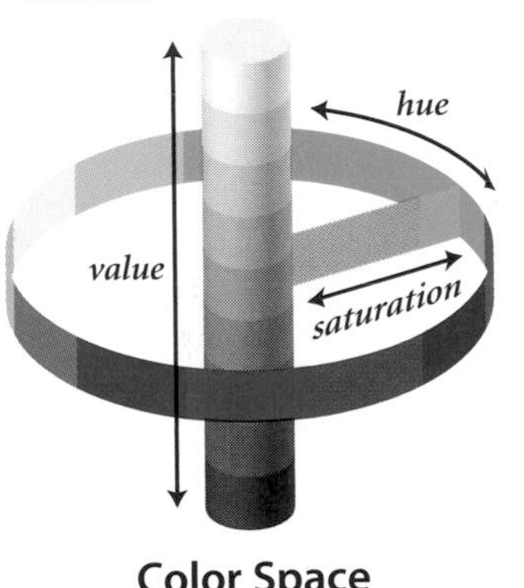

Color Space

color-blind Unable to distinguish certain colors. Humans who are color-blind usually cannot distinguish red from green. Many animals, including cats and dogs, are able to distinguish only a few colors.

co•ma[1] (kō′mə) A state of deep unconsciousness resulting from disease or injury, from which a person cannot be aroused. A person in a coma usually is unable to respond to events taking place outside the body.

coma[2] The brightly shining cloud of gas that encircles the nucleus and makes up the major portion of the head of a comet that is near the sun.

comb jelly (kōm) Any of various invertebrate animals living in the ocean and having transparent, jelly-like bodies. Comb jellies have eight rows of comb-like cilia used for swimming.

com•bus•tion (kəm-bŭs′chən) **1.** The process of burning. **2.** A chemical change, especially through the rapid combination of a substance with oxygen, producing heat and, usually, light. *See also* **spontaneous combustion.**

com•et (kŏm′ĭt) A celestial object that orbits the sun along an elongated path. When close to the sun, a comet has a head made up of a gaseous coma surrounding a solid nucleus of ice, frozen gases, and dust. A long, bright stream of gas and dust forms the tail of a comet. *See Note at* **solar system.**

com•men•sal•ism (kə-mĕn′sə-lĭz′əm) A symbiotic relationship between two organisms of different species in which one derives benefit without harming the other. *See Note at* **symbiosis.**

com•mon cold (kŏm′ən) An infection caused by a virus, in which the membranes lining the mouth, nose, and throat become inflamed. Its symptoms are fever, sneezing, and coughing.

common denominator A quantity into which all the denominators of a set of fractions may be divided without a remainder. The fractions $\frac{1}{3}$ and $\frac{2}{5}$ have a common denominator of 15.

common divisor A number that is a factor of two or more numbers. For example, 3 is a common divisor of both 9 and 15. Also called *common factor.*

common logarithm A logarithm having 10 as its base. *Compare* **natural logarithm.**

common multiple A number divisible by each of two or more numbers without a remainder. A common multiple of 2, 3, 4, and 6 is 12.

com•mu•ni•ca•ble (kə-myo͞o′nĭ-kə-bəl) Capable of being transmitted from person to person. Chickenpox is a communicable disease. *See Note at* **infectious.**

com•mu•ni•ca•tions satellite (kə-myo͞o′nĭ-kā′shənz) An artificial space satellite used to transmit signals, such as television and telephone signals, from one ground station to another.

com•mu•ni•ty (kə-myo͞o′nĭ-tē) A group of plants and animals living and interacting with one another in a particular place. A community can be small and local, as in a pond or city park, or it can be regional or global, as in a rain forest or the ocean.

com•mu•ta•tive property (kŏm′yə-tā′tĭv, kə-myo͞o′tə-tĭv) A property distinguishing some mathematical operations on two objects, such as the addition or multiplication of two numbers, where the order of the objects may be reversed without affecting the result. For example, 2 + 3 gives the same sum as 3 + 2, and 2 × 3 gives the same product as 3 × 2. *See also* **associative property, distributive property.**

com•pact disk *or* **com•pact disc** (kŏm′păkt′) A small optical disk on which data such as music or images is digitally encoded. *See Note at* **disk.**

com•pass (kŭm′pəs) **1.** A device used to determine geographical direction, usually consisting of a magnetic needle mounted on a pivot, aligning itself naturally with the Earth's magnetic field so that it points toward the Earth's geomagnetic north or south pole. **2.** A device for drawing circles and arcs and measuring distances, consisting of two legs hinged together at one end.

com•ple•ment (kŏm′plə-mənt) **1.** A system of proteins found in the serum of the blood that helps antibodies destroy disease-causing bacteria or other foreign substances, especially antigens. **2.** A complementary color.

com•ple•men•ta•ry angles (kŏm′plə-mĕn′tə-rē) Two angles whose sum is 90°.

complementary color A secondary color that, when combined with the primary color whose wavelength it does not contain, produces white light. *See more at* **color.**

com•plex number (kŏm′plĕks′) A number that can be expressed in terms of i (the square root of −1). Mathematically, such a number can be written $a + bi$, where a and b are real numbers. An example is $4 + 5i$.

com•pos•ite number (kəm-pŏz′ĭt) A positive integer that can be divided by at least one other positive integer besides itself and 1 without leaving a remainder. 24 is a composite number since it can be divided by 2, 3, 4, 6, 8, and 12. No prime numbers are composite numbers. *Compare* **prime number.**

com•post (kŏm′pōst′) A mixture of decayed or decaying organic matter used to fertilize soil. Compost is usually made by gathering plant

■ **commensalism**

Barnacles attached to a gray whale gain a home and are harmless to the whale.

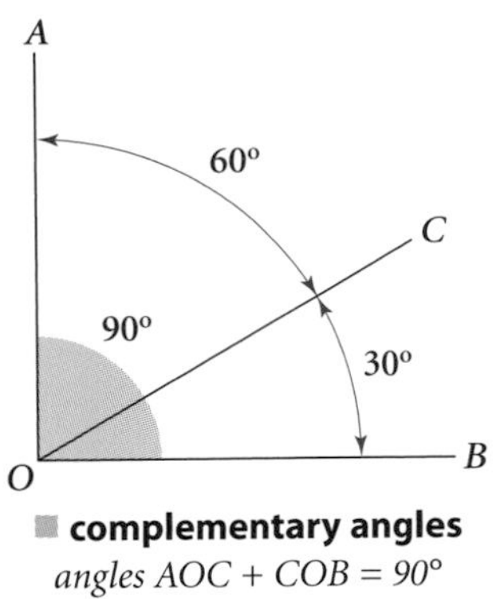

complementary angles
angles AOC + COB = 90°

material, such as leaves, grass clippings, and vegetable peels, into a pile or bin and letting it rot. Manure and other organic substances are often added to enrich the mixture or to speed its decomposition.

com•post•ing toilet (kŏm′pō′stĭng) A toilet that uses little or no water and is connected to a tank in which waste material is decomposed by bacteria. Composting toilets are used especially to conserve water in areas where it is scarce.

com•pound (kŏm′pound′) *Noun.* **1.** *Chemistry.* A substance made up of two or more elements joined by chemical bonds into a molecule. The elements are combined in a definite ratio. Water, for example, is a compound having two hydrogen atoms and one oxygen atom in each molecule. —*Adjective.* **2.** Composed of more than one part, as a compound eye or leaf.

compound eye An eye, as of an insect or crustacean, consisting of hundreds or thousands of tiny light-sensitive parts, with each part creating a portion of an image.

compound leaf A leaf that is composed of two or more leaflets on a common stalk. Clover, roses, sumac, and walnut trees have compound leaves.

compound lens *See* **lens** (sense 2b).

com•pres•sion (kəm-prĕsh′ən) A force that tends to shorten or squeeze something, decreasing its volume.

Comp•ton (kŏmp′tən), **Arthur Holly** 1892–1962. American physicist who proved Albert Einstein's statement that a particle of light has momentum even though it has no mass. Compton's experiments showed that when particles of light (called photons) collide with other particles, such as electrons, they lose energy and

Did You Know?
compound eye

The eyes have it—the important ability to see, that is. But not all eyes are created equal. Insects and other arthropods (which include lobsters and other crustaceans) have *compound eyes,* which are quite different from ours. The compound eye, greatly magnified, looks like a fencer's mask. It consists of many repeating units, called *ommatidia,* each of which is a separate light receptor. Some species' eyes have many ommatidia while others have only a few—the more ommatidia an eye has, the better it can resolve images. But even with many ommatidia, the typical compound eye is poor compared with ours at creating a sharp image. A honeybee, for example, sees only one-sixtieth as clearly as we do. However, the compound eye has other special talents. It is excellent at detecting motion, as the moving object passes from one ommatidium to the next. And some insects see ultraviolet light, which is invisible to us.

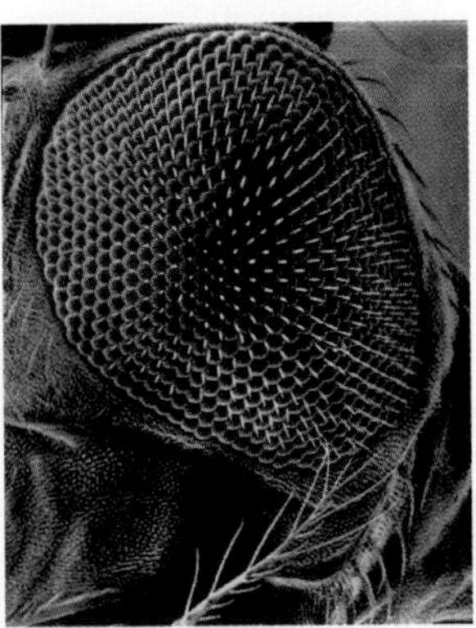

fruit fly eye

Did You Know?

conduction, convection, and radiation

Heat is a form of energy that results in the motion of molecules. Heat travels by conduction, convection, or radiation. In *conduction,* heat spreads through a solid by making its molecules vibrate faster. As faster molecules bump slower ones, the slower ones are made to vibrate faster, and the solid becomes hotter. This is how the handle of a teaspoon sticking out of a cup of hot tea eventually gets hot. When liquids and gases are heated, their molecules, which are free to move about, move farther apart. The hotter portions of the liquid or gas expand, become less dense, and rise, and cooler portions move down to take their place. This movement causes the liquid or gas to circulate in the process called *convection.* The currents of the ocean are convection currents caused by the uneven heating of the ocean waters by the sun. *Radiation* carries heat in the form of waves through space. A hot object, like the hot wire in a heat lamp, gives off energy waves called *infrared rays.* When these rays strike an object, its molecules absorb the rays' energy and vibrate or move faster, and so the object becomes hotter. The sunlight that warms your face has traveled through 93 million miles of space by radiation.

momentum and the light's wavelength increases. This phenomenon became known as the Compton effect.

com•put•er (kəm-pyo͞o′tər) An electronic device capable of processing information according to a set of instructions stored within the device. *See Note at* **program.**

computer science The study of the design and operation of computers and their application to science, business, and the arts. *See A Timeline of Computing, page 80.*

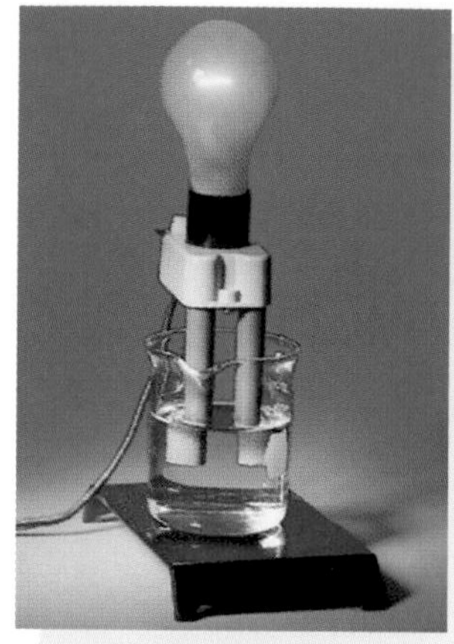

conductivity

Electrons flow through acetic acid, a low-conductivity electrolyte solution, producing a dim light.

con•cave (kŏn′kāv′) Curved inward, like the inside of a circle or sphere.

con•cen•tra•tion (kŏn′sən-trā′shən) The amount of a particular substance in a given amount of another substance, especially a solution or mixture.

con•cep•tion (kən-sĕp′shən) The formation of a cell capable of developing into a new organism by the union of a sperm and egg cell; fertilization.

conch (kŏngk, kŏnch) Any of various tropical mollusks having a large spiral shell with a flared opening.

con•cus•sion (kən-kŭsh′ən) An injury to the brain resulting from shaking or a blow to the head. Symptoms include temporary loss of consciousness and sometimes loss of memory.

con•den•sa•tion (kŏn′dən-sā′shən) The change of a gas or vapor to a liquid, either by cooling or by being subjected to increased pressure. When water vapor cools in the atmosphere, for example, it condenses into tiny drops of water, which form clouds.

con•duc•tance (kən-dŭk′təns) A measure of the ability of a material to carry an electric charge.

con•duc•tion (kən-dŭk′shən) The flow of energy, such as heat or an electric charge, through a substance. In heat conduction, the energy flows by direct contact of the substance's molecules with each other. Although the molecules vibrate, they do not change position in the transfer of

■ **cone**

top: *The volume (V) of a cone can be calculated using the following equation:* $V = \frac{1}{3}\pi r^2 h$.
bottom: *detail of the retina showing cones and rods*

energy. In electrical conduction, energy flows by the movement of electrons or ions.

con•duc•tiv•i•ty (kŏn′dŭk-tĭv′ĭ-tē) The ability or power to transfer heat, electricity, or sound by conduction.

con•duc•tor (kən-dŭk′tər) A material or an object that conducts heat, electricity, light, or sound. Copper is a good conductor of electricity.

con•dyle (kŏn′dīl′) A rounded prominence at the end of a bone.

cone (kōn) **1.** A three-dimensional surface or solid object whose surface rises from a circular base in a continuous series of smaller circles, narrowing to a point (the vertex) at the top. A cone can be defined as the surface covered by a line segment with one end fixed at the vertex, and the other end rotated in a circle. **2.** A rounded or elongated cluster of woody scales enclosing the reproductive structures of conifers such as pines, spruces, and firs. Cones are either male, producing pollen, or female, bearing seeds. Male cones are much smaller than female cones. When the seeds become mature, the female cones expand to release them. **3.** One of the cone-shaped cells in the retina of the eye of many vertebrate animals. Cones are responsible for daylight vision and, in some animals, for the ability to see colors. *Compare* **rod.**

con•gen•i•tal (kən-jĕn′ĭ-tl) Existing at or before birth, as a defect or medical condition. *See Note at* **heritable.**

con•ges•tive heart failure (kən-jĕs′tĭv) Inability of the heart to circulate blood adequately to the lungs and outer body tissues, resulting in weakness and shortness of breath.

con•glom•er•ate (kən-glŏm′ə-rāt′) A coarse-grained sedimentary rock that consists of pebbles, gravel, or seashells cemented together by hardened silt, clay, calcium carbonate, or a similar material. *See Table at* **rock.**

con•gru•ent (kŏng′gro͞o-ənt, kən-gro͞o′ənt) *Geometry.* Having the same size and shape; matching exactly: *congruent triangles.*

con•ic projection (kŏn′ĭk) A method of making a flat map of the Earth by projecting its surface features onto a cone, which is then flattened out so that parallels appear as arcs of circles. *Compare* **homolosine projection, Mercator projection, sinusoidal projection.**

conic section A curve formed by the intersection of a plane with a cone. Conic sections can appear as circles, ellipses, hyperbolas, or parabolas, depending on the angle of the intersecting plane relative to the cone's base.

con•i•fer (kŏn′ə-fər) Any of various trees or shrubs that bear cones. Conifers are dependent on the wind to blow pollen produced by the male cones to the female cones, where seeds develop. Conifers are usually evergreen, often have nee-

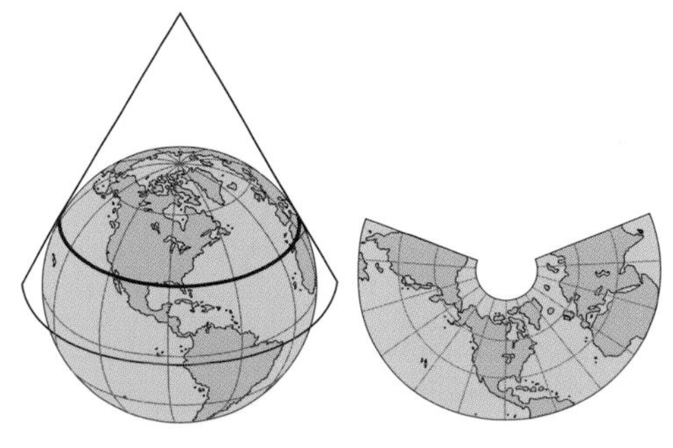

■ **conic projection**

A TIMELINE OF COMPUTING

Throughout recorded history, humans have used devices to help make calculations. Five thousand years ago, people manipulated abacuses with their fingers to add, subtract, multiply, and divide numbers. Much later, mechanical devices were developed for these same tasks. During the twentieth century, the invention of electronics allowed for the development of computer science, making the computation of trillions of calculations per second possible and extending the use of computers into many aspects of people's daily lives. Current research in quantum physics should result in even more powerful computers in the decades to come. Below are some milestones in developing the hardware that has helped people perform calculations through the ages.

YEAR	MILESTONE
3000 BC	The abacus is invented in the Middle East.
1642 AD	Blaise Pascal invents the wheeled calculator.
1694	Wilhem von Leibniz invents the mechanical multiplier.
1842	Charles Babbage designs the Differential Engine (never built) to use steam to perform computations.
1889	Herman Hollerith uses punch cards to tabulate US census, reducing computation time from 10 years to six weeks.
1943	The British complete a secret code-breaking computer called Colossus to decode German war messages.
1944	Mark I, an electronic relay computer half as long as a football field with 500 miles of wiring, is used to create ballistics charts for the US Navy.
1945	The ENIAC computer uses vacuum tubes and resistors to compute at speeds 1,000 times faster than Mark I.
1951	The UNIVAC I computer becomes commercially available. It is the first computer that can store a program in memory.
1955	The first computer to use transistors (which are faster, more compact, and give off less heat than vacuum tubes) becomes available.
1971	Intel designs the first microprocessor. All the components of a central processor are now placed on one chip.
1975	The Altair 8800 personal computer is made available through mail order. Within the next decade the electronic computer will become a tool used by millions of ordinary people in their homes.
1977	Apple Computer unveils the Apple II, the first personal computer to feature color graphics. Radio Shack and Commodore also bring computers to the home market.
1981	IBM introduces the IBM PC, which eventually becomes the standard for desktop computing. Popular applications include word processing and spreadsheets.
1990	Laptop computers become common. During the 1990s, they decrease in size and price.
1991	The World Wide Web offers researchers and students the ability to access electronic files. By the end of the decade, over one hundred million people seek and share information regularly on the Web.
1997	Handheld computers that are small enough to fit in a shirt pocket become widely accepted.

dle-shaped or scale-like leaves, and include the pine, fir, spruce, hemlock, and yew. *See Note at* **pollination.**

con•ju•gate angles (kŏn′jə-gĭt) Two angles whose sum is 360°.

con•ju•ga•tion (kŏn′jə-gā′shən) A type of sexual reproduction in single-celled organisms, such as bacteria and some algae and fungi. In conjugation, two organisms or cells from the same species join together to exchange genetic material before undergoing cell division.

con•junc•ti•va (kŏn′jŭngk-tī′və) The mucous membrane that lines the inside of the eyelid and covers the surface of the eyeball. ❖ Inflammation of the conjunctiva is called **conjunctivitis** (kən-jŭngk′tə-vī′tĭs).

con•nec•tive tissue (kə-nĕk′tĭv) Tissue that forms the framework and supporting structures of the body, including bone, cartilage, mucous membrane, and fat.

con•ser•va•tion (kŏn′sûr-vā′shən) **1.** The protection, preservation, management, or restoration of wildlife and natural resources such as forests and water. **2.** The continuance of a physical quantity, such as mass, in the same amount during a physical or chemical change.

con•stant (kŏn′stənt) **1.** A quantity that is unknown but assumed to have a fixed value in a specified mathematical context. **2.** A theoretical or experimental quantity, condition, or factor that does not vary in specified circumstances. Avogadro's number and Planck's constant are examples of constants.

con•stel•la•tion (kŏn′stə-lā′shən) **1.** A group of stars seen as forming a figure or design in the sky, especially one of 88 recognized groups. **2.** An area of the celestial sphere occupied by one of the 88 recognized constellations.

con•stric•tor (kən-strĭk′tər) Any of various snakes that tightly coil around and suffocate their prey. Boa constrictors, pythons, and anacondas are constrictors.

con•sum•er (kən-sōō′mər) An organism that feeds on other organisms in a food chain. ❖ Herbivores that feed on green plants in a food chain are called **primary consumers,** and carnivores that feed on herbivores are **secondary consumers.** Carnivores that feed on other carnivores are called **tertiary consumers.** *Compare* **producer.**

con•tact (kŏn′tăkt′) **1.** *Electricity.* **a.** A connection between two conductors that allows an electric current to flow. **b.** A part or device that makes or breaks a connection in an electrical circuit. **2.** *Geology.* The place where two different geological layers or rocks come together.

con•ta•gion (kən-tā′jən) **1.** The transmission of disease resulting from contact between individuals: *Lack of sanitary conditions may lead to widespread contagion.* **2.** A disease that is transmitted in this way: *The flu is a common contagion of the winter months.*

con•ta•gious (kən-tā′jəs) Capable of being transmitted by direct or indirect contact; communicable: *a contagious disease. See Note at* **infectious.**

con•tam•i•nate (kən-tăm′ə-nāt′) **1.** To make impure or unclean by mixture or contact. **2.** To cause something to become dangerously radioactive.

con•ti•nent (kŏn′tə-nənt) One of the seven great landmasses of the Earth. The continents are Africa, Antarctica, Asia, Australia, Europe, North America, and South America.

con•ti•nen•tal divide (kŏn′tə-nĕn′tl) A region of high ground, from each side of which the river systems of a continent flow in opposite directions. ❖ In North America, the **Continental Divide** is a series of mountain ridges stretching from Alaska to Mexico.

continental drift The gradual movement of the Earth's continents toward or away from each

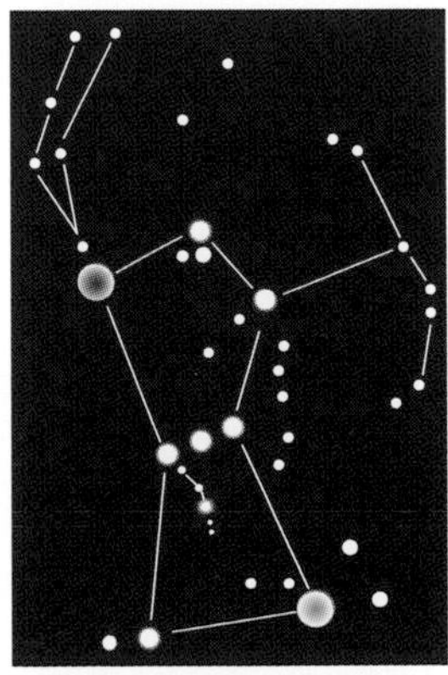

constellation

Diagram of the constellation Orion. Betelgeuse, the large, reddish star, is the coolest star in the constellation; Rigel, the large, bluish-white star, is the hottest. Orion's belt can be seen in the middle of the figure.

other. *See more at* **plate tectonics.** *See Note at* **Gondwanaland.**

continental rise A wide, gentle incline from the ocean bottom to the continental slope. The continental rise consists mainly of silts, muds, and sand, and can be several hundreds of miles wide.

continental shelf The part of the edge of a continent covered by shallow ocean waters and extending to the steep slopes that descend into the deep part of the ocean.

continental slope The sloping region between the continental shelf and the continental rise. The continental slope is typically about 12.5 miles (20 kilometers) wide, consists of muds and silts, and is often crosscut by submarine canyons.

con•tour line (kŏn′to͝or′) A line on a map joining points of the same elevation.

contour map A map that shows elevations above sea level and surface features of the land by means of contour lines.

con•tra•cep•tive (kŏn′trə-sĕp′tĭv) A substance or device capable of preventing pregnancy.

con•trac•tion (kən-trăk′shən) The shortening and thickening of a muscle in action. Contraction of the biceps of the arm causes the elbow to bend.

con•trol (kən-trōl′) Something used as a standard of comparison in a scientific experiment. In an experiment to test the effectiveness of a new drug, for instance, the control is an inactive substance (such as a sugar pill) that is given to one group of people, so that their results can be compared with those of a group who actually took the drug. ❖ An experiment designed to test the effects of a single condition or factor on a system is called a **control experiment.** Only the condition being studied is allowed to vary, and all other conditions are kept constant.

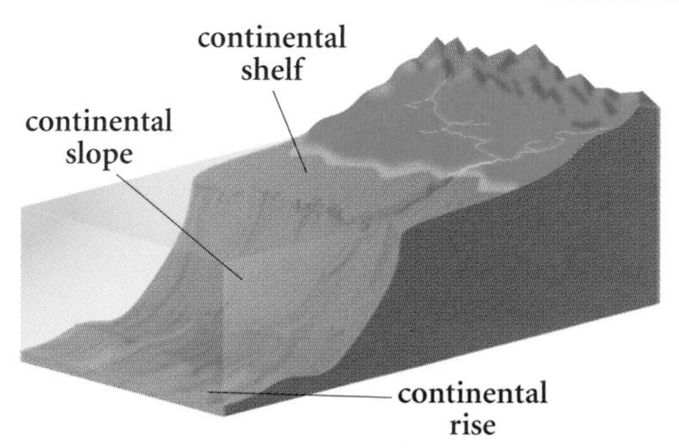

■ **continental shelf**

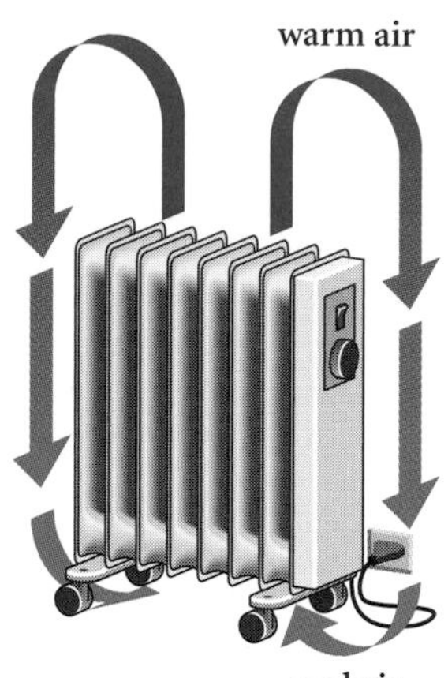

■ **convection**

Air heated by a space heater rises, then cools and falls to be heated and rise again. This cycle creates a convection current that circulates hot air throughout a room.

con•vec•tion (kən-vĕk′shən) The transfer of heat energy through liquids and gases by the movement of molecules. When molecules of the liquid or gas come in contact with a source of heat, they move apart and away from the source of heat, and cooler molecules take their place. Eventually, as the cooler molecules are heated, they move as well, and a convection current forms, transferring the heat. *See Note at* **conduction.**

convection zone The outer part of the inside of a star, especially the sun, where energy travels outward to the photosphere through convection. In this layer, hot gas rises, cools as it nears the surface, and falls to be heated and rise again.

con•verge (kən-vûrj′) **1.** To tend toward or approach an intersecting point. **2.** In calculus, to approach a limit.

con•ver•gence (kən-vûr′jəns) **1.** The act or process of converging; the tendency to meet in one point. **2.** *Mathematics.* The property or manner of approaching a limit, such as a point, line, or value. **3.** *Biology.* The evolution of superficially similar structures in unrelated species as they adapt to similar environments. An example of convergence is the development of fins independently in both fish and whales. Also called *convergent evolution. Compare* **divergence.**

BIOGRAPHY

Nicolaus Copernicus

The man who devised one of astronomy's most important theories wasn't even a trained astronomer: Nicolaus Copernicus practiced medicine, and he wrote the work that made him famous in his spare time. In the first, brief version of his theory, Copernicus set out his heliocentric system, stating that the sun is at the center of the universe and that all the planets and stars revolve around it in circular orbits. In doing so, Copernicus was trying to explain the observed movements of the planets—those that, in the days before telescopes, were visible to the naked eye. These movements did not fit the older, Earth-centered (or geocentric) model of the universe devised by the Greek astronomer Ptolemy. Copernicus's sun-centered model offered a more accurate accounting of planetary movement. He published a longer, more complete account of his theory in 1543, just before he died. Almost all of his contemporaries doubted that his system could be true, and they kept working with the older, geocentric model. After Copernicus died, there were a few people who defended his model, including the astronomers Johannes Kepler and Galileo Galilei. But it took almost 150 years for the Copernican theory to take hold, when Sir Isaac Newton published his theory of universal gravitation.

con•ver•gent plate boundary (kən-vûr′jənt) A tectonic boundary where two plates are moving toward each other. If the two plates are of equal density, they usually push up against each other to form a mountain chain. If they are of unequal density, one plate usually sinks (subducts) beneath the other. Also called *collision zone. See more at* **tectonic boundary.** *Compare* **divergent plate boundary.**

con•vert•er (kən-vûr′tər) **1.** A machine that changes alternating current to direct current or direct current to alternating current. **2.** An electronic device that changes the frequency of a radio or other electromagnetic signal.

con•vex (kŏn′vĕks′) Curving outward, like the outer boundary of a circle or sphere.

co•or•di•nate (kō-ôr′dn-ĭt) One of a set of numbers that determines the position of a point. Only one coordinate is needed if the point is on a line, two if the point is in a plane, and three if it is in space.

coordinate bond A type of covalent bond in which both the shared electrons are contributed by one of the two atoms. Also called *dative bond. See more at* **covalent bond.**

co•pe•pod (kō′pə-pŏd′) Any of various very small crustaceans having an elongated body and a forked tail. Copepods are abundant in both salt and fresh water. They are an important food source for many water animals.

Co•per•ni•cus (kō-pûr′nə-kəs), **Nicolaus** 1473–1543. Polish astronomer whose theory that Earth and other planets revolve around the sun provided the foundation for modern astronomy. He also proposed that the Earth turns once daily on its own axis.

cop•per (kŏp′ər) A reddish-brown, easily shaped metallic element that is an excellent conductor of heat and electricity. It is widely used for electrical wiring, water piping, and rust-resistant parts, either in its pure form or in alloys such as brass and bronze. *Symbol* **Cu.** *Atomic number* 29. *See* **Periodic Table,** pages 262–263. *See Note at* **element.**

co•qui•na (kō-kē′nə) A brittle limestone made of shells and shell fragments.

cor•al (kôr′əl) **1.** Any of numerous small, sedentary animals that often form massive colonies in shallow sea water. They secrete a cup-shaped skeleton of calcium carbonate, which they can retreat into when in danger. Corals are cnidarians and have stinging tentacles radiating around their mouth opening. The tentacles are used in catching prey. **2.** A hard, stony substance consisting of the skeletons of these animals. It is typically white, pink, or reddish and can form large reefs that support an abundance of ocean fish.

coral reef A mound or ridge of coral skeletons and calcium carbonate deposits. Coral reefs form in warm, shallow sea waters and provide food and shelter to a wide variety of fish and invertebrates. They also protect shores against erosion by causing large waves to break and lose some of their force before reaching land.

cor•dil•le•ra (kôr′dl-yâr′ə) A long and wide chain of mountains, especially the main mountain range of a large landmass.

core (kôr) **1.** The hard or stringy central part of certain fruits, such as apples and pears, that contains the seeds. **2.** The central or innermost portion of the Earth below the mantle, probably consisting of iron and nickel. It is divided into a liquid outer core, which begins at a depth of 1,800 miles (2,898 kilometers), and a solid inner core, which begins at a depth of 3,095 miles (4,983 kilometers). **3.** A piece of magnetizable material, such as a rod of soft iron, that is placed inside an electrical coil or transformer to intensify and provide a path for the magnetic field produced by the current running through the wire windings. **4.** The central part of a nuclear reactor where atomic fission occurs. **5.** A long, cylindrical sample of soil, rock, or ice, collected with a drill to study the layers of material that are not visible from the surface.

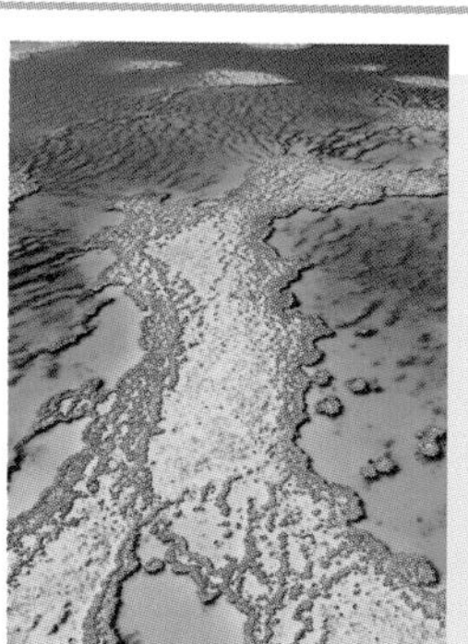

■ **coral reef**

left: *aerial photograph of a portion of Australia's Great Barrier Reef*
right: *undersea photograph of a coral reef*

cork (kôrk) **1.** The outermost layer of tissue that becomes the bark of woody plants. Cork is formed on the outside of the tissue layer known as cork cambium. Once they mature, cork cells die. Also called *phellem.* **2.** The lightweight, elastic outer bark of the cork oak, which grows near the Mediterranean Sea. Cork is used for bottle stoppers, insulation, and other products.

cork cambium A layer of cambium near the outer edge of the stems of woody plants that produces cork to the outside and cortex to the inside. Also called *phellogen. See more at* **cambium.**

corm (kôrm) A fleshy underground stem that is similar to a bulb but stores its food as stem tissue and has fewer and thinner leaf-like scales. The crocus and gladiolus produce new shoots from corms. *Compare* **bulb, rhizome, runner, tuber.**

cor•ne•a (kôr′nē-ə) The tough transparent membrane of the outer layer of the eyeball that covers the iris and the pupil. *See more at* **eye.**

co•rol•la (kə-rŏl′ə, kə-rō′lə) The petals of a flower considered as a group or unit. *See more at* **flower.**

cor•ol•lar•y (kôr′ə-lĕr′ē) A statement that follows with little or no proof required from an already proven statement.

co•ro•na (kə-rō′nə) **1.** The irregular envelope of gas outside the chromosphere of a star, especially the sun. **2.** A faintly colored shining ring appearing around a celestial body, especially the moon or sun, when seen through a haze or thin cloud. **3.** A crown-shaped structure on the inner side of the petals of some flowers, such as the daffodil.

Corona Bo•re•al•is (bôr′ē-ăl′ĭs) A constellation in the Northern Hemisphere between Hercules and Boötes.

cor•o•nar•y (kôr′ə-nĕr′ē) Relating to the heart. ❖ The two arteries that branch from the aorta to supply blood directly to the heart are called the **coronary arteries.**

cor•pus•cle (kôr′pə-səl) Any of various cells or cell-shaped structures in the body, especially a blood cell.

corona

cor•ro•sion (kə-rō′zhən) The breaking down or destruction of a material, especially a metal, through chemical reactions. The most common form of corrosion is rusting, which occurs when iron combines with oxygen and water.

cor•tex (kôr′tĕks′) **1.** The outer layer of an organ or body part, such as the cerebrum or the adrenal glands. **2.** The region of tissue next to the outermost layer of plant stems and roots. The cortex lies between the epidermis (the outermost layer) and the vascular tissue. In roots the cortex transfers water and minerals from the epidermis to the vascular tissue, which distributes them to other parts of the plant. The cortex also stores food manufactured in the leaves.

co•run•dum (kə-rŭn′dəm) An extremely hard mineral composed mainly of aluminum oxide. It occurs in gem varieties such as ruby and sapphire and in a dark-colored variety that is used for polishing and scraping. Corundum is the mineral used to represent a hardness of 9 on the Mohs scale.

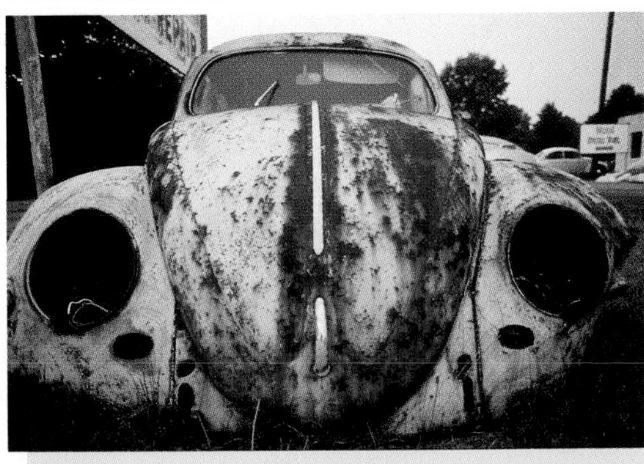
corrosion

cor•ymb (kôr′ĭmb, kôr′ĭm) A flower cluster whose outer flowers have longer stalks than the inner flowers, so that together they form a round cluster that is rather flat on top. Yarrow and the hawthorn have corymbs.

cos Abbreviation of **cosine.**

co•se•cant (kō-sē′kănt′) The ratio of the length of the hypotenuse in a right triangle to the length of the side opposite an acute angle; the inverse of the sine.

co•sine (kō′sīn′) The ratio of the length of the side adjacent to an acute angle of a right triangle to the length of the hypotenuse.

cos•mic (kŏz′mĭk) Relating to the universe or the objects in it.

cos•mol•o•gy (kŏz-mŏl′ə-jē) The branch of astronomy that deals with the origin, evolution, and structure of the universe.

cos•mos (kŏz′məs, kŏz′mōs′) The universe, especially when considered as an orderly and harmonious whole.

cot Abbreviation of **cotangent.**

co•tan•gent (kō-tăn′jənt) The ratio of the length of the adjacent side of an acute angle in a right triangle to the length of the opposite side; the inverse of a tangent.

cot•y•le•don (kŏt′l-ēd′n) A leaf of the embryo of a seed-bearing plant. Most cotyledons emerge, enlarge, and become green after the seed has germinated. Cotyledons either store food for the growing embryo or absorb food that has been stored in the endosperm for eventual distribution to the growing parts of the embryo. Also called *seed leaf. See more at* **dicotyledon, monocotyledon.**

cou•lomb (ko͞o′lŏm′, ko͞o′lōm′) A unit used to measure electric charge. One coulomb is equal to the quantity of charge that passes a point in an electric circuit in one second when a current of one ampere is flowing through the circuit.

Coulomb, Charles Augustin de 1736–1806. French physicist who pioneered research on magnetism and electricity. He is best known for the formulation of Coulomb's law, which he developed as a result of his investigations of Joseph Priestley's work on electrical repulsion. Coulomb also established a law governing the attraction and repulsion of magnetic poles. The coulomb unit of electric charge is named for him.

Coulomb's law A law stating that the strength of the electric field between two charged objects depends on the strength of the charges of the objects and on the distance between them. The greater the charges are, the stronger the field is, and the greater the distance between the charged objects is, the weaker the field is.

Cous•teau (ko͞o-stō′), **Jacques Yves** 1910–1997. French underwater explorer, film producer, and author. Cousteau invented scuba equipment, structures that permit humans to live underwater for prolonged periods of time, and a small submarine known as a diving saucer. He made three feature films and several television series about marine life and later in his career became increasingly involved in biological research and marine conservation.

co•va•lent bond (kō-vā′lənt) A chemical bond formed when electrons are shared between two atoms. Usually each atom contributes one electron to form a pair of electrons that are shared by both atoms. *See more at* **bond, coordinate bond, double bond, ionic bond.**

cow•rie (kou′rē) Any of various tropical marine mollusks having glossy, often brightly marked shells that are rounded on one side and relatively flat on the other. The shells have been used as currency in the South Pacific and Africa.

CPR (sē′pē-är′) Short for *cardiopulmonary resuscitation.* An emergency procedure in which the heart and lungs are made to work by compressing the chest overlying the heart and forcing air into the lungs. CPR is used to maintain circulation when the heart has stopped pumping on its own.

CPU Abbreviation of **central processing unit.**

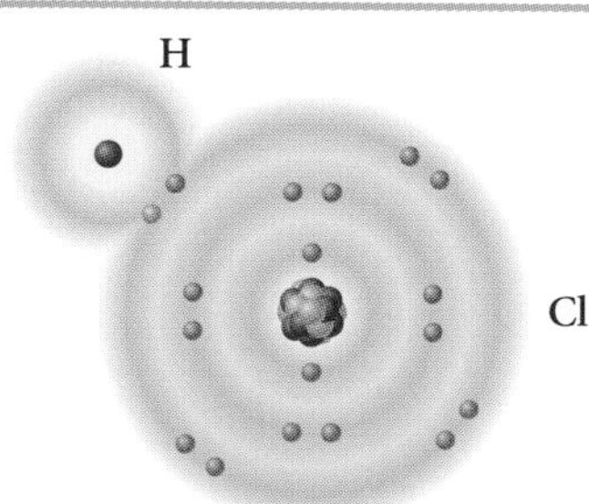

covalent bond

Covalent bonding as seen in a hydrogen chloride molecule. The hydrogen atom (H) shares an electron (yellow) with the chloride atom (Cl).

Cr The symbol for **chromium.**

cra•ni•al (krā′nē-əl) Of or near the skull or cranium.

cranial nerve Any of the 12 pairs of nerves in humans and other mammals that connect the muscles and sensory organs of the head and upper chest directly to the brain. The cranial nerves include the optic nerve and the auditory nerve.

cra•ni•um (krā′nē-əm) The skull of a vertebrate animal. It encloses and protects the brain.

cra•ter (krā′tər) **1.** A bowl-shaped depression at the top of a volcano or at the mouth of a geyser. Volcanic craters can form because of magma explosions, in which a large amount of lava is thrown out from a volcano, leaving a hole, or because the roof of rock over an underground magma pool collapses after the magma has flowed away. **2.** A shallow, bowl-shaped hole in a surface, formed by an explosion or by the impact of a body, such as a meteorite.

cre•o•sote (krē′ə-sōt′) A yellow or brown oily liquid obtained from coal tar and used as a wood preservative and disinfectant.

cres•cent (krĕs′ənt) Partly but less than half illuminated. Used to describe the moon or a planet. *Compare* **gibbous.**

crest (krĕst) The highest part of a wave. *See more at* **wave.**

Cre•ta•ceous (krĭ-tā′shəs) The third and last period of the Mesozoic Era, from about 144 to 65 million years ago, characterized by the development of flowering plants. The Cretaceous Period ended with the sudden mass extinction of dinosaurs and many other forms of life. *See Chart at* **geologic time,** pages 148–149.

Crick (krĭk), **Francis Henry Compton** 1916–2004. British biologist who with James D. Watson identified the structure of DNA. By analyzing the patterns cast by x-rays striking DNA molecules, they discovered that DNA has the structure of a double helix, two spirals linked together by bases, forming ladder-like rungs. Their discovery formed the basis of molecular genetics. Crick continued to work on DNA, later working out how DNA carries its genetic information.

cri•noid (krī′noid′) Any of various invertebrate sea animals having a cup-shaped body, feathery arms, and a stalk by which they attach themselves

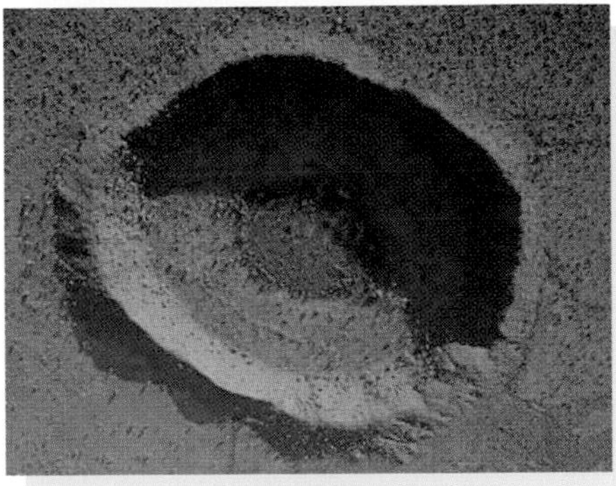

■ **crater**
top: *craters on the moon's surface*
bottom: *Wolf Creek meteorite crater, Australia*

to a surface. Sea lilies and feather stars are types of crinoids.

cris•ta (krĭs′tə) *Plural* **cristae** (krĭs′tē) One of the folds of the inner membrane of a mitochondrion. *See more at* **mitochondrion.**

crit•i•cal angle (krĭt′ĭ-kəl) The smallest angle of incidence at which a light ray can be completely reflected from the boundary between two media.

croc•o•dile (krŏk′ə-dīl′) Any of various large, meat-eating, aquatic reptiles native to tropical and subtropical regions. Crocodiles have longer and slenderer jaws than alligators, and their teeth are visible when they close their jaws.

croc•o•dil•i•an (krŏk′ə-dĭl′ē-ən) Any of various large, lizard-like, meat-eating reptiles having long jaws with sharp teeth, flattened bodies and long tails, and mostly living in or near water. The crocodilians include the crocodiles, alligators, caimans (of South America), and gavial (of India).

Crookes (kro͝oks), Sir **William** 1832–1919. British chemist and physicist who discovered thallium in 1861 and invented the radiometer in 1875. He also investigated cathode rays, demonstrating that they consisted of charged particles.

cross (krôs) *Noun.* **1.** A plant or animal produced by crossbreeding; a hybrid. —*Verb.* **2.** To crossbreed or cross-fertilize plants or animals.

cross•breed (krôs′brēd′) *Verb.* **1.** To produce a hybrid animal or plant by breeding two animals or two plants of different species or varieties. For example, crossbreeding a male donkey with a female horse will produce a mule. —*Noun.* **2.** An animal or a plant produced by breeding two animals or plants of different species or varieties; a hybrid.

cross-fertilization The fertilization that occurs when a male sex cell from one individual joins to a female sex cell from another individual of the same species. In plants, cross-pollination is an example of cross-fertilization. —*Verb* **cross-fertilize.**

cross-pollination The transfer of pollen from the male reproductive organ (an anther or a male cone) of one plant to the female reproductive organ (a stigma or a female cone) of another plant. Insects and wind are agents of cross-pollination. —*Verb* **cross-pollinate.**

crow (krō) Any of various large birds having shiny black feathers and a raucous call. Crows are closely related to ravens and magpies.

cru•ci•ble (kro͞o′sə-bəl) A heat-resistant container used to melt ores, metals, and other materials.

crust (krŭst) The solid, outermost layer of the Earth. ❖ The crust that lies underneath the continents is called **continental crust,** and is approximately 22 to 37 miles (35.4 to 59.6 kilometers) thick. It consists mostly of rocks rich in silica and aluminum, with minor amounts of

■ **Francis Crick**

iron, magnesium, calcium, sodium, and potassium. ❖ The crust that lies underneath the oceans is called **oceanic crust,** and is approximately 3 to 6 miles (4.8 to 9.7 kilometers) thick. It has a similar composition to that of continental crust, but has higher concentrations of iron, magnesium, and calcium. It is denser than continental crust.

crus•ta•cean (krŭ-stā′shən) Any of various arthropods that live mostly in water and have a hard shell, a segmented body, and jointed appendages. Crustaceans include crabs, lobsters, shrimp, and barnacles.

cry•o•gen•ics (krī′ə-jĕn′ĭks) The branch of physics that studies how matter behaves at very low temperatures.

crys•tal (krĭs′təl) A solid composed of atoms, molecules, or ions arranged in regular patterns that are repeated throughout the structure to form a characteristic network. Crystals have straight edges and flat surfaces, and can occur in many sizes and shapes. ❖ The particular arrangement in space of these atoms, molecules, or ions, and the way in which they are joined is called a **crystal lattice.** There are seven crystal groups or systems. Each is defined on the basis of the geometrical arrangement of the crystal lattice. —*Adjective* **crystalline.**

crys•tal•lize (krĭs′tə-līz′) To take on the form of crystals or cause to form crystals.

Cs The symbol for **cesium.**

csc Abbreviation of **cosecant.**

Cu The symbol for **copper.**

cube (kyo͞ob) *Verb.* **1.** To multiply a number or a quantity by itself three times; raise to the third power. For example, five cubed is 5 × 5 × 5. —*Noun.* **2.** The product that results when a number or quantity is cubed. **3.** A solid having six equal square faces or sides.

cube root The number whose cube is equal to a given number. For example, the cube root of 125 is 5, since $5^3 = 125$.

cu•bic (kyo͞o′bĭk) **1.** Referring to a volume unit of measurement: *cubic meter.* **2.** Involving a number or a variable that has been raised to the third power. **3.** Relating to a crystal having three axes of equal length intersecting at right angles. The mineral pyrite has cubic crystals. Also called *isometric. See more at* **crystal.**

cud (kŭd) Food that has been partly digested and brought up from the first stomach to the mouth again for further chewing by ruminants, such as cattle and sheep.

culm (kŭlm) The stem of a grass or similar plant.

cul•ture (kŭl′chər) *Noun.* **1.** A medium for the growth of microorganisms or a batch of cells under specific conditions in a laboratory. **2.** Living material, such as a colony of cells or microorganisms, grown in a culture. —*Verb.* **3.** To grow microorganisms or a batch of cells in a culture.

cu•mu•lo•nim•bus (kyo͞om′yə-lō-nĭm′bəs) A very large cloud with a low, dark base and fluffy masses that billow upward to great heights. Cumulonimbus clouds usually produce heavy rains, thunderstorms, or hailstorms.

cu•mu•lus (kyo͞om′yə-ləs) A white, fluffy cloud often having a flat base. Cumulus clouds form at lower levels of the atmosphere and are generally associated with fair weather. However, large cumulus clouds that billow to higher levels can produce rain showers.

cu•rie (kyo͝or′ē, kyo͝o-rē′) A unit used to measure the rate of radioactive decay. Radioactive decay is measured by the rate at which the atoms making up a radioactive substance are trans-

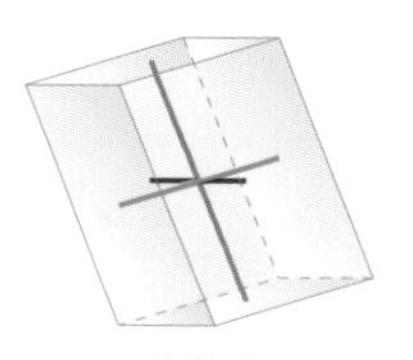
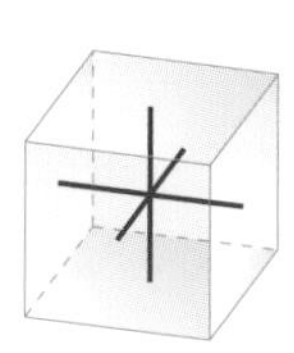
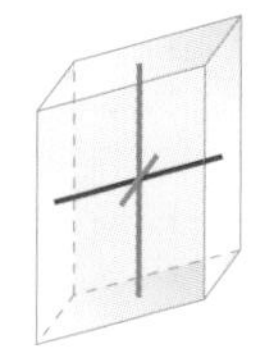
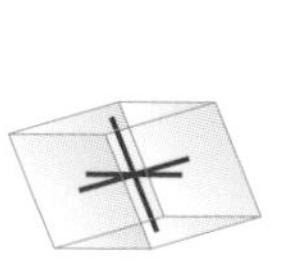
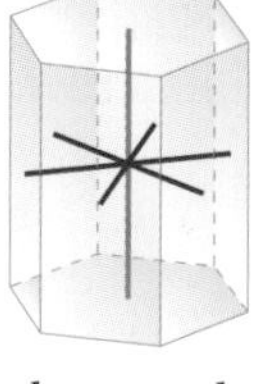
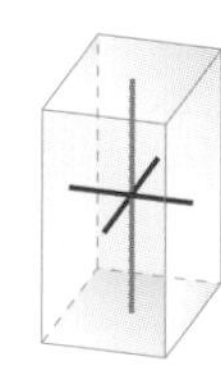

■ **crystal**

Imaginary axes of symmetry in the seven main crystal systems are depicted using different colors. Within each crystal, axes having the same color are of equal length.

Marie and Pierre Curie

formed into different atoms. One curie is equal to 37 billion (3.7×10^{10}) of these transformations per second. Many scientists now measure radioactive decay in becquerels rather than curies.

Curie, Marie 1867–1934. Polish-born French chemist who pioneered research into radioactivity. Following Antoine Henri Becquerel's discovery of radioactivity, she investigated uranium with her husband, **Pierre Curie** (1859–1906). Together they discovered the elements radium and polonium. Marie Curie later isolated pure radium and developed the use of radioactivity in medicine.

cu•ri•um (kyo͝or′ē-əm) A synthetic, silvery-white, radioactive metallic element of the actinide series that is produced artificially from plutonium or americium. Curium isotopes are used to provide electricity for satellites and space probes. Its most stable isotope has a half-life of 16.4 million years. *Symbol* **Cm.** *Atomic number* 96. *See* **Periodic Table,** pages 262–263.

cur•rent (kûr′ənt) **1.** A flowing movement in a liquid or gas, especially one that follows a recognizable course: *a current of cool air flowing through the room.* **2.** A flow of electric charge. *See Note at* **charge. 3.** The amount of electric charge that passes a point in a unit of time, usually expressed in amperes.

curve (kûrv) **1.** A line or surface that bends in a smooth, continuous way without sharp angles. **2.** The graph of a function on a coordinate plane. In this technical sense, straight lines, circles, and waves are all curves.

cu•ta•ne•ous (kyo͞o-tā′nē-əs) Relating to the skin.

Did You Know?

current: direct and alternating

You listen to your portable CD player thanks to direct current, but you turn on the lights thanks to alternating current. *Direct current,* or *DC,* is electricity that flows at a constant voltage directly from a source, such as a battery with a stored electric charge. Batteries are great when you're on the move, but DC has a fundamental problem: electricity is easily lost to resistance and wasted as heat in the wires. *Alternating current,* or *AC,* on the other hand, is what flows from your walls. This is because it can be transmitted at very high voltage with little heat loss. Moreover, the voltage can efficiently be brought down to a low, safe level for home use. AC's name reflects the fact that the current alternates its direction of flow. On average, AC flow in the US switches direction 60 times each second and delivers about 115 volts from an ordinary outlet. Other countries set their own AC standards.

cu•ti•cle (kyo͞o′tĭ-kəl) **1.** The outer layer of skin; the epidermis. **2.** The hard skin around the sides and base of a fingernail or toenail. **3.** *Botany.* A waxy layer that covers the outermost tissue layer of a plant. The cuticle is secreted by the epidermis and helps prevent water loss and infection by parasites.

Cu•vier (kyo͞o′vē-ā′), Baron **Georges Léopold Chrétien Frédéric Dagobert** 1769–1832. French anatomist who is considered the founder of comparative anatomy. He originated a system of zoological classification that grouped animals according to the structures of their skeletons and organs. Cuvier extended his system to fossils, and his reconstructions of the way extinct animals looked, based on their skeletal remains, greatly advanced the science of paleontology.

cy•a•nide (sī′ə-nīd′) Any of a large group of chemical compounds containing the radical CN, especially the very poisonous salts sodium cyanide and potassium cyanide. Cyanides are

Did You Know?

cyclone

Technically, a *cyclone* is nothing more than a region of low pressure around which air flows. In the Northern Hemisphere, the air moves counterclockwise around the low-pressure center, while in the Southern Hemisphere, the air travels clockwise. Meteorologists also refer to *tropical cyclones,* which develop over warm water and can be huge, severe storms. Strong tropical cyclones are better known as hurricanes or typhoons, depending on where in the world they occur. Hurricanes occur in the Atlantic Ocean and Gulf of Mexico, while typhoons occur in the Pacific Ocean. Such storms can be extremely devastating: two cyclones hit a coastal section of India within a few days of each other in 1999, killing an estimated 10,000 people. Because the word *cyclone* broadly defines a kind of air flow, cyclones are not confined to our planet. In 1999, the Hubble Space Telescope photographed a huge cyclone on Mars.

used to make plastics and to extract and treat metals.

cy•a•no•bac•te•ri•um (sī′ə-nō-băk-tîr′ē-əm) A type of bacterium that is capable of photosynthesis and was once thought to be a plant. Many cyanobacteria are able to convert nitrogen into chemical compounds used in cell metabolism. A combination of pigments, including chlorophyll, gives these bacteria their characteristic blue-green color. Also called *blue-green alga.*

cyber– A prefix that means "computer" or "computer network," as in *cyberspace,* the electronic medium in which online communication takes place.

cy•ber•net•ics (sī′bər-nĕt′ĭks) The study of communication and control processes in biological, mechanical, and electronic systems. Research in cybernetics often involves the comparison of these processes in biological and artificial systems.

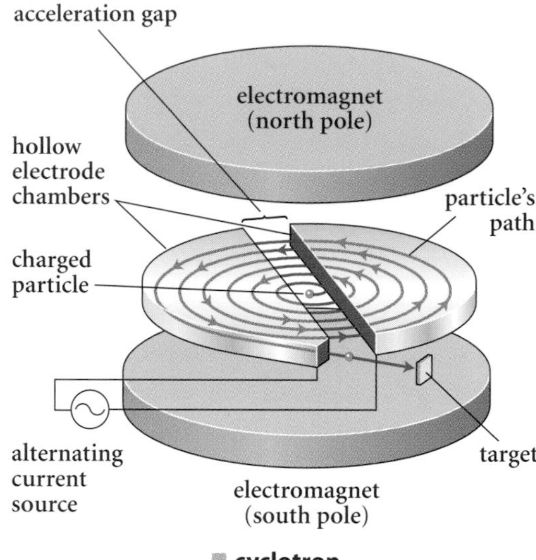

cyclotron

An alternating electric field attracts the particles from one side of the cyclotron to the other. The cyclotron's magnetic field, generated by the two electromagnets, bends each particle's path into a horizontal spiral, forcing it to accelerate in order to keep up with the alternating electric field. When the particle reaches its peak acceleration it is released to collide with the desired target.

cy•cad (sī′kăd′) Any of various cone-bearing evergreen plants that live in warm regions, have large feathery leaves, and resemble palm trees.

cy•clone (sī′klōn′) **1.** A system of winds that spiral in toward a region of low atmospheric pressure, circling counterclockwise in the Northern Hemisphere and clockwise in the Southern Hemisphere. *Compare* **anticyclone. 2.** A violent rotating windstorm, such as a hurricane or tornado.

cy•clo•tron (sī′klə-trŏn′) A device that accelerates charged subatomic particles, such as protons and electrons, in an outwardly spiraling path, greatly increasing their energies. Cyclotrons are used to bring about high-speed particle collisions in order to study subatomic structures. *Compare* **linear accelerator.**

Cyg•nus (sĭg′nəs) A constellation in the Northern Hemisphere near Cepheus and Lyra.

cyl•in•der (sĭl′ən-dər) A three-dimensional surface or solid object bounded by a curved surface and two parallel circles of equal size at the ends. The curved surface is formed by all the line seg-

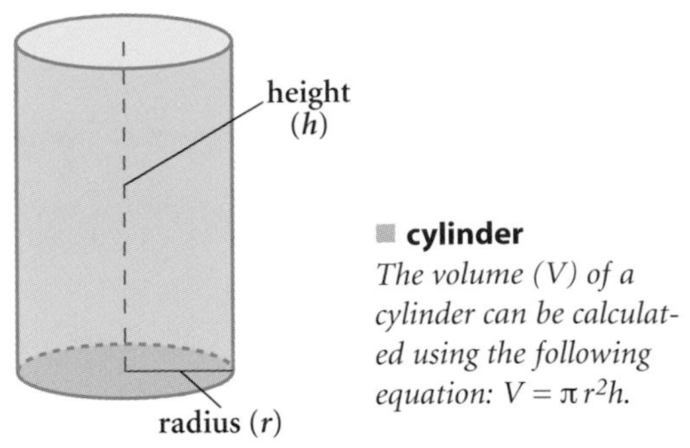

cylinder
The volume (V) of a cylinder can be calculated using the following equation: $V = \pi r^2 h$.

ments joining corresponding points of the two parallel circles.

cyme (sīm) A usually flat-topped or convex flower cluster in which the main stem and each branch end in a flower. Baby's breath and the tomato have cymes.

cyst (sĭst) An abnormal sac in the body, composed of a membrane surrounding a fluid or a soft solid material.

cys•te•ine (sĭs′tə-ēn′) A nonessential amino acid. *See more at* **amino acid.** *See Note at* **keratin.**

cys•tic fi•bro•sis (sĭs′tĭk fī-brō′sĭs) An inherited disease of certain glands, causing them to produce abnormally large amounts of thick mucus. It affects especially the pancreas and the mucus-secreting glands of the lungs, and results in problems with breathing and digestion.

cyto– A prefix meaning "cell," as in the word *cytoplasm.*

cy•to•chrome (sī′tə-krōm′) Any of a class of proteins that are important in cell metabolism and respiration. By comparing different kinds of cytochromes, scientists can trace the evolutionary relationships of the organisms in which they occur.

cy•tol•o•gy (sī-tŏl′ə-jē) The scientific study of the formation, structure, and function of cells.

cy•tom•e•try (sī-tŏm′ə-trē) The counting and measuring of cells, especially cell size and shape. Cytometry is usually performed using a standardized glass slide or small glass chamber of known volume.

cy•to•plasm (sī′tə-plăz′əm) The jelly-like material that makes up much of a cell inside the cell membrane, and, in eukaryotic cells, surrounds the nucleus. The organelles of the cell, such as mitochondria and (in green plants) chloroplasts, are contained in the cytoplasm. The cytoplasm together with the nucleus make up the cell's protoplasm. *See more at* **cell.**

cy•to•sine (sī′tə-sēn′) A base that is a component of DNA and RNA, forming a base pair with guanine.

D

d Abbreviation of **diameter.**

Dal•ton (dôl′tən), **John** 1766–1844. British chemist. His pioneering work on the properties of the atmosphere and gases led him to formulate the atomic theory. It stipulated that all matter is made up of combinations of atoms and that chemical reactions take place through the rearrangement of atoms.

darm•stadt•i•um (därm′shtät′ē-əm) A synthetic, radioactive element, first produced by bombarding lead atoms with nickel atoms. The isotope first synthesized has a half-life of 0.18 milliseconds. *Symbol* **Ds.** *Atomic number* 110. *See* **Periodic Table,** pages 262–263.

Dar•win (där′wĭn), **Charles Robert** 1809–1882. British naturalist who proposed the theory of evolution based on natural selection (1859). Darwin's theory, that random variation of traits within an individual species can lead to the development of new species, revolutionized the study of biology.

da•ta (dā′tə, dăt′ə) *Used with a singular or plural verb.* **1.** Information, especially when it is to be analyzed or used as the basis for a decision. **2.** Information, usually in numerical form, suitable for processing by a computer.

da•tive bond (dā′tĭv) *See* **coordinate bond.**

daugh•ter cell (dô′tər) Either of the two cells formed when a cell undergoes cell division. Daughter cells are genetically identical to the parent cell because they contain the same number and type of chromosomes.

Da•vy (dā′vē), Sir **Humphry** 1778–1829. British chemist who was a pioneer of electrochemistry. Davy used its methods to isolate sodium and potassium (1807) and barium, boron, calcium, and magnesium (1808). He also proved that diamonds are a form of carbon.

dB Abbreviation of **decibel.**

Db The symbol for **dubnium.**

DC Abbreviation of **direct current.**

DDT (dē′dē-tē′) Short for *dichlorodiphenyltrichloroethane.* A powerful insecticide that is also poisonous to humans and animals. It remains active in the environment for many years and has been banned in the United States for most uses since 1972.

deca– A prefix that means "ten," as in *decahedron,* a polygon having ten faces.

dec•a•gon (dĕk′ə-gŏn′) A polygon having ten sides.

dec•a•pod (dĕk′ə-pŏd′) **1.** A crustacean characteristically having ten legs, each joined to a segment of the thorax. Crabs, hermit crabs, lobsters, and shrimp are decapods. **2.** A cephalopod mollusk, such as a squid or cuttlefish, having ten arm-like tentacles.

de•cay (dĭ-kā′) *Verb.* **1.** *Biology.* To break down into component parts through the action of bacteria or fungi; decompose. **2.** *Physics.* To undergo radioactive decay. —*Noun.* **3.** *Biology.* The breaking down or rotting of organic matter through the action of bacteria or fungi; decomposition. **4.** *Physics.* Radioactive decay.

deci– A prefix that means "one tenth," as in *deciliter,* one tenth of a liter.

de•ci•bel (dĕs′ə-bəl) A unit used to measure the loudness or intensity of a sound. The speaking voice of most people ranges from 45 to 75 decibels. *See Note at* **sound**[1]**.**

de•cid•u•ous (dĭ-sĭj′o͞o-əs) **1.** Shedding leaves at the end of a growing season and regrowing them at the beginning of the next growing season. Most deciduous plants bear flowers and have woody stems and broad rather than needle-like leaves. Maples, oaks, elms, and aspens are deciduous. *Compare* **evergreen. 2.** Falling off or shed

John Dalton

BIOGRAPHY

Charles Darwin

During his years as a naturalist at sea on the HMS *Beagle* (1831–1836), Charles Darwin observed many new and wondrous things. But the part of the voyage that would change science forever took place in September 1835, when the *Beagle* reached the Galápagos Archipelago, a group of islands in the Pacific Ocean 650 miles west of Ecuador. Noting that the organisms there were isolated in a unique environment, Darwin wrote, "this archipelago . . . seems to be a little world within itself, the greater number of its inhabitants, both vegetable and animal, being found nowhere else." He observed 26 species of birds (only one of which was known to exist anywhere else), giant tortoises, and other fascinating reptiles. What startled Darwin was the fact that each species was uniquely adapted to the particular island on which it lived. This observation prompted him to ask the questions that became the basis of his theory of evolution, questions he would spend the rest of his life trying to answer. When he returned to England, Darwin refined his notes and continued to make scientific observations, this time of his own garden and the animals his family kept. After 23 years of sustained work, he published his theory in *The Origin of Species by Means of Natural Selection.*

at a particular season or stage of growth: *Deer have deciduous antlers.*

dec•i•mal (dĕs′ə-məl) **1.** A representation of a real number using the base ten and decimal notation, such as 201.4, 3.89, or 0.0006. **2.** A decimal having no digits to the left of the decimal point except zero, such as 0.2 or 0.00354.

USAGE

data

In scientific writing, *data* is usually treated as a singular in much the same way as the word *information* is. We say *When the data comes in, we'll understand what happened.* But because the word is historically the plural of the Latin noun *datum,* it is sometimes used as a plural, as in *These data do not support your conclusions.* The plural use is less frequent than the singular.

decimal fraction A number, such as 0.57, written in decimal notation and having only a zero to the left of the decimal point.

decimal notation A representation of a fraction or other real number using the base ten and consisting of any of the digits 0, 1, 2, 3, 4, 5, 6, 7, 8, 9, and a decimal point. Each digit to the left of the decimal point indicates a multiple of a positive power of ten, while each digit to the right indicates a multiple of a negative power of ten. For example, the number $26\frac{37}{100}$ can be written in decimal notation as 26.37, where 2 represents 2×10, 6 represents 6×1, 3 represents $3 \times \frac{1}{10}$ or $\frac{3}{10}$, and 7 represents $7 \times \frac{1}{100}$ or $\frac{7}{100}$.

decimal place The position of a digit to the right of the decimal point in a number written in decimal notation. In 0.079, for example, 0 is in the first decimal place, 7 is in the second decimal place, and 9 is in the third decimal place.

decimal point A period used in decimal notation to separate whole numbers from fractions, as in the number 1.3, which represents $1 + \frac{3}{10}$.

decimal system A number system based on units of 10 and using decimal notation.

dec•li•na•tion (dĕk′lə-nā′shən) **1.** The position of a celestial object above or below the celestial equator. It is measured as a vertical angle, from 0° at the celestial equator to 90° at one of the celestial poles. Declination and right ascension are the measurements used to map objects on the celestial sphere. *See more at* **celestial sphere. 2.** *See* **magnetic declination.**

de•com•pos•er (dē′kəm-pō′zər) An organism, often a bacterium or fungus, that feeds on and breaks down dead plant or animal matter. Decomposers make essential nutrients available to plants and other organisms in the ecosystem.

de•com•po•si•tion (dē-kŏm′pə-zĭsh′ən) **1.** The separation of a substance into simpler substances or basic elements. **2.** The process of decaying or rotting. Decomposition of dead organic matter is brought about by the activity of certain bacteria and fungi feeding on it.

de•duc•tion (dĭ-dŭk′shən) **1.** The process of reasoning in which a conclusion follows necessarily from the premises; reasoning from the general to the specific. **2.** A conclusion reached by this process.

De•For•est (dĭ-fôr′ĭst), **Lee** 1873–1961. American electrical engineer and inventor who patented more than 300 inventions. In 1907 he patented the triode electron tube, which made it possible to amplify and detect radio waves.

de•for•es•ta•tion (dē-fôr′ĭ-stā′shən) The cutting down and removal of all or most of the trees in a forested area. Deforestation can damage the environment by causing erosion of soils, and it decreases biodiversity by destroying the habitats needed for different organisms.

de•gla•ci•a•tion (dē-glā′shē-ā′shən) The uncovering of land because of the melting of a glacier.

de•gree (dĭ-grē′) **1.** A unit division of a temperature scale. *See Note at* **Celsius. 2a.** A unit for measuring an angle or an arc of a circle. One degree is $\frac{1}{360}$ of the circumference of a circle. **b.** This unit used to measure latitude or longitude on the Earth's surface. **3.** In a polynomial, the degree of the term that has the highest degree. For example, $x^3 + 2xy + x$ is of the third degree.

de•hy•dra•tion (dē′hī-drā′shən) **1.** The process of losing or removing water or moisture. **2.** Excessive loss of water and often salts from the body, as from heavy sweating or illness.

USAGE

deduction/induction

The logical processes known as deduction and induction work in opposite ways. When you use *deduction,* you apply general principles to specific instances. Thus, using a mathematical formula to figure the volume of air that can be contained in a gymnasium is applying deduction. Similarly, you use deduction when applying a law of physics to predict the outcome of an experiment. By contrast, when you use *induction,* you examine a number of specific instances of something and make a generalization based on them. Thus, if you observe hundreds of examples in which a certain chemical kills plants, you might conclude by induction that the chemical is toxic to all plants. Inductive generalizations are often revised as more examples are studied and more facts are known. Certain plants that you have not tested, for instance, may turn out to be unaffected by the chemical, and you might have to revise your thinking. In this way, an inductive generalization is much like a hypothesis.

Del•brück (dĕl′bro͝ok′), **Max** 1906–1981. German-born American biologist who was a pioneer in the study of molecular genetics. He discovered that viruses can exchange genetic material to create new types of viruses.

del•ta (dĕl′tə) A usually triangular mass of sediment, especially silt and sand, deposited at the mouth of a river. Deltas form when a river flows into a body of standing water, such as a sea or lake.

De•moc•ri•tus (dĭ-mŏk′rĭ-təs) 460?–370? B.C. Greek philosopher who developed one of the first atomist theories of the universe, which held that the world consists of an infinite number of very small particles.

den•drite (dĕn′drīt′) **1.** Any of several parts branching from the body of a nerve cell that receive and transmit nerve impulses. **2.** A mineral that has a branching crystal pattern. Dendrites often form within or on the surface of other minerals.

den•dro•chro•nol•o•gy (dĕn′drō-krə-nŏl′ə-jē) The study of annual rings in trees in order to analyze past climate conditions or to determine the date of past events. Trees grow more slowly in periods of drought or other environmental stress than they do under more favorable conditions, and thus the annual rings they produce are smaller. By observing the pattern formed by a tree's rings, scientists can learn about the environmental changes that took place during the period in which it was growing. They can also match up the pattern in trees whose age is known to the pattern in a piece of wood found at an archaeological site, thereby establishing the approximate date of the site.

De•neb (dĕn′ĕb′) A bright star in the constellation Cygnus. It is a supergiant. *See Note at* **Rigel.**

de•nom•i•na•tor (dĭ-nŏm′ə-nā′tər) The number below or to the right of the line in a fraction, indicating the number of equal parts into which one whole is divided. For example, in the fraction $\frac{2}{7}$, 7 is the denominator.

den•si•ty (dĕn′sĭ-tē) A measure of the compactness of a substance. Density is equal to the amount of mass per unit of volume. In general, density increases as pressure increases and temperature decreases.

den•tin (dĕn′tĭn) The main bony part of a tooth beneath the enamel, surrounding the pulp chamber and root canals.

den•tist•ry (dĕn′tĭ-strē) The branch of medicine that deals with the diagnosis, prevention, and treatment of diseases of the teeth, gums, and other structures of the mouth.

den•ti•tion (dĕn-tĭsh′ən) The type, number, and arrangement of teeth in an animal species. In mammals, dentition consists of several different types of teeth, including incisors, canines, and molars. The teeth of toothed fish and reptiles are usually of only one type.

de•ox•y•ri•bo•nu•cle•ic acid (dē-ŏk′sē-rī′bō-no͞o-klē′ĭk) *See* **DNA.**

de•pen•dent variable (dĭ-pĕn′dənt) In mathematics, a variable whose value is determined by the value of some other variable. For example, in the function $y = x + 5$, y is the dependent variable because its value is determined by the value of x.

de•pos•it (dĭ-pŏz′ĭt) Solid material left or laid down by a natural process. For example, deposits can include layers of sand and mud left by streams, an accumulation of stones and debris left by a melting glacier, or a layer of coal formed over many years as decomposing plant material became fossilized. —*Noun* **deposition** (dĕp′ə-zĭsh′ən).

de•riv•a•tive (dĭ-rĭv′ə-tĭv) In calculus, the slope of the tangent line to a curve at a particular point on the curve. Since a curve represents a function, its derivative can also be thought of as the rate of change of the corresponding function at the given point. Derivatives are computed using differentiation.

der•mal (dûr′məl) Relating to the skin.

der•mis (dûr′mĭs) The innermost layer of the skin in vertebrate animals, lying under the epidermis and containing nerve endings and blood and lymph vessels. In mammals, the dermis also contains hair follicles and sweat glands.

de•sal•i•ni•za•tion (dē-săl′ə-nĭ-zā′shən) The removal of salt from something, such as seawater or soil. —*Verb* **desalinize.**

Des•cartes (dā-kärt′), **René** 1596–1650. French mathematician and philosopher. He discovered that the position of a point can be defined by coordinates, a discovery that laid the foundation for analytic geometry.

des•ert (dĕz′ərt) A dry, barren region, usually having sandy or rocky soil and little or no vegetation. Most deserts receive less than 10 inches (25 centimeters) of precipitation each year, con-

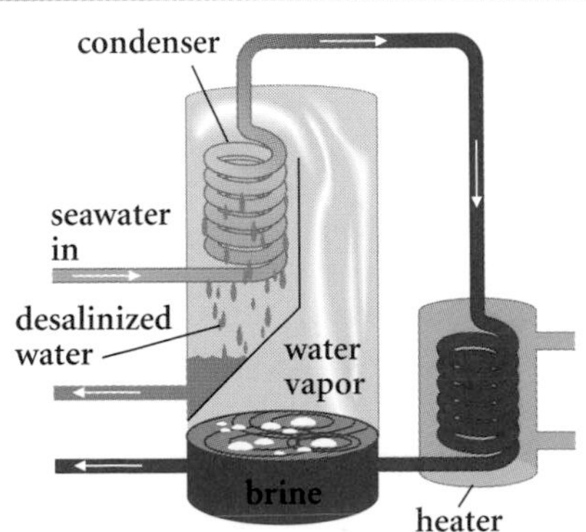

desalinization
a diagram of a distillation process showing how seawater is desalinized

centrated in short bursts. Deserts cover about one fifth of the Earth's surface and are mainly located along the Tropic of Cancer and the Tropic of Capricorn.

de•sert•i•fi•ca•tion (dĭ-zûr′tə-fĭ-kā′shən) The transformation of land once suitable for agriculture into desert. Desertification can result from climate change or from human practices such as cutting down forests or allowing too many animals to graze in a particular area.

des•ic•cate (dĕs′ĭ-kāt′) To remove the moisture from something, or dry it thoroughly.

de•sign•er gene (dĭ-zī′nər) A gene that is created by manipulating the DNA in a cell so that a specific sequence of DNA molecules can be obtained. Designer genes can be used in genetic engineering to help scientists produce substances, such as proteins, needed for research.

de•ter•gent (dĭ-tûr′jənt) A cleaning agent that increases the ability of water to penetrate fabric and break down greases and dirt. Detergents act like soap but are made of chemicals obtained from petroleum products. Their molecules surround particles of grease and dirt, allowing them to be carried away. *Compare* **soap.**

de•tri•tus (dĭ-trī′təs) Loose fragments, such as sand or gravel, that have been worn away from rock.

deu•te•ri•um (do͞o-tîr′ē-əm) An isotope of hydrogen whose nucleus has one proton and one neutron and whose atomic mass is 2. Deuterium is used widely as a tracer for analyzing chemical reactions, and it combines with oxygen to form heavy water. Also called *heavy hydrogen. See more at* **hydrogen.** *See Note at* **heavy water.**

de•vi•a•tion (dē′vē-ā′shən) *Mathematics.* The difference between one number in a set and the mean of the set.

De•vo•ni•an (dĭ-vō′nē-ən) The fourth period of the Paleozoic Era, from about 408 to 360 million years ago, characterized by the appearance of forests, amphibians, and insects. *See Chart at* **geologic time,** pages 148–149.

dew (do͞o) Water droplets that condense from the air onto cool surfaces. Dew usually forms at night, when air near the ground cools and cannot hold as much water vapor as warmer air.

dew•claw (do͞o′klô′) **1.** A small, useless inner claw or toe in some dogs and other animals that does not reach the ground in walking. **2.** The false hoof of deer, hogs, and other hoofed mammals, consisting of two toes.

dew•lap (do͞o′lăp′) A loose fold of skin hanging from the neck of certain animals, such as some dogs or cattle.

Did You Know?
desert

Spell it with two *s*'s (dessert) and it's ice cream. Spell it with one *s* (desert) and it's a place where you'd have trouble finding a glass of water, let alone a scoop of vanilla. A *desert* is defined by the water you won't find there. There's no official standard, but many people say that any place that gets less than 10 inches of precipitation a year qualifies. Deserts do not have to be hot. Even the Sahara Desert in Africa, famous for heat, can get cold at night. And although many people think of the Sahara as the world's biggest desert, that distinction actually belongs to Antarctica, which is incredibly cold and amazingly dry, receiving the frozen equivalent of less than 2 inches of water per year. In spite of this dryness, some animals and plants thrive in deserts. Each desert is therefore a unique ecosystem, a particular environment that includes organisms interacting with it and with each other.

Mojave Desert, California

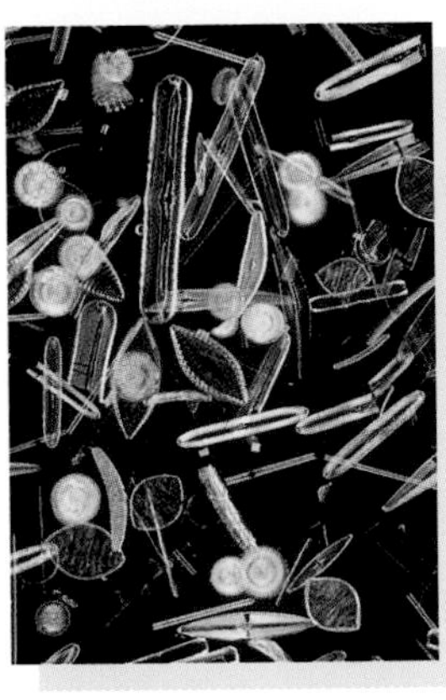

diatom
photograph made through a microscope of a variety of diatoms

dew point The temperature at which air becomes saturated with water vapor and dew forms. The dew point varies depending on how much water vapor is in the air.

dex•trose (dĕk′strōs′) A sugar that is the most common form of glucose, found in plant and animal tissues and also derived from starch.

di– A prefix that means "two," "twice," or "double." It is used commonly in chemistry, as in *dioxide,* a compound having two oxygen atoms.

dia– A prefix meaning "through" or "across," as in *diameter,* the length of a line going through a circle.

di•a•be•tes (dī′ə-bē′tĭs, dī′ə-bē′tēz) A disease marked by abnormal levels of sugar in the blood, caused by the body's inability to produce or use insulin properly. If untreated, it can cause circulatory problems and nerve damage. Diabetes may be treated with medication, insulin injections, and dietary restrictions.

di•ag•no•sis (dī′əg-nō′sĭs) *Plural* **diagnoses** (dī′əg-nō′sēz) The identification by a doctor of a disease or injury, made by examining and taking the medical history of a patient.

di•ag•o•nal (dī-ăg′ə-nəl) *Adjective.* **1.** Connecting two nonadjacent corners in a polygon or two nonadjacent corners in a polyhedron that do not lie in the same face. —*Noun.* **2.** A diagonal line segment.

di•al•y•sis (dī-ăl′ĭ-sĭs) **1.** The separation of the smaller molecules in a solution from the larger molecules by passing the solution through a membrane that does not allow the large molecules through. **2.** The removal of wastes from the bloodstream by a machine that performs dialysis when the kidneys do not function properly.

di•am•e•ter (dī-ăm′ĭ-tər) **1.** A straight line segment that passes through the center of a circle or sphere from one side to the other. **2.** The length of such a line segment.

di•a•mond (dī′ə-mənd) A form of pure carbon that occurs naturally as a clear crystal and is the hardest of all known minerals. It is used as a gemstone in its finer varieties. Poorly crystallized diamonds are used in abrasives and in industrial cutting tools. *See Note at* **carbon.**

di•a•phragm (dī′ə-frăm′) **1.** A muscle that separates the chest cavity from the abdominal cavity. As the diaphragm contracts and expands, it forces air into and out of the lungs. **2.** A thin, flexible disk, especially in a microphone or telephone receiver, that vibrates in response to sound waves to produce electrical signals, or that vibrates in response to electrical signals to produce sound waves.

di•as•to•le (dī-ăs′tə-lē) The period during the normal beating of the heart in which relaxation occurs and the heart's chambers fill with blood. *Compare* **systole.**

di•a•tom (dī′ə-tŏm′) Any of various microscopic one-celled algae that live in water, have hard shells composed mostly of silica, and often live in colonies. Diatom shells are made of two symmetrical parts called valves. —*Adjective* **diatomaceous** (dī′ə-tə-mā′shəs).

Dick (dĭk), **George Frederick** 1881–1967. American medical researcher who collaborated with his wife, **Gladys Henry Dick** (1881–1963), to isolate the bacterium that causes scarlet fever. They developed a serum for the disease in 1923.

di•cot•y•le•don (dī′kŏt′l-ēd′n) *or* **di•cot** (dī′-kŏt′) A flowering plant having two cotyledons that usually appear at germination of the seed. Dicotyledons have leaves with a network of veins radiating from a central main vein, flower parts in multiples of 4 or 5, and a tissue layer known as cambium. Most cultivated plants and many trees are dicotyledons. *See more at* **leaf.** *Compare* **monocotyledon.**

di•e•lec•tric (dī′ĭ-lĕk′trĭk) *Adjective.* **1.** Having little or no ability to conduct electricity. —*Noun.* **2.** A dielectric substance, such as glass or rubber.

die•sel engine (dē′zəl) An internal-combustion engine in which the fuel oil is ignited by the heat of air that has been highly compressed in the cylinder.

dif•fer•ence (dĭf′ər-əns) **1.** The amount by which one number or quantity is greater or less than another. The difference between 10 and 15, for example, is 5. **2.** The amount remaining after one number or quantity is subtracted from another. In the equation 15 – 10 = 5, 5 is the difference.

dif•fer•en•ti•a•tion (dĭf′ə-rĕn′shē-ā′shən) **1.** In calculus, the process of computing the derivative of a function. *Compare* **integration. 2.** The process by which cells or developing body or plant parts change in order to serve a specific function.

dif•frac•tion (dĭ-frăk′shən) The bending or turning of a wave, such as a light wave, when it encounters an obstacle, such as an edge, or a hole whose size is similar to the wavelength of the wave. The patterns made by the diffraction of waves can be useful for understanding the minute structures of objects. The diffraction patterns made by x-rays as they pass between the atoms of a molecule, for example, are studied in order to determine the molecule's overall structure. *See more at* **wave.**

dif•fu•sion (dĭ-fyo͞o′zhən) **1.** The movement of ions or molecules from an area of higher concentration to an area of lower concentration. Small molecules and ions can move across a cell membrane by diffusion. *Compare* **osmosis. 2a.** The reflection of light off an irregular surface in all directions. **b.** The process by which light passes through a transparent substance. **3.** The spreading out of light or other radiation through an area so that its intensity becomes more or less uniform.

di•ges•tion (dī-jĕs′chən) **1.** The process by which food is broken down into simple chemical compounds that can be absorbed and used as nutrients or eliminated by the body. In most animals, nutrients are obtained from food by the action of digestive enzymes. In humans and other higher vertebrates, digestion takes place mainly in the small intestine. **2.** The decomposition of sewage by bacteria.

di•ges•tive tract (dī-jĕs′tĭv) The system of organs of the body that breaks down and absorbs food as nourishment. In higher vertebrates, it consists of the esophagus, stomach, and small and large intestines, together with the glands, such as the salivary glands, liver, and pancreas, that produce substances necessary for digestion. Also called *alimentary canal, gastrointestinal tract.*

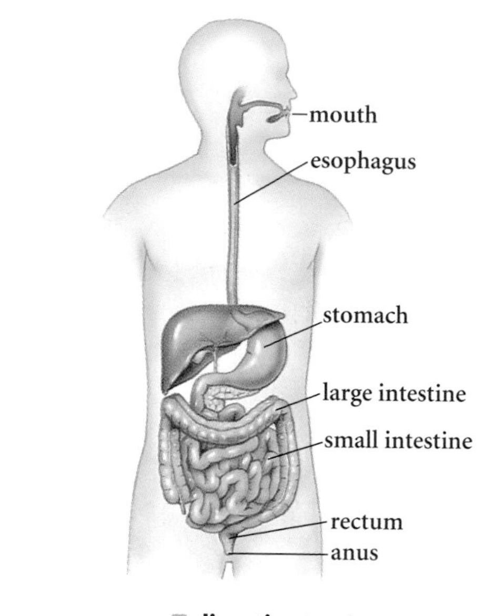

digestive tract

dig•it (dĭj′ĭt) **1.** A finger or toe. **2.** One of the ten Arabic numerals, 0 through 9.

dig•i•tal (dĭj′ĭ-tl) **1.** *Anatomy.* Relating to or resembling a digit, especially a finger. **2.** Expressed in numerical form, especially for use by a computer: *converted the image to a digital form.* **3.** *Computer Science.* Relating to a device that can read, write, or store information represented in numerical form: *a digital computer.*

di•he•dral (dī-hē′drəl) Formed by a pair of planes or sections of planes that intersect: *a dihedral angle.*

dike (dīk) A long mass of igneous rock that cuts across the structure of adjoining rock. It is often of a different composition than the rock it cuts across and can be useful in determining the age relationship between rocks.

di•late (dī-lāt′, dī′lāt′) To widen or expand a body part: *The pupils of the eye dilate in the dark.*

di•lute (dī-lo͞ot′) To make a substance less concentrated by adding a liquid such as water.

di•men•sion (dĭ-mĕn′shən) **1a.** *Mathematics.* Any one of the three physical or spatial properties of length, area, and volume. In geometry, a point is said to have zero dimension; a figure having only length, such as a line, has one dimension; a plane or surface, two dimensions; and a

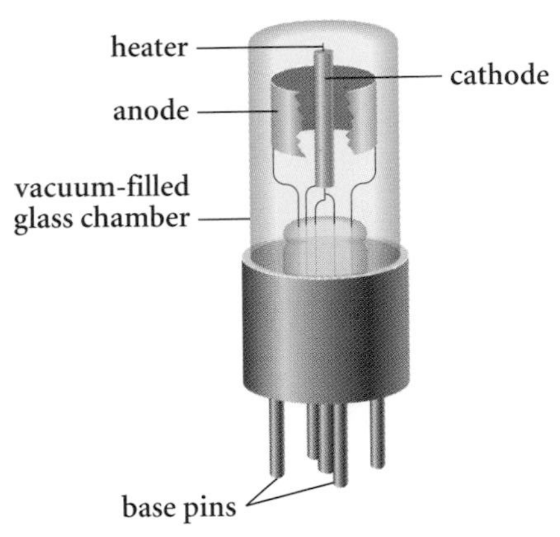

diode

The heated cathode generates a cloud of electrons that are attracted by the anode, causing a current to flow from the cathode to the anode. Because the anode cannot generate electrons of its own, the current cannot flow in the opposite direction.

figure having volume, three dimensions. The fourth dimension is often said to be time, as in the theory of general relativity. Higher dimensions can be dealt with mathematically but cannot be represented visually. **b.** The measurement of a length, width, or thickness: *The dimensions of the window are 2 feet by 4 feet.* **2.** A unit, such as mass, time, or charge, associated with a physical quantity and used as the basis for other measurements, such as acceleration.

di•mer (dī′mər) Any of various chemical compounds made of two smaller, identical molecules (called monomers) that are linked together.

di•met•ro•don (dī-mĕt′rə-dŏn′) An extinct, meat-eating reptile of the Permian Period having a body similar to an alligator's but with a tall, curved sail on its back. The sail had a thick network of blood vessels and may have been used to regulate the animal's body temperature. The dimetrodon belonged to the early group of reptiles that many scientists believe was ancestral to mammals.

di•no•flag•el•late (dī′nō-flăj′ə-lĭt) Any of numerous protozoans found mostly in the ocean, usually having two flagella and an outer covering of cellulose. Dinoflagellates are one of the main components of plankton.

di•no•saur (dī′nə-sôr′) Any of various extinct reptiles that lived mainly during the Mesozoic Era. Dinosaurs were meat-eating or plant-eating, dwelled mostly on land, and varied from the size of a small dog to the largest land animals that ever lived. *See more at* **ornithischian, saurischian.** *See Note at* **bird.**

di•ode (dī′ōd′) An electron tube or a semiconductor that allows current to flow in one direction only. Diodes can be used to convert AC currents into DC currents.

di•oe•cious (dī-ē′shəs) Having male flowers on one plant and female flowers on another plant of the same species. The holly and asparagus plants are dioecious. *Compare* **monoecious.**

di•ox•ide (dī-ŏk′sīd) A compound containing two oxygen atoms per molecule.

diph•the•ri•a (dĭf-thîr′ē-ə, dĭp-thîr′ē-ə) A contagious disease caused by a bacterium and characterized by fever, swollen glands, and the formation of a membrane in the throat that prevents breathing. Diphtheria was once a leading cause of death in children, but now children are routinely immunized against it.

di•plod•o•cus (dĭ-plŏd′ə-kəs) A very large plant-eating dinosaur of the Jurassic Period. Diplodocus had a long, slender neck and tail and a small head with peg-like teeth, and could grow to nearly 90 feet (27 meters) in length. It is one of the longest sauropod dinosaurs known.

dip•loid (dĭp′loid′) Having two sets of each chromosome in a cell or cell nucleus, one set from the female parent and one set from the male parent. In animals, all cells except reproductive cells are diploid. *Compare* **haploid.** *See Note at* **mitosis.**

di•pole (dī′pōl) **1.** A pair of equal and opposite electric charges or magnetic poles, separated by a small distance. **2.** A molecule having two such charges.

Di•rac (dĭ-răk′), **Paul Adrien Maurice** 1902–1984. British mathematician and physicist. He developed a mathematical interpretation of quantum mechanics with which he was able to provide the first correct description of electron behavior.

di•rect current (dĭ-rĕkt′) An electric current flowing in one direction only, as in a battery. *Compare* **alternating current.** *See Notes at* **current, Tesla.**

di•rec•trix (dĭ-rĕk′trĭks) A straight line used in constructing a curve such as a parabola.

USAGE

disk/disc

Have you ever noticed that when you buy a music CD, it is a *compact disc,* but when you buy a CD in a computer store it is usually a *compact disk?* Sometimes spelling varies according to how a word is used. Back in the late 19th century, when people were developing the technology for recording sound on a flat plate (what later became the vinyl phonograph record), the inventors referred to the plates as *discs,* using an alternate spelling of *disk.* The *c* spelling eventually became prevalent in the music industry, known for its *disc jockeys.* When American computer scientists developed flat storage devices back in the 1940s, they chose the common American spelling *disk,* and this is why we have hard disks installed on our computers. When the storage device known as the compact disk was invented, people in the music industry saw them as substitutes for phonograph records, and they referred to them as *compact discs,* despite the fact that these same discs were *compact disks* when they stored nonmusical data.

di•sac•cha•ride (dī-săk′ə-rīd) Any of a class of sugars, including lactose and sucrose, that are composed of two monosaccharides.

dis•charge (dĭs′chärj) A release of matter or energy, especially electrical energy, as from a battery or in a flash of lightning.

disk *or* **disc** (dĭsk) **1.** *Computer Science.* A magnetic disk, such as a hard disk, or an optical disk, such as a compact disk. **2.** *Anatomy. See* **intervertebral disk.**

disk drive *Computer Science.* A device that reads data stored on a magnetic or optical disk and writes data onto the disk for storage.

dis•lo•ca•tion (dĭs′lō-kā′shən) Displacement of a bone from its normal position, especially in a joint.

dis•per•sion (dĭ-spûr′zhən) The separation of light or other radiation into individual components, usually according to frequency and wavelength. When a beam of white light (light that contains all colors) passes through a prism, for example, dispersion causes it to separate into the seven colors of the rainbow.

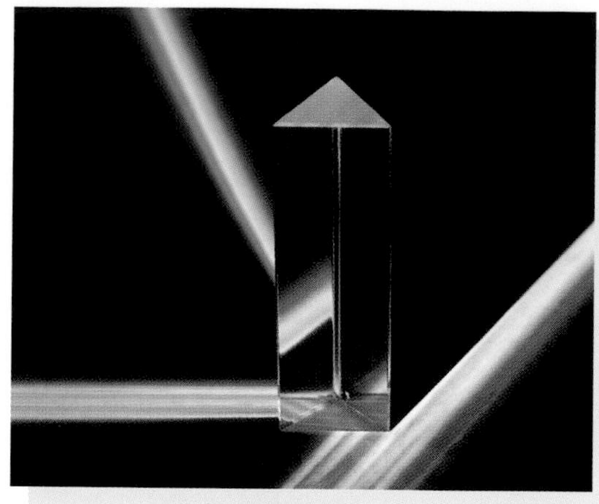

■ **dispersion**

dis•sect (dĭ-sĕkt′, dī′sĕkt′) To cut apart or separate body tissues or parts for study.

dis•so•ci•a•tion (dĭ-sō′sē-ā′shən) The separation of a substance into two or more simpler substances, or of a molecule into atoms or ions, by the action of heat or a chemical process. Dissociation is usually reversible.

dis•solve (dĭ-zŏlv′) To pass or cause to pass into solution: *Salt dissolves in water, and water has the ability to dissolve salt.*

dis•til•la•tion (dĭs′tə-lā′shən) A method of separating a substance that is in solution from its solvent or of separating a liquid from a mixture of liquids having different boiling points. The liquid to be separated is evaporated (as by boiling), and its vapor is then collected after it condenses. Distillation is used to separate fresh water from a salt solution and gasoline from petroleum. ❖ The condensed vapor, which is the purified liquid, is called the **distillate.**

dis•trib•u•tive property (dĭ-strĭb′yə-tĭv) A property distinguishing some pairs of mathematical operations, according to which applying one operation (such as multiplication) to a set of objects combined by another operation (such as addition) gives the same result as applying the first operation to each object in the set individually, and then combining those results using the second operation. Thus $2 \times (3 + 4)$ is equivalent to $(2 \times 3) + (2 \times 4)$, meaning that multiplication is distributive relative to addition. *See also* **associative property, commutative property.**

di•ur•nal (dī-ûr′nəl) **1.** Occurring in a 24-hour period; daily. **2.** Most active during the daytime. Many animals, including the apes, are diurnal. *Compare* **nocturnal. 3.** Having leaves or flowers that open in daylight and close at night. The morning glory and crocus are diurnal.

di•ver•gence (dĭ-vûr′jəns) **1.** *Mathematics.* The property of failing to approach a limit, such as a point, line, or value. **2.** *Biology.* The evolution of different structures in related species as they adapt to different environments. An example of divergence is the development of wings in bats from the same bones that form the arm and hand or paw in most other mammals. Also called *divergent evolution. Compare* **convergence.**

di•ver•gent plate boundary (dĭ-vûr′jənt) A tectonic boundary where two plates are moving away from each other and new crust is forming from magma that rises to the Earth's surface between the two plates. Also called *spreading zone. See more at* **tectonic boundary.** *Compare* **convergent plate boundary.**

div•i•dend (dĭv′ĭ-dĕnd′) A number divided by another. In the equation 15 ÷ 3 = 5, 15 is the dividend.

di•vi•sion (dĭ-vĭzh′ən) **1.** The act, process, or operation of dividing one number or quantity by another; the process of finding out how many times one number or quantity is contained in the other. **2.** A group of plants ranking above a class and below a kingdom, corresponding to a phylum in other kingdoms. *See Table at* **taxonomy.**

di•vi•sor (dĭ-vī′zər) A number used to divide another. In the equation 15 ÷ 3 = 5, 3 is the divisor.

Dje•ras•si (djĕ-rä′sē), **Carl** Born 1923. Austrian-born American chemist who pioneered the development of a contraceptive pill and many commonly used drugs, including antihistamines.

DNA (dē′ĕn-ā′) Short for *deoxyribonucleic acid.* The nucleic acid that is the genetic material determining the makeup of all living cells and many viruses. It consists of two strands of nucleotides linked together in a structure resembling a ladder twisted into a spiral. In eukaryotic cells, the DNA is contained mainly in the nucleus and mitochondria. DNA can replicate itself and synthesize RNA. *Compare* **RNA.** *See Note at* **gene.**

DNA fingerprinting The use of a sample of DNA to determine the identity of a person within a certain probability. DNA fingerprinting is done by analyzing repeating patterns of base pairs in DNA sequences that are known to vary greatly among individuals.

Did You Know?

DNA

One of the wonders of nature is that the complexity and diversity of life can be contained in a molecule with a relatively simple structure. *Deoxyribonucleic acid,* commonly called *DNA,* exists mainly in the nucleus and mitochondria of each cell in an organism. It consists of two long strands linked together in a structure resembling a ladder twisted into a spiral, called a *double helix.* Each rung is made up of two chemical bases, called *nucleotides,* that are joined together by hydrogen bonds. There are four kinds of nucleotides in a DNA molecule: cytosine, guanine, adenine, and thymine—C, G, A, and T, for short. Specific sequences of these bases, known as *genes,* form codes that contain all of an organism's genetic information. When other components of a cell "read" this code, they produce proteins, the building blocks of life.

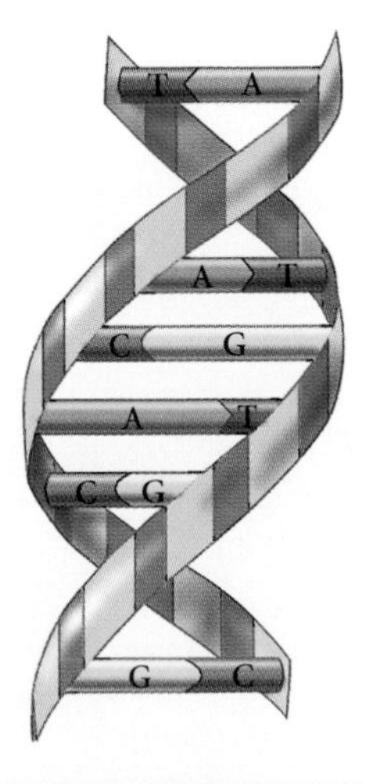

do•dec•a•gon (dō-dĕk′ə-gŏn′) A polygon having 12 sides.

do•dec•a•he•dron (dō′dĕk-ə-hē′drən) A three-dimensional geometric figure having 12 faces. A regular dodecahedron's faces are pentagonal.

dog (dôg) **1.** Any of various meat-eating mammals having a long muzzle and, in nearly all species, a four-toed foot. Many species hunt in packs that have complex social structures. Dogs include the wolf, fox, jackal, and dingo. **2.** The domesticated dog, kept as a pet or work animal since ancient times and probably descended from the wolf. Domesticated dogs are bred in many varieties, though they all belong to the same species.

dol•drums (dōl′drəmz′) A region of the globe found over the oceans near the equator, having weather characterized variously by calm air, light winds, or squalls and thunderstorms. Hurricanes originate in this region.

dol•o•mite (dō′lə-mīt′, dŏl′ə-mīt′) **1.** A gray, pink, or white mineral consisting mainly of a carbonate of calcium and magnesium. Dolomite occurs as rhombohedral crystals with a pearly to

Did You Know?

Doppler effect

When a car rushes past you on the road with the driver holding down the horn, you hear the horn change tone: it's higher pitched than normal as the car approaches and lower pitched as it departs. That's because of the *Doppler effect.* Sound waves spread outward in all directions from the horn. The forward motion of the car compresses the sound waves traveling ahead of the car, making the wavelengths shorter. Sound having shorter wavelengths has higher frequency and therefore higher pitch—what you hear if the car is moving towards you. Behind the car, however, the sound waves are drawn apart. Longer wavelengths mean lower frequency and lower pitch, which is what you hear once the car rushes past. The Doppler effect works on light waves, too; in fact, this was how scientists determined that the universe is expanding. The light from galaxies and other distant celestial objects is shifted toward the red end of the spectrum (a phenomenon called *red shift*). Red light has the longest wavelengths of visible light. The pioneering astronomer Edwin Hubble reasoned that the red shift was due to the Doppler effect: the galaxies are speeding away from us, drawing out the wavelengths of the light emitted behind them, and the universe as a whole is expanding.

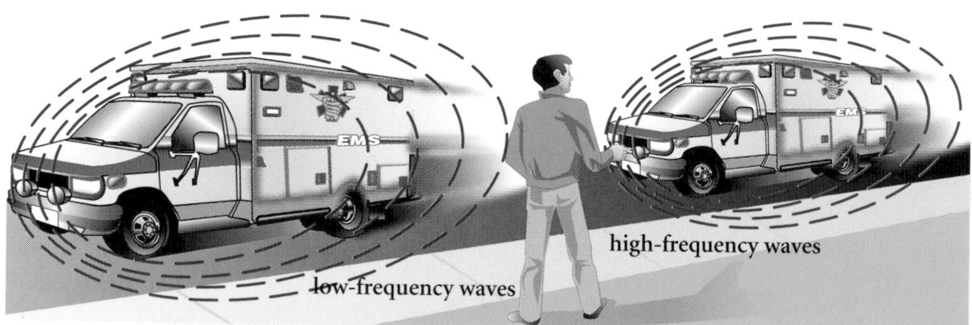

Doppler effect

As the source of sound waves (the ambulance) moves closer to the observer, the frequency of the sound waves and pitch of the sound become higher. As the source moves away from the observer, the frequency and pitch become lower.

glassy luster. It is a common rock-forming mineral. **2.** A sedimentary rock containing more than 50 percent of the mineral dolomite by weight.

dol•phin (dŏl′fĭn) **1.** Any of various, usually ocean-dwelling mammals having a snout shaped like a beak, forelimbs shaped like flippers, and horizontal tail flukes. Dolphins are related to but smaller than whales and are noted for their high intelligence. *Compare* **porpoise. 2.** Either of two edible fish that inhabit warm sea waters and have a fin extending along the back. Dolphins are iridescent when removed from the water.

do•main (dō-mān′) **1.** *Mathematics.* The set of all values that an independent variable of a function can have. In the function $y = 2x$, the set of values that x (the independent variable) can have is the domain. *Compare* **range. 2.** *Biology.* A division of organisms that ranks above a kingdom in systems of classification that are based on shared similarities in DNA sequences rather than shared structural similarities. In these systems, there are three domains: the archaea, the bacteria, and the eukaryotes.

dom•i•nant (dŏm′ə-nənt) **1.** Relating to the form of a gene that expresses a trait, such as hair color, in an individual organism. The dominant form of a gene suppresses the counterpart, or recessive, form located on the other of a pair of chromosomes. *See more at* **inheritance.** *Compare* **recessive. 2.** Being a species that has the greatest effect on other species within its ecological community. For example, in a forest where tall oaks are dominant, the shade they create and the acorns they produce help to determine what other species can thrive there.

Dop•pler effect (dŏp′lər) The apparent change in the frequency of waves, as of sound or light, when the source of the waves is moving toward or away from an observer.

dor•mant (dôr′mənt) **1.** *Biology.* In an inactive state in which growth stops and metabolism is slowed. Many plants survive the winter as dormant seeds or bulbs. Hibernating animals are also in a dormant state. **2.** *Geology.* Not active but capable of renewed activity: *a dormant volcano.*

dor•sal (dôr′səl) Of or on the back or upper surface of an animal: *the dorsal fin of a fish.*

dou•ble bond (dŭb′əl) A type of covalent bond in which two electron pairs are shared between two atoms. Each atom contributes two electrons to the bond. *See more at* **covalent bond.**

drought
corn plants suffering from lack of rain

down (doun) Fine, fluffy feathers that cover a young bird and underlie the outer feathers of certain adult birds. Down feathers are fluffy because they do not have interlocking barbules like adult outer feathers.

Down syndrome A congenital disorder caused by the presence of an extra 21st chromosome. People with Down syndrome have mild to moderate mental retardation, short stature, and a flattened facial profile.

Dra•co (drā′kō) A constellation in the polar region of the Northern Hemisphere near Cepheus and Ursa Major.

drag (drăg) The force that opposes or slows a body's movement through a fluid medium such as air or water. Drag can be reduced by sleek designs that cause less turbulence. *Compare* **lift.** *See Note at* **aerodynamics.**

drag•on•fly (drăg′ən-flī′) Any of various insects having a long slender body and two pairs of many-veined wings that are held outstretched at rest.

Dra•per (drā′pər), **Henry** 1837–1882. American astronomer who developed methods for photographing the heavens and first photographed a stellar spectrum (1872) and a nebula (1880).

drone (drōn) A male bee, especially a honeybee whose only function is to fertilize the queen. Drones have no stingers, do no work, and do not produce honey.

dro•soph•i•la (drō-sŏf′ə-lə) Any of various small fruit flies, one species of which is used extensively in breeding experiments in genetic research to study patterns of inheritance.

drought (drout) A long period of abnormally low rainfall.

drug (drŭg) Any substance that is taken or administered to cause physiological changes, especially one prescribed by a doctor to treat or prevent a medical condition. Drugs that affect the central nervous system are often addictive.

drum•lin (drŭm′lĭn) An extended, oval hill or ridge formed and shaped by a glacier. Drumlins are longer than they are wide and have one steep and one gentle slope along their longest axis.

drupe (dro͞op) A fleshy fruit, such as a peach, usually having a single hard stone that encloses a seed.

dry cell (drī) An electric cell, such as a flashlight battery, in which the chemicals producing the current are made into a paste so that they cannot spill from their container.

dry ice Solid carbon dioxide. Dry ice evaporates without first passing through a liquid state, by a process known as sublimation. It is used for refrigeration. *See Note at* **sublimation.**

dry measure A system of units for measuring dry commodities, such as grains and fruits.

Ds The symbol for **darmstadtium.**

dub•ni•um (do͞ob′nē-əm) A synthetic, radioactive element that is produced from californium, americium, or berkelium. Its most stable isotope has a half-life of 34 seconds. *Symbol* **Db.** *Atomic number* 105. *See* **Periodic Table,** pages 262–263.

Du•bois (do͞o-bwä′), **Eugène** 1858–1940. Dutch paleontologist. In 1891 he discovered fossil hominids that he named *Pithecanthropus erectus* (now called *Homo erectus*), regarded as an ancestor of *Homo sapiens.*

duck-billed dinosaur (dŭk′bĭld′) *See* **hadrosaur.**

Eugène Dubois

dune

left: *A sandstone cliff formed from the sand of ancient dunes in Canyon de Chelly, Arizona.*
right: *A large sand dune in Death Valley, California. The smaller, ripple-like features in the foreground are also dunes.*

duct (dŭkt) A tube or tube-like structure through which something flows, especially a tube in the body for carrying a fluid secreted by a gland.

duc•tile (dŭk′təl) **1.** Easily drawn out into a fine strand or wire. Gold and silver are ductile metals. *Compare* **brittle. 2.** Relating to rock or other materials that are capable of withstanding a certain amount of force by changing form before fracturing or breaking.

dune (do͞on) A hill or ridge of wind-blown sand. Dunes are capable of moving (by the motion of their individual grains) but usually keep the same shape.

du•o•dec•i•mal (do͞o′ə-dĕs′ə-məl) Relating to or based on the number 12; having 12 as the base. In the duodecimal number system, each digit represents a multiple of a power of 12 instead of 10. Thus the duodecimal number 24 represents $(2 \times 12^1) + (4 \times 12^0)$, or 28.

du•o•de•num (do͞o′ə-dē′nəm) The beginning part of the small intestine, starting at the lower end of the stomach and extending to the jejunum.

dwarf•ism (dwôr′fĭz′əm) Abnormally short stature, usually caused by a hereditary disorder.

dwarf planet (dwôrf) A celestial body that orbits the sun, is large enough to have a nearly round shape, does not clear the neighborhood around its orbit, and is not a satellite of a planet.

dwarf star (dwôrf) A small star of low mass that gives off an average or below average amount of light. The sun is a dwarf star.

Dy The symbol for **dysprosium.**

dy•nam•ic (dī-năm′ĭk) **1a.** Relating to energy or to objects in motion. **b.** Relating to the study of dynamics. **2.** Characterized by continuous change or activity.

dy•nam•ics (dī-năm′ĭks) The branch of physics that deals with the effects of forces on the motions of bodies. Also called *kinetics. Compare* **kinematics.**

dy•na•mite (dī′nə-mīt′) A powerful explosive used in blasting and mining. It typically consists of nitroglycerin and a nitrate, combined with an absorbent material that makes it safer to handle.

dy•na•mo (dī′nə-mō′) An electric generator, especially one that produces direct current. *See more at* **generator.**

dyne (dīn) A unit of force equal to the amount of force required to give a mass of one gram an acceleration of one centimeter per second for each second the force is applied.

dys•en•ter•y (dĭs′ən-tĕr′ē) A disease of the lower intestines characterized by severe diarrhea, usually caused by infection with bacteria or parasites.

dys•lex•i•a (dĭs-lĕk′sē-ə) A learning disorder that interferes with a person's ability to recognize and understand written words. *—Adjective* **dyslexic.**

Dy•son (dī′sən), **Freeman John** Born 1923. British-born physicist and writer known for his pioneering work in quantum physics. He has written many articles and books on the subject for the general public.

dys•pla•sia (dĭs-plā′zhə) Abnormal development or growth of tissues, organs, or cells. *—Adjective* **dysplastic.**

dys•pro•si•um (dĭs-prō′zē-əm) A soft, silvery metallic element of the lanthanide series. Because it has a high melting point and absorbs neutrons well, dysprosium is used to help control nuclear reactions. *Symbol* **Dy.** *Atomic number* 66. *See* **Periodic Table,** pages 262–263.

Did You Know?

dwarf star

In the world of stars, even a dwarf is quite large. At 864,000 miles in diameter and more than 330,000 times the mass of Earth, our sun is still a *dwarf star.* But a dwarf star is indeed small compared with certain other kinds of stars, such as red giants. Dwarf stars come in several varieties. The type of star known as a *white dwarf* is in fact the remnant of a red giant that has burned nearly all its fuel. Because of the gravitational attraction of its atoms for each other, the star starts to collapse in on itself. After it contracts and blows its outer layers away, the red giant ends up as a white dwarf. A *black dwarf* is a burned-out white dwarf that no longer gives off detectable radiation. Astronomers also refer to *brown dwarfs,* which are not stars. A brown dwarf is bigger than Jupiter, the biggest planet in our solar system, but too small to carry on the sustained nuclear reactions that are needed in order to become a true star.

E

e (ē) An irrational number, with a numerical value of 2.718281828459. . . . It is mathematically defined as the limit of $(1 + \frac{1}{n})^n$ as n grows infinitely large. It has many applications in science as a natural base for expressions involving exponential growth and decay.

E The symbol for **energy.**

ea•gle (ē′gəl) Any of various large birds of prey having a hooked bill, sharp claws, and long broad wings. Eagles are related to hawks and falcons.

ear[1] (îr) The organ of hearing in humans and other vertebrate animals. The ear also plays an important role in maintaining balance. In many mammals, the ear is composed of three parts: the outer ear, the middle ear, and the inner ear.

ear[2] The seed-bearing spike of a cereal plant, such as corn or wheat.

ear•drum (îr′drŭm′) The thin, oval-shaped membrane that separates the middle ear from the outer ear. It vibrates in response to sound waves, which are then transmitted to the three small bones of the middle ear. Also called *tympanic membrane.*

Earth (ûrth) **1.** The third planet from the sun and the fifth largest. Earth is the only planet known to support life. It is also the only planet on which water in liquid form exists, covering more than 70 percent of its surface. *See Table at* **solar system,** pages 316–317. **2. earth** Dry land; the ground.

earth•quake (ûrth′kwāk′) A sudden movement of the Earth's crust. Earthquakes are caused by the release of built-up stress within rocks along geologic faults or by the movement of magma in volcanic areas. They are usually followed by aftershocks. *See Note at* **fault.**

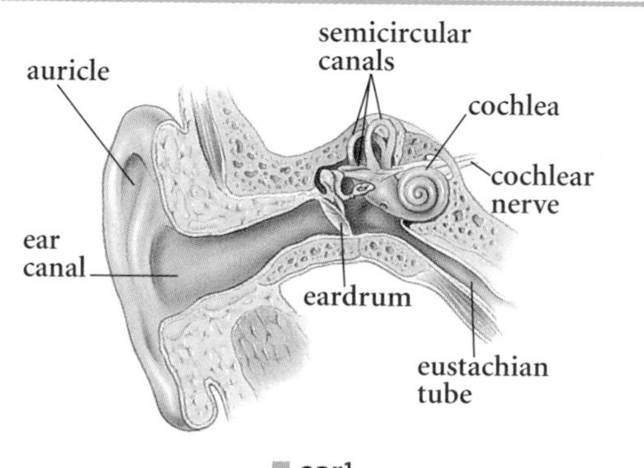

ear[1]

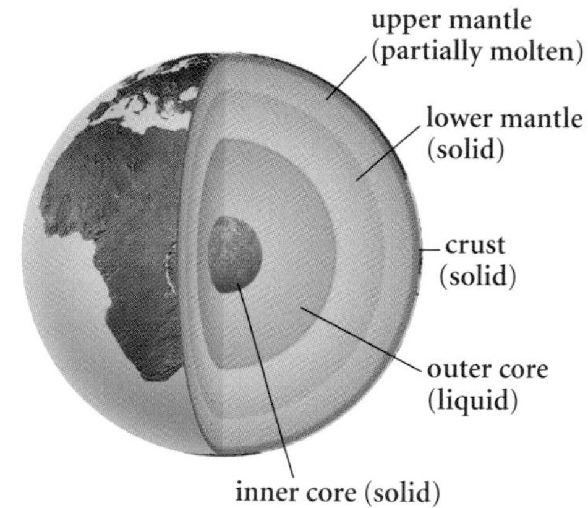

Earth

The inner core and outer core are made up mainly of iron and nickel, the lower and upper mantle mainly of iron and magnesium silicate minerals, and the crust mainly of silicate minerals.

earth science Any of several sciences, such as geology, oceanography, or meteorology, that specialize in the origin, composition, and physical features of the Earth.

earth•worm (ûrth′wûrm′) Any of various segmented worms living in the ground that burrow into and enrich soil. Earthworms are annelids, related to the leeches, and vary in size from a few inches to 11 feet (3 meters) in length. *See Note at* **worm.**

East•ern Hemisphere (ē′stərn) The half of the Earth that includes Europe, Africa, Asia, and Australia.

ebb tide (ĕb) The period between high tide and low tide, during which water flows away from the shore. *Compare* **flood tide.** See more at *tide.*

E•bo•la virus (ĭ-bō′lə) A highly contagious virus that causes fever, bleeding, loss of consciousness, and usually death.

Did You Know?
earthquake

If all the dishes fall out of your cabinet, you may honestly be able to say, "It's the Earth's fault!" Indeed, the Earth has faults, cracks where sections of its outer shell (the lithosphere) slip past each other, causing an *earthquake* when subjected to great forces. Three kinds of waves accompany earthquakes. Primary (P) waves have a push-pull type of vibration. Secondary (S) waves have a side-to-side type of vibration. Both P and S waves travel deep into the Earth, reflecting off the surfaces of its various layers. S waves cannot travel through the liquid outer core. By contrast, surface (L) waves—a third type of wave, named after the 19th-century British mathematician A.E.H. Love—travel along the Earth's surface and do most of the damage associated with an earthquake. The total amount of energy released by an earthquake is measured on the Richter scale. On this scale, each increase by 1 corresponds to a tenfold increase in earthquake strength. Thus an earthquake measuring 5.0 on the Richter scale is 10 times stronger than one measuring 4.0. Earthquakes above 7 on the Richter scale are severe. The famous earthquake that flattened San Francisco in 1906 measured 7.8.

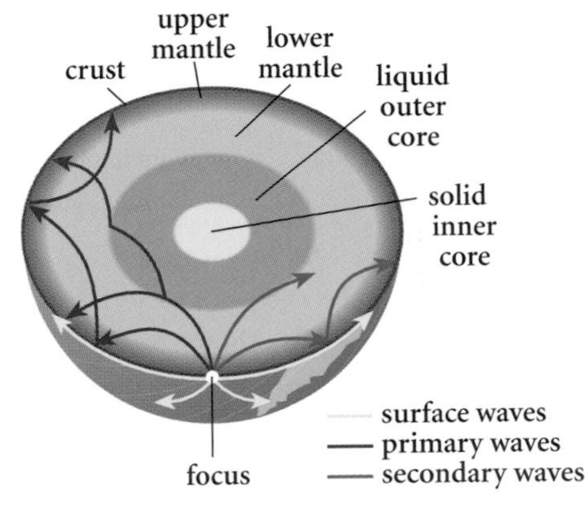

e•chid•na (ĭ-kĭd′nə) Either of two burrowing, egg-laying mammals having a spiny coat, slender snout, and long sticky tongue used for catching ants and termites. Echidnas are toothless and have claws used for digging. They are found in Australia, Tasmania, and New Guinea.

e•chi•no•derm (ĭ-kī′nə-dûrm′) Any of various invertebrate sea animals having a hard spiny outer covering, an internal skeleton, and a radially symmetrical body. Starfish, sea urchins, and sea cucumbers are echinoderms.

ech•o (ĕk′ō) **1.** A repeated sound that is caused by the reflection of sound waves from a surface. The sound is heard more than once because of the time difference between the initial production of the sound waves and their return from the reflecting surface. **2.** A reflected radio wave. Echoes of radio waves are the basis for radar.

ech•o•lo•ca•tion (ĕk′ō-lō-kā′shən) **1.** A sensory system in certain animals, such as bats and dolphins, in which the animals send out high-pitched sounds and use their echoes to determine the position of objects. *See Note at* **bat. 2.** The use of reflected sound waves, as by radar or sonar, to determine the location and size of distant or underwater objects.

Eck•ert (ĕk′ərt) **John Presper** 1919–1995. American engineer who contributed to the development of ENIAC (Electronic Numeral Integrator and Calculator), the first electronic computer (1946).

e•clipse (ĭ-klĭps′) The partial or total blocking of light from one celestial body as it passes behind or through the shadow of another celestial body.

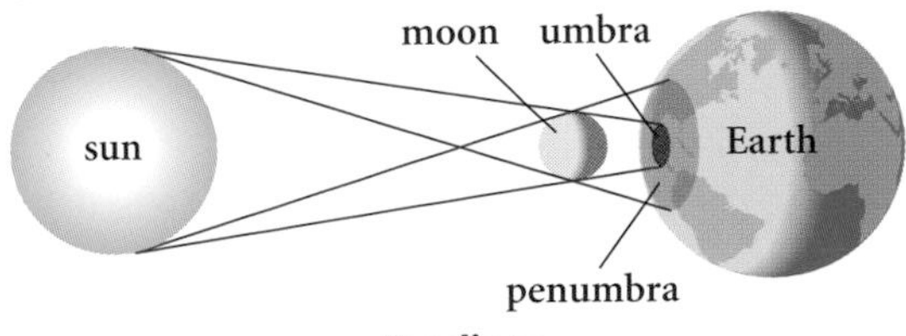

eclipse

A solar eclipse occurs when the moon passes between the sun and the Earth. An observer within the umbra will witness a total solar eclipse, while someone within the penumbra will observe a partial solar eclipse.

Did You Know?
eclipse

Purely by chance, the sun is about 400 times wider than the moon but also 400 times farther from Earth. For this reason, they appear to be almost exactly the same size in the sky. Our unique vantage point makes for the spectacular phenomenon of a *total solar eclipse,* when the moon blocks out the sun. A total solar eclipse reveals the beautiful and delicate corona, wispy tendrils of charged gases that surround the sun but are invisible to the unaided eye in normal sunlight. The orbits of Earth around the sun and of the moon around Earth are not perfect circles. Therefore the sun and moon may vary slightly in how big they appear to us, and the length of total solar eclipses can also vary. The maximum duration of a solar eclipse, however, when Earth is farthest from the sun and the moon is nearest to Earth, is only seven and a half minutes. Since looking at the sun can cause blindness, it is safest to view any solar eclipse indirectly. A good method is to project the image through a pinhole in a piece of paper onto another piece of paper.

❖ In a **solar eclipse** the moon comes between the sun and Earth. ❖ In a **lunar eclipse** the moon enters Earth's shadow.

e•clips•ing binary (ĭ-klĭp′sĭng) A variable binary star whose components pass in front of each other, thereby causing a regular eclipse of one of the stars and changes in brightness.

e•clip•tic (ĭ-klĭp′tĭk) The great circle on the celestial sphere that is made by the plane containing Earth's orbit around the sun. The ecliptic traces the sun's apparent path in the sky in one year, as viewed from Earth.

e•col•o•gy (ĭ-kŏl′ə-jē) **1.** The scientific study of the relationships between living things and their environments. **2.** A system of such relationships: *the fragile ecology of the desert.*

ec•o•sys•tem (ē′kō-sĭs′təm) An ecological community made up of plants, animals, and microorganisms together with their environment. A pond or a rain forest are each examples of complex ecosystems.

ec•ze•ma (ĕk′sə-mə) Inflammation of the skin, often caused by an allergy to a particular substance. Symptoms include itching, scaling, and blistering.

Ed•ding•ton (ĕd′ĭng-tən), Sir **Arthur Stanley** 1882–1944. British mathematician, astronomer, and physicist who founded modern astrophysics. He conducted research on the evolution, structure, and motion of stars and was one of the first scientists to promote the theory of relativity.

ed•dy (ĕd′ē) A current, as of water or air, moving in a direction that is different from that of the main current. Eddies often move in a circular motion.

e•de•ma (ĭ-dē′mə) An excessive accumulation of fluid in body tissue that results in swelling.

e•den•tate (ē-dĕn′tāt′) *Adjective.* **1.** Lacking teeth. —*Noun.* **2.** Any of various mammals having few or no teeth. Sloths, armadillos, and anteaters are edentates.

E•di•a•ca•ran (ē′dē-ä′kə-rən) Relating to a group of fossilized organisms that are the earliest known remains of multicellular life. They are soft-bodied marine life forms that date from between 560 and 545 million years ago, during the late Precambrian Eon.

Ed•i•son (ĕd′ĭ-sən), **Thomas Alva** 1847–1931. American inventor and physicist who took out

Thomas Edison

more than 1,000 patents. His inventions include the telegraph (1869), microphone (1877), and light bulb (1879). During World War I, Edison worked on many military devices, including flamethrowers, periscopes, and torpedoes.

EEG Abbreviation of **electroencephalogram.**

eel (ēl) **1.** Any of various fish having long, snakelike bodies without scales. Eels typically migrate from fresh to salt water to spawn. **2.** Any of several similar fish, such as the lamprey.

ef•fer•ent (ĕf′ər-ənt) Relating to a nerve that carries motor impulses from the central nervous system to the muscles. *Compare* **afferent.**

ef•fer•ves•cence (ĕf′ər-vĕs′əns) The bubbling of a solution due to the escape of gas. The gas may form by a chemical reaction, as in a fermenting liquid, or by coming out of solution after having been under pressure, as in a carbonated drink.

ef•flo•res•cence (ĕf′lə-rĕs′əns) A whitish, powdery deposit on the surface of rocks or soil in dry regions. It is formed as mineral-rich water rises to the surface through capillary action and then evaporates. Efflorescence usually consists of gypsum, salt, or calcite.

egg (ĕg) **1.** The mature reproductive cell of female animals. The nucleus of an egg is capable of fusing with the nucleus of a sperm (the male reproductive cell) to form a new organism. In many species, eggs are produced by the ovaries. An egg carries half as many chromosomes as the other cells of the body. Also called *ovum.* **2.** In many animals, a structure consisting of this reproductive cell together with nourishment for the developing embryo and often a protective covering. It is laid outside the body of the female. **3.** In plants, algae, and certain fungi, the reproductive cell whose nucleus is capable of fusing with the nucleus of a male reproductive cell to form a new organism. An egg has half as many chromosomes as the other cells of the organism. In gymnosperms and angiosperms, eggs are enclosed within ovules.

effervescence

The reaction of baking soda and vinegar produces the gas carbon dioxide.

Paul Ehrlich

egg tooth A hard, tooth-like projection from the beak of embryonic birds, or from the upper jaw of embryonic reptiles, that is used to cut the egg membrane and shell upon hatching and that later falls off.

Ehr•lich (âr′lĭk), **Paul** 1854–1915. German bacteriologist who was a pioneer in the study of the blood and the immune system, and in the development of drugs to fight specific disease-causing agents. Ehrlich theorized that the interactions between cells, antibodies, and antigens were chemical responses, and he developed systematic techniques to search for chemicals that would attack and destroy disease without harming human cells. In the process, he discovered a compound that was effective in combating sleeping sickness and another drug, called salvarsan, that cured syphilis.

Ein•stein (īn′stīn′), **Albert** 1879–1955. German-born American physicist whose theories revolutionized scientific understanding of space and time. His theory of special relativity, published in 1905, showed that bodies moving at high speeds appear to increase in mass and experience time more slowly. His theory of general relativity, published in 1915, stated that the force of gravity is due to the curvature of space-time. Einstein also showed that light is composed of individual

BIOGRAPHY

Albert Einstein

Around 1900, the field of physics had fallen into confusion. The increased precision of new measuring devices had shown that the old laws of motion and gravity established by Galileo and Newton were unable to explain certain phenomena. For example, scientists now knew that the observed orbit of the planet Mercury differed slightly from that predicted by Newton. And new laws describing the movement of electromagnetic waves were shown not to work under certain conditions. A way to solving these problems was opened in 1905 by an unknown 26-year-old office clerk named Albert Einstein. In that year, he published four path-breaking papers that revolutionized physics. Two introduced aspects of his theory of relativity, which broke away from the Newtonian reliance on space and time as unchangeable frames of reference. In one of these papers, Einstein argued that the speed of light is the same for all observers. A third paper showed that light consists of particles called photons. A fourth explained the random movement of particles suspended in a fluid (what is known as Brownian motion). Later, in 1916, he showed that gravity is not just a force, but actually stretches or shrinks distances and even slows down time in relation to someone unaffected by the gravitational field. Einstein's new way of looking at gravity explained the variations in Mercury's orbit, and his theory that light consists not just of waves but of particles led to a more accurate description of electromagnetic radiation. For the next 50 years Einstein devoted himself to unveiling more of the mysteries of the physical world, and he also used his fame to promote peace and humanitarian causes.

particles, later named photons. *See more at* **relativity.**

ein•stein•i•um (īn-stī′nē-əm) A synthetic, radioactive metallic element of the actinide series that is usually produced from plutonium. The most stable isotope of einsteinium has a half-life of 1.3 years. *Symbol* **Es.** *Atomic number* 99. *See* **Periodic Table,** pages 262–263.

EKG Abbreviation of **electrocardiogram.**

e•las•tic•i•ty (ĭ-lă-stĭs′ĭ-tē) The ability of a solid to return to its original shape after being stretched or compressed by a force. Elasticity is a property of most solid materials, including rubber, steel, and many body tissues. —*Adjective* **elastic.**

El•dredge (ĕl′drĕdj), **Niles** Born 1943. American paleontologist who developed the theory of punctuated equilibrium with evolutionary biologist Stephen Jay Gould in 1972.

e•lec•tric (ĭ-lĕk′trĭk) *also* **e•lec•tri•cal** (ĭ-lĕk′trĭ-kəl) Relating to or operated by electricity: *electric power; an electrical appliance. See Note at* **electronic.**

electrical engineering The branch of engineering that specializes in the design, construction, and practical uses of electrical systems.

electric cell A device, such as a battery, that is capable of changing some form of energy, such as chemical or radiant energy, into electricity.

e•lec•tric•i•ty (ĭ-lĕk-trĭs′ĭ-tē) **1.** The collection of physical effects resulting from the existence of charged particles, especially electrons and protons, and their interactions. Particles with like charges repel each other. Particles with opposite charges attract each other. **2.** The electric current generated by the flow of electrons around a circuit and used as a source of power.

e•lec•tro•car•di•o•gram (ĭ-lĕk′trō-kär′dē-ə-grăm′) A recording of the electrical activity of the heart. The electrocardiogram is used by doctors to analyze how well the heart is working and to diagnose abnormal heart rhythms. ❖ The machine used to record an electrocardiogram is called an **electrocardiograph.**

e•lec•tro•chem•is•try (ĭ-lĕk′trō-kĕm′ĭ-strē) The scientific study of chemical reactions that produce an electric current and of the use of electricity to bring about chemical reactions.

e•lec•trode (ĭ-lĕk′trōd′) A piece of metal or carbon through which an electric current enters or leaves a liquid or gas, as in a vacuum tube.

e•lec•tro•dy•nam•ics (ĭ-lĕk′trō-dī-năm′ĭks) The scientific study of electric charges, electric currents, and the forces associated with them. Electrodynamics is a branch of physics.

e•lec•tro•en•ceph•a•lo•gram (ĭ-lĕk′trō-ĕn-sĕf′ə-lə-grăm′) A recording of the electrical activity of the brain. It is used to diagnose abnormalities of the brain. ❖ The machine used to record an electroencephalogram is called an **electroencephalograph.**

e•lec•trol•y•sis (ĭ-lĕk-trŏl′ĭ-sĭs) A process in which a chemical change, especially decomposition, is brought about by passing an electric current through a solution of electrolytes so that the electrolyte's ions move toward the negative and positive electrodes and react with them.

e•lec•tro•lyte (ĭ-lĕk′trə-līt′) **1.** A substance that when dissolved or melted becomes electrically conductive by breaking apart into ions. The movement of ions carries the current. **2.** Any of these ions found in body fluids. Electrolytes are needed by cells to regulate the flow of water molecules across cell membranes.

e•lec•tro•lyt•ic cell (ĭ-lĕk′trə-lĭt′ĭk) A device containing two electrodes immersed in a solution of electrolytes, used to bring about a chemical reaction. Electrolytic cells require an outside source of electricity to initiate the movement of ions between the two electrodes where the chemical change takes place. They have many practical uses including the recovery of pure metal from alloys and the plating of one metal with another. *Compare* **voltaic cell.**

e•lec•tro•mag•net (ĭ-lĕk′trō-măg′nĭt) A device consisting of a coil of insulated wire wrapped around an iron core that becomes magnetized when an electric current flows through the wire. *See Note at* **magnetism.**

Did You Know?

electromagnetic radiation

Many people have heard that light is made up of waves, but what does that mean? The answer seems very abstract: light, and other forms of *electromagnetic radiation,* are made up of wave-shaped electric and magnetic fields that reinforce each other as they travel together. In the 19th century, physicists discovered that a changing electric field can create a magnetic field, and a changing magnetic field can create an electric field. So a wave-shaped electric field (for example, the field created when a charged particle such as an electron moves up and down) can create a wave-shaped magnetic field, which in turn reproduces the wave-shaped electric field. These mutually re-creating fields travel at the speed of light. Electromagnetic radiation can have a variety of properties, depending on its wavelength. Certain wavelengths make up the spectrum of visible light. Infrared light and radio waves have longer wavelengths, whereas ultraviolet light, x-rays, and gamma rays have shorter wavelengths. These wave properties do not tell the full story of electromagnetic radiation, however. Visible light and other forms of electromagnetic radiation also exist as streams of the particles known as *photons.* The energy of the photons increases as the frequency of the waves gets higher.

e•lec•tro•mag•net•ic force (ĭ-lĕk′trō-măg-nĕt′ĭk) The force arising from the attractions and repulsions associated with electric and magnetic fields. The electromagnetic force is one of the four basic forces in nature, being weaker than the strong nuclear force but stronger than the weak nuclear force and gravity.

electromagnetic radiation Energy that moves through space and matter both in the form of

electromagnetic spectrum

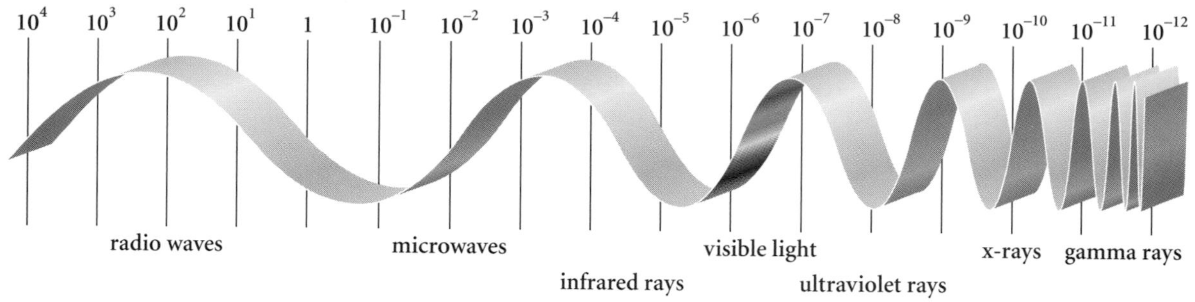

electromagnetic spectrum

The electromagnetic spectrum can be measured in frequencies or in wavelengths. This diagram measures wavelengths in meters, ranging from the longest wavelengths (radio waves) to the shortest (gamma rays). Visible light, which is a band of colors from red to violet, is the only portion of the spectrum that can be seen by the human eye.

magnetic and electric waves and in the form of a stream of particles called photons.

electromagnetic spectrum The entire range of electromagnetic radiation. At one end of the spectrum are gamma rays, which have the shortest wavelengths and high frequencies. At the other end are radio waves, which have the longest wavelengths and low frequencies. Visible light, with intermediate wavelengths and frequencies, is near the center of the spectrum.

electromagnetic wave A wave of energy consisting of oscillating electric and magnetic fields. Radio waves, light waves, and x-rays are electromagnetic waves.

e•lec•tro•mag•net•ism (ĭ-lĕk′trō-măg**′**nĭ-tĭz′-əm) **1.** Magnetism produced by electric charge in motion. *See Note at* **magnetism. 2.** The scientific study of electricity and magnetism and the relationships between them.

e•lec•tro•mo•tive (ĭ-lĕk′trō-mō**′**tĭv) Relating to or producing electric current.

electromotive force 1. The force that makes electrons move to produce an electric current. Electromotive force is supplied by a power source, such as a battery or dynamo. It is measured in volts. **2.** The difference in the potential energies of a cathode and anode immersed in the same solution of electrolytes or connected in another manner.

e•lec•tron (ĭ-lĕk**′**trŏn′) A stable subatomic particle with a negative electric charge. Electrons spin about an atom's nucleus in orbits called shells. Electrons behave both as particles and as waves, and their motion generates electric and magnetic fields. Though the electron is the lightest subatomic particle, its charge is as great as that of a proton. *See more at* **atom.**

e•lec•tron•ic (ĭ-lĕk′trŏn**′**ĭk) Relating to devices that work by the movement of electric charge carriers (such as electrons), especially across a vacuum or a semiconductor. ❖ The scientific study of this movement, along with the development of devices such as televisions and computer circuits that work by controlling this movement, is called **electronics.**

electron microscope An instrument that uses a beam of electrons to view objects that are too small to be seen with an ordinary microscope. As

USAGE

electronic/electric

All electronic devices are electric, but not all electric devices are electronic. An *electric* device is simply one that is powered by electricity. An electric fan usually consists of an electric motor that moves fan blades in a circle. An *electronic* device usually has special components that control the movement of electrons across a vacuum (as in a vacuum tube) or a semiconductor. These components allow a great range of capabilities, from tuning in to radio and television channels, to performing complicated calculations on calculators, to reading the time from a digital watch.

WORD HISTORY

element symbols

The symbols that scientists use for the chemical elements are usually abbreviations of the elements' names. Thus the symbol for hydrogen is H, and the symbol for oxygen is O, both from the first letter of the name. But if you look at the Periodic Table (pages 262–263), you'll notice that some symbols are entirely different from the corresponding element names. The symbol for iron is Fe, and the symbol for tin is Sn, for example. Why is this? It happens that some elements were already known to the ancient Greeks and Romans, such as familiar metals like iron, copper, silver, gold, tin, and lead. For these elements scientists use abbreviations of the Greek and Latin words for them. The Latin words for the six metals listed above are *ferrum, cuprum, argentum, aurum, stannum,* and *plumbum.* From these names come, quite straightforwardly, the chemical symbols Fe, Cu, Ag, Au, Sn, and Pb.

the electrons hit the object being viewed, other electrons are knocked loose from its surface and are picked up by a detector that converts them into a black and white image.

electron tube A sealed glass tube containing either a vacuum or a small amount of gas, in which electrons move from a negatively charged electrode to a positively charged one. With the application and varying of an electric or magnetic field, the direction and number of electrons in the tube can be controlled. Electron tubes are used to amplify signals and change AC currents to DC currents. They have been mostly replaced by transistors but are still used in television screens and computer monitors and in microwave technology. *Compare* **vacuum tube.**

electron volt A unit used to measure the energy of subatomic particles. It is equal to the energy gained by an electron that is accelerated until its electric potential is one volt greater than it was before being accelerated.

e•lec•tro•pho•re•sis (ĭ-lĕk′trō-fə-rē**′**sĭs) The migration of electrically charged particles through a fluid that is under the influence of an electric field. Electrophoresis is used especially to separate colloids for the purpose of studying their components.

e•lec•tro•stat•ic (ĭ-lĕk′trō-stăt**′**ĭk) Relating to or caused by electric charges that do not move. *See more at* **static electricity.**

el•e•ment (ĕl**′**ə-mənt) **1.** A substance that cannot be broken down into simpler substances by chemical means. An element is composed of atoms that have the same atomic number; that is, each atom has the same number of protons in its nucleus as all other atoms of that element. Today 117 elements are known, of which 92 are known to occur in nature, while the remaining ones have only been made with particle accelerators. **2.** *Mathematics.* A member of a set.

el•e•men•ta•ry particle (ĕl′ə-mĕn**′**tə-rē) Any of the smallest known units of matter, such as quarks and neutrinos. Elementary particles are not made up of smaller units.

el•e•phant (ĕl**′**ə-fənt) **1.** A large mammal having thick, nearly hairless skin, a long flexible trunk, and long curved ivory tusks. There are two living species of elephants, the African and the Indian elephant. They can live over 60 years in the wild and display complex social behavior. **2.** Any of various extinct animals, such as the mammoths, that are related to the living elephants.

el•e•va•tion (ĕl′ə-vā**′**shən) The vertical distance between a standard reference point, such as sea level, and the top of an object or point on the Earth, such as a mountain. The summit of Mount Everest is the highest elevation on Earth.

el•lipse (ĭ-lĭps**′**) A closed, symmetric curve shaped like an oval, which can be formed by intersecting a cone with a plane that is not paral-

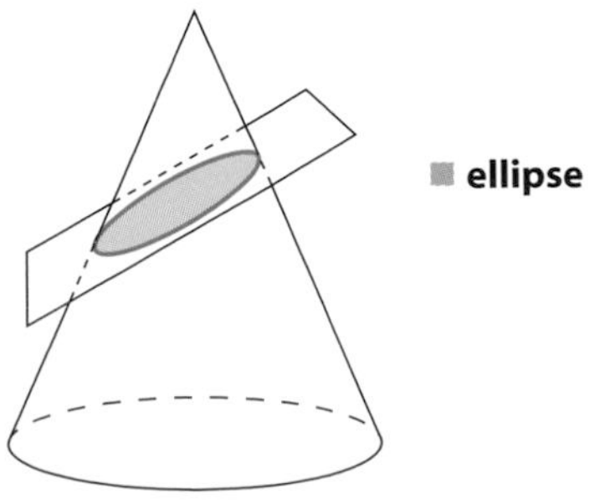

ellipse

lel or perpendicular to the cone's base. The sum of the distances of any point on an ellipse from two fixed points (called the foci) remains constant no matter where the point is on the curve.

el•lip•soid (ĭ-lĭp′soid′) A three-dimensional geometric figure resembling a flattened sphere. Any cross section of an ellipsoid is an ellipse or circle.

elm (ĕlm) Any of various deciduous trees having arching or curving branches and leaves with a saw-toothed edge. The American elm, once widely planted as a shade tree, has largely died off because of disease.

El Ni•ño (ĕl nēn′yō) A warming of the surface water of the eastern and central Pacific Ocean, occurring every 4 to 12 years and causing unusual weather patterns. The warmer water kills fish and plankton, brings heavy rains to western South America, and causes drought in eastern Australia and Indonesia. *Compare* **La Niña.**

el•y•tron (ĕl′ĭ-trŏn′) *Plural* **elytra.** Either of the modified forewings of a beetle or related insect that encase the thin hind wings used in flight.

em•bry•o (ĕm′brē-ō′) **1.** An animal in its earliest stages of development, especially in the uterus of female mammals, or, in egg-laying animals, an animal developing in the egg until it is hatched. **2.** A plant in its earliest stages of development, especially the miniature, partially developed plant contained within a seed. When conditions are right for germination, the embryo begins to grow and bursts through the seed coat. —*Adjective* **embryonic** (ĕm′brē-ŏn′ĭk).

em•bry•ol•o•gy (ĕm′brē-ŏl′ə-jē) The branch of biology that deals with embryos and their development.

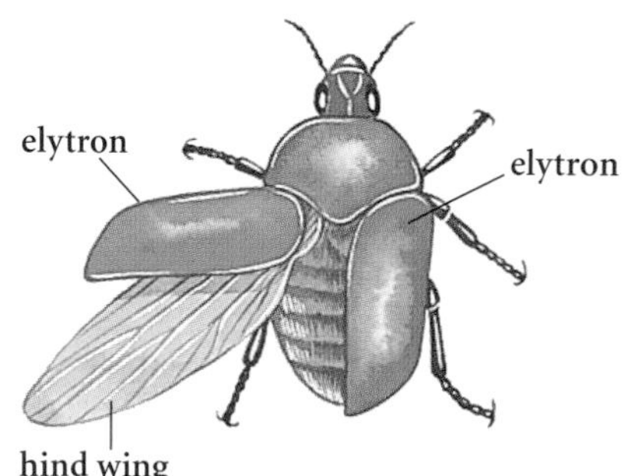

elytron

When closed, the elytron protects the hind wing. The elytra are opened for flight.

embryo sac An oval structure within an ovule of a flowering plant that contains the egg cell. Together with the fertilized egg cell, it develops into a seed.

em•er•ald (ĕm′ər-əld) A transparent, green form of the mineral beryl. It is valued as a gem.

em•er•y (ĕm′ə-rē) A dark mineral that is very hard and is used in a crushed or powdered form for grinding and polishing.

e•mis•sion (ĭ-mĭsh′ən) **1.** The act or process of emitting: *For environmental safety we must seek to reduce the factory's emission of fumes and smoke.* **2.** Something that is emitted: *harmful emissions from automobiles.*

emission spectrum The radiation, such as light, given off by a substance whose atoms have been excited by heat or other radiation. The atoms of different elements give off radiation at specific frequencies as they return to their normal energy level. The radiation can then be passed through a prism, forming a pattern of colored bars (one bar

USAGE

endemic/epidemic

A disease that occurs regularly in a particular area, as malaria does in many tropical countries, is said to be *endemic.* The word *endemic,* built from the prefix *en–,* "in or within," and the Greek word *demos,* "people," means "within the people (of a region)." A disease that affects many more people than usual in a particular area or that spreads into regions in which it does not usually occur is said to be *epidemic.* This word, built from the prefix *epi–,* meaning "upon," and *demos,* means "upon the people." In order for a disease to become epidemic it must be highly contagious, that is, easily spread through a population. Influenza, better known as the flu, has been the cause of many epidemics throughout history. Epidemics of waterborne diseases such as cholera often occur after natural disasters such as earthquakes and severe storms that disrupt or destroy sanitation systems and supplies of fresh water.

Did You Know?
endorphins

In the 1970s, scientists began to wonder why drugs like morphine could kill pain so effectively. Researchers knew that morphine attached to specific body molecules called receptors, so they reasoned that these receptors probably existed because the body itself had natural painkilling compounds that also bonded to those receptors. They searched and finally found proteins called *endorphins,* a word that combines *endogenous,* meaning "naturally occurring within the body," and *morphine.* When your body is under stress, it can produce endorphins so that you can still function under what would otherwise be exceptionally painful conditions. Many long-distance runners, for example, claim that after they run for a while they start to feel exceptionally happy, a condition sometimes called a *runner's high.* High levels of endorphins in response to the strain of running seem to be responsible for this state of mind.

for each frequency). By analyzing these bars, scientists can determine what kinds of atoms the substance is made of. *See more at* **spectroscope.**

em•phy•se•ma (ĕm′fĭ-sē′mə) A chronic disease in which the small air sacs of the lungs (called alveoli) become enlarged and eventually collapse, causing blockage to the flow of air. Symptoms include difficulty breathing and loss of physical endurance. Emphysema can be caused by excessive smoking.

em•pir•i•cal (ĕm-pîr′ĭ-kəl) Relying on or derived from observation or experiment rather than theory: *empirical results prove the theory.*

emp•ty set (ĕmp′tē) *Mathematics.* The set that has no members or elements.

e•mu (ē′myo͞o) A large, flightless Australian bird related to and resembling the ostrich but smaller.

e•mul•sion (ĭ-mŭl′shən) A suspension of tiny droplets of one liquid in a second liquid. By making an emulsion, one can mix two liquids that ordinarily do not mix well, such as oil and water. *Compare* **aerosol, foam.** —*Verb* **emulsify.**

e•nam•el (ĭ-năm′əl) The hard substance covering the exposed portion of a tooth.

en•ceph•a•li•tis (ĕn-sĕf′ə-lī′tĭs) Inflammation of the brain, usually caused by infection with a virus.

en•dan•gered species (ĕn-dān′jərd) A plant or animal species existing in such small numbers that it is in danger of becoming extinct. An organism often becomes endangered because of destruction of its native habitat.

en•dem•ic (ĕn-dĕm′ĭk) **1.** Found in or confined to a particular location, region, or people. Malaria, for example, is endemic to tropical regions. **2.** *Ecology.* Native to a particular region or environment and not occurring naturally anywhere else. The giant sequoia is endemic to California. *Compare* **alien, indigenous.**

en•do•crine gland (ĕn′də-krĭn, ĕn′də-krēn′) Any gland of the body that produces hormones and secretes them directly into the bloodstream. In mammals, the thyroid gland, adrenal gland, and pituitary gland, as well as the ovary, testis, and pancreas are all endocrine glands. ❖ The group of endocrine glands together with the hormones they secrete is known as the **endocrine system.** *See Note at* **hormone.**

en•do•cri•nol•o•gy (ĕn′də-krə-nŏl′ə-jē) The branch of biology or medicine that deals with endocrine glands, their functions, and their diseases.

en•do•me•tri•um (ĕn′dō-mē′trē-əm) The membrane that lines the uterus of a female mammal. A fertilized egg must attach itself to the endometrium to continue to develop.

en•do•plas•mic reticulum (ĕn′də-plăz′mĭk) A network of membranes within the cytoplasm of many cells that is important in protein synthesis and involved in the transport of cellular materials. All organisms except bacteria have at least one endoplasmic reticulum in their cells. *See more at* **cell.**

en•dor•phin (ĕn-dôr′fĭn) Any of a group of substances found in the nervous system, especially in the brain, that regulate the body's response to pain and other stimuli.

en•do•skel•e•ton (ĕn′dō-skĕl′ĭ-tn) A supporting framework in an animal that is contained inside the body. Humans and many other vertebrate animals have bony endoskeletons. Certain

> **WORD HISTORY**
>
> **entomology**
>
> Scientists who study insects (there are close to a million that can be studied!) are called entomologists. Why are they not called "insectologists"? Well, in a way they are. The word *insect* comes from the Latin word *insectum,* meaning "cut up or divided into segments." (The plural of *insectum,* namely *insecta,* is used by scientists as the name of the taxonomic class that insects belong to.) This Latin word was created in order to translate the Greek word for "insect," which is *entomon.* This Greek word also literally means "cut up or divided into segments," and it is the source of the word *entomology.* The Greeks had coined this term for insects because of the clear division of insect bodies into three segments, now called the head, thorax, and abdomen.

invertebrate animals, such as sponges, have endoskeletons made up of needle-like structures called spicules. *Compare* **exoskeleton.**

en•do•sperm (ĕn′də-spûrm′) The tissue that surrounds and provides nourishment to the embryo in plant seeds.

en•do•ther•mic (ĕn′dō-thûr′mĭk) Causing or characterized by absorption of heat: *an endothermic chemical reaction. Compare* **exothermic.**

–ene A suffix used to form the names of hydrocarbons having one or more double bonds, such as *benzene. Compare* **–ane.**

en•er•gy (ĕn′ər-jē) **1.** The capacity or power to do work, such as the capacity to move an object (of a given mass) in a given direction by the application of force. Energy can exist in a variety of forms, such as electrical, mechanical, chemical, thermal, or nuclear, and can be transformed from one form to another. It is measured by the amount of work done, usually in joules or watts. *See more at* **law of conservation of energy. 2.** Usable heat or power: *The school consumed too much energy last year.*

en•gine (ĕn′jĭn) A machine that turns energy into mechanical force or motion, especially one that gets its energy from a source of heat, such as the burning of a fuel. *See more at* **internal-combustion engine, jet engine, steam engine.**

en•gi•neer•ing (ĕn′jə-nîr′ĭng) The application of science to practical uses such as the design of structures, machines, and systems. *See more at* **chemical engineering, civil engineering, electrical engineering, mechanical engineering.**

en•thal•py (ĕn′thăl′pē) The amount of energy contained in a system.

en•to•mol•o•gy (ĕn′tə-mŏl′ə-jē) The scientific study of insects.

en•tro•py (ĕn′trə-pē) A measure of the amount of disorder in a system. Entropy increases as the system's temperature increases. For example, when an ice cube melts and becomes liquid, the energy of the molecular bonds which formed the ice crystals is lost, and the arrangement of the water molecules is more random, or disordered, than it was in the ice cube.

en•vi•ron•ment (ĕn-vī′rən-mənt) All of the physical, chemical, and biological conditions that together act on an organism or an ecological community and influence its growth and development. Soil, air, water, climate, plant and animal life, noise level, and pollution are all components of an environment. To survive, organisms must often adapt to changes in their environments.

en•zyme (ĕn′zīm) Any of the proteins produced in living cells that act as catalysts in the metabolic processes of an organism. For example, enzymes break down the large molecules found in food into smaller molecules so they can be digested.

E•o•cene (ē′ə-sēn′) The second epoch of the Tertiary Period, from about 58 to 37 million years ago, characterized by warm climates and the rise of most modern families of mammals. *See Chart at* **geologic time,** pages 148–149.

e•o•hip•pus (ē′ō-hĭp′əs) *See* **hyracotherium.**

e•on (ē′ŏn′) The longest division of geologic time, containing two or more eras.

ep•i•cen•ter (ĕp′ĭ-sĕn′tər) The point on the Earth's surface that is directly above the focus (the point of origin) of an earthquake.

ep•i•dem•ic (ĕp′ĭ-dĕm′ĭk) An outbreak of a contagious disease that spreads rapidly and widely. *See Note at* **endemic.**

ep•i•de•mi•ol•o•gy (ĕp′ĭ-dē′mē-ŏl′ə-jē) The branch of medicine that deals with the study of

Did You Know?
enzymes

No matter how hard you find chemistry in school, you're still quite good at it: every day your body performs complex biochemistry. Many of the chemical reactions that take place inside you depend on the proteins known as *enzymes.* These large, globular proteins catalyze, or speed up, the reactions sometimes by as much as a million times. Enzymes are structured so that they bond to a second, specific molecule, called a *substrate.* When the enzyme and its substrate come together, at a place on the enzyme called the *active site,* the substrate is modified, for example by combining two different substrate molecules into a single molecule. The enzyme remains unchanged, breaks away, and is free to perform its chemical magic on a fresh substrate molecule. People have found uses for enzymes outside our bodies as well. For example, detergents may include enzymes that break down organic stains on clothing, and enzymes have long been used in making beer, wine, and cheese.

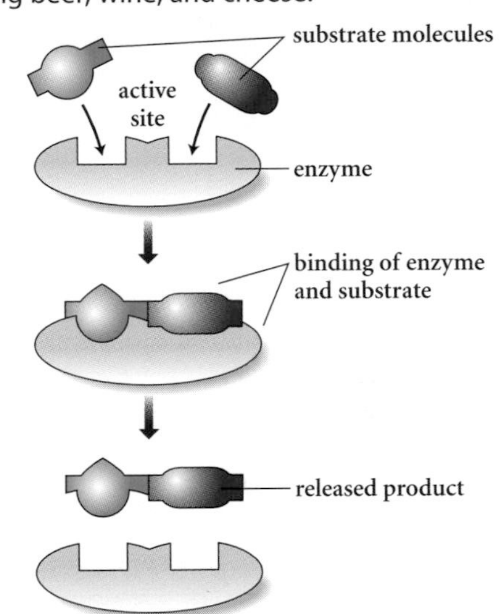

the causes, distribution, and control of disease in populations.

ep•i•der•mis (ĕp′ĭ-dûr′mĭs) **1.** The protective outer layer of the skin of an animal. In invertebrate animals, the epidermis is made up of a single layer of cells. In vertebrates, the epidermis is made up of many layers of cells and overlies the dermis. Hair and feathers grow from the epidermis. **2.** The outer layer of cells of the stems, roots, and leaves of plants. The cells of the epidermis are set close together to protect the plant from water loss, invasion by fungi, and physical damage. *See more at* **photosynthesis.**

■ **epiphyte**
orchids growing on a tree trunk

ep•i•glot•tis (ĕp′ĭ-glŏt′ĭs) A thin, triangular plate of cartilage at the base of the tongue that covers the glottis during swallowing to keep food from entering the trachea.

ep•i•lep•sy (ĕp′ə-lĕp′sē) A disorder characterized by a tendency to have seizures. It is caused by an abnormal discharge of electrical activity in the brain.

ep•i•neph•rine (ĕp′ə-nĕf′rĭn) A hormone secreted by the adrenal gland in response to physical or mental stress, as from fear. The release of epinephrine causes the heart to beat faster and more strongly, the pupils to dilate, and the rate of breathing to increase. Epinephrine also causes an increase in the amount of sugar in the blood, which can be used by the body as fuel when more alertness or greater physical effort is needed. Also called *adrenaline.*

ep•i•phyte (ĕp′ə-fīt′) A plant that grows on another plant and depends on it for support but

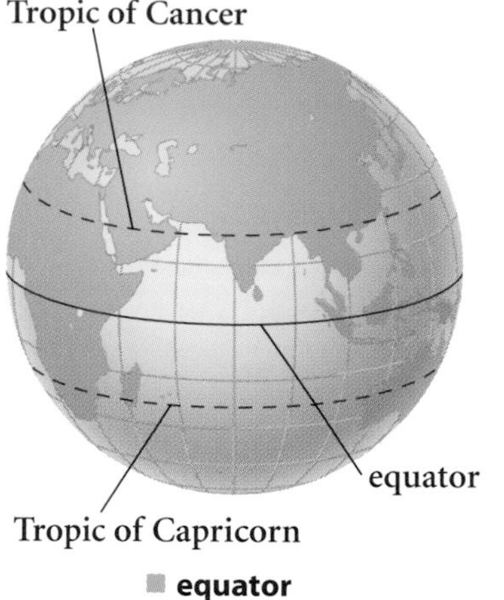

equator

not food. Epiphytes get moisture and nutrients from the air or from small pools of water that collect on the host plant. Spanish moss and many orchids are epiphytes.

ep•i•the•li•um (ĕp′ə-thē′lē-əm) The thin, protective layer of cells that covers most of the outer surface of an animal body and lines the inner surface of many body parts. In vertebrate animals, the outer layer of the skin, called the epidermis, is composed of epithelium.

ep•och (ĕp′ək, ē′pŏk′) The shortest division of geologic time, being a subdivision of a period.

ep•ox•ide (ĕ-pŏk′sīd) A ring-shaped chemical structure or compound consisting of an oxygen atom bonded to two other atoms, usually of carbon, that are already bonded to each other.

ep•ox•y (ĭ-pŏk′sē) Any of various artificial resins that are tough, very adhesive, and resistant to chemicals. Epoxies are used to make protective coatings and glues.

Ep•som salts (ĕp′səm) A bitter, colorless, crystalline salt, used in making textiles, in fertilizers, for medical purposes, and as an additive to bath water to soothe the skin. It consists of hydrated magnesium sulfate.

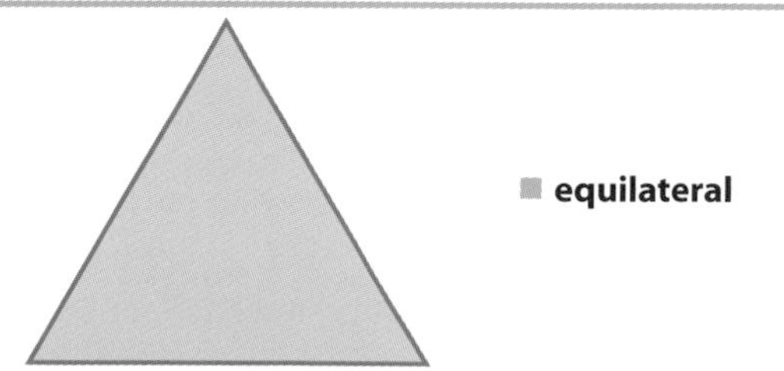
equilateral

e•qua•tion (ĭ-kwā′zhən) **1.** *Mathematics.* A written statement indicating the equality of two expressions. It consists of a sequence of symbols that is split into left and right sides joined by an equal sign. For example, 2 + 3 + 5 = 10 is an equation. **2.** *Chemistry.* A written representation of a chemical reaction, in which the symbols and amounts of the reactants are separated from those of the products by an equal sign, arrow, or a set of opposing arrows. For example, NaOH + HCl = NaCl + H_2O is an equation.

e•qua•tor (ĭ-kwā′tər) **1.** The imaginary line forming a great circle around the Earth's surface halfway between the North and South poles. It divides the Earth into the Northern Hemisphere and the Southern Hemisphere. **2.** A similar circle on the surface of any celestial body.

equi– A prefix that means "equal" or "equally," as in *equidistant.*

e•qui•dis•tant (ē′kwĭ-dĭs′tənt) Equally distant: *two points that are equidistant from a third point.*

e•qui•lat•er•al (ē′kwə-lăt′ər-əl) Having all sides of equal length, as a square or as a triangle that is neither scalene nor isosceles.

e•qui•lib•ri•um (ē′kwə-lĭb′rē-əm) **1.** *Physics.* The state of a body or physical system that is at rest or in constant and unchanging motion. The sum of all forces acting on a body that is in equilibrium is zero (because opposing forces balance each other). A system that is in equilibrium shows no tendency to alter over time. **2.** *Chemistry.* The state of a reversible chemical reaction in which its forward and reverse reactions occur at equal rates so that the concentration of the reactants and products remains the same.

e•quine (ē′kwīn′, ĕk′wīn′) Relating to horses or similar animals, such as donkeys.

e•qui•nox (ē′kwə-nŏks′) **1.** Either of the two moments of the year when the sun crosses the celestial equator. The vernal equinox occurs on March 20 or 21, and the autumnal equinox occurs on September 22 or 23. The days on which an equinox falls have about equal periods of sunlight and darkness. **2.** Either of the two points on the celestial sphere where the apparent path of the sun (known as the ecliptic) crosses the celestial equator. *Compare* **solstice.**

e•quiv•a•lent (ĭ-kwĭv′ə-lənt) **1.** Equal, as in value, meaning, or force. **2.** Having a one-to-one

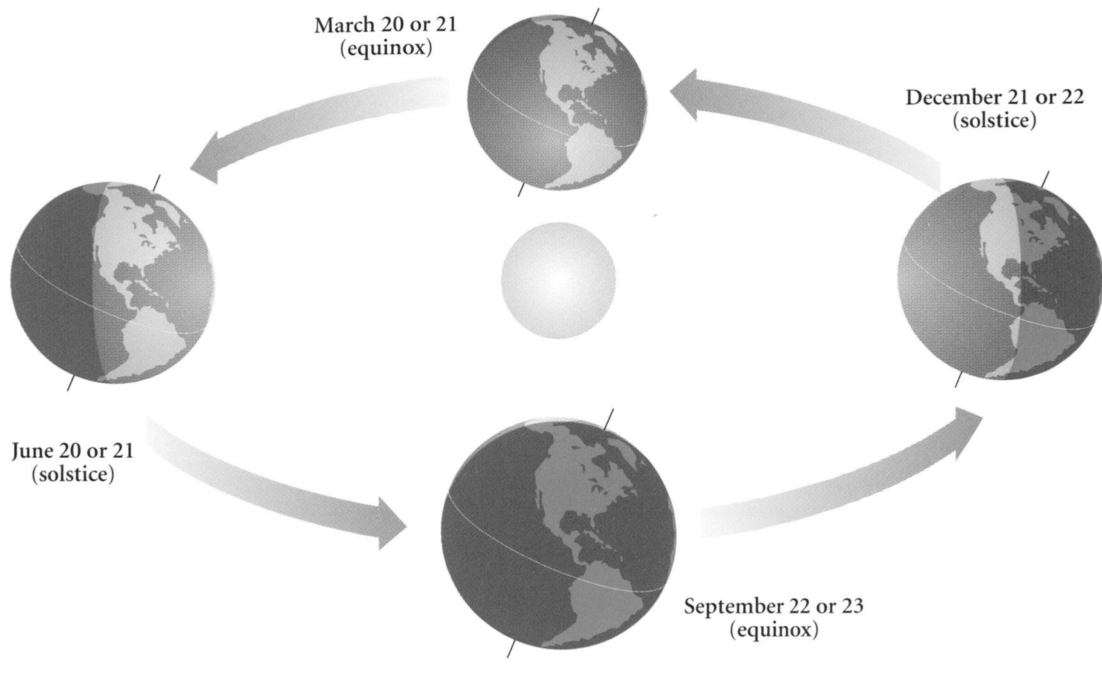

■ **equinox**

Changes in seasons occur as the position of the Earth in relation to the sun changes. Equinoxes and solstices mark the beginning of opposite seasons in the Northern and Southern Hemispheres. For example, the June solstice marks the beginning of summer in the Northern Hemisphere and of winter in the Southern Hemisphere. The September equinox marks the beginning of fall in the Northern Hemisphere and of spring in the Southern Hemisphere.

correspondence, as between parts: *equivalent geometric figures.*

Er The symbol for **erbium.**

e•ra (îr′ə) A division of geologic time, longer than a period and shorter than an eon.

E•ra•tos•the•nes (ĕr′ə-tŏs′thə-nēz′) Third century B.C. Greek mathematician and astronomer. He is best known for making an accurate estimate of the circumference of the Earth by measuring the angle of the sun's rays at two different locations at the same time. Eratosthenes also invented a method for listing the prime numbers that are less than any given number.

er•bi•um (ûr′bē-əm) A soft, silvery, easily shaped metallic element of the lanthanide series. It is used to make light signals stronger in long-distance telephone and computer cables that use fiber optics. *Symbol* **Er.** *Atomic number* 68. *See* **Periodic Table,** pages 262–263.

e•rec•tion (ĭ-rĕk′shən) The hardening or enlargement of certain tissues of the body, especially the penis, when filled with blood.

erg (ûrg) A unit used to measure energy or work, equal to the force of one dyne over a distance of one centimeter. This unit has been mostly replaced by the joule.

er•got (ûr′gət) A fungus that infects rye, wheat, and other grain plants, forming black masses among the seeds. Grain infected with ergot is poisonous and can cause serious illness.

■ **ergot**

left to right: *developing stages of ergot growth on spikes of rye*

erosion

e•ro•sion (ĭ-rō′zhən) The gradual wearing away of land surface materials, especially rocks, sediments, and soils, by the action of water, wind, or a glacier. Usually erosion also involves the transfer of eroded material from one place to another, as from the top of a mountain to an adjacent valley, or from the upstream portion of a river to the downstream portion.

e•rupt (ĭ-rŭpt′) To release gas, ash, molten materials, or hot water into the atmosphere or onto the Earth's surface.

e•ryth•ro•cyte (ĭ-rĭth′rə-sīt′) *See* **red blood cell.**

Es The symbol for **einsteinium.**

Es•a•ki (ĭ-sä′kē), **Leo** Born 1925. Japanese physicist who developed a very fast and very small type of diode that is now widely used in many electronic devices, especially computers.

es•cape velocity (ĭ-skāp′) The velocity that a body, such as a rocket, must achieve to overcome the gravitational pull of the Earth or another celestial body.

es•carp•ment (ĭ-skärp′mənt) A steep slope or long cliff formed by erosion or by vertical movement of the Earth's crust along a fault.

es•ker (ĕs′kər) A long, narrow ridge of coarse sand and gravel deposited by a stream flowing in or under a melting sheet of glacial ice.

e•soph•a•gus (ĭ-sŏf′ə-gəs) The tube of the digestive tract through which food passes from the throat to the stomach.

Es•py (ĕs′pē), **James Pollard** 1785–1860. American meteorologist who is credited with the first correct explanation of the role heat plays in cloud formation and growth. He also developed the use of the telegraph for assembling meteorological observations and tracking storms.

es•ter (ĕs′tər) An organic compound formed when an acid and an alcohol combine and release water. Animal and vegetable fats and oils are esters.

es•ti•va•tion (ĕs′tə-vā′shən) *Zoology.* An inactive state resembling deep sleep, in which some animals living in hot climates, such as certain snails, pass the summer. Estivation protects these animals against the heat and dryness of the summer. *Compare* **hibernation.**

es•tro•gen (ĕs′trə-jən) Any of a group of steroid hormones that primarily regulate the growth, development, and function of the female reproductive system. The main sources of estrogen in the body are the ovaries and the placenta. Estrogens are also formed by certain plants.

es•trous cycle (ĕs′trəs) The series of bodily changes that occur in the female of most mammals from one period of estrus to another. The estrous cycle usually takes place during a specific period known as the breeding season, which ensures that the young are born at a time when the chance of survival is greatest. The length of the cycle varies from species to species.

es•trus (ĕs′trəs) A regularly recurring period during which most female mammals are ready to mate. Also called *heat.*

es•tu•ar•y (ĕs′cho͞o-ĕr′ē) **1.** The wide lower course of a river where it flows into the sea. The water in estuaries is a mixture of fresh water and salt water. **2.** An arm of the sea that extends inland to meet the mouth of a river.

eth•ane (ĕth′ān′) A colorless, odorless, flammable gas, C_2H_6, occurring in natural gas. It is used as a fuel and in refrigeration.

eth•a•nol (ĕth′ə-nôl′) An alcohol, C_2H_6O, obtained from the fermentation of sugars and starches and also made artificially. It is the intoxicating ingredient of alcoholic beverages, and it is also used as a solvent. Also called *ethyl alcohol, grain alcohol.*

eth•ene (ĕth′ēn′) *See* **ethylene.**

e•ther (ē′thər) **1.** An organic compound in which two hydrocarbon groups are linked by an oxygen atom. **2.** A colorless, flammable liquid, $C_4H_{10}O$. It is used as a solvent and was formerly used as an anesthetic. **3.** A hypothetical medium formerly believed to permeate all space and to be the medium through which light and other electromagnetic radiation move. The existence of ether was disproved by the American physicists Albert Michelson and Edward Morley in 1887.

eth•yl (ĕth′əl) The organic group C_2H_5, formed from ethane, having a valence of 1, and occurring in many important chemical compounds.

ethyl alcohol *See* **ethanol.**

eth•yl•ene (ĕth′ə-lēn′) A colorless, flammable gas, C_2H_4, obtained from petroleum and natural gas. It is used as a fuel, in making plastics, and in ripening and coloring fruits. Also called *ethene.*

ethylene gly•col (glī′kôl′) A poisonous, syrupy, colorless alcohol, $C_2H_6O_2$. It is used as an antifreeze in heating and cooling systems that use water.

e•ti•ol•o•gy (ē′tē-ŏl′ə-jē) The cause or origin of a disease.

Eu The symbol for **europium.**

eu•ca•lyp•tus (yo͞o′kə-lĭp′təs) Any of numerous tall trees that are native to Australia. Eucalyptus trees have wood valued as timber and aromatic leaves containing an oil used in medicinal preparations.

Eu•clid (yo͞o′klĭd) Third century B.C. Greek mathematician whose book, *Elements*, was used continuously until the 19th century. In it, he organized and systematized all that was known about geometry. Euclid's systematic use of deductions and axioms was widely regarded as a model working method and influenced mathematicians and scientists for over two thousand years.

eu•gle•na (yo͞o-glē′nə) Any of various one-celled freshwater organisms that move with a long tail called a flagellum, have a reddish eyespot, and often contain chlorophyll like plants. Euglenas are protozoans.

eu•kar•y•ote (yo͞o-kăr′ē-ōt) An organism whose cells contain a nucleus surrounded by a membrane. All organisms except for bacteria, cyanobacteria, and the bacteria-like organisms known as archaea are eukaryotes. *Compare* **prokaryote.**

Eu•ler (oi′lər), **Leonhard** 1707–1783. Swiss mathematician who made many contributions to numerous areas of mathematics. He was one of the first to develop the methods used in calculus, and he introduced much of the basic mathematical notation still used today.

eu•ro•pi•um (yo͞o-rō′pē-əm) A very rare, silvery-white metallic element that is the softest member of the lanthanide series. It is used in making color television tubes and lasers and in scientific research. *Symbol* **Eu.** *Atomic number* 63. *See* **Periodic Table,** pages 262–263.

eu•sta•chian tube (yo͞o-stā′shən) A slender tube that connects the middle ear with the upper part of the pharynx, serving to equalize air pressure on either side of the eardrum.

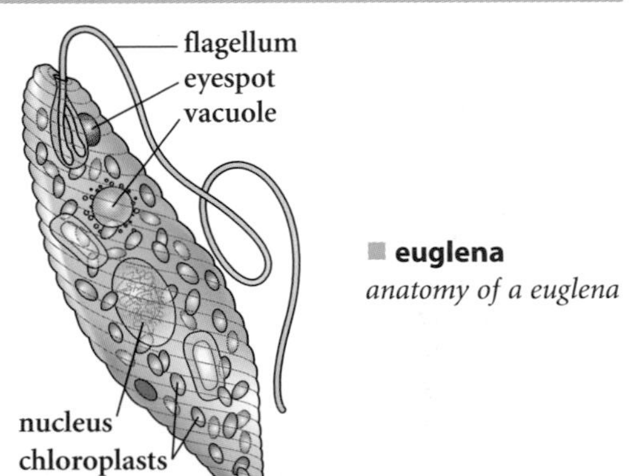

euglena
anatomy of a euglena

Ev•ans (ĕv′ənz), **Herbert McLean** 1882–1971. American biologist who discovered vitamin E in 1922 and conducted research that led to the discovery of the growth hormone in the pituitary gland.

e•vap•o•ra•tion (ĭ-văp′ə-rā′shən) The change of a liquid into a vapor at a temperature below the boiling point.

e•ven (ē′vən) Divisible by 2 with a remainder of 0, such as 12 or 876.

even-toed ungulate *See* **artiodactyl.**

ev•er•green (ĕv′ər-grēn′) *Adjective.* **1.** Having green leaves or needles all year. *Compare* **deciduous.** —*Noun.* **2.** An evergreen tree, shrub, or plant, such as the pine, holly, or rhododendron.

ev•o•lu•tion (ĕv′ə-lo͞o′shən) The process by which species of organisms undergo change over a long period of time through genetic variation and natural selection, resulting in the development of a new species. The evolutionary history of a species can be traced using fossils and recent advances in DNA technology to determine the relationships between it and earlier species to which it is related. *See also* **natural selection.** *See Note at* **Darwin.**

e•volve (ĭ-vŏlv′) **1.** To undergo evolution: *Birds may have evolved from reptiles.* **2.** To develop a characteristic through the process of evolution: *Cats have evolved an extraordinary sense of balance.* **3.** To undergo change or development: *Butterflies evolve from larvae.*

ex•ci•ta•tion (ĕk′sī-tā′shən) The activity produced in an organ, tissue, or cell of the body that is caused by stimulation, especially by a nerve or nerve cell. *Compare* **inhibition.**

Did You Know?

evolution

Darwin's theory of *evolution* by natural selection assumed that tiny adaptations occur in organisms constantly over exceptionally long periods of time. Gradually, a new species develops that is distinct from its ancestors. In the 1970s, however, biologists Niles Eldredge and Stephen Jay Gould proposed that evolution by natural selection was a far more bumpy road. Based on types of fossils that exist around the world, they said that evolution is better described through *punctuated equilibrium.* That is, for long periods of time, species in fact remain virtually unchanged, not even gradually adapting. They are in equilibrium, in a balance with the environment. But when confronted with environmental challenges—sudden climate change, for example—organisms adapt quite quickly, perhaps in only a few thousand years. These active periods are *punctuations,* after which a new equilibrium exists and species remain stable until the next punctuation.

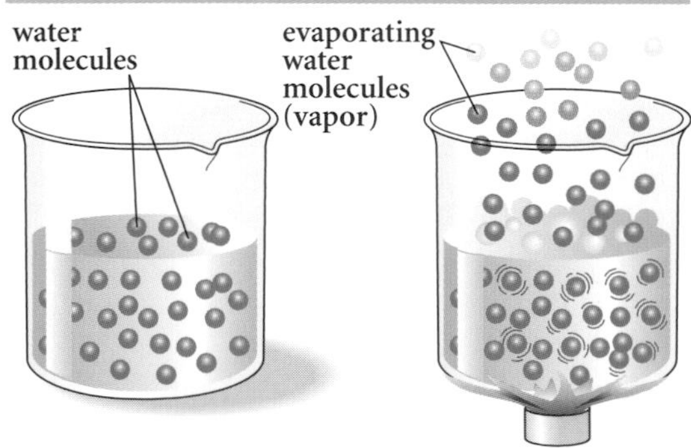

evaporation

On the left is a beaker filled with cool water. On the right, as the water is heated, molecules in the liquid vibrate and move apart. Molecules on the surface of the liquid will escape as vapor.

ex•cre•tion (ĭk-skrē′shən) The elimination by an organism of waste products, such as carbon dioxide and urea, resulting from metabolic processes. Higher animals have specific organs of excretion, such as the lungs and kidneys. In plants and many lower organisms, waste is eliminated by diffusion to the outside environment. —*Verb* **excrete.**

exo– A prefix that means "outside" or "external," as in *exoskeleton.*

ex•o•crine gland (ĕk′sə-krĭn, ĕk′sə-krēn) Any gland of the body that produces secretions and discharges them into a cavity or through a duct to the surface of the body. In mammals, the sweat glands and mammary glands are exocrine glands.

ex•o•skel•e•ton (ĕk′sō-skĕl′ĭ-tn) A hard, protective outer body covering of an animal, such as an insect, crustacean, or mollusk. The exoskeletons of insects and crustaceans are largely made of chitin. *Compare* **endoskeleton.**

ex•o•sphere (ĕk′sō-sfîr′) The outermost region of the Earth's atmosphere, lying beyond the ionosphere and extending indefinitely into space. The air in the exosphere gets thinner and thinner until the lightest particles, such as hydrogen atoms, begin to escape Earth's gravity.

ex•o•ther•mic (ĕk′sō-thûr′mĭk) Releasing heat: *an exothermic chemical reaction. Compare* **endothermic.**

ex•pand•ing universe (ĭk-spăn′dĭng) A model of the universe in which the volume of the universe is expanding. It is based on the idea that the red shift in light from distant galaxies is evidence that all galaxies are moving away from one another. *See Notes at* **big bang, Doppler effect.**

ex•pan•sion (ĭk-spăn′shən) **1.** An increase in size, volume, or quantity, usually due to heating. When substances are heated, the molecular bonds between their particles are weakened, and the particles move faster, causing the substance to expand. **2.** A number or other mathematical expression written in an extended form; for example, $a^2 + 2ab + b^2$ is the expansion of $(a + b)^2$.

ex•pec•to•rant (ĭk-spĕk′tər-ənt) A drug that helps discharge phlegm or mucus from the respiratory tract.

ex•per•i•ment (ĭk-spĕr′ə-mənt) A test or procedure carried out under controlled conditions to determine the validity of a hypothesis or make a discovery. *See Note at* **hypothesis.**

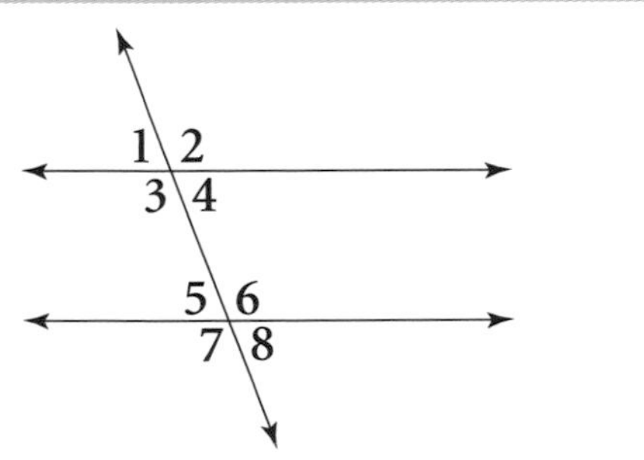

exterior angles

Angles 1, 2, 7, and 8 are exterior angles. Angles 1 and 8 and angles 2 and 7 are alternate exterior angles.

ex•plo•sion (ĭk-splō′zhən) **1.** A violent blowing apart or bursting caused by energy released from a very fast chemical reaction, a nuclear reaction, or the escape of gases under pressure. **2.** A sudden great increase: *a population explosion.*

ex•po•nent (ĕk′spō′nənt, ĭk-spō′nənt) A number or symbol, placed above and to the right of the expression to which it applies, that indicates the number of times the expression is used as a factor. For example, the exponent 3 in 5^3 indicates $5 \times 5 \times 5$; the exponent 2 in $(a + b)^2$ indicates $(a + b) \times (a + b)$.

ex•po•nen•tial (ĕk′spə-nĕn′shəl) Relating to a mathematical expression containing one or more exponents. ❖ Something is said to increase **exponentially** if its rate of change must be expressed using exponents. A graph of such a rate would appear not as a line, but as a curve that becomes steeper and steeper.

ex•ten•sor (ĭk-stĕn′sər) A muscle that extends or straightens a limb or joint. *Compare* **flexor.**

ex•te•ri•or angle (ĭk-stîr′ē-ər) The angle formed between a side of a polygon and an extended adjacent side. *Compare* **interior angle.**

ex•tinct (ĭk-stĭngkt′) **1.** No longer existing or living. Plant and animal species become extinct for many reasons, including climate change, disease, destruction of habitat, and local or worldwide natural disasters. The great majority of species that have ever lived are now extinct. **2.** No longer active or burning: *an extinct volcano. —Noun* **extinction.**

ex•trap•o•late (ĭk-străp′ə-lāt′) To estimate the value of a quantity that falls outside the range in which its values are known.

ex•tra•ter•res•tri•al (ĕk′strə-tə-rĕs′trē-əl) Originating, located, or occurring outside the Earth or its atmosphere: *searching for evidence of extraterrestrial life.*

ex•treme (ĭk-strēm′) Either the first or fourth term of a proportion of four terms. In the proportion $\frac{2}{3} = \frac{4}{6}$, the extremes are 2 and 6. *Compare* **mean** (sense 2).

ex•tru•sion (ĭk-strōō′zhən) The emission of lava onto the surface of the Earth. ❖ Rocks that formed from the cooling of lava are called **extrusive rocks.** *Compare* **intrusion.**

eye (ī) **1.** The organ of the body with which an animal is able to see or sense light. In vertebrate animals, the eye occurs as one of a pair, each consisting of a spherical structure that is filled with fluid. Incoming light is refracted by the cornea and transmitted through the pupil to the lens, which focuses the image onto the retina. *See more at* **compound eye, eyespot. 2.** *Botany.* A bud on a tuber, such as a potato. **3.** The relatively calm area at the center of a hurricane or similar storm. *See more at* **hurricane.**

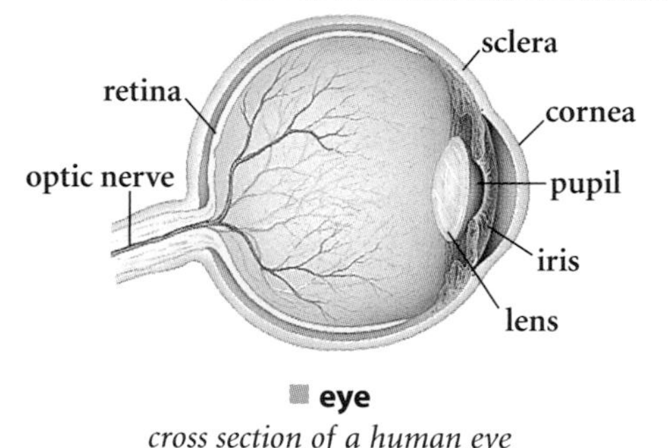

eye
cross section of a human eye

eye•piece (ī′pēs′) The lens or group of lenses closest to the eye in an optical instrument such as a telescope.

eye•spot (ī′spŏt′) **1.** An area that is sensitive to light and functions somewhat like an eye, found in certain single-celled organisms as well as many invertebrate animals. **2.** A round marking resembling an eye, as on the tail feather of a peacock.

eye•stalk (ī′stôk′) A movable stalk having a compound eye on its tip, found on crabs, lobsters, and other crustaceans.

ey•rie (âr′ē) The nest of an eagle or other predatory bird, built on a cliff or other high place.

F

F 1. The symbol for **fluorine. 2.** Abbreviation of **Fahrenheit.**

fac•tor (făk′tər) *Noun.* **1.** One of two or more numbers or expressions that are multiplied to obtain a given product. For example, 2 and 3 are factors of 6, and $a + b$ and $a - b$ are factors of $a^2 - b^2$. **2.** A substance found in the body, such as a protein, that is essential to a biological process. For example, growth factors are needed for proper cell growth and development. —*Verb.* **3.** To find the factors of a number or expression. For example, the number 12 can be factored into 2 and 6, or 3 and 4, or 1 and 12.

fac•to•ri•al (făk-tôr′ē-əl) The product of all of the positive integers from 1 to a given positive integer. It is written as the given integer followed by an exclamation point. For example, the factorial of 4 (written 4!) is $1 \times 2 \times 3 \times 4$, or 24.

Fahr•en•heit (făr′ən-hīt′) Relating to or based on a temperature scale that indicates the freezing point of water as 32° and the boiling point of water as 212° under standard atmospheric pressure. *See Note at* **Celsius.**

Fahrenheit, Gabriel Daniel 1686–1736. German physicist. He invented the mercury thermometer in 1714 and devised the Fahrenheit temperature scale.

fal•con (făl′kən, fôl′kən) Any of various birds of prey having a short curved beak, sharp claws, and long pointed wings. Falcons often eat other birds and are usually smaller than hawks.

fal•lo•pi•an tube (fə-lō′pē-ən) Either of a pair of tubes found in female mammals that carry egg cells from the ovaries to the uterus.

fam•i•ly (făm′ə-lē) A group of organisms ranking above a genus and below an order. *See Table at* **taxonomy.**

fang (făng) A long, pointed tooth in vertebrate animals or a similar structure in spiders, used to seize prey and sometimes to inject venom. The fangs of a poisonous snake, for example, have a hollow groove through which venom flows.

far•ad (făr′əd) A unit used to measure electric capacitance. A capacitor in which a charge of one coulomb can produce a difference of one volt between its two storage plates has a capacitance of one farad.

far•a•day (făr′ə-dā′) A unit of electric charge, equal to about 96,494 coulombs, used to measure the electricity required to break down a compound by electrolysis.

Far•a•day (făr′ə-dā′, făr′ə-dē), **Michael** 1791–1867. British physicist and chemist whose experiments into the connections between electricity, magnetism, and light laid the foundation for modern physics. In 1831 he discovered electromagnetic induction when he produced electricity by moving a magnet inside a wire coil. Faraday invented the electric motor, generator, and transformer, and discovered the carbon compound benzene.

far•sight•ed•ness (fär′sī′tĭd-nĭs) The ability to see distant objects better than objects at close range. It is caused by the eye focusing incoming light behind the retina rather than directly on it. Also called *hyperopia. Compare* **nearsightedness.**

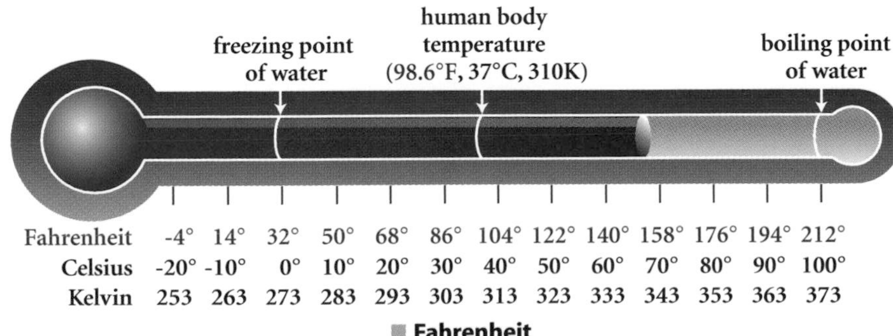

■ **Fahrenheit**

Did You Know?
fat

Millions of Americans are trying to lose adipose tissue, also known as *fat.* It's hard to do, because we love to eat fatty foods, which usually taste good. Many of the chemicals that give food pleasant flavors are easily dissolved in fats—the fattier a food is, the more of these flavorful compounds it may carry. Having some fat is necessary. Just as a city keeps extra water in a reservoir, we store reservoirs of energy most efficiently as fat. An ounce of fat, for example, contains more than twice as much stored energy—calories—as does an ounce of protein or carbohydrates. Fat is also an excellent insulator. Sea mammals, such as whales, have thick layers of fat, called *blubber,* to keep them comfortable in chilly waters. A whale's blubber may be two feet thick—now *that's* fat!

fat (făt) Any of a large number of oily compounds that are widely found in plant and animal tissues and serve mainly as a reserve source of energy. In mammals, fat is deposited beneath the skin and around the internal organs, where it also protects and insulates against heat loss. Fats are made chiefly of triglycerides, each molecule of which contains three fatty acids. *See more at* **saturated fat, unsaturated fat.**

fath•om (făth′əm) A unit of length equal to six feet (1.8 meters), used to measure the depth of water.

fat•ty acid (făt′ē) Any of a large group of organic acids, especially those found in animal and vegetable fats and oils. Fatty acids are mainly composed of long chains of carbon atoms linked to hydrogen atoms. A fatty acid is saturated when the bonds between carbon atoms are all single bonds. It is unsaturated when any of these bonds is a double or triple bond.

fault (fôlt) A crack in a rock mass along which there has been movement. The rock on one side of the crack moves relative to the rock on the other side of the crack. Faults are caused by plate-tectonic forces. *See Note at* **earthquake.**

fau•na (fô′nə) The animals of a particular region or time period: *tropical fauna; prehistoric fauna.*

Fe The symbol for **iron.**

feath•er (fĕth′ər) One of the light, flat structures that cover the skin of birds. A feather has a narrow, hollow shaft bearing flat vanes formed of many parallel barbs. The barbs of outer feathers are formed of even smaller structures (called barbules) that interlock. The barbs of down feathers do not interlock.

feed•back (fēd′băk′) The return of a part of the output of a system or process to the input, especially when used to regulate an electrical system or an electronic process. Computers use feedback to regulate their operations.

feel•er (fē′lər) A slender body part used for touching or sensing. The antennae of insects and the barbels of catfish are feelers.

feld•spar (fĕld′spär′, fĕl′spär′) Any of a group of abundant minerals consisting of silicates of aluminum with potassium, sodium, and calcium. Feldspars range from white, pink, or brown to grayish blue in color. They occur in igneous, sedimentary, and metamorphic rocks and make up more than 60 percent of the Earth's crust.

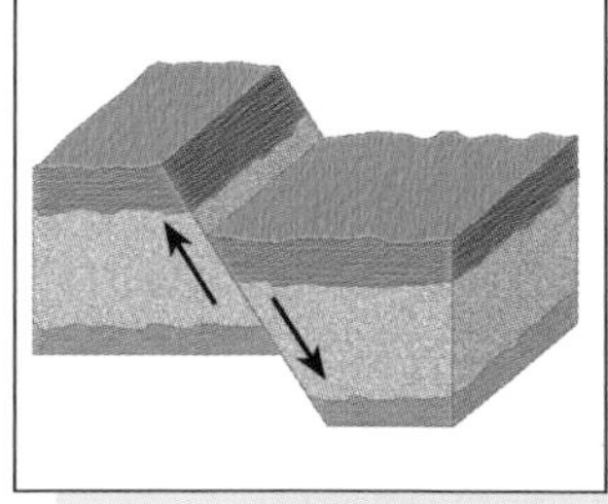
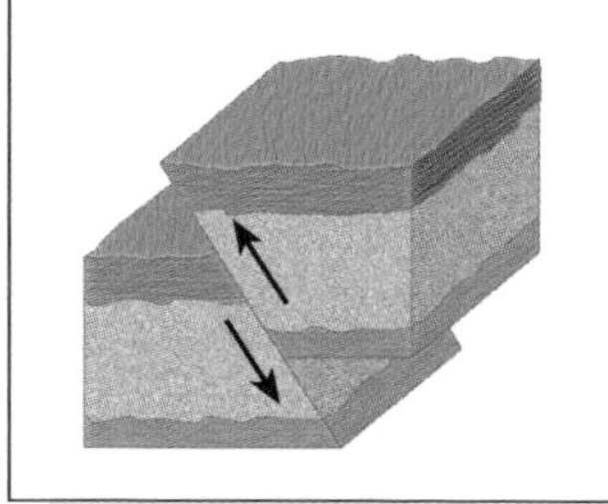
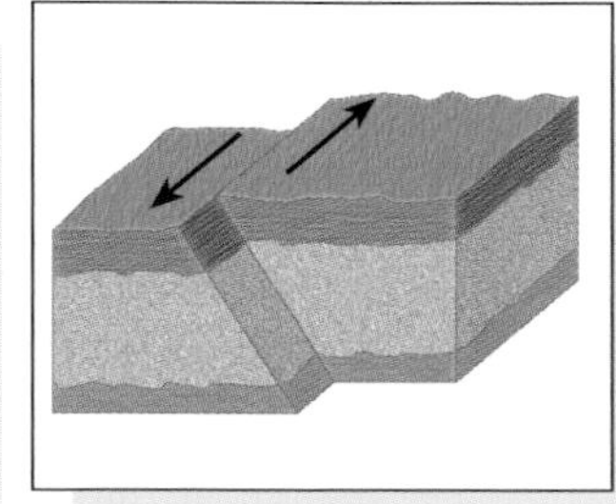

fault
left to right: *normal, reverse, and strike-slip faults*

Did You Know?
faults

Bedrock is often cracked along surfaces known as planes. In some places the cracks extend only a tiny distance; in others they can run for hundreds of miles. When the rocks separated by a crack move past each other, the cracks are known as *faults.* The rocks move because they are pushed or pulled by the forces of plate tectonics. This movement often occurs in sudden jerks known as earthquakes. Geologists study faults to learn the history of the forces that have acted on rocks. *Normal* faults occur when rocks are being pulled apart. In this case, the rocks above the fault plane are moving down relative to the rocks below it. When rocks are pushed together, the opposite happens—the rocks above the plane move upward relative to the rocks below the plane; these types of faults are called *reverse faults. Strike-slip faults* occur when rocks slide past each other; rocks on either side of the crack slide parallel to the fault plane between them. *Transform faults* are a special category of strike-slip faults in which the crack is actually part of a boundary between two enormous tectonic plates. This is the nature of the famous San Andreas Fault in California.

fe•line (fē′līn′) *Adjective.* **1.** Of or belonging to the family of meat-eating mammals that includes the lions, tigers, leopards, and other cats. —*Noun.* **2.** An animal belonging to this family.

fe•male (fē′māl′) *Adjective.* **1.** *Zoology.* **a.** Relating to a female reproductive cell (an egg or ovum). **b.** Being the sex that gives birth or produces offspring. **2.** *Botany.* **a.** Being a reproductive structure, especially a pistil or ovary, that produces a seed or seeds after fertilization. **b.** Bearing a pistil or pistils but not stamens: *female flowers.* —*Noun.* **3.** A female organism.

fe•mur (fē′mər) The long bone of the thigh or of the upper portion of the hind leg. *See more at* **skeleton.**

Fer•mat (fĕr-mä′), **Pierre de** 1601–1665. French mathematician who is best known for his work on probability and on the properties of numbers. He formulated Fermat's last theorem, which remained unsolved for over three hundred years.

Fer•mat's last theorem (fĕr-mäz′) A theorem stating that the equation $a^n + b^n = c^n$ has no solution if a, b, and c are positive integers and if n is an integer greater than 2. The theorem was first stated by the French mathematician Pierre de Fermat around 1630, but not proved until 1994.

fer•men•ta•tion (fûr′mĕn-tā′shən) The process by which complex organic compounds, such as glucose, are broken down by the action of enzymes into simpler compounds when no oxygen is present. Fermentation, which results in the production of energy, occurs in the cells of the body, especially muscle cells, and in plants and some bacteria. Yeasts can convert sugars to alcohol and carbon dioxide by fermentation.

Fer•mi (fĕr′mē), **Enrico** 1901–1954. Italian-born American physicist who is best known for his work on nuclear physics. He discovered over 40 new isotopes and predicted the existence of the neutrino. In 1942, with Leo Szilard, Fermi built the world's first atomic reactor. Fermi also helped to develop the atomic bomb.

fer•mi•um (fûr′mē-əm) A synthetic, radioactive metallic element of the actinide series that is produced from plutonium or uranium. Its most stable isotope has a half-life of about 100 days. *Symbol* **Fm.** *Atomic number* 100. *See* **Periodic Table,** pages 262–263.

fern (fûrn) Any of numerous seedless plants usually having feathery fronds divided into many

■ Enrico Fermi

Did You Know?

fiber optics

In an optical fiber, a beam of light travels within a thin strand of glass or plastic. The light stays within the strand, even if the strand is curved or twisted. That's because the materials the optical fiber is made of—and the way in which the light is aimed into the fiber—are chosen so that when the light beam reaches the strand's outer edge it reflects back into the strand, rather than escaping through the wall. Generally, when a beam of light traveling in one material strikes the boundary of another, some light travels through the boundary and some is reflected back into the original material. But if the speed of light in the material the beam starts out in (the glass) is lower than the speed of light in the other material (the air or insulating material surrounding the fiber), and if the light strikes the boundary of the other material at a shallow enough angle, then all of the light is reflected and none escapes.

leaflets. Ferns have vascular tissue like plants that bear seeds but reproduce by means of spores.

fer•rate (fĕr**′**āt′) A compound containing ferric oxide and another oxide.

fer•ric (fĕr**′**ĭk) Containing iron, especially iron with a valence of 3. *Compare* **ferrous.**

ferric oxide A reddish-brown to silver or black compound, Fe_2O_3, which occurs naturally as the mineral hematite, or as rust. It is often used as a pigment and a metal polish.

fer•rous (fĕr**′**əs) Containing iron, especially iron with a valence of 2. *Compare* **ferric.**

fer•tile (fûr**′**tl) **1.** Capable of producing offspring, seeds, or fruit; able to reproduce. **2.** Capable of developing into a complete organism; fertilized: *a fertile egg.* **3.** Capable of supporting plant life; favorable to the growth of crops and plants: *fertile soil.* —*Noun* **fertility.**

fer•til•i•za•tion (fûr′tl-ĭ-zā**′**shən) **1.** The process by which a female reproductive cell becomes capable of developing into a complete organism by union with a male reproductive cell. In many animals, such as mammals, fertilization occurs inside the body of the female. In fish, eggs are fertilized in the water. In plants, eggs are fertilized inside the parent plant. *See Note at* **pollination. 2.** The process of making soil more productive of plant growth, as by the addition of organic material or fertilizer. —*Verb* **fertilize.**

■ **filtration** *a liquid mixture being poured into a beaker through filter paper*

fe•tus (fē**′**təs) The unborn young of a mammal at the later stages of its development, especially a human embryo from its eighth week of development to its birth. —*Adjective* **fetal.**

fe•ver (fē**′**vər) A body temperature higher than normal. Fever is usually a response by the body's immune system against infection, as by a virus.

Feyn•man (fīn**′**mən), **Richard Phillips** 1918–1988. American physicist who developed many new aspects of quantum theory, especially in regard to electromagnetic energy such as light. He also devised a method of using diagrams to help calculate the interactions of subatomic particles.

fi•ber (fī**′**bər) **1.** The parts of grains, fruits, and vegetables that contain cellulose and are not digested by the body. Fiber helps the intestines function properly by stimulating the muscles of the intestinal walls. **2.** One of the elongated, thick-walled cells that give strength and support to plant tissue. **3a.** A single skeletal muscle cell; a muscle fiber. **b.** The axon of a nerve cell. —*Adjective* **fibrous.**

fi•ber•glass (fī**′**bər-glăs′) A material made up of very fine fibers of glass. Fiberglass is resistant to heat and fire and is used to make various products, such as building insulation and boat hulls.

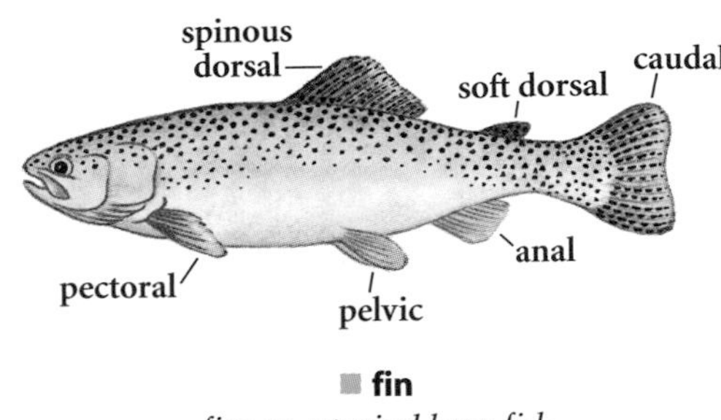

fin

fins on a typical bony fish

fiber optics The technology based on the use of fine glass or plastic fibers that are capable of transmitting light around curves. Fiber optics is used in medicine and for long-distance telephone and computer lines.

Fi•bo•nac•ci (fē′bə-nä**′**chē), **Leonardo** 1170?–1250? Italian mathematician who popularized the modern decimal system and discovered the Fibonacci sequence of integers.

Fibonacci sequence The sequence of numbers, 1, 1, 2, 3, 5, 8, 13, . . . , in which each successive number is equal to the sum of the two preceding numbers. Many shapes occurring in nature, such as certain spirals, have proportions that can be described in terms of the Fibonacci sequence.

fib•ril•la•tion (fĭb′rə-lā**′**shən) A rapid twitching of muscle fibers, as of the heart, caused by the abnormal discharge of electrical nerve impulses.

fi•brin (fī**′**brĭn) A fibrous protein produced in response to bleeding that is the main component of blood clotting.

fib•u•la (fĭb**′**yə-lə) The smaller of the two bones of the lower leg or lower portion of the hind leg. *See more at* **skeleton.**

field (fēld) **1.** A region of space in which a physical force, such as magnetism or gravity, operates. **2.** The area in which an image is visible to the eye or to an optical instrument.

field magnet A magnet used to produce a magnetic field for the operation of an electrical device such as a motor or generator.

fil•a•ment (fĭl**′**ə-mənt) **1.** A fine or slender thread, wire, or fiber. **2.** The part of a stamen that supports the anther of a flower; the stalk of a stamen. *See more at* **flower. 3.** A fine wire that is enclosed in the bulb of an incandescent lamp and gives off light when an electric current is passed through it. **4.** A wire that acts as the cathode in some electron tubes when it is heated with an electric current.

fil•ter (fĭl**′**tər) **1.** A material that has very tiny holes and is used to separate out solid particles contained in a liquid or gas that is passed through it. **2.** A device that allows certain frequencies of energy waves to pass while blocking the passage of others. For example, filters on photographic lenses allow only certain frequencies of light to enter the camera.

filter feeder An aquatic animal, such as a clam or sponge, that feeds by filtering tiny organisms or fine particles of organic material from currents of water that pass through it.

fil•tra•tion (fĭl-trā**′**shən) The act or process of filtering, especially the process of passing a liquid or gas, such as air, through a filter in order to remove solid particles.

fin (fĭn) One of the wing-like or paddle-like parts of a fish, dolphin, or whale that are used for propelling, steering, and balancing in water.

fi•nite (fī**′**nīt′) Having a bound or limit; not infinite or unbounded: *a finite sum; a finite line segment.*

fir (fûr) Any of various evergreen trees that have flat needles and bear cones. Firs generally grow in northern regions or at higher altitudes.

fir

Douglas firs can attain heights of more than 200 feet (61 meters).

fire•ball (fīr′bôl′) A meteor that is as bright or brighter than the brightest planets.

fire•fly (fīr′flī′) Any of various beetles that are active at night and produce a flashing light in the abdomen. The flash is produced by a chemical reaction and enables males and females to find each other for mating.

firth (fûrth) A long narrow inlet of the sea. Firths are usually the lower part of an estuary, but are sometimes fjords.

fish (fĭsh) *Plural* **fish** *or* **fishes.** Any of numerous cold-blooded vertebrate animals that live in water. Fish have gills for obtaining oxygen, a lateral line for sensing pressure changes in the water, and a vertical tail. Most fish are covered with scales and have limbs in the form of fins. *See more at* **bony fish, cartilaginous fish, jawless fish.**

fis•sion (fĭsh′ən) **1.** The splitting of the nucleus of an atom into two or more nuclei. The splitting occurs either spontaneously, because the nucleus has many neutrons and is unstable, or because the nucleus has collided with a free-moving neutron. The splitting of a nucleus releases one or more neutrons and energy in the form of radiation. *Compare* **fusion. 2.** A reproductive process in which a cell splits to form two independent cells that later grow to full size. Bacteria and other single-celled organisms usually reproduce by means of fission. Also called *binary fission.*

fis•sure (fĭsh′ər) A long, narrow crack or opening in the face of a rock. Fissures are often filled with minerals of a different type from those in the surrounding rock.

fixed star (fĭkst) A star so distant from Earth that its position in relation to other stars appears not to change. Its movements can be measured only by precise observations over long periods of time. Sirius is a fixed star.

fjord (fyôrd) A long, narrow inlet from the sea between steep slopes of a mountainous coast. Fjords usually occur where ocean water flows into valleys formed near the coast by glaciers.

flag•el•late (flăj′ə-lāt′) A protozoan that moves by means of a flagellum or flagella. Some flagellates, such as the euglena, can make food by photosynthesis like plants, while others, such as the trypanosomes, are parasitic and cause disease.

fla•gel•lum (flə-jĕl′əm) *Plural* **flagella.** A slender tail or part extending from some single-celled organisms, such as the dinoflagellates, that whips back and forth to produce movement.

flame (flām) The hot, glowing mixture of burning gases and tiny particles that arises from combustion.

fla•min•go (flə-mĭng′gō) Any of several large tropical wading birds having reddish or pinkish plumage, long legs, and a long flexible neck. Flamingoes feed by scooping up water with their heads upside down and filtering the water through tissues in their large bills.

flash point (flăsh) The lowest temperature at which the vapor of a flammable liquid can be made to catch fire in air.

flash tube A device that generates a short, strong burst of light or other radiation by discharging a high voltage of electricity through a substance such as xenon or quartz.

flask (flăsk) A rounded container with a long neck, used in laboratories.

flat•fish (flăt′fĭsh′) Any of numerous bottom-dwelling fish, such as the flounder, halibut, and sole, that have a flattened body. During a flatfish's larval stage, the head twists and one eye migrates to the other side, so that both eyes in the adult are on one side of the body.

flat•worm (flăt′wûrm′) Any of various worms having a flat, unsegmented body that is bilaterally symmetrical. Many flatworms, such as the tapeworm, are parasites. Also called *platyhelminth.*

flea (flē) **1.** Any of various wingless, bloodsucking insects that have legs adapted for jumping and live as parasites on warm-blooded animals. **2.** Any of various small crustaceans, such as the water flea, that resemble or move like fleas.

fledg•ling (flĕj′lĭng) A young bird that has just grown the feathers needed to fly and is capable of surviving outside the nest.

Flem•ing (flĕm′ĭng), Sir **Alexander** 1881–1955. Scottish bacteriologist who discovered penicillin in 1928. The drug was developed and purified 11 years later by Howard Florey and Ernst Chain. Fleming was also the first to administer typhoid vaccines to humans.

Fleming, Sir **John Ambrose** 1849–1945. British physicist and electrical engineer who invented the vacuum tube in 1904. His invention was essential to the development of radio. Fleming also helped develop electric devices designed for large-scale use, such as the electric lamp.

A CLOSER LOOK

Fission

Nuclear fission occurs when a heavy, unstable atomic nucleus splits into two or more lighter nuclei. For example, the nucleus of U-235 (an isotope of uranium) undergoes fission when it is struck by an unattached neutron. When this happens, the U-235 nucleus becomes so unstable that it splits into two or more fragments and releases two or three free neutrons. The combined mass of these fragments is less than that of the original nucleus and the neutron that produced them. The missing mass is changed into energy in the form of heat and gamma rays.

The free neutrons flying from the split nucleus may collide with other U-235 nuclei, causing them to break apart. This is the start of a chain reaction, where, within a few millionths of a second, the number of fission events multiplies rapidly. In nuclear reactors, the neutrons are slowed down or absorbed to control the reaction. In nuclear weapons, the chain reaction develops uncontrollably to produce the largest amount of energy possible.

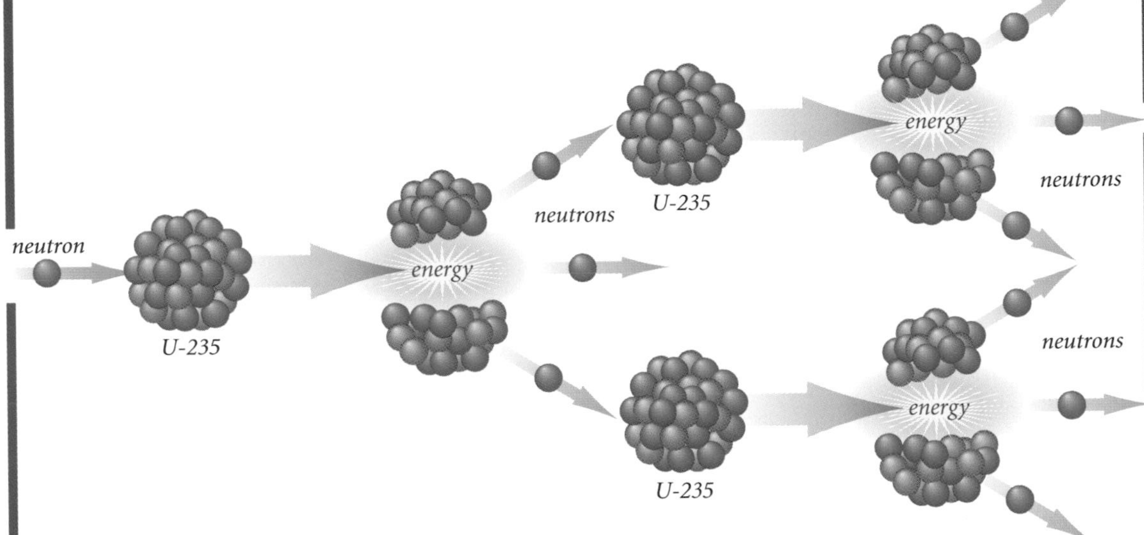

Fusion

Nuclear fusion is basically the opposite of fission, but produces some similar results.

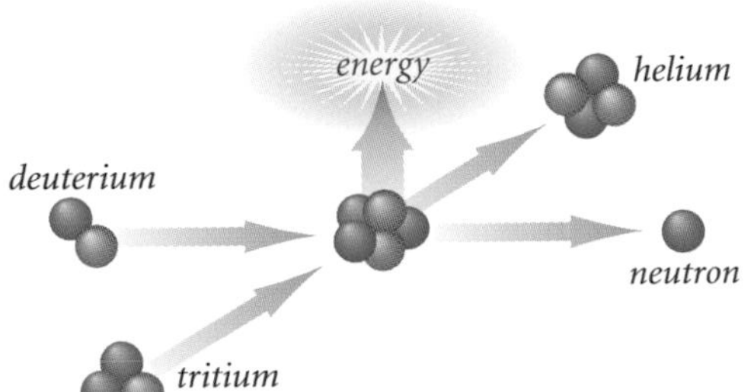

Fusion occurs, for example, when two types of hydrogen atoms (deuterium and tritium) collide and turn into a single atom of helium and an extra neutron. As in fission, this process releases energy that is quickly multiplied as millions of these collisions occur in a fraction of a second. Nuclear fusion powers the sun and other stars, and it is the type of chain reaction that occurs in thermonuclear weapons.

flex•or (flĕk′sər) A muscle that bends or flexes a joint. *Compare* **extensor.**

flint (flĭnt) A very hard, gray to black sedimentary rock that makes sparks when it is struck with steel. Flint is a type of chert.

flip•per (flĭp′ər) A wide, flat limb adapted for swimming, found on aquatic animals such as whales, seals, and sea turtles. Flippers evolved from legs.

float (flōt) *Verb.* **1.** To remain suspended within or on the surface of a fluid without sinking. —*Noun.* **2.** An air-filled sac in certain aquatic organisms, such as kelp, that helps maintain buoyancy. Also called *air bladder, air vesicle.*

floe (flō) A mass or sheet of floating ice.

flood•plain (flŭd′plān′) Flat land bordering a river and made up of sediments such as sand, silt, and clay deposited during floods.

flood tide (flŭd) The period between low tide and high tide, during which water flows toward the shore. *Compare* **ebb tide.** *See more at* **tide.**

flop•py disk (flŏp′pē) *Computer Science.* A flexible plastic disk coated with magnetic material and covered by a protective jacket, used for storing data.

flo•ra (flôr′ə) The plants of a particular region or time period: *desert flora; prehistoric flora.*

Flo•rey (flôr′ē), Sir **Howard Walter.** Baron Florey of Adelaide 1898–1968. Australian-born British pathologist who developed and purified penicillin, with Ernst Chain. Florey also helped to develop a way to manufacture the drug in large quantities and was involved in the first tests of its effects on humans.

flow chart (flō) **1.** A diagram that shows the order of operations or sequence of tasks for solving a problem or managing a complex project. **2.** A schematic representation of a sequence of operations.

flow•er (flou′ər) *Noun.* **1.** The reproductive structure of the seed-bearing plants known as angiosperms. The female reproductive part is the pistil, including the ovary, style, and stigma, and the male reproductive part is the stamen, including the filament and anther. The organs are enclosed in an outer envelope of petals and sepals. *See Note at* **pollination. 2.** A flowering plant that is grown mainly for its brightly colored petals. —*Verb.* **3.** To produce flowers; bloom. *See A Closer Look, page 134.*

flower head 1. A dense cluster of short flowers that together look like part of a single flower, as in the daisy or dandelion. **2.** A dense grouping of flower buds, as in broccoli and cauliflower.

flow•er•ing plant (flou′ər-ĭng) A plant that produces flowers and fruit; an angiosperm.

fl. oz. Abbreviation of **fluid ounce.**

flu (flo͞o) *See* **influenza.**

flu•id (flo͞o′ĭd) A substance, such as air or water, in which the atoms or molecules can freely move past one another. Fluids flow easily and take on the shape of their containers. All liquids and gases are fluids. —*Noun* **fluidity** (flo͞o-ĭd′ĭ-tē).

fluid dram A unit equal to $\frac{1}{8}$ of a fluid ounce (3.70 milliliters).

fluid ounce A liquid measure equal to $\frac{1}{16}$ of a pint (29.57 milliliters). *See Table at* **measurement.**

fluke (flo͝ok) Either of the two flattened fins of a whale's tail.

fluo•res•cence (flo͝o-rĕs′əns) **1.** The giving off of light by a substance when it is exposed to electromagnetic radiation, such as visible light or x-rays. Light is emitted only as long as the electromagnetic radiation continues to bombard the substance. *Compare* **phosphorescence** (sense 1). **2.** The light produced in this way.

fluo•res•cent lamp (flo͝o-rĕs′ənt) A lamp that produces light by exciting the atoms of a mixture of argon gas and mercury vapor with electric current. Ultraviolet rays produced by the excited atoms strike a phosphor coating on the interior surface of the bulb, causing it to emit visible light. Fluorescent lamps are much more efficient than incandescent lamps because the excited atoms give off little of their energy as heat. *Compare* **incandescent lamp.**

fluor•i•date (flo͝or′ĭ-dāt′) To add fluorine or a fluoride to something, especially to drinking water in order to prevent tooth decay.

fluor•ide (flo͝or′īd′) A compound containing fluorine and another element or radical.

fluor•ine (flo͝or′ēn′) A pale-yellow, poisonous, gaseous halogen element that is highly corrosive. It is used to separate certain isotopes of uranium and to make refrigerants and high-temperature plastics. It is also added in fluoride form to the water supply to prevent tooth decay. *Symbol* **F.** *Atomic number* 9. *See* **Periodic Table,** pages 262–263.

Did You Know?
fluorescence

Have you ever stood in a room illuminated by a "black light" and wondered why your white T-shirt, your shoelaces, and your teeth appear to glow? These objects appear so bright under ultraviolet light because they contain fluorescent materials that absorb the black light's ultraviolet rays (which are not visible to the human eye) and re-emit some of their energy as visible light. Therefore, these objects give off more visible light than is being shone on them, seemingly making something out of nothing. Many fabric whiteners leave fluorescent pigments behind in treated clothes; the clothes then look very bright because they absorb ultraviolet light from the environment and emit some of the absorbed energy as visible light.

fluor•ite (flo͝or′īt′) A mineral consisting of calcium fluoride. Fluorite occurs in many colors (especially yellow and purple), usually in crystals shaped like cubes or octahedrons, and is often fluorescent in ultraviolet light. It is the mineral used to represent a hardness of 4 on the Mohs scale.

fluor•o•car•bon (flo͝or′ō-kär′bən) An inert, liquid or gaseous organic compound similar to a hydrocarbon but having fluorine atoms in the place of hydrogen atoms. Fluorocarbons are used in aerosol propellants and refrigerants. ❖ Fluorocarbons containing chlorine, known as **chlorofluorocarbons**, are destructive to the Earth's ozone layer. For this reason, the production and use of chlorofluorocarbons has been sharply reduced in recent years.

fluo•ros•co•py (flo͝o-rŏs′kə-pē) A technique for viewing internal organs in which a continuous series of x-rays is taken, and the images are processed by a computer before being projected onto a display screen. Fluoroscopy makes it possible to see moving images of the body system being examined.

flux (flŭks) **1.** A substance used in a smelting furnace to make metals melt more easily. **2.** The rate of flow of fluids, particles, or energy across a given surface or area. **3.** *See* **magnetic flux.**

fly (flī) Any of numerous insects having one pair of wings and large compound eyes. Flies include the houseflies, horseflies, and mosquitoes. Many species feed on other insects or as scavengers.

Fm The symbol for **fermium.**

FM Abbreviation of **frequency modulation.**

foam (fōm) **1.** A mass of small, frothy bubbles formed in or on the surface of a liquid, as from fermentation or shaking. **2.** A colloid in which particles of a gas are dispersed throughout a liquid. *Compare* **aerosol, emulsion.**

fo•cal length (fō′kəl) The distance from the surface of a lens or mirror to the point where the light rays converge to form an image (the point of focus).

fo•cus (fō′kəs) *Plural* **focuses** *or* **foci** (fō′sī′, fō′kī′) **1.** A point at which rays of light come together or from which they appear to spread apart, as after passing through a lens. **2.** The degree of clarity with which an eye or optical instrument produces an image: *a telescope with excellent focus.* **3.** A central point or region, such as the point at which an earthquake starts. **4.** *Mathematics.* A fixed point or one of a pair of fixed points used in constructing a curve such as an ellipse, a parabola, or a hyperbola.

fog (fôg) A dense layer of cloud lying close to the surface of the ground or water.

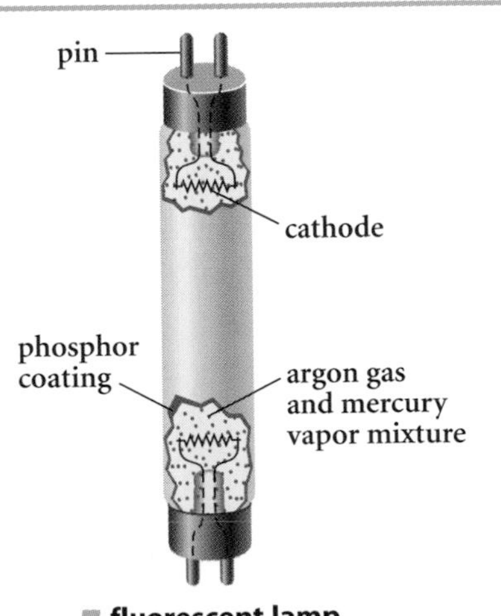

fluorescent lamp

A CLOSER LOOK

Flower

Most flowers, like the Asiatic lily shown here, have both male and female organs. The anthers of the male organs release pollen that is transferred to the stigma, usually on a flower of another plant, by the wind or by pollinating animals such as insects and hummingbirds.

Certain species, such as the corn plant and birch tree, have flowers with only male organs and flowers with only female organs growing on the same plant. Some other species, such as the holly, have flowers with male organs growing on one plant, and flowers with female organs growing on another.

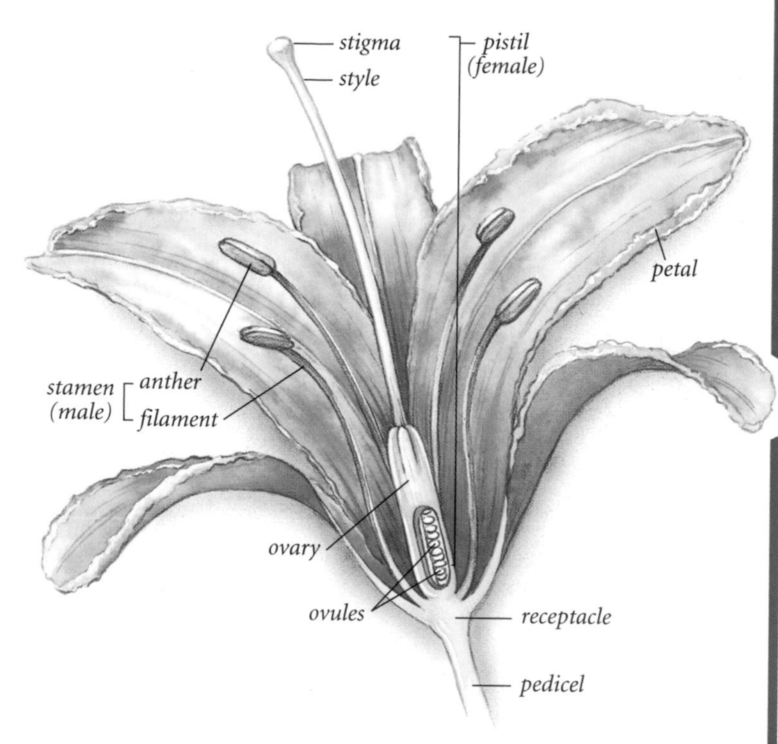

clematis

wild rye

Not all flowers occur as large individual blooms attached to a stem, as in the Asiatic lily and clematis. The flowers of rye grass, for example, are very small. Some plants, such as clover, have groups of flowers growing in clusters as flower heads. Certain trees, like the alder, produce blossoms in elongated clusters known as catkins. The sausage-like part of the cattail is actually a head of densely packed female flowers. The cattail's male flowers grow on the more slender tip or "tail" that extends at the top.

European alder

white clover

cattail

■ **fold**
folded rock strata in Dorset, England

fold (fōld) A bend in a layer or in several layers of rock. Folds occur in rocks when they are compressed by plate-tectonic forces.

fo•lic acid (fō′lĭk, fŏl′ĭk) A vitamin belonging to the vitamin B complex that is important in cell growth and metabolism. It is found especially in green leafy vegetables and fresh fruit. Lack of folic acid can cause anemia because it is necessary for the formation of red blood cells.

fol•li•cle (fŏl′ĭ-kəl) **1.** A small, protective sac in the body. In most vertebrate animals, fertilized eggs develop in follicles located in the ovaries. In mammals, hair develops and grows from follicles in the skin. **2.** A dry fruit that has a single chamber and splits open along only one seam to release its seeds. Milkweed pods are follicles.

food chain (fo͞od) The sequence of the transfer of food energy from one organism to another in an ecological community. In a typical food chain, plants are eaten by herbivores, which are then eaten by carnivores. These carnivores are in turn eaten by other carnivores. ❖ Many species of animals in an ecological community feed on both plants and animals, creating a complex system of interrelated food chains known as a **food web.** *See more at* **consumer, producer.**

Food Guide Pyramid A diagram of the nutritional needs of humans that is shaped like a pyramid. Grains and cereals represent the pyramid's base. Above these are fruits and vegetables, and then meats and dairy products. Fats and sweets are at the peak.

food web A group of interrelated food chains in a particular ecological community.

fool's gold (fo͞olz) Any of several minerals, especially pyrite and chalcopyrite, sometimes mistaken for gold.

foot (fo͝ot) *Plural* **feet** (fēt) A unit of length equal to $\frac{1}{3}$ of a yard or 12 inches (about 30.5 centimeters). *See Table at* **measurement.**

foot-and-mouth disease A highly contagious disease of cattle and other hoofed animals that is caused by a virus. Symptoms include fever and the presence of blisters around the mouth and hooves.

foot-pound A unit of work equal to the work or energy needed to lift a one-pound weight a distance of one foot against the force of the Earth's gravity.

foot•wall (fo͝ot′wôl′) The block of rock lying under an inclined fault. *See more at* **fault.** *Compare* **hanging wall.**

force (fôrs) **1.** Something that causes a body to move, changes its speed or direction, or distorts its shape. One force may be counteracted by another, so that there is no change or distortion. **2.** Any of the four natural phenomena exerting

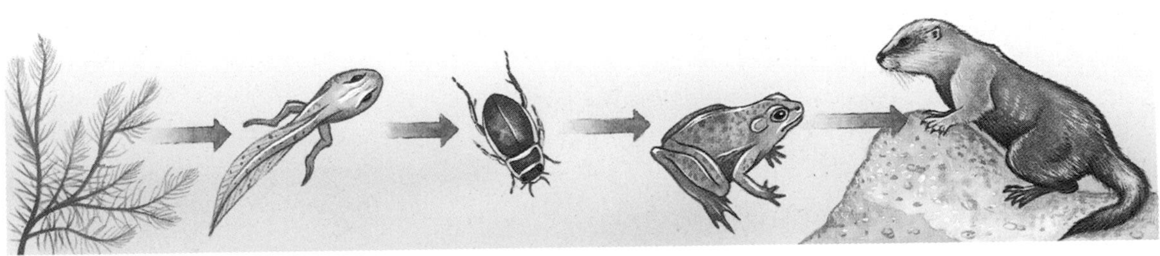

■ **food chain**
A typical food chain in a water community would include a plant that is eaten by tadpoles, a great diving beetle that eats tadpoles, a bullfrog that eats great diving beetles, and a river otter that consumes frogs.

Did You Know?
force

The verb *force* might make you think of pushing really hard on a stuck door or of banging the bottom of a stubborn ketchup bottle. The scientific meaning of the noun *force* also involves getting an object to move. In the mid-1600s, the great English physicist Isaac Newton figured out that the amount of force needed to move an object was directly related to both the mass of the object and how it is accelerated. (Pushing a pebble clearly takes less force than pushing a boulder, and pushing a boulder quickly obviously takes more force than pushing it slowly.) What is now known as Newton's second law of motion sets down this relationship quantitatively: Force equals mass times acceleration, or $F = ma$. You see this equation in action every time you step on a scale. Your weight is actually the downward force that results from your body mass being pulled—accelerated—by gravity. Remember that acceleration here means a change in direction or in speed, either faster or slower. A boat that bumps a dock comes momentarily to a standstill. That rapid decrease in speed multiplied by the mass of the boat is the force with which the boat hits the dock.

an influence between particles of matter. From the strongest to the weakest, these four forces are the strong nuclear force, the electromagnetic force, the weak nuclear force, and gravity.

fore•brain (fôr′brān′) The forwardmost part of the brain in vertebrate animals. In humans, it consists of the thalamus, the hypothalamus, and the cerebrum. *Compare* **hindbrain, midbrain.**

fo•ren•sic medicine (fə-rĕn′sĭk) The branch of medicine that interprets or establishes the facts in civil or criminal law cases.

for•est (fôr′ĭst) A dense growth of trees and usually bushes or other plants covering a large area. Forests exist in all regions of the Earth except for regions of extreme cold or dryness. ❖ The science of cultivating and managing forests is called **forestry.**

for•mal•de•hyde (fôr-măl′də-hīd′) A colorless gas, CH_2O, having a sharp, suffocating odor. It is used in making plastics and is mixed with water to form a solution used to preserve biological specimens.

for•ma•tion (fôr-mā′shən) A long layer of sediments or rocks that look alike and were formed at the same time. Formations are shown on geological maps, much as highways are shown on road maps.

for•mic acid (fôr′mĭk) A colorless, caustic, fuming liquid, CH_2O_2, that occurs naturally as the poison of ants and stinging nettles. It is used in making textiles and paper and in insecticides.

for•mu•la (fôr′myə-lə) **1.** A set of symbols showing the composition of a chemical compound. A formula lists the elements contained within it and indicates the number of atoms of each element with a subscript numeral if the number is more than 1. For example, H_2O is the formula for water, where H_2 indicates two atoms of hydrogen and O indicates one atom of oxygen. **2.** A set of symbols that expresses a mathematical rule or principle; for example, the formula for the area of a rectangle is $a = lw$, where a is the area, l the length, and w the width.

For•res•ter (fôr′ĭs-tər), **Jay Wright** Born 1918. American computer engineer who developed computer storage devices, including the first core memory for an electronic digital computer (1949).

Fos•sey (fŏs′ē), **Dian** 1932–1985. American zoologist who conducted extensive studies of

Dian Fossey

■ **fossil**
fossilized fish from the Eocene Epoch, found in the Green River Formation, Wyoming

mountain gorillas in Rwanda, Africa. Her research brought about a new understanding of the gorilla's behavior and habitat and supported conservation efforts in Africa.

fos•sil (fŏs′əl) The hardened remains or imprint of a plant or animal that lived long ago. Fossils are often found in layers of sedimentary rock and along the beds of rivers that flow through them. Other sources of fossils include tar pits, ice, and amber. ❖ Petroleum, coal, and natural gas, which are derived from the accumulated remains of ancient plants and animals, are called **fossil fuels.** —*Verb* **fossilize.**

Fou•cault (fo͞o-kō′), **Jean Bernard Léon** 1819–1868. French physicist who measured the velocity of light (1850) and proved that light moves more slowly in water than in air. In 1857 he constructed the first gyroscope.

fowl (foul) **1.** A bird, such as a chicken, duck, or dove, that is raised or hunted for food. **2.** In scientific usage, any of various birds having large heavy bodies, short wings, and legs built for running and scratching the ground. Most fowl nest on the ground. The turkey, pheasant, quail, grouse, partridge, and chicken are fowl.

fox (fŏks) Any of various meat-eating mammals related to the dogs and wolves. Foxes usually have upright ears, a pointed snout, and a long bushy tail.

Fr The symbol for **francium.**

frac•tal (frăk′təl) A geometric pattern repeated at ever smaller scales to produce irregular shapes and surfaces that cannot be represented by standard geometry. Even the most minute details of a fractal's pattern repeat elements of the overall geometric pattern. Fractals are widely used in computer modeling of irregular patterns and structures in nature, such as the patterns of seasonal weather. They are also considered to be a visual representation of chaos. *See more at* **chaos.**

frac•tion (frăk′shən) A number that compares part of an object or a set with the whole, especially the quotient of two whole numbers written in the form $\frac{a}{b}$. The fraction $\frac{1}{2}$, which means 1 divided by 2, can represent such things as 10 pencils out of a box of 20, or 50 cents out of a dollar. *See also* **decimal fraction, improper fraction, proper fraction.**

frac•tion•a•tion (frăk′shə-nā′shən) The separation of a chemical compound into components, as by distillation or crystallization.

frac•ture (frăk′chər) A break or crack in a bone, usually also involving injury to surrounding structures. A fracture occurs when a force greater than the strength of the bone is applied, as in a fall.

fran•ci•um (frăn′sē-əm) An extremely unstable, radioactive element that is the heaviest alkali metal. Francium occurs in nature, but less than one ounce (30 grams) is present in the Earth's crust at any time. The most stable of its several isotopes has a half-life of 21 minutes. *Symbol* **Fr.** *Atomic number* 87. *See* **Periodic Table,** pages 262–263.

Frank•lin (frăngk′lĭn), **Benjamin** 1706–1790. American public official, scientist, inventor, and writer. He conducted experiments with electricity, established the direction of the prevailing storm track in North America, and determined the existence of the Gulf Stream. Franklin also

■ **fractal**

invented bifocals and a type of stove that was widely used for indoor heating.

Franklin, Rosalind 1920–1958. British chemist whose diffraction images, made by directing x-rays at DNA, provided crucial information that led to the discovery of its structure as a double helix. Franklin's work was never publicly acknowledged in her lifetime.

freeze (frēz) To change from a liquid to a solid state by cooling or being cooled to the freezing point.

freeze-dry To preserve something by freezing it rapidly and then placing it in a vacuum chamber. The ice is then forced out, through sublimation, in the form of water vapor.

freez•ing point (frē′zĭng) The temperature at which a liquid becomes a solid. For a given substance, the freezing point of its liquid form is the same as the melting point of its solid form. The freezing point of water is 32°F (0°C); that of liquid nitrogen is –345.75°F (–209.89°C).

fre•quen•cy (frē′kwən-sē) **1.** *Physics.* The number of complete cycles of a wave, such as a radio wave, that occur per second. See more at *wave.* **2.** *Mathematics.* The ratio of the number of occurrences of some event to the number of opportunities for its occurrence.

frequency modulation A method of radio broadcasting in which the frequency of the wave that carries the sound signal changes to reflect the various sounds that are to be reproduced, while the amplitude of the wave remains the same. Frequency modulation reduces static in radio transmission. *Compare* **amplitude modulation.**

fresh•wa•ter (frĕsh′wô′tər) Consisting of or living in water that is not salty: *a freshwater pond; a freshwater fish.*

Fres•nel (frā-nĕl′), **Augustin Jean** 1788–1827. French physicist whose investigations of the properties of light were fundamental to the establishment of the theory that light moves in a wave-like motion. Fresnel also made great contributions to the field of optics, including the development of a compound lens for use in lighthouses.

fric•tion (frĭk′shən) The resistance to movement that occurs when two objects are in contact. It is friction, for example, that slows down a ball rolling on grass and causes the blade of a saw cutting wood to get hot. There is less friction between smooth surfaces than between rough surfaces. Friction can be reduced by using a lubricant such as oil or silicone.

Frig•id Zone (frĭj′ĭd) Either of two zones of the Earth of extreme latitude, the **North Frigid Zone,** extending north of the Arctic Circle, or the **South Frigid Zone,** extending south of the Antarctic Circle.

frog (frôg) Any of numerous amphibians typically having smooth, moist skin, webbed feet,

BIOGRAPHY

Benjamin Franklin

Scientist, inventor, statesman, printer, philosopher, musician, and economist: Benjamin Franklin was all of these during his long life, but most of all he was curious. His curiosity about things led him to investigate the way they work, and sometimes to invent ways to make them work better. For example, he had poor vision and needed glasses to read. He got tired of constantly taking them off and putting them back on, so he figured out a way to make his glasses let him see both near and far. He had two pairs of spectacles cut in half and put half of each lens in a single frame. Today, we call glasses like these bifocals. In his role as a statesman, Franklin sailed to Europe many times. These voyages piqued his curiosity about ocean currents, and from the data he collected while onboard ship he created the first map of the Gulf Stream.

long hind legs used for leaping, and no tail when fully grown. Frogs mostly live in or around water, but some species, such as tree frogs, live on land. *Compare* **toad.**

frond (frŏnd) **1.** A leaf of a fern, usually consisting of multiple leaflets. **2.** A large, fan-like leaf of a palm tree. **3.** A large, leaf-like structure on a seaweed.

front (frŭnt) The boundary between two air masses that have different temperatures. Fronts are often accompanied by rain or unsettled weather. *See more at* **cold front, warm front.**

fron•tal (frŭn′tl) **1.** *Anatomy.* Relating to the forehead. **2.** *Meteorology.* Relating to a front.

frontal bone A bone of the skull, consisting of a part that corresponds to the forehead and a part that forms the roof of the eye sockets and cavities of the nose.

frontal lobe The largest and forwardmost part of each cerebral hemisphere. It controls voluntary muscle activity and contains, usually on the left side, the area that controls the ability to produce speech.

frost (frôst) A deposit of tiny ice crystals on a surface. Frost is formed when water vapor in the air condenses at a temperature below freezing.

frost•bite (frôst′bīt′) Damage to a part of the body as a result of exposure to freezing temperatures. It is caused by a loss of blood supply and the formation of ice crystals in the affected body part.

fruc•tose (frŭk′tōs′) A simple sugar found in honey, many fruits, and some vegetables. Fructose is similar to glucose, is sweeter than table sugar, and is an important source of energy for cellular processes.

USAGE

fruit/vegetable

To most of us, a *fruit* is a plant part that is eaten as a dessert or snack because it is sweet, but to someone who studies botany a fruit is a mature ovary of a plant, and as such it may or may not taste sweet. All species of flowering plants produce fruits that contain seeds. A peach, for example, contains a pit that can grow into a new peach tree, while the seeds known as peas can grow into another pea vine. To a botanist, apples, peaches, peppers, tomatoes, pea pods, cucumbers, and winged maple seeds are all fruits. A *vegetable* is simply part of a plant that is grown primarily for food. Thus, the leaf of spinach, the root of a carrot, the flower of broccoli, and the stalk of celery are all vegetables. In everyday, nonscientific talk we make the distinction between sweet plant parts (fruits) and nonsweet plant parts (vegetables). This is why we speak of peppers and cucumbers and squash—all fruits in the eyes of a botanist—as vegetables.

fruit (fro͞ot) The ripened ovary of a flowering plant that contains the seeds. Fruits can be dry or fleshy. Berries, nuts, grains, pods, and drupes are fruits. *See Note at* **berry.** ❖ Fruits that consist of ripened ovaries alone, such as the tomato and pea pod, are called **true fruits.** ❖ Fruits that consist of ripened ovaries and other parts such as the

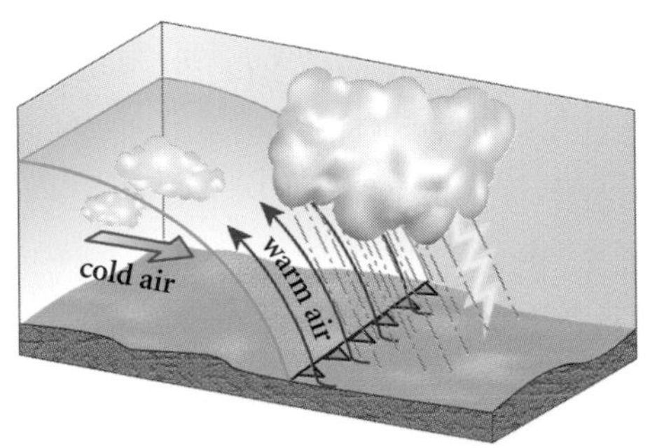

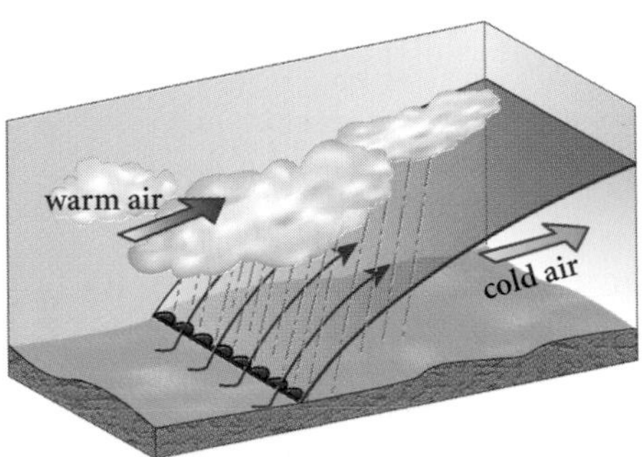

■ **front**
cold front (left) *and warm front* (right)

receptacle or bracts, as in the apple and the cucumber, are called **accessory fruits** or **false fruits.**

fruit•ing body (fro͞o′tĭng) A specialized spore-producing structure, especially of a fungus. A mushroom is the fruiting body of a fungus.

ft. Abbreviation of **foot.**

fu•el (fyo͞o′əl) A substance that produces useful energy when it undergoes a chemical or nuclear reaction. Fuel such as coal, wood, oil, or gas provides energy when burned. Compounds in the body such as glucose are broken down into simpler compounds to provide energy for metabolic processes. Some radioactive substances, such as plutonium and tritium, provide energy by undergoing nuclear fission or fusion.

fuel cell A device that produces electricity by combining a fuel with oxygen. Fuel cells are used in space shuttles, where an electric current is produced by oxidizing hydrogen gas (the fuel) in an electrolyte cell.

ful•crum (fo͝ol′krəm) The point or support on which a lever turns.

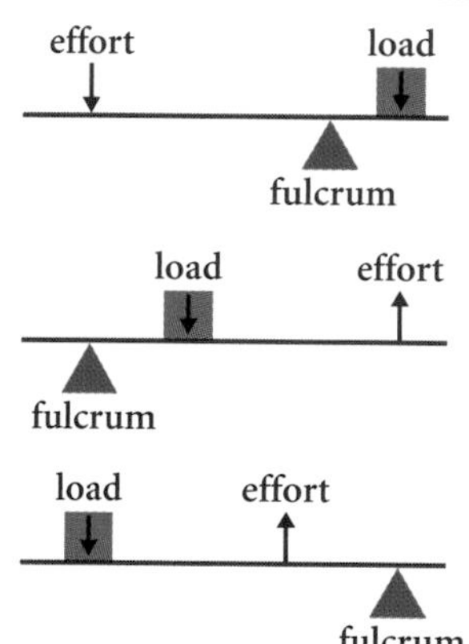

fulcrum
This diagram shows the relative position of the fulcrum in the three basic types of levers, with arrows indicating the direction of the effort and the downward force of the load.
top: *The effort and load are on opposite sides of the fulcrum, as in a crowbar.*
middle: *The load is between the fulcrum and effort, as in a wheelbarrow.*
bottom: *The effort is between the fulcrum and load, as in a person's forearm, where the fulcrum is the elbow and the load is something held in the hand.*

Did You Know?
fungus

There's a *fungus* among us, as they say. And it's true—they are everywhere. You have no doubt eaten mushrooms, which are fungi. And you have eaten bread, made with yeast, another fungus. Old bread may grow mold, still another fungus. Athlete's foot and a variety of other infections are caused by fungi, but, on the good side, a fungus also produces the medicine penicillin. About 100,000 different species of fungi exist. When you see a light-colored splat on a tree or rock in the woods, it is probably a lichen, which is a fungus and an alga living in a symbiotic relationship, benefiting each other. Fungi are neither plants nor animals; scientists classify them as their own unique kingdom.

full moon (fo͝ol) The phase of the moon in which it is visible as a fully illuminated disk. This phase occurs when the moon is on the opposite side of Earth as the sun and is not in Earth's shadow. *See more at* **moon.** *Compare* **new moon.**

Ful•ton (fo͝ol′tən), **Robert** 1765–1815. American engineer and inventor who developed the first useful submarine and torpedo (1800) and produced the first practical steamboat (1807).

fu•ma•role (fyo͞o′mə-rōl′) A hole in the Earth's surface that hot smoke and gases escape from. Fumaroles are found on or near volcanoes.

fumarole
Steam fumarole near Spirit Lake, Washington

fume (fyo͞om) Smoke, vapor, or gas, especially if irritating, harmful, or smelly.

func•tion (fŭngk′shən) **1.** A relationship between two sets that matches each member of the first set with a unique member of the second set. Functions are often expressed as an equation, such as $y = x + 5$, meaning that y is a function of x such that for any value of x, the value of y will be 5 greater than x. **2.** A quantity whose value depends on the value given to one or more related quantities. For example, the area of a square is a function of the length of its sides.

fun•gi•cide (fŭn′jĭ-sīd′, fŭng′gĭ-sīd′) A chemical used to kill fungal diseases. *Compare* **herbicide, insecticide, pesticide.**

fun•gus (fŭng′gəs) *Plural* **fungi** (fŭn′jī, fŭng′gī) Any of a wide variety of organisms that reproduce by spores, including the mushrooms, molds, yeasts, and mildews. The spores of most fungi grow a network of slender tubes called hyphae that spread into and feed off of living organisms or dead organic matter. The hyphae also produce reproductive structures, such as mushrooms and other growths. Fungi are grouped as a separate kingdom in taxonomy. *See Table at* **taxonomy.** —*Adjective* **fungal.**

fun•nel (fŭn′əl) A utensil with a wide opening at one end and a tube at the other, used to pour liquids or other substances into a container with a small mouth.

fuse (fyo͞oz) *Noun.* **1.** A safety device that protects an electric circuit from becoming overloaded. Fuses contain a length of thin wire that melts and breaks the circuit if too much current flows through it. Fuses have largely been replaced by circuit breakers. —*Verb.* **2.** To melt something, such as metal or glass, by heating. **3.** To blend two or more substances by melting: *Bronze is made by fusing copper and tin.*

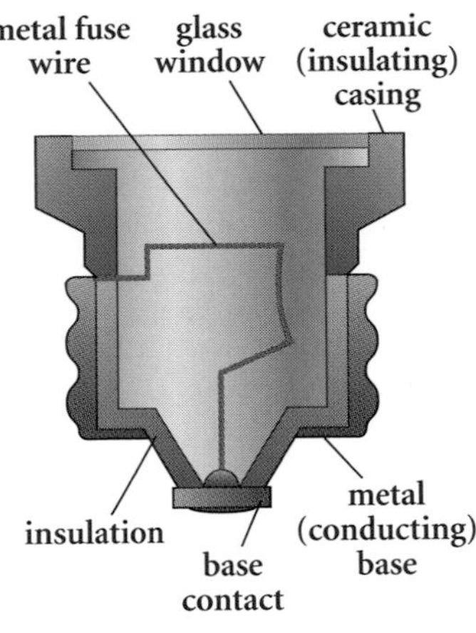

fuse
a typical household fuse

fu•sion (fyo͞o′zhən) **1.** The joining together of light atomic nuclei, especially hydrogen nuclei, to form a heavier nucleus, especially a helium nucleus. Fusion occurs when light nuclei are heated to extremely high temperatures, forcing them to collide at great speed. The collision releases one or more neutrons and energy in the form of radiation. Fusion reactions power the sun and other stars. *See more at* **fission. 2.** A mixture or blend formed by fusing two or more things: *An alloy is a fusion of two or more metals.*

G

g 1. Abbreviation of **gram. 2.** The symbol for **acceleration of gravity. 3.** A symbol for **g-force.**

G 1. A symbol for **g-force. 2.** The symbol for **gravitational constant.**

Ga The symbol for **gallium.**

gab•bro (găb′rō) A usually dark, coarse-grained igneous rock composed mostly of plagioclase and pyroxene. It is mineralogically similar to basalt but has larger crystals. *See Table at* **rock.**

Ga•bor (gä′bôr, gə-bôr′), **Dennis** 1900–1979. Hungarian-born British physicist who invented the technique of holography in 1947.

gad•o•lin•i•um (găd′l-ĭn′ē-əm) A silvery-white, easily shaped metallic element of the lanthanide series that occurs in nature as a mix of seven isotopes. It is used to improve the heat and corrosion resistance of iron, chromium, and various alloys. *Symbol* **Gd.** *Atomic number* 64. *See* **Periodic Table,** pages 262–263.

■ **galaxy**

The Whirlpool (top) *and Sombrero* (bottom) *galaxies are both spiral galaxies. The Sombrero galaxy is viewed from the side.*

gal. Abbreviation of **gallon.**

gal•ax•y (găl′ək-sē) Any of numerous large-scale collections of stars, gas, and dust that make up the universe. A galaxy may range in diameter from 1,500 to 300,000 light-years.

Ga•len (gā′lən) A.D. 130?–200? Greek anatomist, physician, and writer. He developed numerous theories about the structures and functions of the human body, many of which were based on information he gained from dissecting animals. Galen's theories formed the basis of European medicine until the Renaissance.

ga•le•na (gə-lē′nə) A gray, metallic mineral consisting of lead and sulfur. Galena usually occurs in cube-shaped crystals within veins of igneous rock or in sedimentary rocks.

Ga•li•le•o Ga•li•lei (găl′ə-lā′ō găl′ə-lā′) 1564–1642. Italian astronomer, mathematician, and physicist who was the first to use a telescope to study the stars and planets. He discovered that Jupiter has moons and that Venus has phases like those of Earth's moon, suggesting that Venus orbits the sun.

gall (gôl) An abnormal swelling of plant tissue, caused by insects, microorganisms, or injury.

gall•blad•der (gôl′blăd′ər) A small, pear-shaped muscular sac in which bile is stored. The gallbladder is located beneath the liver and secretes bile into the small intestine.

gal•li•um (găl′ē-əm) A rare, silvery metallic element that is found as a trace element in coal, bauxite, and several minerals. It melts just above room temperature and is used in thermometers and semiconductors. *Symbol* **Ga.** *Atomic number* 31. *See* **Periodic Table,** pages 262–263.

gal•lon (găl′ən) A unit of volume or capacity used for measuring liquids, equal to 4 quarts (3.79 liters). *See Table at* **measurement.**

gal•van•ic (găl-văn′ĭk) Relating to electricity that is produced by chemical reaction.

gal•va•nom•e•ter (găl′və-nŏm′ĭ-tər) An instru-

BIOGRAPHY

Galileo Galilei

In 1609 Galileo heard of the invention of the spyglass, a tube with a piece of glass at each end that made objects appear closer and larger when you looked through it. He set about making his own. One night Galileo used his telescope (as they began to be called) to look up at the moon. He was astonished to see its mountains and valleys, since the moon was believed to be perfectly smooth. Galileo continued to observe the heavens, and a few months later he discovered Jupiter's four largest moons. As he studied them, he realized that they were orbiting Jupiter, not Earth. Galileo's observations convinced him that Copernicus had been right when he stated that Earth and all the planets orbit the sun. Many people feared Copernicus's theory, which overthrew the long-held belief that Earth was the center of the universe. Because he openly supported Copernicus's theory, Galileo was called before Church authorities and forced to declare that the theory was false. He was then put under house arrest on his own farm, where he was nonetheless allowed to continue his scientific work until the end of his life.

ment that detects, measures, and determines the direction of small electric currents.

gam•ete (găm′ēt′) *See* **reproductive cell.**

ga•me•to•phyte (gə-mē′tə-fīt′) In plants, algae, and certain other kinds of organisms, the individual organism or generation of organisms that produces reproductive cells (called gametes). Each cell of a gametophyte has only one set of chromosomes, just as its gametes do. In nonvascular plants like mosses, the gametophyte is the main plant form. In ferns, the gametophyte is a very small independent plant. The gametophytes of gymnosperms and flowering plants are even smaller—the pollen grain and the egg-containing structure inside an ovule. They depend entirely on the main plant for nutrients as they develop inside it. *Compare* **sporophyte.**

gam•ma globulin (găm′ə) A class of proteins in the blood plasma of humans and other mammals that function as part of the body's immune system. Antibodies are gamma globulins.

gamma ray A stream of electromagnetic radiation having wavelengths shorter than those of x-rays and therefore greater energy and penetrating power. Gamma rays are given off by unstable nuclei during radioactive decay. ❖ The emission of gamma rays by a nucleus is called **gamma decay.** Gamma decay does not change the atomic number or the mass number of an element. *See more at* **radiation, radioactive decay.**

gan•gli•on (găng′glē-ən) *Plural* **ganglia.** A compact group of nerve cells having a specific function. In invertebrate animals, pairs of ganglia occur at intervals along the axis of the body, with the forwardmost pair functioning like a brain. In vertebrates, ganglia are usually located outside the brain or spinal cord and control the functioning of the body's internal organs.

gan•grene (găng′grēn′) Death of tissue in a living body, especially in a limb, caused by a bacterial infection resulting from a stoppage of the blood supply to the affected tissue.

gar•net (gär′nĭt) Any of several common, usually red or black minerals consisting of aluminum or calcium silicate. Garnets occur in igneous, metamorphic, and sedimentary rocks, and are used as gemstones.

WORD HISTORY

gastropod

Snails, conchs, whelks, and many other similar animals with shells are all called gastropods by scientists. The word *gastropod* comes from Greek and means "stomach foot," a name that owes its existence to the unusual anatomy of snails. While they don't have feet like ours, exactly, snails have a broad flat "foot" used for support and for forward movement. This foot runs along the underside of the animal—essentially along its belly. The Greek elements *gastro–*, "stomach," and *-pod,* "foot," are found in many other scientific names, such as *gastritis* (an inflammation of the stomach) and *sauropod* ("lizard foot," a type of dinosaur).

gas (găs) One of the three basic forms of matter, composed of molecules in constant random motion. Unlike a solid, a gas has no fixed shape and will take on the shape of the space available. Unlike a liquid, it has no fixed volume and will expand to fill the space available. —*Adjective* **gaseous** (găs′ē-əs, găsh′əs).

gas exchange The movement of gases from an area of higher concentration to an area of lower concentration, especially the exchange of oxygen and carbon dioxide between an organism and its environment. In plants, gas exchange takes place during photosynthesis. In animals, gases are exchanged during respiration.

gas•o•line (găs′ə-lēn′) A highly flammable mixture of liquid hydrocarbons that are derived from petroleum. Gasoline is used as a fuel for internal-combustion engines in automobiles, motorcycles, and small trucks.

gas•tric (găs′trĭk) Relating to the stomach.

gastric juice A fluid secreted by glands lining the inside of the stomach. It contains hydrochloric acid and enzymes, such as pepsin, that aid in digestion.

gas•tro•in•tes•ti•nal tract (găs′trō-ĭn-tĕs′tə-nəl) *See* **digestive tract.**

gas•tro•pod (găs′trə-pŏd′) Any of various mollusks having a head with eyes and feelers, usually a coiled shell, and a muscular foot on the underside of its body with which it moves. Gastropods include both land-dwelling forms, like land snails and slugs, and aquatic species, like conchs, cowries, and whelks.

gas•tru•la (găs′trə-lə) *Plural* **gastrulas** *or* **gastrulae** (găs′trə-lē′) An embryo at the stage following the blastula, in which the cells are distributed into layers that eventually develop into the organs of the body. *Compare* **blastula.**

Gauss (gous), **Karl Friedrich** 1777–1855. German mathematician, astronomer, and physicist. He brought about significant and rapid advances to mathematics with his contributions to algebra, geometry, statistics, and number theory.

Gay-Lus•sac (gā′lə-săk′), **Joseph Louis** 1778–1850. French chemist and physicist who developed a law governing the combination of gases. He discovered boron, with Louis Jacques Thénard, in 1808.

Gd The symbol for **gadolinium.**

Ge The symbol for **germanium.**

gear (gîr) A wheel with teeth around its rim that mesh with the teeth of another wheel to transmit motion. Gears are used to transmit power (as in a car transmission) or change the direction of motion in a mechanism (as in a differential axle). Speed in various parts of a machine is usually determined by the arrangement of gears.

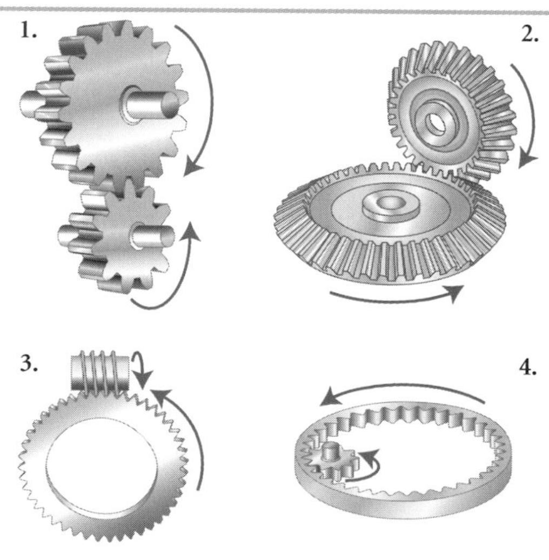

gear

Gears can be used to reverse (1) or otherwise change (2,3) the direction of rotation. Gears of different size (1–4) change the speed of rotation.

Gei•ger (gī′gər), **Hans Wilhelm** 1882–1945. German physicist who was a pioneer in nuclear physics. He invented numerous instruments and techniques used to detect charged particles, including the Geiger counter (1908).

Geiger counter An electronic instrument that detects and measures nuclear radiation, such as x-rays or gamma rays. The Geiger counter consists of a gas-filled tube with an electrode connected to a counter. As radiation passes through the gas, ions are produced, making pulses of electric current that are registered by the counter.

gel•a•tin (jĕl′ə-tn) An odorless, colorless protein substance obtained by boiling a mixture of water and the skin, bones, and tendons of animals. The preparation forms a gel when allowed to cool. It is used in foods, drugs, glue, and film.

Gell-Mann (gĕl′măn′), **Murray** Born 1929. American physicist who studied the interactions of subatomic particles and helped develop a system for classifying them. He also introduced the concept of quarks.

Gem•i•ni (jĕm′ə-nī′) A constellation in the Northern Hemisphere near Cancer and Auriga. It contains the bright stars Pollux and Castor.

gem•ma (jĕm′ə) A bud-like outgrowth on certain organisms, such as the liverworts and mosses, that separates from the parent organism and develops into a new individual.

gene (jēn) A segment of DNA, occupying a specific place on a chromosome, that is the basic unit of heredity. Genes act by directing the synthesis of proteins, which are the main components of cells and are the catalysts of all cellular processes. Physical traits, such as the shape of a plant leaf, the coloration of an animal's coat, and the texture of a person's hair, are all determined by genes. *See also* **dominant, recessive.** *See Notes at* **DNA, Mendel.**

gen•er•a•tor (jĕn′ə-rā′tər) A machine that converts movement, or mechanical energy, into electrical energy. Generators create an electric current by means of a coiled electric wire that rotates between two magnets. When the wire turns inside the magnetic field, an electric current flows through it.

gene therapy The treatment of disease, especially one caused by the inheritance of a defective gene, by replacing defective genes with healthy ones through genetic engineering.

Did You Know?

genes

What makes a human different from a chimpanzee? Much of the answer lies in the *genes*, the basic units of heredity. Each gene is a specific segment of DNA, occupying a fixed place on a chromosome. Genes contain the chemical information needed to create different kinds of proteins. These proteins are used to repair cells and make new ones. The kinds of proteins, the amounts, and the order in which they are made all help determine how one type of cell differs from another and, ultimately, how one species of organism differs from another. Just how different are the genes making up different life forms? In the case of the human and the chimp, not much: about 98 percent of the DNA in a chimpanzee cell is identical to the DNA in a human cell. Because of this close similarity, scientists think that it is the sequence of genes, as well as the types of genes themselves, that account for most of the differences between the two species. However, not all differences between species can be explained by gene differences alone. How closely matching sets of genes can belong to entirely different species is one of the great mysteries of modern biology.

ge•net•ic code (jə-nĕt′ĭk) The sequence of organic bases (called nucleotides) in DNA and RNA that determines the structure of amino acids in a protein.

genetic engineering The science of altering and cloning genes to produce a new trait in an organism or to make a biological substance, such as a protein or hormone. Genetic engineering mainly involves the creation of recombinant DNA, which is then inserted into the genetic material of a cell or virus.

genetic map *or* **gene map** A graphic representation of the arrangement of genes on a chromosome. A genetic map is used to locate and identify the gene or genes that determine a particular inherited trait. ❖ Locating and identifying genes in a genetic map is called **genetic mapping.**

ge•net•ics (jə-nĕt′ĭks) The scientific study of the principles of heredity and the variation of inherited traits among related organisms. Genetics is a branch of biology.

gen•i•tals (jĕn′ĭ-tlz) The organs of reproduction in animals, especially the external sex organs.

ge•nome (jē′nōm) The total amount of genetic information in the chromosomes of an organism, including its genes and DNA sequences. The genome of eukaryotes is made up of a single, haploid set of chromosomes that is contained in the nucleus of every cell and exists in two copies in the chromosomes of all cells except reproductive cells. The human genome is made up of about 30,000 genes. ❖ The scientific study of genomes is called **genomics** (jə-nō′mĭks).

gen•o•type (jĕn′ə-tīp′, jē′nə-tīp′) The genetic makeup of an organism as distinguished from its physical characteristics. *Compare* **phenotype.**

ge•nus (jē′nəs) *Plural* **genera** (jĕn′ər-ə) A group of organisms ranking above a species and below a family. *See Table at* **taxonomy.**

geo– *or* **ge–** A prefix that means "earth," as in *geochemistry,* the study of the Earth's chemistry.

ge•o•cen•tric (jē′ō-sĕn′trĭk) **1.** Relating to or measured from the Earth's center. **2.** Relating to a model of the solar system or universe having the Earth as the center. *Compare* **heliocentric.**

ge•o•chem•is•try (jē′ō-kĕm′ĭ-strē) The study of the chemistry of the Earth, including its layers, waters, and atmosphere.

ge•ode (jē′ōd′) A small, hollow, usually rounded rock lined on the inside with inward-pointing crystals. Geodes form when mineral-rich water entering a cavity in a rock undergoes a sudden change in pressure or temperature, causing crystals to form from the solution and line the cavity's walls.

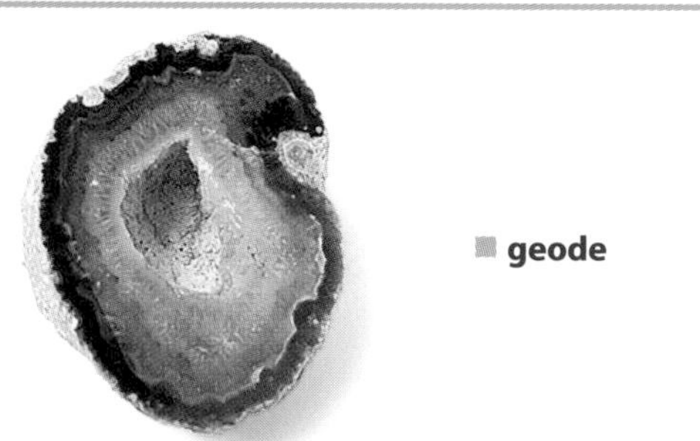

■ **geode**

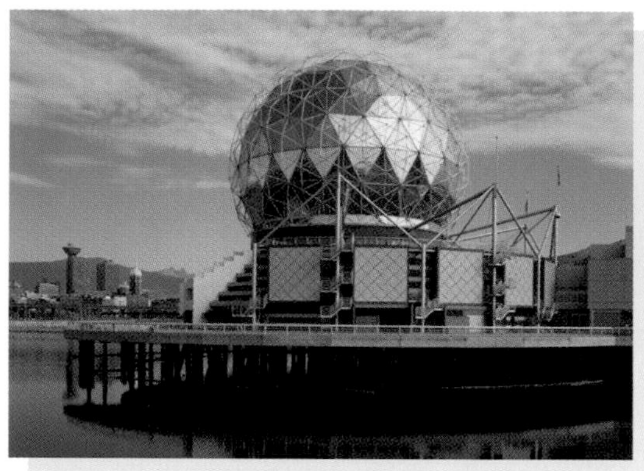

■ **geodesic dome**
Science World geodesic dome, Vancouver, Canada

ge•o•des•ic dome (jē′ə-dĕs′ĭk, jē′ə-dē′sĭk) A structure having the shape of a dome or partial sphere but made of flat triangular pieces that fit rigidly together.

ge•o•graph•ic north (jē′ə-grăf′ĭk) The direction from any point on Earth toward the North Pole. Also called *true north. Compare* **magnetic north.**

ge•og•ra•phy (jē-ŏg′rə-fē) The scientific study of the Earth's surface and its various climates, countries, peoples, and natural resources.

ge•o•log•ic time (jē′ə-lŏj′ĭk) The period of time covering the formation and development of the Earth, from about 4.6 billion years ago to today. *See chart,* pages 148–149.

ge•ol•o•gy (jē-ŏl′ə-jē) **1.** The scientific study of the origin of the Earth along with its rocks, minerals, and land forms, and of the history of the changes these have undergone. **2.** The structure of a specific region of the Earth, including its rocks, soils, mountains, fossils, and other features.

ge•o•mag•ne•tism (jē′ō-măg′nĭ-tĭz′əm) The magnetic properties of the Earth. ❖ The magnetic field surrounding the Earth is called the **geomagnetic field.**

ge•o•met•ric progression (jē′ə-mĕt′rĭk) A sequence of numbers in which each number is multiplied by the same factor to obtain the next number in the sequence; a sequence in which the ratio of any two adjacent numbers is the same. An example is 5, 25, 125, 625, . . . , where each number is multiplied by 5 to obtain the following number, and the ratio of any number to the next number is always 1 to 5. *Compare* **arithmetic progression.**

ge•om•e•try (jē-ŏm′ĭ-trē) The mathematical study of the properties, measurement, and relationships of points, lines, planes, surfaces, angles, and solids.

ge•o•phys•ics (jē′ō-fĭz′ĭks) The application of physics to the scientific study of the Earth and its environment.

ge•o•ther•mal (jē′ō-thûr′məl) Relating to the internal heat of the Earth. The water of hot springs and geysers is heated by geothermal sources. ❖ Power that is generated using the Earth's internal heat is called **geothermal energy.**

ge•ot•ro•pism (jē-ŏt′rə-pĭz′əm) The growth of an organism in response to gravity. The downward growth of plant roots is an example of geotropism. —*Adjective* **geotropic** (jē′ə-trō′pĭk, jē′ə-trŏp′ĭk).

germ (jûrm) **1.** A microscopic organism or substance, especially a bacterium or a virus, that causes disease. **2.** The earliest living form of an organism; a seed, spore, or bud.

Ger•main (zhĕr-măn′), **Sophie** 1776–1831. French mathematician who made significant advances in theoretical mathematics.

ger•ma•ni•um (jər-mā′nē-əm) A brittle, crystalline, grayish-white nonmetallic element that is found in coal, zinc ores, and other minerals. It is widely used as a semiconductor and in wide-angle lenses. *Symbol* **Ge.** *Atomic number* 32. *See* **Periodic Table,** pages 262–263.

■ **geothermal**
clouds of steam rising from Morning Glory hot spring, Yellowstone National Park

USAGE

germ/microbe/pathogen

You've heard it many times. Some food falls on the floor, and someone (usually an adult) says, "Don't eat that now. It has germs on it." The word *germ* has been used to refer to invisible agents of disease since the 19th century, when scientists were first learning about the nature of disease. Similarly, the term *microbe,* which comes from the Greek prefix *mikro–,* "small," and word *bios,* "life," is a term that arose in the late 19th century in reference to the microscopic organisms that caused disease. The terms *germ* and *microbe* thus became associated with an early era of scientific research in which knowledge was very limited, and they are no longer used much by scientists. Thanks to generations of research, scientists today can usually identify the specific agents of disease, such as individual species of bacteria or viruses. When they want to refer generally to agents of disease, they use the term *pathogen,* which comes from Greek *pathos,* "suffering," and the suffix *–gen,* "producer." The term *microorganism* is used to refer to any one-celled microscopic organism, whether it causes disease or is harmless.

Ger•man measles (jûr′mən) A contagious disease caused by a virus in which symptoms, such as skin rash and fever, are usually mild. German measles can cause congenital defects if contracted by a woman during early pregnancy. Also called *rubella.*

germ cell A reproductive cell of a plant or animal; a gamete. In mammals, germ cells are eggs or sperm.

ger•mi•na•tion (jûr′mə-nā′shən) The beginning of growth, as of a seed, spore, or bud. The germination of most seeds and spores occurs in

GEOLOGIC TIME

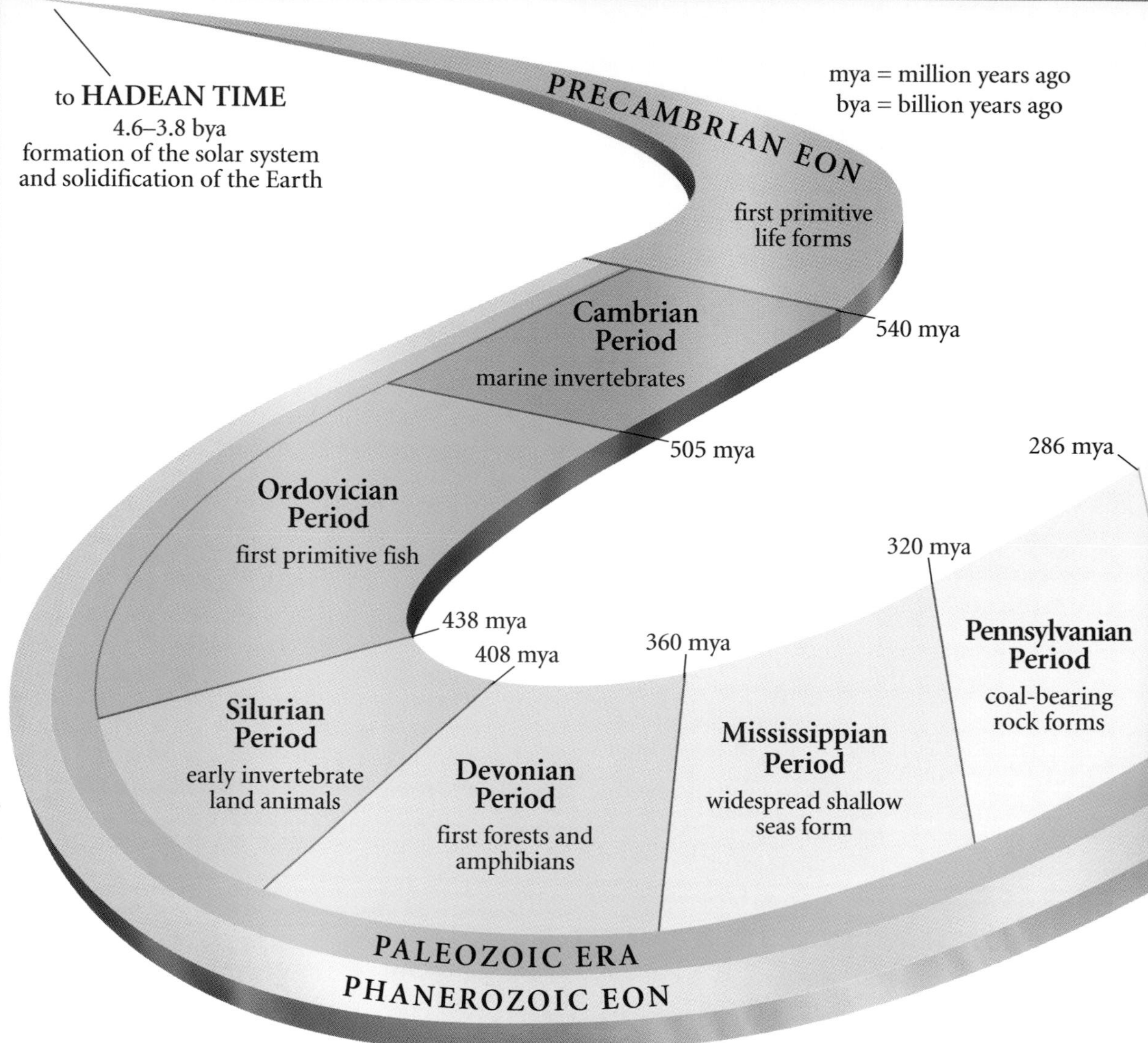

The Earth formed approximately 4.6 billion years ago. For the purpose of studying its history, scientists have separated these 4.6 billion years into a set of divisions, much as a year is divided into months, weeks, and days. The first 800 million years of the Earth's history are referred to as Hadean Time. During this time the solar system was forming and the Earth was solidifying. The 3.8 billion years after Hadean time are subdivided into eons, eras, periods, and epochs. Eons are the longest divisions of time, and epochs are the shortest. Most of the boundaries between the divisions correspond to visible changes in the types of life forms preserved as fossils in the corresponding rocks.

Because our understanding of the Earth's history is based on what we learn by studying its rocks and the fossils within them, we know a lot more about the Earth's recent history than we do about its earlier history. This is why most of the geologic time divisions correspond to the last 540 million years (the Phanerozoic Eon), even though most of the Earth's history occurred before that time.

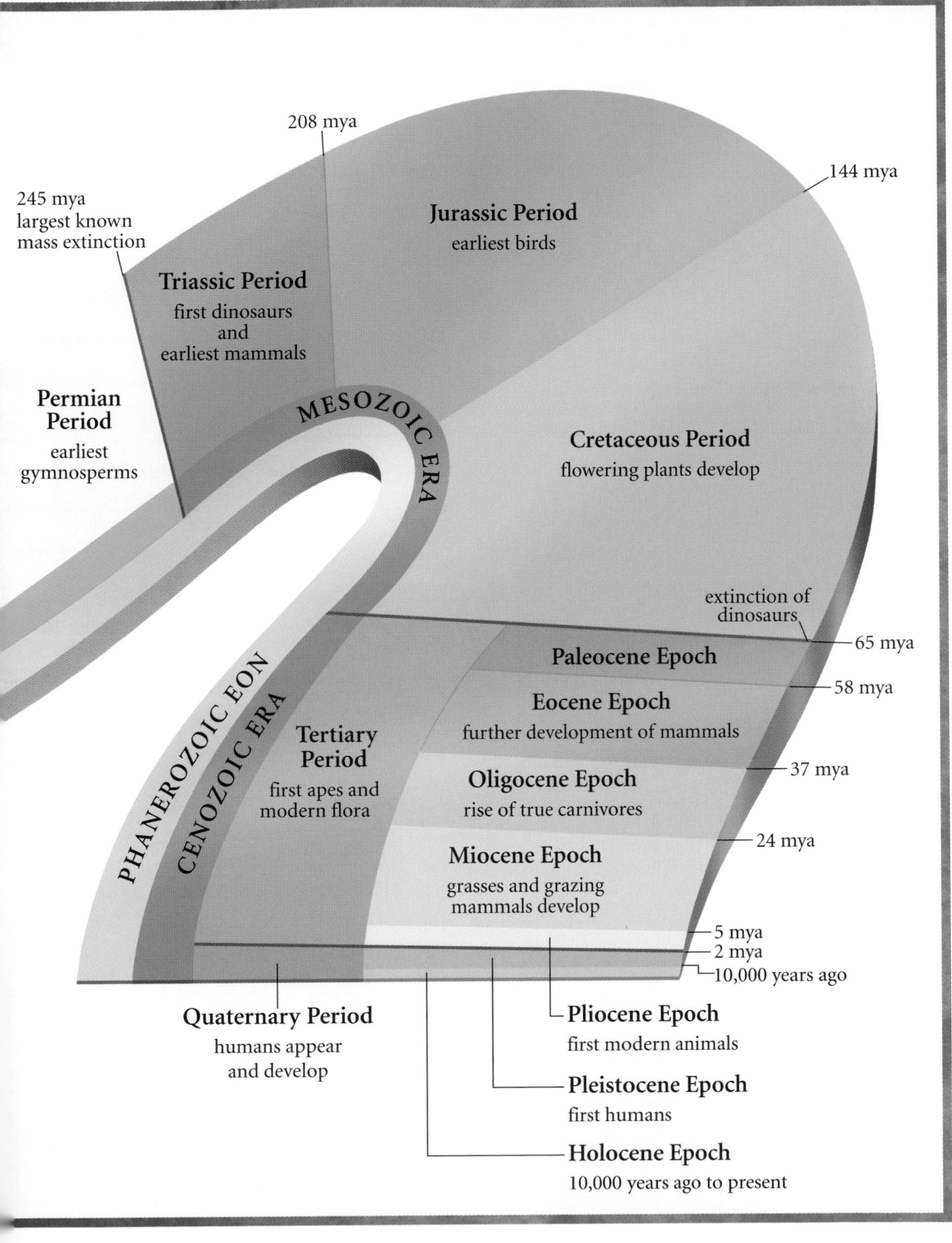
208 mya
144 mya
245 mya
largest known
mass extinction
Jurassic Period
earliest birds
Triassic Period
first dinosaurs
and
earliest mammals
Permian
Period
earliest
gymnosperms
MESOZOIC ERA
Cretaceous Period
flowering plants develop
extinction of
dinosaurs
65 mya
Paleocene Epoch
58 mya
Eocene Epoch
further development of mammals
PHANEROZOIC EON
CENOZOIC ERA
Tertiary
Period
first apes and
modern flora
Oligocene Epoch
rise of true carnivores
37 mya
24 mya
Miocene Epoch
grasses and grazing
mammals develop
5 mya
2 mya
10,000 years ago
Quaternary Period
humans appear
and develop
Pliocene Epoch
first modern animals
Pleistocene Epoch
first humans
Holocene Epoch
10,000 years ago to present

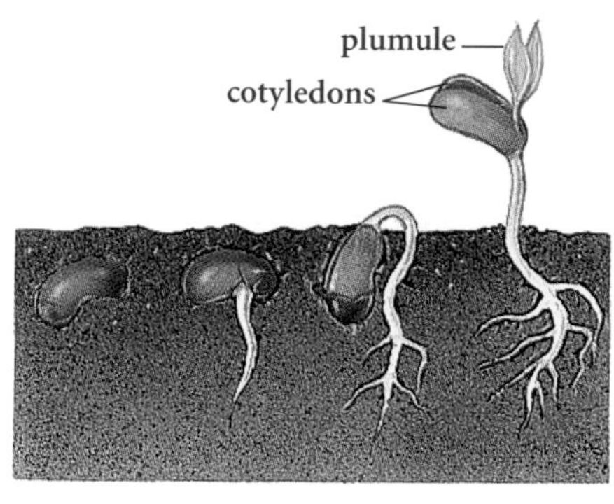

germination
germination of a bean seed

response to warmth and water. —*Verb* **germinate.**

ges•ta•tion (jĕ-stā′shən) The period of time spent in the uterus by the young of an animal before being born. Gestation in humans is about nine months.

gey•ser (gī′zər) A natural hot spring that regularly ejects a spray of steam and boiling water into the air. The water is heated by coming in contact with hot rock or steam underground.

g-force A measure of force acting on a body, expressed as a multiple of the force that the Earth's gravity at sea level would exert on the body (equal to 1 G). The force of gravity on Jupiter, for example, is 2.5 Gs. Other forces of acceleration, such as those exerted on jet pilots making sharp turns, are also expressed in Gs.

gi•ant star (jī′ənt) A very large, very bright star having high mass and low density.

gib•bous (gĭb′əs) More than half but less than fully illuminated. Used to describe the moon or a planet. *Compare* **crescent.**

Gibbs (gĭbz), **Josiah Willard** 1839–1903. American mathematician and physicist known especially for his investigations of thermodynamics. He developed methods for analyzing the thermodynamic properties of substances, and his findings established the basic theory for physical chemistry.

giga– A prefix that means: **1.** One billion (10^9), as in *gigahertz,* one billion hertz. **2.** 2^{30} (that is, 1,073,741,824), which is the power of 2 closest to a billion, as in *gigabyte. See Table at* **measurement.**

gig•a•byte (gĭg′ə-bīt′) **1.** A unit of computer memory or data storage capacity equal to 1,024 megabytes (2^{30} bytes). **2.** One billion bytes. *See Note at* **megabyte.**

Gil•bert (gĭl′bərt), **William** 1544–1603. English court physician and physicist whose book *De Magnete* (1600) was the first comprehensive scientific work published in England. Gilbert demonstrated that the Earth itself is a magnet, with lines of force running between the North and South Poles. He theorized that magnetism and electricity were two types of a single force and was the first to use the words *electricity* and *magnetic pole.*

gill (gĭl) **1.** The organ that enables most aquatic animals to take oxygen from the water. It consists of a series of membranes that have many small blood vessels. Oxygen passes into the bloodstream and carbon dioxide passes out of it as water passes across the membranes. **2.** One of the thin, plate-like structures on the underside of the cap of a mushroom or similar fungus.

gin•gi•va (jĭn′jə-və) The gums of the mouth. ❖ Inflammation of the gums is called **gingivitis** (jĭn′jə-vī′tĭs).

gink•go (gĭng′kō) A deciduous tree originally native to China, having fan-shaped leaves and

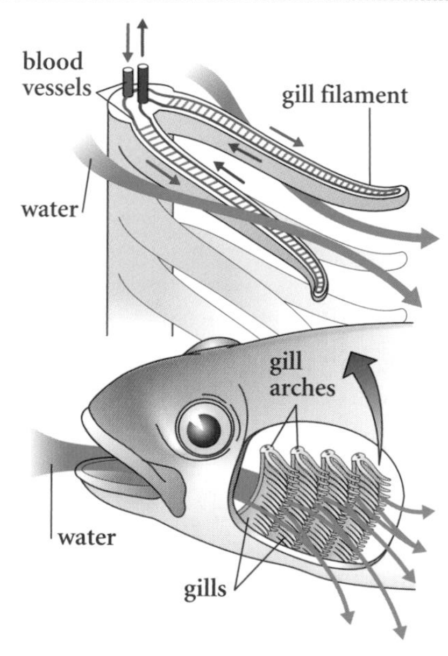

gill
Fish breathe by swallowing water and passing it through gill slits on each side of their head. Blood-filled filaments on the gills extract oxygen from the water as it flows through.

fleshy yellow seeds. Ginkgoes are gymnosperms and do not have flowers.

giz•zard (gĭz′ərd) A muscular pouch behind the stomach in birds. It has a thick lining and often contains swallowed sand or grit, which helps to break food into small pieces.

gla•cier (glā′shər) A large mass of ice flowing very slowly through a valley or spreading outward from a center. Glaciers form over many years from packed snow in areas where snow accumulates faster than it melts. A glacier is always moving, but when its forward edge melts faster than the ice behind it advances, the glacier as a whole shrinks backward.

gland (glănd) An organ in the body of an animal that produces and secretes a specific substance, such as a hormone. *See also* **endocrine gland, exocrine gland.**

glass (glăs) A transparent or translucent material that has no crystalline structure and that usually breaks or shatters easily. It is made by melting a silicate, such as sand, with soda and lime. The soda causes the silicate particles to fuse, and the lime acts as a stabilizer.

glau•co•ma (glou-kō′mə, glô-kō′mə) An eye disease in which the pressure of fluid inside the eyeball becomes abnormally high. The pressure can damage the optic nerve and lead to partial or complete loss of vision.

Did You Know?

glass

Windows, television screens, and eyeglasses all take advantage of the fact that we can see through *glass.* Like common sand, glass is made of silicon dioxide. But if they are made of the same chemical, why should sand be impossible to see through and glass be transparent? The startling see-through property of glass owes its existence to another amazing fact: although glass is hard, it is not truly a solid. Some scientists think of glass as a sort of frozen liquid, whereas others talk about glass as being a disordered kind of solid. Glass is thus different from what we usually think of as either a solid or a liquid. Rather than having the orderly arrangement of most hard matter, the microscopic structure of glass resembles a liquid, stuck in time. The interiors of true solids have boundaries that scatter light, causing it to bounce off. Glass's liquid-like lack of these boundaries lets the light through.

glacier
Athabasca Glacier, Jasper National Park, Alberta, Canada

Glob•al Positioning System (glō′bəl) A system that determines latitude and longitude of a particular location on the Earth by calculating the difference in the time it takes for signals sent from different satellites to reach a receiver at that location.

global warming An increase in the average temperature of the Earth's atmosphere, especially a sustained increase great enough to cause changes in the global climate. Many scientists believe that the Earth has been in a period of global warming for the past century or more, due in part to the increased production of greenhouse gases related to human activity. *See more at* **greenhouse effect.**

glob•u•lar cluster (glŏb′yə-lər) A dense system of very old stars that has a more or less spherical structure. Globular clusters contain from ten thousand to one million stars. *Compare* **open cluster.**

glob•u•lin (glŏb′yə-lĭn) A major class of proteins found in the seeds of plants and in the blood, muscle, and milk of animals. *See also* **gamma globulin.**

glot•tis (glŏt′ĭs) The space between the vocal cords at the upper part of the larynx.

glu•cose (glo͞o′kōs′) A crystalline sugar having the formula $C_6H_{12}O_6$, found in plant and animal tissue and essential to the animal diet. It is transported by blood and lymph to all the cells of the body, where it is broken down to produce ATP, the main source of energy for cellular processes.

glue (glo͞o) A thick, sticky substance made of gelatin or other substances, such as epoxy, resin, or polyethylene. Glues are used to join things together.

glu•tam•ic acid (glo͞o-tăm′ĭk) A nonessential amino acid. *See more at* **amino acid.**

glu•ta•mine (glo͞o′tə-mēn′) A nonessential amino acid. *See more at* **amino acid.**

glyc•er•in *also* **glyc•er•ine** (glĭs′ər-ĭn) *See* **glycerol.**

glyc•er•ol (glĭs′ə-rôl′) A sweet, syrupy liquid obtained from animal fats and oils or by the fermentation of glucose. It is used as a solvent, sweetener, and antifreeze and in making explosives and soaps. Also called *glycerin.*

gly•co•gen (glī′kə-jən) A carbohydrate stored in the liver and muscles of animals that is converted to glucose for energy when glucose levels in the blood are depleted.

gly•col•y•sis (glī-kŏl′ə-sĭs) The process in cell metabolism by which carbohydrates and sugars, especially glucose, are broken down, producing ATP and pyruvic acid.

gnat (năt) Any of various small biting flies.

gneiss (nīs) A type of metamorphic rock consisting of light-colored layers, usually of quartz and feldspar, alternating with dark-colored layers of other minerals. The layers are often folded into curves. *See Table at* **rock.**

goat (gōt) Any of various hoofed ruminant mammals related to the sheep and having hollow, curved horns and a beard. Goats are raised in many parts of the world for wool, milk, and meat.

God•dard (gŏd′ərd), **Robert Hutchings** 1882–1945. American physicist who developed and launched the first successful liquid-fueled rocket in 1926. He also invented numerous rocketry devices.

Gö•del (gŭd′l), **Kurt** 1906–1978. Austrian-born American mathematician. He worked out the most important axiom in modern mathematics, known as Gödel's proof. It states that in any finite mathematical system, there will always be statements that cannot be proved or disproved. Gödel's proof ended efforts by mathematicians to find a mathematical system that was entirely consistent in itself.

Goep•pert-May•er (gŭp′ûrt-mā′ər), **Maria** 1906–1972. German-born American physicist. She developed a model of the atomic nucleus that explained why certain nuclei were stable and had an unusual number of stable isotopes.

goi•ter (goi′tər) An enlarged thyroid gland, visible as a swelling at the front of the neck. It is often associated with a diet that contains too little iodine.

gold (gōld) A soft, shiny, yellow element that is the most easily shaped metal. It occurs in veins and in alluvial deposits. Because it is very durable, resistant to corrosion, and a good conductor of heat and electricity, gold is used as a plating on electrical and mechanical components. It is also an international monetary standard and is used to make jewelry and decoration. *Symbol* **Au.** *Atomic number* 79. *See* **Periodic Table,** pages 262–263. *See Note at* **element.**

Did You Know?

Gondwanaland

Sometimes a suggested solution to a scientific problem can raise more questions than it answers. So it was with Austrian geologist Eduard Suess's hypothesis explaining why identical groups of fossil plants occur in India, South America, southern Africa, Australia, and Antarctica. These plants, known as the *Glossopteris flora,* had seeds that were too large to have blown across wide oceans. In 1885 Suess proposed that the plant fossils were common to all of the landmasses because the landmasses were actually connected when the plants first developed, eventually breaking apart into separate continents. Suess named this huge landmass *Gondwanaland,* after a region of central India called Gondwana. Few believed Suess's idea because most people could not see what would cause such a giant supercontinent to break apart. In the early 1900s, Alfred Wegener, a German meteorologist, noticed other kinds of evidence for Gondwanaland, including similarities in animal fossils, rock types, and marks left by glaciers across the continents of the Southern Hemisphere. Wegener used this evidence to propose the idea of *continental drift,* which says that the continents are always moving toward or away from one another. But it wasn't until the 1960s that Wegener's ideas or the concept of Gondwanaland were finally accepted, when the theory of *plate tectonics* was put forward to explain how the internal workings of the Earth could cause continents to move about.

Gold•ber•ger (gōld′bər-gər), **Joseph** 1874–1924. Hungarian-born American physician. He investigated the cause and treatment of pellagra, a widespread and often fatal disease. Goldberger demonstrated that it was caused by a poor diet and introduced an effective method of prevention.

Gol•gi apparatus *or* **Gol•gi body** (gōl′jē) A structure within many cells that is composed of a series of sacs, called vesicles, and is thought to play a role in the synthesis and transport of proteins. All organisms except bacteria have at least one Golgi apparatus in their cells. *See more at* **cell.**

go•nad (gō′năd′) An organ in animals that produces reproductive cells; an ovary or testis.

Gond•wa•na•land (gŏnd-wä′nə-lănd′) A supercontinent of the Southern Hemisphere comprising the landmasses that currently correspond to India, Australia, Antarctica, and South America. According to the theory of plate tectonics, Gondwanaland formed at the end of the Paleozoic Era and broke up in the middle of the Mesozoic Era. *Compare* **Laurasia.**

gon•or•rhe•a (gŏn′ə-rē′ə) A sexually transmitted disease caused by a bacterial infection that causes inflammation of the genitals and urinary tract.

Good•all (go͝od′ôl), **Jane** Born 1934. British zoologist whose study of the behavior and habitat of the chimpanzee has greatly increased understanding of primate behavior. She established a research center in Tanzania, Africa, and has been a leader in international conservation efforts.

goo•gol (go͞o′gôl′, go͞o′gəl) The number 10 raised to the 100th power, written as 10^{100} or as 1 followed by 100 zeros.

Gor•gas (gôr′gəs), **William Crawford** 1854–1920. American army surgeon. He directed pro-

Jane Goodall

grams to eradicate the mosquito spreading yellow fever in Havana, Cuba (1898), and in the Panama Canal Zone (1904–1913).

gorge (gôrj) A deep, narrow passage with steep sides, often with a stream flowing through it.

go•ril•la (gə-rĭl′ə) The largest and most powerful of the apes, found in central African forests and mountains. Gorillas have a heavy, stocky body with dark hair, dwell on the ground, and feed mainly on leaves and stems. They live in close-knit groups and have elaborate social interactions.

Gould (go͞old), **Stephen Jay** Born 1941. American evolutionary biologist and historian of science. He developed the theory of punctuated equilibrium with Niles Eldredge in 1972.

gout (gout) A hereditary disorder caused by painful deposits of crystals in the joints, especially of the big toe, knee, or elbow. It is caused by abnormally high levels of uric acid in the blood.

gra•da•tion (grā-dā′shən) *Geology.* The process by which the land is leveled off, as through the action of wind or water.

gra•di•ent (grā′dē-ənt) **1.** The degree to which something inclines; a slope. A mountain road with a gradient of ten percent rises one foot for every ten feet of horizontal length. **2.** The rate at which a physical quantity, such as temperature or pressure, changes over a distance.

grad•u•al•ism (grăj′o͞o-ə-lĭz′əm) The theory that new species evolve from existing species through gradual, often imperceptible changes rather than through abrupt, major changes. The small changes are believed to result in perceptible changes over long periods of time. *Compare* **punctuated equilibrium.**

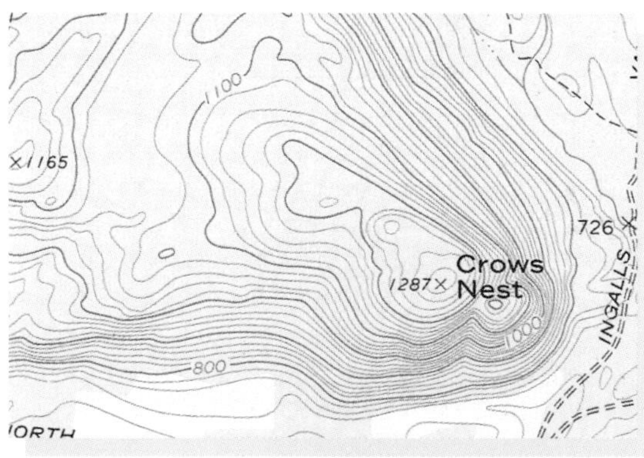

gradient

Closely spaced contour lines on the right indicate a steeper gradient than the more loosely spaced lines on the left.

grad•u•at•ed (grăj′o͞o-ā′tĭd) Divided into or marked with intervals indicating measures, as of length, volume, or temperature.

graft (grăft) *Noun.* **1.** A shoot or bud of one plant that is inserted into or joined to the stem, branch, or root of another plant so that the two grow together as a single plant. Grafts are used to strengthen or repair plants, create dwarf trees, produce seedless fruit, and increase fruit yields without requiring plants to mature from seeds. **2.** A transplant of body tissue, especially skin or bone, from one part to another. —*Verb.* **3.** To join a graft to another plant. **4.** To transplant tissue from one part of the body to another.

grain (grān) **1.** A small, dry, one-seeded fruit, especially of wheat, corn, rice, or another cereal plant. **2.** A small particle of something, such as salt, pollen, or sand. **3.** A unit of weight equal to 0.002 ounce (0.07 gram). *See Table at* **measurement.**

grain alcohol *See* **ethanol.**

gram (grăm) A unit of mass or weight in the metric system, equal to about 0.04 ounces. *See Table at* **measurement.**

Gram (gräm, grăm), **Hans Christian Joachim** 1853–1938. Danish bacteriologist. He developed a method of staining bacteria with dyes, an important tool used to identify and classify bacteria and treat infections.

gram-negative Relating to a group of bacteria that generally are resistant to the effects of antibiotics or the actions of the body's immune cells. Gram-negative bacteria have relatively thin cell walls and, when subjected to a specialized laboratory staining method, do not change color. *Compare* **gram-positive.**

gram-positive Relating to a group of bacteria that generally are sensitive to the destructive effects of antibiotics or the actions of the body's immune cells. Gram-positive bacteria have relatively thick cell walls and, when subjected to a specialized laboratory staining method, turn a dark-blue color. *Compare* **gram-negative.**

grand unified theory (grănd) *See* **unified field theory.**

gran•ite (grăn′ĭt) A usually light-colored, coarse-grained igneous rock composed mostly of quartz, feldspar, and mica. It is one of the most common rocks in the crust of continents. *See Table at* **rock.**

gran•u•lo•cyte (grăn′yə-lō-sīt′) Any of various white blood cells that contain granular material in the cytoplasm and are important in the body's defense against infection. Granulocytes are the most numerous of the white blood cells in humans.

graph (grăf) **1.** A diagram showing the relationship of quantities, especially such a diagram in which lines, bars, or proportional areas represent how one quantity depends on or changes with another. **2.** A curve or line showing a mathematical function or equation, typically drawn in a Cartesian coordinate system.

graph•i•cal user interface (grăf′ĭ-kəl) *See* **GUI.**

graph•ics (grăf′ĭks) **1.** The representation of data in a way that includes images in addition to text. Computer-aided design, typesetting, and video games, for example, involve the use of graphics. **2.** The process by which a computer displays information in the form of images.

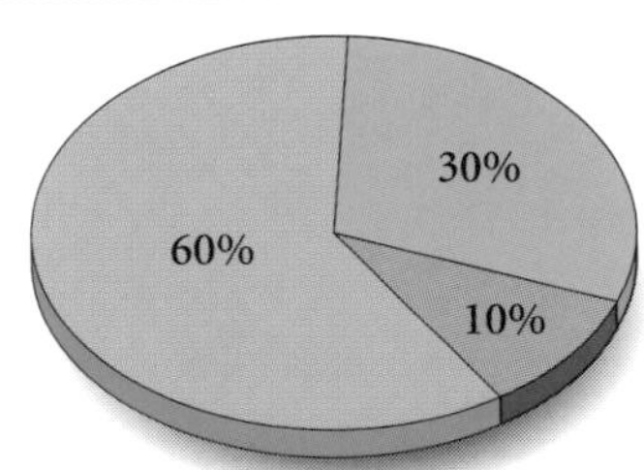

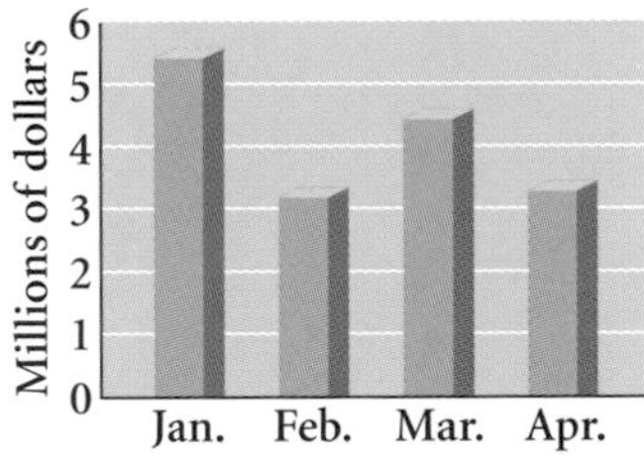

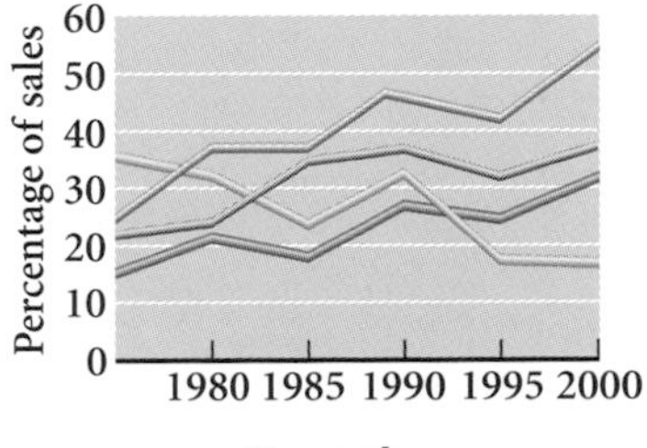

graph

top to bottom: *examples of a pie chart, bar graph, and line graph*

graph•ite (grăf′īt′) A naturally occurring steel-gray to black, crystalline form of carbon. The carbon atoms in graphite are strongly bonded together in sheets. Because the bonds between the sheets are weak, other atoms can easily fit between them, causing the graphite to be soft and slippery to the touch. Graphite is used in pencils and paints and as a lubricant and electrode. It is also used to control chain reactions in nuclear reactors because of its ability to absorb neutrons. *See Note at* **carbon.**

grass (grăs) Any of various plants having narrow leaves, hollow stems, and clusters of very small flowers. Grasses include many varieties of plants used for food and fodder and grown as lawns. Wheat, corn, sugar cane, and bamboo are grasses. *See more at* **leaf.**

grass•hop•per (grăs′hŏp′ər) Any of numerous large insects typically having two pairs of wings and long hind legs for jumping. Grasshoppers feed on plants and can be very destructive to plants. They are closely related to cockroaches, crickets, and praying mantises.

grass•land (grăs′lănd′) An area, such as a prairie or steppe, of grass or grass-like vegetation.

gra•vim•e•ter (gră-vĭm′ĭ-tər) **1.** An instrument used to measure specific gravity. **2.** An instrument used to measure variations in a gravitational field.

grav•i•ta•tion (grăv′ĭ-tā′shən) The force of attraction that tends to draw together any two objects in the universe. Gravitation increases as the mass of the objects increases and as their distance from each other decreases.

grav•i•ta•tion•al constant (grăv′ĭ-tā′shə-nəl) A number used to calculate the force of the gravitational attraction between two bodies in Newton's law of gravitation. The gravitational constant equals 6.67×10^{-11} cubic meters per kilogram per second squared. *See more at* **Newton's law of gravitation.**

grav•i•ty (grăv′ĭ-tē) **1.** The attraction that objects have for each other merely because they have mass and occupy space. Gravity is the weakest of the four basic forces in nature, being weaker than the strong nuclear force, the electromagnetic force, and the weak nuclear force. *See more at* **acceleration, relativity. 2.** This force as

Did You Know?

gravity

Isaac Newton discovered *gravity,* which he saw as the mutual attraction that two masses have for each other. Newton developed an equation that showed that any two objects in the universe, no matter how far apart or how small, exert an instantaneous gravitational effect on each other. These effects diminish, however, as the distance between the objects gets larger and as the masses of the objects get smaller, so that for many distant objects or objects with barely any mass, the effects of gravity are very small. Newton seemed to have the last word on gravity, until Albert Einstein came along. He noted that gravity's effects could not be instantaneous, since they would have to travel at infinite velocities, violating his theory of relativity, which states that nothing can travel faster than light. He also showed that gravity and acceleration are related. Imagine, he said, that you are an astronaut standing in a stationary rocket on Earth: because of Earth's gravity your feet are pressed against the rocket's floor with a force equal to your weight. Now imagine that you are in the same rocket, in outer space, in an area that has no gravitational pull. Even though you are weightless, if the rocket is accelerating and its floor is pushing against your feet, you feel as if you are being acted upon by a gravitational field. Unless you look out the window you have no idea whether the rocket is at rest on Earth or accelerating through space.

it operates in and around the Earth and other massive objects (such as the planets).

gray (grā) A unit used to measure the energy absorbed from radiation. One gray is equal to one joule per kilogram, or 100 rads.

gray matter The brownish-gray tissue of the brain and spinal cord in vertebrate animals, made up chiefly of the cell bodies of neurons. *Compare* **white matter.**

Did You Know?

graywater

White water is what you go rafting on. If you ever rafted on *graywater,* well, you'd need a good shower (in fresh water) at the end of the day to get rid of the smell. To understand graywater, it's best to first define something even smellier: *blackwater.* Blackwater is, quite simply, the water that gets flushed down the toilet, complete with the reasons *why* you flushed the toilet. Blackwater can also include water with other organic wastes—from the sink or garbage disposal, for example. Graywater is still not drinkable, but it's less nasty than blackwater. Graywater is the stuff that goes down the drain from other uses, such as showering or laundry. Because it is relatively clean, graywater can be recycled in areas where water is scarce, to irrigate flower beds or to be fed into toilets to become blackwater. These uses conserve fresh water for drinking and bathing.

gray•wa•ter (grā′wô′tər) Wastewater from household baths and washing machines that is recycled, especially for use in gardening or for flushing toilets.

great circle (grāt) A circle on the surface of a sphere whose plane passes through the center of the sphere. The Earth's equator is a great circle on the sphere of the globe.

green•house effect (grēn′hous′) The trapping of the sun's radiation in the Earth's atmosphere due to the presence of greenhouse gases.

greenhouse gas Any of the atmospheric gases that contribute to the greenhouse effect. Greenhouse gases include carbon dioxide, water vapor, methane, and nitrous oxide.

Green•wich Mean Time (grĕn′ĭch) *See* **universal time.**

ground (ground) **1.** The solid surface of the Earth; land. **2.** A connection between an electri-

A CLOSER LOOK

Greenhouse Effect

A greenhouse is designed to trap the sun's energy. Sunlight can penetrate its glass roof to warm the soil, but the heat given off by the soil can't pass back through the glass, so it remains inside to warm the air.

A similar process takes place on the Earth as a whole. Sunlight penetrates the atmosphere to warm the Earth's surface, which then radiates heat into the lower level of the atmosphere. Although some of this heat passes out into space, much of it is absorbed by water vapor, carbon dioxide, and other gases in the air. These gases act like the glass roof of a greenhouse, trapping the infrared heat energy and warming the atmosphere.

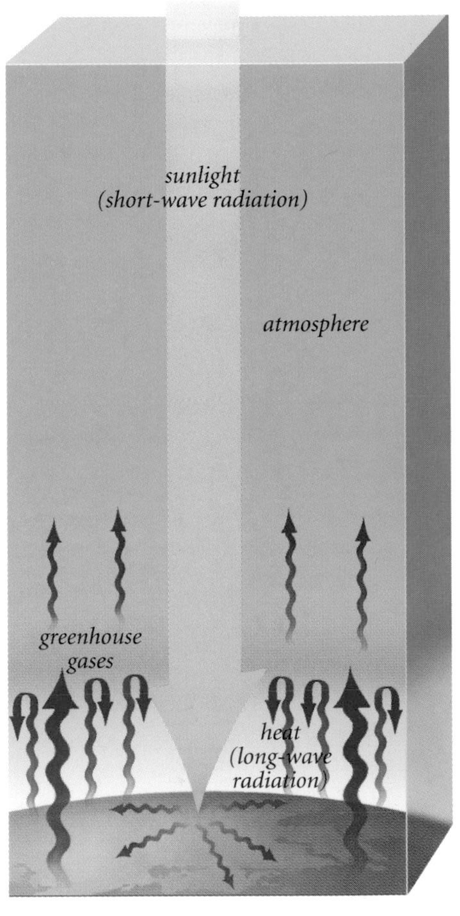

cal conductor and the Earth. **3.** A point in an electrical system where the voltage is zero.

ground state The state of lowest possible energy, especially of atoms. Physical systems that are not in a ground state, such as excited electrons orbiting an atom, tend to return to their ground state, giving off radiation.

ground•wa•ter (ground′wô′tər) Water that flows or collects beneath the Earth's surface. Groundwater originates from rain and from melting snow and ice. It sinks into the ground, filling the small empty spaces in soil, sediment, and porous rocks. Aquifers, springs, and wells are supplied by the flow of groundwater.

group (gro͞op) **1.** Two or more atoms bound together that act as a unit in a number of chemical compounds: *a hydroxyl group.* **2.** In the Periodic Table, a vertical column that contains elements having the same number of electrons in the outermost shell of their atoms. Elements in the same group have similar chemical properties. *See* **Periodic Table,** pages 262–263.

growth (grōth) An increase in size, amount, or volume, usually as a result of an increase in the number of cells. Growth of an organism may stop at maturity, as in the case of humans and other mammals, or it may continue throughout life, as in many plants.

growth ring A layer of wood formed in a plant during a single period of growth. Growth rings are visible as concentric circles of varying width when a tree is cut crosswise. They represent layers of cells produced by the tissue known as vascular cambium. ❖ Most growth rings reflect a full year's growth and are called **annual rings.** But abrupt changes in the environment, especially in the availability of water, can cause a plant to produce more than one growth ring in a year. *See more at* **dendrochronology.**

gua•nine (gwä′nēn′) A base that is a component of DNA and RNA, forming a base pair with cytosine.

gua•no (gwä′nō) A substance composed chiefly of the partly decomposed dung of sea birds or bats. It is used as a fertilizer.

guard cell (gärd) One of the paired cells that control the opening and closing of a stoma of a leaf. When swollen with water, guard cells pull apart from each other, opening the stoma to allow the escape of water vapor and the exchange of gases. When drier, guard cells move closer together, allowing the plant to conserve water. *See more at* **cell.**

GUI (go͞o′ē) Short for *graphical user interface.* An interface that is used to issue commands to a computer by means of a device such as a mouse that manipulates and activates onscreen images.

gulf (gŭlf) A large body of ocean or sea water that is partly surrounded by land.

Gulf Stream A warm ocean current of the northern Atlantic Ocean off eastern North America. It flows northward and eastward from the Gulf of Mexico, eventually dividing into several branches. A major branch continues eastward to warm the coast and moderate the climate of northwest Europe.

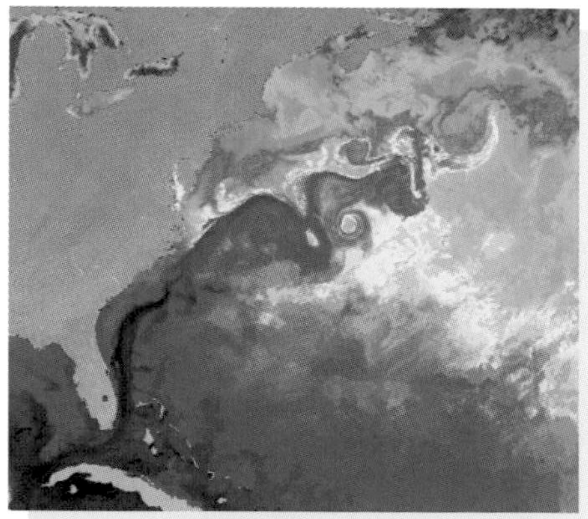

Gulf Stream

A sea surface temperature satellite image indicates the warmer waters of the Gulf Stream in red.

gyroscope

gul•ly (gŭl′ē) A narrow, steep-sided channel formed in loose earth by running water. A gully is usually dry except after periods of heavy rainfall or after the melting of snow or ice.

gum[1] (gŭm) A sticky substance that is produced by certain plants and trees and dries into a brittle solid that dissolves in water.

gum[2] The firm connective tissue that surrounds and supports the bases of the teeth.

gut (gŭt) The digestive tract, especially of an invertebrate animal or an embryo of a vertebrate animal.

gym•no•sperm (jĭm′nə-spûrm′) Any of a group of plants that produce seeds that are not enclosed in a fruit or ovary. Most gymnosperms are cone-bearing trees or shrubs. Seeds develop next to the inside surface of the scales of female cones. Gymnosperms include the conifers, the cycads, and the ginkgo. *Compare* **angiosperm.**

gy•ne•col•o•gy (gī′nĭ-kŏl′ə-jē) The branch of medicine that deals with the female reproductive system, its diseases, and their treatment.

gyp•sum (jĭp′səm) A colorless, white, or pinkish mineral consisting of calcium sulfate. Gypsum occurs as individual blade-shaped crystals or as massive beds in sedimentary rocks. It is used in manufacturing plasterboard, cement, and fertilizers. It is the mineral used to represent a hardness of 2 on the Mohs scale.

gy•ro•scope (jī′rə-skōp′) An instrument consisting of a disk or wheel that spins rapidly about an axis like a top. The spinning motion keeps the axis fixed even if the base is turned in any direction, making the gyroscope an accurate navigational instrument and an effective stabilizing device in ships and airplanes.

H The symbol for **hydrogen.**

Ha•ber (hä′bər), **Fritz** 1868–1934. German chemist who was the first to produce ammonia synthetically, in 1908–1909.

hab•it (hăb′ĭt) **1.** The characteristic shape of a crystal: *the cubic habit of pyrite.* **2.** The characteristic manner of growth of a plant: *a low plant with a creeping habit.*

hab•i•tat (hăb′ĭ-tăt′) The area or natural environment in which an animal or plant normally lives, such as a desert, coral reef, or freshwater lake. A habitat can often be home to many different organisms.

hack•le (hăk′əl) **1.** One of the long, slender, often glossy feathers on the neck of a bird, especially a rooster. **2. hackles** The hairs along the back of the neck of an animal, especially a dog, that can stand out and bristle in displaying aggression or fear.

Ha•de•an Time (hā-dē′ən) The period of time between 4.6 and 3.8 billion years ago, when the solar system was forming and the Earth was solidifying. No rocks are known from this time, as they were probably eroded or drawn deep into the Earth and melted through the processes of plate tectonics. *See Chart at* **geologic time,** pages 148–149.

had•ro•saur (hăd′rə-sôr′) Any of various medium-sized to large plant-eating dinosaurs of the Cretaceous Period that had a duck-like bill, hoofed feet, and many series of rough grinding teeth. The hadrosaurs were the last group of ornithopod dinosaurs. Also called *duck-billed dinosaur.*

Haeck•el (hĕk′əl), **Ernst Heinrich** 1834–1919. German biologist who was one of the first scientists to publicly support Darwin's theory of evolution. His own ideas about evolution attracted popular attention, and though they were later disproved, they helped to stimulate biological research.

haf•ni•um (hăf′nē-əm) A bright, silvery metallic element that occurs in zirconium ores. Because hafnium absorbs neutrons better than any other metal and is resistant to corrosion, it is used to control nuclear reactions. *Symbol* **Hf.** *Atomic number* 72. *See* **Periodic Table,** pages 262–263.

hag•fish (hăg′fĭsh′) Any of various jawless fish that resemble eels and may be related to the lampreys. Hagfish have several hearts, glands that produce slime, and tentacles around the mouth. They do not have eyes, a backbone, or a stomach. Hagfish often feed on dead or dying fish by boring into them and eating them from the inside.

Hahn (hän), **Otto** 1879–1968. German chemist who investigated radioactive elements and helped discover several new ones. His work on uranium and thorium led to the discovery of nuclear fission.

hah•ni•um (hä′nē-əm) *An earlier name for* **dubnium.**

hail (hāl) Precipitation in the form of rounded pellets of ice and hard snow that usually falls during thunderstorms. Hail forms when raindrops are blown up and down within a cloud, passing repeatedly through layers of warm and freezing air and collecting layers of ice until they are too heavy for the winds to keep them from falling.

hair (hâr) **1.** One of the fine strands that grow from the skin of humans and other mammals.

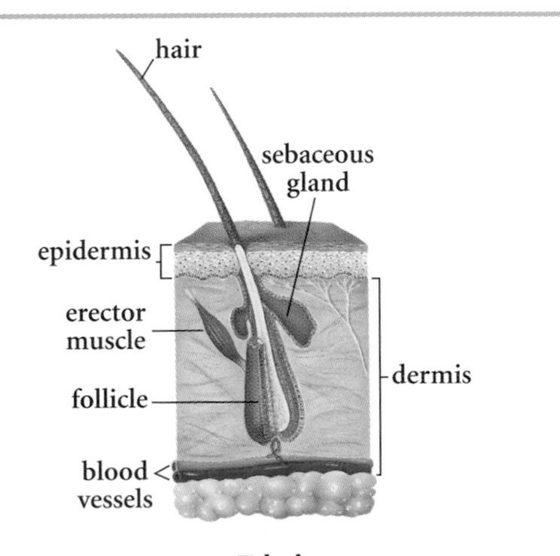

hair

Hair provides insulation against the cold in most mammals. Specialized hairs, such as porcupine quills, provide protection. **2.** A slender growth resembling a mammalian hair, found on insects and other animals. **3.** *Botany.* A fine, thread-like growth from the outer layer of plants.

half-life (hăf′līf′) The average time needed for half the nuclei in a sample of a radioactive substance to undergo radioactive decay. The half-life of a substance does not equal half of its full duration of radioactivity. For example, if one starts with 100 grams of radium 229, whose half-life is 4 minutes, then after 4 minutes only 50 grams of radium will be left in the sample, after 8 minutes 25 grams will be left, after 12 minutes 12.5 grams will be left, and so on.

hal•ide (hăl′īd′, hā′līd′) A chemical compound consisting of a halogen and another element, especially one such as sodium or potassium that readily shares electrons. Salt is a halide.

hal•ite (hăl′īt′, hā′līt′) A colorless or white mineral consisting of sodium chloride and occurring as cubic crystals. Halite is found in dried lakebeds in arid climates and is used as table salt.

Hal•ley (hăl′ē), **Edmund** 1656–1742. English astronomer who is best known for his study of comets. He accurately predicted that a comet observed in 1583 would return in 1758, 1835, and 1910. This comet is now named for him. Halley was also the first to catalog the stars in the Southern Hemisphere (1679).

Hal•ley's comet (hăl′ēz, hā′lēz) A comet that makes one complete orbit around the sun in approximately 76 years. It is visible to the unaided eye and last appeared in 1986.

hal•lu•cin•o•gen (hə-lo͞o′sə-nə-jən) A drug or chemical that causes a person to see, hear, or otherwise sense something that is not real.

■ **halite**

ha•lo (hā′lō) A hazy ring of colored light in the sky around the sun, the moon, or a similar bright object. It is caused by the reflection and refraction of light through ice crystals suspended in the upper atmosphere.

hal•o•gen (hăl′ə-jən) Any of a group of five nonmetallic elements with similar properties. The halogens are fluorine, chlorine, bromine, iodine, and astatine. Because they are missing an electron from their outermost shell, they react readily with most metals to form salts. The halogens are located in the column of the Periodic Table that is second from the right. *See* **Periodic Table,** pages 262–263.

hal•o•phyte (hăl′ə-fīt′) A plant adapted to living in salty soil, as along the seashore. The mangrove and grasses that grow in salt marshes are halophytes.

Hal•sted (hôl′stĕd′), **William Stewart** 1852–1922. American surgeon. In 1885 he discovered the technique of local anesthesia by injecting cocaine into specific nerves. He administered what is believed to be the first blood transfusion in the US in 1881. Halsted also developed important new surgical procedures and introduced the use of rubber gloves during surgery.

ham•string (hăm′strĭng′) A powerful group of muscles with strong tendons at the back of the thigh or hind leg.

hang•ing wall (hăng′ĭng) The block of rock lying above an inclined fault. *See more at* **fault.** *Compare* **footwall.**

hap•loid (hăp′loid′) Relating to or having a single set of each chromosome in a cell or cell nucleus. In animals, only the reproductive cells are haploid. *Compare* **diploid.** *See Note at* **mitosis.**

hard disk (härd) A rigid magnetic disk fixed within a disk drive and used for storing computer data. Hard disks hold more data than floppy disks, and data on a hard disk can be accessed faster than data on a floppy disk.

hard drive A disk drive that reads data stored on hard disks.

hard•ness (härd′nĭs) A measure of how easily a mineral can be scratched. Hardness is measured on the Mohs scale.

hard palate *See under* **palate.**

hard•ware (härd′wâr′) A computer, its components, and its related equipment. Hardware

BIOGRAPHY

William Harvey

In the second century A.D., the Greek physician Galen theorized that blood is created in the liver, passes once through the heart, and is then absorbed by bodily tissues. Galen's ideas went unchallenged until 1628, when William Harvey published a book describing the circulation of blood throughout the body. Through his observations of human and animal dissections, Harvey saw that blood flows from one side of the heart to the other and that it flows through the lungs and returns to the heart to be pumped elsewhere. There was one missing part of the cycle: How did the blood pumped to distant body tissues get into the veins to be carried back to the heart? As an answer, Harvey offered his own, unproven theory, one that has since been shown to be true: blood passes from small, outlying arteries through tiny vessels called capillaries into the outlying veins. Harvey's views were so controversial at the time that many of his patients left his care, but his work became the basis for all modern research on the heart and blood vessels.

includes disk drives, integrated circuits, display screens, cables, modems, speakers, and printers. *Compare* **software.**

hare (hâr) Any of various mammals similar to rabbits but having longer ears and legs and giving birth to active, furred young. Most hares are burrowing animals but do not make extensive warrens the way rabbits do.

Har•vey (här′vē), **William** 1578–1657. English physician and physiologist who was the first to demonstrate the function of the heart and the circulation of blood throughout the human body (1628).

has•si•um (hä′sē-əm) A synthetic, radioactive element that is produced by bombarding lead with iron ions. Its most stable isotope has a half-life of two milliseconds. *Symbol* **Hs.** *Atomic number* 108. *See* **Periodic Table,** pages 262–263.

hawk (hôk) Any of various birds of prey having a short hooked bill, broad wings, and strong claws for seizing prey. Hawks are usually smaller than eagles and larger than falcons.

Haw•king (hô′kĭng), **Stephen William** Born 1942. British physicist noted for his study of black holes and the origin of the universe, especially the big bang theory. His work has provided much of the mathematical basis for scientific explanations of the physical properties of black holes.

hay fever (hā) An allergic reaction to pollen that results in sneezing, itching, and watery eyes. Hay fever occurs during pollination season and can be caused by the pollens of many different plants, especially ragweed and certain trees and grasses.

haz•ard•ous waste (hăz′ər-dəs) A used or discarded material that can damage the environment and be harmful to health. Certain chemicals left over from industrial processes, and the radioactive remains of fuel used in nuclear power plants, are examples of hazardous waste.

He The symbol for **helium.**

heart (härt) **1.** The hollow, muscular organ that pumps blood through the body of a vertebrate animal by contracting and relaxing. In humans and other mammals, it has four chambers, consisting of two atria and two ventricles. The right side of the heart collects blood with low oxygen levels from the veins and pumps it to the lungs. The left side receives blood with high oxygen levels from the lungs and pumps it into the aorta, which carries it to all of the arteries of the body. The heart in other vertebrates functions similarly but often has fewer chambers. **2.** A similar but simpler organ in invertebrate animals.

heart attack A sudden interruption in the normal functioning of the heart that is often accompanied by severe pain. Heart attacks are usually caused by an insufficient supply of blood to part of the heart muscle resulting from blockage of a coronary artery.

heat (hēt) **1.** A form of energy produced by the motion of molecules. The heat of a substance is the total energy produced by the motion of its molecules. *See Note at* **temperature. 2.** *See* **estrus.**

heat exchanger A device used to transfer heat from one fluid to another without direct contact of the fluids. Heat exchangers contain a hot fluid that flows through one part of the exchanger and transfers its heat either to a cool fluid (water or air, for example) in another part or to the air outside of the exchanger. A car radiator is a heat exchanger, transferring the heat in a liquid that has circulated through the engine to the air.

heav•y hydrogen (hĕv′ē) *See* **deuterium.**

heavy water Water formed of oxygen and deuterium. Heavy water is much like ordinary water but has higher freezing and boiling points. It is used in certain nuclear reactors to help promote fission reactions and to prevent the reactor core from getting overheated.

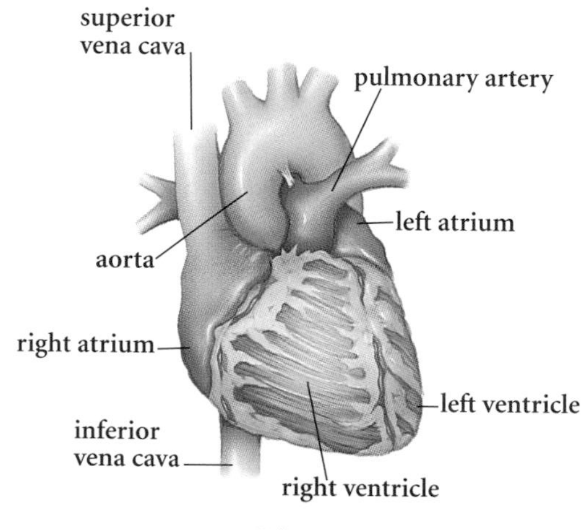

heart
adult human heart

Did You Know?
heavy water

How can one drop of water be heavier than another? The answer lies at the atomic level. Normal hydrogen has a nucleus consisting entirely of one proton, around which whirls one electron. However, in a variety of hydrogen called *heavy hydrogen* or *deuterium,* a neutron accompanies the proton in the nucleus. Deuterium thus weighs about twice as much as standard hydrogen. The substance we call *heavy water* is H_2O in which many of the hydrogen atoms are replaced by deuterium. Heavy water has many uses in nuclear energy. Most importantly, it tends to slow down neutrons that result from nuclear fission reactions without absorbing them. For this reason it is used in some nuclear power plants to encourage fission. When a fuel atom absorbs a neutron, it splits, releasing energy and more neutrons. But these neutrons move too fast to be absorbed by other fuel atoms. The heavy water slows the neutrons down so that they are more easily absorbed, adding to the chain reaction.

Hei•sen•berg (hī′zən-bûrg′), **Werner Karl** 1901–1976. German physicist who was a founder of quantum mechanics. He discovered the uncertainty principle, which states that the more accurately one knows the position of a particle such as an electron, the less accurately one can know its velocity, and the more accurately one knows a particle's velocity, the less accurately one can know its position. *See more at* **uncertainty principle.**

he•li•o•cen•tric (hē′lē-ō-sĕn′trĭk) **1.** In relation to the sun as seen from the sun's center: *the heliocentric position of a planet.* **2.** Relating to a model of the solar system or universe having the sun as the center. *Compare* **geocentric.** *See Note at* **Copernicus.**

he•li•ot•ro•pism (hē′lē-ŏt′rə-pĭz′əm) The growth or movement of a fixed organism, especially a plant, toward or away from sunlight.

—*Adjective* **heliotropic** (hēl′ē-ə-trō′pĭk, hēl′ē-ə-trŏp′ĭk).

he•li•um (hē′lē-əm) A very lightweight, colorless, odorless element that is a noble gas and occurs in natural gas, in radioactive ores, and in small amounts in the atmosphere. It has the lowest boiling point of any substance and is the second most abundant element in the universe. Helium is used to provide lift for balloons and blimps and to create artificial air that will not chemically react. *Symbol* **He.** *Atomic number* 2. *See* **Periodic Table,** pages 262–263.

he•lix (hē′lĭks) **1.** A three-dimensional spiral curve. In mathematical terms, a helix can be described as a curve turning about an axis on the surface of a cylinder or cone while rising at a constant upward angle from a base. **2.** Something, such as a strand of DNA, having a spiral shape.

Helm•holtz (hĕlm′hōlts′), **Hermann Ludwig Ferdinand von** 1821–1894. German physicist and physiologist. He was a founder of the law of conservation of energy. Helmholtz did pioneering research on vision and invented an instrument for examining the interior of the eye in 1851.

he•ma•tite (hē′mə-tīt′) A reddish-brown to silver-gray mineral consisting of iron oxide. Hematite occurs in igneous, metamorphic, and sedimentary rocks and is the most abundant iron ore. It is usually slightly magnetic.

he•ma•to•ma (hē′mə-tō′mə) The abnormal buildup of blood in an organ or other tissue of the body, caused by a break in a blood vessel. A bruise is a type of hematoma.

heliotropism *A houseplant bends toward the sunlight in the window.*

WORD HISTORY

helium

A lot of elements are named after the place they were first discovered—even if that place is 93 million miles away, as is the case with the element helium. In 1868 astronomers were studying a solar eclipse with a spectroscope, an instrument that breaks up light into a spectrum. When an element is heated hot enough to glow, the light emitted will produce a unique spectrum (pattern of lines) when refracted through a prism. The astronomers noticed that the spectrum of the sun's corona, which is only visible during an eclipse, contained some lines produced by an unknown element. The element was then named *helium,* from *helios,* the Greek word for "sun." We now know that helium is produced abundantly by the nuclear fusion in all stars, and is also found in smaller amounts on Earth. The Greek word *helios* gives us many other words pertaining to the sun, such as *heliocentric* and *perihelion.*

hemi– A prefix meaning "half," as in *hemisphere,* half a sphere.

hem•i•ple•gia (hĕm′ĭ-plē′jə) Paralysis of one side of the body, usually resulting from injury to the brain.

hem•i•sphere (hĕm′ĭ-sfîr′) **1.** One half of a sphere, formed by a plane that passes through the center of the sphere. **2.** Either the northern or southern half of the Earth as divided by the equator, or the eastern or western half as divided by a meridian. **3.** One half of the celestial sphere. **4.** *See* **cerebral hemisphere.**

hem•lock (hĕm′lŏk′) **1.** Any of various coniferous evergreen trees of North America and eastern Asia, having small cones and short, flat leaves with two white bands underneath. **2.** Any of several poisonous European plants that have small, white flowers.

hemo– A prefix meaning "blood," as in *hemophilia,* a disorder in which blood fails to clot.

he•mo•glo•bin (hē′mə-glō′bĭn) An iron-containing protein in the blood of many animals that, in vertebrates, carries oxygen from the lungs to the tissues of the body and carries carbon dioxide from the tissues to the lungs. Hemoglobin is contained in the red blood cells of vertebrates and gives these cells their characteristic color. Hemoglobin is also found in many invertebrates, where it circulates freely in the blood. *See Note at* **red blood cell.**

he•mo•phil•i•a (hē′mə-fĭl′ē-ə) An inherited disease in which the blood does not clot properly, causing excessive bleeding. Hemophilia usually only affects males.

hem•or•rhage (hĕm′ər-ĭj) Bleeding, especially in excessive amounts.

hen•ry (hĕn′rē) A unit used to measure electrical inductance. When a current varies at the rate of one ampere per second and induces an electromotive force of one volt, the circuit has an inductance of one henry.

Henry, Joseph 1797–1878. American physicist who studied electromagnetic phenomena. He constructed the first electromagnetic motor in 1829. The henry unit of inductance is named for him.

he•pat•ic (hĭ-păt′ĭk) Relating to the liver.

hep•a•ti•tis (hĕp′ə-tī′tĭs) Inflammation of the liver, usually caused by infection with a virus. It is characterized by jaundice, fever, and weakness throughout the body.

hep•ta•gon (hĕp′tə-gŏn′) A polygon having seven sides.

her•bi•cide (hûr′bĭ-sīd′, ûr′bĭ-sīd′) A chemical used to kill weeds. *Compare* **fungicide, insecticide, pesticide.**

her•bi•vore (hûr′bə-vôr′, ûr′bə-vôr′) An animal that feeds mainly or only on plants. *Compare* **carnivore.** —*Adjective* **herbivorous.**

Her•cu•les (hûr′kyə-lēz′) A constellation in the Northern Hemisphere near Lyra and Corona Borealis.

he•red•i•tar•y (hə-rĕd′ĭ-tĕr′ē) Passed or capable of being passed from parent to offspring by means of genes: *a hereditary trait.*

he•red•i•ty (hə-rĕd′ĭ-tē) The passage of biological traits or characteristics from parents to offspring through the inheritance of genes.

USAGE

heritable/congenital

The words *heritable* and *congenital* are often confused when used in describing medical conditions or diseases. A heritable disease is one that results from a variation or defect in the genetic makeup of an individual. Because of their genetic nature, heritable diseases, such as hemophilia, can be passed from one generation to the next. In this regard the diseases are no different from other genetic traits. A congenital disease is simply one that appears at birth (*congenital* comes from Latin *com–*, meaning "together," and *genitus,* meaning "born"). Congenital diseases may be heritable ones, but they may also result from some factor, such as a drug, infection, or injury, that has upset the careful timing and balance of the developmental process in the uterus.

her•i•ta•ble (hĕr′ĭ-tə-bəl) Capable of being passed from one generation to the next through the genes; hereditary.

her•maph•ro•dite (hər-măf′rə-dīt′) An organism, such as an earthworm or flowering plant, having both male and female reproductive organs in a single individual.

her•ni•a (hûr′nē-ə) A condition in which an organ or other structure of the body protrudes through an abnormal opening in the body structure that normally contains it.

He•ro (hē′rō) First century A.D. Greek mathematician who invented many water-driven and steam-driven machines and developed a formula for determining the area of a triangle.

her•pes (hûr′pēz) Any of several infections caused by a virus, characterized by the eruption of painful blisters on the skin or a mucous membrane.

her•pe•tol•o•gy (hûr′pĭ-tŏl′ə-jē) The scientific study of reptiles and amphibians.

Her•schel (hûr′shəl) Family of British astronomers. Sir **William Herschel** (1738–1822) discovered Uranus (1781) and cataloged more

BIOGRAPHY

William and Caroline Herschel

Both William and Caroline Herschel began their professional careers as musicians. They were born in Germany and later moved to England, where Caroline became a soprano soloist in performances conducted by her brother. William's background in music theory spurred him to study mathematics and astronomy, and he taught his sister in turn. Each produced a string of important discoveries. William was the first astronomer to study binary stars. His careful observations and his skill at mapping the stars led him to discover the planet Uranus in 1781. It was the first new planet to be discovered since ancient times. He further discovered two satellites of Uranus, Titania and Oberon (1787), and two of Saturn, Mimas and Enceladus (1789–1790). King George III appointed William his Astronomer Royal in 1787, and Caroline was made his assistant. Caroline observed her first comet in 1786 and later discovered seven others, as well as nebulae and star clusters. After her brother's death in 1822, Caroline reorganized and published his catalog of nebulae. She also continued her own observations up to the end of her life.

than 800 binary stars and 2,500 nebulae. His sister **Caroline Herschel** (1750– 1848) discovered 8 comets and several nebulae and star clusters, and published a star catalog in 1798. His son Sir **John Frederick William Herschel** (1792–1871) discovered 525 nebulae and pioneered celestial photography. *See Note at* **infrared.**

hertz (hûrts) A unit used to measure the frequency of vibrations and waves. One hertz is equal to one cycle per second. Radio waves are usually measured in megahertz, or millions of hertz.

Hertz•sprung-Rus•sell diagram (hĕrts′sprŏŏng-rŭs′əl) A graph of the natural brightness of stars plotted against their surface temperature or color. It is used in the study of the life cycles of stars.

Hess (hĕs), **Harry Hammond** 1906–1969. American geologist who studied the sea floor and developed the theory of sea-floor spreading. He theorized that sea floors were constantly renewed by the flow of magma from the Earth's mantle through the oceanic rifts. Hess's hypothesis became an important component of the theory of plate tectonics.

het•er•o•troph•ic (hĕt′ər-ə-trŏf′ĭk) Relating to an organism that cannot manufacture its own food and instead obtains its food and energy by taking in organic substances, usually plant or animal matter. All animals, protozoans, fungi, and most bacteria are heterotrophic. ❖ An organism that consumes organic matter or other organisms for food is called a **heterotroph** (hĕt′ər-ə-trŏf′). *Compare* **autotrophic.**

het•er•o•zy•gous (hĕt′ər-ə-zī′gəs) Having a contrasting pair of genes, as for tallness and shortness, at corresponding positions on the chromosomes of an organism. *Compare* **homozygous.**

Hew•ish (hyōō′ĭsh), **Antony** Born 1924. British astronomer. In 1967, working with the astronomer Susan Bell Burnell, he discovered the first pulsar.

hex•a•gon (hĕk′sə-gŏn′) A polygon having six sides.

hex•ag•o•nal (hĕk-săg′ə-nəl) **1.** Having six sides. **2.** Relating to a crystal having three axes of equal length intersecting at angles of 60° in one plane, and a fourth axis of a different length that is perpendicular to this plane. The mineral calcite has hexagonal crystals. *See more at* **crystal.**

Hf The symbol for **hafnium.**

Hg The symbol for **mercury.**

hi•ber•na•tion (hī′bər-nā′shən) An inactive state resembling deep sleep in which certain animals living in cold climates pass the winter. In hibernation, the body temperature is lowered and breathing and heart rates slow down. Hibernation protects the animal from cold and reduces the need for food during the season when food is scarce. *Compare* **estivation.**

hic•cup (hĭk′əp) A sudden and uncontrolled contraction of the diaphragm, causing the breath to be quickly drawn in and then immediately cut off by a closing of the throat.

high blood pressure (hī) A condition in which the pressure of the blood, especially in the arteries, is abnormally high. High blood pressure can increase the risk of heart attack or stroke. Also called *hypertension.*

high-tension Having a high voltage: *high-tension wires.*

high tide The time at which the tide reaches its highest level.

hi•lum (hī′ləm) A mark or scar on a seed, such as a bean, showing where it was formerly attached to the plant.

hind•brain (hīnd′brān′) The rearmost part of the brain in vertebrate animals. In humans, it consists of the pons and the medulla oblongata. *Compare* **forebrain, midbrain.**

hip•bone (hĭp′bōn′) Either of two large, flat bones, each forming one of the outer borders of the pelvis and consisting of the fused ilium, ischium, and pubis.

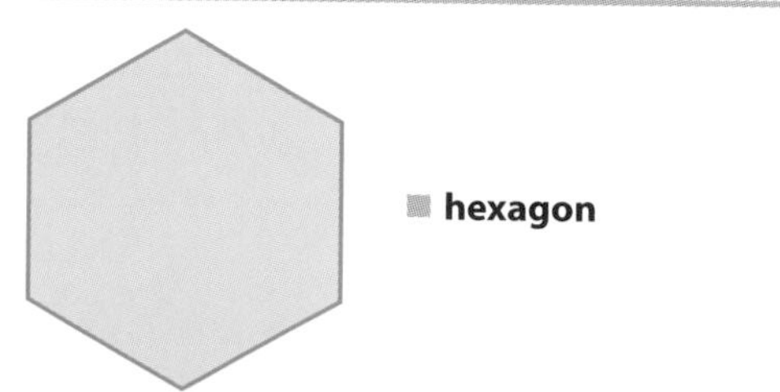

hexagon

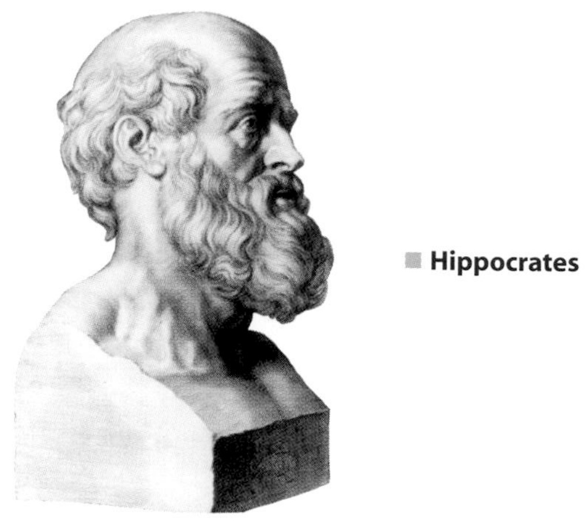

Hippocrates

Hip•par•chus (hĭ-pär′kəs) Second century B.C. Greek astronomer who mapped the position of 850 stars in the earliest known star chart. His observations of the heavens formed the basis of Ptolemy's Earth-centered model of the universe.

Hip•poc•ra•tes (hĭ-pŏk′rə-tēz′) 460?–377? B.C. Greek physician who is credited with establishing the foundations of scientific medicine. He and his followers worked to distinguish medicine from superstition and magic beliefs by basing their treatment of illness on close observation and rational deduction.

hip•po•pot•a•mus (hĭp′ə-pŏt′ə-məs) A large, chiefly aquatic African mammal having a barrel-shaped body, thick skin, short legs, and a wide-mouthed muzzle. Because its skin loses water quickly when exposed to the air, the hippopotamus must spend the day in water. It feeds at night on land grasses. *See Note at* **rhinoceros.**

his•ta•mine (hĭs′tə-mēn′) An organic compound found widely in animals and plants. In humans and other mammals, histamine is released as part of the body's immune response, causing a variety of changes in the body including enlargement of the blood vessels, tightening of the airways, and faster beating of the heart. The itchiness and sneezing typical of an allergic reaction are caused by the release of histamine.

his•ti•dine (hĭs′tĭ-dēn′) An essential amino acid. *See more at* **amino acid.**

his•tol•o•gy (hĭ-stŏl′ə-jē) The scientific study of the microscopic structure of plant and animal tissues.

his•tone (hĭs′tōn′) Any of several proteins that, together with DNA, make up most of the chromatin in a cell nucleus.

HIV (āch′ī-vē′) Short for *human immunodeficiency virus.* The virus that causes AIDS by infecting the body's immune system.

hive (hīv) **1.** A structure for housing bees, especially honeybees. **2.** A colony of bees living in such a structure.

hives (hīvz) Itchy welts on the skin that are redder or paler than the surrounding skin. Hives may result from an allergic reaction, but often the cause is unknown.

Ho The symbol for **holmium.**

Hodg•kin (hŏj′kĭn), **Dorothy Mary Crowfoot** 1910–1994. British chemist. Using x-ray techniques, she determined the structure of several complex molecules, including penicillin and vitamin B_{12}.

Holmes (hōmz, hōlmz), **Arthur** 1890–1965. British geologist who pioneered a method of determining the age of rocks by measuring their radioactive components.

hol•mi•um (hōl′mē-əm) A soft, silvery, easily shaped metallic element of the lanthanide series. When exposed to a magnetic field, holmium becomes highly magnetic. It is mainly used in scientific research but has also been used to make electronic devices. *Symbol* **Ho.** *Atomic number* 67. *See* **Periodic Table,** pages 262–263.

Hol•o•cene (hŏl′ə-sēn′, hō′lə-sēn′) The more recent of the two epochs of the Quaternary Period, beginning at the end of the last Ice Age, about 10,000 years ago. It is characterized by the development of human civilizations. Also called *Recent. See Chart at* **geologic time,** pages 148–149.

hive

Did You Know?
hologram

If you tear an ordinary photograph in two, each piece shows only a part of the original image. If you break a *hologram* in two, however, you end up with two holograms, each of which shows the entire original scene, although from slightly different points of view. That's because each spot on a hologram contains enough information to show how the entire scene would look if it were viewed from a particular vantage point. Imagine looking at a room through a peephole set in a solid door. What you see depends on where in the door the peephole is placed. Each piece of the hologram is a "peephole" view, and that's what makes the image look three-dimensional: as you move the hologram around or look at different parts of it, you see the original object from different angles, just as if it were a truly three-dimensional object and you were walking around it. The amount of information contained in holograms makes them very useful. They are much harder to copy than simple two-dimensional images, since to forge a hologram you'd have to know what the original object looked like from many angles. That's why credit cards, CDs, and other items include holographic stickers as indicators of authenticity.

hol•o•gram (hŏl′ə-grăm′, hō′lə-grăm′) A three-dimensional image of an object made by holography.

ho•log•raph•y (hō-lŏg′rə-fē) A method of making a three-dimensional image of an object by using a divided beam of light from a laser. The laser light is directed by mirrors so that one beam reflects off the object onto a photographic plate or film while the other beam is aimed directly at

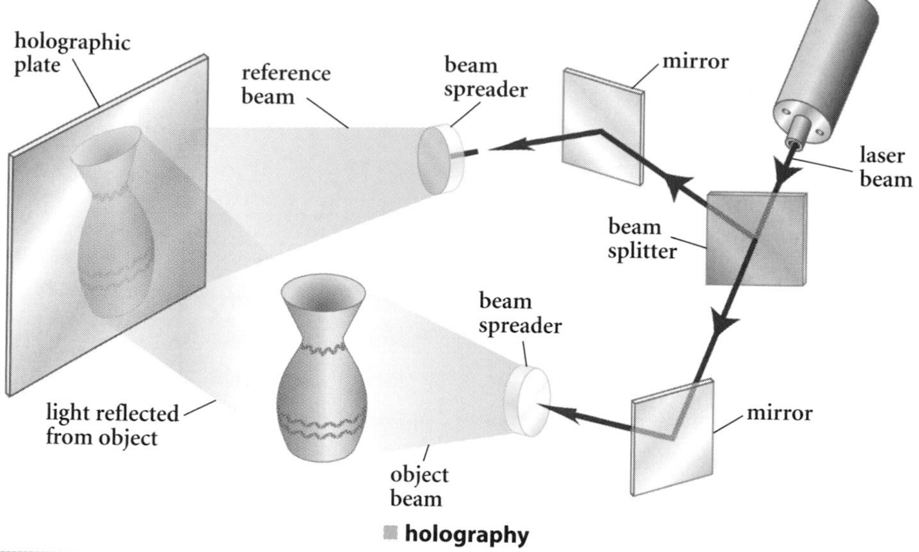

■ **holography**

the plate or film. The two beams are combined to form a three-dimensional image of the object.

ho•me•op•a•thy (hō′mē-ŏp′ə-thē) A system for treating disease in which patients are given tiny doses of a drug that, when given in large amounts to healthy people, produces symptoms like those of the disease itself. Homeopathy is a kind of alternative medicine.

ho•me•o•sta•sis (hō′mē-ō-stā′sĭs) The tendency of an organism or cell to regulate the chemical processes that take place internally so as to maintain health and functioning, regardless of outside conditions. The ability to maintain a steady body temperature is an example of homeostasis.

hom•i•nid (hŏm′ə-nĭd) A member of the family of primates whose only living members are modern humans. All earlier hominids, such as australopithecines and members of the species *Homo erectus,* are now extinct.

Ho•mo e•rec•tus (hō′mō ĭ-rĕk′təs) An extinct species of humans that lived during the Pleistocene Epoch from about 1.6 million years ago to 250,000 years ago. *Homo erectus* was the first species of humans to master fire, and its remains have been found in Africa, Europe, and Asia. It is widely thought to be the direct ancestor of modern humans.

Homo hab•i•lis (hăb′ə-ləs) An extinct species of humans considered to be an ancestor of modern humans and the earliest hominid to make tools. This species existed between about 2.0 and 1.5 million years ago.

ho•mol•o•gous (hə-mŏl′ə-gəs) **1.** Similar in structure and evolutionary origin but having different functions, as a human's arm and a seal's flipper. *Compare* **analogous. 2.** Being a set of two pairs of chromosomes, one pair from the female parent and one from the male parent, having genes for the same trait in the same positions. Genes on homologous chromosomes may not have the same form, however. For example, one set of homologous chromosomes may contain a gene for brown eyes and the other for blue eyes.

ho•mol•o•sine projection (hō-mŏl′ə-sīn′) A method of making a flat map of the Earth's surface with interruptions in the oceans so that the continents appear with the most accurate area and shape possible. *Compare* **conic projection, Mercator projection, sinusoidal projection.**

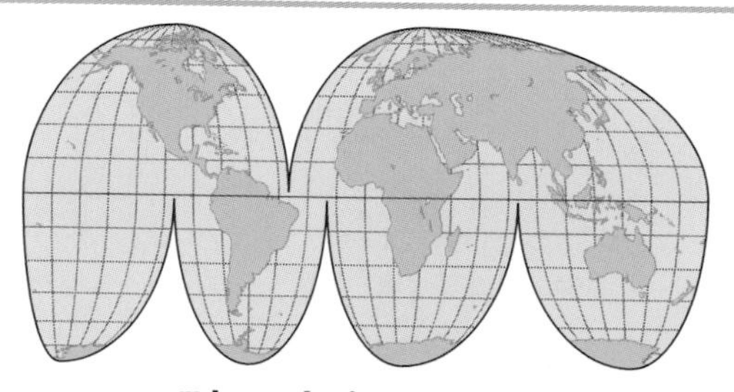

■ **homolosine projection**

Grace Hopper

Homo sa•pi•ens (sā′pē-ənz) The modern species of humans. *Homo sapiens* evolved probably between 250,000 and 100,000 years ago in Africa. The closest living relative of *Homo sapiens* is the chimpanzee.

ho•mo•zy•gous (hō′mō-zī′gəs) Having two like genes for a hereditary trait such as tallness at corresponding positions on the chromosomes. *Compare* **heterozygous.**

Hooke (ho͝ok), **Robert** 1635–1703. English physicist, inventor, and mathematician. With Robert Boyle, Hooke demonstrated that both combustion and respiration require air and that sound will not travel in a vacuum. He studied numerous objects under microscopes and was the first to use the word *cell* to describe the patterns he observed.

Hooke's law A law in physics stating that the extent to which an elastic material will change size and shape under stress is directly proportional to the amount of stress applied to it. If a spring is stretched to a length of 6 inches (15.2 centimeters) by a force of 1 newton, for example, it will be stretched to a length of 12 inches (30.4 centimeters) by a force of 2 newtons.

hook•worm (ho͝ok′wûrm′) Any of numerous parasitic worms that have a hooked mouthpart by which they fasten themselves to the inside wall of the intestines of various animals, including humans.

Hop•per (hŏp′ər), **Grace Murray** 1906–1992. American mathematician and computer programmer who is noted for her development of programming languages.

ho•ri•zon (hə-rī′zən) The circle on the celestial sphere along which the Earth and the sky appear to meet.

Did You Know?

hormones

On the inside, humans are bathing in a sea of *hormones,* chemical compounds that regulate many essential activities in the body. A lot of hormones are produced in glands known as *endocrine glands,* such as the thyroid gland, pancreas, and ovaries, and travel from there through the bloodstream before arriving at their target sites of action. Specialized cells of the nervous system also produce hormones. Hormones are not found only in humans, but also in all other animals and plants. The variety of different functions hormones have is astounding. Insulin, secreted by the pancreas, regulates the absorption of sugars in the body. Thyroid hormones regulate the rate of cell metabolism and affect many other processes, including reproduction. Growth hormone, secreted by the pituitary gland, controls growth of the body. Estrogen and testosterone control sexual development. Some of the hormones released in the brain, known as *endorphins,* act as natural painkillers. When the amounts of these or other hormones are abnormal, disease can result. Too little insulin causes diabetes, too little estrogen weakens the bones of older women, and too much growth hormone causes people to grow without stopping. Fortunately, these diseases can usually be treated, either with hormones made artificially in laboratories or by operating on the affected gland.

hor•mone (hôr′mōn′) A substance produced in one part of the body, especially in an endocrine gland, that has an effect on another part of the body, to which it is usually carried in the bloodstream. Hormones regulate many biological processes, including growth and metabolism.

horn (hôrn) **1.** Either of the bony growths projecting from the upper part of the head of certain hoofed mammals, such as cattle, sheep, and goats. The horns of these animals are never shed, and they consist of bone covered by a hard substance called keratin. **2.** A hard growth that looks like a horn, such as an antler or a growth on the head of a giraffe or rhinoceros. Unlike true horns, antlers are shed yearly and have a velvety covering, and the horns of a rhinoceros are made not of bone but of hairy skin fused with keratin. **3.** The hard durable substance that forms the outer covering of true horns. It consists of keratin. *See Note at* **keratin.**

horn•blende (hôrn′blĕnd′) A common, green to black mineral found in many metamorphic and igneous rocks. It is composed of iron, calcium, magnesium, and other metals.

ho•rol•o•gy (hô-rŏl′ə-jē) The science of measuring time.

horse (hôrs) **1.** A large hoofed mammal having a short-haired coat, a long mane, and a long tail. Horses have been domesticated for riding and for drawing or carrying loads since ancient times. Because they have a single broad hoof on each foot, horses run not on entire feet but on single toes. **2.** Any living or extinct equine mammal.

horse latitudes Either of two regions of the globe found over the oceans about 30 degrees north and south of the equator. Because winds are generally light and unsteady in the horse latitudes, sailing ships were often caught in them for days without enough wind to move.

horse•pow•er (hôrs′pou′ər) A unit used to measure the power of engines and motors. One unit of horsepower is equal to the power needed to lift 550 pounds one foot in one second. This unit has been widely replaced by the *watt* in scientific usage.

horse•shoe crab (hôrs′sho͞o′) Any of various marine arthropods that have a large rounded shell that covers the body, two large compound eyes on the shell, and a stiff pointed tail. Horseshoe crabs are not in fact crabs, but belong to an ancient order of arthropods related to the spiders and extinct trilobites.

hor•ti•cul•ture (hôr′tĭ-kŭl′chər) The science or art of raising and tending plants, especially flowers, fruits, and vegetables.

host (hōst) A cell or organism, such as a plant, animal, or alga, on or in which another organism lives or feeds. For example, a cat may be a host to fleas that feed on its blood, or a cell in the human respiratory tract may be a host to a flu virus.

hot spot (hŏt) A volcanic area, usually 60 to 120 miles (97 to 193 kilometers) across, believed to lie above a rising plume of hot magma within the Earth. The source of the heat is thought to be the decay of radioactive elements deep within the Earth. The Hawaiian Islands are believed to have formed as the result of a tectonic plate moving over a hot spot. *See more at* **tectonic boundary.**

hot spring A spring of warm water, usually having a temperature greater than that of the human body.

Hs The symbol for **hassium.**

Hub•ble (hŭb′əl), **Edwin Powell** 1889–1953. American astronomer. He demonstrated that there are galaxies beyond our own and that they are receding from ours, bolstering the theory that the universe is expanding. Hubble also established the first measurements for the age

WORD HISTORY

humor

Doctors in ancient times and in the Middle Ages thought the human body contained a mixture of four substances, called humors, that determined a person's health and character. The humors were fluids (*humor* means "fluid" in Latin), namely blood, phlegm, black bile, and yellow bile. Illnesses were thought to be caused by an imbalance in the humors, as were defects in personality. Too much black bile, for example, was thought to make one gloomy, and too much yellow bile was thought to make one short-tempered. Modern English has words referring to these moods that come from the Greek words for the relevant humors. We call a gloomy person *melancholic,* from the Greek term for "black bile," and we call a short-tempered person *choleric,* from the Greek word for "yellow bile." Our word *humorous,* in fact, originally meant "having changeable moods due to the influence of different humors."

and radius of the known universe. His methods for determining them remain in use today. *See Note at* **Doppler effect.**

hue (hyo͞o) The property of colors by which they are seen as ranging from red through yellow, green, and blue, as determined by the dominant wavelength of the light. *See more at* **color.**

hull (hŭl) **1.** The dry outer covering of a fruit, seed, or nut; a husk. **2.** The enlarged calyx of a fruit, such as a strawberry, that is usually green and easily detached.

hu•man (hyo͞o′mən) **1.** A member of the species *Homo sapiens;* a human being. **2.** A member of any of the extinct species of the genus *Homo,* such as *Homo erectus* or *Homo habilis,* that are considered ancestral or closely related to modern humans.

Human Genome Project A scientific research project designed to study and identify all of the genes in the human genome, to determine the base-pair sequences in human DNA, and to store this information in computer databases. The Human Genome Project began in the United States in 1990.

Hum•boldt (hŭm′bōlt′), Baron **(Friedrich Heinrich) Alexander von** 1769–1859. German naturalist and writer. He undertook scientific expeditions in South America, Asia, and Europe and published works recording his observations. Humboldt made important contributions to the study of volcanoes, mountain ranges, ocean currents, and the relation of climate to plant growth.

hu•mer•us (hyo͞o′mər-əs) The bone of the upper arm or the upper portion of the foreleg. *See more at* **skeleton.**

hu•mid•i•ty (hyo͞o-mĭd′ĭ-tē) *See* **absolute humidity, relative humidity.**

hu•mor (hyo͞o′mər) One of the four fluids of the body—blood, phlegm, black bile, and yellow bile—whose relative proportions were thought in ancient and medieval medicine to determine general health and character.

hu•mus (hyo͞o′məs) A dark-brown or black organic substance made up of decayed plant or animal matter. Humus provides nutrients for plants and increases the ability of soil to retain water.

hur•ri•cane (hûr′ĭ-kān′) A severe, rotating tropical storm with heavy rains and cyclonic winds exceeding 74 miles (119 kilometers) per hour. Hurricanes originate in the tropical parts of the Atlantic Ocean or the Caribbean Sea and move generally northward. They lose force when they move over land or colder ocean waters. *See Note at* **cyclone.**

hus•band•ry (hŭz′bən-drē) The application of scientific principles to agriculture, especially to animal breeding.

husk (hŭsk) The dry outer covering of certain seeds or fruits, as of an ear of corn or a nut.

Hut•ton (hŭt′n), **James** 1726–1797. Scottish geologist whose theories of rock and land formation laid the foundation for modern geology. He showed that, over long periods of time, the erosion of rocks produces sediments, which are transported by water, ice and air to locations at or near sea level. These sediments eventually become solidified into other rocks. He also showed that the Earth's heat causes igneous rocks to form and mountains to form through the

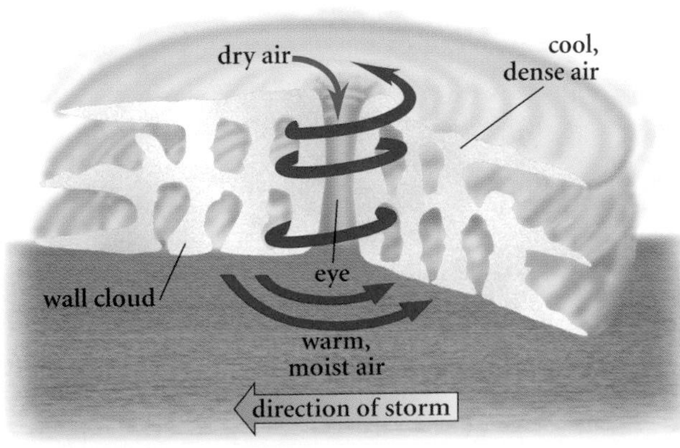

hurricane
A hurricane forms when clusters of thunderstorms converge over warm water. Warm, moist air is drawn up into the clouds, creating tunnels as the air rises. The strongest winds and heaviest rains center around the eye of the storm, while the eye itself remains calm.

BIOGRAPHY

James Hutton

As a gentleman farmer in late 18th-century Scotland, James Hutton noticed that farmers' soil is carried away, ultimately to the oceans, by the wind and rain. Hutton was a religious man, and he imagined that a God who was benevolent would create a way to recreate this lost soil. He theorized that the soil must be replaced when older rocks are pushed upward, forming new mountains, which are then eroded by the weather into soil. Hutton proposed heat as the source of this mountain-building: as it built up inside the Earth, it forced rocks to move upward and created newer rocks from lava. He called this process Plutonism, in honor of Pluto, the Greek god of the underworld. Because the cycle of uplift and erosion had to take a very long time, Hutton concluded the Earth must be very old. It was not until the 20th century that geologists, using a technique called radiometric dating, demonstrated that the Earth is in fact over four billion years old. Because of his groundbreaking insights, Hutton is known as the father of geology.

upheaval of rock layers. Hutton demonstrated that the geological processes that created the landforms on the Earth are ongoing.

Huy•gens (hī′gənz, hoi′gĕns), **Christiaan** 1629–1695. Dutch physicist and astronomer. In 1655 he discovered Saturn's rings and its fourth satellite, using a telescope he made himself. He made the first pendulum clock in 1657. Huygens also proposed that light consists of waves that vibrate up and down perpendicular to the direction in which it travels. This theory, which explained light better than Newton's theory, was made public in 1690.

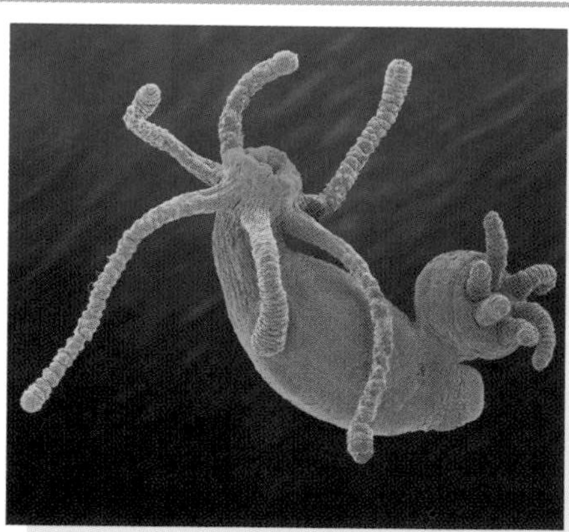

hydra

A hydra photographed through a microscope. On the right, an immature hydra can be seen budding from the parent.

hy•brid (hī′brĭd) A plant or animal that has parents of different species or varieties. A mule, which is the offspring of a male donkey and a female horse, is an example of a hybrid. Hybrid animals are usually unable to reproduce.

hy•dra (hī′drə) Any of several small freshwater polyps having a simple cylindrical body with a mouth-like opening surrounded by tentacles. The young develop from eggs or from buds.

hy•drate (hī′drāt′) *Noun.* **1.** A compound produced by combining a substance chemically with water. Many minerals and crystalline substances are hydrates. —*Verb.* **2.** To combine a compound with water, especially to form a hydrate. **3.** To supply water to a person in order to restore or maintain a balance of fluids.

hy•drau•lic (hī-drô′lĭk) **1.** Operated by the pressure of water or other liquids in motion, especially when forced through an opening: *a hy-*

draulic brake; a hydraulic jack. **2.** Relating to hydraulics. **3.** Capable of hardening under water: *hydraulic cement.*

hy•drau•lics (hī-drô′lĭks) The scientific study of water and other liquids, their uses in engineering, and the forces and pressures associated with them.

hy•dride (hī′drīd′) A compound of hydrogen with another element or radical.

hydro– A prefix that means: **1.** Water, as in *hydroelectric.* **2.** Hydrogen, as in *hydrocarbon.*

hy•dro•car•bon (hī′drə-kär′bən) Any of numerous organic compounds, such as benzene, that contain only carbon and hydrogen.

hy•dro•chlo•ric acid (hī′drə-klôr′ĭk) A solution of hydrogen chloride in water. It is a very strong, poisonous, and corrosive acid with a sharp odor and is used in food processing, metal cleaning, and dyeing. Small amounts of hydrochloric acid are also secreted by the stomachs of animals for digestion.

hy•dro•chlo•ride (hī′drə-klôr′īd′) A salt containing the group HCl.

hy•dro•dy•nam•ics (hī′drō-dī-năm′ĭks) The scientific study of the forces exerted by fluids in motion.

hy•dro•e•lec•tric (hī′drō-ĭ-lĕk′trĭk) Generating electricity through the use of the energy of running water: *a hydroelectric power station.*

hy•dro•gen (hī′drə-jən) A colorless, odorless, highly flammable gaseous element that is the lightest and most abundant element in the universe. It occurs in water in combination with oxygen, in most organic compounds, and in small amounts in the atmosphere as a gaseous mixture of its three isotopes (protium, deuterium, and tritium). In the sun and other stars, the conversion of hydrogen into helium by nuclear fusion produces heat and light. Hydrogen is used to make rocket fuel, synthetic ammonia, and methanol, to hydrogenate fats and oils, and to refine petroleum. *Symbol* **H.** *Atomic number* 1. *See* **Periodic Table,** pages 262–263. *See Note at* **oxygen.**

hy•dro•gen•ate (hī′drə-jə-nāt′, hī-drŏj′ə-nāt′) To treat or combine chemically with hydrogen. Liquid vegetable oils are often hydrogenated to turn them into solids.

hydrogen bomb An extremely destructive bomb whose explosive power is derived from the energy released when hydrogen atoms are fused to form helium. A hydrogen bomb uses an atomic bomb to compress the hydrogen atoms and is much more powerful than an atomic bomb.

hydrogen bond A chemical bond in which a hydrogen atom that is already bonded to an atom in a molecule forms a second bond with another

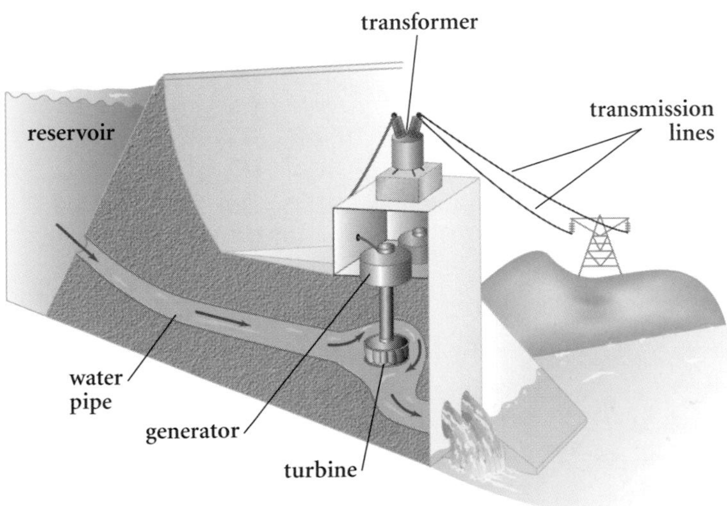

hydroelectric

Hydroelectric power uses the force of moving water to turn turbines. The turbines drive generators that convert the mechanical energy of moving water to electrical energy. Electricity is then changed by a transformer to the appropriate voltage and sent along transmission lines to consumers.

atom, either in the same molecule or in a different one. The second atom is usually of a type that strongly attracts electrons, such as nitrogen or oxygen.

hydrogen chloride A colorless, corrosive, suffocating gas, HCl, used in making plastics and in many industrial processes. When mixed with water, it forms hydrochloric acid.

hydrogen cyanide A colorless, flammable, extremely poisonous liquid, HCN. It is used to make dyes, poisons, and plastics. A solution of hydrogen cyanide in water forms a colorless acid that has a characteristic smell of bitter almonds.

hydrogen peroxide A colorless, dense liquid, H_2O_2, that is often used as a bleach or is diluted with water for use as an antiseptic.

hydrogen sulfide A colorless, poisonous gas, H_2S, that smells like rotten eggs. It is formed naturally by decaying organic matter and is found in volcanic gases. It has many industrial uses.

hy•dro•log•ic cycle (hī-drə-lŏj**′**ĭk) *See* **water cycle.**

hy•drol•o•gy (hī-drŏl**′**ə-jē) The scientific study of the properties, distribution, and effects of water on the Earth's surface, in the soil and underlying rocks, and in the atmosphere. —*Adjective* **hydrologic** (hī′drə-lŏj**′**ĭk).

hy•drol•y•sis (hī-drŏl**′**ĭ-sĭs) The splitting of a chemical compound into two or more new compounds by reacting with water. Hydrolysis plays a role in the breakdown of food in the body, as in the conversion of starch to glucose.

hy•drom•e•ter (hī-drŏm**′**ĭ-tər) An instrument used to measure the density of a liquid as compared to that of water. Hydrometers consist of a calibrated glass tube ending in a weighted glass sphere that makes the tube stand upright. The lower the density of the liquid, the deeper the tube sinks.

hy•dro•pho•bi•a (hī′drə-fō**′**bē-ə) *See* **rabies.**

hy•dro•phyte (hī**′**drə-fīt′) A plant that grows wholly or partly submerged in water. The lotus, water lily, and cattail are hydrophytes.

hy•dro•pon•ics (hī′drə-pŏn**′**ĭks) The growing of plants in water supplied with nutrients rather than in soil.

hy•dro•sphere (hī**′**drə-sfîr′) All of the Earth's water, including surface water (water in oceans, lakes, and rivers), groundwater (water beneath the Earth's surface), ice, and water vapor in the atmosphere. *Compare* **asthenosphere, atmosphere, lithosphere.**

hy•dro•stat•ics (hī′drə-stăt**′**ĭks) The branch of physics that deals with the study of fluids at rest and the forces and pressures associated with them.

hy•dro•ther•mal (hī′drə-thûr**′**məl) **1.** Relating to hot water, especially water heated by the Earth's internal heat. ❖ Power that is generated using the Earth's hot water is called **hydrothermal energy. 2.** *Geology.* Relating to the rocks, ore deposits, and springs produced by hot water or magma.

hy•drot•ro•pism (hī-drŏt**′**rə-pĭz′əm) The growth or movement of a fixed organism, especially a plant, toward or away from water. —*Adjective* **hydrotropic** (hī′drə-trō**′**pĭk, hī′drə-trŏp**′**ĭk).

hy•drous (hī**′**drəs) *Chemistry.* Containing water: *a hydrous salt.*

hy•drox•ide (hī-drŏk**′**sīd′) An inorganic chemical compound containing a hydroxyl radical, OH. Metal hydroxides are bases and nonmetal hydroxides are acids.

hy•drox•yl (hī-drŏk**′**sĭl) The group OH. It has a valence of 1 and is present in bases, certain acids, hydroxides, and alcohols.

hy•e•na (hī-ē**′**nə) Any of several meat-eating, dog-like mammals of Africa and Asia that feed mainly in groups as scavengers. Hyenas have very

WORD HISTORY

hydrophobia

Hydrophobia is an older term for the disease rabies, and it means "fear of water." Because of this name, many people think that rabies makes one afraid of water. In fact, this is not the case (although rabies does cause mental confusion of other kinds). The name hydrophobia comes from the fact that animals and people with rabies get spasms in their throat muscles that are so painful that they cannot eat or drink, and so will refuse water in spite of being very thirsty.

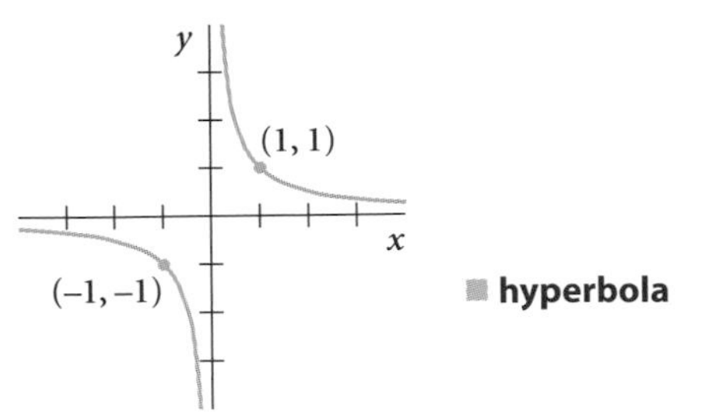

■ hyperbola

powerful jaws, a thick neck, and relatively short hind limbs.

hy•grom•e•ter (hī-grŏm′ĭ-tər) An instrument that measures the humidity of the air.

hy•gro•scope (hī′grə-skōp′) An instrument that records changes in the humidity of the air.

hy•men (hī′mən) A membrane that partly closes the opening of the vagina.

Hy•pa•tia (hī-pā′shə) A.D. 370?–415. Greek philosopher, mathematician, and astronomer whose writings on mathematics and astronomy were used as textbooks. She also invented instruments used to view the stars.

hyper– A prefix that means "excessively," as in *hypertension,* excessively high blood pressure.

hy•per•ac•tiv•i•ty (hī′pər-ăk-tĭv′ĭ-tē) **1.** A condition of greater than normal activity. **2.** An abnormally high level of activity or excitement shown by a person, especially a child, that interferes with the ability to concentrate or interact with others.

hy•per•bo•la (hī-pûr′bə-lə) A plane curve having two separate parts or branches, formed when two cones that point toward one another are intersected by a plane that is parallel to the axes of the cones.

hy•per•o•pi•a (hī′pə-rō′pē-ə) *See* **farsightedness.**

hy•per•ten•sion (hī′pər-tĕn′shən) *See* **high blood pressure.**

hy•per•text (hī′pər-tĕkst′) A computer-based text retrieval system that enables a user to access particular locations in webpages or other electronic documents by clicking on links within specific webpages or documents.

hy•pha (hī′fə) *Plural* **hyphae** (hī′fē) One of the long slender tubes that form the structural parts of the body of a fungus. Masses of hyphae make up the mycelium.

hyp•no•sis (hĭp-nō′sĭs) A trance-like state resembling sleep in which a person becomes very responsive to suggestions from another. Hypnosis is brought on by having one fix one's attention on a particular object, and it can be self-induced through concentration and relaxation.

hypo– *or* **hyp–** A prefix that means "beneath" or "below," as in *hypodermic,* below the skin. It also means "less than normal," as in *hypoglycemia,* having a level of sugar that is less than normal in the blood.

hy•po•chon•dri•a (hī′pə-kŏn′drē-ə) A condition in which a person often believes that he or she is ill without actually being ill, or worries so much about becoming ill that it affects his or her life. ❖ A person with hypochondria is called a **hypochondriac.**

hy•po•der•mic needle (hī′pə-dûr′mĭk) A hollow needle used in medical syringes to inject a fluid beneath the skin.

hy•po•gly•ce•mi•a (hī′pō-glī-sē′mē-ə) An abnormally low level of sugar in the blood, usually caused by too much insulin and resulting in weakness and dizziness.

hy•pot•e•nuse (hī-pŏt′n-o͞os′) The side of a right triangle opposite the right angle. It is the longest side, and the square of its length is equal to the sum of the squares of the lengths of the other two sides.

hy•po•thal•a•mus (hī′pō-thăl′ə-məs) The part of the brain in vertebrate animals that lies below the thalamus. It regulates many biological processes, including body temperature, thirst, hunger, and sleeping. The hypothalamus also controls hormone production of the pituitary gland.

hy•po•ther•mi•a (hī′pə-thûr′mē-ə) Abnormally low body temperature, often caused by prolonged exposure to cold.

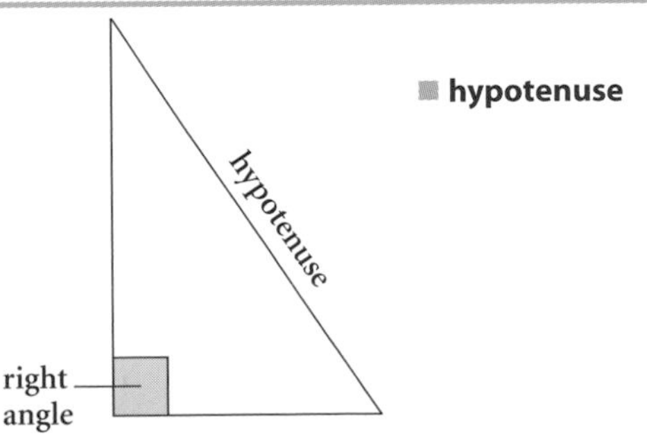

■ hypotenuse

USAGE

hypothesis/law/theory

The words *hypothesis, law,* and *theory* refer to different kinds of statements that scientists make about natural phenomena. A *hypothesis* is a statement that attempts to explain a set of facts. It forms the basis for an experiment that is designed to test whether it is true. Suppose your friend Smedley's room is a mess; your hypothesis might be that Smedley makes the room messy. You could test this hypothesis with an experiment: tidy up the room and see if it becomes messy again after Smedley returns. A scientific *law* is a statement that is believed to be true all the time for a set of conditions. If Smedley's room is always a mess when he is in it, you might propose a "Smedley's Mess Law" stating that whenever Smedley is in his room, he will always make it messy. Laws have the power to predict what will happen under the conditions they apply to. Thus, "Smedley's Mess Law" predicts that Smedley's room will be messy anytime Smedley is in it. A *theory* is a set of principles or statements devised to explain a whole group of observations or phenomena. A theory thus tries to account for a wider variety of events than a law does. Broad acceptance of a theory comes when it has been repeatedly tested experimentally on new data and makes accurate predictions about them. If people noticed that it became messy everywhere Smedley went, it might lead to the theory that Smedley brings messiness wherever he goes. This theory could be tested by bringing Smedley somewhere he's never been.

hy•poth•e•sis (hī-pŏth′ĭ-sĭs) *Plural* **hypotheses** (hī-pŏth′ĭ-sēz′) A statement that explains a set of facts and can be tested to determine if it is false or inaccurate.

hy•poth•e•size (hī-pŏth′ĭ-sīz) To form a hypothesis.

hy•po•thet•i•cal (hī′pə-thĕt′ĭ-kəl) Relating to or based on a hypothesis: *a hypothetical state of matter that has not yet been shown to exist.*

hy•ra•co•the•ri•um (hī′rə-kō-thîr′ē-əm) *Plural* **hyracotheria.** A small primitive horse that lived about 50 million years ago during the early Eocene Epoch. It had three or four hoofed toes on each foot and is sometimes considered the ancestor of modern horses. It is sometimes called the "dawn horse," a translation of its earlier scientific name, *Eohippus.*

Hz Abbreviation of **hertz.**

I

i (ī) The number whose square is equal to –1. Numbers expressed in terms of *i* are called imaginary or complex numbers.

I The symbol for **iodine.**

Ibn al-Hay•tham (ĭb′ən ĕl-hī′thəm) *Latin name* **Al•haz•en** (ăl-hăz′ən) 965?–1040? Arab mathematician who is best known for his book on optics, which became very influential in Europe after it was translated in the 12th century. It contained a detailed description of the eye and disproved the older Greek idea that vision is the result of the eye sending out rays to the object being looked at.

Ibn Si•na (ĭb′ən sē′nä), **Hakim** *Also known as* **Av•i•cen•na** (ăv′ĭ-sĕn′ə) 980–1037. Persian physician and philosopher whose medical textbook, *Canons of Medicine,* greatly influenced European medical studies until the 17th century.

i•bu•pro•fen (ī′byo͞o-prō′fən) A medicine used to reduce fever, pain, or inflammation.

ice (īs) Water frozen solid, normally at or below a temperature of 32°F (0°C).

ice age 1. Any of several cold periods during which glaciers covered much of the Earth. **2. Ice Age.** The most recent glacial period, which occurred during the Pleistocene Epoch and ended about 10,000 years ago. During the Pleistocene Ice Age, great sheets of ice up to two miles thick covered most of Greenland, Canada, and the northern United States as well as northern Europe and Russia.

ice•berg (īs′bûrg′) A massive body of floating ice that has broken away from a glacier. Most of an iceberg lies underwater, but because ice is not quite as dense as water, about one ninth of it remains above the surface.

iceberg

iguana
common iguana

ice•cap (īs′kăp′) **1.** A glacier spreading out from a center and covering a large area. **2.** A polar cap.

ich•thy•ol•o•gy (ĭk′thē-ŏl′ə-jē) The scientific study of fish.

ich•thy•o•saur (ĭk′thē-ə-sôr′) Any of various extinct sea reptiles of the Mesozoic Era having a long beak, four flippers, a dolphin-like body, and a tail with a large fin.

–ide A suffix used to form the names of various chemical compounds, especially the second part of the name of a compound that has two members (such as sodium *chloride*) or the name of a general type of compound (such as *polysaccharide*).

i•de•al gas (ī-dē′əl) A gas in which there is no interaction between the individual molecules. Such a gas would obey the gas laws (such as Charles's law) exactly. No known gas qualifies as an ideal gas.

ig•ne•ous (ĭg′nē-əs) Relating to rocks formed by the cooling and hardening of magma or molten lava. Basalt and granite are examples of igneous rocks. *See Table at* **rock.**

i•gua•na (ĭ-gwä′nə) Any of various large tropical American lizards, often having spiny projections along the back.

il•e•um (ĭl′ē-əm) The lower part of the small intestine, connecting the jejunum to the cecum of the large intestine.

il•i•um (ĭl′ē-əm) The uppermost of the three bones that fuse together to form each of the hipbones in many vertebrate animals. *See more at* **skeleton.**

i•mag•i•nar•y number (ĭ-măj′ə-nĕr′ē) A type of complex number in which the multiple of *i* (the square root of –1) is not equal to zero. Examples of imaginary numbers include 4*i* and 2 – 3*i*, but not 3 + 0*i* (which is just 3). *See more at* **complex number.**

i•ma•go (ĭ-mā′gō) An insect in its sexually mature adult stage after metamorphosis. *Compare* **larva, nymph, pupa.**

im•mis•ci•ble (ĭ-mĭs′ə-bəl) Incapable of being mixed or blended together. Immiscible liquids that are shaken together eventually separate into layers. Oil and water are immiscible.

im•mune response (ĭ-myo͞on′) A response of the body to a foreign substance, called an antigen, especially a microorganism or virus that causes disease. The immune response involves the action of white blood cells called lymphocytes, which work to deactivate foreign antigens, often by stimulating the production of antibodies.

immune system The system in humans and other animals that provides immunity by protecting against disease-causing agents, such as bacteria, viruses, parasites, and fungi. The immune system is composed of the skin and mucous membranes, which provide an external barrier to infection, and the cells involved in the body's immune response, such as lymphocytes.

im•mu•ni•ty (ĭ-myo͞o′nĭ-tē) Resistance of the body to infection by a disease-causing agent, such as a bacterium or virus. Immunity is usually provided by the body's own immune system, which is determined by the action of one's genes. It may also be brought about by having had a disease or infection in the past and recovering from it. Immunity can also be induced artificially, especially by vaccination.

im•mu•ni•za•tion (ĭm′yə-nĭ-zā′shən) **1.** The production of immunity to an infectious disease in an individual through inoculation or vaccination. **2.** A specific inoculation or vaccination. —*Verb* **immunize.**

im•mu•no•de•fi•cien•cy (ĭm′yə-nō-dĭ-fĭsh′ən-sē, ĭ-myo͞o′nō-dĭ-fĭsh′ən-sē) The inability to produce a normal immune response, usually as a result of a disease or inherited disorder.

im•mu•no•glob•u•lin (ĭm′yə-nō-glŏb′yə-lĭn, ĭ-myo͞o′nō-glŏb′yə-lĭn) *See* **antibody.**

im•mu•nol•o•gy (ĭm′yə-nŏl′ə-jē) The scientific study of the structure and function of the immune system.

im•ped•ance (ĭm-pēd′ns) A measure of the opposition to the flow of an electric current through a circuit of alternating current. Impedance is measured in ohms.

im•per•me•a•ble (ĭm-pûr′mē-ə-bəl) Relating to a material through which substances, such as liquids or gases, cannot pass: *an impermeable cell wall.*

im•pe•ti•go (ĭm′pĭ-tī′gō) A contagious disease often affecting children, characterized by the formation of pimples and thick yellow crusts on the skin.

im•prop•er fraction (ĭm-prŏp′ər) A fraction in which the numerator is greater than or equal to the denominator, such as $\frac{3}{2}$. *Compare* **proper fraction.**

im•pulse (ĭm′pŭls′) **1.** A usually sudden flow of electrical current in one direction. Impulses typically occur as single events. **2.** An electrical signal traveling along the axon of a nerve cell. Nerve impulses excite or inhibit activity in other nerve cells or in the tissues of the body, such as muscles and glands.

in. Abbreviation of **inch.**

In The symbol for **indium.**

in•breed (ĭn′brēd′) To breed by continued mating of closely related individuals.

in•can•des•cent lamp (ĭn′kən-dĕs′ənt) A lamp that produces light by heating up a filament of wire inside a bulb with an electric current. Because the filament, usually made of tungsten, would burn from the heat, the bulb is filled with a nonreactive gas, such as argon, which protects the wire from burning. *Compare* **fluorescent lamp.**

inch (ĭnch) A unit of length equal to $\frac{1}{12}$ of a foot (2.54 centimeters). *See Table at* **measurement.**

in•ci•sor (ĭn-sī′zər) A tooth having a sharp edge adapted for cutting or gnawing, located in mam-

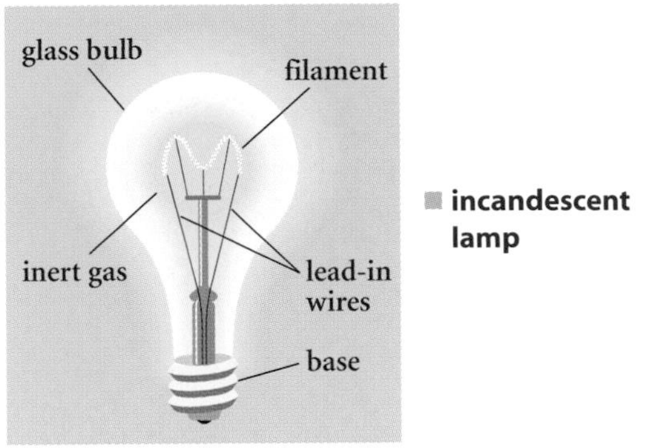

■ **incandescent lamp**

mals in the front of the mouth between the canine teeth.

in•clined plane (ĭn**′**klīnd′) A plane surface, such as a ramp, set at an acute angle to a horizontal surface. It is a simple machine because it requires less force to slide or roll a body up the plane than to raise the body vertically. Many tools are based on the principle of the inclined plane, such as the ax, screw, wedge, and chisel.

in•cu•bate (ĭn**′**kyə-bāt′) **1.** To warm and hatch eggs by bodily heat; to brood. **2.** To keep an organism, a cell, or cell cultures in conditions favorable for growth and development. ❖ The **incubation** of a disease is the period between the time of infection and the time the first symptoms appear. ❖ An **incubator** is an insulated device in which organisms, cells, or cell cultures are kept at a constant temperature and humidity.

in•cus (ĭng**′**kəs) One of the three small bones, called ossicles, in the middle ear. The incus is also called the anvil.

in•de•pen•dent variable (ĭn′dĭ-pĕn**′**dənt) *Mathematics.* A variable whose value determines the value of other variables. For example, in the function $y = x - 4$, x is the independent variable because its value determines the value of y.

in•dex of refraction (ĭn**′**dĕks′) The ratio of the speed of light in a vacuum to the speed of light in another medium, such as water or oil.

in•di•ca•tor (ĭn**′**dĭ-kā′tər) A chemical compound that changes color and structure when exposed to certain conditions and is therefore useful for chemical tests. Litmus, for example, becomes red in the presence of acids and blue in the presence of bases.

indicator species A species whose presence, absence, or relative well-being in a given environment is a sign of the overall health of its ecosystem. By monitoring the condition and behavior of an indicator species, scientists can determine how changes in the environment are likely to affect other species that are more difficult to study.

in•dig•e•nous (ĭn-dĭj**′**ə-nəs) *Ecology.* Native to a particular region or environment but occurring naturally in other places as well. The American black bear is indigenous to many different parts of North America. *Compare* **alien, endemic.**

in•di•um (ĭn**′**dē-əm) A soft, easily shaped, silvery-white metallic element that occurs mainly in ores of zinc and lead. It is used in the manufacturing of semiconductors and bearings for aircraft engines and as a plating over silver in making mirrors. *Symbol* **In.** *Atomic number* 49. *See* **Periodic Table,** pages 262–263.

in•dri•co•the•ri•um (ĭn′drə-kō-thîr**′**ē-əm) *Plural* **indricotheria.** A large, extinct land mammal of the Oligocene and Miocene Epochs, related to the rhinoceros. It stood 18 feet (5.5 meters) high at the shoulder and weighed 4 times as much as an elephant. The indricotherium is thought to have been the largest land mammal ever.

in•duc•tance (ĭn-dŭk**′**təns) The property of an electric circuit that makes it possible for an electromotive force to be created in a nearby circuit by a change of current in either circuit.

in•duc•tion (ĭn-dŭk**′**shən) **1a.** The process of deriving general principles from particular facts or instances. **b.** A conclusion reached by this pro-

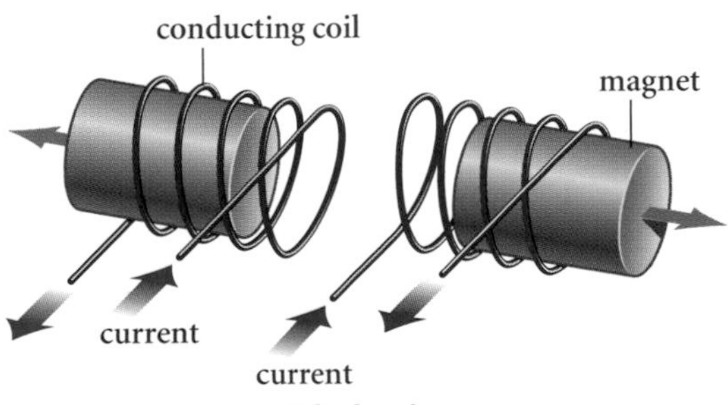

■ **induction**

When a magnet moves through a conducting coil, it induces a voltage across the coil that can cause electric current to flow. The direction of the current depends on the direction in which the magnet moves. In the diagram on the left, the current runs from right to left. In the diagram on the right, the current moves from left to right.

cess. *See Note at* **deduction. 2a.** The generation of an electric current in a conductor, such as a copper wire, by moving the conductor through a magnetic field or by moving or varying a magnetic field that already affects the conductor. **b.** The generation of an electric current in a conductor, such as a copper wire, by exposing it to the electric field of an electrically charged conductor. **3.** *See* **magnetic induction.**

induction coil A type of transformer that changes a low-voltage direct current to a high-voltage alternating current. Induction coils are used for many purposes, such as firing spark plugs in automobile engines and starting oil burners.

in•ert (ĭn-ûrt′) Not chemically reactive.

inert gas *See* **noble gas.**

in•er•tia (ĭ-nûr′shə) The tendency of a body at rest to remain at rest, or of a body in motion to continue moving in a straight line at a constant speed unless a force is applied to it. Mass is a measure of a body's inertia.

inflorescence
top left: *umbel*
top right: *corymb*
bottom left: *panicle*
bottom right: *raceme*

USAGE

infectious/communicable/contagious

A *contagious* or *communicable* disease is one that can be transmitted from one living being to another through direct or indirect contact. Thus the flu, which can be transmitted by coughing, and cholera, which is often acquired by drinking contaminated water, are contagious (or communicable) diseases. Modern medicine also uses the word *infectious* to refer to such diseases. *Infectious* has a slightly different meaning. It refers to diseases caused by *infectious agents*—agents such as viruses and bacteria that are not normally present in the body and can cause an infection. While the notion of contagiousness goes back to ancient times, the idea of infectious diseases is more modern, coming from the germ theory of disease, which was not proposed until the later 19th century. *Contagious* and *infectious* are also used to refer to people who have communicable diseases at a stage at which transmission to others is likely.

in•fec•tion (ĭn-fĕk′shən) The invasion of the body by microorganisms that can cause disease or by a virus. Microorganisms that can cause infection include bacteria, fungi, and protozoans.

in•fec•tious (ĭn-fĕk′shəs) Capable of causing infection: *an infectious disease.*

WORD HISTORY

influenza

Since ancient times, influenza has periodically swept the world. In just a few years during the early 1900s, 20 million people worldwide died from influenza, which we commonly call the flu. Until recently, people could not tell how this illness could spread so widely. Before people knew that organisms cause disease, they thought the stars influenced the spread of influenza. The name for this illness, in fact, reflects that belief. *Influenza* comes eventually from the Latin word *influentia,* meaning "influence of the stars." Today, however, the stars are no longer blamed for the flu. Modern medicine has found that inhaling certain viruses, called influenza viruses, causes the spread of this illness.

Did You Know?
infrared

In 1800 the astronomer Sir William Herschel discovered *infrared light* when he was exploring the relationship between heat and light. Herschel used a prism to split a beam of sunlight into a rainbow of colors (red, orange, yellow, green, blue, indigo, and violet) and measured how hot a thermometer got when it was placed in each of the various bands. Then he tried placing the thermometer just outside the red band, where there was no visible color at all. The thermometer heated up, just as if light were shining on it. Further experiments showed that this invisible form of light behaved just like visible light in many ways; for example, it could be reflected by a mirror. We now call this form of light infrared light. Another kind of invisible light, ultraviolet light, is found just beyond the violet end of the spectrum.

in•fer•tile (ĭn-fûr′tl) **1.** Not capable of producing offspring, seeds, or fruit; unable to reproduce. **2.** Not capable of developing into a complete organism: *infertile eggs.* **3.** Not capable of supporting plant life; unfavorable to the growth of crops and plants: *infertile soil.* —*Noun* **infertility.**

in•fin•i•ty (ĭn-fĭn′ĭ-tē) A space, extent of time, or quantity that has no limit.

in•flam•ma•tion (ĭn′flə-mā′shən) The reaction of a part of the body to injury or infection, characterized by swelling, heat, and pain. Inflammation increases the amount of blood flow to the injured area, bringing in more white blood cells and often healing the damaged tissue.

in•flo•res•cence (ĭn′flə-rĕs′əns) A group of flowers growing from a common stem, often in a characteristic arrangement.

in•flu•en•za (ĭn′flo͞o-ĕn′zə) A contagious disease caused by a virus that is characterized by fever, inflammation of the airways, and muscle pain. It commonly occurs in epidemics, one of which killed 20 million people between 1917 and 1919.

in•for•ma•tion technology (ĭn′fər-mā′shən) The development, installation, and use of computer systems and applications.

in•fra•red (ĭn′frə-rĕd′) Relating to the invisible part of the electromagnetic spectrum with wavelengths longer than those of visible red light but shorter than those of microwaves. *See more at* **electromagnetic spectrum.**

in•fra•sound (ĭn′frə-sound′) Sound whose wave frequency is too low (under 20 hertz) to be heard by humans.

in•her•i•tance (ĭn-hĕr′ĭ-təns) The process by which traits or characteristics pass from parents to offspring through the genes.

in•hi•bi•tion (ĭn′hə-bĭsh′ən) The blocking or limiting of the action of an organ, tissue, or cell of the body that is caused by the activity of certain nerves or by the release of a particular substance, such as a hormone or enzyme. *Compare* **excitation.**

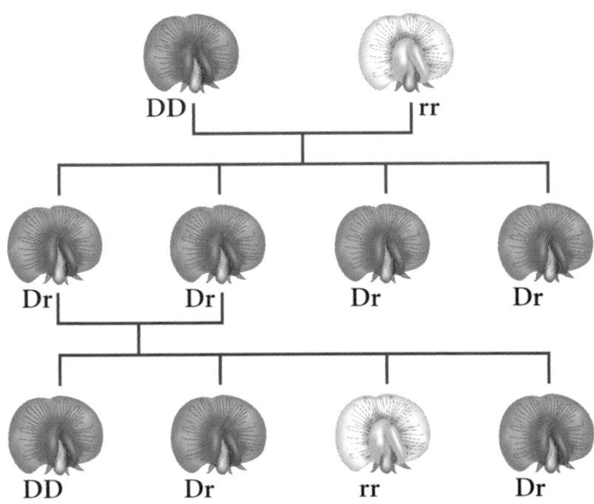

inheritance

In this diagram, pink pea flowers are produced by dominant genes (D) *and white pea flowers are produced by recessive genes* (r). *When flowers having two dominant genes are mated with flowers having two recessive genes* (top row), *the first generation of plants* (middle row) *all have one dominant and one recessive gene* (Dr). *Since dominant genes suppress recessive ones, all the flowers in the first generation will be pink. In the second generation* (bottom row), *one of the four plants will have two recessive genes. Therefore, three of the flowers in the second generation will be pink and one will be white.*

ink (ĭngk) A dark liquid ejected for protection by most cephalopods, including the octopus and squid.

in•ner ear (ĭn′ər) The innermost part of the ear in many vertebrate animals, consisting of the cochlea and semicircular canals. It transmits sound vibrations to the brain and is also the organ of balance. *See more at* **ear.**

in•oc•u•la•tion (ĭ-nŏk′yə-lā′shən) **1.** The production of immunity in an individual through injection with a vaccine. **2.** An injection of a specific vaccine. —*Verb* **inoculate.**

in•or•gan•ic (ĭn′ôr-găn′ĭk) **1.** Not involving organisms or the products of their life processes. **2.** Relating to chemical compounds that do not contain carbon (and especially hydrocarbons). Inorganic compounds occur mainly outside of living or once living organisms. Some inorganic compounds, such as carbon dioxide, contain carbon, but most do not. Salt (NaCl) and ammonia (NH_3) are typical inorganic compounds.

inorganic chemistry The branch of chemistry that deals with inorganic compounds.

in•put (ĭn′po͝ot′) *Noun.* **1.** The energy, power, or work put into a system or device. **2.** The data or programs put into a computer. —*Verb.* **3.** To enter data or a program into a computer.

in•sect (ĭn′sĕkt′) Any of numerous small arthropods that have six segmented legs in the adult stage and a body divided into three parts. The three parts are the head, thorax, and abdomen, and the thorax often has a pair of wings. Flies, bees, grasshoppers, beetles, butterflies, and moths are all insects. More than 600,000 species are known, most of them beetles. *See Notes at* **biomass, bug, entomology.**

in•sec•ti•cide (ĭn-sĕk′tĭ-sīd′) A chemical used to kill insects. *Compare* **fungicide, herbicide, pesticide.**

in•sec•ti•vore (ĭn-sĕk′tə-vôr′) **1.** An animal or plant that feeds mainly on insects. **2.** Any of an order of mammals that are small, eat insects and other invertebrate animals, and are usually active at night. The moles, shrews, and hedgehogs are examples of insectivores. —*Adjective* **insectivorous.**

in•sol•u•ble (ĭn-sŏl′yə-bəl) Not capable of being fully dissolved; not soluble.

in•stinct (ĭn′stĭngkt′) An inherited tendency of an organism or species to behave in a certain way that is usually a reaction to something in the environment and that fulfills a basic need. Examples of behaviors that are the result of instinct include nest-building in birds, spawning in fish, and food-gathering in insects.

in•su•late (ĭn′sə-lāt′) To cover or surround with a material that prevents the loss or transfer of heat, electricity, or sound: *We insulated our attic to keep out the cold.* —*Noun* **insulation.** —*Noun* **insulator.**

in•su•lin (ĭn′sə-lĭn) **1.** A hormone produced in the pancreas that acts to regulate the amount of sugar in the blood by causing cells, especially liver and muscle cells, to absorb glucose from the bloodstream. **2.** A drug containing this hormone, obtained from the pancreas of animals or produced synthetically and used in treating diabetes.

in•te•ger (ĭn′tĭ-jər) A positive or negative whole number or zero. The numbers 4, –876, and 5,280 are all integers.

in•te•gral (ĭn′tĭ-grəl) **1.** Involving or expressed as an integer or integers. **2.** In calculus, the result of integration.

in•te•grat•ed circuit (ĭn′tĭ-grā′tĭd) A device made of interconnected electronic components that are etched or imprinted onto a tiny slice of a semiconducting material, such as silicon or germanium. An integrated circuit smaller than a fingernail can hold millions of circuits. Also called *chip.*

in•te•gra•tion (ĭn′tĭ-grā′shən) In calculus, the inverse of differentiation. Integrating a given

interference
interference between waves on a lake surface

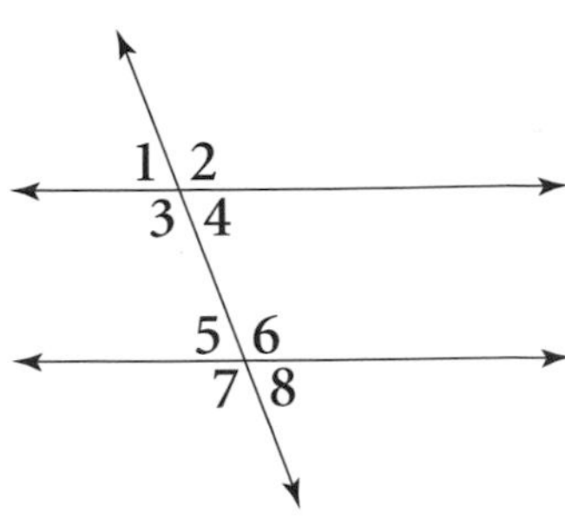

interior angle

Angles 3, 4, 5, and 6 are interior angles.

function results in a function whose derivative is the given function. Integration is used to compute such things as the areas and volumes of irregular shapes and solids. *Compare* **differentiation.**

in•teg•u•ment (ĭn-tĕg′yo͞o-mənt) A natural outer covering of an animal or a plant, such as skin, a seed coat, or a shell.

inter– A prefix meaning "between" or "among," as in *interplanetary,* located between planets.

in•ter•cel•lu•lar (ĭn′tər-sĕl′yə-lər) Located between or among cells: *intercellular fluid.*

in•ter•cept (ĭn′tər-sĕpt′) *Mathematics.* In a Cartesian coordinate system, the coordinate of a point at which a line, curve, or surface intersects a coordinate axis. If a curve intersects the x-axis at (4,0), then 4 is the curve's x-intercept; if the curve intersects the y-axis at (0,2), then 2 is its y-intercept.

in•ter•course (ĭn′tər-kôrs′) *See* **sexual intercourse.**

in•ter•fer•ence (ĭn′tər-fîr′əns) **1.** The wave that forms when two or more waves of the same or different frequencies come together. The amplitude of the resulting wave will be either larger or smaller than the amplitude of the individual waves, depending on whether or not their peaks and troughs match up. ❖ If the peaks of the waves match up, the amplitude of the resulting wave will be larger than that of the individual waves. This is called **constructive interference.** ❖ If the peaks and troughs of the individual waves do not match up, the resulting amplitude is smaller. This interference is called **destructive interference.** *See more at* **wave. 2.** In electronics, the distortion or interruption of one broadcast signal by others.

in•ter•fer•on (ĭn′tər-fîr′ŏn′) Any of a group of proteins that are produced by animal cells in response to infection by a virus and that, in many cases, prevent replication of the virus. Some interferons trigger an immune response in the body. They have been investigated as treatment for many diseases, including certain cancers.

in•te•ri•or angle (ĭn-tîr′ē-ər) **1.** Any of the four angles formed inside two straight lines when these lines are intersected by a third straight line. **2.** An angle formed by two adjacent sides of a polygon and included within the polygon. *Compare* **exterior angle.**

in•ter•nal-com•bus•tion engine (ĭn-tûr′nəl-kəm-bŭs′chən) An engine whose fuel is burned inside the engine itself rather than in an outside furnace or burner. Gasoline and diesel engines are internal-combustion engines; a steam engine is not.

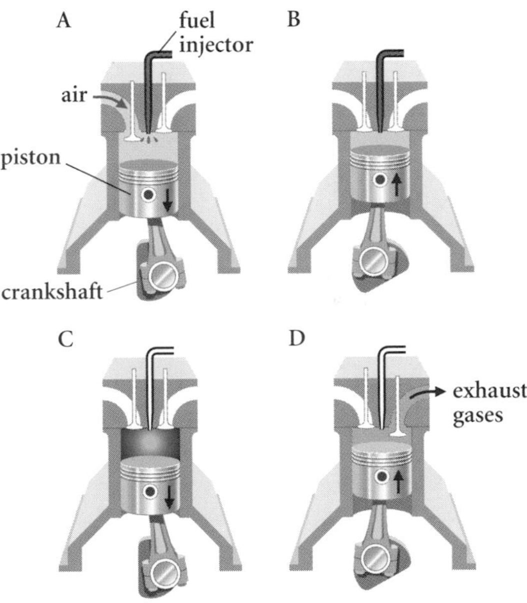

internal-combustion engine

cycles of a four-stroke diesel engine
A. intake stroke: *the piston moves down, drawing air and fuel into the cylinder*
B. compression stroke: *the piston moves up, compressing and heating the air and fuel mixture*
C. power stroke: *the hot air and fuel mixture ignites, forcing the piston down*
D. exhaust stroke: *the piston moves up, forcing the exhaust gases out of the cylinder*

internal medicine The branch of medicine that deals with the diagnosis and treatment of diseases affecting the internal organs of the body, especially in adults.

In•ter•na•tion•al Date Line (ĭn′tər-năsh′ə-nəl) An imaginary line through the Pacific Ocean roughly along the 180th meridian, agreed upon as the place where each new calendar day begins. The calendar day to the east of the line is one day earlier than it is to the west of the line.

International System A decimal system of units used mainly in scientific work, in which the basic quantities are length, mass, time, electric current, temperature, amount of matter, and luminous intensity. *See Table at* **measurement.**

international unit A unit for measuring a biologically active substance, such as a hormone or vitamin.

In•ter•net (ĭn′tər-nĕt′) A system connecting computers around the world using a common software protocol for transmitting and receiving data. This protocol is known as TCP/IP, which stands for Transmission Control Protocol/Internet Protocol.

in•ter•phase (ĭn′tər-fāz′) The stage of a cell immediately following the completion of cell division (mitosis), during which complete development of the daughter cells takes place.

in•ter•sec•tion (ĭn′tər-sĕk′shən) **1.** *Geometry.* The point or set of points where one line, surface, or solid crosses another. **2.** *Mathematics.* The set that contains only those elements shared by two or more sets. The intersection of the sets {3,4,5,6} and {4,6,8,10} is the set {4,6}.

in•ter•ver•te•bral disk (ĭn′tər-vûr′tə-brəl) A broad disk of cartilage that separates adjacent vertebrae and acts as a shock absorber during movement.

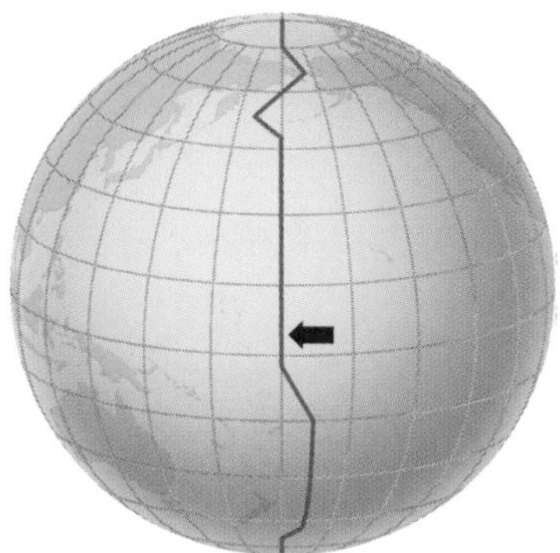

International Date Line

Did You Know?

Internet

Although the *Internet* is an immense global network that reaches millions of homes and businesses, it began as a relatively simple computer network called ARPANET, funded by a Department of Defense research agency. ARPANET linked educational institutions and research facilities. Users could transfer files, send e-mail, and post messages in a forum called USENET. Later, the development of HTTP (hypertext transfer protocol) allowed users to make connections from one electronic document to others by using hyperlinks. Such hyperlinked electronic documents (called *webpages*) can consist of text, pictures, and sound files. Over a billion of these webpages form the World Wide Web. The transmission of webpages, e-mails, files, and similar electronic data takes place on the massive network known as the Internet. What began as a simple way for military and educational researchers to communicate has developed into an international means of communicating ideas, as well as transmitting text, pictures, sound files, and even entire movies.

in•tes•tine (ĭn-tĕs′tĭn) The part of the digestive tract that extends from the stomach to the anus, consisting of the small intestine and large intestine. The intestine is a muscular tube in which most of the processes of digestion take place.

intra– A prefix meaning "inside" or "within," as in *intravenous,* within a vein.

in•tra•ve•nous (ĭn′trə-vē′nəs) Within or into a vein: *an intravenous injection.*

in•tru•sion (ĭn-tro͞o′zhən) The movement of magma through underground rocks within the Earth, usually in an upward direction. ❖ Rocks that formed from the underground cooling of magma are called **intrusive rocks.** *Compare* **extrusion.**

in•verse *Adjective.* (ĭn-vûrs′) **1.** Relating to a mathematical operation whose nature or effect is the opposite of another operation. For example, addition and subtraction are inverse operations, as are multiplication and division. —*Noun.* (ĭn′vûrs′) **2.** An inverse operation. Subtraction is the inverse of addition. **3.** Either of two numbers or quantities that cancel each other out under a given mathematical operation. For example, the inverse of 5 under multiplication is $\frac{1}{5}$, since $5 \times \frac{1}{5} = 1$. The inverse of 5 under addition is –5, since $5 + -5 = 0$.

inverse-square law A principle in physics dealing with forces that spread equally in all directions (such as sound, light, and gravity) and describing how the strength of these forces weakens over increasing distance. According to this principle, the effect of the force on an object changes by the inverse square of the distance between the object and the force's source. For example, an object placed three feet away from a light source will receive only one-ninth ($\frac{1}{3^2}$, the inverse of 3 squared) as much illumination as an object placed one foot from the light.

in•ver•te•brate (ĭn-vûr′tə-brĭt, ĭn-vûr′tə-brāt′) *Adjective.* **1.** Having no backbone or spinal column. —*Noun.* **2.** An animal, such as a coral, insect, or worm, that has no backbone. Most animals are invertebrates.

in vi•tro (ĭn vē′trō) In an artificial environment, such as a test tube; not inside a living organism: *grow tissue in vitro. Compare* **in vivo.**

in vi•vo (ĭn vē′vō) Inside a living organism rather than in an artificial environment: *test a new drug in vivo. Compare* **in vitro.**

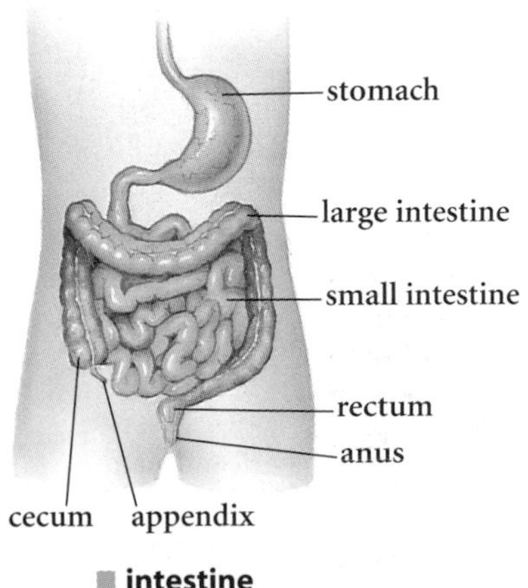

intestine

in•vol•un•tar•y (ĭn-vŏl′ən-tĕr′ē) Not under conscious control. Most of the biological processes in animals that are vital to life, such as contraction of the heart, blood flow, breathing, and digestion, are involuntary and controlled by the autonomic nervous system.

i•o•dide (ī′ə-dīd′) A chemical compound consisting of iodine together with another element or radical.

i•o•dine (ī′ə-dīn′) A shiny, grayish-black halogen element that is corrosive and poisonous. It occurs in very small amounts in nature but is abundant in seaweed. Iodine compounds are used in medicine, antiseptics, and dyes. *Symbol* **I.** *Atomic number* 53. *See* **Periodic Table,** pages 262–263.

i•on (ī′ən, ī′ŏn′) An atom or a group of atoms that has an electric charge. Positive ions, or cations, are formed by the loss of electrons; negative ions, or anions, are formed by the gain of electrons. *See Note at* **charge.**

i•on•ic bond (ī-ŏn′ĭk) A chemical bond formed between two ions with opposite charges. Ionic bonds form when one atom gives up one or more electrons to another atom. These bonds can form between a pair of atoms or between molecules and are the type of bond found in salts. *See more at* **bond, coordinate bond, covalent bond.**

i•on•ize (ī′ə-nīz′) **1.** To add an electron to, or remove an electron from, an atom or group of atoms so as to give it an electric charge. **2.** To form ions in a substance. Lightning ionizes air, for example.

i•on•o•sphere (ī-ŏn′ə-sfîr′) A region of the Earth's atmosphere in which atoms are often ionized (electrically charged) by radiation from the sun. The ionosphere lies mostly in the lower thermosphere, from about 43 to 250 miles (69 to 402.5 kilometers) above the Earth. Radio waves, which normally travel in a straight line, can be transmitted long distances over the curved surface of the Earth because they bounce off certain layers of the ionosphere and return to Earth instead of continuing into space.

Ir The symbol for **iridium.**

i•rid•i•um (ĭ-rĭd′ē-əm) A rare, whitish-yellow element that is the most corrosion-resistant metal known. It is very dense, hard, and brittle. Iridium is used to make hard alloys of platinum for jewelry, pen points, and electrical contacts.

Did You Know?

iridium

In 1978 geologist Walter Alvarez found an unusually high concentration of the element *iridium* in a layer of clay. This layer formed at the time dinosaurs and many other organisms went extinct. The iridium deposits were a great surprise, since iridium is very rare at the Earth's surface. Most surface iridium is believed to come from outer space—from dust left over after meteors disintegrate in the atmosphere or smash into the Earth. Walter's father, the physicist Luis Alvarez, suggested that the iridium came from the impact of a meteor about 6 miles (10 kilometers) across. He argued that such an impact would have caused an enormous explosion, sending huge clouds of dust into the atmosphere. The dust, blocking out the sun and causing acid rain for years, would have caused a worldwide ecological disaster. Many scientists think that such a disaster caused the extinction of dinosaurs and at least 70 percent of all other species alive at the time, including most of the Earth's land plants. Geologists have since found iridium deposits in rocks of a similar date in over 100 places worldwide. In the early 1990s, a large impact crater of the same age as the iridium deposits was identified in the Yucatan peninsula of central Mexico. It is 125 miles (200 kilometers) wide and may well have been caused by the impact hypothesized by Alvarez.

Symbol **Ir.** *Atomic number* 77. *See* **Periodic Table,** pages 262–263.

i•ris (ī′rĭs) The colored part around the pupil of the eye in vertebrate animals, located between the cornea and lens. Contraction and expansion of the muscular iris controls the size of the pupil, thereby regulating the amount of light reaching the retina.

i•ron (ī′ərn) A silvery-white, hard, brittle metallic element that occurs abundantly in minerals such as hematite and magnetite. It can be magnetized and is used to make steel and other alloys important in construction and manufacturing. Iron is a component of hemoglobin, which allows red blood cells to carry oxygen and carbon dioxide through the body. *Symbol* **Fe.** *Atomic number* 26. *See* **Periodic Table,** pages 262–263. *See Note at* **element.**

ir•ra•di•ate (ĭ-rā′dē-āt′) To expose to or treat with radiation so as to bring about a chemical or biological change. For example, meat sold as food is often irradiated to kill bacteria.

ir•ra•tion•al number (ĭ-răsh′ə-nəl) A number that cannot be expressed as a ratio between two integers and is not an imaginary number. If written in decimal notation, an irrational number would have an infinite number of digits to the right of the decimal point, without repetition. Pi and the square root of 2 ($\sqrt{2}$) are irrational numbers.

is•chi•um (ĭs′kē-əm) The lowest or rearmost of the three bones that fuse together to form each of the hipbones in many vertebrate animals. *See more at* **skeleton.**

is•land arc (ī′lənd) A usually curved chain of volcanic islands occurring at a subduction zone. The chain occurs in the plate that rides over the subducting plate. It is curved because of the curvature of the Earth.

is•lets of Lang•er•hans (ī′lĭts əv läng′ər-häns′) Irregular clusters of endocrine cells that are scattered throughout the tissue of the pancreas and secrete insulin.

iso– A prefix that means "equal," as in *isometric,* "having equal measurements."

i•so•bar (ī′sə-bär′) A line drawn on a weather map connecting places having the same atmospheric pressure.

i•so•leu•cine (ī′sə-lo͞o′sēn′) An essential amino acid. *See more at* **amino acid.**

i•so•mer (ī′sə-mər) One of two or more compounds composed of the same chemical elements in the same proportions but having a different arrangement of atoms. Isomers differ from one another in at least one physical or chemical property. Lactose and sucrose are isomers.

i•so•met•ric (ī′sə-mĕt′rĭk) *See* **cubic** (sense 3).

i•sos•ce•les (ī-sŏs′ə-lēz′) Having at least two sides of equal length: *an isosceles triangle.*

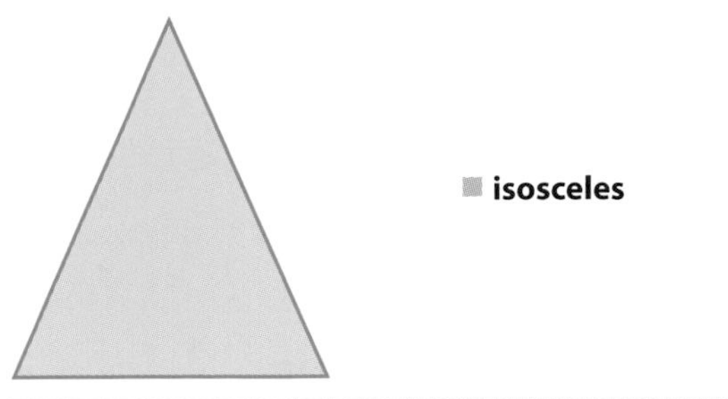

i•so•therm (ī′sə-thûrm′) A line drawn on a weather map connecting places having the same average temperature.

i•so•tope (ī′sə-tōp′) One of two or more atoms that have the same number of protons but a different number of neutrons. Carbon 12, the most common form of carbon, has six protons and six neutrons, whereas carbon 13 has six protons and seven neutrons.

–ite 1. A suffix used to form the names of minerals, such as *hematite* and *malachite.* **2.** A suffix used to form the name of a salt or ester of a specified acid whose name ends in *–ous.* Such salts or esters have one oxygen atom fewer than corresponding salts or esters with names ending in *–ate.* For example, a *nitrite* is a salt of nitrous acid and contains the group NO_2, while a nitrate contains NO_3. *Compare* **–ate.**

–itis A suffix meaning "inflammation," as in *bronchitis,* inflammation of the bronchial tubes.

i•vo•ry (ī′və-rē) The hard, smooth, yellowish-white substance forming the teeth and tusks of certain animals, such as the tusks of elephants and walruses and the teeth of certain whales.

J

Ja•cob (zhä-kôb′), **François** Born 1920. French geneticist who studied how genes control cellular activity by directing the synthesis of proteins. With Jacques Monod, he theorized that there are genes that regulate the activity of other, neighboring genes. They also proposed the existence of messenger RNA.

jade (jād) A hard mineral that is pale green or white and is often used as a gemstone. Jade usually forms within metamorphic rocks.

jas•per (jăs′pər) A reddish, brown, or yellow variety of opaque quartz.

jaun•dice (jôn′dĭs) Yellowish discoloration, as of the skin and whites of the eyes, that is a symptom of diseases like hepatitis that interfere with the normal processing of bile.

jaw (jô) **1.** Either of two bony or cartilaginous structures that in most vertebrate animals form the framework of the mouth, hold the teeth, and are used for biting and chewing food. The lower, movable part of the jaw is called the mandible. The upper, fixed part is called the maxilla. **2.** Any of various structures of invertebrate animals, such as the pincers of spiders or mites, that function similarly to the jaws of vertebrates.

jaw•less fish (jô′lĭs) Any of several primitive fish that lack a jaw and resemble the eels. Jawless fish include the lampreys and hagfish. *Compare* **bony fish, cartilaginous fish.**

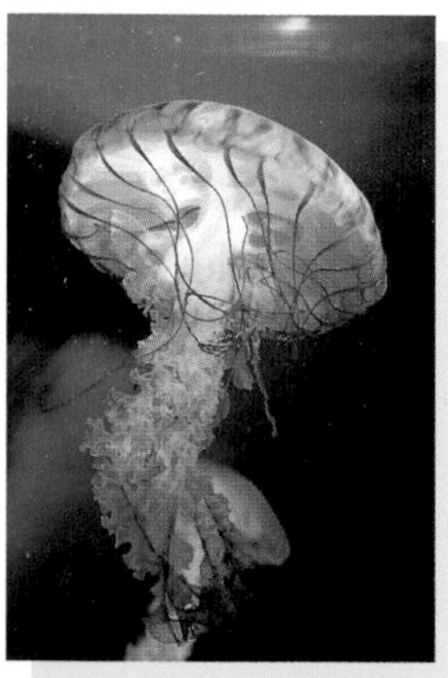

jellyfish
The West Coast sea nettle is a common jellyfish whose tentacles deliver a mild sting.

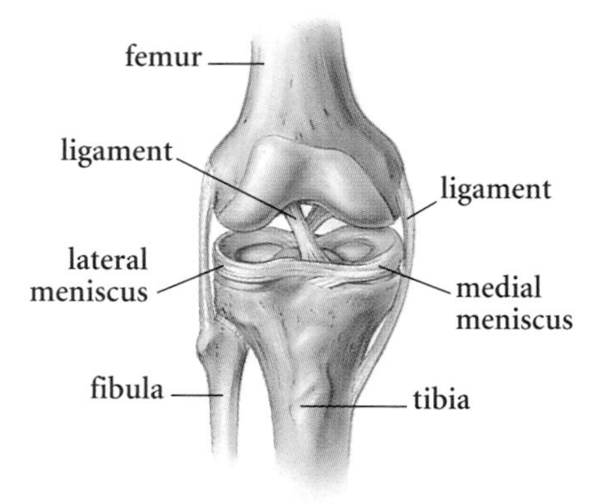

joint
a human knee joint

je•ju•num (jə-jo͞o′nəm) The middle part of the small intestine, connecting the duodenum and the ileum.

jel•ly•fish (jĕl′ē-fĭsh′) Any of numerous invertebrate marine animals having a soft, often umbrella-shaped body with stinging tentacles around a central mouth. Jellyfish are cnidarians and are related to the hydras and corals. *See also* **medusa, polyp.**

Jen•ner (jĕn′ər), **Edward** 1749–1823. British physician who pioneered the practice of vaccination. His experiments proved that people who had been inoculated with matter from cowpox, a mild skin disease of cattle, were immune to smallpox. Jenner's discovery laid the foundations for the science of immunology.

jet (jĕt) **1.** A rapid stream of liquid or gas forced through a small opening or nozzle under pressure: *A jet of water shot out of the hose.* **2.** An aircraft or other vehicle propelled by a jet engine. **3.** A jet engine.

jet engine An engine that develops thrust by ejecting a jet of hot gases from fuel burned in a combustion chamber. *See more at* **turbojet.**

jet propulsion 1. The driving of an aircraft by the powerful thrust developed when a jet of gas is forced out of a jet engine. **2.** Propulsion by means of any fluid that is forced out in a stream

BIOGRAPHY

Edward Jenner

In 1980 the World Health Organization declared that the deadly disease smallpox had been eradicated, thanks to the success of the smallpox vaccine. This triumph of medicine goes back over 200 years, to the British physician Edward Jenner. Jenner based his work on a piece of folk wisdom from the countryside that few doctors had taken seriously: if a person got cowpox, a mild disease of cattle, the person never got smallpox. Jenner proved scientifically that this was true in a famous experiment he did on an eight-year-old boy, James Phipps, in 1796. He exposed the boy to a person with cowpox, then two months later exposed the boy to smallpox (something that would be considered unethical by today's standards). Luckily, as Jenner expected, the boy warded off the smallpox with no problem. Before Jenner, a kind of vaccination against smallpox did exist in the form of exposing people to a mild form of the disease. While this often worked quite well, it was risky, and the exposed person sometimes died. Through further experiments Jenner refined his new method and soon set up the first successful vaccination program in history. Because of his work, systematic vaccination as a way of preventing disease became a central part of medicine.

in the opposite direction. Squids, octopuses, and cuttlefish, for example, jet their way through the ocean by taking in and then quickly expelling water.

jet stream A narrow current of strong wind circling the Earth from west to east at altitudes of about 6 to 9 miles (10 to 15 kilometers) above sea level. There are usually four distinct jet streams, two each in the Northern and Southern Hemispheres.

joint (joint) **1.** A usually movable body part in which adjacent bones are joined by ligaments and other fibrous tissues. **2.** *Botany.* A point on a plant stem from which a leaf or branch grows.

Jo•liot-Cu•rie (zhô-lyō′kyŏŏr′ē), **Irène** 1897–1956. French physicist. With her husband, **Frédéric Joliot-Curie** (1900–1958), she made the first artificial radioactive isotope. They also contributed to the discovery of the neutron and the development of nuclear reactors.

joule (jo͞ol, joul) A unit used to measure energy or work. One joule is equal to the work done when a force of one newton acts over a distance of one meter.

Joule, James Prescott 1818–1889. British physicist. His work established the law of conservation of energy, stating that energy is never destroyed but may be converted from one form into another. The joule unit of energy is named for him.

jug•u•lar vein (jŭg′yə-lər) Either of the two large veins on either side of the neck that drain blood from the head.

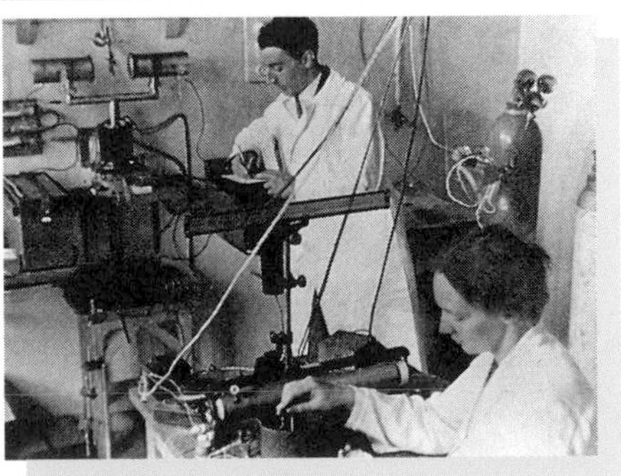

Frédéric and Irène Joliot-Curie

Jul•ian (jo͞ol′yən), **Percy Lavon** 1899–1975. American physician noted for developing cortisone (a synthetic hormone used to treat arthritis) and a drug used to treat glaucoma and memory loss.

jun•gle (jŭng′gəl) An area of tropical, forested land having high humidity and a dense growth of trees, bushes, and vines.

Ju•pi•ter (jo͞o′pĭ-tər) The fifth planet from the sun and the largest, with a diameter about 11 times that of Earth. It turns on its axis faster than any other planet in the solar system, taking less than ten hours to complete one rotation. *See Table at* **solar system,** pages 316–317. *See Note at* **planet.**

Jupiter

Ju•ras•sic (jo͝o-răs′ĭk) The second and middle period of the Mesozoic Era, from about 208 to 144 million years ago, during which dinosaurs were the dominant form of land life and the earliest birds appeared. *See Chart at* **geologic time,** pages 148–149.

ju•ve•nile (jo͞o′və-nīl′) An animal or plant that is not fully grown or developed.

K 1. The symbol for **potassium. 2.** Abbreviation of **kelvin.**

kan•ga•roo (kăng′gə-ro͞o′) Any of various plant-eating marsupials of Australia and nearby islands having short forelimbs, large hind limbs adapted for leaping, and a long tapered tail. Female kangaroos have pouches in which their young, born tiny, blind, and hairless, are suckled and grow.

ka•o•lin (kā′ə-lĭn) A soft, fine, whitish sedimentary rock made of clay minerals, especially kaolinite. Kaolin forms from the weathering of other rocks that are rich in aluminum.

ka•o•lin•ite (kā′ə-lĭ-nīt′) An aluminum-rich silicate mineral that is the main component of kaolin.

kar•y•o•type (kăr′ē-ə-tīp′) The number and shape of chromosomes in the nucleus of a cell. Scientists prepare karyotypes by staining cell nuclei, placing them on slides, and then photographing them through a microscope. Images of the chromosomes can then be grouped by size using a computer. Karyotypes are used to study the genetic makeup of an individual.

Ke•ku•lé von Stra•do•nitz (kā′ko͞o-lā′ fôn shträ′dō-nĭts), **Friedrich August** 1829–1896. German chemist who was a founder of organic chemistry. His discovery of the structure of benzene, a basic unit of organic chemistry, was fundamental to understanding many other organic compounds. *See Note at* **benzene.**

kelp (kĕlp) Any of various brown, often very large seaweeds that live in colder ocean regions. Kelp are varieties of brown algae. Some species grow over 200 feet (61 meters) long.

kel•vin (kĕl′vĭn) A unit of absolute temperature having the same value as one Celsius degree. It is used in the Kelvin scale. *See more at* **Celsius.** *See Table at* **measurement.**

Kelvin, First Baron. *Title of* **William Thomson.** 1824–1907. British mathematician and physicist known especially for his work on heat and electricity. In 1848 he proposed a scale of temperature independent of any physical substance, which became known as the Kelvin scale.

Kelvin scale A scale of temperature beginning at absolute zero (–273.15°C). Each degree, or kelvin, has the same value as one degree on the Celsius scale. On the Kelvin scale water freezes at 273.15 K and boils at 373.15 K. *See Note at* **Celsius.**

Kep•ler (kĕp′lər), **Johannes** 1571–1630. German astronomer and mathematician who was the first to accurately describe the elliptical orbits of Earth and the planets around the sun. He also demonstrated that planets move fastest when they are closest to the sun and that a planet's distance from the sun can be calculated if its period of revolution is known.

ker•a•tin (kĕr′ə-tĭn) A tough, fibrous protein that is the main structural component of hair, nails, horns, feathers, and hooves.

Did You Know?

keratin

Nature ingeniously uses the same chemicals to perform a wide variety of functions in living things. An example is the group of closely related proteins known as the *keratins.* When nature wants something hard and tough for an animal, it turns to keratins. Your nails and hair are made mostly of a kind of keratin, and so are a dog's claws, a bird's beak, and a goat's horns. Even the hard material called baleen that some whales have in their mouths to help them eat is made of a variety of keratin. All proteins are strings of amino acids, and the keratins' secret is the amino acid known as cysteine. This amino acid tends to form strong bonds with other cysteines in the protein. The different keratins vary in hardness, depending on how many cysteine bonds are present. The bonds are what make the keratins tough as, well, nails.

ker•nel (kûr′nəl) **1.** A grain or seed, especially of a cereal plant such as corn or wheat, that is enclosed in a husk. **2.** The inner, often edible part of a nut or stone of a fruit, such as a peach or plum.

ker•o•sene (kĕr′ə-sēn′) A thin, light-colored oil that is obtained from petroleum and used mainly as a fuel in lamps, home heaters and furnaces, and jet engines.

ke•tone (kē′tōn′) Any of a class of organic compounds, such as acetone, having a group consisting of a carbon and an oxygen atom (CO) joined on either side to a carbon atom of a hydrocarbon radical.

ket•tle (kĕt′l) A steep, bowl-shaped hollow in ground once covered by a glacier. Kettles are believed to form when a block of ice left by a glacier becomes covered by sediments and later melts, leaving a hollow.

kg Abbreviation of **kilogram.**

Kho•ra•na (kō-rä′nə), **Har Gobind** Born 1922. Indian-born American biochemist. He developed one of the first artificial genes and determined the sequence of nucleic acids for each of the amino acids in the body.

Khwa•riz•mi (kwär′ĭz-mē), **al-** *Full name* **Muhammad ibn-Musa al-Khwarizmi.** 780?–850? Arab mathematician and astronomer. His work was widely translated into Latin, introducing Arabic numerals and algebraic concepts to Western mathematics. The word *algorithm* is derived from his name. *See Note at* **algebra.**

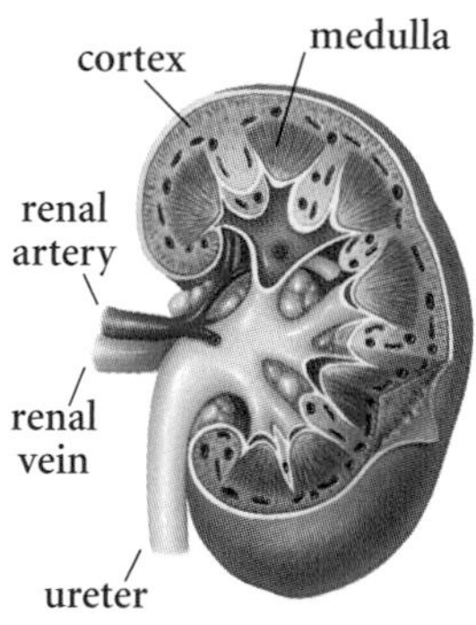

kidney

Blood that flows through a kidney is filtered to remove waste, such as urea and excess water. This process results in the byproduct urine, which travels through the ureter to the bladder, where it is stored until emptied by urination.

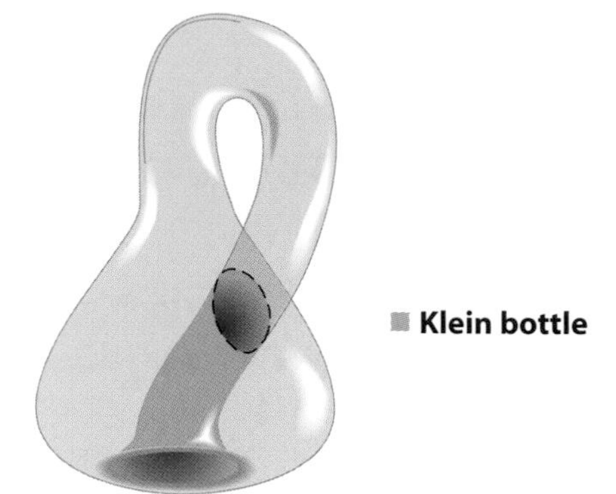

Klein bottle

kid•ney (kĭd′nē) Either of a pair of organs that are located in the rear of the abdominal cavity of vertebrate animals and that regulate the amount of water in the body and filter out wastes from the bloodstream in the form of urine. Each kidney is connected to the bladder by a muscular tube called a ureter.

kill•er whale (kĭl′ər) *See* **orca.**

kilo– A prefix that means: **1.** One thousand, as in *kilowatt,* one thousand watts. **2.** 2^{10} (that is, 1,024), which is the power of 2 closest to 1,000, as in *kilobyte.*

kil•o•bit (kĭl′ə-bĭt′) *Computer Science.* **1.** One thousand bits. **2.** 1,024 (that is, 2^{10}) bits. *See Note at* **megabyte.**

kil•o•byte (kĭl′ə-bīt′) **1.** A unit of computer memory or data storage capacity equal to 1,024 (that is, 2^{10}) bytes. **2.** One thousand bytes. *See Note at* **megabyte.**

kil•o•cal•o•rie (kĭl′ə-kăl′ə-rē) *See* **calorie** (sense 2a).

kil•o•gram (kĭl′ə-grăm′) The basic unit of mass in the metric system, equal to 1,000 grams (2.2 pounds). *See Table at* **measurement.** *See Note at* **weight.**

kil•o•hertz (kĭl′ə-hûrts′) A unit of frequency equal to 1,000 cycles per second. It is used to express the frequency of radio waves.

kil•o•me•ter (kĭ-lŏm′ĭ-tər, kĭl′ə-mē′tər) A unit of length in the metric system, equal to 1,000 meters (0.62 mile). *See Table at* **measurement.**

kil•o•watt (kĭl′ə-wŏt′) A unit of power equal to 1,000 watts.

■ Robert Koch

kilowatt-hour A unit used to measure energy, especially electrical energy. One kilowatt-hour is equal to one kilowatt acting for a period of one hour.

kin•e•mat•ics (kĭn′ə-măt′ĭks) The branch of physics that deals with the characteristics of motion without regard for the effects of forces or mass. *Compare* **dynamics.**

ki•net•ic energy (kə-nĕt′ĭk) The energy possessed by a body as a result of being in motion. Kinetic energy is dependent upon the mass and velocity of the object. *Compare* **potential energy.**

ki•net•ics (kə-nĕt′ĭks) *See* **dynamics.**

king•dom (kĭng′dəm) The highest classification into which living organisms are grouped, ranking above a phylum. One widely accepted system of classification divides life into five kingdoms: prokaryotes, protists, fungi, plants, and animals. *See Table at* **taxonomy.**

Kirch•hoff (kîr′kôf′), **Gustav Robert** 1824–1887. German chemist who with Robert Bunsen discovered the elements cesium and rubidium. He also investigated the solar spectrum and researched electrical circuits and the flow of currents.

Klebs (klāps), **Edwin** 1834–1913. German bacteriologist. With Friedrich Löffler, he isolated the bacillus that causes diphtheria (1884). Klebs also demonstrated the presence of bacteria in infected wounds and showed that tuberculosis can be transmitted through infected milk.

Klein bottle (klīn) A theoretical surface in topology that has no inside or outside. It can be pictured in ordinary space as a tube that bends back upon itself, entering through the side and joining with the open end. A true Klein bottle would not actually intersect itself. *Compare* **Möbius strip.**

km Abbreviation of **kilometer.**

knee•cap (nē′kăp′) *See* **patella.**

ko•a•la (kō-ä′lə) A tree-dwelling Australian marsupial that resembles a small bear. Koalas have grayish fur, large ears, and sharp claws, and they feed exclusively on leaves and shoots of the eucalyptus tree.

Koch (kôk), **Robert** 1843–1910. German bacteriologist who demonstrated that specific diseases are caused by specific microorganisms. He identified the bacilli that cause anthrax, tuberculosis, and cholera, and he showed that fleas and rats are responsible for transmission of the bubonic plague and that the tsetse fly is responsible for transmitting sleeping sickness.

Köh•ler (kŭ′lər), **Georges Jean Franz** 1946–1995. German scientist who investigated the immune system. With Cesar Milstein he developed a method of producing antibodies that fight specific cells. The antibodies are used to diagnose and treat specific forms of cancer and other diseases.

Ko•mo•do dragon (kə-mō′dō) An Indonesian monitor lizard that is the largest living lizard. It can grow up to 10 feet (3 meters) long, has dark skin, and feeds on eggs and small animals.

Kov•a•lev•sky (kŏv′ə-lĕv′skē), **Sonya** 1850–1891. Russian mathematician. She made important contributions to calculus, and her mathematical description of the shape of Saturn's rings became a model for other scientists.

■ Komodo dragon

Kr The symbol for **krypton.**

Krebs (krĕbz), Sir **Hans Adolf** 1900–1981. German-born British biochemist who discovered the Krebs cycle in 1936.

Krebs cycle A series of chemical reactions in most aerobic organisms in which cells break down glucose and other molecules in the presence of oxygen to produce carbon dioxide and energy in the form of ATP. The Krebs cycle occurs in the mitochondria of all organisms except bacteria. Also called *citric acid cycle.*

krill (krĭl) Small crustaceans that float in the ocean in huge numbers and are one of the most important parts of zooplankton. Krill are the main food of baleen whales.

kryp•ton (krĭp′tŏn′) A colorless, odorless element that is a noble gas. It is used in certain fluorescent lamps and photographic flash lamps. *Symbol* **Kr.** *Atomic number* 36. *See* **Periodic Table,** pages 262–263.

Kui•per belt (kī′pər) A disk-shaped region in the outer solar system, containing thousands of small, icy celestial bodies. Comets that make one complete orbit of the sun in less than 200 years come from this area. The Kuiper belt lies beyond the orbit of Neptune and includes Pluto, which was traditionally classed with the planets. In 2006, the International Astronomical Union declared Pluto to be a dwarf planet that resides in the Kuiper belt. *Compare* **Oort Cloud.**

kwa•shi•or•kor (kwä′shē-ôr′kôr′) A disease, usually of children, caused by lack of protein in the diet and resulting in swelling of the limbs, enlargement of the liver, potbelly, reduced growth, and change skin and hair color.

Kwo•lek (kwŏl′ĕk′), **Stephanie** Born 1923. American chemist who pioneered the use of polymers to make synthetic fibers. She developed the first liquid crystal polymer fiber, now used to make many products, including bulletproof vests.

L

l Abbreviation of **liter.**

La The symbol for **lanthanum.**

la•bor (lā′bər) The process by which the birth of a mammal occurs, beginning with contractions of the uterus and ending with the delivery of the fetus or infant and the placenta.

lab•o•ra•to•ry (lăb′rə-tôr′ē) A room or building equipped for scientific research and for conducting experiments, especially under controlled conditions.

lab•y•rinth (lăb′ə-rĭnth′) The system of tubes and spaces that make up the inner ear of many vertebrate animals.

lac•ri•mal (lăk′rə-məl) Relating to or producing tears: *the lacrimal glands.*

lac•tase (lăk′tās′) An enzyme that is found in the small intestine, liver, and kidneys of mammals and catalyzes the breakdown of lactose into simpler sugars, such as glucose.

lac•ta•tion (lăk-tā′shən) The secretion or production of milk by the mammary glands, occurring in female mammals after giving birth.

lac•tic acid (lăk′tĭk) An organic acid produced when milk sours or various fruits ferment. It is used as a flavoring and preservative for foods. Lactic acid is also produced by muscle tissue during exercise, especially when oxygen supply is limited, and can cause cramping pains.

lac•tose (lăk′tōs′) A white crystalline sugar that is found in milk. It is used in the manufacture of various foods. ❖ The inability to properly digest lactose is called **lactose intolerance.** This condition is caused by a lack of the enzyme lactase and can cause stomach cramps and other symptoms.

la•goon (lə-go͞on′) **1.** A shallow body of salt water close to the sea but separated from it by a narrow strip of land, such as a barrier island, or by a coral reef. **2.** A shallow pond or lake close to a larger lake or river but separated from it by a barrier such as a levee.

La•grange (lə-grānj′, lə-gränj′), Comte **Joseph Louis** 1736–1813. French mathematician and astronomer who made important contributions to algebra and calculus. His work on celestial mechanics extended scientific understanding of planetary and lunar motion.

■ **lagoon**
Moorea, French Polynesia

lake (lāk) A large inland body of standing fresh or salt water.

lam•i•na (lăm′ə-nə) **1.** *Botany.* The expanded area of a leaf or petal; a blade. **2.** A thin layer of bone, membrane, or other tissue. **3.** *Geology.* A thin layer of sediment.

lam•i•nar flow (lăm′ə-nər) Movement of a fluid in which the motion of the particles of fluid is very orderly and all particles move along straight lines in the same direction. Laminar flow is common in viscous fluids, especially those moving at low velocities. *Compare* **turbulent flow.**

lam•prey (lăm′prē) Any of various fish having a body like an eel, a skeleton made of cartilage, and a jawless sucking mouth. Lampreys attach to other fish in order to feed on their blood.

lance•let (lăns′lĭt) Any of various small, transparent, fish-like animals that live in water and have a structure similar to that of vertebrates, but with a notochord instead of a true backbone. Lancelets are cephalochordates. Also called *amphioxus.*

land bridge (lănd) A neck of land that connects two landmasses; an isthmus.

land•fill (lănd′fĭl′) A disposal site where solid waste, such as paper, glass, and metal, is buried

■ landslide

between layers of dirt and other materials in such a way as to reduce contamination of the surrounding land. Modern landfills are often lined with layers of absorbent material and sheets of plastic to keep pollutants from leaking into the soil and water. Also called *sanitary landfill.*

land•form (lănd′fôrm′) Any recognizable, naturally formed feature on the Earth's surface. Landforms have a characteristic shape and can include such large features as plains, plateaus, mountains, and valleys, as well as smaller features such as hills, eskers, and canyons.

land•mass (lănd′măs′) A large, continuous area of land, such as a continent or a very large island.

land•slide (lănd′slīd′) **1.** The downward sliding of a relatively dry mass of earth and rock. **2.** The mass of soil and rock that moves in this way.

Land•stein•er (lănd′stī′nər), **Karl** 1868–1943. Austrian-born American pathologist who discovered human blood types. *See Note at* **blood type.**

La Ni•ña (lä nēn′yä) A cooling of the surface water of the eastern and central Pacific Ocean, occurring every 4 to 12 years and causing unusual weather patterns. The cooler water brings drought to western South America and heavy rains to eastern Australia and Indonesia. *Compare* **El Niño.**

lan•o•lin (lăn′ə-lĭn) A yellowish-white, fatty substance obtained from wool and used in soaps, cosmetics, and ointments.

lan•tha•nide (lăn′thə-nīd′) Any of a series of 15 naturally occurring metallic elements. The lanthanides include elements having atomic numbers 57 through 71. They are grouped apart from the rest of the elements in the Periodic Table because they all behave in a similar way in chemical reactions. Also called *rare-earth element. See* **Periodic Table,** pages 262–263.

lan•tha•num (lăn′thə-nəm) A soft, easily shaped, silvery-white metallic element of the lanthanide series. It is used to make glass for lenses and lights for movie and television studios. *Symbol* **La.** *Atomic number* 57. *See* **Periodic Table,** pages 262–263.

large calorie (lärj) *See* **calorie** (sense 2a).

large intestine The wide lower section of the intestine that extends from the end of the small intestine to the anus. In most vertebrate animals, it includes the cecum, colon, and rectum.

lar•va (lär′və) *Plural* **larvae** (lär′vē) *or* **larvas. 1.** An animal in an early stage of development that differs greatly in appearance from its adult stage. Larvae are adapted to a different environment and way of life than adults and go through a process of metamorphosis in changing to adults. Tadpoles are the larvae of frogs and toads. **2.** The immature, wingless, and usually worm-like feeding form of those insects that undergo three stages of metamorphosis, such as butterflies, moths, and beetles. Insect larvae hatch from eggs, later turn into pupae, and finally turn into adults. *Compare* **imago, nymph, pupa.**

lar•yn•gi•tis (lăr′ĭn-jī′tĭs) Inflammation of the larynx, usually caused by a virus.

lar•ynx (lăr′ĭngks) The upper part of the trachea in most vertebrate animals, containing the vocal cords. Air passes through the larynx on the way to the lungs. Also called *voice box.*

la•ser (lā′zər) A device that emits a very narrow and intense beam of light or other radiation. The light is generated by exciting electrons in the atoms of some substance. As the electrons fall back to their normal lower energy, they give off light that strikes other excited electrons, which then fall back as well, producing light of a precise frequency. Lasers are used for many purposes, such as cutting hard substances and destroying diseased tissue.

la•tent heat (lāt′nt) The quantity of heat absorbed or released by a substance undergoing a change of state, such as ice changing to water or water changing to ice, at constant temperature and pressure.

latent period The incubation period of a dis-

Did You Know?

laser

A *laser* emits a thin, intense beam of light that can travel long distances without diffusing. Light beams consist of many waves traveling in roughly the same direction, but in laser light, each light wave, or photon, is precisely in step with every other. Such light is called *coherent.* Lasers produce coherent light through a process called *stimulated emission.* A laser contains a chamber in which atoms of a medium such as a synthetic ruby rod or a gas are excited to a high energy state by a flash tube. When an atom drops to a lower energy state, it gives off the extra energy as a photon with a specific frequency. If this photon hits another excited atom, it will stimulate it to emit another photon that has the same frequency as the first, and is in phase with it. The photons bounce back and forth between mirrors on either end of the chamber, stimulating other atoms to emit still more coherent photons. One of the mirrors is partially transparent, allowing the laser beam to exit from that end of the chamber.

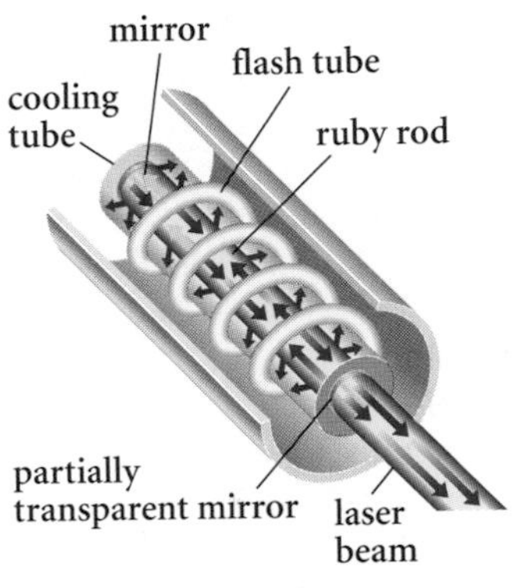

ease; the time elapsing between an infection and the appearance of symptoms.

lat•er•al line (lăt′ər-əl) A series of tube-like canals along the head and sides of fish and some amphibians by which vibrations, as from water currents, and changes in pressure are detected.

la•tex (lā′tĕks′) **1.** The colorless or milky sap of certain trees and plants, such as the milkweed and the rubber tree, that hardens when exposed to the air. Latex usually contains gum resins, waxes, and oils. **2.** An emulsion of rubber or plastic droplets in water that looks like the latex of plants. It is used in paints, adhesives, and synthetic rubber products.

lat•i•tude (lăt′ĭ-to͞od′) Distance north or south on the Earth's surface, measured in degrees from the equator, which has a latitude of 0°. The distance of a degree of latitude is about 69 statute miles (111 kilometers) or 60 nautical miles. Latitude and longitude are the coordinates used to identify any point on the Earth's surface. *Compare* **longitude.**

lat•tice (lăt′ĭs) An arrangement of objects separated in space, such as the pattern of intersecting lines on graph paper or the pattern of atoms in a crystal.

Laur•a•sia (lô-rā′zhə) A supercontinent of the Northern Hemisphere made up of the landmasses that currently correspond to North America, Greenland, Europe, and Asia (except India). According to the theory of plate tectonics, Laurasia formed at the end of the Paleozoic Era and broke up in the middle of the Mesozoic Era. *Compare* **Gondwanaland.**

la•va (lä′və) **1.** Molten rock that flows from a volcano or from a crack in the Earth. *See more at* **magma. 2.** The igneous rock formed when this substance cools and hardens.

La•voi•sier (lä-vwä-zyā′), **Antoine Laurent** 1743–1794. French chemist who is regarded as one of the founders of modern chemistry. In 1778 he discovered that air consists of a mixture of two gases, which he called oxygen and nitrogen. Lavoisier also discovered the law of conservation of mass and devised the modern method of naming chemical compounds. His wife, **Marie** (1758–1836), assisted him with his laboratory

BIOGRAPHY

Antoine Lavoisier

Although Antoine Lavoisier made many fundamental contributions to the science of chemistry, rather than being known for major experiments or discoveries, he is best known for being the first scientist to collect and publish everything that was known about chemistry in his time. His *Elementary Treatise of Chemistry,* published in 1789, is regarded as the first textbook on modern chemistry. In it, Lavoisier presented a systematic and unified view of new theories and established a system for naming chemical compounds. Lavoisier also put to rest an important and longstanding theory about combustion, a mysterious process that had baffled the greatest minds since antiquity. For centuries it was believed that a substance called *phlogiston,* thought to be a volatile part of all combustible substances, was released during the process of combustion. By repeating the experiments of Joseph Priestley, Lavoisier demonstrated that combustion is a process in which the burning substance combines with a constituent of the air, the gas he named *oxygen.*

work and translated a number of important chemistry texts. *See Notes at* **oxygen, Priestley.**

law (lô) A statement that describes what will happen in all cases under a specified set of conditions. Laws describe an invariable relationship among phenomena. Boyle's law, for instance, describes what will happen to the volume of a gas if its pressure changes and its temperature remains the same. *See Note at* **hypothesis.**

law of conservation of energy The principle that energy can neither be created nor be destroyed, now part of the first law of thermodynamics. The term is also used as a synonym for the first law of thermodynamics. *See Note at* **thermodynamics.**

law of conservation of mass The principle that matter can neither be created nor be destroyed, now part of the first law of thermodynamics. *See Note at* **thermodynamics.**

law of gravitation *or* **law of universal gravitation** *See* **Newton's law of gravitation.**

Law•rence (lôr′əns), **Ernest Orlando** 1901–1958. American physicist who built the first cyclotron, a type of particle accelerator, in 1929.

law•ren•ci•um (lô-rĕn′sē-əm) A synthetic, radioactive metallic element of the actinide series that is produced by bombarding californium with boron ions. Its most stable isotope has a half-life of 3.6 hours. *Symbol* **Lr.** *Atomic number* 103. *See* **Periodic Table,** pages 262–263.

laws of motion *See* **Newton's laws of motion.**

laws of thermodynamics Three laws that state how energy is transformed from one form into another. *See Note at* **thermodynamics.**

lb. Abbreviation of **pound.**

LCD (ēl′sē-dē′) Short for *liquid-crystal display.* A low-power, flat-panel display used in many digital devices to display numbers or images. It is made up of a substance that is almost liquid, but also has a crystal structure like a solid, sandwiched between filtering layers of glass or plastic. When the device is turned on, the molecules of the "liquid crystal" twist so that they can either reflect or transmit light that falls on them to produce the number or image indicated by a computer.

leach (lēch) To remove the soluble materials from a substance, such as ash or rock, by passing

A CLOSER LOOK

Leaf

Flowering plants are classified as monocotyledons or dicotyledons. The leaves of monocotyledons have parallel veins and are often sessile (attached directly to the stem without a stalk). The leaves of dicotyledons have net veins and are usually attached to the plant by a leafstalk.

Leaves have a shape and structure adapted to the specific habitat of each kind of plant. Leaves that are narrow and needle-like are designed to limit water loss. Broad leaves are designed for wetter climates and make maximum use of sunlight for photosynthesis.

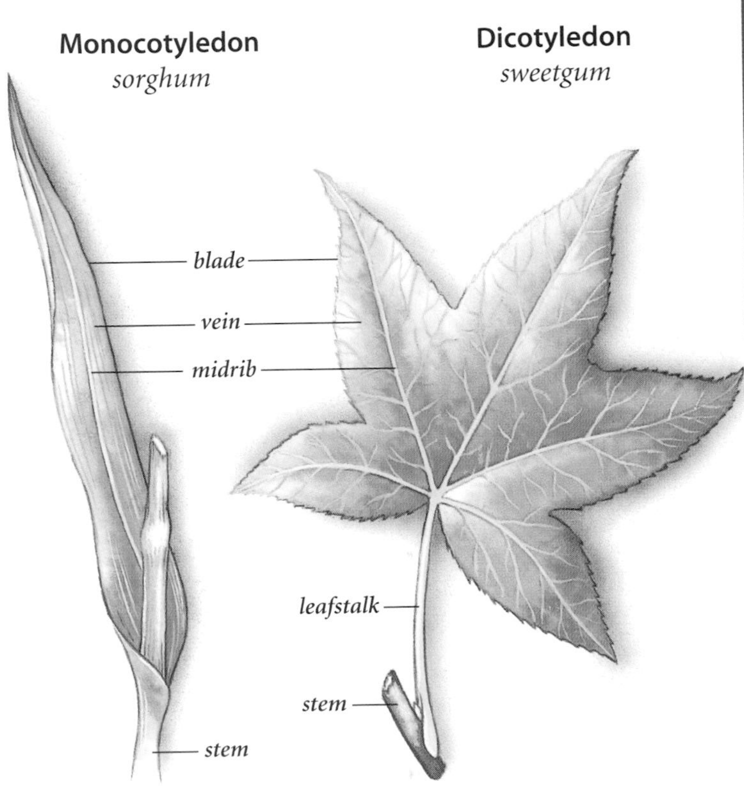

Broad leaf
sugar maple

Grass
wheat grass

Needle
shore pine

Spine
cactus

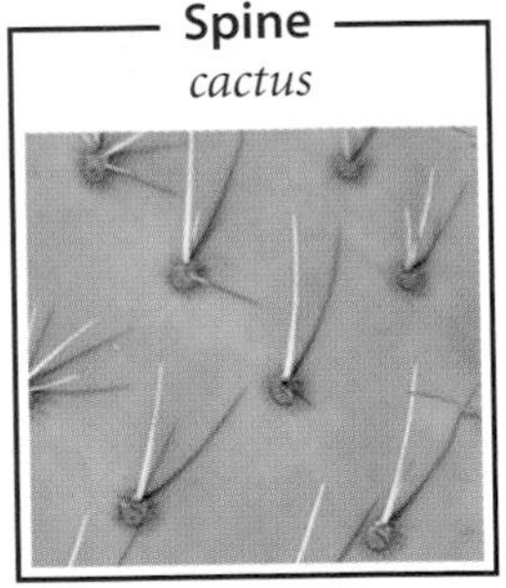

a liquid through or over it: *Heavy rains leached minerals from the soil.*

lead (lĕd) A soft, easily shaped, heavy, bluish-gray metallic element that is extracted chiefly from galena. It is very durable and resistant to corrosion and is a poor conductor of electricity. Lead is used to make radiation shielding and containers for corrosive substances. *Symbol* **Pb.** *Atomic number* 82. *See* **Periodic Table,** pages 262–263. *See Note at* **element.**

leaf (lēf) *Noun.* **1.** A flat, usually green plant part that grows on the stem and takes in carbon dioxide and sunlight to manufacture food by photosynthesis. Leaves consist of an outer tissue layer (the epidermis) through which water and gases are exchanged, a spongy inner layer of cells that contain chloroplasts, and veins that supply water and minerals and carry out food. Some leaves are simple, while others are compound, consisting of multiple leaflets. —*Verb.* **2.** To produce leaves.

leaf•let (lē′flĭt) A small leaf or leaf-like part, especially one of the blades or divisions of a compound leaf.

leaf•stalk (lēf′stôk′) The stalk by which the leaves of most plants are attached to a stem. Also called *petiole.*

Lea•key (lē′kē) Family of British scientists. **Louis** (1903–1972) is known for fossil discoveries of early humans made in close collaboration with his wife, **Mary** (1913–1996). In 1959, while working in Tanzania, Africa, Mary Leakey uncovered skull and teeth fragments of a species called *Zinjanthropus,* now thought to be about 1.75 million years old. The next year the Leakeys discovered remains of a larger-brained species, called *Homo habilis.* Their discoveries provided powerful evidence that human ancestors were of greater age than was previously thought, and that they had evolved in Africa rather than in Asia. Their son **Richard** (born 1944) and his wife **Meave** (born 1942) have continued the family's research and discoveries. In 2001 Meave Leakey discovered a skull belonging to an entirely new genus, called *Kenyanthropus platyops* and believed to be 3.5 million years old.

learn•ing disability (lûr′nĭng) Any of various disorders of attention, memory, or reasoning that interfere with the ability to learn.

Leav•itt (lē′vĭt), **Henrietta Swan** 1868–1921. American astronomer who discovered four novae and over 2,400 variable stars. She also developed a mathematical formula used to measure intergalactic distances.

lec•i•thin (lĕs′ə-thĭn) A fatty substance containing phosphorus that is present in most plant and animal tissues and is an important structural part of cell membranes. Lecithin is used commercially in foods, cosmetics, paints, and plastics for its ability to form emulsions.

■ **Mary and Louis Leakey**

BIOGRAPHY

Anton van Leeuwenhoek

As a young man, Anton van Leeuwenhoek worked in a drapery store, where he used magnifying glasses to examine the quality of the cloth. This led him to begin building microscopes as a hobby, which he used to examine hair, blood, insects, and other things, keeping detailed records and drawings of his observations. Eventually, van Leeuwenhoek made hundreds of microscopes, each one for a different investigation, with specimens permanently mounted so he could study them as long as he wanted to. Some of the discoveries he made with his microscopes include protozoans (1674), bacteria (1676), blood cells (1674), and the structure of nerves (1717). Van Leeuwenhoek lived a very long life, and he remained active and curious throughout it. By the time of his death at the age of 90, he had made more than 400 microscopes.

LED (ĕl′ē-dē′, lĕd) Short for *light-emitting diode.* An electronic semiconductor device that emits light when an electric current passes through it. LEDs are used for indicator lights, such as those on the front of a disk drive.

leech (lēch) Any of various worms that live in water and suck blood from other animals, including humans. One species, the medicinal leech, has been used in bloodletting and in helping to heal wounds and surgical grafts. Leeches are annelids, related to earthworms.

Leeu•wen•hoek (lā′vən-ho͝ok′), **Anton van** 1632–1723. Dutch naturalist and pioneer of microscopic research. He was the first to describe protozoa, bacteria, and spermatozoa. He also made observations of yeasts, red blood cells, and blood capillaries, and traced the life histories of various animals, including the flea, ant, and weevil.

leg•ume (lĕg′yo͞om′, lə-gyo͞om′) **1.** Any of a variety of plants having pods that contain seeds. Because of a symbiotic relationship with bacteria that live in nodules on their roots, legumes are able to take nitrogen from the air and convert it into compounds that enrich soils. Beans, peas, clover, and alfalfa are all legumes. **2.** The pod or seed of such a plant, used as food.

Leib•niz (līb′nĭts), Baron **Gottfried Wilhelm von** 1646–1716. German philosopher and mathematician. He invented the mathematical processes of differentiation and integration, which greatly expanded the field of calculus. Leibniz also established the foundations of probability theory and designed a practical calculating machine.

le•mur (lē′mər) Any of several small nocturnal mammals of the island of Madagascar. Lemurs have large eyes, soft fur, and a long tail, and live in trees. They are distantly related to monkeys.

Le•noir (lĕ-nwär′), **Jean-Joseph-Étienne** 1822–1900. French inventor who designed and assembled the first practical internal-combustion engine (1859).

lens (lĕnz) **1.** A transparent structure behind the iris of the eye that focuses light entering the eye on the retina. **2a.** A piece of glass or plastic shaped so as to focus or spread parallel light rays that pass through it to form an image. **b.** A combination of two or more such lenses used to form an image, as in a camera or telescope. Also called *compound lens.*

Le•o (lē′ō) A constellation in the Northern Hemisphere near Cancer and Virgo.

Le•o•nar•do da Vin•ci (lē′ə-när′dō də vĭn′chē) 1452–1519. Italian artist, scientist, and inventor whose scientific insights were far ahead of their time. He investigated anatomy, geology, botany, hydraulics, optics, mathematics, meteorology, and mechanics. Leonardo designed the first helicopter, parachute, and bicycle, all of which were made, centuries after his death, using modern materials and technology.

lep•ro•sy (lĕp′rə-sē) A disease caused by a bacterium that damages nerves, skin, and mucous membranes. Leprosy progresses slowly, but if untreated it can destroy the affected body tissues.

leu•cine (lo͞o′sēn′) An essential amino acid. *See more at* **amino acid.**

leu•ke•mi•a (lo͞o-kē′mē-ə) Any of several cancers of the blood in which abnormal white blood cells multiply uncontrollably, eventually crowding out normal cells in the bone marrow.

leu•ko•cyte *also* **leu•co•cyte** (lo͞o′kə-sīt′) *See* **white blood cell.**

lev•ee (lĕv′ē) A long ridge of sand, silt, and clay built up by a river along its banks, especially during floods.

lev•er (lĕv′ər) A simple machine consisting of a bar that pivots on a fixed support, the fulcrum, and is used to transmit force. For example, a lever with the fulcrum positioned between the two ends can raise or move a heavy weight at one end as the bar is pushed down at the other. *See more at* **fulcrum.**

Ley•den jar (līd′n) An early device for storing electric charge. It consists of a glass jar with conductive metal foil covering most of the inner and outer surfaces (all except the top parts). A metal rod or wire, used to draw electric charge into the jar, touches the inner foil and then exits through an insulating stopper in the neck.

Leonardo da Vinci

■ **lichen**
rock orange lichen

Li The symbol for **lithium.**

Li•bra (lē′brə) A constellation in the Southern Hemisphere near Scorpius and Virgo.

li•chen (lī′kən) An organism that consists of a fungus and an alga living together in a symbiotic relationship. The alga supplies nutrients by photosynthesis, while the fungus shades the alga from excessive sunlight and supplies water by absorbing water vapor from the air. Lichens often live on rocks and tree bark and can thrive in extreme environments, such as mountaintops and the polar regions.

Lie•big (lē′bĭg), Baron **Justus von** 1803–1873. German chemist who contributed to many areas of chemistry. He was one of the first to investigate organic compounds and to develop techniques for their analysis. Liebig also established one of the first teaching laboratories, where many 19th-century chemists were trained.

life (līf) **1.** The property or quality that distinguishes living organisms from dead organisms and nonliving matter. Life is shown in an organism that has the ability to grow, carry on metabolism, respond to stimuli, and reproduce. **2.** Living organisms considered as a group: *plant life; marine life.*

life cycle The series of changes in the growth and development of an organism from its beginning as an independent life form to its mature state in which offspring are produced. In simple organisms, such as bacteria, the life cycle begins when an organism is produced by fission and ends when that organism in turn divides into two new ones. In more complex organisms, the life cycle starts with the fusion of reproductive cells and ends when that organism produces its own reproductive cells, which then may go on to reproduce.

life science Any of several branches of science, such as biology, medicine, or ecology, that studies living organisms and their organization, life processes, and relationships to each other and their environment. *Compare* **physical science.**

lift (lĭft) An upward force acting on an object. Lift can be caused because an object, such as an air balloon, contains a type of gas that weighs less than air, or because of a low-pressure area above an object, such as a wing, that is moving through a fluid. *Compare* **drag.** *See Note at* **aerodynamics.**

lig•a•ment (lĭg′ə-mənt) A sheet or band of tough fibrous tissue that connects two bones or holds an organ of the body in place.

light (līt) **1.** A form of electromagnetic energy that can be perceived by the human eye. It is made up of electromagnetic waves that travel at a speed of about 186,282 miles (299,728 kilometers) per second. **2.** Electromagnetic energy that cannot be perceived by the human eye, as infrared light and ultraviolet light. *See Note at* **electromagnetic radiation.**

light-emitting diode *See* **LED.**

Did You Know?
lightning

The energy within a bolt of *lightning* is so great that it heats the air around it to temperatures up to five times greater than that of the surface of the sun, or 55,000°F (30,000°C). The rapid expansion of this superheated air is what creates the sounds we call thunder. The sounds travel to us more slowly than the light from lightning, so it is possible to estimate how far away a lightning strike is by timing the gap between when you see the lightning and when you hear the thunder it has produced. Count the seconds from when you see the flash until you hear the thunder, and divide this number by five. The result will be the number of miles you are from the point of the strike.

USAGE

light-year

It is important to remember that a *light-year* is a measure of distance, not time. A light-year is the length of empty space that light can traverse in a year, close to six trillion miles. When scientists calculate how many light-years the stars are from Earth or from one another, they are calculating their distance, not their age.

light•ning (līt′nĭng) A flash of light in the sky caused by an electrical discharge between clouds or between a cloud and the Earth's surface. The flash heats the air and usually causes thunder. Lightning may appear as a jagged streak, a bright sheet, or, in rare cases, a glowing red ball.

light-year (līt′yîr′) The distance that light travels in a vacuum in one year, equal to about 5.88 trillion miles (9.48 trillion kilometers).

lig•nin (lĭg′nĭn) A complex organic compound that binds to cellulose fibers and hardens and strengthens the cell walls of plants. It is the chief noncarbohydrate constituent of wood.

lig•nite (lĭg′nīt′) A soft, brownish-black form of coal having more carbon than peat but less carbon than bituminous coal. Lignite is easy to mine but does not burn as well as other forms of coal. *Compare* **anthracite, bituminous coal.**

lime (līm) A white, lumpy powder made of calcium oxide (CaO). It is made by heating limestone, bones, or shells, and is used to make glass, paper, steel, and building plaster. It is also added to soil to lower its acidity.

lime•stone (līm′stōn′) A sedimentary rock consisting primarily of calcium carbonate, often in the form of the mineral calcite. Limestones can occur in many colors but are usually white, gray, or black. They often contain fossil shells and other marine organisms. *See Table at* **rock.**

line (līn) A geometric figure formed by a point moving in a fixed direction and in the reverse direction. The intersection of two planes is a line. ❖ The part of a line that lies between two points on the line is called a **line segment.**

lin•e•ar (lĭn′ē-ər) Of or resembling a line. ❖ A **linear equation** is an algebraic equation, such as $y = 4x + 3$, in which the variables are of the first degree (that is, raised only to the first power). The graph of such an equation is a straight line.

linear accelerator A device that accelerates charged subatomic particles, such as protons and electrons, in a straight line by means of alternating negative and positive impulses from electric fields. Linear accelerators are used to bring about high-speed particle collisions in order to study subatomic structures. *Compare* **cyclotron.**

line of force A line used to show the direction of force of an electric or magnetic field. *See Note at* **magnetism.**

Lin•nae•us (lĭ-nē′əs, lĭ-nā′əs) 1707–1778. Swedish naturalist who founded the modern classification system for the naming of plants and animals. He introduced the use of two names including a designation of genus and species in 1749. *See more at* **binomial nomenclature.**

lip•ase (lĭp′ās′, lī′pās′) An enzyme that promotes the decomposition of fats to form glycerol and fatty acids.

lip•id (lĭp′ĭd) Any of a large group of organic compounds composed of fats and fatty compounds that are oily to the touch and insoluble in water. Lipids include fatty acids, oils, waxes, sterols, and triglycerides. They are a source of stored energy and are a component of cell membranes.

liq•ue•fac•tion (lĭk′wə-făk′shən) **1.** *Chemistry.* The act or process of turning a gas into a liquid. **2.** *Geology.* The process by which sediment that is very wet starts to behave like a liquid. Liquefaction is often caused by severe shaking, as in earthquakes.

Carolus Linnaeus

liq•uid (lĭk′wĭd) One of the three basic forms of matter, composed of molecules that can move short distances. Unlike a solid, a liquid has no fixed shape, but instead has a characteristic readiness to flow and therefore takes on the shape of any container. Unlike a gas, a liquid usually has a volume that remains constant or changes only slightly under pressure.

liquid-crystal display *See* **LCD.**

Lis•ter (lĭs′tər), **Joseph.** First Baron Lister 1827–1912. British surgeon who introduced strict standards of hygiene to hospitals to help combat infection. As a young doctor, Lister observed that patients with compound fractures (fractures with bone protruding through the skin) often died of infection. He became convinced that infection was spread by contact with the air and demonstrated that keeping wounds clean and covered decreased infection. In 1865 he read about Pasteur's germ theory of disease and established a system of antiseptic measures that dramatically decreased the number of deaths caused by infection. Lister's practices were gradually adopted by hospitals throughout Europe.

li•ter (lē′tər) The basic unit of volume in the metric system, equal to about 1.06 liquid quarts or 0.91 dry quart. *See Table at* **measurement.**

lith•i•um (lĭth′ē-əm) A soft, silvery metallic element that is an alkali metal and occurs in small amounts in some minerals. It is the lightest of all metals and is highly reactive. Lithium is used to make alloys, batteries, glass for large telescopes, and ceramics. *Symbol* **Li.** *Atomic number* 3. *See* **Periodic Table,** pages 262–263.

lith•o•sphere (lĭth′ə-sfîr′) The outer part of the Earth, consisting of the crust and upper mantle. It is approximately 62 miles (100 kilometers) thick. *Compare* **asthenosphere, atmosphere, hydrosphere.**

Joseph Lister

litmus

Red litmus paper turns blue when it comes in contact with an alkaline, or basic, solution.

lit•mus (lĭt′məs) A colored powder, obtained from certain lichens, that changes to red in an acid solution and to blue in an alkaline solution. ❖ Litmus is typically added to paper to make **litmus paper,** which is used to determine whether a solution is basic or acidic.

Lit•tle Dipper (lĭt′l) A group of seven stars in the constellation Ursa Minor that form the outline of a dipper.

lit•to•ral (lĭt′ər-əl) *Adjective.* **1.** Of or on a shore, especially a seashore: *the littoral zone.* —*Noun.* **2.** The zone between the limits of high and low tides.

liv•er (lĭv′ər) **1.** A large glandular organ in the abdomen of vertebrate animals that is essential to many metabolic processes. The liver secretes bile, stores fat and sugar as reserve energy sources, converts harmful substances to less toxic forms, and regulates the amount of blood in the body. **2.** A similar organ of invertebrate animals.

liv•er•wort (lĭv′ər-wûrt′, lĭv′ər-wôrt′) Any of numerous small, green plants that lack vascular tissue and do not bear seeds. Liverworts usually grow in the tropics in moist soil and on damp rocks and tree trunks. They are related to the mosses.

liz•ard (lĭz′ərd) Any of numerous reptiles having a scaly, often slender body, a tapering tail, and usually four legs. Lizards typically have movable eyelids, unlike most other reptiles. The iguana and chameleon are lizards.

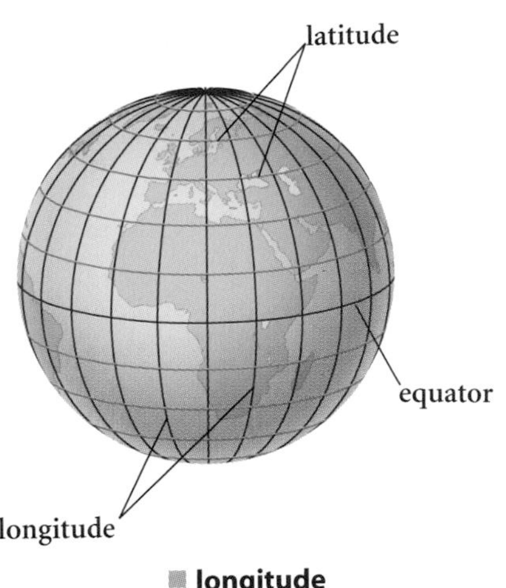

■ **longitude**

load (lōd) **1.** The resistance that a machine must overcome in order to work. **2.** The power output of a generator or power plant.

loam (lōm) Soil composed of approximately equal quantities of sand, silt, and clay. It typically also contains decayed plant matter.

Lo•ba•chev•ski (lō′bə-chĕf′skē), **Nikolai Ivanovich** 1792–1856. Russian mathematician who developed two systems of geometry that were not based on Euclid's axioms.

lobe (lōb) **1.** A rounded projection, as on a leaf or body part. **2.** An anatomical division of an organ of the body, such as the liver or lungs, bounded by fissures and connective tissue.

lobe-finned fish Any of various bony fish with fins that are rounded and fleshy, suggesting limbs. The lobe-finned fish are thought by some to be ancestors of amphibians and other land-dwelling vertebrate animals. They first appeared in the Ordovician Period and are extinct except for the coelacanth and lungfish.

lo•co•mo•tion (lō′kə-mō′shən) The ability of an animal to move from place to place. In many animals, locomotion is produced by the action of limbs or other appendages, such as wings or flagella. Other organisms, such as snakes, propel themselves by thrusting the body sideways against a hard surface. Fish move through the water by means of wave-like muscle contractions that course through the body from head to tail.

lode•stone *also* **load•stone** (lōd′stōn′) A piece of the mineral magnetite that acts like a magnet.

lo•ess (lō′əs, lĕs, lŭs) A very fine-grained silt or clay, thought to be deposited as dust blown by the wind. Most loess is believed to have originated during the Pleistocene Epoch from areas of land covered by glaciers and from desert surfaces.

Löf•fler (lŭf′lər), **Friedrich** 1852–1915. German bacteriologist. With Edwin Klebs, he isolated the bacillus that causes diphtheria (1884).

log (lôg) A logarithm.

log•a•rithm (lô′gə-rĭth′əm) The power to which some base number must be raised to produce a given number. For example, if the base is 10, then the logarithm of 1,000 (written $\log_{10} 1{,}000$) is 3, because $10^3 = 1{,}000$. Natural logarithms are represented with the notation *ln* such that *ln(x)* means "the natural logarithm of *x*."

log•ic (lŏj′ĭk) The study of the principles of reasoning.

lon•gi•tude (lŏn′jĭ-to͞od′) Distance east or west on the Earth's surface, measured in degrees from a certain meridian, usually the prime meridian at Greenwich, England, which has a longitude of 0°. The distance of a degree of longitude is about 69 statute miles (111 kilometers) or 60 nautical miles at the equator, narrowing to zero at the poles. Longitude and latitude are the coordinates used to identify any point on the Earth's surface. *Compare* **latitude.**

lon•gi•tu•di•nal wave (lŏn′jĭ-to͞od′n-əl) A wave in which the particles of the medium through which the wave moves vibrate in the same direction as the wave travels. Sound waves are a type of longitudinal wave. *See more at* **wave.** *Compare* **transverse wave.**

long ton (lông) *See* **ton** (sense 2).

Lons•dale (lŏnz′dāl′), Dame **Kathleen Yardley** 1903–1971. Irish physicist. In 1929 her x-ray analysis showed that the carbon atoms in the benzene ring are arranged hexagonally and are in the same plane.

louse (lous) *Plural* **lice** (līs) Any of numerous small, wingless insects that often live as parasites on the bodies of other animals, including humans. Lice have mouthparts that are adapted for biting or sucking, and they often feed on blood.

low•est common denominator (lō′ĭst) The least common multiple of the denominators of a set of fractions. For example, the lowest common denominator of $\frac{1}{3}$ and $\frac{3}{4}$ is 12.

low tide (lō) The time at which the tide reaches its lowest level.

Lr The symbol for **lawrencium.**

Lu The symbol for **lutetium.**

lum•bar (lŭm′bər) Relating to, located at, or located near the part of the back lying between the lowest ribs and the hips: *lumbar vertebrae; the lumbar spine.*

lu•men (lo͞o′mən) **1.** *Anatomy.* The central space in a tubular organ, such as a blood vessel or intestine. **2.** *Physics.* A unit used to measure the amount of light passing through a given area per second. One lumen is equal to the amount of light that passes through a given area (shaped like a cone) that is illuminated by a light with a brightness of one candela.

lu•mi•nes•cence (lo͞o′mə-nĕs′əns) **1.** The emission of light as a result of the excitation of atoms by a source of energy other than heat. Bioluminescence, fluorescence, and phosphorescence are examples of luminescence that can be produced by biological or chemical processes. **2.** The light produced in this way.

lu•nar (lo͞o′nər) **1.** Relating to the moon: *a lunar mountain.* **2.** Measured by the revolution of the moon: *a lunar month.*

lunar eclipse *See under* **eclipse.**

lung (lŭng) **1.** Either of two spongy organs in the chest of air-breathing vertebrate animals that serve as the organs of gas exchange. Blood flowing through the lungs picks up oxygen from inhaled air and releases carbon dioxide, which is exhaled. Air enters and leaves the lungs through the bronchial tubes. **2.** A similar organ found in some invertebrates.

lungfish
African lungfish

lung•fish (lŭng′fĭsh′) Any of several tropical freshwater fish that, in addition to having gills, have lung-like organs for breathing air. Lungfish have a long, narrow body, and certain species can survive periods of drought inside a mucus-lined cocoon in the mud. The lungfish and the coelacanths are the only living lobe-finned fishes.

Lu•ri•a (lo͝or′ē-ə), **Salvador Edward** 1912–1991. Italian-born American biologist whose research on gene mutation and bacteria increased scientific understanding of the role of DNA in bacterial viruses.

lus•ter (lŭs′tər) The shine from the surface of a mineral. Luster is important in describing different kinds of minerals. It is usually characterized as metallic, glassy, pearly, or dull.

lu•te•ti•um (lo͞o-tē′shē-əm) A silvery-white metallic element of the lanthanide series that is used in nuclear technology. Its radioactive isotope is used to find the age of meteorites. *Symbol* **Lu.** *Atomic number* 71. *See* **Periodic Table,** pages 262–263.

lux (lŭks) A unit used to measure illumination. One lux is equal to one lumen per square meter.

L wave *See* **surface wave.** *See Note at* **earthquake.**

Lwoff (lwôf), **André Michel** 1902–1994. French microbiologist who studied the genetics of bacterial viruses and explained how they reproduce. His findings have been important in cancer research and in understanding how viruses resist drugs.

lye (lī) A strong alkaline solution of potassium hydroxide or sodium hydroxide, made by allowing water to wash through wood ashes. It is used to make soap.

Ly•ell (lī′əl), Sir **Charles** 1797–1875. Scottish geologist who is considered one of the founders of modern geology. His *Principles of Geology* (1830–1833) had a powerful influence on the science of his day.

Lyme disease (līm) A disease caused by bacteria that is transmitted by a species of tick called a deer tick. It begins as a large red spot at the site of the tick bite and is usually followed by chills, fever, and fatigue, often lasting for several weeks.

lymph (lĭmf) The clear fluid flowing through the lymphatic system that serves mainly to bathe and nourish the tissues of the body. It is composed of blood plasma that has leaked out through the capillaries into the tissues.

lym•phat•ic system (lĭm-făt′ĭk) A network of vessels, tissues, and organs in vertebrate animals that helps the body regulate fluid balance and fight against disease. The vessels of the lymphatic system drain excess fluid (called lymph) from the tissues and return it to the circulating blood. Lymphocytes circulate throughout the lymphatic system.

lymph node A bean-shaped mass of tissue found along the vessels of the lymphatic system. Lymph nodes act to filter foreign substances from the blood.

lym•pho•cyte (lĭm′fə-sīt′) Any of various white blood cells that function in the body's immune system by recognizing and deactivating specific foreign substances called antigens. Certain lymphocytes (called B cells) act by stimulating the production of antibodies. Others (T cells) contain receptors on their cell surfaces that are capable of recognizing and binding to specific antigens.

Ly•ra (lī′rə) A constellation in the Northern Hemisphere near Cygnus and Hercules.

ly•sine (lī′sēn′) An essential amino acid. *See more at* **amino acid.**

ly•sis (lī′sĭs) The disintegration of a cell that results from destruction of the cell membrane by a specific substance, especially an antibody or toxin.

ly•so•some (lī′sə-sōm′) A structure in the cytoplasm of many cells that is surrounded by a membrane and contains enzymes that digest food molecules. *See more at* **cell.**

m **1.** Abbreviation of **mass. 2.** Abbreviation of **meter.**

ma•chine (mə-shēn′) **1.** A simple device that applies force or changes the direction of a force in order to perform a task. The lever, pulley, inclined plane, screw, wedge, and the wheel and axle are all simple machines. **2.** A device made of simple machines and used to perform a task: *a washing machine.*

Mach number (mäk) The ratio of the speed of a body to the speed of sound in a particular medium. For example, an aircraft flying through air at twice the speed of sound has a Mach number of 2.

macro– A prefix that means "large," as in *macronucleus,* a large kind of nucleus.

mac•ro•cli•mate (măk′rō-klī′mĭt) The climate of a large geographic area.

mac•ro•mol•e•cule (măk′rō-mŏl′ĭ-kyo͞ol′) A large molecule, such as a protein, consisting of many smaller molecules linked together.

mac•ro•phage (măk′rə-fāj′) Any of the large white blood cells in many vertebrates that engulf and break down foreign particles and bacteria in blood or lymph. Macrophages are important in the body's defense against disease and are found mainly in the spleen, lymph nodes, and liver.

mac•u•la (măk′yə-lə) An area near the center of the retina in vertebrate animals where vision is sharpest.

mad cow disease (măd) A disease of cattle in which the tissues of the brain deteriorate and take on a spongy appearance, resulting in abnormal behaviors and loss of muscle control. Mad cow disease is thought to be caused by infection-causing agents called prions. A form of the disease is thought to be transmitted to humans through the eating of infected meat. Also called *bovine spongiform encephalopathy.*

Mag•el•lan•ic Clouds (măj′ə-lăn′ĭk) Two small, irregularly shaped galaxies that are the galaxies closest to the Milky Way. They are faintly visible near the south celestial pole.

mag•ma (măg′mə) The molten rock material that originates under the Earth's crust and forms igneous rock when it has cooled. When magma cools and solidifies beneath the Earth's surface, it forms what are known as intrusive rocks. When it reaches the Earth's surface, it flows out as lava and forms extrusive (or volcanic) rocks.

mag•ne•sia (măg-nē′zhə) A white powder, MgO, used in heat-resistant materials because of its very high melting point. It is also used in medicine as an antacid or laxative.

mag•ne•si•um (măg-nē′zē-əm) A lightweight, moderately hard, silvery-white metallic element that is an alkaline-earth metal and burns with an intense white flame. It is an essential component of chlorophyll and is used in lightweight alloys, flash photography, and fireworks. *Symbol* **Mg.** *Atomic number* 12. *See* **Periodic Table,** pages 262–263.

mag•net (măg′nĭt) **1.** A rock, piece of metal, or other solid that has the property of attracting iron or steel. A lodestone is a natural magnet, but most magnets today are made by inducing magnetism in a material such as steel or a metal alloy. Magnets have two magnetic poles, called north and south. **2.** An electromagnet.

mag•net•ic (măg-nĕt′ĭk) Having the properties of a magnet; showing magnetism.

magnetic declination The horizontal angle between the true geographic North Pole and the magnetic north pole, as figured from a specific point on the Earth.

magnetic disk A memory device, such as a floppy disk or a hard disk, that is covered with a magnetic coating. Digital information is stored on magnetic disks in the form of microscopically small, magnetized needles.

magnetic field The area around a magnet in which its magnetism can affect other objects. *See Note at* **magnetism.**

magnetic flux A measure of the strength of the magnetic field around a magnet or an electric current, based on the total number of magnetic lines of force that pass through a specific area.

magnetic force **1.** The force that exists between two magnets, caused by the interaction of their magnetic fields. This force causes the magnets to attract or repel one another. **2.** The force that

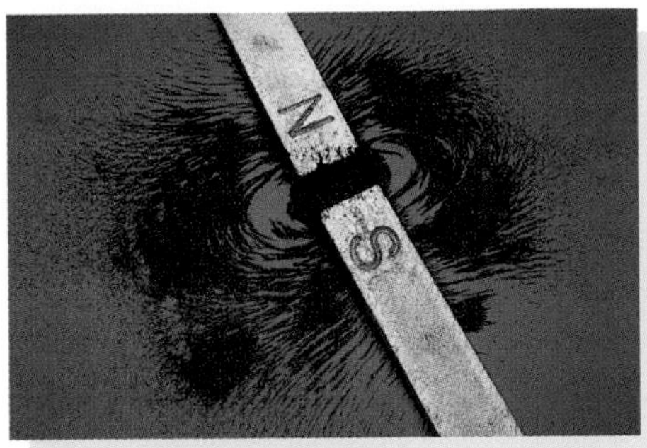

■ **magnetic field**

Iron filings show the magnetic field surrounding opposite poles.

exists between two moving, electrically charged particles, causing them to attract or repel one another.

magnetic induction The process by which a substance, such as iron, becomes magnetized by a magnetic field.

magnetic north The direction toward which the north-seeking arrow of a compass points. ❖ The **magnetic north pole** is the northern pole of the Earth's magnetic field and changes slightly in response to variations in the Earth's magnetism. The current magnetic north pole is located in the Arctic Islands of Canada. *Compare* **geographic north.**

magnetic pole 1. Either of two areas of a magnet where the magnetic field is strongest. *See Note at* **magnetism. 2.** Either of two locations on the Earth's surface toward which a compass needle points; either the magnetic north pole or the magnetic south pole. The location of the magnetic poles, which are found near to but not exactly at the geographic poles, changes gradually over time.

magnetic resonance imaging The use of nuclear magnetic resonance to produce images of the molecules that make up a substance, especially the soft tissues of the human body. Magnetic resonance imaging is used in medicine to diagnose disorders of body structures that do not show up well on x-rays. *See more at* **nuclear magnetic resonance.**

magnetic storm A disturbance or fluctuation in the Earth's magnetic field, caused by streams of charged particles given off by solar flares.

mag•net•ism (măg′nĭ-tĭz′əm) **1.** The force produced by a magnetic field. **2.** The properties or effects of magnets: *Magnetism causes a compass needle to point north.*

Did You Know?
magnetism

The force known as *magnetism* is caused by the motion of electrons. As these tiny, negatively charged particles revolve around an atomic nucleus, they create an electric current that produces a *magnetic field.* This invisible field is made up of closed loops called *lines of force* that surround and run through the atom like tiny raceways. The places where these lines of force come together are strongly magnetic and are called north and south *poles.* In some substances, these tiny magnetic fields naturally align, and the entire substance acts like a magnet—with north and south poles and a magnetic field. These naturally magnetic substances are called *permanent magnets.* Other things, such as a coil of wire, can be made magnetic by running electric current through them. These electrically produced magnets, called *electromagnets,* are used in many devices, such as the one that translates electric signals into the voice you hear on the telephone.

mag•net•ite (măg′nĭ-tīt′) A usually brown to black, magnetic mineral composed of iron and magnesium oxide. Magnetite occurs in many different types of rocks, commonly as small octahedrons. It is an important source of iron.

mag•net•ize (măg′nĭ-tīz′) To cause an object to become magnetic. For example, a nail can be magnetized by wrapping it in a wire that will carry an electric current and connecting the wire to a battery.

mag•ne•tom•e•ter (măg′nĭ-tŏm′ĭ-tər) An instrument for measuring the magnitude and direction of a magnetic field. Magnetometers are often used in archaeological and geological investigations to determine the intensity and direction of the Earth's magnetic field at various times in the past.

mag•ne•tron (măg′nĭ-trŏn′) An electron tube that produces microwave radiation by applying magnetic and electric fields to a stream of electrons emitted by a heated filament. Magnetrons are used in radar and in microwave ovens.

mag•ni•tude (măg′nĭ-to͞od′) **1.** The brightness of a star or another celestial body as seen from the Earth, measured on a numerical scale in which lower numbers mean greater brightness. The dimmest stars visible to the unaided eye have magnitude 6, while the brightest star outside our solar system, Sirius, has magnitude –1.4. The moon has magnitude –12.7, and the sun has magnitude –26.8. **2.** A measure of the total amount of energy released by an earthquake, as indicated on the Richter scale.

mai•a•sau•ra (mī′ə-sôr′ə) *or* **mai•a•saur** (mī′ə-sôr′) A duck-billed dinosaur of the late Cretaceous Period of North America. Its remains suggest that the adults lived in herds and cared for their young in large nesting sites.

Mai•man (mā′mən), **Theodore Harold** 1927–2007. American physicist who constructed the first working laser, in 1960.

main•frame (mān′frām′) A large, powerful computer, often serving many terminals and usually used by large, complex organizations.

mal•a•chite (măl′ə-kīt′) A bright-green copper carbonate mineral found in copper veins and used as a copper ore. Malachite often occurs together with the mineral azurite.

ma•lar•i•a (mə-lâr′ē-ə) An infectious disease of tropical areas that is caused by a parasite transmitted by mosquitoes. It causes repeated attacks of chills, fever, and sweating.

mammoth
skeleton on display at The Mammoth Site, Hot Springs, South Dakota

manatee

male (māl) *Adjective.* **1.** *Zoology.* **a.** Relating to a male reproductive cell (a sperm cell). **b.** Being the sex that can fertilize egg cells and father offspring: *a male kangaroo.* **2.** *Botany.* **a.** Being a structure, especially a stamen or anther, that produces reproductive cells or nuclei that are capable of fertilizing a female reproductive cell. **b.** Bearing stamens but not pistils: *male flowers.* —*Noun.* **3.** A male organism.

ma•lig•nant (mə-lĭg′nənt) Likely to spread or get worse: *a malignant tumor.*

mal•le•a•ble (măl′ē-ə-bəl) Capable of being shaped or formed in its solid state, especially by pressure or hammering. Gold is the most malleable substance known.

mal•le•us (măl′ē-əs) The largest and outermost of the three small bones (called ossicles) in the middle ear. It is also called the hammer.

mal•nu•tri•tion (măl′no͞o-trĭsh′ən) Poor nourishment caused by lack of essential foods or by disease.

mal•oc•clu•sion (măl′ə-klo͞o′zhən) A condition in which the upper and lower teeth do not meet properly; a faulty bite.

Mal•pi•ghi (măl-pē′gē), **Marcello** 1628–1694. Italian anatomist who was the first to use a microscope in the study of anatomy. He discovered the capillary system, extending the work of William Harvey.

mal•tose (môl′tōs′) A sugar made by the action of various enzymes on starch. It is formed in the body during digestion.

mam•mal (măm′əl) Any of various warm-blooded vertebrate animals whose young feed on milk that is produced by the mother's mammary glands. Unlike other vertebrates, mammals have

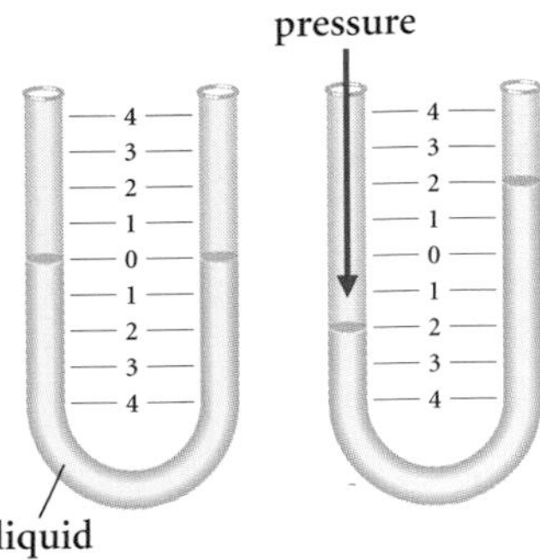

manometer

To calculate pressure in a U-tube manometer, add the sum of the readings above and below zero. The manometer on the left is at equilibrium. The manometer on the right shows readings of 2 above zero and 2 below zero, indicating a pressure of 4.

a diaphragm that separates the heart and lungs from the other internal organs, red blood cells that lack a nucleus, and usually hair or fur. All mammals but the monotremes bear live young. Dogs, mice, whales, and humans are mammals.

mam•ma•ry gland (măm′ə-rē) One of the glands in female mammals that produces milk. It is present but undeveloped in the male. In most animals, the gland opens onto the surface by means of a nipple or teat.

mam•mo•gram (măm′ə-grăm′) An x-ray image of the human breast, used to detect tumors or other abnormalities.

mam•moth (măm′əth) Any of various extinct elephants of very large size that had long, upwardly curving tusks and thick hair. Mammoths lived throughout the Northern Hemisphere during the Ice Age.

man•a•tee (măn′ə-tē′) Any of various plant-eating water mammals living in rivers and bays along the tropical Atlantic Ocean. Manatees avoid contact with humans, have flippers shaped like paddles, and are more closely related to elephants than they are to dolphins or whales.

man•di•ble (măn′də-bəl) **1.** The lower part of the jaw in vertebrate animals. *See more at* **skeleton. 2.** One of the pincer-like mouthparts of insects and other arthropods.

man•ga•nese (măng′gə-nēz′) A grayish-white, hard, brittle metallic element that occurs in several different minerals. It is used to increase the hardness and strength of steel and other important alloys. *Symbol* **Mn.** *Atomic number* 25. *See* **Periodic Table,** pages 262–263.

ma•nom•e•ter (mə-nŏm′ĭ-tər) An instrument that measures the pressure exerted by liquids and gases.

man•tis•sa (măn-tĭs′ə) The part of a logarithm to the base ten that is to the right of the decimal point. For example, if 2.749 is a logarithm, .749 is the mantissa. *Compare* **characteristic.**

man•tle (măn′tl) **1.** The layer of the Earth between the crust and the core. It consists mainly of silicate minerals and has an upper, partially molten part and a lower, solid part. The upper mantle is the source of magma and volcanic lava. **2.** The layer of soft tissue that covers the body of a clam, oyster, or other mollusk and secretes the material that forms the shell.

mar•ble (mär′bəl) A metamorphic rock consisting primarily of calcite and dolomite. Marble is formed by the action of heat and pressure on limestone. Although it is usually white to gray in color, it often has irregularly colored marks due to impurities. *See Table at* **rock.**

Mar•co•ni (mär-kō′nē), **Guglielmo** 1874–1937. Italian physicist and inventor. In 1901 he used radio waves to transmit signals in Morse code across the Atlantic Ocean. Soon after his experiment, radio waves became established as a medium for communications.

ma•re (mä′rā) *Plural* **maria** (mä′rē-ə) Any of the large, dark areas on the moon or on Mars or other planets.

ma•rine (mə-rēn′) Relating to or living in the sea: *marine ecosystems; marine animals.*

Guglielmo Marconi

■ **Mars**
view of Mars's surface recorded by the Imager for Mars Pathfinder (IMP)

marine biology The scientific study of organisms living in or dependent on the oceans.

mar•row (măr′ō) *See* **bone marrow.**

Mars (märz) The fourth planet from the sun and the third smallest, with a diameter about half that of Earth. Mars has seasons similar to but much longer than Earth's. *See Table at* **solar system,** pages 316–317. *See Note at* **planet.**

marsh (märsh) An area of low-lying wet land, often having an abundance of reeds and rushes.

mar•su•pi•al (mär-so͞o′pē-əl) Any of various mammals whose young are very undeveloped when born and continue developing outside their mother's body attached to one of her nipples. Most marsupials have longer hindlegs than forelimbs, and the females usually have pouches in which they carry their young. Kangaroos, opossums, and koalas are marsupials.

ma•ser (mā′zər) Any of several devices that amplify or generate microwaves. Masers are similar to lasers but emit microwaves instead of light.

mass (măs) A measure of the amount of matter contained in a physical body. Mass is independent of gravity and is therefore different from weight. *See Note at* **weight.**

mass-energy equivalence The principle that mass and energy can be converted into each other and that a particular quantity of mass is equivalent to a particular quantity of energy. The principle was stated mathematically by Albert Einstein as $E = mc^2$, where E is the energy in ergs, m is the mass in grams, and c is the speed of light in centimeters per second.

mass number The total number of protons and neutrons in the nucleus of an atom. For example, nitrogen has 7 protons and 7 neutrons in its nucleus, giving it a mass number of 14.

mass spectroscope Any of various devices that use electric or magnetic fields to determine the masses of atoms or molecules in a sample. A beam of ions (electrically charged atoms or molecules) is passed through the electric or magnetic field. The field deflects the ions at different angles depending on their masses, thereby breaking the beam into separate bands. ❖ Each different element, isotope, or ion has a unique series of bands, called a **mass spectrum,** that can be used to identify it.

mas•ti•ca•tion (măs′tĭ-kā′shən) The chewing or grinding of food by the teeth.

mas•to•don (măs′tə-dŏn′) Any of several extinct mammals similar to elephants and mammoths except in the shape of their molar teeth. Like elephants, mastodons had a pair of long, curved tusks growing from their upper jaw, but they also sometimes had a second pair from the lower jaw. They lived from the Oligocene Epoch to the end of the Ice Age.

mas•toid (măs′toid′) A protruding area of bone in the lower part of the skull that is located behind the ear in humans and many other vertebrates.

math•e•mat•ics (măth′ə-măt′ĭks) The study of the measurement, relationships, and properties of quantities and sets, using numbers and symbols. Arithmetic, algebra, geometry, and calculus are branches of mathematics.

ma•trix (mā′trĭks) A substance within which something is contained or embedded. The mineral grains of a rock in which fossils are embedded make up a matrix. Bone cells are embedded in a matrix of collagen fibers and mineral salts.

mat•ter (măt′ər) Something that occupies space, has mass, and can exist ordinarily as a solid, liquid, or gas.

mat•u•ra•tion (măch′ə-rā′shən) The process of becoming fully developed or ripe, as when a reproductive cell, such as an egg or a sperm, becomes capable of fertilization.

Mau•ry (môr′ē), **Matthew Fontaine** 1806–1873. American naval officer and oceanographer who charted the currents and winds of the Atlantic, Pacific, and Indian Oceans and wrote *Physical Geography of the Sea* (1855).

max•il•la (măk-sĭl′ə) The upper part of the jaw in vertebrate animals.

max•i•mum (măk′sə-məm) *Plural* **maxima. 1.** The greatest known or greatest possible number, measure, quantity, or degree. **2.** *Mathematics.* The greatest value of a function, if it has such a value.

Max•well (măks′wĕl′), **James Clerk** 1831–1879. Scottish physicist who developed four laws of electromagnetism showing that light is composed of electromagnetic waves. He determined that Saturn's rings are composed of a large number of tiny particles and investigated color vision, producing the first color photograph (1861).

Mayr (mī′ər), **Ernst** 1904–2005. German-born American zoologist whose work expanded scientific understanding of the formation of species and how they adapt to their environment.

Mc•Clin•tock (mə-klĭn′tək), **Barbara** 1902–1992. American geneticist who proved that genes can change position on chromosomes. By studying the chromosomes found in corn, McClintock discovered that the genes for specific traits, such as kernel color, did not remain in the same place on the chromosomes. Much of her work investigated the ways chromosomes reacted to damage, as from exposure to x-rays. She also did pioneering research in the ways that humans breed new varieties of plants, showing how the history of the cultivation of corn by different cultures could be traced by looking at the genes of different strains.

Md The symbol for **mendelevium.**

Barbara McClintock

mean (mēn) **1.** A number or quantity having a value that is intermediate between other numbers or quantities, especially an arithmetic mean or average. *See more at* **arithmetic mean. 2.** Either the second or third term of a proportion of four terms. In the proportion $\frac{2}{3} = \frac{4}{6}$, the means are 3 and 4. *Compare* **extreme.**

mean time Time measured with reference to an imaginary sun that lies in the same plane as the Earth's equator and that the Earth orbits at a constant speed. Using this convention results in equal, 24-hour days throughout the year. If days were measured by the actual movement of the sun, they would vary slightly in length at different times of the year.

mea•sles (mē′zəlz) A highly contagious disease that is caused by a virus and usually occurs in childhood. Symptoms include fever, coughing, and a rash that begins on the face and then spreads to other parts of the body.

meas•ure•ment (mĕzh′ər-mənt) A method for determining quantity, capacity, or dimension. All systems of measurement use units whose amounts have been arbitrarily set and agreed upon by a group of people. Several systems of measurement are in common use, notably the United States Customary System and the metric system. The metric system has been officially adopted as the international standard for use in science, providing scientists all over the world with an efficient way of comparing the results of experiments conducted at different times and in different places. *See Table, next page.*

me•chan•i•cal engineering (mĭ-kăn′ĭ-kəl) The branch of engineering that specializes in the design, production, and uses of machines.

MEASUREMENT TABLE

INTERNATIONAL SYSTEM

The International System is an expanded and modified version of the metric system made up of base units from which all others in the system are derived. Larger or smaller multiples of any base unit are formed by adding a prefix to the unit and multiplying it by the appropriate factor. For example, to get a kilometer (multiplying factor = 10^3), you would multiply one meter by **1,000.** Similarly, to get a centimeter (multiplying factor = 10^{-2}), you would multiply one meter by **0.01.**

BASE UNITS

Unit	Quantity	Symbol
meter	length	m
kilogram	mass	kg
second	time	s
ampere	electric current	A
kelvin	temperature	K
mole	amount of matter	mol
candela	luminous intensity	cd

PREFIXES

Prefix	Symbol	Multiplying Factor	Prefix	Symbol	Multiplying Factor
tera-	T	10^{12} = 1,000,000,000,000	deci-	d	10^{-1} = 0.1
giga-	G	10^{9} = 1,000,000,000	centi-	c	10^{-2} = 0.01
mega-	M	10^{6} = 1,000,000	milli-	m	10^{-3} = 0.001
kilo-	k	10^{3} = 1,000	micro-	μ	10^{-6} = 0.000,001
hecto-	h	10^{2} = 100	nano-	n	10^{-9} = 0.000,000,001
deca-	da	10 = 10	pico-	p	10^{-12} = 0.000,000,000,001

US CUSTOMARY SYSTEM

Unit	Relation to Other US Customary Units
LENGTH	
inch	1/12 foot
foot	12 inches or 1/3 yard
yard	36 inches or 3 feet
rod	16½ feet or 5½ yards
furlong	220 yards or 1/8 mile
mile (statute)	5,280 feet or 1,760 yards
mile (nautical)	6,076 feet or 2,025 yards

Unit	Relation to Other US Customary Units
LIQUID VOLUME OR CAPACITY	
ounce	1/16 pint
gill	4 ounces
pint	16 ounces
quart	2 pints or ¼ gallon
gallon	128 ounces or 8 pints

Unit	Relation to Other US Customary Units
WEIGHT	
grain	1/7000 pound
dram	1/16 ounce
ounce	16 drams
pound	16 ounces
ton (short)	2,000 pounds
ton (long)	2,240 pounds

CONVERSION BETWEEN METRIC AND US CUSTOMARY SYSTEMS

FROM US CUSTOMARY TO METRIC

When you know	multiply by	to find
inches	25.4	millimeters
	2.54	centimeters
feet	30.48	centimeters
yards	0.91	meters
miles	1.61	kilometers
fluid ounces	29.57	milliliters
pints	0.47	liters
quarts	0.95	liters
gallons	3.79	liters
ounces	28.35	grams
pounds	0.45	kilograms

FROM METRIC TO US CUSTOMARY

When you know	multiply by	to find
millimeters	0.04	inches
centimeters	0.39	inches
meters	3.28	feet
	1.09	yards
kilometers	0.62	miles
milliliters	0.03	fluid ounces
liters	1.06	quarts
	0.26	gallons
	2.12	pints
grams	0.035	ounces
kilograms	2.20	pounds

TEMPERATURE CONVERSION BETWEEN CELSIUS AND FAHRENHEIT

$°C = (°F - 32) \div 1.8$

Condition	Fahrenheit	Celsius
Boiling point of water	212°	100°
Normal body temperature	98.6°	37°

$°F = (°C \times 1.8) + 32$

Condition	Fahrenheit	Celsius
Freezing point of water	32°	0°
Lowest temperature Gabriel Fahrenheit could obtain mixing salt and ice	0°	-17.8°

USAGE

megabyte

Usually the prefix *kilo–* means "one thousand," and the prefix *mega–* means "one million." But in the calculation of data storage these prefixes have a different meaning. Data storage capacity (measured in bytes) is based on powers of 2 because of the binary nature of bits (1 byte is 8, or 2^3, bits). Here, the prefix *mega–* refers to the power of 2 closest to 1,000,000, which is 2^{20}, or 1,048,576. Thus, a megabyte is 1,048,576 bytes, although it is also used less technically to refer to a million bytes. Similarly, the prefix *kilo–* refers either to 1,000 or to 2^{10} (1,024). Measuring the transmission of data is somewhat different from measuring its storage. Since a bit of transmitted data is considered as one signal pulse rather than an either/or unit, it is natural to count transmitted bits using ordinary numbers instead of the binary system. Thus a megabyte of transmitted data usually refers to a million (not 1,048,576) bits. Other prefixes for greater amounts, such as *giga–* and *tera–,* follow similar rules for data storage and transmission.

me•chan•ics (mĭ-kăn′ĭks) **1.** The branch of physics that focuses on motion and on the effects of forces and energy on solids, liquids, and gases at rest or in motion. **2.** The functional aspect of a system: *the mechanics of blood circulation.* **3.** The development, production, and use of machines or mechanical devices.

me•di•an (mē′dē-ən) **1.** In a sequence of numbers arranged from smallest to largest: **a.** The middle number, when such a sequence has an odd number of values. For example, in the sequence 3, 4, 14, 35, 280, the median is 14. **b.** The average of the two middle numbers, when such a sequence has an even number of values. For example, in the sequence 4, 8, 10, 56, the median is 9 (the average of 8 and 10). *Compare* **arithmetic mean, average, mode. 2.** A line joining a vertex of a triangle to the midpoint of the opposite side.

med•i•cine (mĕd′ĭ-sĭn) **1.** The scientific study of diagnosing, treating, or preventing disease and injury to the body or mind. **2.** A drug or other substance used to treat a disease or injury.

me•di•um (mē′dē-əm) *Plural* **media. 1.** A substance, such as agar, in which bacteria or other microorganisms are grown for scientific purposes. **2.** A substance through which energy, especially in waves, is transmitted. Sound waves, for example, can travel through the medium of a solid (such as wood or steel), a liquid (such as water), or a gas (such as air). In contrast, seismic waves can travel through the Earth's solid layers and in some cases its liquid layer (the outer core) as well, but they cannot travel through air. *See more at* **wave.**

me•dul•la (mĭ-dŭl′ə, mĭ-do͞o′lə) **1.** *See* **medulla oblongata. 2.** The central core of an anatomical structure, such as the adrenal gland or the kidney.

medulla ob•lon•ga•ta (ŏb′lông-gä′tə) The lowermost portion of the brainstem in humans and other mammals. It regulates many involuntary functions, such as breathing and circulation.

me•du•sa (mĭ-do͞o′sə) A cnidarian in its free-swimming stage. Medusas are bell-shaped, with tentacles hanging down around a central mouth. Jellyfish are medusas, while corals and sea anemones lack a medusa stage and exist only as polyps. *Compare* **polyp.**

mega– A prefix that means: **1.** Large, as in *megatherium,* large animal. **2.** One million, as in *megahertz,* one million hertz. **3.** 2^{20} (that is, 1,048,576), which is the power of 2 closest to a million, as in *megabyte.*

meg•a•bit (mĕg′ə-bĭt′) *Computer Science.* **1.** One million bits. **2.** 1,048,576 (that is, 2^{20}) bits. *See Note at* **megabyte.**

meg•a•byte (mĕg′ə-bīt′) **1.** A unit of computer memory or data storage capacity equal to 1,024 kilobytes (2^{20} bytes). **2.** One million bytes.

meg•a•dose (mĕg′ə-dōs′) An exceptionally large dose, as of a drug or vitamin.

meg•a•fau•na (mĕg′ə-fô′nə) Large or relatively large animals of a particular place or time period. Saber-toothed tigers and mastodons belong to the extinct megafauna of the Oligocene and Pleistocene Epochs.

meg•a•hertz (mĕg′ə-hûrts′) A unit of frequen-

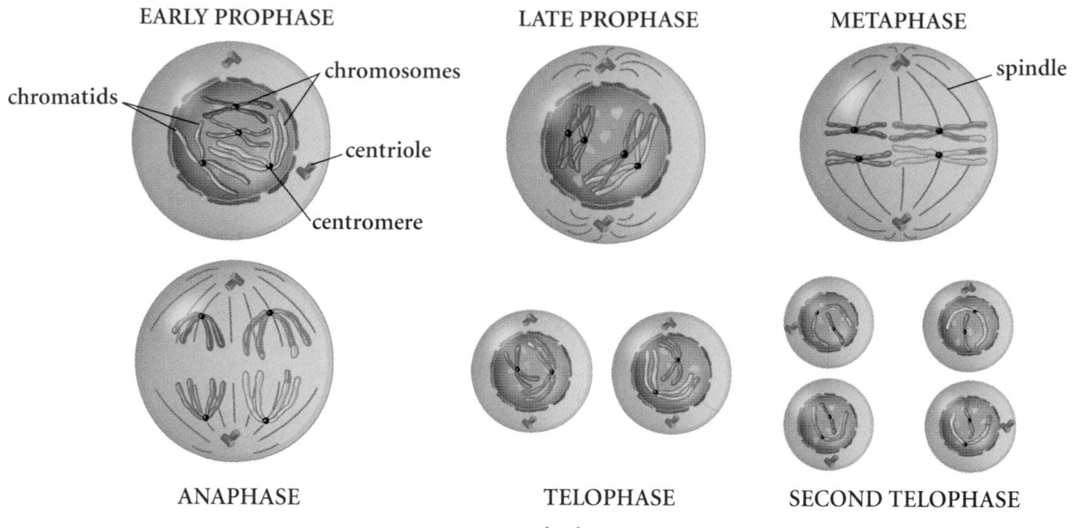

meiosis

In early prophase, chromosomes line up to form pairs, centrioles move toward opposite ends of the cell, and the membrane surrounding the nucleus disappears. In late prophase, the chromatids line up along the center of the cell. During metaphase, each member of a chromatid pair becomes attached to spindle fibers from opposite ends of the cell. In anaphase, the chromosomes from each chromatid pair separate and begin to move toward opposite ends of the cell. During telophase, the cell divides into two new daughter cells, each with half the original number of chromosomes. In second telophase, each of the two daughter cells from the first division divides again to produce a total of four daughter cells, each having just a single set of chromosomes.

cy equal to one million cycles per second, used to express the frequency of radio waves.

meg•a•par•sec (mĕg′ə-pär′sĕk) One million parsecs.

meg•a•the•ri•um (mĕg′ə-thîr′ē-əm) A large, extinct ground sloth that lived from the Miocene through the Pleistocene Epochs, primarily in South America. It was as large as an elephant, had long curved claws, and ate plants.

meg•a•vi•ta•min (mĕg′ə-vī′tə-mĭn) A dose of a vitamin that is much greater than the amount required to maintain health.

meg•a•volt (mĕg′ə-vōlt′) One million volts.

meg•a•watt (mĕg′ə-wŏt′) One million watts.

mei•o•sis (mī-ō′sĭs) A type of cell division, occurring in two phases, that reduces the number of chromosomes in reproductive cells to half the original number. It results in the production of reproductive cells (called gametes) in animals and the formation of spores in plants, fungi, and most algae. The first phase of meiosis involves duplication and then separation of the chromosomes, followed by division into two daughter cells that each contain half the number of chromosomes as the original cell. In the second phase, each daughter cell divides to form an additional reproductive cell. *See Note at* **mitosis.**

Meit•ner (mīt′nər), **Lise** 1878–1968. Austrian-born Swedish physicist who was the first to describe the process of nuclear fission. Her contributions to the field of nuclear fission led to the development of the atomic bomb and nuclear energy.

meit•ner•i•um (mīt-nûr′ē-əm) A synthetic, radioactive element that is produced by bombarding bismuth with iron ions. Its most stable isotope has a half-life of 70 milliseconds. *Symbol* **Mt.** *Atomic number* 109. *See* **Periodic Table,** pages 262–263.

mel•a•nin (mĕl′ə-nĭn) A dark pigment found in the skin, hair, scales, feathers, and eyes of animals. It provides protection against the sun's rays by absorbing ultraviolet light.

mel•a•nism (mĕl′ə-nĭz′əm) Dark coloration of the skin, hair, fur, or feathers because of a high concentration of melanin.

mel•a•no•ma (mĕl′ə-nō′mə) A type of skin cancer that arises from the cells that produce

BIOGRAPHY

Gregor Mendel

Gregor Mendel entered a monastery at the age of 21, later becoming a priest. He was sent to a university to study mathematics and science. When he returned to the monastery, he combined his interests in math and botany by experimenting with garden peas. Mendel cross-pollinated plants of different sizes and shapes as well as plants that produced different colors of flowers or peas. He analyzed each generation of new plants that were produced by this cross-pollination. He observed that some characteristics remained constant in every generation, while others remained hidden, or recessive, and became apparent only in later generations. We now refer to the element that determines each characteristic as a *gene,* and know that genes are parts of chromosomes and are made of DNA—things Mendel had no knowledge of. Mendel proved that two genes exist for each trait and that each gene comes from a different parent. A recessive trait becomes visible only when both genes for the trait are present, but a dominant trait is visible even when only one dominant gene is present. Mendel summarized his discoveries in 1865 in laws that became fundamental to the study of human heredity.

melanin, usually appearing as a dark-colored spot or mole.

melt (mĕlt) To change from a solid to a liquid state by heating or being heated to the melting point.

melt•down (mĕlt′doun′) Severe overheating of a nuclear reactor core, resulting in melting of the core and escape of radiation.

melt•ing point (mĕl′tĭng) The temperature at which a solid becomes a liquid. For a given substance, the melting point of its solid form is the same as the freezing point of its liquid form. The melting point of ice is 32°F (0°C); that of iron is 2,797°F (1,535°C).

melt•wa•ter (mĕlt′wô′tər) Water that comes from melting snow or ice, especially from a glacier.

mem•ber (mĕm′bər) *Mathematics.* **1.** A quantity that belongs to a set; an element of a set. **2.** The expression on either side of an equality sign.

mem•brane (mĕm′brān′) **1.** A thin, flexible layer of tissue that covers, lines, separates, or connects cells or parts of an organism. **2.** *See* **cell membrane. 3.** *Chemistry.* A thin sheet of natural or synthetic material that is permeable to substances in solution.

mem•bra•nous (mĕm′brə-nəs) **1.** Relating to, made of, or similar to a membrane. **2.** Characterized by the formation of a membrane or a layer like a membrane.

mem•o•ry (mĕm′ə-rē) **1.** The ability to remember past experiences or learned information. **2a.** A unit of a computer in which data is stored for later use. **b.** A computer's capacity for storing information: *How much memory does this computer have?*

me•nar•che (mə-när′kē) The first menstrual period.

Men•del (mĕn′dl), **Gregor Johann** 1822–1884. Austrian botanist and founder of the science of genetics. He formulated the important principles, known as Mendel's laws, that formed the basis of modern genetics.

Men•de•le•ev (mĕn′də-lā′əf), **Dmitri Ivanovich** 1834–1907. Russian chemist. He devised

Dmitri Mendeleev

the Periodic Table, which shows the relationships between the chemical elements. It was first published in 1869.

men•de•le•vi•um (mĕn′də-lē′vē-əm) A synthetic, radioactive metallic element of the actinide series that is produced by bombarding einsteinium with helium ions. Its most stable isotope has a half-life of about two months. *Symbol* **Md.** *Atomic number* 101. *See* **Periodic Table,** pages 262–263.

Men•del's law (mĕn′dlz) Any of the principles first proposed by Gregor Mendel to describe the inheritance of traits passed from one generation to the next. The first (also called the law of segregation) states that during the formation of reproductive cells (gametes), pairs of hereditary factors (genes) for a specific trait separate so that offspring receive one factor from each parent. The second (also called the law of independent assortment) states that chance determines which factor for a particular trait is inherited. The third (also called the law of dominance) states that one of the factors for a pair of inherited traits will be dominant and the other recessive, unless both factors are recessive. *See more at* **inheritance.**

me•nin•ges (mə-nĭn′jēz) The membranes enclosing the brain and spinal cord.

men•in•gi•tis (mĕn′ĭn-jī′tĭs) Inflammation of the membranes (meninges) that enclose the brain and spinal cord, usually resulting from a bacterial infection.

me•nis•cus (mə-nĭs′kəs) **1.** A lens that is concave on one side and convex on the other. **2.** The curved upper surface of a column of liquid. The surface is concave if the molecules of the liquid are attracted to the container walls and convex if they are not. **3.** A piece of cartilage shaped like a crescent and located at the junction of two bones in a joint, such as the knee. *See more at* **joint.**

men•o•pause (mĕn′ə-pôz′) The time at which menstruation ceases, occurring usually between 45 and 55 years of age in humans.

men•ses (mĕn′sēz) *See* **menstruation.**

men•stru•al cycle (mĕn′stro͞o-əl) The series of bodily changes in women and other female primates in which the lining of the uterus thickens to allow for implantation of a fertilized egg. The cycle takes about a month to complete, with ovulation usually occurring around the midway point. If the egg produced is not fertilized, the lining of the uterus breaks down and is discharged during menstruation.

men•stru•a•tion (mĕn′stro͞o-ā′shən) The monthly flow of blood from the uterus that begins at puberty in girls and in the females of other primates. Also called *menses.*

men•tal illness (mĕn′tl) Any of various disorders or diseases characterized by abnormal patterns of thought and behavior.

mental retardation Below-average intellectual ability resulting from genetic defect, brain injury, or disease, and usually present from birth or early infancy.

men•thol (mĕn′thôl′) A white, crystalline compound obtained from peppermint oil. It is used as a flavoring and as a mild anesthetic.

Mer•ca•tor projection (mər-kā′tər) A method of making a flat map of the Earth's surface so that the meridians and parallels appear as straight lines that cross at right angles. In a Mercator projection, the areas farther from the equator appear larger, making the polar regions

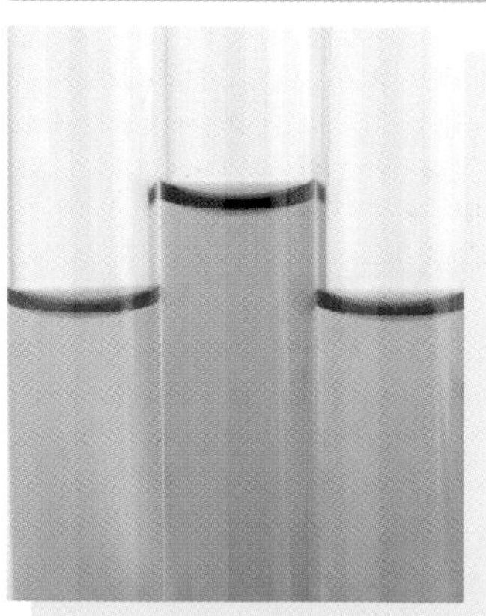

meniscus
The liquid in each tube forms a concave meniscus.

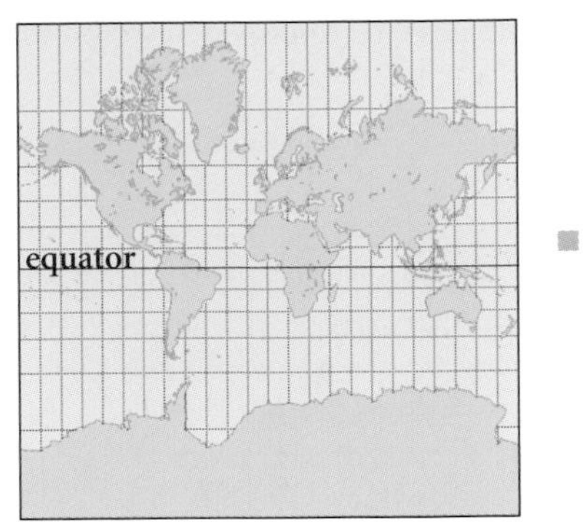

Mercator projection

greatly distorted. *Compare* **conic projection, homolosine projection, sinusoidal projection.**

mer•cu•ry (mûr′kyə-rē) A silvery-white, dense, poisonous metallic element that is a liquid at room temperature. It is used to make thermometers and pesticides. *Symbol* **Hg.** *Atomic number* 80. *See* **Periodic Table,** pages 262–263.

Mercury The planet closest to the sun and the second smallest, with a diameter about two-fifths that of Earth. Mercury's surface is covered with mountains, craters, ridges, and valleys. It orbits the sun once every 88 days, the shortest amount of time for any planet. *See Table at* **solar system,** pages 316–317. *See Note at* **planet.**

me•rid•i•an (mə-rĭd′ē-ən) **1a.** An imaginary line forming a great circle that passes through the North and South Poles. **b.** Either half of such a circle from pole to pole. All the places on the same meridian have the same longitude. *See more at* **longitude. 2.** *Astronomy.* A great circle passing through the poles of the celestial sphere and the point on the celestial sphere that is directly above the observer. *See more at* **celestial sphere.**

mer•i•stem (mĕr′ĭ-stĕm′) Plant tissue whose cells actively divide to produce new tissues that cause the plant to grow. The cells of the meristem are not specialized but can become specialized to form the tissues of roots, leaves, and other plant parts. The growing tips of roots and stems and the tissue layer known as cambium are part of a plant's meristem.

me•sa (mā′sə) An area of high land with a flat top and two or more steep, cliff-like sides. Mesas are larger than buttes and smaller than plateaus, and are common in the southwest United States.

Mes•o•lith•ic (mĕz′ə-lĭth′ĭk) The cultural period of the Stone Age between the Paleolithic and Neolithic, beginning at different times in different parts of the world, about 40,000 to 10,000 years ago. The Mesolithic is marked by the appearance of small-bladed stone tools and weapons and by the beginnings of settled communities. *Compare* **Neolithic, Paleolithic.**

mes•o•phyll (mĕz′ə-fĭl′) The tissues of a leaf that carry on photosynthesis, consisting of the palisade layer and the spongy parenchyma.

WORD HISTORY

mercury

Like a few other elements, mercury has a chemical symbol, Hg, that bears no resemblance to its name. This is because Hg is an abbreviation of the Latin name of the element, which was *hydrargium.* This word in turn was taken over from Greek, where it literally meant "water-silver." With this name the Greeks were referring to the fact that mercury is a silvery liquid at room temperature, rather than a solid like other metals. Similarly, an older English name for this element is *quicksilver,* which means "living silver," referring to its ability to move like a living thing. (The word *quick* used to mean "alive," as in the Biblical phrase "the quick and the dead.") The name *mercury* refers to the fact that the element flows about quickly: the name comes from the Roman god Mercury, who was the swift-footed messenger of the gods.

mesa
North Caineville Mesa, Utah

mes•o•sphere (mĕz′ə-sfîr′) The layer of the Earth's atmosphere lying above the stratosphere and below the thermosphere, from about 31 to 50 miles (50 to 80 kilometers) above the Earth's surface. In the mesosphere, temperatures decrease with increasing altitude.

Mes•o•zo•ic (mĕz′ə-zō′ĭk) The era of geologic time from about 245 to 65 million years ago. The Mesozoic Era was characterized by the development of flowering plants and by the appearance and extinction of dinosaurs. *See Chart at* **geologic time,** pages 148–149.

mes•sen•ger RNA (mĕs′ən-jər) *See under* **RNA.**

me•tab•o•lism (mĭ-tăb′ə-lĭz′əm) The chemical processes by which cells produce the substances and energy needed to sustain life. In metabolism, organic compounds are broken down to provide heat and energy, while simpler molecules are used to build complex compounds like proteins for growth and repair of tissues. Many metabolic processes are brought about by the action of enzymes. —*Adjective* **metabolic.**

met•a•car•pal (mĕt′ə-kär′pəl) Any of the bones of the hand lying between the carpal bones and the bones of the fingers or digits (phalanges). *See more at* **skeleton.**

met•al (mĕt′l) **1.** Any of a large group of elements, including iron, gold, copper, lead, and magnesium, that conduct heat and electricity well. Metals can be hammered into thin sheets or drawn into wires. They are usually shiny and opaque. All metals except mercury are solid at room temperature. **2.** An alloy, such as steel or bronze, made of two or more metals.

me•tal•lic bond (mə-tăl′ĭk) The chemical bonding that holds the atoms of a metal together. This bond is formed from the attraction between mobile electrons and fixed, positively charged metallic atoms. Whereas most chemical bonds are localized between specific neighboring atoms, metallic bonds extend over the entire molecular structure. *See more at* **bond.**

met•al•loid (mĕt′l-oid′) **1.** An element that is not a metal but that has some properties of metals. Arsenic, for example, is a metalloid that looks like a metal, but is a poor conductor of electricity. **2.** A nonmetallic element, such as carbon, that can form alloys with metals.

met•al•lur•gy (mĕt′l-ûr′jē) The science and technology of extracting metals from their ores, refining them for use, and creating alloys and useful objects from them.

USAGE

metal

We think of metals as hard, shiny materials used to make things like paper clips and cars. But for chemists, a *metal* is a chemical element that loses electrons in a chemical reaction. Metal atoms do this because of the structure of their electron shells—the layers in which electrons are arranged around an atom's nucleus. If an element's outermost electron shell is filled, the element is stable and does not react easily. But if the shell contains only a few electrons, the atom will try to share them with another atom in a chemical reaction, thereby becoming stable. Elements having only one electron in their outermost shell are the most reactive; all they have to do to become stable is lose this electron. Such elements are *alkali metals* like sodium and potassium, and they are listed in the left-hand column of the Periodic Table, pages 262–263. The metals farther toward the right side of the Periodic Table, such as tin and lead, have more electrons in their outermost shell and are not as reactive because sharing or losing all these electrons would require more energy. The elements that fall between these extremes are somewhat reactive and are called *transition elements.* They include elements like iron, copper, tungsten, and silver.

met•a•mor•phic (mĕt′ə-môr′fĭk) **1.** *Zoology.* Relating to metamorphosis. **2.** *Geology.* Relating to metamorphism. Metamorphic rocks are formed when igneous, sedimentary, or other metamorphic rocks undergo a physical change due to extreme heat and pressure. These changes often produce folded layers and veins in the rocks, and they can also cause pockets of precious minerals to form. *See Table at* **rock.**

met•a•mor•phism (mĕt′ə-môr′fĭz′əm) The process by which rocks are changed in composition, texture, or structure by extreme heat and pressure.

met•a•mor•pho•sis (mĕt′ə-môr′fə-sĭs) Dramatic change in the form and often the habits of an animal during its development after birth or hatching. The transformation of a maggot into an adult fly, and of a tadpole into an adult frog, are examples of metamorphosis. The young of such animals are called larvae.

met•a•phase (mĕt′ə-fāz′) The stage of cell division in which the spindle forms and chromosomes line up along the center of the cell. In mitosis, metaphase is preceded by prophase and followed by anaphase. *See more at* **meiosis, mitosis.**

me•tas•ta•sis (mə-tăs′tə-sĭs) The spread of cancerous cells from one area of the body to other areas. —*Verb* **metastasize.**

met•a•tar•sal (mĕt′ə-tär′səl) Any of the bones of the foot lying between the tarsal bones and the bones of the toes or digits (phalanges). *See more at* **skeleton.**

met•a•zo•an (mĕt′ə-zō′ən) A multicellular animal, especially one having a body made up of many cells arranged in tissues and organs.

me•te•or (mē′tē-ər) **1.** A bright trail or streak of light that appears in the night sky when a meteoroid enters the Earth's atmosphere. The friction with the air causes the rock to glow with heat. **2.** A rocky body that produces such light. Most meteors burn up before reaching the Earth's surface. *See Note at* **solar system.** ❖ A **meteor shower** occurs when a large number of meteors appear together and seem to come from the same area in the sky.

metamorphosis
development of a monarch butterfly from egg to larva (caterpillar) to pupa (cocoon) to imago (adult)

USAGE

meteor/meteorite/meteoroid

The streaks of light we sometimes see in the night sky and call *meteors* were not identified as interplanetary rocks until the 19th century. Before then, the streaks of light were considered only one of a variety of atmospheric phenomena, all of which bore the name *meteor.* Rain was an *aqueous meteor,* winds and storms were *airy meteors,* and streaks of light in the sky were *fiery meteors.* This general use of *meteor* survives in our word *meteorology,* the study of the weather and atmospheric phenomena. Nowadays, astronomers use any of three words for rocks from interplanetary space, depending on their stage of descent to the Earth. A *meteoroid* is a rock in space that has the potential to collide with the Earth's atmosphere. Meteoroids range in size from a speck of dust to a chunk about 100 meters in diameter, though most are smaller than a pebble. Thus if a small or tiny asteroid or fragment of a comet is floating in orbit near the Earth, it is called a meteoroid. When a meteoroid enters the atmosphere, it becomes a *meteor.* The light that it gives off when heated by friction with the atmosphere is also called a *meteor.* If the rock is not obliterated by the friction and lands on the ground, it is called a *meteorite.* For this term, scientists borrowed the *–ite* suffix used in the names of minerals like malachite and pyrite.

me•te•or•ite (mē′tē-ə-rīt′) A meteor that reaches the Earth's surface without completely burning up due to friction.

me•te•or•oid (mē′tē-ə-roid′) A rocky celestial body that travels through interplanetary space in an orbit that crosses the Earth's orbit. *See Note at* **meteor.**

me•te•or•ol•o•gy (mē′tē-ə-rŏl′ə-jē) The scientific study of the atmosphere and of atmospheric conditions, especially as they relate to weather.

me•ter (mē′tər) The basic unit of length in the metric system, equal to 39.37 inches. *See Table at* **measurement.**

meter-kilogram-second Relating to a system of measurement in which the meter, the kilogram, and the second are the basic units of length, mass, and time.

meth•ane (mĕth′ān′) A colorless, odorless, flammable gas that is the simplest of the hydrocarbons, having the formula CH_4. It is the major constituent of natural gas and is released during the decomposition of plant or other organic compounds, as in marshes and coal mines.

meth•a•nol (mĕth′ə-nôl′) A colorless, toxic, flammable liquid, CH_4O, used as an antifreeze, a general solvent, and a fuel. Also called *methyl alcohol, wood alcohol.*

me•thi•o•nine (mə-thī′ə-nēn′) An essential amino acid. *See more at* **amino acid.**

meth•yl (mĕth′əl) The organic radical CH_3, derived from methane. The methyl group occurs in many important chemical compounds such as methyl alcohol.

methyl alcohol *See* **methanol.**

met•ric (mĕt′rĭk) Relating to the meter or the metric system. *See Table at* **measurement.**

metric system A decimal system of weights and measures based on the meter as a unit of length, the kilogram as a unit of mass, and the liter as a unit of volume. *See Table at* **measurement.**

metric ton A unit of mass or weight equal to 1,000 kilograms (2,205 pounds). *See Table at* **measurement.**

mg Abbreviation of **milligram.**

Mg The symbol for **magnesium.**

MHz An abbreviation of **megahertz.**

mi. Abbreviation of **mile.**

mi•ca (mī′kə) Any of a group of aluminum silicate minerals that can be split easily into thin, partly transparent sheets. Mica is common in igneous and metamorphic rocks. It is highly resistant to heat and is used in electric fuses and other electrical equipment.

Mi•chel•son (mī′kəl-sən), **Albert Abraham** 1852–1931. German-born American physicist. With Edward Morley he disproved the existence of ether, the hypothetical medium of electromagnetic waves.

micro– A prefix that means: **1.** Small, as in *microorganism,* a very small organism. **2.** One millionth, as in *microgram,* one millionth of a gram.

mi•crobe (mī′krōb′) A microorganism, especially a bacterium that causes disease. *See Note at* **germ.**

mi•cro•bi•ol•o•gy (mī′krō-bī-ŏl′ə-jē) The scientific study of the structure and function of microorganisms.

mi•cro•cli•mate (mī′krō-klī′mĭt) The climate of a small, specific place within a larger area. An area as small as a yard or park can have several different microclimates depending on how much sunlight, shade, or exposure to the wind there is at a particular spot.

mi•cro•cline (mī′krō-klīn′) A type of feldspar consisting of potassium aluminum silicate. Microcline is white, pink, red-brown, or green.

mi•cro•graph (mī′krə-grăf′) A photograph of an object viewed through a microscope.

mi•crom•e•ter[1] (mī-krŏm′ĭ-tər) A device for measuring very small distances, angles, or objects.

mi•cro•me•ter[2] (mī′krō-mē′tər) A unit of length in the metric system equal to one millionth (10^{-6}) of a meter. Also called *micron.*

mi•cron (mī′krŏn′) *See* **micrometer**[2]**.**

mi•cro•or•gan•ism (mī′krō-ôr′gə-nĭz′əm) An organism that can be seen only with the aid of a microscope. Microorganisms include bacteria, protozoans, algae, and fungi. *See Note at* **germ.**

mi•cro•scope (mī′krə-skōp′) An instrument used to magnify objects that are hard to see or invisible to the naked eye. Optical microscopes consist of a lens or combination of lenses. Others such as the electron microscope, use other means of magnification, such as beams of electrons.

mi•cro•sec•ond (mī′krō-sĕk′ənd) A unit of time equal to one millionth (10^{-6}) of a second.

mi•cro•tu•bule (mī′krō-to͞o′byo͞ol) Any of the tube-shaped structures that help cells maintain their shape and assist in forming the cell spindle during cell division. Microtubules are found in the cytoplasm of the cells of all organisms except bacteria.

mi•cro•wave (mī′krō-wāv′) **1.** A high-frequency radio wave used in radio broadcasting and radar. *See more at* **electromagnetic spectrum. 2.** An oven in which food is cooked, warmed, or thawed by means of microwaves.

mid•brain (mĭd′brān′) The middle part of the brain in vertebrate animals. In most animals except mammals, the midbrain processes sensory information. In mammals, it serves mainly to connect the forebrain with the hindbrain. *Compare* **forebrain, hindbrain.**

mid•dle ear (mĭd′l) The part of the ear in most mammals that contains the eardrum and three small bones, called ossicles, which transmit sound vibrations from the eardrum to the inner ear. *See more at* **ear.**

mid-o•cean ridge (mĭd′ō′shən) A long mountain range on the ocean floor, extending almost continuously through the North and South Atlantic Oceans, the Indian Ocean, and the South Pacific Ocean. A deep rift valley is located at its center, from which magma flows and forms new oceanic crust. As the magma cools and hardens it becomes part of the mountain range. *See more at* **tectonic boundary.**

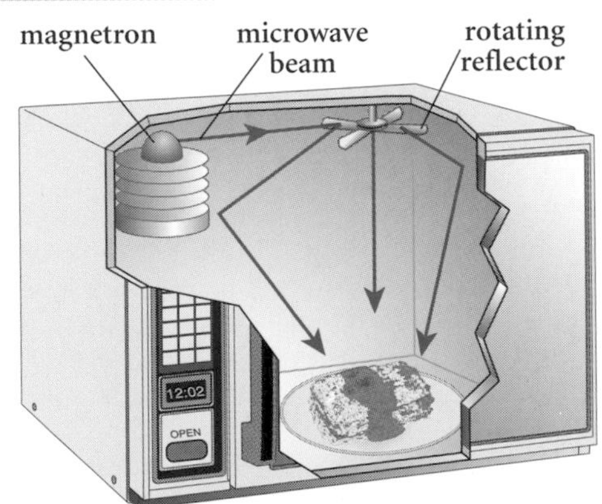

microwave

A microwave oven is activated when an electric current causes a magnetron to emit a beam of microwaves. The beam is distributed throughout the unit by a rotating reflector. The microwaves agitate water molecules in the food, generating enough heat to cook it.

Milky Way

photograph of the Milky Way's central region

mid•rib (mĭd′rĭb′) The central or main vein of a leaf. *See more at* **leaf.**

mi•graine (mī′grān′) A severe, throbbing headache, often accompanied by nausea, that usually affects only one side of the head and tends to recur.

mi•gra•to•ry (mī′grə-tôr′ē) Traveling from one place to another at regular times of year, often over long distances. Salmon, whales, and swallows are all migratory animals.

mil (mĭl) A unit of length equal to 0.001 of an inch (0.03 millimeter), used chiefly to measure the diameter of wires.

mil•dew (mĭl′do͞o′) Any of various fungi that form a white or grayish coating on surfaces, such as plant leaves, cloth, or leather, especially under damp, warm conditions.

mile (mīl) **1.** A unit of length equal to 5,280 feet or 1,760 yards (about 1,609 meters). Also called *statute mile.* **2.** *See* **nautical mile.** *See Table at* **measurement.**

milk (mĭlk) A white liquid produced by the mammary glands of female mammals for feeding their young. Milk contains proteins, fats, vitamins, minerals, and sugars, especially lactose.

Milk•y Way (mĭl′kē) The galaxy containing the solar system. It is visible as a broad band of faint light in the night sky.

milli– A prefix that means "one thousandth," as in *millimeter,* one thousandth of a meter.

mil•li•bar (mĭl′ə-bär′) A unit of atmospheric pressure equal to 0.001 bar.

Did You Know?

mimicry

Many species have evolved to improve their chances of survival by *mimicry,* the imitation of the looks, sounds, actions, or other characteristics of other species. For example, the similar red and black wing markings of two butterfly species, the monarch and the viceroy, protect them from being eaten by birds. The monarch contains chemicals that birds find distasteful, and scientists once thought that the viceroy lacked these chemicals but had evolved to resemble the monarch. In this view, a bird that had tried a monarch ought to be reluctant to try a viceroy. Recently scientists tested this idea by removing the wings from monarchs, viceroys, and another species of butterfly and feeding the bodies to birds. The birds found monarchs and viceroys equally distasteful. Thus these two species evolved to resemble each other, since it is easier for birds to associate bad taste with one wing pattern instead of two.

mil•li•gram (mĭl′ĭ-grăm′) A unit of mass or weight in the metric system equal to 0.001 gram. *See Table at* **measurement.**

mil•li•li•ter (mĭl′ə-lē′tər) A unit of fluid volume or capacity in the metric system equal to 0.001 liter. *See Table at* **measurement.**

mimicry
The viceroy (top) *and monarch* (bottom) *butterflies mimic each other to warn birds of their foul taste.*

mirage
an illusion of water produced on a desert highway

mil•li•me•ter (mĭl′ə-mē′tər) A unit of length in the metric system equal to 0.001 meter. *See Table at* **measurement.**

mil•li•pede (mĭl′ə-pēd′) Any of various wormlike arthropods having a body composed of many narrow segments, most of which have two pairs of legs. Millipedes feed on plants and, unlike centipedes, do not have venomous pincers. *Compare* **centipede.**

Mil•stein (mĭl′stēn′), **Cesar** 1927–2002. British-born Argentinian immunologist. With Georges Köhler he developed a method of producing antibodies that fight specific cells. The antibodies are used to diagnose and treat specific forms of cancer and other diseases.

milt (mĭlt) Fish sperm, together with the milky liquid that contains them.

mim•ic•ry (mĭm′ĭ-krē) The resemblance of one organism to another or to an object in its surroundings for concealment or protection from predators.

min•er•al (mĭn′ər-əl) **1.** A naturally occurring, solid, inorganic element or compound having a uniform composition and a specific crystal structure. Minerals typically have a characteristic hardness and color, or range of colors, by which they can be recognized. **2.** A natural substance of commercial value, such as iron ore, coal, or petroleum, that is obtained by mining, quarrying, or drilling.

min•er•al•o•gy (mĭn′ə-rŏl′ə-jē) The scientific study of minerals, their composition and properties, and the places where they are likely to occur.

mineral oil A colorless, odorless, tasteless oil distilled from petroleum. It is used as a lubricant

Did You Know?

mirrors

The earliest mirrors, some dating to over 3,000 years ago, were highly polished pieces of bronze or another metal. Later on, in the Middle Ages, the technique of covering one side of a piece of glass with a sheet of reflective metal came into being. Nowadays, mirrors are usually coated with an extremely thin layer of silver or aluminum. While you may use mirrors just to look at yourself in the bathroom each morning, in science they have many important uses. Mirrors are used in microscopes, telescopes, and lasers, as well as in devices that collect light for solar power and the devices that make holograms. For instance, a common type of telescope called a *reflecting telescope* has a concave mirror (curved inward) at one end. This mirror, unlike your bathroom mirror, is coated on the front side with the reflecting layer; if light were allowed to pass through the glass first, it could get distorted and interfere with accurate observation. Light waves hitting the curved surface are reflected so that they all come together at a single point—the *focus*. The larger the mirror, the more powerful the telescope; the very largest ones are over 30 feet (9 meters) wide.

and, in medicine, as a laxative.

min•i•mum (mĭn′ə-məm) **1.** The lowest known or lowest possible number, measure, quantity, or degree. **2.** *Mathematics.* The lowest value of a function, if it has such a value.

min•u•end (mĭn′yo͞o-ĕnd′) A number from which another is subtracted. For example, in the numerical expression 100 – 23 = 77, the minuend is 100.

min•ute (mĭn′ĭt) **1.** A unit of time equal to $\frac{1}{60}$ of an hour or 60 seconds. **2.** A unit of angular measurement that is equal to $\frac{1}{60}$ of a degree or 60 seconds.

Mi•o•cene (mī′ə-sēn′) The fourth epoch of the Tertiary Period, from about 24 to 5 million years ago, characterized by the development of grasses and grazing mammals. *See Chart at* **geologic time,** pages 148–149.

mi•rage (mĭ-räzh′) An optical illusion in which nonexistent bodies of water and upside-down reflections of objects appear in the distance. A mirage occurs when light is bent after entering a low layer of hot air at an angle.

mir•ror (mĭr′ər) A surface that is able to reflect light, often used to form an image of an object placed in front of it.

mis•ci•ble (mĭs′ə-bəl) Relating to two or more substances, such as water and alcohol, that can be mixed together in any proportion without separating.

Mis•sis•sip•pi•an (mĭs′ĭ-sĭp′ē-ən) The fifth period of the Paleozoic Era, from about 360 to 320 million years ago, during which shallow seas spread over former land areas. The first primitive conifers appeared during the Mississippian. *See Chart at* **geologic time,** pages 148–149.

Mitch•ell (mĭch′əl), **Maria** 1818–1889. American astronomer and educator noted for her study of sunspots and nebulae and for the discovery of a comet (1847).

mite (mīt) Any of various very small arachnids that often live as parasites on other animals or plants. Like ticks and unlike spiders, mites have no division between the cephalothorax and abdomen.

mi•to•chon•dri•on (mī′tə-kŏn′drē-ən) *Plural* **mitochondria.** A structure in the cytoplasm of all cells except bacteria in which food molecules are broken down in the presence of oxygen and converted to energy in the form of ATP.

Maria Mitchell

Mitochondria contain their own DNA. *See more at* **cell.**

mi•to•sis (mī-tō′sĭs) The process in cell division in which the nucleus divides to produce two new nuclei, each having the same number and type of chromosomes as the original. Early in mitosis, each chromosome duplicates itself to form two identical strands (called chromatids), which then line up along the center of the cell by attaching to the fibers of the cell spindle. The pairs of chromatids then separate, each strand of a pair moving to an opposite end of the cell. When a new membrane forms around each of the two groups of chromosomes, division of the nucleus is complete. The four main phases of mitosis are prophase, metaphase, anaphase, and telophase.

mixed number (mĭkst) A number, such as $7\frac{3}{8}$, consisting of a whole number and a fraction.

mix•ture (mĭks′chər) A composition of two or more substances that are not chemically combined with each other and are capable of being separated.

ml *or* **mL** Abbreviation of **milliliter.**

mm Abbreviation of **millimeter.**

Mn The symbol for **manganese.**

Mo The symbol for **molybdenum.**

mo•a (mō′ə) Any of various flightless, wingless, ostrich-like birds of New Zealand that have been extinct for over a century. One species grew to 13 feet (4 meters) in height, making it the largest bird of modern times.

Mö•bi•us strip (mō′bē-əs) A continuous one-sided surface formed from a rectangular strip by rotating one end 180° and attaching it to the other end. *Compare* **Klein bottle.**

mode (mōd) The value that occurs most frequently in a data set. For example, in the set 125, 140, 172, 164, 140, 110, the mode is 140. *Compare* **arithmetic mean, average, median.**

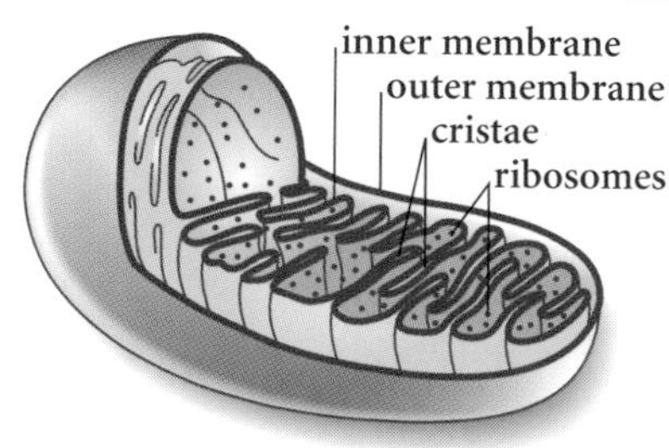

mitochondrion

USAGE

mitosis/meiosis

Mitosis and *meiosis* are easily confused, since both words refer to processes of cell division. Most cells have two full sets of chromosomes and are technically called *diploid* cells. When such a cell divides, it must first duplicate its chromosomes so as to produce two daughter cells that are also diploid. This type of cell division is called *mitosis,* and all somatic cells—that is, cells used for the maintenance, functioning, and growth of an organism—reproduce in this way. By contrast, reproductive cells, or gametes, are created by another kind of cell division, called *meiosis.* Meiosis also starts out by duplicating the chromosomes, but there are two divisions instead of one, with the result that four daughter cells are produced rather than two. Since the number of chromosomes is halved with each division, each daughter cell has just a single set of chromosomes and is called a *haploid* cell. During reproduction, the union of a female gamete with a male gamete restores the two full sets of chromosomes in a new organism.

mod•el (mŏd′l) A description or concept of a system or set of observable events that accounts for all its known properties in a reasonable way.

mo•dem (mō′dəm) A device for transmitting and receiving data, usually in digital form, over telephone wires. Modems send data by converting it into an audio signal and receive it by converting audio signals into data.

mod•er•a•tor (mŏd′ə-rā′tər) A substance, such as graphite or water, placed in a nuclear reactor to slow neutrons down to speeds at which they are likely to cause additional nuclear fission.

mod•i•fi•ca•tion (mŏd′ə-fĭ-kā′shən) A change in an organism resulting from external influences, and not inheritable.

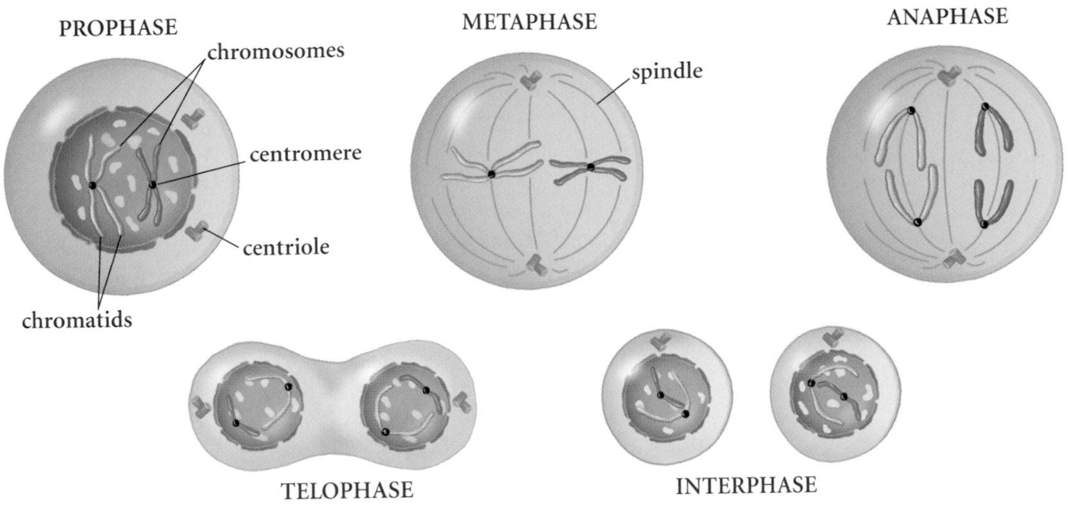

mitosis

During prophase, chromosomes thicken, centrioles move to opposite ends of a cell, and the membrane around the nucleus disappears. In metaphase, a spindle is formed to which the centromeres attach, lining up the chromosomes at the center. In anaphase, the chromatids split, and the chromosomes from each chromatid pair move to opposite ends of the spindle. In telophase, the spindle disappears, and a nuclear membrane forms around the chromosomes at each end of the cell. The cytoplasm of the dividing cell begins to separate during mitosis and ends after division of the nucleus is complete. During interphase, the daughter cells develop and the chromosomes duplicate.

mod•u•late (mŏj′ə-lāt′) To vary the amplitude, frequency, or some other characteristic of electromagnetic waves in a way that makes them correspond to a signal or to information that is to be transmitted.

Mo•ho•ro•vi•čić discontinuity (mō′hə-rō′və-chĭch) The boundary between the Earth's crust and mantle. The Mohorovičić discontinuity is located at an average depth of 5 miles (8 kilometers) under the oceans and 20 miles (32 kilometers) under the continents. Scientists discovered this boundary because they noticed that the velocity of seismic waves increases sharply as the waves pass from the Earth's crust into the mantle.

Mohs scale (mōz) A scale used to measure the relative hardness of a mineral by its resistance to scratching. There are ten standard minerals on this scale, ranging from talc, the softest (measuring 1 on the scale), to diamond, the hardest (measuring 10 on the scale).

Möbius strip

mo•lar[1] (mō′lər) *Chemistry.* **1.** Relating to a mole. **2.** Containing one mole of solute per liter of solution.

molar[2] Any of the teeth located toward the back of the jaws, having broad crowns for grinding food. Adult humans have 12 molars.

mold (mōld) Any of various fungi that often form a fuzzy growth on the surface of organic matter. Some molds cause food to spoil, but others are beneficial, such as those used to make certain cheeses and those from which drugs like penicillin were developed.

mole[1] (mōl) A small, usually dark growth on the skin.

mole[2] Any of various small mammals that have silky fur, strong forefeet for burrowing, and poor vision. Moles usually live underground and eat insects and earthworms.

mole[3] The amount of an element or substance that has a mass in grams numerically equal to the atomic or molecular weight of the substance. For example, carbon dioxide, CO_2, has a molecular weight of 44; therefore, one mole of it weighs 44 grams. The number of atoms or molecules making up a mole is Avogadro's number.

mo•lec•u•lar formula (mə-lĕk′yə-lər) A chemical formula that shows the total number and kinds of atoms in a molecule, but not their structural arrangement. For example, the molecular formula of aspirin is $C_9H_8O_4$. *Compare* **structural formula.**

molecular weight The sum of the atomic weights of the atoms contained in a molecule. For example, since the atomic weight of hydrogen is 1 and the atomic weight of oxygen is 16, the molecular weight of water (H_2O) is 1 + 1 + 16, or 18.

mol•e•cule (mŏl′ĭ-kyo͞ol′) A group of two or more atoms linked together by sharing electrons in a chemical bond.

mol•lusk *or* **mol•lusc** (mŏl′əsk) Any of numerous soft-bodied invertebrate animals, usually living in water and frequently having a hard outer shell. Mollusk bodies have a muscular foot, a well-developed circulatory and nervous system, and often complex eyes. Mollusks include gastropods (snails and shellfish), slugs, octopuses, and squids.

molt (mōlt) To shed an outer covering, such as skin or feathers, for replacement by a new growth. Many snakes, birds, and arthropods molt.

mo•lyb•de•num (mə-lĭb′də-nəm) A hard, silvery-white metallic element that resists corrosion and remains strong at high temperatures. It is used to harden and toughen steel and to make wire that can withstand high temperatures. Molybdenum is an essential trace element in plant metabolism. *Symbol* **Mo.** *Atomic number* 42. *See* **Periodic Table,** pages 262–263.

molt

an insect undergoing its final molt and changing from a nymph to adult

mo•men•tum (mō-mĕn′təm) A quantity used to measure the motion of a body, equal to the product of its mass and velocity. Any change in the speed or direction of a body changes its momentum.

mo•ne•ran (mə-nîr′ən) *See* **prokaryote.**

mon•goose (mŏng′go͞os′) Any of various mammals of Asia and Africa that resemble weasels and are noted for their ability to kill poisonous snakes such as cobras.

mon•i•tor (mŏn′ĭ-tər) **1.** A device that accepts video signals from a computer and displays information on a screen. *See Note at* **pixel. 2.** Any of various meat-eating lizards living in tropical regions of Asia and Africa, and in Australia and New Guinea. Monitors range in length from about an inch to 10 feet (2.5 centimeters to 3 meters), the largest being the Komodo dragon of Indonesia.

mon•key (mŭng′kē) Any of various primates of medium size that have long tails. Most monkeys live in trees in tropical or subtropical regions. Baboons, macaques, mandrills, and marmosets are monkeys. *Compare* **ape.**

mono– A prefix that means "one, only, single," as in *monochromatic,* having only one color. It is often found in chemical names where it means "containing just one" of the specified atom or group, as in *carbon monoxide,* which is carbon attached to a single oxygen atom.

mon•o•chro•mat•ic (mŏn′ə-krō-măt′ĭk) **1.** Having or appearing to have only one color: *monochromatic light.* **2.** Consisting of a single wavelength of light or other radiation: *monochromatic x-rays.*

mon•o•clin•ic (mŏn′ə-klĭn′ĭk) Relating to a crystal having three axes of different lengths. Two of the axes are at oblique angles to each other, and the third axis is perpendicular to the plane that is made by the other two. The mineral gypsum has monoclinic crystals. *See more at* **crystal.**

mon•o•cot•y•le•don (mŏn′ə-kŏt′l-ēd′n) *or* **mon•o•cot** (mŏn′ə-kŏt′) Any of various flowering plants having a single cotyledon in the seed. Monocotyledons have leaves with parallel veins and flower parts in multiples of 3. Grasses, palms, lilies, and irises are monocotyledons. *See more at* **leaf.** *Compare* **dicotyledon.**

mon•o•cyte (mŏn′ə-sīt′) Any of various large white blood cells that circulate in the blood and mature into macrophages. Monocytes engulf and break down microorganisms capable of causing infection.

Mo•nod (mô-nō′), **Jacques Lucien** 1910–1976. French biochemist. With François Jacob, he proposed the existence of messenger RNA. They also studied how genes control cellular activity by directing the synthesis of proteins.

mon•o•dac•tyl (mŏn′ə-dăk′təl) An animal having only one toe, digit, or claw on each limb.

mo•noe•cious (mə-nē′shəs) Having separate male flowers and female flowers on the same plant. Maize and oaks are monoecious plants. *Compare* **dioecious.**

mon•o•mer (mŏn′ə-mər) A molecule that can combine with others of the same kind to form a polymer. Glucose molecules, for example, are monomers that can combine to form the polymer cellulose.

mo•no•mi•al (mŏ-nō′mē-əl) An algebraic expression consisting of a single term, such as $4x$.

mon•o•nu•cle•o•sis (mŏn′ō-no͞o′klē-ō′sĭs) A contagious disease caused by a virus and characterized by fever, sore throat, swollen lymph nodes, and tiredness. The symptoms may last for several weeks.

mon•o•sac•cha•ride (mŏn′ə-săk′ə-rīd′) Any of a class of simple carbohydrates that cannot be broken down to simpler sugars by hydrolysis. Fructose is a monosaccharide.

mon•o•so•di•um glu•ta•mate (mŏn′ə-sō′dē-əm glo͞o′tə-māt′) A white, crystalline salt used to flavor food, especially in China and Japan. It occurs naturally in tomatoes, Parmesan cheese, and seaweed.

mon•o•treme (mŏn′ə-trēm′) The most primitive type of living mammal. Monotremes lay eggs, and the females have no teats but provide milk directly through the skin to their young. Monotremes include only the duck-billed platypus, found in Australia and New Guinea, and the echidnas, found only in New Guinea.

mon•o•un•sat•u•rat•ed (mŏn′ō-ŭn-săch′ə-rā′tĭd) Relating to an organic compound, especially an oil or fatty acid, having only one double or triple bond per molecule. *See more at* **unsaturated.**

Did You Know?

moons

We earthlings usually think of our moon as *the* moon, but any planet's natural satellites are properly called moons. Jupiter has at least 28 moons, while Saturn has 30, and additional small ones around these and other planets may yet be discovered. Earth's moon is also not necessarily typical of other moons in the solar system. No water exists on our moon, but some scientists think that one of Jupiter's moons, Europa, may have liquid water that might support life under a thick layer of ice. Titan, a moon of Saturn, is also thought to have an environment that can support primitive life: an ocean of ethane instead of water. Earth's moon is also very quiet, geologically. By comparison, Io, another of Jupiter's moons, is a violent cauldron of geologic activity. It is covered with huge volcanoes that emit plumes of sulfur so enormous that they can be seen by the Hubble Space Telescope orbiting Earth.

mon•ox•ide (mə-nŏk′sīd′) A compound consisting of two elements, one of which is a single oxygen atom. Carbon monoxide, for example, contains a carbon atom bound to a single oxygen atom.

mon•soon (mŏn-so͞on′) **1.** A system of winds that influences the climate of a large area and that reverses direction with the seasons. Monsoons are caused primarily by the seasonal changes in temperature over large areas of land and water. **2.** In southern Asia, a wind that blows from the southwest in summer and usually brings heavy rains.

moon (mo͞on) **1.** Often **Moon.** The natural satellite of Earth, visible by reflection of sunlight and traveling around Earth in a slightly elliptical orbit at an average distance of about 237,000 miles (381,500 kilometers). The moon's average diameter is 2,160 miles (3,475 kilometers), and its mass is about $\frac{1}{80}$ that of Earth. **2.** A natural satellite revolving around a planet: *the moons of Jupiter.* **3.** The moon as it appears at a particular time in its cycle of phases: *a half moon.*

mo•raine (mə-rān′) A mass of boulders, pebbles, sand, and mud deposited in the form of a long ridge along the front or sides of a glacier. Moraines typically form because of the plowing effect of a moving glacier, which causes it to pick up rock fragments and sediments as it moves, and because of the periodic melting of the ice, which causes the glacier to deposit these materials during warmer intervals. ❖ A moraine that forms in front of a glacier is a **terminal moraine.** ❖ A moraine that forms along the side of a glacier is a **lateral moraine.**

Mor•gan (môr′gən), **Thomas Hunt** 1866–1945. American zoologist who investigated heredity. In experiments with fruit flies, he demonstrated that hereditary traits are carried by genes on chromosomes and that traits can cross over from one chromosome to another.

Mor•ley (môr′lē), **Edward Williams** 1838–1923. American chemist and physicist who with Albert Michelson disproved the existence of ether, the hypothetical medium of electromagnetic waves.

mor•phine (môr′fēn′) A drug extracted from opium, used in medicine to relieve severe pain and for its sedative effects. It can be highly addictive.

mor•phol•o•gy (môr-fŏl′ə-jē) The size, shape, and structure of an organism or one of its parts. Biologists usually describe the morphology of an organism separately from its physiology.

Morse (môrs), **Samuel Finley Breese** 1791–1872. American inventor who developed a telegraphic code for transmitting messages, which became known as Morse code.

mos•qui•to (mə-skē′tō) Any of various winged insects related to the flies whose females suck blood through a tubular piercing organ called a proboscis. Some kinds transmit diseases such as malaria and yellow fever.

moss (môs) **1.** Any of numerous small, green plants that lack vascular tissue and do not bear seeds. Mosses usually live in moist, shady areas and grow in clusters or mats on the ground, rocks, and tree trunks. **2.** Any of a number of plants that look like mosses but are not related to them. For instance, reindeer moss is a lichen, Irish moss is an alga, and Spanish moss is a flowering plant.

moth (môth) Any of various insects that resemble butterflies but are nocturnal and have smaller and less brightly colored wings, stouter bodies,

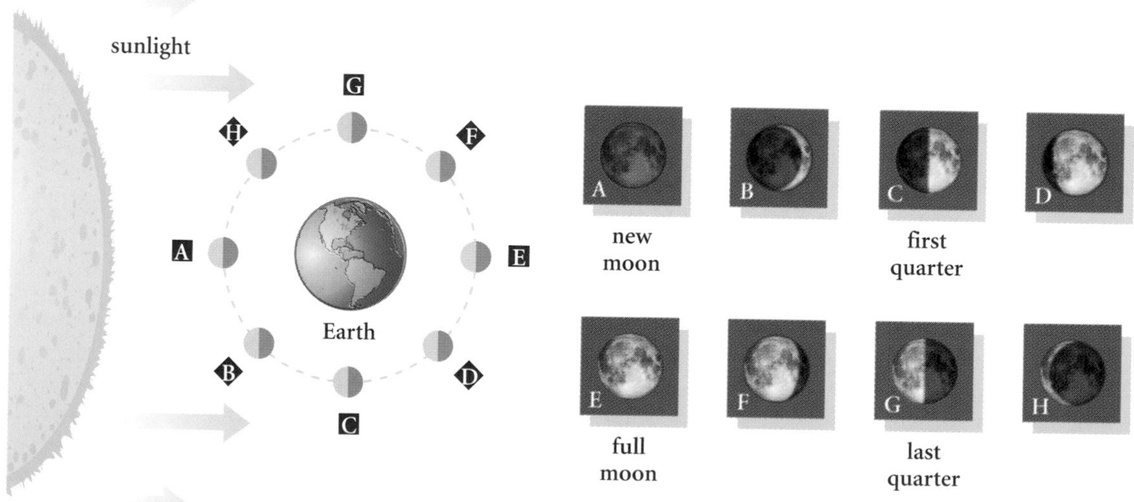

moon
Half of the moon is always in sunlight, as seen on the left. The relative positions of Earth, the moon, and the sun determine how much of the lighted half can be seen from Earth, as seen on the right. These forms in which the moon appears are known as phases.

■ Samuel Morse

and hair-like or feathery antennae. Unlike butterflies, moths tend to hold their wings out horizontally when at rest. *Compare* **butterfly.**

moth•er•board (mŭ*th*′ər-bôrd′) The main circuit board of a computer, usually containing the central processing unit and main system memory as well as circuitry that controls the disk drives, keyboard, monitor, and other peripheral devices.

moth•er-of-pearl (mŭ*th*′ər-əv-pûrl′) The hard, smooth, pearly layer on the inside of certain seashells, such as abalones and certain oysters. It is used to make buttons and jewelry. Also called *nacre.*

mo•tile (mōt′l, mō′tīl′) Moving or able to move by itself. Sperm and certain spores are motile. —*Noun* **motility** (mō-tĭl′ĭ-tē).

mo•tor (mō′tər) *Noun.* **1.** A machine that uses a form of energy, such as electric energy or the explosive power of a fuel, to produce mechanical motion. —*Adjective.* **2.** Involving the muscles or the nerves that are connected to them: *motor control; a motor nerve. Compare* **sensory.**

moun•tain (moun′tən) A generally massive and usually steep-sided, raised portion of the Earth's surface. Mountains can occur as single peaks or as part of a long chain. They can form through volcanic activity, by erosion, or by the collision of two tectonic plates. The Himalayas, which are the highest mountains in the world, formed when the plate carrying the landmass of India collided with the plate carrying the landmass of China.

mouse (mous) *Plural* **mice** (mīs) **1.** Any of numerous small rodents usually having a pointed snout, rounded ears, and a long narrow tail. Some kinds live in or near human dwellings. **2.** A movable hand-held device that is connected to a computer and is moved about on a flat surface to direct the cursor on a screen. A mouse also has buttons for activating computer functions.

mouth•part (mouth′pärt′) Either of the appendages occurring in pairs in insects and other arthropods that extend from the head and are used for feeding.

MRI Abbreviation of **magnetic resonance imaging.**

Mt The symbol for **meitnerium.**

mu•cous membrane (myo͞o′kəs) Any of the membranes lining the passages of the body that open onto the outside, such as the respiratory and digestive tracts. Cells in the mucous membranes secrete mucus, which lubricates the membranes and protects against infection.

mu•cus (myo͞o′kəs) The slimy substance secreted by mucous membranes to lubricate and protect them.

multi– A prefix that means "many" or "much," such as *multicellular,* having many cells.

mul•ti•cel•lu•lar (mŭl′tē-sĕl′yə-lər) Having or consisting of many cells: *multicellular organisms. Compare* **unicellular.**

mul•ti•ple (mŭl′tə-pəl) A number that may be divided by another number with no remainder. For example, 4, 10, and 32 are multiples of 2.

multiple scle•ro•sis (sklə-rō′sĭs) A disease of unknown cause in which the sheaths around nerve fibers become damaged. The nerves in the brain, spinal cord, and eye are most commonly affected, causing weakness, loss of balance and coordination, and visual disturbances.

multiple star A system of three or more stars that usually orbit a common center of mass. The group appears as a single star to the unaided eye. Alpha Centauri is a multiple star.

mul•ti•pli•cand (mŭl′tə-plĭ-kănd′) A number that is multiplied by another number.

mul•ti•pli•ca•tion (mŭl′tə-plĭ-kā′shən) **1.** The mathematical operation that consists of adding a number (the multiplicand) to itself a specified number of times. Thus multiplying 6 by 3 means adding 6 to itself three times. **2.** A mathematical operation performed on a pair of numbers in order to derive a third number called a product. It is sometimes convenient to consider multiplication as repeated addition in which one number indicates how many times the other is to be added together. For example, $3 \times 4 = 4 + 4 + 4 = 4 \times 3 = 3 + 3 + 3 + 3 = 12$.

mul•ti•pli•er (mŭl′tə-plī′ər) The number by which another number is multiplied.

mul•ti•ply (mŭl′tə-plī′) To perform multiplication on a pair of quantities.

mumps (mŭmps) A contagious disease, usually affecting children, that is caused by a virus. Symptoms include inflammation of the salivary glands, especially those at the back of the jaw.

mus•cle (mŭs′əl) A body tissue composed of elongated cells (called muscle fibers) that contract to produce movement. In vertebrate animals, voluntary movement is produced by the action of muscles on bone. Movement of the muscles of the heart and other organs is involuntary and controlled by the autonomic nervous system. —*Adjective* **muscular.**

mus•co•vite (mŭs′kə-vīt′) A usually colorless to pale-gray mineral composed mostly of a silicate of potassium and aluminum. Muscovite is one of the most common forms of mica.

mus•cu•lar dys•tro•phy (mŭs′kyə-lər dĭs′trə-fē) Any of several hereditary diseases in which a person's muscles gradually deteriorate, causing progressive weakness.

mush•room (mŭsh′ro͞om′) Any of various fungi having a stalk topped by a fleshy, often umbrella-shaped cap. Some mushrooms are edible; others are poisonous.

mu•ta•tion (myo͞o-tā′shən) A change in the genes or chromosomes of an organism. Mutations occurring in the reproductive cells, such as an egg or sperm, can be passed from one generation to the next. Most mutations have harmful effects, but some can increase an organism's ability to survive. A mutation that benefits a species may evolve by means of natural selection into a trait shared by all members. *See Note at* **sickle cell anemia.**

mutualism
tickbirds perched on a black rhinoceros

mu•tu•al•ism (myo͞o′cho͞o-ə-lĭz′əm) A symbiotic relationship between two organisms of different species in which each member benefits. *See Note at* **symbiosis.**

my•ce•li•um (mī-sē′lē-əm) *Plural* **mycelia.** The mass of fine branching tubes (called hyphae) that forms the main growing structure of a fungus. Visible structures like mushrooms are reproductive structures produced by the mycelium.

my•col•o•gy (mī-kŏl′ə-jē) The scientific study of fungi.

my•e•lin (mī′ə-lĭn) A whitish, fatty substance that forms a sheath around many nerve fibers. Myelin insulates the nerves and permits nerve impulses to travel more rapidly. The white matter of the brain is composed of nerve fibers covered in myelin.

my•o•pi•a (mī-ō′pē-ə) *See* **nearsightedness.**

N

N The symbol for **nitrogen.**

Na The symbol for **sodium.**

na•cre (nā′kər) *See* **mother-of-pearl.**

na•dir (nā′dər) The point on the celestial sphere that is directly below the observer.

nano– A prefix that means: **1.** One billionth, as in *nanosecond,* one billionth of a second. **2.** Very small or at a microscopic level, as in *nanotube.*

nan•o•tube (năn′ə-to͞ob′) A type of carbon molecule in which the carbon atoms form a cylindrical or donut-like shape.

naph•tha (năf′thə) Any of several products made by refining petroleum or by breaking down coal tar. Naphtha is usually flammable, and is used as a solvent and as an ingredient in gasoline. It is also used to make plastics.

naph•tha•lene (năf′thə-lēn′) A white crystalline compound made from coal tar or petroleum and used to make dyes, moth repellents, explosives, and solvents.

nar•cot•ic (när-kŏt′ĭk) Any of a group of drugs used to relieve pain and cause drowsiness. Narcotics are highly addictive.

na•sal (nā′zəl) Relating to the nose: *the nasal passages.*

nat•u•ral gas (năch′ər-əl) A mixture of hydrocarbon gases that occurs naturally beneath the Earth's surface, often with or near petroleum deposits. Natural gas contains mostly methane, but also has varying amounts of ethane, propane, butane, and nitrogen. It is used as a fuel and in making organic compounds.

natural history The study and description of living things and natural objects, especially their origins, evolution, and relationships to one another. Natural history includes the sciences of zoology, botany, geology, and paleontology.

nat•u•ral•ist (năch′ər-ə-lĭst) A person who specializes in natural history, especially in the study of plants and animals in their natural surroundings.

nat•u•ral•ize (năch′ər-ə-līz′) To adapt or accustom a plant or animal to living in a region to which it is not native. Eucalyptus trees are native to Australia but have become naturalized in many other parts of the world.

natural logarithm A logarithm whose base is the irrational number *e*. Natural logarithms are frequently used in calculus. *See more at* **e.** *Compare* **common logarithm.**

natural number A positive integer.

natural resource Something, such as a forest, a mineral deposit, or fresh water, that is found in nature and is necessary or useful to humans.

natural selection The principle that only organisms best suited to their environment survive long enough to pass on their genetic characteristics to their offspring. According to this principle, the proportion of the species having these characteristics increases with each generation. Natural selection results from random variation of genetic traits in a species and forms the basis of the process of evolution. *See Notes at* **adaptation, evolution.**

na•ture (nā′chər) **1.** The world and its naturally occurring phenomena, together with all of the physical laws that govern them. **2.** Living organisms and their environments.

nau•ti•cal mile (nô′tĭ-kəl) A unit of length used in air and sea navigation, equal to about 6,076 feet (1,852 meters). *See Table at* **measurement.**

nau•ti•lus (nôt′l-əs) A tropical sea mollusk having a spiral shell with alternating white and light-

nautilus

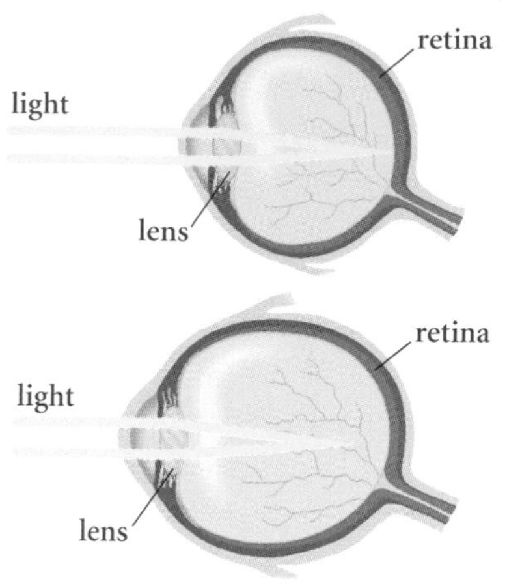

nearsightedness

top: *A normal eye focuses light on the retina.*
bottom: *An elongated eyeball causes light to focus in front of the retina.*

brown bands on the outside and many chambers on the inside. The nautilus is related to the squids and octopuses.

Nb The symbol for **niobium.**

Nd The symbol for **neodymium.**

Ne The symbol for **neon.**

Ne•an•der•thal (nē-ăn′dər-thôl′, nē-ăn′dər-tôl′) *or* **Ne•an•der•tal** (nē-ăn′dər-tôl′) An extinct variety of human that lived throughout Europe and in parts of Asia and Africa during the late Pleistocene Epoch, until about 30,000 years ago. Neanderthals had a stocky build and large skulls with thick eyebrow ridges and big teeth. They usually lived in caves, made stone tools, and were the earliest humans known to bury their dead. Neanderthals were either a subspecies of modern humans or a separate, closely related species.

neap tide (nēp) A tide in which the difference between high and low tide is the least. Neap tides occur twice a month when the sun and moon are at right angles to the Earth. When this is the case, their total gravitational pull on the Earth's water is weakened because it comes from two different directions. *Compare* **spring tide.** *See more at* **tide.**

near•sight•ed•ness (nîr′sī′tĭd-nĭs) The ability to see objects at close range better than distant objects. Nearsightedness is caused by the eye focusing light in front of the retina instead of directly on it, usually as a result of an elongated eyeball or a misshapen cornea. Also called *myopia. Compare* **farsightedness.**

neb•u•la (nĕb′yə-lə) *Plural* **nebulae** (nĕb′yə-lē′) *or* **nebulas.** A thinly spread cloud of interstellar gas and dust. It will appear as a bright patch in the night sky if it reflects light from nearby stars, emits its own light, or re-emits ultraviolet radiation from nearby stars as visible light. If it absorbs light, the nebula appears as a dark patch. In dark nebulae, stars form from clumps of hydrogen gas. *See more at* **star.**

neb•u•lar hypothesis (nĕb′yə-lər) An explanation of the origin of the solar system according to which a rotating nebula cooled and contracted, flattening into a disk shape with a central bulge. The matter in the disk condensed into the planets, their moons, asteroids, and comets, while the great mass at the center became the sun.

nec•tar (nĕk′tər) A sweet liquid secreted by certain flowers that is consumed by pollinating insects and birds and is gathered by bees to make honey.

nee•dle (nēd′l) **1.** A narrow, stiff leaf, as of firs, pines, and other conifers. The reduced surface area of needles minimizes water loss and allows needle-bearing plants to live in dry climates. *See more at* **leaf. 2.** *See* **hypodermic needle.**

neg•a•tive (nĕg′ə-tĭv) **1.** Less than zero, as –3. **2.** Having the electric charge of an electron. The symbol for a negative charge is a minus sign. **3.** Having more electrons than protons. Negatively charged bodies, such as atoms or molecules,

nebula
Trifid Nebula

neon
neon signs

repel other negatively charged bodies but attract positively charged bodies. **4.** Not showing the presence of a suspected disease or microorganism, as in a blood test.

nem•a•to•cyst (nĕm′ə-tə-sĭst′, nĭ-măt′ə-sĭst′) One of the stinging cells in the tentacles of a jellyfish, hydra, or related animal, used to capture prey and ward off attackers.

nem•a•tode (nĕm′ə-tōd′) Any of several slender cylindrical worms, usually of tiny size, that live in great numbers in water, soil, plants, and animals. They have a simple structure, with a long hollow gut separated from the body wall by a fluid-filled space. Several nematodes are parasites on animals and humans and cause disease.

ne•o•dym•i•um (nē′ō-dĭm′ē-əm) A shiny, silvery metallic element of the lanthanide series that exists in two forms. It is used to make glass for welders' goggles and purple glass for lasers. *Symbol* **Nd.** *Atomic number* 60. *See* **Periodic Table,** pages 262–263.

Ne•o•lith•ic (nē′ə-lĭth′ĭk) The period of human culture that began around 10,000 years ago in the Middle East and later in other parts of the world. It is characterized by the beginning of farming, the domestication of animals, the development of crafts such as pottery and weaving, and the making of polished stone tools. *Compare* **Mesolithic, Paleolithic.**

ne•on (nē′ŏn′) A rare element that is a noble gas and occurs naturally in extremely small amounts in the atmosphere. It is colorless but glows reddish orange when electricity passes through it, such as in a tube in an electric sign. Neon is also used for refrigeration. *Symbol* **Ne.** *Atomic number* 10. *See* **Periodic Table,** pages 262–263.

ne•o•prene (nē′ə-prēn′) A tough synthetic rubber that is resistant to the effects of oils, solvents, heat, and weather.

ne•phri•tis (nə-frī′tĭs) Inflammation of the kidneys.

neph•ron (nĕf′rŏn) One of the units of the kidney that filter waste products from the blood and produce urine.

Nep•tune (nĕp′to͞on′) The eighth planet from the sun and the fourth largest, with a diameter almost four times that of Earth. Neptune has a very active weather system with extremely long and powerful storms. It is the coldest planet in the solar system, with an average surface temperature of –330°F (–201°C). *See Table at* **solar system,** pages 316–317. *See Note at* **planet.**

nep•tu•ni•um (nĕp-to͞o′nē-əm) A silvery, radioactive metallic element of the actinide series. It occurs naturally in trace amounts in uranium ores and is produced artificially as a by-product of plutonium production. The most stable isotope of neptunium has a half-life of 2.1 million years. *Symbol* **Np.** *Atomic number* 93. *See* **Periodic Table,** pages 262–263.

nerve (nûrv) Any of the bundles of fibers made up of nerve cells that carry information in the form of electrical impulses throughout the body. Nerves send sensory information to the brain and spinal cord and carry impulses to the muscles, organs, and glands.

nerve cell Any of the cells of the nervous system. Nerve cells typically consist of a cell body, which contains a nucleus and receives incoming nerve impulses, and an axon, which carries impulses away from the cell body. Also called *neuron. See more at* **cell.**

nerve fiber *See* **axon.**

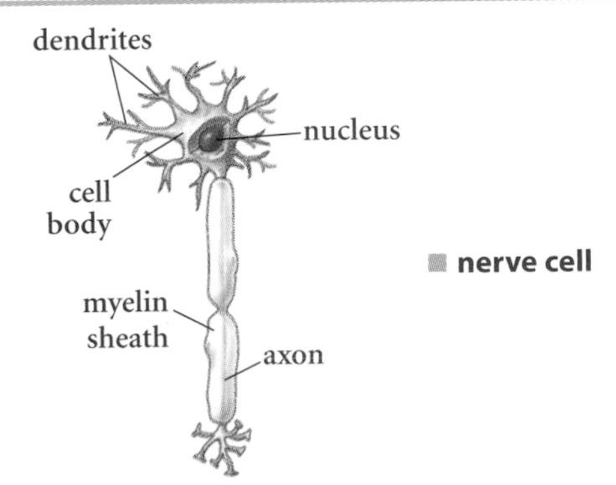

nerve cell

nerv•ous system (nûr′vəs) The system of nerve cells and tissues that regulates the actions and responses of vertebrate and many invertebrate animals. The nervous system of vertebrates consists mainly of the brain, spinal cord, and nerves. The nervous systems of invertebrates vary from a simple network of nerves to a complex nerve network under the control of a primitive brain. *See also* **autonomic nervous system, central nervous system, peripheral nervous system.**

Neu•mann (noi′män′), **John von** 1903–1957. Hungarian-born American mathematician who contributed to mathematical theories about numbers and games. He was a leader in the design and development of high-speed electronic computers. Von Neumann also contributed to cybernetics, a term he created.

neu•ral (no͝or′əl) Relating to the nerves or nervous system.

neu•rol•o•gy (no͝o-rŏl′ə-jē) The branch of medicine that deals with the diagnosis and treatment of disorders of nerves and the nervous system.

neu•ron (no͝or′ŏn′) *See* **nerve cell.**

neu•ro•trans•mit•ter (no͝or′ō-trănz′mĭt-ər) A chemical substance that helps transmit nerve impulses from one nerve cell to another.

neu•tral (no͞o′trəl) **1.** Neither acid nor alkaline. **2.** Having positive electric charges exactly balanced by negative electric charges.

neu•tral•ize (no͞o′trə-līz′) To cause to be neither acid nor alkaline: *neutralize a solution.*

neu•tri•no (no͞o-trē′nō) Any of three electrically neutral subatomic particles that travel at the speed of light. Neutrinos are thought to have a mass that is too close to zero, when they are not moving, to be measured.

neu•tron (no͞o′trŏn′) An electrically neutral subatomic particle that is part of the nucleus of an atom and has a mass slightly greater than that of a proton. Beams of neutrons from nuclear reactors are used to bombard the atoms of various elements to produce fission and other nuclear reactions and to determine the atomic arrangements in molecules. *See more at* **atom.**

neutron star A celestial object consisting of an extremely dense mass of neutrons, formed by the forcing together of protons and electrons in the collapse of a massive star. Most neutron stars rotate very rapidly. Many have powerful magnetic fields that focus radio waves, light, and other radiation into two beams that point outward from the magnetic poles. *See more at* **star.**

Did You Know?

neutrinos

Neutrinos were not observed until 1955, roughly a quarter of a century after the physicist Wolfgang Pauli first proposed, on theoretical grounds, that they might exist. Pauli was studying certain radioactive decay processes in which it seemed that energy somehow mysteriously disappeared. He suggested that the energy was carried away by a very small, electrically neutral particle that was not being detected. (He originally wanted to name the particle a neutron but didn't publish the suggestion, and a few years later the particle we now know as the neutron was discovered and named in print. The Italian physicist Enrico Fermi then coined the term neutrino, which means "little neutron" in Italian.) Neutrinos are hard to detect because they interact only very weakly with other forms of matter. Most of the neutrinos that reach the Earth from space pass right through and go out the other side. Even a chunk of iron a few light-years thick would stop only about half of the neutrinos that struck it.

New•co•men (no͞o′kə-mən), **Thomas** 1663–1729. English inventor who developed an early steam engine (1711) that was used successfully to pump water.

new moon (no͞o) The phase of the moon that occurs when it passes between Earth and the sun, making it either invisible or visible only as a thin crescent at sunset. *See more at* **moon.** *Compare* **full moon.**

newt (no͞ot) Any of several small salamanders that live both on land and in the water. The water-dwelling species have smooth skin, while the land-dwelling species have rough skin.

new•ton (no͞ot′n) A unit used to measure force. One newton is equal to the force needed to accel-

newt
immature red-spotted newt

erate a mass of one kilogram one meter per second per second.

Newton, Sir **Isaac** 1642–1727. English mathematician and scientist. He invented a form of calculus and formulated the law of universal gravitation, a theory about the nature of light, and three laws of motion. His treatise on gravitation, presented in *Principia Mathematica* (1687), was in his own account inspired by the sight of a falling apple.

Newton's law of gravitation The principle that two bodies exert a gravitational attraction for each other that increases as their masses increase and as the distance between them decreases. In mathematical terms, the force equals the product of the two masses multiplied by the gravitational constant and divided by the square of the distance. Also called *law of gravitation, law of universal gravitation. See Note at* **gravity.**

Newton's laws of motion The three laws proposed by Sir Isaac Newton to define the concept of force and describe motion, used as the basis of classical mechanics. The first law states that a body at rest tends to stay at rest, and a body in motion tends to stay in motion at a constant speed in a straight line, unless acted upon by a force. The second law states that the total force acting on a body is equal to the body's mass times its acceleration. The third law states that whenever one body exerts a force on a second body, the second body exerts an equal but opposite force on the first.

Ni The symbol for **nickel.**

ni•a•cin (nī′ə-sĭn) A vitamin belonging to the vitamin B complex that is important in carbohydrate metabolism. It is found in liver, fish, and whole-grain foods.

niche (nĭch, nēsh) The function or position of a species within an ecological community. A species' niche includes the physical environment to which it has become adapted as well as its role as producer and consumer of food resources.

BIOGRAPHY

Isaac Newton

Issac Newton's college classes were suspended for a time in 1665 because of an outbreak of the plague. During his days away from school, Newton conducted his own studies. He was especially interested in light. His experiments with prisms demonstrated that sunlight contains all the colors of the spectrum. During this time he made his famous observation of an apple falling from a tree. The force of gravity acting on the apple, he proposed, was the same force that caused the Moon to remain in orbit around the Earth. Newton showed mathematically how this law of gravitation could apply everywhere in the universe. Newton also explored and defined new concepts of mass, weight, force, inertia, and acceleration, demonstrating the mathematical relationships between them. These concepts still have great power to predict how matter will behave under many different conditions.

nick•el (nĭk′əl) A silvery, hard, easily shaped metallic element that occurs in ores along with iron or magnesium. It resists oxidation and corrosion and is used to make alloys such as stainless steel. It is also used as a coating for other metals. *Symbol* **Ni.** *Atomic number* 28. *See* **Periodic Table,** pages 262–263.

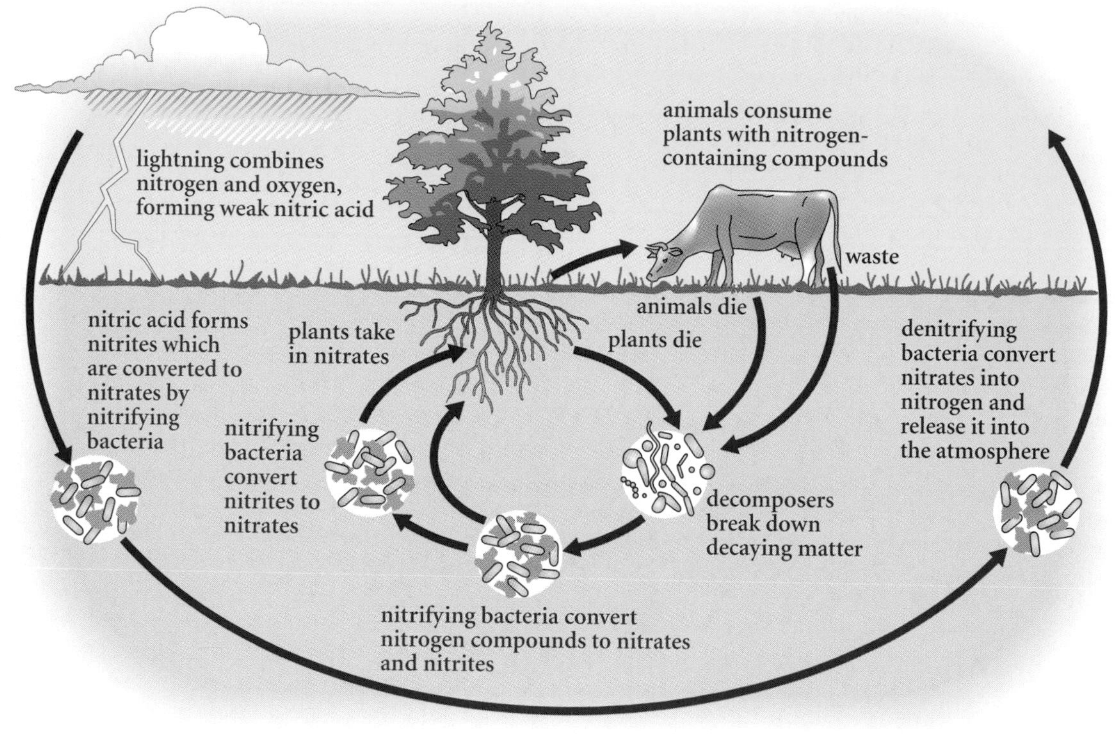
lightning combines nitrogen and oxygen, forming weak nitric acid
animals consume plants with nitrogen-containing compounds
waste
animals die
plants die
nitric acid forms nitrites which are converted to nitrates by nitrifying bacteria
plants take in nitrates
nitrifying bacteria convert nitrites to nitrates
denitrifying bacteria convert nitrates into nitrogen and release it into the atmosphere
decomposers break down decaying matter
nitrifying bacteria convert nitrogen compounds to nitrates and nitrites

■ **nitrogen cycle**

nic•o•tine (nĭk′ə-tēn′) A poisonous compound occurring naturally in the tobacco plant. It is used in medicine and as an insecticide. Nicotine can be addictive.

nic•ti•tat•ing membrane (nĭk′tĭ-tā′tĭng) A transparent inner eyelid in birds, reptiles, amphibians, and some mammals that protects and moistens the eye without blocking vision.

nim•bo•strat•us (nĭm′bō-străt′əs) A low, gray, dark cloud formation often covering the entire sky. Nimbostratus clouds usually produce steady rain, sleet, or snow.

nim•bus (nĭm′bəs) A rain cloud.

ni•o•bi•um (nī-ō′bē-əm) A soft, silvery, easily shaped metallic element that usually occurs in nature together with the element tantalum. It is used to build nuclear reactors, to make steel alloys, and to allow magnets to conduct electricity with almost no resistance. *Symbol* **Nb.** *Atomic number* 41. *See* **Periodic Table,** pages 262–263.

nip•ple (nĭp′əl) A small projection near the center of the mammary gland, as of the human breast, containing in females the outlets of the milk ducts.

ni•ter (nī′tər) A naturally occurring mineral form of potassium nitrate, used to make gunpowder.

ni•trate (nī′trāt′) A salt or ester of nitric acid; a compound containing the group NO_3. Nitrates dissolve extremely easily in water and are an important component of the nitrogen cycle. *Compare* **nitrite.**

ni•tric (nī′trĭk) Containing nitrogen, especially with a valence of 5. *Compare* **nitrous.**

nitric acid A clear, colorless to yellow liquid, HNO_3. It is very corrosive and is used to make fertilizers, explosives, dyes, and rocket fuels. Nitric acid can dissolve most metals.

ni•tri•fi•ca•tion (nī′trə-fĭ-kā′shən) The process by which bacteria in soil oxidize ammonia and form nitrates and nitrites. Because the nitrates and nitrites can be absorbed by the roots of green plants, nitrification is an important step in the nitrogen cycle.

nit•ri•fy•ing bacteria (nī′trə-fī′ĭng) Any of various soil bacteria that change ammonium compounds into nitrites or change nitrites into nitrates as part of the nitrogen cycle.

ni•trite (nī′trīt′) A salt or ester of nitrous acid; a compound containing the group NO_2. Nitrites are important in the nitrogen cycle and are used as food preservatives. *Compare* **nitrate.**

ni•tro•gen (nī′trə-jən) A nonmetallic element that makes up about 78 percent of the atmosphere by volume, occurring as a colorless, odorless gas. It is a component of all proteins, making it essential for life, and it is also found in various minerals. Nitrogen is used to make ammonia, nitric acid, TNT, and fertilizers. *Symbol* **N.** *Atomic number* 7. *See* **Periodic Table,** pages 262–263. *See Note at* **oxygen.**

nitrogen cycle The continuous process by which nitrogen is exchanged between organisms and the environment. Some of the atmosphere's free nitrogen combines with other elements to form compounds that are deposited in the soil. These are then converted by bacteria, in a process called nitrification, into nutrients that are absorbed by the roots of green plants. Nitrogen is then passed into the food chain and returned to the soil by the metabolism and decay of plants and animals.

nitrogen fixation The process by which free nitrogen from the air is combined with other elements to form organic compounds that plants can use as nutrients. Cyanobacteria and certain other forms of bacteria, especially those that live in the roots of legumes, convert gaseous nitrogen into organic compounds.

ni•tro•glyc•er•in (nī′trō-glĭs′ər-ĭn) A thick, pale-yellow, explosive liquid formed by treating glycerin with nitric and sulfuric acids. It is used to make dynamite, and in medicine to dilate blood vessels.

ni•trous (nī′trəs) Containing nitrogen, especially with a valence of 3. *Compare* **nitric.**

nitrous acid A weak acid, HNO_3, that exists only in solution or in the form of nitrites.

nitrous oxide A colorless, sweet-smelling gas, N_2O. It is used as a mild anesthetic, in which use it is often called *laughing gas.* Nitrous oxide occurs naturally in the atmosphere and is a greenhouse gas.

No The symbol for **nobelium.**

no•bel•i•um (nō-bĕl′ē-əm) A synthetic, radioactive metallic element in the actinide series that is produced by bombarding curium with carbon ions. Its most stable isotope has a half-life of about three minutes. *Symbol* **No.** *Atomic number* 102. *See* **Periodic Table,** pages 262–263.

WORD HISTORY

noble gas

What makes a noble gas so noble? The noble gases are a group of six chemical elements, normally occurring in gaseous form, that do not react chemically with other elements except very rarely. Helium and neon are two familiar examples. The fact that the noble gases do not mix with other elements became the basis for a comparison with nobility. The nobility—the class that rules many societies and includes royalty—usually keep to themselves and do not mix with common folk.

no•ble gas (nō′bəl) Any of the six gases helium, neon, argon, krypton, xenon, and radon. Because the outermost electron shell of atoms of these gases is full, they do not react chemically with other substances except under certain special conditions. Also called *inert gas. See* **Periodic Table,** pages 262–263.

noc•tur•nal (nŏk-tûr′nəl) **1.** Occurring at night. **2.** Most active at night. Many animals, such as owls and bats, are nocturnal. *Compare* **diurnal.** **3.** Having flowers that open during the night and close at daylight. Nocturnal plants are often pollinated by moths.

Nod•dack (nŏd′ăk′), **Ida Eva Tacke** 1896–1979. German chemist who with her husband, **Walter Karl Friedrich Noddack** (1893–1960), discovered rhenium and an element they called masurium (later named technetium) in 1925.

node (nōd) **1.** *Anatomy.* A small mass or lump of body tissue that either occurs naturally, as in the case of lymph nodes, or is a result of disease. **2.** *Botany.* **a.** A point on a stem where a leaf is attached or has been attached. **b.** A swelling or lump on a tree; a knob or knot. **3.** *Physics.* A point or region of a vibrating or oscillating system, such as the standing wave of a vibrating guitar string, at which the amplitude of the vibration or oscillation is zero. *Compare* **antinode.** **4.** *Astronomy.* **a.** Either of the two points at which the orbit of a planet intersects the ecliptic. **b.** Either of the two points at which the orbit of a satellite intersects the plane of orbit of a planet.

nod•ule (nŏj′o͞ol) **1.** *Anatomy.* A small, usually hard mass of tissue. **2.** *Botany.* A small knob-like outgrowth found on the roots of many plants that are legumes. *See more at* **legume.**

Noe•ther (nŭ′tər), **Amalie** *Known as* **Emmy.** 1882–1935. German mathematician who contributed to the development of modern algebra and geometry.

non•re•new•a•ble (nŏn′rĭ-no͞o′ə-bəl) Relating to a natural resource, such as oil or iron ore, that cannot be replaced once it has been used. *Compare* **renewable.**

nor•mal fault (nôr′məl) A geologic fault in which the hanging wall has moved downward relative to the footwall. Normal faults occur where two blocks of rock are pulled apart, as by tension. *See more at* **fault.**

North•ern Hemisphere (nôr′*th*ərn) **1.** The half of the Earth north of the equator. **2.** *Astronomy.* The half of the celestial sphere north of the celestial equator.

northern lights *See* **aurora borealis.**

North Pole (nôrth) The northern end of the Earth's axis of rotation, a point in the Arctic Ocean.

North Star *See* **Polaris.**

no•to•chord (nō′tə-kôrd′) A flexible rod-like structure that forms the main support of the body in the embryos of vertebrate animals, later developing into a true backbone. Primitive relatives of the vertebrates, known as lancelets and tunicates, only have a notochord and never develop a backbone. Animals having a notochord during some stage of their development are called chordates.

Amalie Noether

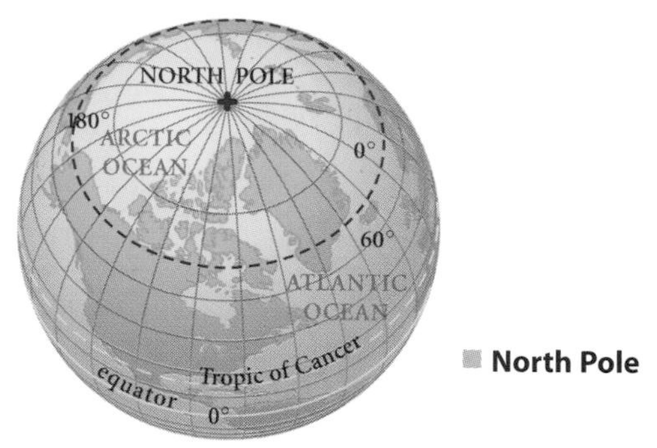

North Pole

no•va (nō′və) *Plural* **novae** (nō′vē) *or* **novas.** A white dwarf star that suddenly becomes extremely bright as a result of the explosion on its surface of material taken from a nearby star. It gradually returns to its original brightness over a period of weeks to years. *Compare* **supernova.**

Np The symbol for **neptunium.**

nu•cle•ar (no͞o′klē-ər) **1.** Relating to or forming a cell nucleus. **2.** Relating to atomic nuclei. **3.** Using energy derived from the nuclei of atoms: *a nuclear power plant.*

USAGE

nuclear/atomic

The words nuclear and atomic mean the same thing when referring to weapons or to the making of power: We say nuclear (or atomic) weapons and nuclear (or atomic) energy. But in most scientific uses nuclear and atomic mean different things. Nuclear is used to refer to the nucleus of an atom, where the protons and neutrons are located. When a radioactive element gives off a neutron, for example, we call this a nuclear event. Atomic, by contrast, is used to refer to the outer layers of the atom, where the electrons that orbit about the nucleus are located. So when two or more atoms share electrons to form a covalent bond, we call this an atomic interaction.

Did You Know?

nuclear reactor

The cylindrical core of a nuclear reactor consists of fuel rods containing pellets of fissionable material, usually uranium 235 or plutonium 239. These are unstable isotopes that readily split apart and release free neutrons that strike other isotopes, causing them to split. The fuel rods contain enough fissionable material that is close enough together to start what is called a chain reaction. If left unaltered, the chain reaction would cause the fuel rods to overheat and melt. To prevent this, and to regulate the reaction, the fuel rods are interspersed with control rods made of a material (usually boron or cadmium) that absorbs some of the neutrons given off by the fuel. Inserting the control rods deeper into the reactor core slows down the reaction. If the control rods are fully inserted, the reaction will stop. The chain reaction releases enormous amounts of heat which is transferred, through a closed loop of radioactive water, to a separate, nonradioactive water system. The heat turns the nonradioactive water into pressurized steam. The steam then drives turbines that turn generators, producing electricity. Nuclear power is by far the most efficient means of generating electricity in the world today. It remains controversial, however, because much of the equipment needed to generate it, including the used-up fuel rods and the water inside the container vessels, remains radioactive for thousands of years. So far there is little agreement about how to store this material safely.

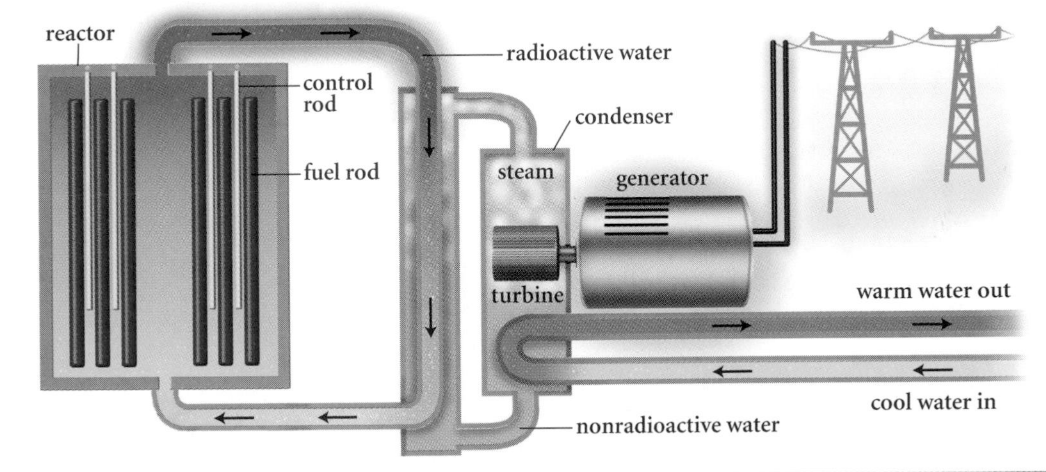

nuclear energy 1. The energy released during a nuclear reaction. **2.** Electricity generated by a nuclear reactor.

nuclear magnetic resonance The absorption of energy (as specific frequencies of radio waves) by the nuclei of atoms that are placed within a strong magnetic field. Because certain atoms absorb specific frequencies, nuclear magnetic resonance is used to analyze substances in spectroscopy and to examine soft body tissues in magnetic resonance imaging (MRI).

nuclear physics The scientific study of the properties of atomic nuclei, including their structure and reactions.

nuclear reaction A reaction, as in fission, fusion, or radioactive decay, that changes the energy or structure of an atomic nucleus. *See more at* **fission, fusion.**

nuclear reactor A device in which a nuclear chain reaction is started and controlled, producing heat which is usually used to generate electricity.

nuclear weapon A weapon whose destructive power comes from nuclear energy; an atomic bomb or a hydrogen bomb. Also called *thermonuclear weapon.*

nu•cle•ic acid (no͞o-klē′ĭk) Any of a group of organic compounds found in living cells and viruses that control the hereditary material of a cell or virus by regulating the synthesis of proteins. The two main nucleic acids are DNA and RNA.

nu•cle•o•lus (no͞o-klē′ə-ləs) A usually round structure located in the nucleus of a cell and involved in the formation of ribosomes, the sites of protein synthesis in cells.

nu•cle•on (no͞o′klē-ŏn′) A proton or a neutron, especially as part of an atomic nucleus.

nu•cle•o•tide (no͞o′klē-ə-tīd′) Any of a group of organic compounds composed of one of several nitrogen bases linked to a sugar and a phosphate group. The nucleic acids DNA and RNA are made up of chains of nucleotides. *See Note at* **DNA.**

nu•cle•us (no͞o′klē-əs) *Plural* **nuclei** (no͞o′klē-ī′) **1.** *Chemistry.* The positively charged central region of an atom, composed of protons and neutrons and containing most of the mass of the atom. *See more at* **atom. 2.** *Biology.* The structure in the cytoplasm of a living cell that contains the cell's DNA and controls its metabolism, growth, and reproduction. A nucleus surrounded by a membrane is found in almost all the cells of eukaryotes and thus sets them apart from the cells of prokaryotes, such as bacteria, which do not contain nuclei. *See more at* **cell. 3.** *Astronomy.* The solid central part of a comet, composed of ice, frozen gases, and dust.

nu•di•branch (no͞o′də-brăngk′) *See* **sea slug.**

nu•mer•al (no͞o′mər-əl) A symbol or mark used to represent a number.

nu•mer•a•tor (no͞o′mə-rā′tər) A number written above or to the left of the line in a common fraction to indicate the number of parts of the whole. For example, 2 is the numerator in the fraction $\frac{2}{7}$.

nu•tri•ent (no͞o′trē-ənt) A substance that provides nourishment. Plants absorb nutrients mainly from the soil in the form of minerals and other inorganic compounds. Animals obtain nutrients from the foods they eat or take in. The three most important nutrients for animals are proteins, carbohydrates, and fats.

nu•tri•tion (no͞o-trĭsh′ən) The process by which an organism obtains the nutrients needed for growth and metabolism.

ny•lon (nī′lŏn′) Any of various very strong, elastic, artificial resins. Nylon can be formed into fibers, sheets, or bristles, and is used to make fabrics and plastics.

nymph (nĭmf) The immature form of those insects that do not pass through a pupal stage. Nymphs usually resemble the adults, but are smaller, lack fully developed wings, and are sexually immature. *Compare* **imago, larva, pupa.**

O The symbol for **oxygen.**

oak (ōk) Any of numerous trees that bear acorns and often have leaves that are irregularly notched or lobed.

o•a•sis (ō-ā′sĭs) *Plural* **oases** (ō-ā′sēz) A small area in a desert that has a supply of water and is able to support vegetation. An oasis forms when groundwater lies close enough to the surface to form a spring or to be reached by wells.

ob•jec•tive (əb-jĕk′tĭv) The lens or group of lenses that first receives light from the object in an optical instrument such as a telescope.

ob•ser•va•tion (ŏb′zər-vā′shən) **1.** The act of perceiving and recording something with instruments. **2.** The result or record of such notation: *a meteorological observation.*

ob•sid•i•an (ŏb-sĭd′ē-ən) A shiny, usually black, volcanic glass. Obsidian forms from lava that cools so quickly that minerals do not have a chance to form within it.

ob•stet•rics (ŏb-stĕt′rĭks) The branch of medicine that deals with the care of women during pregnancy and childbirth.

ob•tuse angle (ŏb-to͞os′) An angle whose measure is between 90° and 180°. *Compare* **acute angle.**

oc•cip•i•tal lobe (ŏk-sĭp′ĭ-tl) The rearmost lobe of each cerebral hemisphere, containing the main visual centers of the brain.

oasis
Skeleton National Park, Namibia

USAGE

ocean/sea

The word *ocean* refers to one of the Earth's four distinct, large areas of salt water, the Pacific, Atlantic, Indian, and Arctic Oceans. The word can also mean the entire network of water that covers almost three quarters of our planet. It comes from the Greek *Okeanos,* a river believed to circle the globe. The word *sea* can also mean the vast ocean covering most of the world. But it more commonly refers to large landlocked or almost landlocked salty waters smaller than the great oceans, such as the Mediterranean Sea or the Bering Sea. Sailors have long referred to all the world's waters as the seven seas. Although the origin of this phrase is not known for certain, many people believe it referred to the Red Sea, the Mediterranean Sea, the Persian Gulf, the Black Sea, the Adriatic Sea, the Caspian Sea, and the Indian Ocean, which were the only waters of interest to Europeans before Columbus.

oc•clu•sion (ə-klo͞o′zhən) **1.** An obstruction in a passageway, especially of the body. **2.** The manner in which the upper and lower sets of teeth fit together.

oc•cul•ta•tion (ŏk′ŭl-tā′shən) The passage of a celestial object between an observer and another celestial object, blocking the second object from view. An occultation occurs when the moon moves between Earth and the sun in a solar eclipse.

o•cean (ō′shən) **1.** The continuous saltwater body that covers about 72 percent of the surface of the Earth. **2.** Any of the principal divisions of this body of water, including the Atlantic, Pacific, Indian, and Arctic Oceans.

o•cean•og•ra•phy (ō′shə-nŏg′rə-fē) The scientific study of oceans, the life that inhabits them, and their physical characteristics, including the depth and extent of ocean waters, their movement and chemical makeup, and the topography and composition of the ocean floors. Oceanography also includes ocean exploration.

o•cel•lus (ō-sĕl′əs) *Plural* **ocelli** (ō-sĕl′ī′) **1.** A small, simple eye or eyespot, found in many invertebrates. **2.** A marking that resembles an eye, as on the wings of some butterflies.

oc•ta•gon (ŏk′tə-gŏn′) A polygon having eight sides.

oc•ta•he•dron (ŏk′tə-hē′drən) A three-dimensional geometric figure with eight triangular faces.

oc•tane (ŏk′tān′) Any of several hydrocarbon compounds having the formula C_8H_{18}. Octane is commonly added to gasoline to prevent uneven burning of fuel in internal-combustion engines.

oc•to•pus (ŏk′tə-pəs) *Plural* **octopuses** *or* **octopi** (ŏk′tə-pī) Any of numerous sea mollusks having a soft rounded body and eight tentacles, each having two rows of suckers used for grasping and holding. Octopuses have large and highly developed eyes and a sharp beak-like mouth. They are considered to be the most intelligent invertebrate animals.

oc•u•lar (ŏk′yə-lər) **1.** Of or having to do with the eye or the sense of vision. **2.** The eyepiece of a microscope, telescope, or other optical instrument.

odd (ŏd) Divisible by 2 with a remainder of 1, such as 17 or –103.

odd-toed ungulate *See* **perissodactyl.**

Oer•sted (ûr′stĕd′), **Hans Christian** 1777–1851. Danish physicist who founded the science of electromagnetism with his discovery (1820) of the magnetic effect produced by an electric current.

ohm (ōm) A unit used to measure the electrical resistance of a material. One ohm is equal to the resistance of a conductor through which a current of one ampere flows when a potential difference of one volt is applied to it.

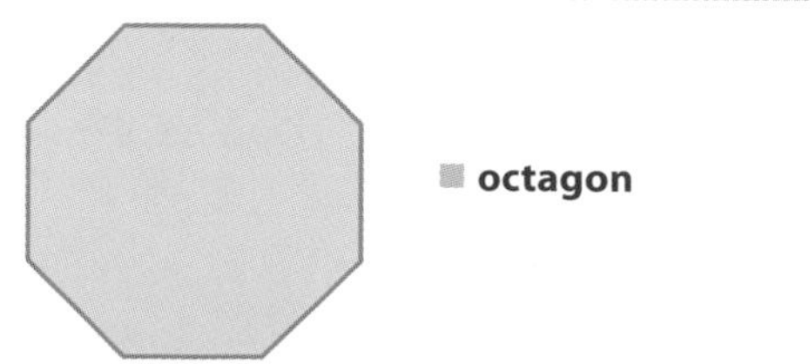

octagon

octopus
giant Pacific octopus

Ohm, Georg Simon 1789–1854. German physicist who discovered the relationship between voltage, current, and resistance in an electrical circuit. His discovery is now known as Ohm's law. The unit of electrical resistance is named for him.

Ohm's law A law stating that the current in an electric circuit is equal to the voltage divided by the resistance. The current increases as the voltage increases, but decreases as the resistance increases.

-oid A suffix meaning "like" or "resembling," as in *ellipsoid,* a geometric solid that resembles an ellipse.

oil (oil) **1.** Any of a large class of liquid or easily melted substances that are typically very slippery and greasy. Oils are flammable, do not mix with water, and include animal and vegetable fats as well as substances of mineral or synthetic origin. They are used in food, soap, and candles, and make good lubricants and fuels. **2.** Petroleum.

-ol A suffix used to form the names of chemical compounds having a hydroxyl (OH) group, such as *ethanol.*

o•le•fin (ō′lə-fĭn) *See* **alkene.**

ol•fac•to•ry (ŏl-făk′tə-rē, ōl-făk′tə-rē) Relating to the sense of smell or the organs of smell.

olfactory nerve The nerve that carries sensory information on smell from the nose to the brain. The olfactory nerve is a cranial nerve.

Ol•i•go•cene (ŏl′ĭ-gō-sēn′) The third epoch of the Tertiary Period, from about 37 to 24 million years ago, characterized by the continued development of modern mammalian groups and the rise of the first cats, dogs, and related mammals. *See Chart at* **geologic time,** pages 148–149.

ol•i•vine (ŏl′ə-vēn′) An olive-green to brownish-green mineral consisting primarily of iron, magnesium, and silica. Olivine is a common mineral in the igneous rocks, such as basalt and gabbro, that make up most of the Earth's crust beneath the oceans.

o•ma•sum (ō-mā′səm) The third division of the stomach in ruminant animals. It removes excess water from food and further reduces the size of food particles before passing them to the abomasum for digestion by enzymes. *See more at* **ruminant.**

om•ma•tid•i•um (ŏm′ə-tĭd′ē-əm) *Plural* **ommatidia.** One of the tiny light-sensitive parts of the compound eye of insects and other arthropods. An ommatidium resembles a single simplified eye. *See more at* **compound eye.**

om•ni•vore (ŏm′nə-vôr′) An organism that eats both plants and animals. —*Adjective* **omnivorous.**

on•co•gene (ŏn′kə-jēn) A gene containing a mutation in its DNA that causes normal cells to turn into cancerous ones. *See Note at* **cancer.**

on•col•o•gy (ŏn-kŏl′ə-jē) The branch of medicine that deals with the diagnosis and treatment of cancer.

–one A suffix used to form the names of chemical compounds containing an oxygen atom attached to a carbon atom, such as *acetone.*

on•yx (ŏn′ĭks) A type of quartz that occurs in bands of different colors, often black and white.

Oort cloud (ôrt, ōrt) A sphere-shaped mass of comets that makes up the outer edge of the solar system, surrounding the Kuiper belt and the planets. The more than 100 billion comets in this region orbit the sun at a distance of one to two light-years. Comets from this area that come into the inner solar system take more than 200 years to make one complete orbit. *Compare* **Kuiper belt.**

o•pac•i•ty (ō-păs′ĭ-tē) The quality or condition of being opaque.

o•pal (ō′pəl) A usually transparent mineral consisting of hydrous silica. Opal can occur in almost any color, but it is often pinkish white with a milky or pearly appearance. It typically forms within cracks in igneous rocks, in limestones, and in mineral veins. It also occurs in the silica-rich shells of certain marine organisms.

o•paque (ō-pāk′) Not letting light pass through; neither transparent nor translucent. Metals and many minerals are opaque.

o•pen circuit (ō′pən) An electric circuit through which current cannot flow because the path is broken or interrupted by an opening.

open cluster A loose group of approximately 100 to several thousand young stars that formed from the same nebula at about the same time. The Pleiades is an open cluster. *Compare* **globular cluster.**

open universe A model of the universe in which there is not enough matter, and therefore not enough gravitational force, to stop the expansion started by the big bang. *See Note at* **big bang.**

op•er•at•ing system (ŏp′ə-rā′tĭng) Software designed to control the hardware of a specific data-processing system in order to allow users and programs to make use of the system.

o•per•cu•lum (ō-pûr′kyə-ləm) A lid or flap covering an opening, such as the gill cover in some fish or the horny flap covering the opening of a snail.

oph•thal•mol•o•gy (ŏf′thəl-mŏl′ə-jē, ŏp′thəl-mŏl′ə-jē) The branch of medicine that deals with the eye, its diseases, and their treatment.

o•pi•um (ō′pē-əm) A highly addictive, yellowish-brown drug obtained from the pods of a variety of poppy, from which other drugs, such as morphine, are prepared.

o•pos•sum (ə-pŏs′əm) Any of various rat-like mammals that mostly dwell in trees and have thick fur, a long snout, and a long hairless tail. The tail is often used to hang from branches. Opossums are marsupials and carry their young in a pouch until they grow older, when they cling to their mother's back or tail with their tails. When attacked by predators, opossums "play dead" or "play possum" by collapsing and lying still.

Op•pen•hei•mer (ŏp′ən-hī′mər), **J(ulius) Robert** 1902–1967. American physicist who

J. Robert Oppenheimer

made discoveries in the field of quantum theory. Oppenheimer also directed the laboratory at Los Alamos, New Mexico, during the development of the first atomic bomb (1942–1945).

op•pos•a•ble thumb (ə-pō′zə-bəl) A thumb that can be placed opposite the fingers of the same hand. Opposable thumbs allow the digits to grasp and handle objects, and are characteristic of primates.

op•tic (ŏp′tĭk) Relating to the eye or vision.

op•ti•cal (ŏp′tĭ-kəl) **1.** Relating to sight; visual. **2.** Relating to optics. **3.** Relating to or using visible light: *optical astronomy.*

optical disk *or* **optical disc** A plastic-coated disk that stores digital data, such as music or text, as tiny pits etched into its surface. Optical disks are read with a laser scanning the surface.

optical fiber A flexible, transparent, and very thin fiber that is made of pure glass or plastic and is used to carry light signals. Optical fibers are used especially in telecommunication and in instruments for seeing inside hollow body structures. They can be as thin as one-hundredth of a millimeter. *See more at* **fiber optics.**

optic nerve The nerve that carries sensory information on vision from the retina of the eye to the brain. The optic nerve is a cranial nerve.

op•tics (ŏp′tĭks) The scientific study of light and vision.

o•ral (ôr′əl) Relating to the mouth.

o•rang•u•tan (ô-răng′ə-tăn′) A large ape of the islands of Borneo and Sumatra, having long arms and a reddish-brown coat. Orangutans are highly intelligent and usually solitary.

or•bit (ôr′bĭt) *Noun.* **1a.** The path of a celestial body or an artificial satellite as it revolves around another body. **b.** One complete revolution of such a body. *See Note at* **solar system. 2.** The path of a body in a field of force surrounding another body; for example, the path of an electron in relation to the nucleus of an atom. **3.** Either of two bony hollows in the skull containing the eye and its associated structures. —*Verb.* **4.** To move in an orbit around another body. **5.** To put into an orbit: *orbit a satellite.*

or•bi•tal (ôr′bĭ-tl) The region within the shell of an atom in which an electron is most likely to be found. One or more orbitals make up each electron shell.

or•ca (ôr′kə) A large dolphin found in all the world's oceans, having a black body with a white underside and a tall, triangular dorsal fin. Orcas grow up to 30 feet (9.1 meters) in length. Also called *killer whale.*

or•chid (ôr′kĭd) Any of numerous tropical and subtropical plants that grow on the ground or in trees as epiphytes. Orchids have irregularly shaped flowers with one petal larger than the others.

or•der (ôr′dər) A group of organisms ranking above a family and below a class. *See Table at* **taxonomy.**

or•di•nal number (ôr′dn-əl) A number, such as 3rd, 11th, or 412th, used in counting to indicate position in a series but not quantity. *Compare* **cardinal number.**

or•di•nate (ôr′dn-ĭt) The distance of a point from the x-axis on a graph in the Cartesian coordinate system. It is measured parallel to the y-axis. For example, a point having coordinates (2,3) has 3 as its ordinate. *Compare* **abscissa.**

Or•do•vi•cian (ôr′də-vĭsh′ən) The second period of the Paleozoic Era, from about 505 to 438 million years ago, characterized by the appearance of primitive fishes. *See Chart at* **geologic time,** pages 148–149.

ore (ôr) A mineral or rock from which a valuable or useful substance, especially a metal, can be extracted at a reasonable cost.

or•gan (ôr′gən) A distinct part of an organism that performs one or more particular functions. Examples of organs are the eyes, ears, lungs, and heart of an animal, and the roots, stems, and leaves of a plant.

or•gan•elle (ôr′gə-nĕl′) A structure or part that is enclosed within its own membrane inside a cell and has a particular function. Organelles are found only in eukaryotic cells and are absent from the cells of prokaryotes like bacteria. The nucleus, mitochondrion, and chloroplast are examples of organelles.

or•gan•ic (ôr-găn′ĭk) **1.** Involving organisms or the products of their life processes. **2.** Relating to chemical compounds containing carbon, especially hydrocarbons. **3.** Using or produced with fertilizers or pesticides that are strictly of animal or vegetable origin. *See Table on* page 248.

organic chemistry The branch of chemistry that deals with carbon and carbon compounds. *See Table on* page 248.

or•gan•ism (ôr′gə-nĭz′əm) An individual form of life, such as a bacterium, fungus, plant, or animal, that is capable of growing and reproducing. Organisms are composed of one or more cells.

or•i•gin (ôr′ə-jĭn) The point at which the axes of a Cartesian coordinate system intersect. The coordinates of the origin are (0,0) in two dimensions and (0,0,0) in three dimensions.

O•ri•on (ō-rī′ən) A constellation in the region of the celestial equator near Gemini and Taurus. It contains the bright stars Betelgeuse and Rigel.

or•nith•is•chi•an (ôr′nə-thĭs′kē-ən) One of the two main types of dinosaurs. Ornithischians have a pelvis similar to that of modern birds, and include all the plant-eating dinosaurs except the sauropods. They include armor-plated, horned, and duck-billed varieties. *Compare* **saurischian.**

or•ni•thol•o•gy (ôr′nə-thŏl′ə-jē) The scientific study of birds.

or•nith•o•pod (ôr-nĭth′ə-pŏd′) One of the main types of ornithischian dinosaurs, including the hadrosaurs. Ornithopods walked on their hind legs and had three blunt toes on each foot. They lived from the late Triassic Period until the end of the Cretaceous Period.

or•tho•clase (ôr′thə-klās′) A type of feldspar consisting of potassium aluminum silicate. Orthoclase is typically white, pink, yellow, or brown, but it can also be colorless. It is especially common in igneous rocks.

or•tho•pe•dics (ôr′thə-pē′dĭks) The branch of medicine that deals with the correction or treatment of disorders or injuries of the bones, joints, and associated muscles.

or•tho•rhom•bic (ôr′thō-rŏm′bĭk) Relating to a crystal having three axes of different lengths intersecting at right angles. The mineral topaz has orthorhombic crystals. *See more at* **crystal.**

Os The symbol for **osmium.**

os•cil•la•tion (ŏs′ə-lā′shən) **1.** A steady, uninterrupted, backward and forward swinging about a central point. *Compare* **vibration. 2.** A single cycle of motion about a central position.

os•cil•lo•scope (ə-sĭl′ə-skōp′) An electronic instrument used to measure changing electric voltages. It displays the waveforms of electric oscillations on a screen.

–ose A suffix used to form the chemical names of carbohydrates, such as *glucose.*

–osis A suffix that means: **1.** Diseased condition, as in *tuberculosis.* **2.** Condition or process, as in *osmosis.*

os•mi•um (ŏz′mē-əm) A hard, brittle, bluish-white metallic element. Osmium is the densest naturally occurring element. It is used to make very hard alloys for fountain pen points and electrical contacts. *Symbol* **Os.** *Atomic number* 76. *See* **Periodic Table,** pages 262–263.

os•mo•sis (ŏz-mō′sĭs) The movement of a solvent through a membrane separating two solutions of different concentrations. The solvent

oscillation

The time it takes the pendulum to swing from **a** *to* **b** *and back to* **a** *is known as its period. The dashed red line from the central point represents the position of the pendulum at rest.*

ORGANIC COMPOUNDS

Chemical compounds containing one or more carbon atoms are called **organic compounds.** Hundreds of thousands of organic compounds are found in nature or have been artificially made. They range from the very simple, like methane, with its five atoms, to the very complex, like DNA, which has millions of atoms.

A very common class of organic compounds, called the **alkanes,** all have one or more carbon atoms arranged in a row, or chain. Atoms are attached to each other in a molecule by sharing electrons; these attachments are called **bonds.** Because of its particular structure, a carbon atom (C) must share a total of four electrons with other atoms. In an alkane, each carbon in the chain shares one electron with its neighboring carbon, forming what are called **single bonds** (indicated by single lines between the element symbols in the diagrams below). The remaining electrons are shared with hydrogen atoms (H). Below are illustrated the first four compounds in the alkane series—methane, ethane, propane, and butane:

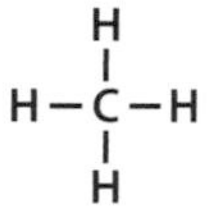

methane
CH_4

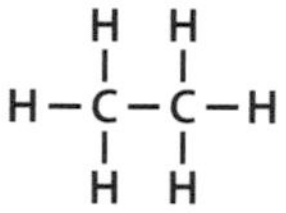

ethane
C_2H_6

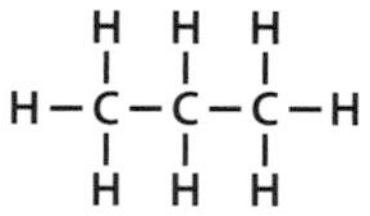

propane
C_3H_8

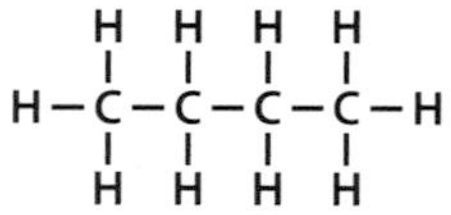

butane
C_4H_{10}

A large number of compounds can be created by modifying these basic alkanes. For example, replacing one of the hydrogen atoms at the end of an ethane molecule with a group containing an oxygen atom and a hydrogen atom (OH) produces ethanol, the most familiar form of alcohol:

ethanol
C_2H_6O

A slightly more complicated modification of a basic alkane, shown below, produces acetic acid, the acid occurring in vinegar. The double line between the carbon and the upper oxygen atom indicates that two electrons (rather than one) are shared between the two atoms, forming what is called a **double bond:**

acetic acid
$C_2H_4O_2$

The carbon atoms in organic molecules can also be joined to each other by double bonds, or (more rarely) **triple bonds,** in which three electrons are shared. Two such molecules are ethylene, with a double bond between the carbon atoms, and acetylene, with a triple bond:

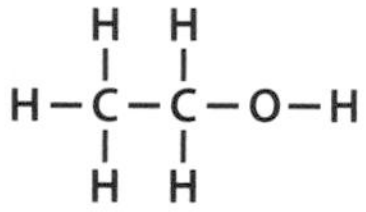

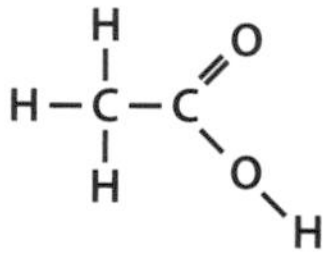

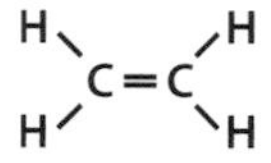

ethylene
C_2H_4

H−C≡C−H

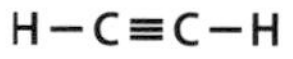

acetylene
C_2H_2

Very often, chains of carbon atoms loop to form rings. The basic ring compound in organic chemistry is benzene, which has six carbon and six hydrogen atoms. The carbon atoms are joined to each other by alternating single and double bonds:

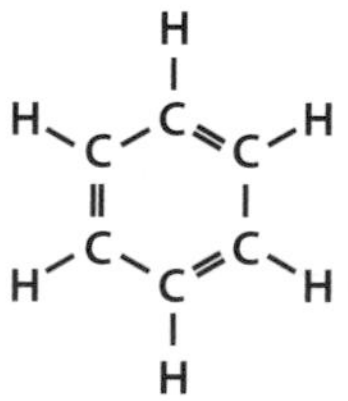

benzene
C_6H_6

from the side of weaker concentration usually moves to the side of the stronger concentration, diluting it, until the concentrations of the solutions are equal on both sides of the membrane. ❖ The pressure exerted by the molecules of the solvent on the membrane they pass through is called **osmotic pressure.** Osmotic pressure is the energy driving osmosis and is important for living organisms because it allows water and nutrients dissolved in water to pass through cell membranes.

os•si•cle (ŏs′ĭ-kəl) A small bone, especially one of the three located in the middle ear (the incus, malleus, and stapes) that transmit sound vibrations from the eardrum to the inner ear.

os•si•fi•ca•tion (ŏs′ə-fĭ-kā′shən) The process of bone formation, brought about by the action of specialized bone cells called osteoblasts.

os•te•o•ar•thri•tis (ŏs′tē-ō-är-thrī′tĭs) A form of arthritis that is characterized by wearing down of the cartilage of the joints.

os•te•o•blast (ŏs′tē-ə-blăst′) A cell that produces the collagen needed for the development of new bone. As new bone grows and hardens, osteoblasts become embedded in the bone matrix. Once embedded, they are no longer able to secrete collagen and are called osteocytes.

os•te•o•cyte (ŏs′tē-ə-sīt′) A cell with branching parts that is embedded in the matrix of bone.

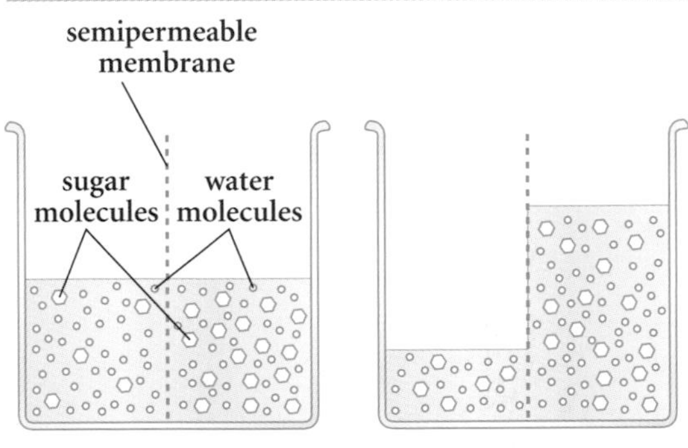

osmosis

left: *The concentration of sugar molecules is greater on the right side of the membrane than on the left. The water molecules are small enough to move across the membrane, but the larger sugar molecules cannot pass through.*
right: *The water molecules move across the membrane until the water and sugar molecules are of equal concentration on both sides. This lowers the water level on the left side and raises it on the right side.*

Osteocytes, which are derived from osteoblasts, regulate the metabolism of bone tissue.

os•te•o•po•ro•sis (ŏs′tē-ō-pə-rō′sĭs) A condition in which the bones become porous and weak from loss of minerals, especially calcium.

os•trich (ŏs′trĭch) A very large African bird having a small head, a long neck, and long, strong legs. Ostriches cannot fly but can run very fast, and are the largest living species of bird.

ot•ter (ŏt′ər) Any of various meat-eating mammals that live in or near water and have webbed feet and thick brown fur. Otters are related to the weasels.

ounce (ouns) **1.** A unit of weight equal to $\frac{1}{16}$ of a pound and containing 16 drams or 437.5 grains. *See Table at* **measurement. 2.** A unit of volume or capacity used to measure liquids, equal to $\frac{1}{16}$ of a pint and containing 8 fluid drams or 1.8 cubic inches. *See Table at* **measurement.**

out•crop (out′krŏp′) An area of visible bedrock that is not covered with soil.

out•er ear (ou′tər) The part of the ear in many mammals that is made chiefly of cartilage and includes the passage leading to the eardrum. The outer ear gathers and focuses incoming sound waves and transmits them to the inner ear. *See more at* **ear.**

out•put (out′po͝ot′) **1.** The energy, power, or work produced by a system or device: *the output of an engine.* **2.** The information that a computer produces by processing a specific input.

o•va•ry (ō′və-rē) **1.** The reproductive organ in female animals that produces eggs and the sex hormones estrogen and progesterone. In most vertebrate animals, the ovaries occur in pairs. **2.** The part of a flower pistil that contains ovules. The ovary is located at the base of the pistil and ripens into a fruit after fertilization of one or more of the ovules. *See more at* **flower.** —*Adjective* **ovarian** (ō-vâr′ē-ən).

o•vi•duct (ō′vĭ-dŭkt′) A tube through which eggs or egg cells are carried to the uterus in mammals or to the outside of the body in other animals. The fallopian tubes are oviducts.

o•vip•a•rous (ō-vĭp′ər-əs) Producing eggs that hatch outside the body. Amphibians, birds, and most insects, fish, and reptiles are oviparous. *Compare* **ovoviviparous, viviparous.**

oxbow

o•vi•pos•i•tor (ō′və-pŏz′ĭ-tər) A tube in many female insects that extends from the end of the abdomen and is used to lay eggs.

o•vo•vi•vip•a•rous (ō′vō-vī-vĭp′ər-əs) Producing eggs that hatch within the female's body. Some fish and reptiles are ovoviviparous. *Compare* **oviparous, viviparous.**

o•vu•la•tion (ō′vyə-lā′shən, ŏv′yə-lā′shən) The release of eggs or egg cells from the ovary in female animals, regulated in mammals by hormones of the pituitary gland. In humans and most other primates, ovulation usually occurs midway through the menstrual cycle.

o•vule (ō′vyo͞ol, ŏv′yo͞ol) A small part in a seed-bearing plant that becomes a seed after its egg cell has been fertilized by a male cell. *See more at* **flower.**

o•vum (ō′vəm) *Plural* **ova.** *See* **egg** (sense 1).

owl (oul) Any of various birds of prey that are usually active at night and have a large head, large forward-facing eyes, a short hooked bill, and a flat round face.

ox•al•ic acid (ŏk-săl′ĭk) A poisonous, crystalline acid found in a number of plants. It is used for many industrial purposes, including rust removal and bleaching.

ox•bow (ŏks′bō′) A sharp, U-shaped bend in a river. ❖ When a river changes its course and cuts through the strip of land in the middle of an oxbow, the water that remains in the former oxbow loop is called an **oxbow lake.**

ox•i•da•tion (ŏk′sĭ-dā′shən) **1.** The chemical combination of a substance with oxygen. **2.** A chemical reaction in which an atom or ion loses electrons, thus undergoing an increase in valence. Removing an electron from an iron atom having a valence of +2 changes the valence to +3. *Compare* **reduction.**

WORD HISTORY

oxygen, hydrogen, and nitrogen

In 1786, the French chemist Antoine Lavoisier coined a term for the element *oxygen* (*oxygène* in French). He used Greek words for the coinage: *oxy–* means "sharp," and *–gen* means "producing." Oxygen was called the "sharp-producing" element because it was thought to be essential for making acids. Lavoisier also coined the name of the element *hydrogen,* the "water-producing" element, in 1788. Soon after, in 1791, another French chemist, J. A. Chaptal, introduced the word *nitrogen,* the "niter-producing" element, referring to its discovery from an analysis of nitric acid.

Did You Know?

oxidation

If you've ever seen rust, you've seen oxidation. If you've ever watched a candle burn, you've seen oxidation. And if you've ever breathed, which is a good bet, you've experienced oxidation. In all these cases, oxygen is added to another substance. Rust is oxygen reacting with iron, and both burning and breathing involve oxygen reacting with carbon to free up energy stored in chemical bonds. Perhaps you have seen movies in which people are trapped in a confined space like a mine. They might light a match to see, but the burning flame uses up the same oxygen they need to survive. Rust can be thought of as burning that happens incredibly slowly. Oxygen takes electrons from whatever it is oxidizing, so chemists also use the word oxidation to describe what happens to any substance that loses electrons to another substance.

Did You Know?

ozone

For the Earth's organisms, including people, ozone can be a lifesaver or a threat to health, depending on how high it is found in the atmosphere. The ozone that lingers in the lower atmosphere is a pollutant and contributes to respiratory diseases like asthma. But in the upper atmosphere, ozone protects us from the more severe forms of the sun's radiation. The region of the atmosphere in which ozone is most concentrated is known as the ozone layer, which lies from about 10 to 20 miles (16 to 32 kilometers) above the Earth. Because ozone absorbs certain wavelengths of harmful ultraviolet radiation, this layer acts as an important protection for life on the Earth. In recent years the ozone has thinned or disappeared in parts of the ozone layer, creating an ozone hole that lets in dangerous amounts of ultraviolet radiation. Ozone holes are created in part by the presence of certain industrial or commercial chemicals released into the atmosphere.

oxidation-reduction A chemical reaction in which an atom or ion loses electrons to another atom or ion.

ox•ide (ŏk**′**sīd′) A compound of oxygen and another element or radical. Water (H_2O) is an oxide.

ox•i•dize (ŏk**′**sĭ-dīz′) To undergo or cause to undergo oxidation.

ox•y•gen (ŏk**′**sĭ-jən) A nonmetallic element that exists in its free form as a colorless, odorless gas and makes up about 21 percent of the Earth's atmosphere. It is the most abundant element in the Earth's crust and occurs in many compounds, including water, carbon dioxide, and iron ore. Oxygen combines with most elements, is required for combustion, and is essential for life in most organisms. *Symbol* **O.** *Atomic number* 8. *See* **Periodic Table,** pages 262–263.

ox•y•gen•ate (ŏk**′**sĭ-jə-nāt′) To combine or mix with oxygen, as in a physical, chemical, or biological system. Blood is oxygenated in the lungs.

ox•y•he•mo•glo•bin (ŏk′sē-hē**′**mə-glō′bĭn) The compound formed when a molecule of hemoglobin binds with a molecule of oxygen. In vertebrate animals, oxyhemoglobin forms in the red blood cells as they take up oxygen in the lungs.

oys•ter (oi**′**stər) Any of several mollusks of shallow waters, having a rough, irregularly shaped, double-hinged shell. Many kinds of oysters are used as food, and some kinds produce pearls inside their shells.

oz. Abbreviation of **ounce.**

o•zone (ō**′**zōn′) A poisonous, blue form of oxygen that has three atoms per molecule rather than the usual two. It is produced by electricity passing through air, as in a lightning strike, and also by the sun's radiation reacting with ordinary oxygen or with the pollutants in smog. Ozone is used commercially in water purification, in air conditioning, and as a bleach.

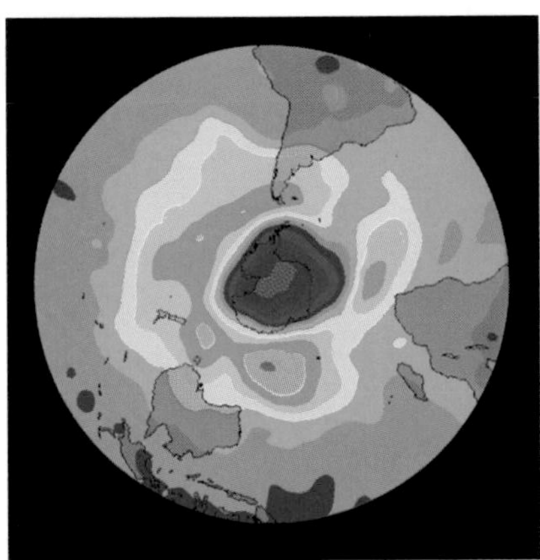

ozone

This image of the Southern Hemisphere was generated by a satellite instrument that measures infrared radiation from the Earth. The irregular circles of purple, red, and gray over Antarctica indicate an ozone hole, where ozone levels are progressively thinner.

P

P The symbol for **phosphorus.**

Pa The symbol for **protactinium.**

pace•mak•er (pās′mā′kər) An electronic device that is surgically implanted to regulate the heartbeat.

pach•y•ceph•a•lo•sau•rus (păk′ĭ-sĕf′ə-lə-sôr′-əs) A medium-sized, plant-eating dinosaur of the late Cretaceous Period having a domed skull up to 10 inches (25.4 centimeters) thick.

pach•y•derm (păk′ĭ-dûrm′) Any of various large, thick-skinned mammals, such as the elephant, rhinoceros, or hippopotamus.

pack ice (păk) *Oceanography.* A large area of floating ice consisting of a mixture of ice fragments packed or squeezed together.

Pag•et (păj′ĭt), Sir **James** 1814–1899. British surgeon and researcher who was a pioneer of modern pathology. He discovered the cause of trichinosis in 1834.

pa•hoe•hoe (pə-hoi′hoi′, pə-hō′ē-hō′ē) Lava with a smooth, swirled surface. It is highly fluid and spreads out in shiny sheets. *Compare* **aa.** *See Table at* **rock.**

WORD HISTORY

pahoehoe and aa

The islands that make up Hawaii were born and bred from volcanoes that rose up over thousands of years from the sea floor. Volcanoes are such an important part of the Hawaiian landscape and environment that the people who originally settled Hawaii, the Polynesians, worshiped a special volcano goddess, Pele. Not surprisingly, two words have entered English from Hawaiian that are used by scientists in naming different kinds of lava flows. One, *pahoehoe,* refers to lava with a smooth, shiny, or swirled surface and comes from the Hawaiian verb *hoe,* "to paddle" (since paddles make swirls in the water). The other, *aa,* refers to lava having a rough surface and comes from the Hawaiian word meaning "to burn."

pahoehoe
volcanic lava flows: pahoehoe (foreground) *and aa* (background)

pal•ate (păl′ĭt) The roof of the mouth in vertebrate animals, separating the mouth from the passages of the nose. ❖ The bony part of the palate is called the **hard palate.** ❖ A soft, flexible, rear portion of the palate, called the **soft palate,** is present in mammals only and serves to close off the mouth from the nose during swallowing.

paleo– A prefix that means: **1.** Prehistoric, as in *Paleocene.* **2.** Early or primitive, as in *Paleolithic.*

Pa•le•o•cene (pā′lē-ə-sēn′) The earliest epoch of the Tertiary Period, from about 65 to 58 million years ago, characterized by the appearance of placental mammals and the formation of the Rocky Mountains and Himalayas. *See Chart at* **geologic time,** pages 148–149.

Pa•le•o•lith•ic (pā′lē-ə-lĭth′ĭk) The cultural period of the Stone Age that began about 2 million years ago, marked by the earliest use of tools made of chipped stone. The Paleolithic Period ended at different times in different parts of the world, between about 40,000 and 10,000 years ago. *Compare* **Mesolithic, Neolithic.**

pa•le•on•tol•o•gy (pā′lē-ŏn-tŏl′ə-jē) The scientific study of life in the geologic past, especially through the study of animal and plant fossils.

Pa•le•o•zo•ic (pā′lē-ə-zō′ĭk) The era of geologic time from about 540 to 245 million years ago.

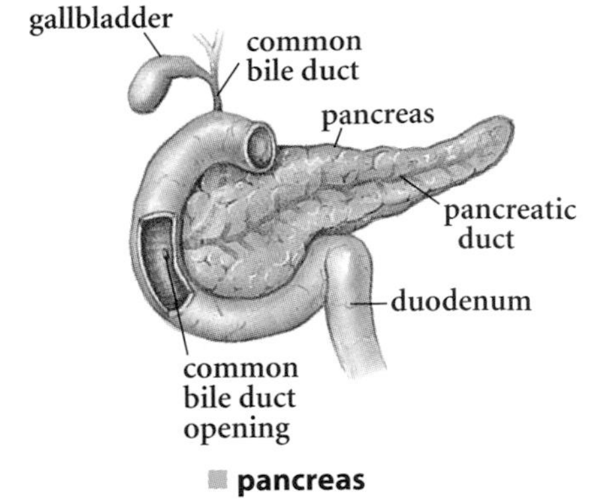

pancreas

The Paleozoic Era is characterized by the appearance of marine invertebrate animals, primitive fish and reptiles, and land plants. *See Chart at* **geologic time,** pages 148–149.

pal•i•sade layer (păl′ĭ-sād′) A layer of cells just below the upper surface of most leaves, consisting of cylindrical cells that contain many chloroplasts and stand at right angles to the leaf surface. Also called *palisade parenchyma. See more at* **photosynthesis.**

pal•i•sades (păl′ĭ-sādz′) *Geology.* A line of high cliffs, especially of basalt, usually along a river.

pal•la•di•um (pə-lā′dē-əm) An easily shaped, grayish-white metallic element that occurs naturally with platinum. Because it can absorb large amounts of hydrogen, it is used as a catalyst in reactions involving hydrogen. Palladium and its alloys are used to make electrical contacts and jewelry. *Symbol* **Pd.** *Atomic number* 46. *See* **Periodic Table,** pages 262–263.

palm (päm) Any of various evergreen trees of tropical and subtropical regions, usually having a branchless trunk with a group of large, featherlike or fan-shaped leaves at the top.

pal•mate (păl′māt′, päl′māt′) **1.** Having a shape similar to that of a hand with the fingers extended. Some kinds of coral and the antlers of moose and certain deer are palmate. **2.** *Botany.* Having three or more veins, leaflets, or lobes radiating from one point. Maples have palmate leaves. **3.** *Zoology.* Having webbed toes, as the feet of many swimming and diving birds do.

palp (pălp) A segmented organ extending from the mouthparts of arthropods, used for touch or taste.

pam•pa (păm′pə) An extensive, treeless grassland of southern South America.

pan•cre•as (păng′krē-əs) A long, irregularly shaped gland in vertebrate animals that is located behind the stomach. It secretes insulin and produces enzymes needed for digestion, which are secreted into the gut or small intestine.

pan•dem•ic (păn-dĕm′ĭk) An epidemic that spreads over a very wide area, such as a whole country or continent.

Pan•gae•a (păn-jē′ə) A supercontinent made up of all the world's present landmasses as they are thought to have been joined during the Permian and Triassic Periods. According to the theory of plate tectonics, Pangaea later broke up into Laurasia and Gondwanaland, which eventually broke up into the continents we know today.

pan•i•cle (păn′ĭ-kəl) A branched cluster of flowers in which the branches are racemes. Oats have panicles.

pan•to•then•ic acid (păn′tə-thĕn′ĭk) A vitamin belonging to the vitamin B complex that is important in the metabolism of fats and carbohydrates. It is found in liver, yeast, and many vegetables.

pa•pil•la (pə-pĭl′ə) *Plural* **papillae** (pə-pĭl′ē) A small projection from a body surface, especially a taste bud on the tongue.

pa•rab•o•la (pə-răb′ə-lə) The curve formed by the set of points in a plane that are all equally distant from both a given line (called the directrix) and a given point (called the focus) that is not on the line.

par•af•fin (păr′ə-fĭn) A waxy, white or colorless solid mixture made from petroleum and used to make candles, wax paper, lubricants, and waterproof coatings.

par•al•lax (păr′ə-lăks′) An apparent change in the position of an object, such as a star, caused by a change in the observer's position that provides a new line of sight. The parallax of nearby stars caused by observing them from opposite points

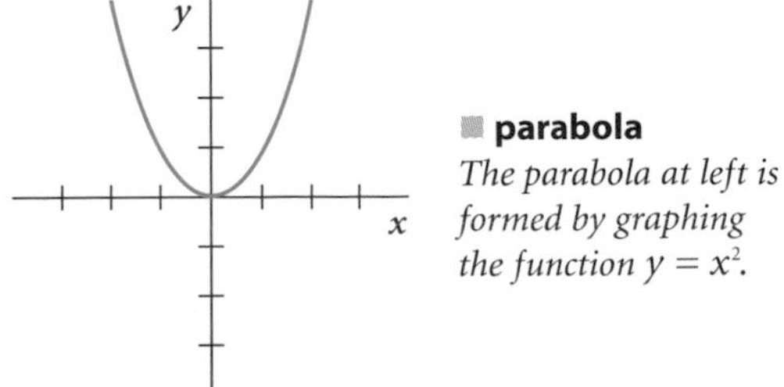

parabola
The parabola at left is formed by graphing the function $y = x^2$.

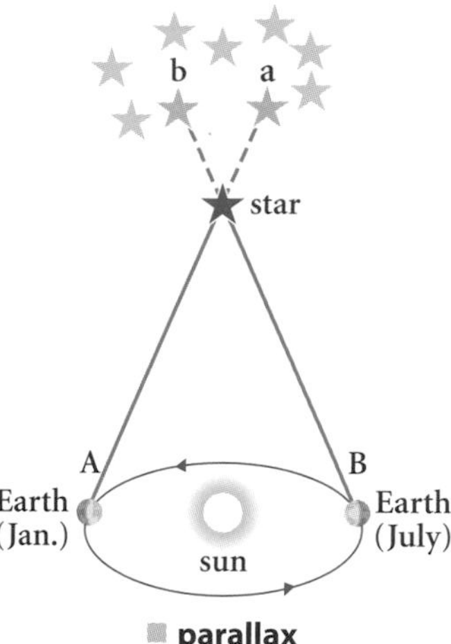

parallax

*Viewed from point **A**, a nearby star appears to occupy position **a** against a background of more distant stars. Six months later, from point **B**, the star appears to occupy position **b**.*

in Earth's orbit around the sun is used in estimating the stars' distance from Earth.

par•al•lel (păr′ə-lĕl′) *Adjective.* **1.** Relating to lines or surfaces that are separated everywhere from each other by the same distance. —*Noun.* **2.** Any of the imaginary lines encircling the Earth's surface parallel to the plane of the equator, used to represent degrees of latitude. *See more at* **longitude.**

parallel circuit *See under* **circuit.**

par•al•lel•e•pi•ped (păr′ə-lĕl′ə-pī′pĭd) A solid geometric figure having six faces, each one being a parallelogram.

par•al•lel•o•gram (păr′ə-lĕl′ə-grăm′) A four-sided plane geometric figure in which each pair of opposite sides is parallel.

par•a•me•ci•um (păr′ə-mē′sē-əm) *Plural* **paramecia** *or* **parameciums.** Any of various freshwater protozoans that are usually oval in shape and that move by means of cilia.

pa•ram•e•ter (pə-răm′ĭ-tər) A quantity whose value can vary in general but is fixed when the quantity is used in a specific mathematical expression involving one or more other variables. For example, in finding the area of a circle, one needs to know the length of the circle's radius; that length is a parameter that will have different values for circles of different sizes.

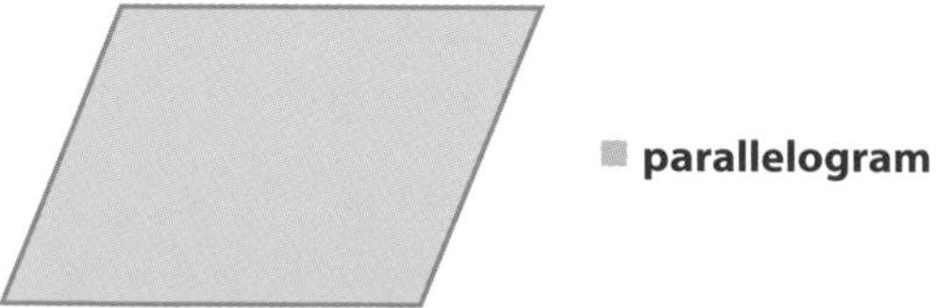

parallelogram

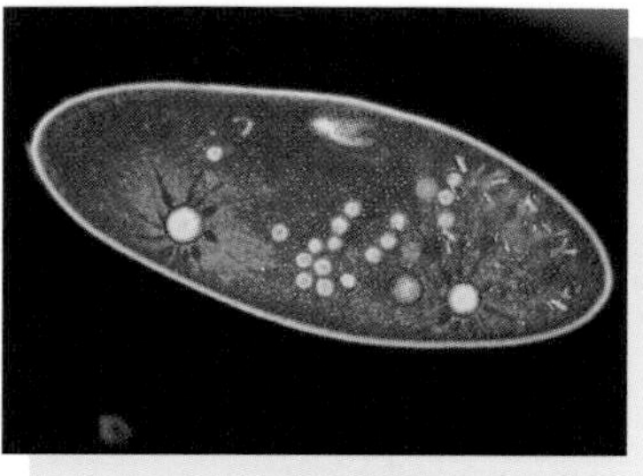

paramecium
photographed through a microscope

par•a•ple•gi•a (păr′ə-plē′jē-ə) Paralysis of the lower part of the body, caused by injury to the spinal cord.

par•a•site (păr′ə-sīt′) An organism that lives in or on a different kind of organism (called the host) from which it gets some or all of its nourishment. Parasites are generally harmful to their hosts, and in some cases they may even destroy the other organism, although more often the damage they do is minor. Lice and tapeworms are parasites of humans.

par•a•sit•ism (păr′ə-sĭ-tĭz′əm) A symbiotic relationship between two organisms of different species in which one organism benefits and the other is generally harmed. *See Note at* **symbiosis.**

par•a•sym•pa•thet•ic nervous system (păr′ə-sĭm′pə-thĕt′ĭk) The part of the autonomic nervous system that tends to act in opposition to the sympathetic nervous system, as by slowing down the heart and dilating the blood vessels. It also regulates the function of many glands, such as those that produce tears and saliva.

par•a•thy•roid gland (păr′ə-thī′roid) Any of four kidney-shaped glands located behind or within the thyroid gland of many vertebrate animals. The parathyroid glands secrete a hormone (called parathyroid hormone) that regulates the amount of calcium in the blood.

pa•ren•chy•ma (pə-rĕng′kə-mə) The basic tissue of plants, consisting of thin-walled, nonspecialized cells that sometimes adapt to specialized functions. The internal layers of leaves, the cortex and pith of the stem, and the soft parts of

parasite
color-enhanced photograph through an electron microscope of a louse on a human scalp

fruits are made of parenchyma. In higher plants, parenchyma supports the plant body, roots, and leaves; it also stores water and contains chloroplasts in which photosynthesis takes place.

pa•ri•e•tal lobe (pə-rī′ĭ-təl) The middle portion of each cerebral hemisphere, where sensory information from the body is processed.

Par•kin•son's disease (pär′kĭn-sənz) A disease of the brain, usually in older people, that tends to become more severe over time. Symptoms include shaking, slowed movement, and rigid muscles.

par•sec (pär′sĕk′) A unit of astronomical length equal to 3.26 light-years. It is based on the distance from Earth at which a star would have a parallax of one second of arc.

par•the•no•gen•e•sis (pär′thə-nō-jĕn′ĭ-sĭs) Reproduction in which an egg develops without fertilization, as in certain insects such as aphids. —*Adjective* **parthenogenetic** (pär′thə-nō-jə-nĕt′ĭk).

par•tial product (pär′shəl) A product formed by multiplying the multiplicand by one digit of the multiplier when the multiplier has more than one digit. For example, the product of 67 multiplied by 12 is 134 (that is, 67 × 2) + 670 (that is, 67 × 10), or 804. In this example 134 and 670 are partial products.

par•ti•cle (pär′tĭ-kəl) **1.** A very small piece of solid matter; a speck: *particles of dust.* **2.** An elementary or subatomic particle.

particle accelerator Any of several machines, such as the cyclotron and synchrotron, that increase the speed of protons, electrons, or other subatomic particles, and cause them to collide with other particles. The collisions often release new particles and can be studied to determine the structure of the colliding particles. Particle accelerators are also used to bombard atomic nuclei with neutrons, creating new isotopes. *See Note at* **subatomic particle.**

par•tic•u•late (pər-tĭk′yə-lĭt) *Adjective.* **1.** Formed of very small, separate particles. Dust and soot are forms of particulate matter. —*Noun.* **2.** A very small particle, as of dust or soot. Particulates that are given off by the burning of oil, gasoline, and other fuels can remain suspended in the atmosphere for long periods, where they are a major component of air pollution and smog.

pas•cal (pă-skăl′, pä-skäl′) A unit used to measure pressure. One pascal is equal to one newton per square meter.

Pascal, Blaise 1623–1662. French mathematician, physicist, and philosopher. He invented the mechanical calculator and the syringe. With Pierre de Fermat, he developed the mathematical theory of probability.

Pascal's law The principle that if a fluid is under pressure from the outside, the pressure is distributed evenly throughout the fluid.

pas•ser•ine (păs′ə-rīn′) Belonging to the order of perching birds, including more than half of all living birds. Passerine birds are of small to medium size, have three toes pointing forward and one pointing back, and are often brightly colored. The songbirds are passerines.

Pas•teur (păs-tûr′), **Louis** 1822–1895. French chemist who founded modern microbiology. His early work with fermentation led him to invent the process of pasteurization. Pasteur established that germs cause communicable diseases and

Blaise Pascal

BIOGRAPHY

Louis Pasteur

In the mid-19th century, most people believed that disease was caused by a process of spontaneous generation. According to this belief, disease-causing parasites arose spontaneously in an organism (that is, all by themselves, without any outside cause), much as maggots were thought to arise spontaneously in rotting meat. In the 1860s, the chemist Louis Pasteur demonstrated in a series of experiments that the fermentation of wine to vinegar was caused by living agents—germs—that entered the wine from outside it. That is, the agents of fermentation were not generated within the substance but were carried to it by the air and then reproduced inside it. He became convinced that, if agents from the air could cause a substance to undergo fermentation, they could also enter and cause disease in animals and plants. Pasteur believed that if the agents of fermentation in substances could be identified and destroyed, they could be identified and destroyed in the body as well. He spent the rest of his life working to isolate the organisms that cause specific diseases and to find treatments to prevent them. Although Pasteur's germ theory of disease was not immediately accepted, thanks to the work of other pioneering scientists like Robert Koch, it eventually provided the foundation for modern medicine.

infections. He developed vaccines for anthrax, chicken cholera, and rabies.

pas•teur•i•za•tion (păs′chər-ĭ-zā′shən) A process in which an unfermented liquid, such as milk, or a partially fermented one, such as beer, is heated to a specific temperature for a certain amount of time in order to kill harmful germs or prevent further fermentation. During pasteurization, the liquid is not allowed to reach its boiling point so as to avoid changing its molecular structure.

pa•tel•la (pə-tĕl′ə) The small, flat, movable bone at the front of the knee in most mammals. Also called *kneecap. See more at* **skeleton.**

path•o•gen (păth′ə-jən) An agent that causes infection or disease, especially a microorganism, such as a bacterium or protozoan, or a virus. *See Note at* **germ.**

pa•thol•o•gy (pə-thŏl′ə-jē) **1.** The scientific study of disease and its causes, processes, and effects. **2.** The physical changes in the body and its functioning as a result of illness or disease.

Pau•li (pou′lē), **Wolfgang** 1900–1958. Austrian-born American physicist. He formulated a principle stating that no two electrons in an atom can have identical energy, masses, and angular momentums at the same time. This principle is known as the Pauli Exclusion Principle.

Pau•ling (pô′lĭng), **Linus Carl** 1901–1994. American chemist noted for his work on the structure and nature of chemical bonding. After studying in Europe with Niels Bohr and other physicists, Pauling applied quantum physics to chemistry. He discovered the structure of many molecules found in living tissue, especially proteins and amino acids. While studying the structure of hemoglobin, Pauling discovered the genetic defect that causes sickle cell anemia.

Pav•lov (păv′lôv′, păv′lôf′), **Ivan Petrovich** 1849–1936. Russian physiologist who studied the digestive system of dogs. His experiments showed that if a bell is rung whenever food is presented to a dog, the dog will eventually salivate when it hears the bell, even if no food is pre-

BIOGRAPHY

Linus Pauling

Linus Pauling is as well known for his efforts to make the world a better place as for advancing the frontiers of scientific knowledge. After devoting two decades to investigating chemical bonding, he made one of his most important discoveries one day while he was sick in bed. He lay there playing with pieces of paper, imagining them as molecules, and in a few hours he had figured out how amino acids are arranged in proteins. For this and related work he won the Nobel Prize in Chemistry in 1954. Pauling also worked tirelessly on behalf of world peace. He studied the harmful effects of nuclear fallout from atomic weapons and concluded that they should be banned, a position that got him into trouble. He was accused of being a Communist and was prevented from traveling abroad for a while, almost missing the award ceremony for his Nobel Prize. Pauling did not give in, however. He helped get a petition signed by thousands of scientists calling for an end to nuclear testing. In 1962 he won the Nobel Peace Prize for his efforts. He is the only person ever to receive two unshared Nobel Prizes. Pauling devoted much of his later life to researching the health benefits of large doses of vitamins and minerals, especially vitamin C.

sented. This demonstration of what is known as the conditioned response prompted later scientific studies of human and animal behavior.

Pb The symbol for **lead.**

Pd The symbol for **palladium.**

pearl (pûrl) A smooth, slightly iridescent, white or grayish rounded growth inside the shells of some mollusks. A pearl, which forms as a reaction to the presence of a foreign particle, consists of thin layers of mother-of-pearl that are deposited around the particle. The pearls of oysters are often valued as gems.

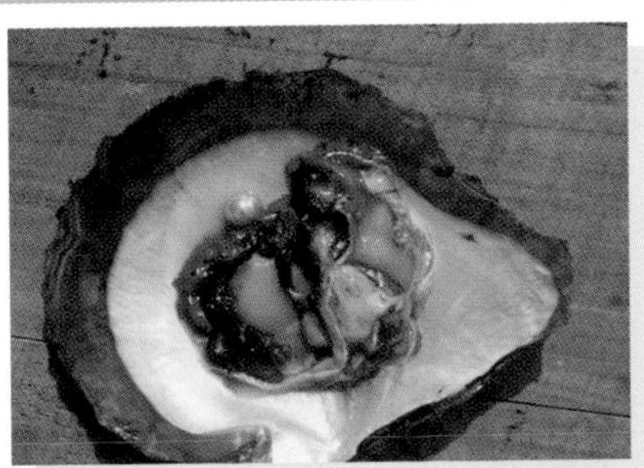

pearl
half shell of an oyster containing a pearl

peat (pēt) Partially decayed vegetable matter, especially mosses, found in bogs. Peat is burned as a fuel and is also used as a fertilizer.

pec•tin (pĕk′tĭn) Any of a group of substances that are found in ripe fruits and can be made to form gels. Pectins are derived from carbohydrates. They are used in certain medicines and cosmetics and in making jellies.

pec•to•ral (pĕk′tər-əl) Located in or attached to the chest: *a pectoral muscle; the pectoral fin.*

pe•di•at•rics (pē′dē-ăt′rĭks) The branch of medicine that deals with the care of infants and children.

ped•i•cel (pĕd′ĭ-səl) A small stalk supporting a single flower in a plant.

pe•dun•cle (pĭ-dŭng′kəl, pē′dŭng′kəl) **1.** *Botany.* The stalk of a single flower or flower cluster. *See more at* **flower. 2.** *Zoology.* A stalk supporting an animal organ, such as the eyestalk of a lobster.

Peg•a•sus (pĕg′ə-səs) A constellation in the Northern Hemisphere near Aquarius and Andromeda.

peg•ma•tite (pĕg′mə-tīt′) Any of various coarse-grained igneous rocks that often occur as wide veins cutting across other types of rock. Pegmatites form from magma or lava that is rich in water and cools slowly, allowing the crystals to grow to large sizes.

pel•i•can (pĕl′ĭ-kən) Any of various large, web-footed water birds of warm regions, having a large expandable pouch under the lower bill. The pouch is used for scooping up water and fish.

pel•lag•ra (pə-lăg′rə, pə-lā′grə) A disease caused by a lack of niacin in the diet. It causes skin and digestive disorders and mental deterioration.

pel•vis (pĕl′vĭs) The basin-shaped structure in vertebrate animals that joins the spine and lower or hind limbs. In primates, the pelvis is composed of the two hipbones joined to the sacrum. It contains and supports the intestines, bladder, and internal reproductive organs.

pen•du•lum (pĕn′jə-ləm) A mass hung from a fixed support so that it is able to swing freely under the influence of gravity. Pendulums are often used to regulate the action of various devices, especially clocks.

Pen•field (pĕn′fēld′), **Wilder Graves** 1891–1976. American-born Canadian neurosurgeon. His research on patients with epilepsy greatly expanded scientific understanding of brain functions, brain disease, and speech.

pen•guin (pĕng′gwĭn) Any of various flightless sea birds having white feathers in front and black feathers in back and living mostly in or near Antarctica. With their webbed feet, narrow flipper-like wings, and scale-like feathers, penguins are adapted for swimming underwater, where they feed on fish and other sea animals. On land, they have an upright posture.

pen•i•cil•lin (pĕn′ĭ-sĭl′ĭn) Any of a group of antibiotics obtained from penicillium molds, used to treat or prevent infections caused by a wide variety of bacteria.

pen•i•cil•li•um (pĕn′ĭ-sĭl′ē-əm) Any of various green and blue-green fungi that grow as molds on citrus fruits, cheeses, and bread, including several species used to produce penicillin and certain other antibiotics.

peninsula

pen•in•su•la (pə-nĭn′syə-lə) A piece of land that projects into a body of water and is connected with a larger landmass.

pe•nis (pē′nĭs) **1.** The male reproductive organ of mammals and some reptiles and birds. In mammals, the penis contains the urethra, which carries urine from the bladder and releases sperm during reproduction. **2.** A similar organ found in the males of some invertebrate animals.

Penn•syl•va•nian (pĕn′səl-vān′yən) The sixth period of the Paleozoic Era, from about 320 to 286 million years ago, whose rock deposits are rich in coal. Reptiles first appeared in the Pennsylvanian Period. *See Chart at* **geologic time,** pages 148–149.

Pen•rose (pĕn′rōz′), **Roger** Born 1931. British mathematician and physicist. With Stephen Hawking he studied the physics of black holes.

pen•ta•gon (pĕn′tə-gŏn′) A polygon having five sides.

pe•num•bra (pĭ-nŭm′brə) **1.** A partial shadow between regions of complete shadow and complete illumination, especially as cast by Earth, the moon, or another body during an eclipse. **2.** The grayish outer part of a sunspot. *Compare* **umbra.**

pep•sin (pĕp′sĭn) A powerful enzyme that breaks down proteins in the stomach of vertebrate animals.

pep•tic (pĕp′tĭk) Relating to or caused by the process of digestion or the secretions associated with it.

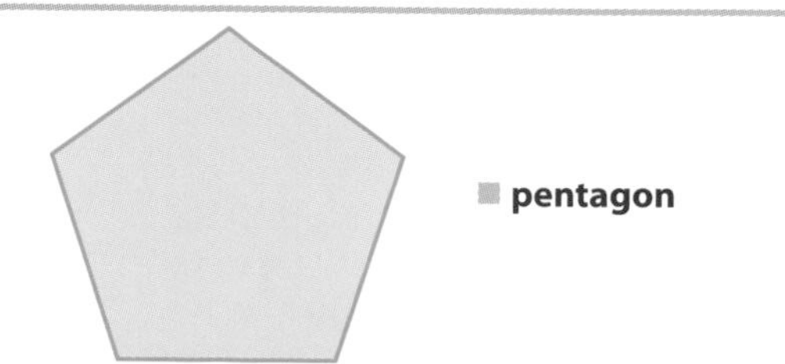

pentagon

Marguerite Perey

pep•tide (pĕp′tīd′) A chemical compound that is composed of a chain of two or more amino acids and is usually smaller than a protein. Some hormones and antibiotics are peptides.

per•cent *also* **per cent** (pər-sĕnt′) One part in a hundred. For example, 62 percent (also written 62%) means 62 parts out of 100.

per•cen•tile (pər-sĕn′tīl′) Any of the 100 equal parts into which the range of the values of a set of data can be divided in order to show the distribution of those values. The percentile of a given value is determined by the percentage of the values that are smaller than that value. For example, a test score that is higher than 95 percent of the other scores is in the 95th percentile.

per•chlo•rate (pər-klôr′āt′) A salt of perchloric acid, containing the group ClO_4.

per•chlo•ric acid (pər-klôr′ĭk) A clear, colorless liquid, $HClO_4$, that is very corrosive and, under some conditions, extremely explosive. It is a powerful oxidant and is used as a catalyst and in explosives.

per•en•ni•al (pə-rĕn′ē-əl) *Botany. Adjective.* **1.** Living for three or more years. —*Noun.* **2.** A perennial plant. Asters, irises, and peonies are some examples of perennials.

Pe•rey (pĕ-rā′), **Marguerite Catherine** 1909–1975. French physicist who discovered the element francium (1939).

per•fect number (pûr′fĭkt) A positive integer that equals the sum of all of its divisors other than itself. An example is 28, whose divisors (not counting itself) are 1, 2, 4, 7, and 14, which added together give 28.

peri– A prefix that means: **1.** Around, as in *pericardium,* the membrane around the heart. **2.** Near, as in *perihelion,* the point at which a planet is nearest the sun.

per•i•anth (pĕr′ē-ănth′) The outer envelope of a flower, consisting of the sepals or the petals or both.

per•i•car•di•um (pĕr′ĭ-kär′dē-əm) The membrane sac that encloses the heart in vertebrate animals.

per•i•derm (pĕr′ĭ-dûrm′) The outer, protective layers of tissue of woody roots and stems, consisting of the cork cambium and the tissues produced by it. *See more at* **cork cambium.**

per•i•gee (pĕr′ə-jē) **1.** The point nearest Earth's center in the orbit of the moon or an artificial satellite. **2.** The point in the orbit of a body, such as a satellite, where it is nearest the body around which it revolves, such as a planet. *Compare* **apogee.**

per•i•he•li•on (pĕr′ə-hē′lē-ən) The point nearest the sun in the orbit of a body, such as a planet or comet, that travels around the sun.

pe•rim•e•ter (pə-rĭm′ĭ-tər) **1.** The sum of the lengths of the segments that form the sides of a polygon. **2.** The total length of any closed curve, such as the circumference of a circle.

pe•ri•od (pîr′ē-əd) **1.** A division of geologic time, longer than an epoch and shorter than an era. **2.** The time it takes for a regularly recurring action or event to be repeated; a cycle. **3.** An instance or occurrence of menstruation. **4.** *Chemistry.* In the Periodic Table, any of the seven horizontal rows that contain elements arranged in order of increasing atomic number. All the elements in a particular period have the same number of electron shells in their atoms. *See* **Periodic Table,** pages 262–263.

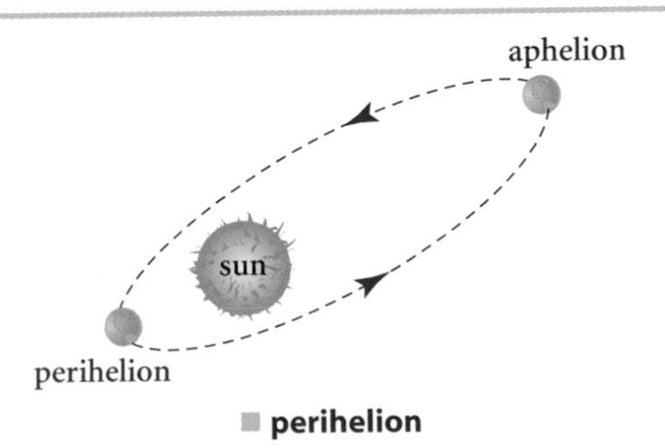

perihelion

Pe•ri•od•ic Table (pîr′ē-ŏd′ĭk) A table in which the chemical elements are arranged in order of increasing atomic number. Elements with similar properties are arranged in the same column (called a group), and elements with the same number of electron shells are arranged in the same row (called a period). See Table on pages 262–263.

pe•riph•er•al nervous system (pə-rĭf′ər-əl) In vertebrate animals, the part of the nervous system that lies outside of the brain and spinal cord. It includes the nerves that extend to the limbs. *Compare* **central nervous system.**

per•i•scope (pĕr′ĭ-skōp′) An instrument that has angled mirrors or prisms and allows objects not in the direct line of sight to be seen.

pe•ris•so•dac•tyl (pə-rĭs′ō-dăk′təl) Any of various hoofed mammals having an odd number of toes. Horses, tapirs, and rhinoceroses are perissodactyls. Also called *odd-toed ungulate.*

per•i•stal•sis (pĕr′ĭ-stôl′sĭs) The wave-like muscle contractions in the organs of the digestive tract that push food into the stomach and to the intestines. Peristalsis starts in the esophagus and ends when digested food is eliminated as waste.

per•i•to•ne•um (pĕr′ĭ-tn-ē′əm) The membrane that lines the inside of the abdomen and encloses the abdominal organs.

per•ma•frost (pûr′mə-frôst′) A layer of permanently frozen subsoil, reaching depths up to 5,000 feet (1,524 meters). Permafrost is found throughout most of the polar regions.

per•me•a•ble (pûr′mē-ə-bəl) Capable of being passed through or permeated, especially by liquids or gases: *a permeable membrane.*

Per•mi•an (pûr′mē-ən) The seventh and last period of the Paleozoic Era, from about 286 to 245 million years ago. The Permian Period was characterized by the formation of the supercontinent Pangaea, by the rise of modern conifers, and by the diversification of reptiles. It ended with the largest known mass extinction in the history of life. *See Chart at* **geologic time,** pages 148–149.

per•ox•ide (pə-rŏk′sīd′) **1.** A compound containing the group O_2. When any peroxide is combined with an acid, one of the products is hydrogen peroxide. **2.** Hydrogen peroxide.

per•pen•dic•u•lar (pûr′pən-dĭk′yə-lər) *Adjective.* **1.** Intersecting at or forming a right angle or right angles. —*Noun.* **2.** A line or plane that is perpendicular to a given line or plane.

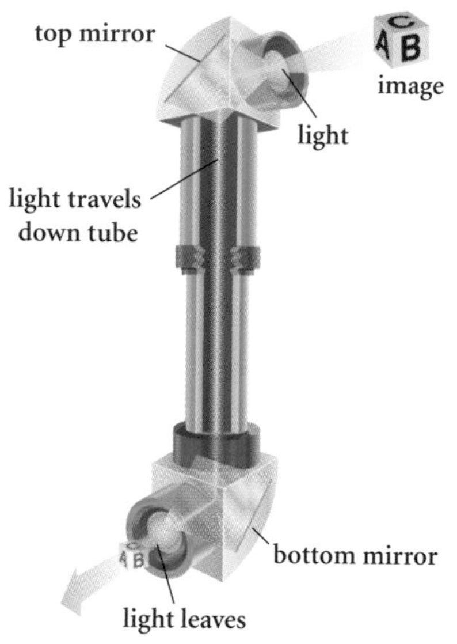

periscope

Light enters the top lens of the periscope, reflects off a mirror set at a 45° angle, travels down the periscope tube, and reflects off a second mirror, also set at a 45° angle. The light that reflects off the second mirror exits through the bottom lens and into the eye of the user.

Per•se•us (pûr′sē-əs) A constellation in the Northern Hemisphere near Andromeda and Auriga.

per•tus•sis (pər-tŭs′ĭs) *See* **whooping cough.**

Per•utz (pə-ro͞ots′, pĕr′əts), **Max Ferdinand** 1914–2002. Austrian-born British biochemist who determined the structure of hemoglobin, demonstrating that it is composed of four chains of molecules.

pes•ti•cide (pĕs′tĭ-sīd′) A chemical used to kill harmful animals or plants. *Compare* **fungicide, herbicide, insecticide.**

pet•al (pĕt′l) One of the often brightly colored parts of a flower surrounding the reproductive organs. Petals may be separate or joined at their bases. As a group, the petals are called the corolla. *See more at* **flower.**

pet•i•ole (pĕt′ē-ōl′) *See* **leafstalk.**

pe•tri dish (pē′trē) A shallow, circular dish with a loose cover, used to grow cultures of microorganisms.

pet•ri•fac•tion (pĕt′rə-făk′shən) *also* **pet•ri•fi•ca•tion** (pĕt′rə-fĭ-kā′shən) The process by

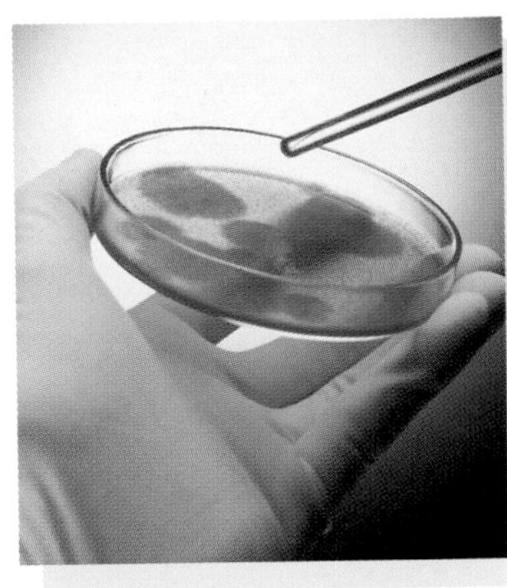

■ petri dish

which organic materials are turned into rock. Petrifaction occurs when water that is rich with inorganic minerals, such as calcium carbonate or silica, passes slowly through organic matter, such as wood, replacing its cellular structure with minerals.

pet•ro•chem•i•cal (pĕt′rō-kĕm′ĭ-kəl) Any of a large number of chemicals made from petroleum or natural gas. Important petrochemicals include benzene, ammonia, acetylene, and polystyrene. Petrochemicals are used to produce a wide variety of materials, such as plastics, explosives, fertilizers, and synthetic fibers.

pe•tro•le•um (pə-trō′lē-əm) A thick, black to yellow, flammable liquid mixture of hydrocarbons. Petroleum occurs naturally, mainly below the Earth's surface, and is believed to originate from the accumulated remains of ancient plants and animals. It is the source of petrochemicals and is used to make gasoline, lubricating oils, plastics, and many other products.

pe•trol•o•gy (pə-trŏl′ə-jē) The scientific study of the origin, composition, and structure of rocks.

pH (pē′āch′) A numerical measure of the acidity or alkalinity of a solution, usually measured on a scale of 0 to 14. Neutral solutions have a pH of 7, acidic solutions have a pH lower than 7, and alkaline solutions have a pH higher than 7.

phag•o•cyte (făg′ə-sīt′) An organism or specialized cell that engulfs and ingests other cells or particles. Phagocytes in vertebrate animals include white blood cells called macrophages, which help the body fight disease by breaking down foreign particles and bacteria. ❖ The process by which phagocytes engulf and break down bacteria or particles, as of food, is called **phagocytosis** (făg′ə-sī-tō′sĭs). Single-celled organisms such as amoebas ingest food by the process of phagocytosis.

pha•lan•ges (fə-lăn′jēz) The small bones of the fingers or toes in humans or the digits in other primates. *See more at* **skeleton.**

Phan•e•ro•zo•ic (făn′ər-ə-zō′ĭk) The period of geologic time from about 540 million years ago to the present, including the Paleozoic, Mesozoic, and Cenozoic Eras. The Phanerozoic Eon is marked by an abundance of fossil evidence of life, especially more complex forms. *See Chart at* **geologic time,** pages 148–149.

phar•ma•col•o•gy (fär′mə-kŏl′ə-jē) The scientific study of drugs and their effects, especially in the treatment of disease.

phar•ynx (făr′ĭngks) The passage that leads from the cavities of the nose and mouth to the larynx (voice box) and esophagus.

phase (fāz) **1.** Any of the forms, recurring in cycles, in which the moon or a planet appears. **2.** *See* **state of matter. 3.** *Physics.* A condition in which two or more patterns of oscillatory motion, such as two or more waves, are in step with each other. Two waves are said to be in phase when their peaks and troughs line up. *See more at* **wave.**

phel•lem (fĕl′əm) *See* **cork** (sense 1).

phel•lo•derm (fĕl′ə-dûrm′) The tissue produced on the inside of the cork cambium in woody plants. It forms a secondary cortex. *See more at* **cork cambium.**

phel•lo•gen (fĕl′ə-jən) *See* **cork cambium.**

phe•nol (fē′nôl′, fē′nōl′) A poisonous, white, crystalline compound used as a disinfectant and to make plastics and drugs. Also called *carbolic acid.*

phe•nol•o•gy (fĭ-nŏl′ə-jē) The scientific study of cyclical biological events, such as flowering, breeding, and migration, in relation to climatic conditions.

phe•nol•phthal•ein (fē′nōl-thăl′ēn′) A white or pale-yellow, crystalline powder used as an indicator for acid and basic solutions. It is also used as a laxative and in making dyes.

phe•no•type (fē′nə-tīp′) The physical appearance of an organism as distinguished from its genetic makeup. The phenotype of an organism depends on which genes are dominant and on

PERIODIC TABLE OF THE ELEMENTS

The Periodic Table is a systematic arrangement of the chemical elements according to their atomic structure. The elements are arranged so that their **atomic numbers**—the number of protons in each element's nucleus—increase as you read across each row from left to right. Thus hydrogen (atomic number 1) comes first in the Table, helium (atomic number 2) comes second, lithium (atomic number 3) comes third, and so on.

The first Periodic Table was designed by Dmitri Mendeleev in 1869. At that time only 63 of the elements were known. Today we know a total of 117. When Mendeleev made the first table he knew that other elements would eventually be discovered, and he left empty spaces so that the new elements could be added as they were found.

Key	
1	atomic number
H	symbol
Hydrogen	
1.00794	atomic weight (or mass number of most stable isotope if in parentheses)

	Group 1	Group 2	Group 3	Group 4	Group 5	Group 6
Period 1	1 H Hydrogen 1.00794					
Period 2	3 Li Lithium 6.941	4 Be Beryllium 9.0122				
Period 3	11 Na Sodium 22.9898	12 Mg Magnesium 24.305				
Period 4	19 K Potassium 39.098	20 Ca Calcium 40.08	21 Sc Scandium 44.956	22 Ti Titanium 47.87	23 V Vanadium 50.942	24 Cr Chromiu 51.996
Period 5	37 Rb Rubidium 85.47	38 Sr Strontium 87.62	39 Y Yttrium 88.906	40 Zr Zirconium 91.22	41 Nb Niobium 92.906	42 Mo Molybden 95.96
Period 6	55 Cs Cesium 132.905	56 Ba Barium 137.33	57–71* Lanthanides	72 Hf Hafnium 178.49	73 Ta Tantalum 180.948	74 W Tungste 183.84
Period 7	87 Fr Francium (223)	88 Ra Radium (226)	89–103** Actinides	104 Rf Rutherfordium (267)	105 Db Dubnium (262)	106 Sg Seaborgiu (266)

* LANTHANIDES	57 La Lanthanum 138.91	58 Ce Cerium 140.12	59 Pr Praseodymium 140.908	60 Nd Neodymi 144.24
** ACTINIDES	89 Ac Actinium (227)	90 Th Thorium 232.038	91 Pa Protactinium 231.036	92 U Uraniur 238.03

Periods

The elements are placed into seven rows, or **periods,** according to the number of electron shells in their atoms. Each atom consists of a nucleus of neutrons and protons surrounded by one or more energy levels, or shells, in which electrons are continuously orbiting. The smallest atoms have only one electron shell. Larger atoms have as many as seven shells, each one successively larger than the one inside it. Hydrogen and helium have only one electron shell and are therefore placed in Period 1, while sodium and chlorine have three shells and are placed in Period 3. By noting the period in which an element is located, you can immediately know how many electron shells it has.

Lanthanides and Actinides

The elements of the **lanthanide series** (elements 57–71) and the **actinide series** (elements 89–103) all behave in a manner similar to that of the elements in Group 3. But since they have different atomic numbers, they are separated from the main Periodic Table to make it easier to read.

roups

he elements are organized into 18 separate olumns, or **groups,** according primarily to the umber of electrons occupying their outermost ell. This number is important because it rongly affects the way an element will behave in chemical reaction. Since the elements in each roup have the same number of electrons in their uter shell, they share certain chemical behaviors ich as the ability to combine with other elements to form compounds. In the case of the rger elements in Periods 4 through 7, the numer of electrons in some of the inner shells also ffects their behavior and thus determines where heir groups are placed in the Table.

oup 7	Group 8	Group 9	Group 10	Group 11	Group 12	Group 13	Group 14	Group 15	Group 16	Group 17	Group 18
											2 He Helium 4.0026
						5 B Boron 10.811	6 C Carbon 12.011	7 N Nitrogen 14.0067	8 O Oxygen 15.9994	9 F Fluorine 18.9984	10 Ne Neon 20.18
						13 Al Aluminum 26.9815	14 Si Silicon 28.086	15 P Phosphorus 30.9738	16 S Sulfur 32.066	17 Cl Chlorine 35.453	18 Ar Argon 39.948
25 Mn ganese 9380	26 Fe Iron 55.845	27 Co Cobalt 58.9332	28 Ni Nickel 58.69	29 Cu Copper 63.546	30 Zn Zinc 65.38	31 Ga Gallium 69.72	32 Ge Germanium 72.64	33 As Arsenic 74.9216	34 Se Selenium 78.96	35 Br Bromine 79.904	36 Kr Krypton 83.80
43 Tc netium 98)	44 Ru Ruthenium 101.07	45 Rh Rhodium 102.905	46 Pd Palladium 106.4	47 Ag Silver 107.868	48 Cd Cadmium 112.41	49 In Indium 114.82	50 Sn Tin 118.71	51 Sb Antimony 121.76	52 Te Tellurium 127.60	53 I Iodine 126.9045	54 Xe Xenon 131.29
75 Re enium 86.2	76 Os Osmium 190.2	77 Ir Iridium 192.2	78 Pt Platinum 195.08	79 Au Gold 196.967	80 Hg Mercury 200.59	81 Tl Thallium 204.38	82 Pb Lead 207.2	83 Bi Bismuth 208.98	84 Po Polonium (209)	85 At Astatine (210)	86 Rn Radon (222)
107 Bh hrium 264)	108 Hs Hassium (277)	109 Mt Meitnerium (268)	110 Ds Darmstadtium (281)	111 Rg Roentgenium (285)	112† (285)	113† (284)	114† (289)	115† (287)	116† (293)		118† (294)

61 Pm nethium 145)	62 Sm Samarium 150.36	63 Eu Europium 151.96	64 Gd Gadolinium 157.25	65 Tb Terbium 158.925	66 Dy Dysprosium 162.50	67 Ho Holmium 164.930	68 Er Erbium 167.26	69 Tm Thulium 168.934	70 Yb Ytterbium 173.04	71 Lu Lutetium 174.97
93 Np tunium 237)	94 Pu Plutonium (244)	95 Am Americium (243)	96 Cm Curium (247)	97 Bk Berkelium (247)	98 Cf Californium (251)	99 Es Einsteinium (252)	100 Fm Fermium (257)	101 Md Mendelevium (258)	102 No Nobelium (259)	103 Lr Lawrencium (262)

Until official names are given to new elements, names ased on a Latin translation of the atomic number are used; .g. *ununbium* (Latin *unus* '1' + *unus* '1' + *bi-* '2') for lement 112.

Alkali metals	Actinide series	Transition elements	Nonmetals
Alkaline-earth metals	Other metals	Lanthanide series (rare-earth elements)	Noble gases

the interaction between genes and environment. *Compare* **genotype.**

phen•yl (fĕn′əl, fē′nəl) The organic radical C_6H_5, made by removing one hydrogen atom from benzene.

phen•yl•al•a•nine (fĕn′əl-ăl′ə-nēn′) An essential amino acid. *See more at* **amino acid.**

pher•o•mone (fĕr′ə-mōn′) A chemical that is secreted by an animal and influences the behavior or development of other animals of the same species. For example, the male and female of many species establish territory and attract mates by means of pheromones. Queen bees give off a substance that prevents other females in the hive from becoming sexually mature, with the result that only the queen bee mates and lays eggs.

phlegm (flĕm) Mucus produced by the mucous membranes of the respiratory tract.

phlo•em (flō′ĕm′) A tissue in vascular plants that conducts food from the leaves to the other plant parts. Phloem consists primarily of tubelike cells that have porous openings. In mature woody plants it forms a sheath-like layer of tissue in the stem, just inside the bark. *See more at* **cambium, photosynthesis.** *Compare* **xylem.**

phlo•gis•ton (flō-jĭs′tən) A colorless, odorless, weightless substance once believed to be the combustible part of all flammable substances and to be given off as flame during burning. In the 18th century, Antoine Lavoisier proved that phlogiston does not exist. *See Note at* **Lavoisier.**

phos•phate (fŏs′fāt′) A compound containing the group PO_4. Phosphates are important in metabolism and are frequently used in fertilizers.

phos•phor (fŏs′fər) A substance that can emit light after absorbing some form of radiation. The insides of television screens and fluorescent lamp tubes are coated with phosphors. *See Note at* **cathode-ray tube.**

phos•pho•res•cence (fŏs′fə-rĕs′əns) **1.** The giving off of light by a substance as a result of having absorbed energy from a form of electromagnetic radiation, such as visible light or x-rays. Unlike fluorescence, phosphorescence continues for a short while after the source of radiation is removed. *Compare* **fluorescence** (sense 1). **2.** The light produced in this way.

phos•pho•rus (fŏs′fər-əs) A highly reactive, poisonous nonmetallic element occurring naturally in phosphates and existing in white (or sometimes yellow), red, and black forms. It is an essential component of protoplasm. Phosphorus is used to make matches, fireworks, and fertilizers and to protect metal surfaces from corrosion. *Symbol* **P.** *Atomic number* 15. *See* **Periodic Table,** pages 262–263. —*Adjective* **phosphoric.**

photo– A prefix that means "light," as in *photoreceptor.*

pho•to•de•grad•a•ble (fō′tō-dĭ-grā′də-bəl) Capable of being chemically decomposed by light. For example, photodegradable plastic becomes brittle and breaks into smaller pieces when exposed to sunlight, helping reduce litter and environmental damage.

pho•to•e•lec•tric (fō′tō-ĭ-lĕk′trĭk) Relating to the electrical effects of light. For example, exposure to light can bring about the emission of electrons from a material, the generation of an electric current, or a change in the electrical resistance of a material. ❖ The emission of electrons from a material, such as a metal, as a result of being struck by photons (light) is called the **photoelectric effect.**

pho•tom•e•try (fō-tŏm′ĭ-trē) The measurement of the intensity, brightness, or other properties of light.

pho•to•mi•cro•graph (fō′tō-mī′krə-grăf′) A photograph made through a microscope.

pho•ton (fō′tŏn′) The smallest unit of light or other electromagnetic energy, having no mass and no electric charge. Photons behave both as particles and waves. *See Note at* **electromagnetic radiation.**

pho•to•re•cep•tor (fō′tō-rĭ-sĕp′tər) A specialized structure or cell that is sensitive to light. In vertebrate animals, the photoreceptors are the rods and cones of the eye's retina. *See Note at* **circadian rhythm.**

pho•to•sphere (fō′tə-sfîr′) The thin, outer layer that forms the visible surface of a star, especially the sun.

pho•to•syn•the•sis (fō′tō-sĭn′thĭ-sĭs) The process by which green plants, algae, and certain forms of bacteria make carbohydrates from carbon dioxide and water in the presence of chlorophyll, using light as energy. Photosynthesis normally releases oxygen as a byproduct. *Compare* **chemosynthesis.** *See Note at* **transpiration.**

A CLOSER LOOK

Photosynthesis

A leaf is a plant's food factory. It makes food by photosynthesis, a two-stage process that converts the energy of sunlight into chemical energy. In the first stage, light from the sun strikes leaf cells that contain special structures called chloroplasts. The chloroplasts contain chlorophyll, the catalyst that makes photosynthesis possible. Supplied with water brought up from the soil, the chloroplasts convert the light energy into chemical energy in the form of ATP. The water is split into hydrogen and oxygen, with the oxygen being given off as a waste product. In the second stage, which does not require light, the chloroplasts use the chemical energy stored in the ATP to combine the hydrogen with carbon dioxide from the air to make glucose. The glucose is then distributed throughout the plant as food.

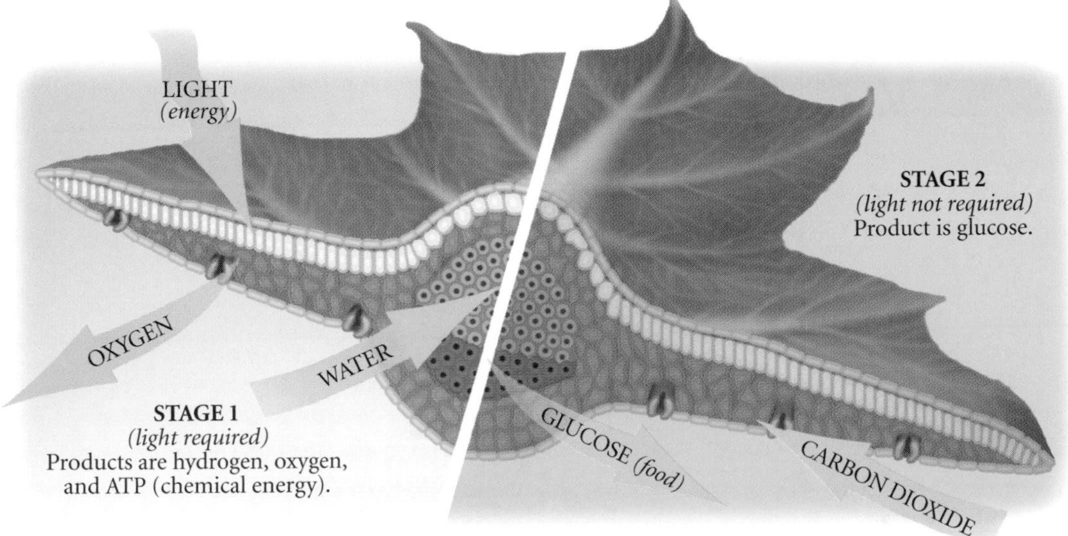

Photosynthesis takes place in the column-like cells of the palisade layer and in the irregularly shaped cells of the spongy parenchyma. Chloroplasts are present in both kinds of cells, but are especially numerous in the palisade layer. The cells receive carbon dioxide from air that enters the leaf through holes called stomata. The stomata also allow oxygen produced by photosynthesis to escape. Water from the roots is supplied by the vascular tissue known as xylem. Glucose made by the leaf is distributed to the rest of the plant by the vascular tissue known as phloem.

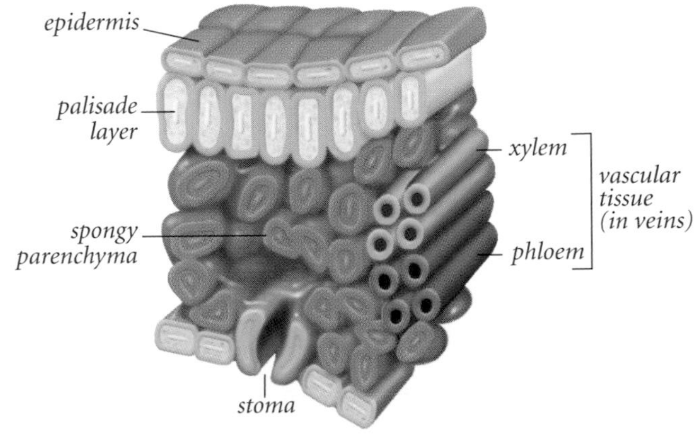

pho•tot•ro•pism (fō-tŏt′rə-pĭz′əm) The growth or movement of a fixed organism, especially a plant, toward or away from light. *—Adjective* **phototropic** (fō′tə-trō′pĭk, fō′tə-trŏp′ĭk).

pho•to•vol•ta•ic cell (fō′tō-vŏl-tā′ĭk) *See* **solar cell.**

phre•nol•o•gy (frĭ-nŏl′ə-jē) The study of the shape of the skull as a means of determining character and intelligence. Phrenology has been disproven as a science.

phy•lum (fī′ləm) *Plural* **phyla.** A group of organisms ranking above a class and below a kingdom. *See Table at* **taxonomy.**

phys•i•cal chemistry (fĭz′ĭ-kəl) The branch of chemistry that is concerned with the physical structure of chemical compounds, the amount of energy they have, the way they react with other compounds, and the bonds that hold their atoms together.

physical science Any of several branches of science, such as physics, chemistry, or geology, that studies the nature and properties of energy and nonliving matter. *Compare* **life science.**

phys•ics (fĭz′ĭks) The scientific study of matter and energy and the relations between them.

phys•i•ol•o•gy (fĭz′ē-ŏl′ə-jē) The scientific study of an organism's vital functions, such as circulation, respiration, and digestion.

phy•to•plank•ton (fī′tō-plăngk′tən) Plankton consisting of plants and plant-like organisms, such as algae. Phytoplankton are a major source of food for aquatic animals and fix large amounts of carbon, which would otherwise be released as carbon dioxide.

pi (pī) An irrational number that has a numerical value of 3.141592653589. . . and is represented by the symbol π. It expresses the ratio of the circumference to the diameter of a circle and appears in many mathematical expressions.

Pick•er•ing (pĭk′ər-ĭng), **Edward Charles** 1846–1919. American astronomer who made many innovations in the equipment used to observe and measure the distance of stars. His brother **William Henry Pickering** (1858–1938) discovered Phoebe, the ninth moon of Saturn (1899), and predicted the existence of Pluto (1919).

pi•e•zo•e•lec•tric effect (pī-ē′zō-ĭ-lĕk′trĭk) The generation of an electric charge in certain nonconducting materials, such as quartz crystals and ceramics, when they are subjected to mechanical stress (such as pressure or vibration), or the generation of vibrations in such materials when they are subjected to an electric field.

pig•ment (pĭg′mənt) **1.** An organic compound that gives a characteristic color to plant or animal tissues and is involved in vital processes. Chlorophyll and hemoglobin are examples of pigments. **2.** A substance or material used as coloring.

pin•cers (pĭn′sərz) A jointed grasping claw of certain animals, such as lobsters or scorpions.

pine (pīn) Any of various evergreen trees that bear cones and have clusters of leaves that are shaped like needles. Pines are found chiefly in cooler temperate regions in the Northern Hemisphere.

pin•e•al gland (pĭn′ē-əl, pī′nē-əl) A small gland that is located near the brain and is involved in the regulation of hormones. In many animals, the pineal gland controls metabolism, hibernation, and sexual development.

pin•nate (pĭn′āt′) Having parts or divisions arranged on each side of a common axis in the manner of a feather. Ash, hickory, and walnut trees have pinnate leaves.

pin•ni•ped (pĭn′ə-pĕd′) Any of various carnivorous, aquatic mammals having long, smooth bodies and fin-like flippers for swimming. Pinnipeds include the seals and walruses.

pint (pīnt) **1.** A unit of volume or capacity used in liquid measure, equal to 16 fluid ounces or 28.88 cubic inches (about 0.47 liter). **2.** A unit of volume or capacity used in dry measure, equal to $\frac{1}{2}$ of a quart or 34.6 cubic inches (about 0.55 liter). *See Table at* **measurement.**

pi•pette (pī-pĕt′) A narrow glass tube that is open at both ends and often marked to show volume. It is used for transferring liquids.

Pi•sces (pī′sēz) A constellation in the Northern Hemisphere near Aries and Pegasus.

pis•til (pĭs′təl) The female reproductive organ of a flower, consisting of the ovary, style, and stigma. *See more at* **flower.**

pis•til•late (pĭs′tə-lāt′) **1.** Having one or more pistils. **2.** Having pistils but no stamens. Female flowers are pistillate.

pis•ton (pĭs′tən) A solid cylinder or disk that fits snugly into a hollow cylinder and moves back

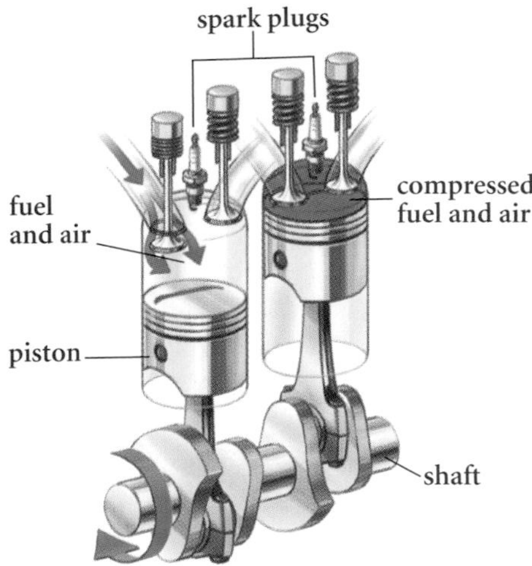

piston

The fuel-air mixture in the left-hand chamber expands when ignited by the spark plug, pushing the piston down and turning the shaft to which it is attached. The turning shaft drives the piston in the right-hand cylinder upward. It will then be pushed down in the same way when the fuel-air mixture enters that chamber and is ignited. The alternating action of the two pistons keeps the shaft turning.

and forth under the pressure of a fluid, as in many engines, or moves or compresses a fluid, as in a pump or compressor.

pit (pĭt) The hard, central part of certain fruits, such as a peach or cherry, usually containing a single seed; a stone.

pitch (pĭch) **1.** A thick, tar-like substance used for roofing, waterproofing, and paving. **2.** Any of various natural bitumens, such as asphalt, having similar uses. **3.** A resin derived from the sap of a cone-bearing tree, such as a pine.

pitch•blende (pĭch**′**blĕnd′) A brown to black, often crusty mineral that is a principal ore of uranium. It is highly radioactive.

pith (pĭth) The soft, spongy tissue in the center of the stems of most flowering plants. Composed of parenchyma cells, the pith is gradually compressed by the inward growth of the vascular tissue known as xylem. As the plant grows older, the pith dries out and often disintegrates, leaving the stem hollow.

pi•tu•i•tar•y gland (pĭ-to͞o**′**ĭ-tĕr′ē) A gland at the base of the brain in vertebrate animals that regulates the function of most of the body's hormone-producing glands and organs, including the thyroid and adrenal glands. The pituitary gland also controls overall body growth.

Did You Know?

pixels

If you look at a panel in a comic book very closely, you will see that colored or shaded areas are often made of very tiny dots. Images on computer screens are also composed of very tiny dots known as *pixels.* (Pixel is a shortening of *picture element.*) The computer controls each pixel individually. Most monitors have hundreds of thousands or millions of pixels that are lit or dimmed to create an image. The colors on a monitor consist of arrangements of red, blue, and green pixels that adjust in intensity to create all of the colors that you see on a screen. Pixels vary in size according to the model of monitor. Monitors with the smallest pixels have the sharpest images, but they require more memory to store data about the color and intensity of each pixel.

pit viper Any of various venomous snakes having a small pit below each eye that is used to sense heat. Their fangs are hollow and folded back in the mouth when the snake is not striking prey. Pit vipers are mostly found in the Western Hemisphere and include the cottonmouth and rattlesnakes.

pix•el (pĭk**′**səl) The most basic unit of an image on a computer or television screen. Pixels are arranged in rows and columns and are lit up in a specific pattern to create an image.

pla•ce•bo (plə-sē**′**bō) A substance resembling a drug but containing only inactive ingredients, used especially in scientific experiments to test the effectiveness of a drug. Researchers give one group of people a real drug and another group a placebo and then determine whether the people taking the drug get better results than the people taking the placebo.

pla•cen•ta (plə-sĕn**′**tə) **1.** The sac-shaped organ that attaches the embryo or fetus to the uterus during pregnancy in most mammals. It supplies the fetus with oxygen and nutrients and is expelled after birth. **2.** *Botany.* The part of the ovary of a flowering plant to which the ovules are attached. —*Adjective* **placental.**

plac•er (plăs′ər) A deposit of minerals, such as gold or magnetite, left by a river. The minerals are usually concentrated in one area because they are relatively heavy and therefore settle out of the river's currents more quickly than lighter sediments such as silt and sand. When mineral prospectors pan for gold, they look for placer deposits.

pla•gi•o•clase (plā′jē-ə-klās′) Any of a series of common feldspar minerals, consisting of mixtures of sodium and calcium aluminum silicates. Plagioclase is typically white, yellow, or reddish-gray, but it can also be blue to black. It is especially common in igneous rocks.

plague (plāg) **1.** Any highly infectious, usually fatal epidemic disease. **2.** An often fatal disease caused by a bacterium transmitted to humans usually by fleas that have bitten infected rats or other rodents. The most common form of plague is bubonic plague, though plague can also exist as a highly contagious form infecting the lungs and as an extremely severe form infecting the blood.

plain (plān) **1.** An extensive, level, usually treeless area of land. **2.** A broad, level expanse, such as an area of the sea floor or a lunar mare.

Planck (plängk), **Max Karl Ernst Ludwig** 1858–1947. German physicist who formulated quantum theory (1900), which explained and predicted certain phenomena that could not be accounted for in classical physics.

Max Planck

WORD HISTORY

planet names

To learn the origins of the names of the planets is to have a little lesson in Roman mythology. Mercury moves fastest through the sky and was named after the swift-footed messenger of the gods, Mercury. Venus, the morning and evening star, was named after the Roman goddess of love because of its beauty and the pure brightness of its light. The reddish appearance of Mars reminded early astronomers of the color of blood, so Mars was named after the Roman god of war. Jupiter is the largest of the planets and was named after the king of the gods. Jupiter's father was Saturn, the name given to the next planet after Jupiter. To continue that logic, the name of Saturn's own father, Uranus, was given to the next planet after Saturn. Viewed through a telescope, the planet Neptune appears sea-green, and it gets its name from the Roman god of the sea. Finally, the darkest reaches of the solar system are the home of the frozen object Pluto, traditionally considered a planet, and named after the god of the cold world of the dead, the underworld.

plane (plān) A two-dimensional surface, any two of whose points can be joined by a straight line that lies entirely in the surface.

plane geometry The mathematical study of geometric figures whose parts lie in the same plane, such as polygons, circles, and lines.

plan•et (plăn′ĭt) A celestial body that does not produce its own light, is larger than an asteroid, and is illuminated by light from a star, such as the sun, around which it revolves. In our solar system there are eight planets: Mercury, Venus, Earth, Mars, Jupiter, Saturn, Uranus, and Neptune. Pluto was considered a planet until 2006, when it was reclassified as a dwarf planet. —*Adjective* **planetary.**

plan•e•tar•y nebula (plăn′ĭ-tĕr′ē) A nebula consisting of an expanding shell of gas, mostly hydrogen, that surrounds a hot, compact central star. *See more at* **star.**

plank•ton (plăngk′tən) Small organisms that float or drift in great numbers in bodies of salt or fresh water. Plankton is a primary food source for many animals, and consists of bacteria, protozoans, certain algae, cnidarians, tiny crustaceans such as copepods, and many other organisms.

plant (plănt) Any of a wide variety of multicellular organisms, most of which manufacture their own food by means of photosynthesis. Plants have cells with cell walls made of cellulose, cannot move about under their own power, and have no nervous system. They range in size from a few millimeters to trees that stand over 300 feet (91.4 meters) tall. Plants are grouped as a separate kingdom in taxonomy.

plant kingdom The category of living organisms that includes all plants. The scientific name of this kingdom is Plantae. Also called *vegetable kingdom. See Table at* **taxonomy.**

plaque (plăk) **1.** A film of mucus and bacteria on the surface of the teeth. **2.** A deposit of fatty material on the inner lining of an artery wall, characteristic of atherosclerosis.

plas•ma (plăz′mə) **1.** *See* **blood plasma. 2.** Protoplasm or cytoplasm. **3.** A state of matter similar to a gas but consisting of positively charged ions with most or all of their detached electrons moving freely about. Because the concentrations of free electrons and positively charged ions are nearly equal, a plasma is electrically neutral. Plasmas are produced by very high temperatures, as in the sun and other stars, and also by the ionization resulting from exposure to an electric current, as in a fluorescent light bulb or a neon sign.

■ **plankton**
photographed through a microscope

plasma cell A cell that produces antibodies as part of an immune response. B cells develop into plasma cells. *See Note at* **antibody.**

plas•mo•di•al slime mold (plăz-mō′dē-əl) *See under* **slime mold.**

plas•mo•di•um (plăz-mō′dē-əm) *Plural* **plasmodia. 1.** A mass of protoplasm having many cell nuclei but not divided into separate cells. It is formed by the combination of many amoeba-like cells and is characteristic of the active, feeding phase of certain slime molds. **2.** Any of various single-celled organisms (called protozoans) that exist as parasites in vertebrate animals, one of which causes malaria.

plas•ter of Paris (plăs′tər) A form of calcium phosphate derived from the mineral gypsum. It is mixed with water to make casts and molds.

plas•tic (plăs′tĭk) *Noun.* **1.** Any of numerous artificial compounds formed by linking simple chemical units into giant molecules called polymers. Plastics are soft or liquid when heated. They can be molded into objects, pressed into thin layers, and drawn into fibers for use in textiles. *—Adjective.* **2.** Capable of being molded or formed into a shape.

plas•tid (plăs′tĭd) A structure found in plant cells, green algae, and certain protozoans. Some plastids, such as the chloroplasts in plant leaves, contain pigments.

plate (plāt) *Noun.* **1.** A thin, flat sheet of metal or other material, especially one used as an electrode in a storage battery or capacitor. **2.** In plate tectonics, one of the sections of the Earth's lithosphere (crust and upper mantle) that is in constant motion along with other sections. *See more at* **tectonic boundary.** *—Verb.* **3.** To coat or cover with a thin layer of metal.

pla•teau (plă-tō′) An elevated, comparatively level expanse of land.

plate•let (plāt′lĭt) Any of the numerous small round structures found in the blood of mammals that function in the clotting of blood. Platelets are formed in the bone marrow, contain no nuclei, and ingest and absorb foreign particles, including viruses.

plate tectonics In geology, a theory that the Earth's lithosphere (crust and upper mantle) is divided into a number of large, plate-like sections that move as distinct masses. *See Notes at*

Did You Know?
plate tectonics

Have you ever noticed that the Earth's continents seem to fit together like pieces of a puzzle? This observation is what led the German meteorologist Alfred Wegener to propose the theory of continental drift in 1915. Since rocks and fossils were found to match up in parts of different continents, it seemed that they must have once been joined, but no one could explain how such large landmasses could move so far apart. This problem was not solved until the 1960s, when the theory of *plate tectonics* was proposed. According to this theory, the continents move apart by riding piggyback on plates—huge slabs of the Earth's lithosphere—that are much larger than the continents themselves. The plates move like parts of a conveyor belt powered by huge convection currents of molten rock that many geologists believe is heated by the decay of radioactive elements deep within the Earth. Although they only move a few inches per year, over hundreds of millions of years the continents are carried thousands of miles. Along their boundaries, the plates crumple, scrape, or pull apart from one another, giving rise to volcanoes and earthquakes and creating and destroying rock on the ever-changing surface of the planet.

fault, Gondwanaland. *See more at* **tectonic boundary.**

plat•form (plăt′fôrm′) The basic technology of a computer system's hardware and software, defining how a computer is operated and determining what other kinds of software can be used. Additional software or hardware must be compatible with the platform.

plat•i•num (plăt′n-əm) A soft, easily shaped, silver-white metallic element that occurs worldwide with similar metals. It has a high melting point and does not corrode in air. Platinum is used as a catalyst and in making jewelry, electrical contacts, and dental crowns. *Symbol* **Pt.** *Atomic number* 78. *See* **Periodic Table,** pages 262–263.

plat•y•hel•minth (plăt′ĭ-hĕl′mĭnth) *See* **flatworm.**

plat•y•pus (plăt′ĭ-pəs) An egg-laying mammal of Australia and Tasmania that spends much of its life in water. Platypuses have a broad flat tail, webbed feet, and a snout resembling a duck's bill.

pla•ya (plī′ə) A dry lake bed at the bottom of a desert basin, sometimes temporarily covered with water. Playas have no vegetation and are among the flattest geographical features in the world.

Ple•ia•des (plē′ə-dēz′) A loose collection of several hundred stars in the constellation Taurus, at least six of which are visible to the unaided eye.

Pleis•to•cene (plīs′tə-sēn′) The earlier of the two epochs of the Quaternary Period, from about 2 million to 10,000 years ago. The Pleistocene Epoch was characterized by the formation of widespread glaciers in the Northern Hemisphere and by the appearance of humans. *See Chart at* **geologic time,** pages 148–149.

pleu•ra (plo͝or′ə) A membrane that encloses each lung and lines the chest cavity.

Pli•o•cene (plī′ə-sēn′) The fifth and last epoch of the Tertiary Period, from about 5 to 2 million years ago, characterized by the appearance of distinctly modern animals. *See Chart at* **geologic time,** pages 148–149.

plum•age (plo͞o′mĭj) The covering of feathers on a bird.

plume (plo͞om) **1.** *Zoology.* A feather, especially a large one. **2.** *Geology.* A body of magma that rises from the Earth's mantle into the crust. ❖ If a plume rises to the Earth's surface, it erupts as

platypus

lava. ❖ If it remains below the Earth's surface, it eventually solidifies into a body of rock known as a **pluton. 3.** *Ecology.* An area in air, water, soil, or rock containing pollutants released from a single source. A plume often spreads in the environment due to the action of wind, currents, or gravity.

plu•mule (plo͞om′yo͞ol) The developing bud of a plant embryo, situated just above the cotyledons and often containing immature leaves.

Plu•to (plo͞o′tō) A dwarf planet that until 2006 was classified as the ninth planet in our solar system. Its diameter is about $\frac{1}{6}$ that of Earth. It orbits the sun once every 248 years. Its orbit crosses that of Neptune. Its average surface temperature is –369°F (–223°C). *See Table at* **solar system,** pages 316–317. *See Note at* **planet.**

plu•toid (plo͞o′toid′) A dwarf planet that orbits the sun at a greater distance on average than Neptune.

plu•ton (plo͞o′tŏn′) A large body of igneous rock formed when a plume of magma cools underground. Although most plutons are deep within the Earth's crust, some become exposed at the surface due to plate-tectonic processes.

plu•to•ni•um (plo͞o-tō′nē-əm) A silvery, radioactive metallic element of the actinide series that has the highest atomic number of all naturally occurring elements. It can be found in trace amounts in uranium ores and is produced artificially by bombarding uranium with neutrons. It is absorbed by bone marrow and is highly poisonous. Plutonium is used in nuclear weapons and as a fuel in nuclear reactors. Its most stable isotope has a half-life of 76 million years. *Symbol* **Pu.** *Atomic number* 94. *See* **Periodic Table.**

plu•vi•al (plo͞o′vē-əl) **1.** Relating to rain; rainy: *During the Pleistocene Epoch there were many pluvial periods.* **2.** Caused by rain: *pluvial lakes.*

Pm The symbol for **promethium.**

pneu•mat•ic (no͞o-măt′ĭk) **1.** Relating to air or another gas: *pneumatic pressure.* **2.** Filled with or operated by compressed air: *a pneumatic drill.*

pneu•mo•nia (no͞o-mōn′yə) Any of several infections resulting in inflammation of the lungs, caused by bacteria or viruses.

Po The symbol for **polonium.**

pod (pŏd) A fruit or seed case that splits along two seams to release its seeds when it matures. Legumes, such as peas and beans, produce pods.

-pod A suffix meaning "foot." It is used in the scientific names of the members of many groups of organisms, such as *arthropod,* an organism having "jointed feet," and *sauropod,* a dinosaur having "lizard feet."

point (point) A geometric object having no dimensions and no property other than its location. The intersection of two lines is a point.

po•lar bond (pō′lər) A type of covalent bond between two atoms in which electrons are shared unequally. Because of this, one end of the molecule has a slightly negative charge and the other a slightly positive charge. *See more at* **covalent bond.**

polar cap 1. The mass of permanent ice that covers either of the Earth's polar regions. **2.** The mass of frozen carbon dioxide and water that covers either of Mars's polar regions.

polar circle The Arctic Circle or the Antarctic Circle.

polar coordinate system A system of coordinates in which the location of a point is determined by its distance from a fixed point at the center of the coordinate space (called the pole), and by the measurement of the angle formed by a fixed line (the polar axis, corresponding to the x-axis in Cartesian coordinates) and a line from the pole through the given point. The polar coordinates of a point are given as (r, θ), where r is the distance of the point from the pole, and θ is the measure of the angle.

Po•lar•is (pə-lăr′ĭs) A bright star at the end of the handle of the Little Dipper and almost at the north celestial pole. Also called *North Star.*

po•lar•i•ty (pō-lăr′ĭ-tē) The condition of having poles or being aligned with or directed toward poles, especially magnetic or electric poles.

po•lar•ize (pō′lə-rīz′) **1.** To cause the positive and negative electric charges in an object, such as an atom or molecule, to become separated from each other. This is typically done by placing the object in an electric field. **2.** To control the direction of the vibration of electromagnetic waves. Polarized light, for example, consists of electromagnetic waves that vibrate in a single plane, rather than in all directions as in ordinary light.

pole (pōl) **1.** *Mathematics.* **a.** Either of the points at which an axis that passes through the center of a sphere intersects the surface of the sphere. **b.**

The fixed point used as a reference in a system of polar coordinates. It corresponds to the origin in the Cartesian coordinate system. **2a.** *Geography.* Either of the points at which the Earth's axis of rotation intersects the Earth's surface; the North Pole or South Pole. **b.** Either of the two similar points on another planet. **3.** *Physics.* A magnetic pole. **4.** *Electricity.* Either of two oppositely charged terminals, such as the two electrodes of an electrolytic cell or the electric terminals of a battery. —*Adjective* **polar.**

po•li•o (pō′lē-ō′) A contagious disease, caused by a virus, that mainly affects the nerve cells of the spinal cord and brain, often leading to muscle weakness and paralysis. The name is a shortening of **poliomyelitis** (pō′lē-ō-mī′ə-lī′tĭs).

pol•len (pŏl′ən) Powdery grains that contain the male reproductive cells of most plants. In flowering plants, pollen is produced by the anthers of stamens.

pollen tube The slender tube formed by the pollen grain that penetrates an ovule after pollination and releases the male gametes.

pol•li•na•tion (pŏl′ə-nā′shən) The process by which plant pollen is transferred from the male reproductive organs to the female reproductive organs to form seeds. In flowering plants, pollen is transferred from the anther to the stigma, often by the wind or by insects. In cone-bearing plants, male cones release pollen that is usually borne by the wind to the ovules of female cones. —*Verb* **pollinate.**

pol•lut•ant (pə-lo͞ot′nt) A substance, especially a waste material, that contaminates air, water, or soil.

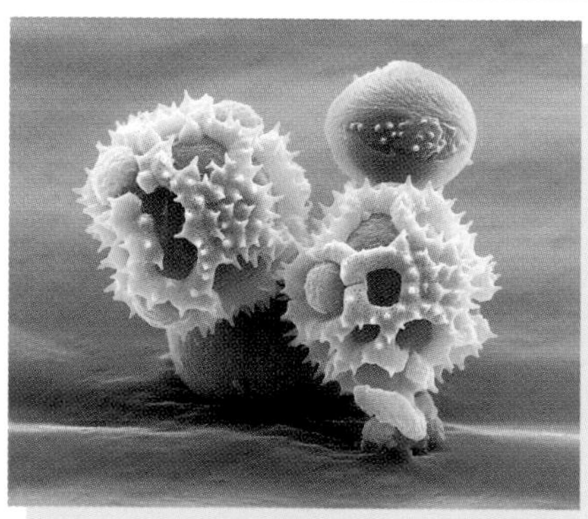

pollen

dandelion (larger) *and horse chestnut* (smaller) *pollen photographed through a scanning electron microscope*

Did You Know?

pollination and fertilization

When a pollen grain lands on or is carried to the receptive tissue of a pistil known as the stigma, the flower has been *pollinated.* But this is only the first step in a complicated process that, if successful, leads to *fertilization.* The pollen grain contains two nuclei—a generative nucleus and a tube nucleus. The generative nucleus divides in two to form two sperm nuclei. The tube nucleus grows down into the pistil until it reaches one of the ovules contained in the ovary. The two sperm nuclei travel down the tube and enter the ovule. There, one sperm nucleus unites with the egg nucleus, fertilizing the egg. The other sperm nucleus combines with two other nuclei that exist in the ovule. The fused nuclei then develop into the endocarp, the tissue that feeds the embryo. The ovule itself develops into a seed that is contained in the flower's ovary (which we know as a fruit). In conifers, the ovule is exposed (that is, not contained in an ovary), and the pollen produced by male cones lands directly on the ovule in female cones. Fertilization in conifers is not as quick as in flowering plants—the pollen nuclei often take as long as a year to reach the ovule.

pol•lu•tion (pə-lo͞o′shən) The contamination of air, water, or soil by substances that are harmful to living things. ❖ Light from cities and towns at night that interferes with astronomical observations is known as **light pollution.** It can also disturb natural rhythms of growth in plants and other organisms. ❖ Continuous noise that is loud enough to be annoying or physically harmful is known as **noise pollution.** ❖ Heat from hot water that is discharged from a factory into a river or lake, where it can kill or endanger aquatic life, is known as **thermal pollution.**

Pol•lux (pŏl′əks) A bright giant star in the constellation Gemini.

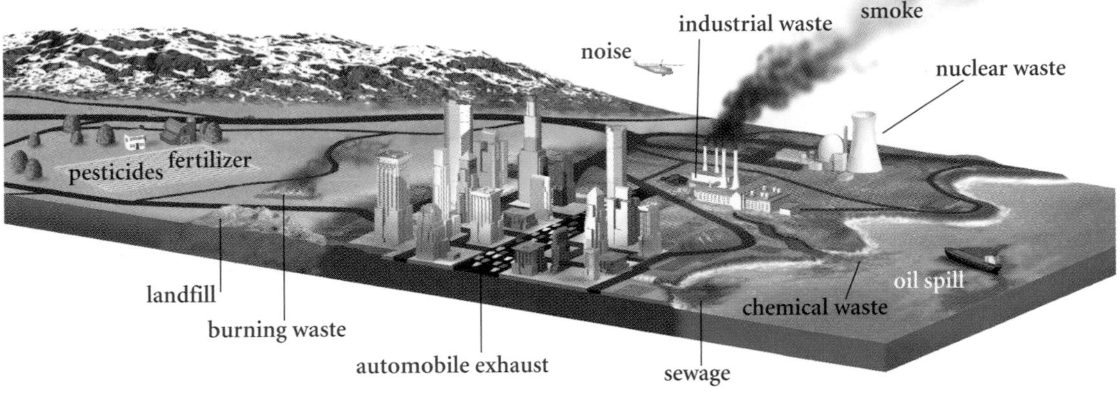

pollution

Pollution can affect air, water, or land and can threaten the health of humans, wildlife, and plants.

po•lo•ni•um (pə-lō′nē-əm) A very rare, naturally radioactive, silvery-gray or black metallic element. It is produced in extremely small amounts by the radioactive decay of radium or the bombardment of bismuth or lead with neutrons. *Symbol* **Po.** *Atomic number* 84. *See* **Periodic Table,** pages 262–263.

poly– A prefix meaning "many," as in *polygon,* a figure having many sides.

pol•y•chaete (pŏl′ĭ-kēt′) Any of various often brightly colored, meat-eating worms that are related to earthworms and leeches and usually live in the ocean. Each segment of a polychaete has a pair of fleshy appendages that are tipped with bristles, used for swimming or burrowing.

pol•y•chro•mat•ic (pŏl′ē-krō-măt′ĭk) **1.** Of or having many colors. **2.** Consisting of radiation of more than one wavelength.

polymorphism

two forms of carbon: diamonds and graphite (in powdered form and in its common use as the "lead" in pencils)

pol•y•es•ter (pŏl′ē-ĕs′tər) Any of various synthetic resins that are light, strong, and resistant to weather. Polyesters are long chains of esters and are used to make plastics and fibers.

pol•y•eth•yl•ene (pŏl′ē-ĕth′ə-lēn′) An artificial resin that is easily molded and is resistant to other chemicals. It can be repeatedly softened and hardened by heating and cooling, and it is used for many purposes, such as making containers, tubes, and packaging.

pol•y•gon (pŏl′ē-gŏn′) A closed plane figure having three or more sides. Triangles, rectangles, and octagons are all examples of polygons.

pol•y•he•dron (pŏl′ē-hē′drən) A three-dimensional geometric figure whose sides are polygons. A tetrahedron, for example, is a polyhedron having four triangular sides.

pol•y•mer (pŏl′ə-mər) Any of various chemical compounds made of smaller, identical molecules (called monomers) linked together. Some polymers, like cellulose, occur naturally, while others, like nylon, are artificial. Polymers have extremely high molecular weights, make up many of the tissues of organisms, and are used to make such materials as plastics, concrete, glass, and rubber. ❖ The process by which molecules are linked together to form polymers is called **polymerization** (pə-lĭm′ər-ĭ-zā′shən).

pol•y•mor•phism (pŏl′ē-môr′fĭz′əm) **1.** The existence of two or more different forms in an adult organism of the same species, as of an insect. In bees, the presence of queen, worker, and drone is an example of polymorphism. Differences between the sexes and between breeds of domesticated animals are not considered examples of polymorphism. **2.** The crystallization of a compound in at least two distinct forms. Diamond and graphite, for example, are polymorphs of the element carbon. They both consist entirely of carbon but have different crystal structures and different physical properties.

pol•y•no•mi•al (pŏl′ē-nō′mē-əl) An algebraic expression that is the sum of two or more terms, where each term consists of a variable raised to some power and multiplied by some constant. The expressions $x^2 - 4$ and $5x^4 + 2x^3 - x + 7$ are both polynomials.

pol•yp (pŏl′ĭp) A cnidarian in its sedentary stage. Polyps have hollow, tube-shaped bodies with a central mouth on top surrounded by tentacles. Some cnidarians, such as corals and sea anemones, only exist as polyps, while others turn into medusas as adults or lack a polyp stage completely. *Compare* **medusa.**

pol•y•sac•cha•ride (pŏl′ē-săk′ə-rīd′) Any of a class of carbohydrates that are made of long chains of simple carbohydrates (called monosaccharides). Starch and cellulose are polysaccharides.

pol•y•sty•rene (pŏl′ē-stī′rēn) A plastic polymer that is transparent, hard, and rigid. It has a wide variety of uses, including as a solid foam for insulation.

pol•y•un•sat•u•rat•ed (pŏl′ē-ŭn-săch′ə-rā′tĭd) Relating to an organic compound, especially a fat, in which more than one pair of carbon atoms are joined by double or triple bonds. *See more at* **unsaturated.**

pol•y•u•re•thane (pŏl′ē-yo͝or′ə-thān′) Any of various resins used to make tough resistant coatings, adhesives, and electrical insulation.

pond (pŏnd) An inland body of standing water that is smaller than a lake.

pons (pŏnz) A thick band of nerve fibers in the brainstem of mammals that links the brainstem to the cerebellum and upper portions of the brain. It is a major pathway for the transmission of nerve impulses among different portions of the brain.

pop•u•la•tion (pŏp′yə-lā′shən) A group of individuals of the same species occupying a specific habitat, community, or other defined area: *the elk population in their winter range.*

pore (pôr) **1.** A tiny opening, as one in an animal's skin or on the surface of a plant leaf or stem, through which liquids or gases may pass. **2.** A space in soil, rock, or loose sediment that is not occupied by mineral matter and allows the passage or absorption of fluids, such as water or air.

po•rif•er•an (pə-rĭf′ər-ən) *See* **sponge** (sense 1).

po•rous (pôr′əs) Having many pores or other small spaces that allow a gas or liquid to pass through. —*Noun* **porosity** (pə-rŏs′ĭ-tē).

por•phy•ry (pôr′fə-rē) A fine-grained igneous rock containing some relatively large crystals, especially of feldspar.

por•poise (pôr′pəs) Any of several small, toothed whales having a blunt snout and a triangular dorsal fin. *Compare* **dolphin.**

pos•i•tive (pŏz′ĭ-tĭv) **1.** Greater than zero, as 12. **2.** Having the electric charge of a proton. The symbol for a positive charge is a plus sign. **3.** Showing the presence, as in a blood test, of a suspected disease or microorganism.

pos•i•tron (pŏz′ĭ-trŏn′) A subatomic particle that is the antiparticle of the electron.

post– A prefix that means "after," as in *postoperative,* after an operation, or "behind," as in *postnasal,* behind the nose or nasal passages.

pos•tu•late (pŏs′chə-lĭt) A principle that is accepted as true without proof; an axiom.

pot•ash (pŏt′ăsh′) Any of several compounds that contain potassium, especially potassium carbonate (K_2CO_3), a strongly alkaline material obtained from wood ashes and used in fertilizers.

po•tas•si•um (pə-tăs′ē-əm) A soft, highly reactive, silvery-white metallic element that is an alkali metal and occurs in nature only in compounds. It is essential for the growth of plants and is used especially in fertilizers and soaps. *Symbol* **K.** *Atomic number* 19. *See* **Periodic Table,** pages 262–263.

potassium hydroxide A white, corrosive, solid compound, KOH, used in bleaches and to make soaps and detergents. It is soluble in water and very soluble in alcohol. In solution, it forms lye.

potassium nitrate A white, crystalline compound and strong oxidizing agent, KNO_3. It is used in gunpowder and fertilizer, and in making glass. Also called *saltpeter. See also* **niter.**

po•ten•tial (pə-tĕn′shəl) **1.** The work required to move a charged particle, a magnetic pole, or an amount of mass from one specific point to another in an unchanging electric, magnetic, or gravitational field. **2.** The difference in voltage between two points in an electric circuit.

potential energy The energy possessed by a body as a result of its position or condition rather than its motion. A raised weight, coiled spring, or charged battery has potential energy. *Compare* **kinetic energy.**

po•ten•ti•om•e•ter (pə-tĕn′shē-ŏm′ĭ-tər) **1.** An adjustable resistor used to control the magnitude of the voltage that is applied to an electric circuit. Potentiometers are used in the volume controls of radios and televisions. **2.** An instrument for measuring an unknown voltage by comparison with a known voltage, such as that of a generator.

pound (pound) A unit of weight equal to 16 ounces (about 453.6 grams). *See Table at* **measurement.** *See Note at* **weight.**

pow•er (pou′ər) **1.** The energy by which a machine or system is operated: *trains that run on steam power; ships that use nuclear power.* **2.** *Physics.* The rate at which work is done with respect to time, measured in units such as watts or horsepower. *Compare* **energy, work. 3.** *Mathematics.* The number of times a number or an expression is multiplied by itself, as shown by an exponent. Thus ten to the sixth power, or 10^6, equals one million. **4.** A number that represents the magnification of an optical instrument, such as a microscope or telescope. A 500-power microscope can magnify something 500 times.

Pr The symbol for **praseodymium.**

prai•rie (prâr′ē) An extensive area of flat or rolling grassland, especially the large plain of central North America.

pra•se•o•dym•i•um (prā′zē-ō-dĭm′ē-əm) A soft, silvery, easily shaped metallic element of the lanthanide series that develops a green tarnish in air. It is used to color glass and ceramics yellow and to make glass used in goggles for welders. *Symbol* **Pr.** *Atomic number* 59. *See* **Periodic Table,** pages 262–263.

pray•ing man•tis (prā′ĭng măn′tĭs) Any of various predatory insects that are usually pale green and have two pairs of walking legs and a pair of strong grasping forelimbs. Praying mantises are related to cockroaches, and the female often eats her mate.

pre– A prefix that means "earlier, before," or "in advance," as in *prenatal,* before birth.

Pre•cam•bri•an (prē-kăm′brē-ən, prē-kām′brē-ən) The span of geologic time between Hadean Time and the Phanerozoic Eon, from about 3.8 billion to 540 million years ago. During the Precambrian Eon, which is divided into the Archean and Proterozoic, primitive forms of life first appeared on Earth. *See Chart at* **geologic time,** pages 148–149.

pre•ces•sion (prē-sĕsh′ən) **1.** The motion of the axis of a spinning body, such as the wobbling of a spinning top, that arises when an external force acts on the axis. **2.** The motion of this kind made by the Earth's axis, caused mainly by the gravitational pull of the sun, moon, and other planets. ❖ The **precession of the equinoxes** is the slow westward shift of the autumnal and vernal equinoxes along the ecliptic, resulting from precession of the Earth's axis. A complete precession of the equinoxes takes 25,800 years.

pre•cip•i•tate (prĭ-sĭp′ĭ-tāt′) *Verb.* **1.** To cause water vapor to condense from the atmosphere and fall as rain or snow. **2.** To separate chemically from a solution in the form of a solid. —*Noun.* **3.** A solid material separated from a solution by chemical means: *an insoluble precipitate.*

pre•cip•i•ta•tion (prĭ-sĭp′ĭ-tā′shən) A form of water, such as rain, snow, or sleet, that condenses from the atmosphere and falls to the Earth's surface.

pred•a•tor (prĕd′ə-tər) An animal that lives by capturing and eating other animals.

preg•nan•cy (prĕg′nən-sē) **1.** The condition of being pregnant. **2.** The time during which one is pregnant; gestation.

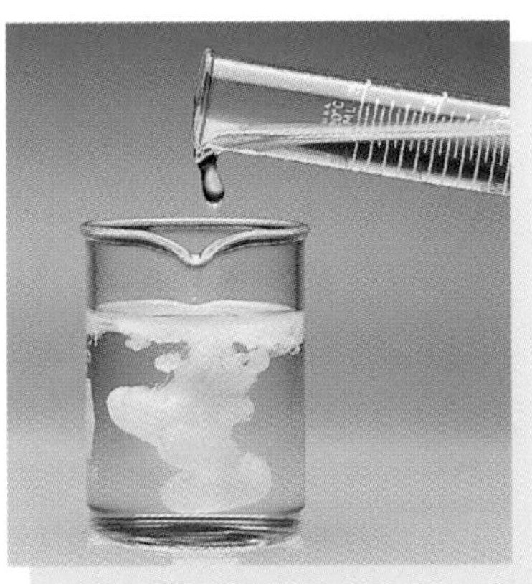

precipitate

When aqueous potassium chromate is added to a colorless barium nitrate solution, yellow barium chromate precipitates.

BIOGRAPHY

Joseph Priestley

When Joseph Priestley met Benjamin Franklin in 1766, it was the beginning of a friendship that would have an enormous impact on science. Franklin's enthusiasm about his experiments with electricity convinced Priestley to conduct his own experiments. Priestley developed an improved technique for isolating gases in a sealed glass vessel. Using a magnifying glass to focus the rays of the sun on a piece of mercuric oxide, he discovered a gas that made a candle burn more brightly, while all the other gases he tested put out the candle's flame. Priestley did not appreciate the full implications of his discovery, however. When he told the French chemist Antoine Lavoisier about his discovery, Lavoisier repeated Priestley's experiments and was able to prove that air was not an element but was made up of various parts, and that combustion required the presence of Priestley's gas. Lavoisier gave the element its name, *oxygen.*

pre•hen•sile (prē-hĕn′səl) Adapted for seizing, grasping, or holding, especially by wrapping around an object. The feet of many birds and the tails of monkeys are prehensile.

pre•mo•lar (prē-mō′lər) Any of eight bicuspid teeth in mammals, arranged in pairs on both sides of the upper and lower jaws between the canines and molars. Premolars are used to tear and grind food.

pres•sure (prĕsh′ər) Continuous force applied to a gas, liquid, or solid by another gas, liquid, or solid. Pressure is expressed as the amount of force applied per unit of area.

Priest•ley (prēst′lē), **Joseph** 1733–1804. British chemist who discovered oxygen (1774) and ten other gases, including hydrogen chloride, sulphur dioxide, and ammonia.

pri•mar•y (prī′mĕr′ē) **1.** Relating to a primary color. **2.** *Botany.* Relating to plant tissues in the tips of roots and shoots whose cells divide to cause the plant to grow lengthwise.

primary color Any of a group of colors from which all other colors can be made by mixing. *See more at* **color.**

primary wave An earthquake wave in which rock particles vibrate parallel to the direction of wave travel. Primary waves can travel through both solids and liquids. Also called *P wave. See Note at* **earthquake.**

pri•mate (prī′māt′) Any of various mammals having a highly developed brain, eyes facing forward, a shortened nose and muzzle, and opposable thumbs. Primates usually live in groups with complex social systems, and their high intelligence allows them to adapt their behavior successfully to different environments. Lemurs, monkeys, apes, and humans are primates.

prime meridian (prīm) The meridian with a longitude of 0°, used as a reference line from which longitude east and west is measured. It passes through Greenwich, England.

prime number An integer greater than 1 that can be divided only by itself and 1 without leaving a remainder. Examples of prime numbers are 7, 23, and 67. *Compare* **composite number.**

prim•i•tive (prĭm′ĭ-tĭv) **1.** Relating to an early or original stage: *a primitive form of life.* **2.** Having evolved very little from an early type. Lampreys and sturgeon are primitive fishes.

pri•on (prē′ŏn) A particle composed of protein, similar to a virus but lacking DNA or RNA. Prions are thought to be the agent of infection of some diseases of the nervous system.

prism (prĭz′əm) **1.** A geometric solid whose bases are congruent polygons lying in parallel planes and whose sides are parallelograms. **2.** A solid of

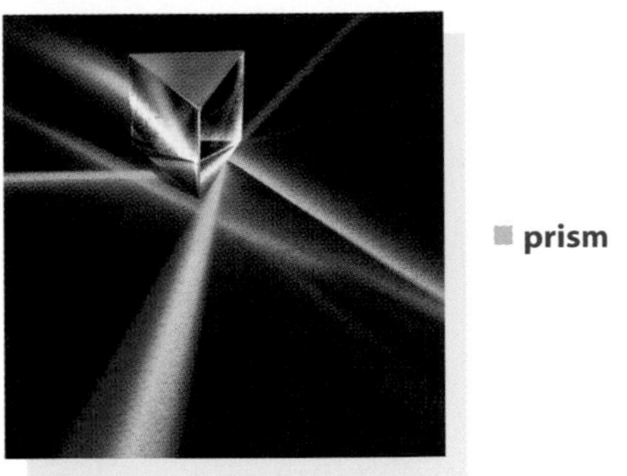

prism

this type, often made of glass with triangular ends, used to disperse light and break it up into a spectrum.

prob•a•bil•i•ty (prŏb′ə-bĭl′ĭ-tē) A number expressing the likelihood of the occurrence of a given event, especially a fraction expressing how many times the event will happen in a given number of tests or experiments. For example, when rolling a six-sided die, the probability of rolling a particular side is 1 in 6, or $\frac{1}{6}$.

pro•bos•cis (prō-bŏs′ĭs) **1.** A long, flexible snout or trunk, as of an elephant. **2.** The slender, tubular feeding and sucking organ of certain invertebrates, such as butterflies and mosquitoes.

Pro•cy•on (prō′sē-ŏn′) A very bright binary star in the constellation Canis Minor.

pro•duc•er (prə-dōō′sər) An organism that serves as a source of food for other organisms in a food chain. Producers include green plants, which produce food through photosynthesis, and certain bacteria that are capable of converting inorganic substances into food through chemosynthesis. *Compare* **consumer.**

prod•uct (prŏd′əkt) A number or quantity obtained by multiplication. For example, the product of 3 and 7 is 21.

pro•ges•ter•one (prō-jĕs′tə-rōn′) A steroid hormone that prepares the uterus for pregnancy, maintains pregnancy, and promotes development of the mammary glands. The main sources of progesterone are the ovary and the placenta.

pro•gram (prō′grăm′) **1.** The set of steps, including the collection and processing of data and the presentation of results, that is necessary for a computer to solve a problem. **2.** The set of instructions that a computer must execute in carrying out these steps.

pro•kar•y•ote (prō-kăr′ē-ōt′) Any of a wide variety of one-celled organisms that lack a distinct cell nucleus or other structures bound by a membrane and that have DNA that is not organized into chromosomes. Prokaryotes reproduce asexually, are the most primitive and ancient known forms of life, and include the bacteria and blue-green algae. Prokaryotes are grouped as a separate kingdom in taxonomy. Also called *moneran. Compare* **eukaryote.** *See Table at* **Taxonomy.**

pro•line (prō′lēn′) A nonessential amino acid. *See more at* **amino acid.**

pro•me•thi•um (prə-mē′thē-əm) A radioactive metallic element of the lanthanide series. Promethium does not occur in nature, but it can be found as a product of the fission of uranium. It has 17 isotopes, one of which can be used to make miniature batteries that work at extreme temperatures for up to five years. *Symbol* **Pm.**

Did You Know?

program

When you program a VCR, you are making a set of instructions that tell the VCR what to do. Similarly, when programmers write computer *programs,* they are creating a set of instructions that make a computer perform particular tasks or functions. Modern programs are typically created on a computer in a special program called an *application development environment.* This program includes a blank screen and various methods for adding words, pictures, and buttons to the screen. Using an artificial language consisting of a set of words and grammatical rules for stringing them together, the programmer writes instructions describing what the program will do when the user enters a command or clicks on a button, for example. The application development environment stores the programmer's instructions and translates them into instructions that the computer can understand and perform.

Atomic number 61. *See* **Periodic Table,** pages 262–263.

prom·i·nence (prŏm′ə-nəns) A burst of flaming gas that erupts from the sun's surface.

proof (pro͞of) A demonstration of the truth of a mathematical or logical statement, based on axioms and theorems derived from these axioms.

pro•pane (prō′pān′) A colorless, gaseous hydrocarbon, C_3H_8, found in petroleum and natural gas. It is widely used as a fuel.

pro•pel•ler (prə-pĕl′ər) A device consisting of a series of twisted blades mounted around a shaft and spun to force air or water in a specific direction and thereby move an aircraft or boat.

prop•er fraction (prŏp′ər) A fraction in which the numerator is less than the denominator, such as $\frac{1}{2}$. *Compare* **improper fraction.**

pro•phase (prō′fāz′) The first stage of cell division. Before prophase begins, the chromosomes duplicate to form two long, thin strands called chromatids. During prophase, the chromatids thicken and the membrane surrounding the nucleus disappears. In mitosis, metaphase follows prophase. *See more at* **meiosis, mitosis.**

pros•ta•glan•din (prŏs′tə-glăn′dĭn) Any of a group of substances that are derived from fatty acids and have a wide range of effects in the body. Prostaglandins influence the contraction of the muscles lining many internal organs and can lower or raise blood pressure.

pros•tate gland (prŏs′tāt′) A gland in male mammals at the base of the bladder that opens into the urethra. It secretes a fluid that is a major component of semen.

pro•tac•tin•i•um (prō′tăk-tĭn′ē-əm) A rare, extremely toxic, radioactive metallic element of the actinide series that occurs in uranium ores. Its most common isotope has a half-life of 32,500 years. *Symbol* **Pa.** *Atomic number* 91. *See* **Periodic Table,** pages 262–263.

pro•te•ase (prō′tē-ās′) Any of various enzymes that bring about the breakdown of proteins into peptides or amino acids by hydrolysis. Pepsin is an example of a protease.

pro•tein (prō′tēn′) One of a large class of complex organic chemical compounds that are essential for life. Proteins play a central role in biological processes and form the basis of living tissues. They consist of long, looping or folding chains of smaller compounds called amino acids. Enzymes, antibodies, and hemoglobin are examples of proteins.

pterodactyl

Prot•er•o•zo•ic (prŏt′ər-ə-zō′ĭk) The later of the two divisions of the Precambrian Eon, from about 2.5 billion to 540 million years ago. The Proterozoic was characterized by the buildup of oxygen in the atmosphere and the appearance of the first multicellular eukaryotes. *See Chart at* **geologic time,** pages 148–149.

pro•tist (prō′tĭst) Any of a large variety of usually one-celled organisms, including the protozoans, most algae, and the slime molds. Protists are eukaryotes (they have cell nuclei) and live in water or in watery tissues of organisms. They are grouped as a separate kingdom in taxonomy. Also called *protoctist. See Table at* **taxonomy.**

pro•ti•um (prō′tē-əm, prō′shē-əm) The most abundant isotope of hydrogen, having an atomic mass of 1. Its nucleus consists of a single proton. *See more at* **hydrogen.**

pro•to•col (prō′tə-kôl′) A standard procedure for regulating data transmission between computers.

pro•toc•tist (prə-tŏk′tĭst) *See* **protist.**

pro•ton (prō′tŏn′) A stable subatomic particle that has a positive electric charge and is part of the nucleus of an atom. Its charge is opposite to that of an electron but is equal in magnitude. A proton's mass is 1,836 times that of an electron. *See more at* **atom.**

pro•to•plasm (prō′tə-plăz′əm) A substance resembling jelly that forms the living matter in all plant and animal cells. Protoplasm is made up of

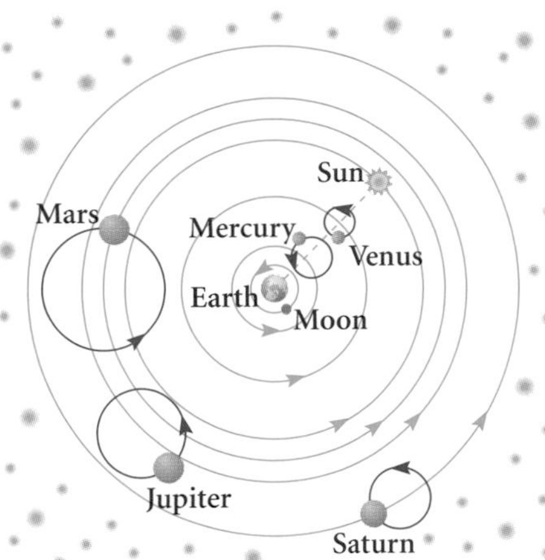

Ptolemaic system

Ptolemy believed that Earth was at the center of the universe and that the sun and planets orbited Earth (with the planets also moving in smaller circles called epicycles). In this system, the centers of Mercury's and Venus's epicycles always lie on the line shown in the diagram between Earth and the sun.

proteins, fats, and other substances suspended in water. It includes the nucleus and cytoplasm.

pro•to•zo•an (prō′tə-zō′ən) Any of a large group of one-celled organisms that have a cell nucleus and live in water or as parasites. Many protozoans move about by means of appendages known as cilia or flagella. Protozoans include the amoebas and paramecia and are classified as protists.

Prox•i•ma Centauri (prŏk′sə-mə) *See under* **Alpha Centauri.**

pseu•do•pod (so͞o′də-pŏd′) *also* **pseu•do•po•di•um** (so͞o′də-pō′dē-əm) *Plural* **pseudopods** *or* **pseudopodia.** A temporary foot-like extension of the protoplasm of a one-celled organism, such as an amoeba, used for moving about and for surrounding and taking in food.

psy•chi•a•try (sĭ-kī′ə-trē) The branch of medicine that deals with the study and treatment of mental illness.

psy•chol•o•gy (sī-kŏl′ə-jē) The scientific study of mental processes and behavior.

psy•cho•sis (sī-kō′sĭs) *Plural* **psychoses** (sī-kō′sēz) A mental illness so severe that a person loses the ability to think logically, to communicate, and to relate to others. A person with a psychosis loses contact with reality and often shows dramatic changes in behavior. Psychoses can be caused by diseases affecting the brain. —*Adjective* **psychotic** (sī-kŏt′ĭk).

Pt The symbol for **platinum.**

pter•an•o•don (tə-răn′ə-dŏn′) Any of several large, extinct, flying reptiles of the Cretaceous Period, having a long pointed head, no teeth, and a wingspan of 20 feet (6.1 meters) or more.

pter•o•dac•tyl (tĕr′ə-dăk′təl) Any of various small, extinct, flying reptiles of the late Jurassic and Cretaceous Periods. The pterodactyls were about the size of small to mid-sized birds.

pter•o•saur (tĕr′ə-sôr′) Any of various extinct, flying reptiles of the Jurassic and Cretaceous Periods with wings consisting of a flap of skin supported by an elongated fourth digit on each forelimb. Pterosaurs had wingspans ranging from less than a foot (0.3 meter) to close to 50 feet (15.2 meters).

Ptol•e•ma•ic system (tŏl′ə-mā′ĭk) The astronomical system of Ptolemy, in which Earth is at the center of the universe and all celestial bodies revolve around it. The sun, moon, and planets revolve at different levels in circular orbits, and the stars lie in fixed locations on a sphere that revolves beyond these orbits.

Ptol•e•my (tŏl′ə-mē) Second century A.D. Greek astronomer and mathematician who based his astronomy on the belief that all heavenly bodies revolve around Earth. *See more at* **Copernicus.**

pty•a•lin (tī′ə-lĭn) An enzyme found in saliva that breaks down starches into sugars.

Pu The symbol for **plutonium.**

Ptolemy

pu•ber•ty (pyo͞o′bər-tē) The stage in the development of humans and other primates marked by maturing of the reproductive organs and by the start of menstruation in females and sperm production in males. During puberty, the production of sex hormones causes other physical changes, including breast development in females and deepening of the voice in males.

pu•bis (pyo͞o′bĭs) The forwardmost of the three bones that fuse together to form each of the hipbones. *See more at* **skeleton.** —*Adjective* **pubic.**

pul•ley (po͝ol′ē) A simple machine consisting of a wheel over which a pulled rope or chain runs to change the direction of the pull used for lifting a load. Combinations of two or more pulleys working together reduce the force needed to lift a load. *See also* **block and tackle.**

pul•mo•nar•y (po͝ol′mə-nĕr′ē) Relating to the lungs: *a pulmonary infection.*

pulmonary artery An artery that carries blood with low levels of oxygen from the right ventricle of the heart to the lungs.

pulmonary vein A vein that carries blood with high levels of oxygen from the lungs to the left atrium of the heart.

pul•sar (pŭl′sär′) A spinning neutron star that emits radiation, usually radio waves, in very short and very regular pulses. Because a pulsar's magnetic poles do not align with the poles of its axis, its beams of radiation sweep around like the beacon of a lighthouse.

pulse (pŭls) The rhythmical expansion and contraction of the arteries as blood is pumped through them by the beating of the heart.

pum•ice (pŭm′ĭs) A usually light-colored, porous, lightweight rock of volcanic origin. The pores form when water vapor and gases escape from the lava during its quick solidification into rock.

pump (pŭmp) A machine for raising or transferring fluids. Most pumps function either by compression or suction.

punc•tu•at•ed equilibrium (pŭngk′cho͞o-ā′tĭd) The theory that new species evolve suddenly over relatively short periods of time, followed by longer periods in which little genetic change occurs. Punctuated equilibrium is a revision of Darwin's theory that evolution takes place at a slow, constant rate over millions of years. *Compare* **gradualism.** *See Note at* **evolution.**

Did You Know?

pulsar

When a very large star goes off like a giant bomb in an explosion called a supernova, the core of the star collapses into either a neutron star or a black hole. In 1054, one of these explosions could be seen in the sky during both day and night for 23 days. Chinese astronomers took note of this "guest star," and rock paintings and pottery found in Arizona and New Mexico suggest that Native Americans recorded it, too. In the 18th century, astronomers discovered in the constellation Taurus the leftovers that had been blown away by this explosion, the bright cloud called the Crab Nebula. In the late 1960s, 900 years after the supernova, astronomers found a source of rapidly pulsing radio waves, with 30 flashes per second, near the center of this nebula. The source of this pulsating radiation is an object that was named a *pulsar.* We now know that a pulsar is a rapidly rotating neutron star whose radiation is emitted like a spinning flashlight. Over 700 pulsars have now been detected, with rates of rotation ranging from once every 4 seconds to more than 600 times per second.

pu•pa (pyo͞o′pə) *Plural* **pupae** (pyo͞o′pē) An insect in the nonfeeding stage of development between the larva and adult, during which it typically undergoes a complete transformation within a protective cocoon or hardened case. Only certain kinds of insects, such as moths, butterflies, ants, and beetles, develop as larvae and pupae. *Compare* **imago, larva, nymph.** —*Adjective* **pupal.**

pu•pil (pyo͞o′pəl) The opening in the center of the iris through which light enters the eye.

pu•rine (pyo͝or′ēn′) Any of a group of organic compounds containing two rings of alternating

pyrite

carbon and nitrogen atoms. Purines include caffeine and uric acid, as well as the two bases adenine and guanine, which are components of DNA and RNA.

pus (pŭs) A thick, yellowish-white liquid that forms in infected body tissues. It consists mainly of dead white blood cells.

P wave *See* **primary wave.** *See Note at* **earthquake.**

pyr•i•dox•ine (pĭr′ĭ-dŏk**′**sēn) *See under* **vitamin B complex.**

py•rim•i•dine (pī-rĭm**′**ĭ-dēn′) Any of a group of organic compounds having a single ring with alternating carbon and nitrogen atoms. Pyrimidines include the bases cytosine, thymine, and uracil, which are components of nucleic acids.

py•rite (pī**′**rīt′) A silver to yellow, metallic mineral consisting of iron and sulfur. Pyrite often crystallizes in cubes or octahedrons but also occurs as shapeless masses of grains. It is used as a source of iron and in making sulfur dioxide. Because of its shiny look and often yellow color, it is sometimes mistaken for gold and for this reason is also called *fool's gold.*

py•rox•ene (pī-rŏk**′**sēn′) Any of a series of rock-forming minerals consisting of mixtures of calcium, sodium, magnesium, or iron silicates. Pyroxenes vary in color from white to dark green or black and are characterized by a rectangular-shaped cross section. They occur in igneous and metamorphic rocks.

py•ru•vic acid (pī-ro͞o**′**vĭk) A colorless organic liquid formed by the breakdown of carbohydrates and sugars during cell metabolism. It is the final product of the process known as glycolysis and has the formula $C_3H_4O_3$.

Py•thag•o•ras (pĭ-thăg**′**ər-əs) Sixth century B.C. Greek philosopher who theorized that numbers constitute the essence of all natural things. He developed the Pythagorean theorem and was one of the first to apply mathematical order to observations of the stars.

Py•thag•o•re•an theorem (pĭ-thăg′ə-rē**′**ən) A theorem stating that the square of the length of the hypotenuse (the longest side) of a right triangle is equal to the sum of the squares of the lengths of the other sides. It is mathematically stated as $c^2 = a^2 + b^2$, where c is the length of the hypotenuse and a and b the lengths of the other two sides.

py•thon (pī**′**thŏn′) Any of various very large and colorful snakes of Africa, Asia, and Australia. Pythons are not poisonous, but coil around and suffocate their prey, which can be as large as wild deer.

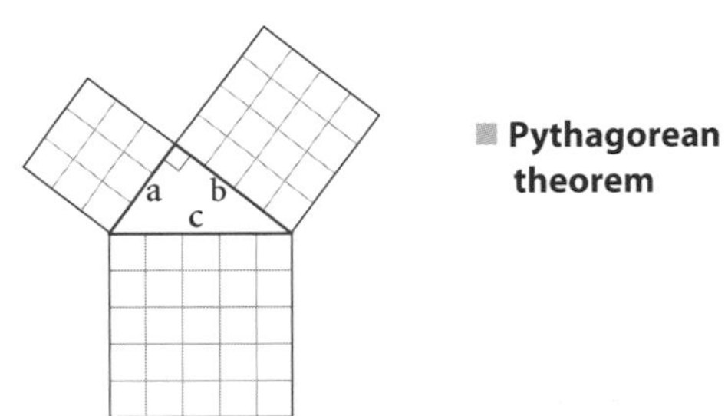

Pythagorean theorem

qt. Abbreviation of **quart.**

quad•rant (kwŏd′rənt) **1.** An arc equal to one quarter of the circumference of a circle; an arc of 90°. **2.** Any of the four regions into which a plane is divided by the axes of a Cartesian coordinate system. The quadrants are numbered counterclockwise one through four, beginning with the quadrant in which both the x- and y-coordinates are positive (usually the upper right quadrant). **3.** An instrument with an arc of 90°, used to measure the angle between a celestial object and the horizon.

quad•rat•ic (kwŏ-drăt′ĭk) Relating to a mathematical expression containing a term of the second degree, such as $x^2 + 2$. ❖ A **quadratic equation** is an equation having the general form $ax^2 + bx + c = 0$, where *a, b,* and *c* are constants. ❖ The **quadratic formula** is

$$x = \frac{-b \pm \sqrt{b^2 - 4ac}}{2a}$$

It is important in algebra, where it is used to calculate the roots of quadratic equations.

quad•ri•ceps (kwŏd′rĭ-sĕps′) The large, four-part muscle at the front of the thigh that acts to extend the leg.

quad•ri•lat•er•al (kwŏd′rə-lăt′ər-əl) A polygon that has four sides, such as a rectangle or rhombus.

quad•ri•ple•gi•a (kwŏd′rə-plē′jē-ə) Paralysis of the body from the neck down, caused by injury to the spinal cord.

quad•ru•man•ous (kwŏ-dro͞o′mə-nəs) Having four feet and using all four feet as hands, as primates other than humans do.

quad•ru•ped (kwŏd′rə-pĕd′) An animal having four feet, such as most reptiles and mammals.

quan•ti•ta•tive analysis (kwŏn′tĭ-tā′tĭv) A test performed on a substance or mixture to find out the amounts and proportions of its chemical components.

quan•ti•ty (kwŏn′tĭ-tē) *Mathematics.* Something, such as a number or symbol that represents a number, on which a mathematical operation is performed.

quan•tum (kwŏn′təm) *Plural* **quanta.** A unit of energy, especially electromagnetic energy, that is the smallest physical quantity that can exist on its own. A quantum acts both like a particle and like an energy wave. Photons are examples of quanta.

quantum mechanics 1. The properties of an object or physical system of objects as described by quantum theory. **2.** *See* **quantum theory.**

quantum physics The branch of physics that uses quantum theory to describe and predict the properties of a physical system.

quantum theory A theory in physics in which matter and energy have properties of both waves and particles. In quantum theory, many physical phenomena come in discrete units called quanta. For example, photons are the quanta of electromagnetic energy. In quantum theory, the behavior of matter and energy is described in terms of probability. For example, exactly when a radioactive atom will decay cannot be known; only the probability of its decay can be known. Quantum theory is especially important for physics at the scale of atoms and subatomic particles. Also called *quantum mechanics.*

quark (kwôrk, kwärk) Any of a group of elementary particles supposed to be the fundamental units that combine in threes to make up protons and neutrons. *See Note at* **subatomic particle.**

quart (kwôrt) A unit of volume or capacity used in liquid measure, equal to $\frac{1}{4}$ of a gallon or 32 ounces (0.95 liter). *See Table at* **measurement.**

quartz (kwôrts) A hard, transparent mineral composed of silicon dioxide. Quartz is the most

quartz

Did You Know?

quasar

"The universe is not only stranger than we imagine," Albert Einstein said. "It is stranger than we *can* imagine." In the 1960s, astronomers found some very strange objects that we now call *quasars* in the far reaches of the universe. A quasar is like a far-off floodlight. It appears to be an extremely distant star putting out huge amounts of energy. In fact, just one of these objects can be a trillion times brighter than the sun. All of the radiation that a quasar gives off comes from a small area at its center, and many astronomers believe that the source of the energy is an enormous black hole rotating at the center of a young galaxy. Quasars are among the most distant celestial objects known. Some are more than ten billion light-years away, meaning their radiation has taken ten billion years to reach us. So when we look at quasars, we're observing these objects as they were billions of years ago, and we're able to see part of the early history of the universe.

common of all minerals. It occurs as a component of rocks such as sandstone and granite, and separately in a variety of forms such as rock crystal, flint, and agate. Some crystalline forms, such as amethyst, are considered gemstones. Quartz is the mineral used to represent a hardness of 7 on the Mohs scale.

quartz•ite (kwôrt′sīt′) A metamorphic rock consisting entirely of quartz. Quartzite forms when quartz crystals in sandstone or chert grow into larger crystals during metamorphism.

qua•sar (kwā′zär′) An extremely distant, compact, star-like celestial object. The power output of a quasar is several thousand times that of the Milky Way galaxy.

Qua•ter•nar•y (kwŏt′ər-nĕr′ē) The second and last period of the Cenozoic Era, from about 2 million years ago to the present, characterized by the appearance of humans. *See Chart at* **geologic time,** pages 148–149.

queen (kwēn) The fertile, fully developed female in a colony of social bees, ants, or termites. The queen's sole function is to lay eggs.

quick•sand (kwĭk′sănd′) A deep bed of loose sand mixed with water, forming a soft, shifting mass that yields easily to pressure and tends to swallow objects resting on its surface.

quill (kwĭl) The hollow shaft of a feather, the bottom of which attaches to the bird's skin.

qui•nine (kwī′nīn′) A bitter-tasting, colorless drug derived from cinchona bark, used to treat malaria. *See Note at* **aspirin.**

quo•tient (kwō′shənt) The number that results when one number is divided by another. If 6 is divided by 3, the quotient can be represented as 2, or as $6 \div 3$, or as the fraction $\frac{6}{3}$.

r 1. *Mathematics.* Abbreviation of **radius. 2.** or **R** *Electricity.* Abbreviation of **resistance.**

Ra The symbol for **radium.**

rab•bit (răb′ĭt) Any of various long-eared, short-tailed mammals that have long hind legs adapted for quick movement by hopping. Rabbits eat mainly plants and dig many-chambered burrows known as warrens. They have been domesticated since ancient times.

ra•bies (rā′bēz) A usually fatal viral disease of warm-blooded animals that causes inflammation of the brain and spinal cord. It is transmitted by the bite of an infected animal and can be prevented in humans by a vaccine. *See Note at* **hydrophobia.**

ra•ceme (rā-sēm′) A flower cluster in which each flower grows on its own stalk from a common stem. The lily of the valley and snapdragon have racemes.

rad (răd) A unit used to measure energy absorbed by a material from radiation. One rad is equal to 100 ergs per gram of material. Many scientists now measure this energy in grays rather than in rads.

radial symmetry

ra•dar (rā′där) **1.** A method of detecting distant objects and determining their position, speed, or other characteristics by causing radio waves to be reflected from them and analyzing the reflected waves. **2.** The equipment used in doing this.

radar gun A usually hand-held device that measures the velocity of a moving object by sending out a continuous radio wave and measuring the frequency of reflected waves.

ra•di•al symmetry (rā′dē-əl) The arrangement of similar forms or features around a central

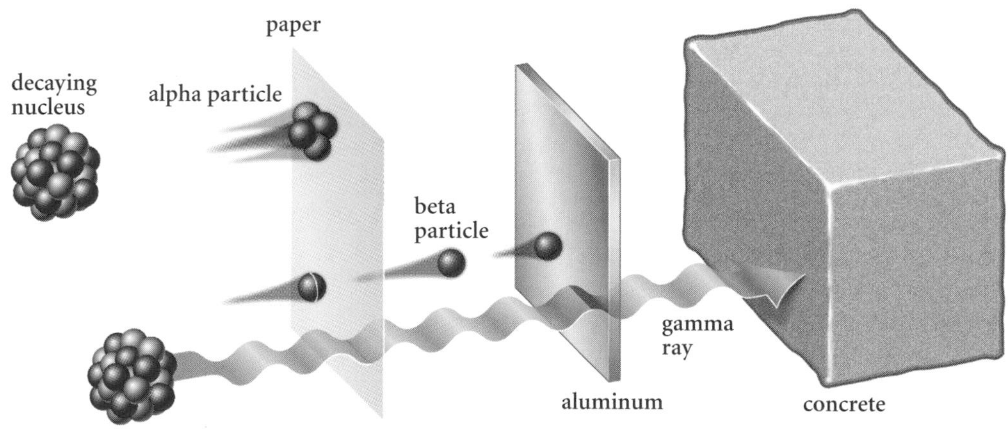

radiation

As the nucleus of a radioactive element decays, it releases alpha particles, beta particles, or gamma rays. Alpha rays (a stream of alpha particles) are the weakest form of radiation and can be stopped by paper. Beta rays (a stream of beta particles) are able to pass through paper but not through aluminum. Gamma rays (a form of electromagnetic radiation) are the strongest. They are able to pass through paper and aluminum, but not through a block of lead or concrete.

Did You Know?

radioactivity

Within the nuclei of stable atoms, such as those of lead, the force binding the protons and neutrons to each other individually is great enough to hold the nuclei together as a whole. In the nuclei of other atoms, especially of heavy ones such as uranium atoms, this energy is not great enough, and the nuclei are unstable. An unstable nucleus gives off particles and energy in a process known as *radioactivity.* When enough particles and energy have been given off to create a new, stable nucleus (often the nucleus of an entirely different element), the radioactivity ceases. For example, uranium 238, a very unstable element, goes through 18 different stages of decay before finally turning into a stable isotope of lead, lead 206. (Some of the intermediate stages include the heavier elements thorium, radium, radon, and polonium.) All known elements with an atomic number greater than 83 (bismuth) are radioactive, and many isotopes of elements with lower atomic numbers are radioactive too.

point. The bodies of echinoderms, such as starfish and sea urchins, are radially symmetrical. *Compare* **bilateral symmetry.**

ra•di•an (rā′dē-ən) A unit of angular measure equal to a little more than 57°. This is the measure of an angle whose vertex is the center of a circle and whose two rays intersect the circle so as to form an arc with the same length as the circle's radius.

ra•di•ant (rā′dē-ənt) **1.** Sending forth light, heat, or other radiation: *a radiant star.* **2.** Consisting of or transmitted as radiation.

radiant energy Energy in the form of waves, especially electromagnetic waves. Radio waves, x-rays, and visible light are all forms of radiant energy.

ra•di•a•tion (rā′dē-ā′shən) **1a.** Energy in the form of electromagnetic waves or streams of particles, such as photons or electrons. Radiation is given off by nuclear reactions (as in fission) and by radioactive decay. **b.** The emission or movement of such energy through space or a medium, such as air. *See Notes at* **conduction, electromagnetic radiation. 2.** The use of such energy, especially x-rays, in medical diagnosis and treatment.

ra•di•a•tive zone (rā′dē-ə-tĭv) The layer of a star, especially the sun, that lies just outside the core, where energy is transferred by means of radiation. In this layer, photons travel around in random movements until they enter the convection zone.

rad•i•cal (răd′ĭ-kəl) **1.** A root, such as $\sqrt{2}$, especially as indicated by a radical sign ($\sqrt{}$). **2.** A group of atoms that behaves as a unit in chemical reactions and is often not stable except as part of a molecule. The hydroxyl, ethyl, and phenyl radicals are examples. Radicals are unchanged by chemical reactions.

rad•i•cand (răd′ĭ-kănd′) The number or expression written under a radical sign, such as the 3 in $\sqrt{3}$.

ra•di•o (rā′dē-ō) *Noun.* **1.** The equipment used to generate, alter, transmit, and receive radio waves so that they carry information. —*Adjective.* **2.** Involving the emission of radio waves: *radio frequency.*

ra•di•o•ac•tive decay (rā′dē-ō-ăk′tĭv) The spontaneous breakdown of a radioactive nucleus into a lighter nucleus. Radioactive decay causes the release of radiation in the form of alpha particles, beta particles, or gamma rays. The end result of radioactive decay is the creation of a stable atomic nucleus.

ra•di•o•ac•tiv•i•ty (rā′dē-ō-ăk-tĭv′ĭ-tē) The emission of radiation by unstable atomic nuclei undergoing radioactive decay.

radio astronomy The branch of astronomy dealing with the detection of objects in space by means of the radio waves that these objects emit.

ra•di•o•car•bon (rā′dē-ō-kär′bən) A radioactive isotope of carbon, especially carbon 14.

radiocarbon dating A technique for measuring the age of organic remains based on the rate of decay of carbon 14. The carbon 14 present in an organism at the time of its death decays at a steady rate, and so the age of the remains can be

Did You Know?
radiocarbon dating

The cells of all living things contain carbon atoms that they take in from their environment. Back in the 1940s, the American chemist Willard Libby used this fact to determine the ages of organisms long dead. Most carbon atoms have six protons and six neutrons in their nuclei and are called carbon 12. Carbon 12 is very stable. But a tiny percentage of carbon is made of carbon 14, or *radiocarbon,* which has six protons and eight neutrons and is not stable: half of any sample of it decays into other atoms after 5,700 years. Carbon 14 is continually being created in the Earth's atmosphere by the interaction of nitrogen and gamma rays from outer space. Since atmospheric carbon 14 arises at about the same rate that the atom decays, the Earth's levels of carbon 14 have remained constant. In living organisms, which are always taking in carbon, the levels of carbon 14 likewise stay constant. But in a dead organism, no new carbon is coming in, and its carbon 14 gradually begins to decay. So by measuring carbon 14 levels in an organism that died long ago, researchers can figure out when it died. The procedure of radiocarbon dating can be used for remains that are up to 50,000 years old.

calculated from the amount of carbon 14 that is left.

radio frequency A frequency at which radio waves can be transmitted, ranging from extremely low frequency (below 3000 hertz) to extremely high frequency (between 30 and 300 gigahertz).

ra•di•o•i•so•tope (rā′dē-ō-ī′sə-tōp′) A radioactive isotope of a chemical element.

ra•di•ol•o•gy (rā′dē-ŏl′ə-jē) The branch of medicine that deals with the use of x-rays and other forms of radiation in diagnosis and treatment.

ra•di•om•e•ter (rā′dē-ŏm′ĭ-tər) A device used to detect and measure radiation. Radiometers consist of a glass bulb containing a partial vacuum in which four diamond-shaped paddles are mounted on a central axis. Each paddle is black on one side and silvery on the other. When radiation, such as sunlight, strikes them, the black side absorbs radiation and the silvery side reflects it, resulting in a temperature difference between the two sides that causes the paddles to spin. The stronger the radiation, the faster the paddles spin.

ra•di•o•met•ric dating (rā′dē-ō-mĕt′rĭk) A method for determining the age of an object based on the concentration of a particular radioactive isotope contained within it. The amount of the isotope in the object is compared to the amount of the isotope's decay products. The object's approximate age can then be figured out using the known rate of decay of the isotope. Radiocarbon dating is one kind of radiometric dating, used for determining the age of organic remains that are less than 50,000 years old. For inorganic matter and for older materials, isotopes of other elements, such as potassium, uranium, and strontium, are used.

ra•di•o•sonde (rā′dē-ō-sŏnd′) An instrument that is carried into the atmosphere, usually by balloon, to gather and transmit information about the weather.

radio wave An electromagnetic wave having a low frequency and long wavelength. Radio waves are used for the transmission of both radio and television broadcasts. They also include the microwaves used for cooking. Some celestial objects, such as pulsars, also emit radio waves. *See more at* **electromagnetic spectrum.**

ra•di•um (rā′dē-əm) A rare, bright-white, highly radioactive element that is an alkaline-earth metal and gives off its own light. It occurs naturally in very small amounts in ores and minerals containing uranium. Radium is used as a source of radon gas for the treatment of disease and as a neutron source for scientific research. The most common of its several isotopes has a half-life of 1,622 years. *Symbol* **Ra.** *Atomic number* 88. *See* **Periodic Table,** pages 262–263.

ra•di•us (rā′dē-əs) *Plural* **radii** (rā′dē-ī′) *or* **radiuses. 1.** A line segment that joins the center of a circle or sphere with any point on the circumference of the circle or the surface of the sphere. It is half the length of the diameter. **2.** The shorter and thicker of the two bones of the

Did You Know?

rain forest

Rain forests are, not surprisingly, forests where it rains a lot—between 160 and 400 inches (406.4 and 1,016 centimeters) a year. Most of the world's rain forests lie near the equator and have tropical climates with temperatures that remain around 80°F (26.6°C) all year long. However, there are also cooler rain forests, such as the one in the Pacific Northwest region of the United States and Canada. The largest rain forest in the world is the one located in the Amazon River basin in South America. Rain forests are extremely important because they help regulate the world's climate and because they host such extraordinary diversity of life. Scientists believe that as many as half of the Earth's different species of plants and animals are found only in the rain forests, which take up a mere 7 percent of the world's landmass. Among other benefits, this biodiversity supports important biological research. For example, many of the natural chemicals used in prescription drugs are found in plants that grow only in rain forests. Unfortunately, the demand for agriculture is causing many people to turn rain forests into farms and grazing land, and by some estimates, more than half of the Earth's original rain forests have already been burned or cut down.

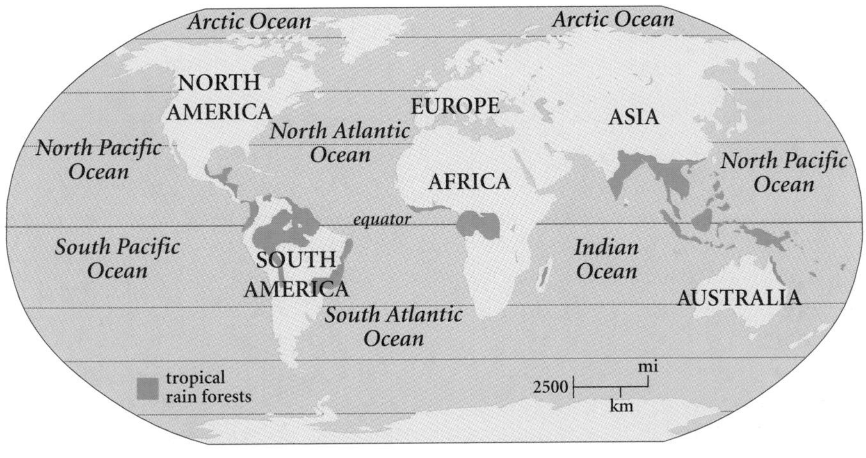

forearm or the lower portion of the foreleg. *See more at* **skeleton.**

ra•don (rā′dŏn) A colorless, odorless, radioactive element that is a noble gas. It is produced by the radioactive decay of radium and occurs in minute amounts in soil, rocks, and the air near the ground. Radon is used as a source of radiation for the treatment of cancer and other diseases. Its most stable isotope has a half-life of about four days. *Symbol* **Rn.** *Atomic number* 86. *See* **Periodic Table,** pages 262–263.

rain (rān) Water that condenses from vapor in the atmosphere and falls to earth as separate drops from clouds.

rain•bow (rān′bō′) An arc-shaped spectrum of color seen in the sky opposite the sun, especially after rain, caused by the refraction and reflection of sunlight by droplets of water suspended in the air.

rain forest A dense evergreen forest with an annual rainfall of at least 160 inches (406.4 centimeters).

RAM (răm) Short for *random access memory.* The main memory of a computer, in which data can be accessed by the central processing unit in any order without having to go through other data first. The random access of data greatly increases processing speed and efficiency.

William Ramsay

Ram•say (răm′zē), Sir **William** 1852–1916. British chemist who discovered the inert gases argon, neon, xenon, and krypton.

ran•dom-ac•cess memory (răn′dəm-ăk′sĕs) *See* **RAM.**

range (rānj) **1.** The set of all values that a given function may have. *Compare* **domain. 2.** The difference between the smallest and largest values in a set of data. If the lowest test score of a group of students is 54 and the highest is 94, the range is 40.

rap•id eye movement (răp′ĭd) *See* **REM.**

rap•tor (răp′tər) **1.** A bird of prey, such as a hawk, eagle, or owl. **2.** Any of various mostly small, slender, meat-eating dinosaurs of the Cretaceous Period. Raptors had hind legs that were adapted for leaping and large, curved claws used for grasping and tearing at prey. Raptors were probably related to birds, and some even had feathers.

rare-earth element (râr′ûrth′) *See* **lanthanide.**

ra•tio (rā′shō, rā′shē-ō′) A relationship between two quantities, normally expressed as the quotient of one divided by the other. For example, if a box contains six red marbles and four blue marbles, the ratio of red marbles to blue marbles is 6 to 4, also written 6:4. A ratio can also be expressed as a decimal or percentage.

ra•tion•al number (răsh′ə-nəl) A number that can be expressed as an integer or a quotient of integers. For example, 2, –5, and $\frac{1}{2}$ are rational numbers.

ray (rā) **1.** *Physics.* A thin line or narrow beam of light or other radiation. **2.** *Mathematics.* A geometric figure consisting of the part of a line that is on one side of a point on the line. **3.** *Botany.* A narrow flower resembling a petal, such as one of those surrounding the disk-shaped flower cluster of a daisy or sunflower.

Rb The symbol for **rubidium.**

Re The symbol for **rhenium.**

re•ac•tant (rē-ăk′tənt) A substance participating in a chemical reaction, especially one present at the start of the reaction.

re•ac•tion (rē-ăk′shən) **1.** A rearrangement of the atoms or molecules of two or more substances that come into contact with each other, resulting in the formation of one or more new substances. Chemical reactions are caused by electrons of one substance interacting with those of another. The reaction of an acid with a base, for example, results in the creation of a salt and water. Some, but not all, reactions can be reversed. **2.** A change to the structure of an atomic nucleus; a nuclear reaction. **3.** An action that results directly from or counteracts another action, especially the change in a body's motion as a result of a force applied to it. Some reactions counteract forces and are not readily apparent. When an object rests on a surface, such as a table, for example, the downward force it applies to the surface is counteracted by an equal but upwards force, or reaction, applied by the surface. *See more at* **Newton's laws of motion.**

read-on•ly memory (rēd′ōn′lē) *See* **ROM.**

re•a•gent (rē-ā′jənt) Any substance involved in a chemical reaction, especially one used to detect, measure, or produce another substance. *Compare* **agent.**

reaction

reaction of a nickel sulfate solution with an ammonia solution

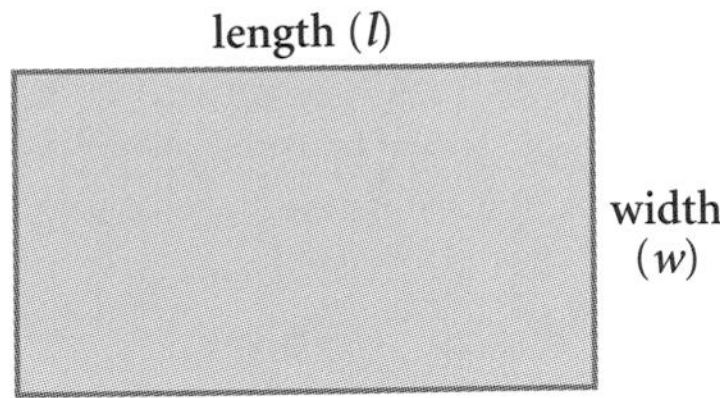

rectangle

To calculate the area of a rectangle, multiply the length by the width. A rectangle with a length of 10 feet and a width of 5 feet has an area of 50 square feet.

re•al number (rē′əl) A number that is rational or irrational and not imaginary. The numbers 2, –12.5, $\frac{3}{7}$, and pi are all real numbers.

re•ceiv•er (rĭ-sē′vər) A device, as in a radio or telephone, that converts incoming radio or microwave signals to a form, such as sound or light, that can be perceived by humans.

Re•cent (rē′sənt) *See* **Holocene.**

re•cep•ta•cle (rĭ-sĕp′tə-kəl) The enlarged upper end of a flower stalk that bears the flower or group of flowers. *See more at* **flower.**

re•cep•tor (rĭ-sĕp′tər) **1.** A nerve ending specialized to sense or receive stimuli. Skin receptors respond to stimuli such as touch and pressure and signal the brain by activating portions of the nervous system. Receptors in the nose detect odors. **2.** A cell structure or site that is capable of combining with a hormone, antigen, or other chemical substance.

re•ces•sive (rĭ-sĕs′ĭv) Relating to the form of a gene that is not expressed as a trait in an individual unless two such genes are inherited, one from each parent. In an organism having two different genes for a trait, the recessive form is suppressed by its counterpart, or dominant, form located on the other of a pair of chromosomes. *See more at* **inheritance.** *Compare* **dominant.**

re•cip•ro•cal (rĭ-sĭp′rə-kəl) Either of a pair of numbers whose product is 1. For example, the number 3 is the reciprocal of $\frac{1}{3}$.

re•com•bi•nant DNA (rē-kŏm′bə-nənt) A form of DNA produced by combining genetic material from two different sources by means of genetic engineering. Recombinant DNA can be used to change the genetic makeup of a cell, as in adding a gene to make a bacterial cell produce insulin.

rec•tan•gle (rĕk′tăng′gəl) A four-sided plane figure with four right angles. A rectangle whose sides are equal is a square.

Did You Know?

red blood cells

Blood contains many cell types, but the distinctive red color comes from the aptly named *red blood cells* (RBCs). RBCs have their rich red color because of a vitally important iron-containing protein called hemoglobin. The protein picks up oxygen molecules as the blood exchanges gases in the lungs. The RBCs then carry oxygen to the far reaches of the body, where it is released for use by other cells, such as those of the brain and muscles. Just as importantly, after the RBC drops off its load of oxygen, its hemoglobin picks up carbon dioxide, the waste product of those brain and muscle cells, and brings it back to the lungs to be breathed out. All animals have some oxygen distribution system, but only vertebrate animals use RBCs. In some invertebrate animals, such as the earthworm, oxygen is transported using hemoglobin that is freely dissolved in the blood. Other invertebrates don't use hemoglobin at all. The horseshoe crab, for instance, uses copper instead of iron, making its blood blue instead of red.

rec•ti•lin•e•ar (rĕk′tə-lĭn′ē-ər) Relating to, consisting of, or moving in a straight line or lines: *a rectilinear path.*

rec•tum (rĕk′təm) The lower end of the digestive tract, extending from the colon to the anus.

re•cy•cle (rē-sī′kəl) To collect and usually reprocess discarded materials for reuse, often in another form. For example, newspaper and other paper waste can be reprocessed to make cardboard or insulation, and plastics can be melted down and molded into new products. Recycling helps reduce pollution and conserve natural resources.

red blood cell (rĕd) Any of the disc-shaped cells that circulate in the blood of vertebrate animals, contain hemoglobin, and give blood its red color. The hemoglobin binds to oxygen, which is then transported by the cells to all of the tissues of the

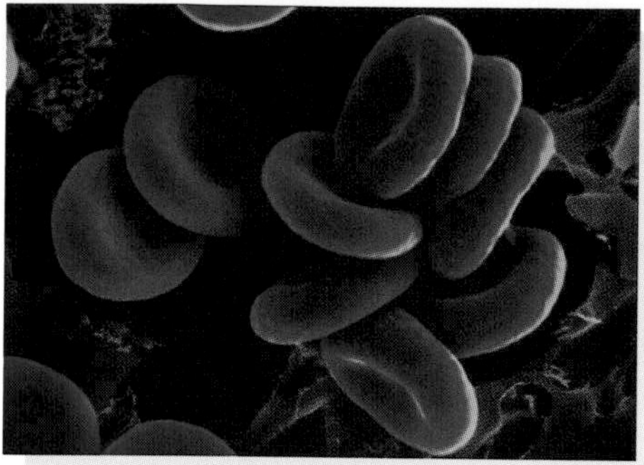

red blood cell

body. The red blood cells of mammals have no nucleus. Red blood cells are formed in the bone marrow. Also called *erythrocyte. See more at* **cell.**

red dwarf A star that is cool, small, and very faint. Red dwarfs burn very slowly and live for about 100 billion years. Although they are difficult to see, they are likely the most abundant type of star. Proxima Centauri is a red dwarf star.

red giant A star of great size and brightness that has a relatively low surface temperature, making it appear red. The sun will become a red giant in several billion years. *See more at* **star.** *See Note at* **dwarf star.**

red shift An increase in the wavelength of radiation emitted by a receding celestial body as a result of the Doppler effect. Objects appear reddish because the longer wavelengths of light are at the red end of the visible spectrum. *Compare* **blue shift.** *See Note at* **Doppler effect.**

red tide A population explosion of certain species of dinoflagellates, a kind of protozoan found in plankton. The dinoflagellates color the water red or reddish-brown, and secrete a toxin that kills fish. Red tide usually occurs in warm coastal waters.

re•duc•tion (rĭ-dŭk′shən) **1.** *Mathematics.* The changing of a fraction into a simpler form, especially by dividing the numerator and denominator by a common factor. For example, the fraction $\frac{8}{12}$ can be reduced to $\frac{4}{6}$, which can be further reduced to $\frac{2}{3}$, in each case by dividing both the numerator and denominator by 2. **2.** *Chemistry.* A chemical reaction in which an atom or ion gains electrons, thus undergoing a decrease in valence. If an iron atom having a valence of +3 gains an electron, the valence decreases to +2. *Compare* **oxidation.**

red•wood (rĕd′wo͝od′) A very tall, cone-bearing evergreen tree that grows along the coast of northwest California and southern Oregon. Redwoods can grow to a height of over 300 feet (91.4 meters).

Reed (rēd), **Walter** 1851–1902. American physician and army surgeon who proved that yellow fever was transmitted by the *Aedes aegypti* mosquito.

reef (rēf) An irregular mass of rock or coral that rises up to or near the surface of a body of water. *See more at* **coral reef.**

USAGE

refraction/reflection

The words *refraction* and *reflection* describe two different ways that a light wave, sound wave, or other wave can move when it encounters a boundary between two media. The media can be two different substances, such as glass and air, or they can be regions of a single substance that are in different states, such as regions of air that are at different temperatures. Reflection occurs when a wave hits the boundary and returns immediately to its original medium. Refraction occurs when a wave passes from one medium to another and is bent; that is, the wave deviates from the straight-line path it would have otherwise followed. For example, light passing through a prism is bent when it enters the prism and again when it leaves the prism. The light is therefore *refracted.* Light striking a mirror bounces off the silver backing without entering it. The light is therefore *reflected.* The boundary between the media does not have to be abrupt for reflection or refraction to occur. On a hot day, the air over the surface of an asphalt road is warmer than the air above it. Because light travels at different speeds in these two regions, we see an image that shimmers because its light waves are refracted.

■ **refraction**

Light waves bend as they pass from one substance to another. This pencil appears to be bent at various angles as the light passes through air only; through air and glass; through water, air, and glass; and through water and glass.

re•fin•er•y (rĭ-fī′nə-rē) An industrial plant for purifying a substance, such as petroleum or sugar, or converting it to a form that is more useful. These processes are carried out by mechanical and chemical means.

re•flect•ing telescope (rĭ-flĕk′tĭng) A telescope in which light from an object is gathered and focused by a concave mirror. *See more at* **telescope.** *See Note at* **mirror.**

re•flec•tion (rĭ-flĕk′shən) **1.** The turning back of a wave, such as a light or sound wave, when it encounters a boundary. Reflected waves return immediately to their original medium instead of entering the medium they encounter. ❖ According to the **law of reflection,** the angle of reflection of a reflected wave is equal to its angle of incidence. *See more at* **wave.** *Compare* **refraction. 2.** Something, such as sound, light, or heat, that is reflected.

re•flex (rē′flĕks′) An automatic, involuntary response to a stimulus, as the withdrawal of a body part from a painful stimulus such as burning heat.

re•fract•ing telescope (rĭ-frăk′tĭng) A telescope in which light from an object is gathered and focused by lenses. *See more at* **telescope.**

re•frac•tion (rĭ-frăk′shən) **1.** The bending or turning of a wave, such as a light or sound wave, when it passes from one medium to another medium of different density. *See more at* **wave.** *Compare* **reflection. 2.** The apparent change in position of a celestial body caused by the bending of light as it enters the Earth's atmosphere.

re•frig•er•ant (rĭ-frĭj′ər-ənt) A substance, such as ice or ammonia, used to cool something by absorbing heat from it. Refrigerants are usually substances that evaporate quickly. In the process of evaporation they draw heat from surrounding substances.

re•gen•er•a•tion (rĭ-jĕn′ə-rā′shən) Regrowth of lost or destroyed parts or organs. Certain lizards, for example, can regenerate their tails if they lose them to a predator, and a number of invertebrate animals, such as starfish, can be cut into several pieces that will each regenerate into a whole new organism. Regeneration is common in plants, where cuttings can grow into a new plant.

reg•o•lith (rĕg′ə-lĭth′) The layer of soil and loose rock resting on bedrock, constituting the surface of most land.

reg•u•lar (rĕg′yə-lər) Having all sides or faces equal. A square is a regular polygon, and a cube is a regular polyhedron.

Reg•u•lus (rĕg′yə-ləs) A bright binary star in the constellation Leo.

re•gur•gi•ta•tion (rē-gûr′jĭ-tā′shən) **1.** The return of undigested food from the stomach to the mouth. **2.** The food so returned.

rel•a•tive humidity (rĕl′ə-tĭv) The ratio of the actual amount of water vapor present in the air at a given temperature to the maximum amount that the air could hold at that temperature. Relative humidity is expressed as a percentage. *Compare* **absolute humidity.**

rel•a•tiv•i•ty (rĕl′ə-tĭv′ĭ-tē) The two-part theory of physical laws developed by Albert Einstein. The first part, called the **theory of special relativity,** states that the laws of physics apply equally to any body or system of bodies having unchanging motion, and that the speed of light is always constant. The second part, the **theory of general relativity,** extends the first part to bodies in accelerated motion, such as bodies in gravitational fields. Among the many consequences of the theory are that measurements of speed and time depend on the motion of the observer, that mass and energy are equivalent, and that

Did You Know?
relativity

Developed as part of the theory of special relativity, Einstein's formula $E=mc^2$ expresses the equivalence of energy and mass. Energy (E) equals mass (m) multiplied by the square of the speed of light (c). Since the speed of light is a large number (186,000 miles per second), the formula shows that even small amounts of mass contain enormous amounts of energy. A mass weighing one-thirtieth of a milligram, if converted into energy, would equal the heat and light put out by a 100-watt light bulb over an entire year! This energy is stored in the mass itself and in the energy that holds it together, such as the energy that keeps the protons and neutrons together in the atomic nucleus. Einstein's formula opened the way to the discovery of nuclear energy, the energy that is released when atomic nuclei break apart or fuse together.

time and space form a continuum called space-time. *See Notes at* **acceleration, Einstein, gravity, space-time.**

re•lay (rē′lā) An electrical switch that is operated by an electromagnet, such as a solenoid. When a small current passes through the electromagnet's coiled wire, it causes a movable iron bar to pivot and open or close the switch.

REM (rĕm) Short for *rapid eye movement.* A stage of sleep characterized by twitching movements of the muscles of the eyes and face, faster heartbeat, and increased circulation to the brain. Dreaming takes place during REM sleep.

re•main•der (rĭ-mān′dər) *Mathematics.* In division, the difference between the dividend and the product of the quotient and divisor.

re•mis•sion (rĭ-mĭsh′ən) A lessening or disappearance of the symptoms of a disease, especially cancer.

rem•o•ra (rĕm′ər-ə) Any of several fish having a sucking disk on their head with which they attach themselves to sharks and other larger fish. They feed mainly on scraps of food left over from the sharks' meals.

re•nal (rē′nəl) Relating to the kidneys: *renal disease.*

re•new•a•ble (rĭ-no͞o′ə-bəl) Relating to a natural resource, such as solar energy or wood, that is never used up or that can be replaced by new growth. *Compare* **nonrenewable.**

re•pro•duc•tion (rē′prə-dŭk′shən) The process by which cells and organisms produce other cells and organisms of the same kind. Cell reproduction usually involves division of a cell into two identical parts by means of mitosis or into four different parts by meiosis. ❖ The reproduction of organisms by the union of male and female reproductive cells (gametes) is called **sexual reproduction.** Most multicellular animals reproduce sexually. ❖ Reproduction in which offspring are produced by a single parent, without the union of reproductive cells, is called **asexual reproduction.** The fission (splitting) of bacterial cells is a form of asexual reproduction. Many plants and fungi are capable of reproducing both sexually and asexually, as are some animals, such as sponges.

re•pro•duc•tive cell (rē′prə-dŭk′tĭv) A cell whose nucleus unites with that of a cell of the opposite sex to form a new organism. A reproductive cell contains only a single (haploid) set of chromosomes. Animal egg and sperm cells, the nuclei in grains of pollen, and egg cells in plant ovules are all reproductive cells. Also called *gamete, sex cell. See Note at* **mitosis.**

reproductive system The system of organs involved with the reproduction of an organism,

reservoir
Hollywood Reservoir, Los Angeles

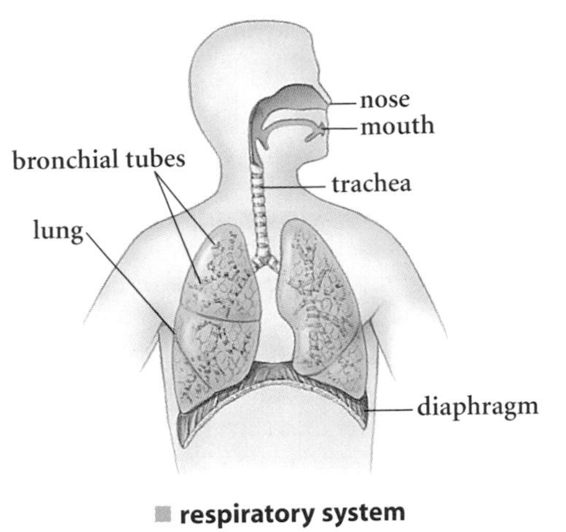

respiratory system

especially sexual reproduction. In flowering plants, for example, the reproductive system consists of pistils and stamens. In mammals, it consists mainly of the ovaries, uterus, and vagina in females and the testes and penis in males.

rep•tile (rĕp′tīl′) Any of various cold-blooded vertebrate animals that have skin covered with scales or horny plates, breathe air with lungs, and usually have a three-chambered heart. Reptiles include the crocodiles, snakes, turtles, and lizards.

res•er•voir (rĕz′ər-vwär′) **1.** A natural or artificial pond or lake used for the storage of water. **2.** An underground mass of rock or sediment that is porous and permeable enough to allow oil or natural gas to accumulate in it.

res•in (rĕz′ĭn) **1.** Any of numerous clear or translucent, yellowish or brownish substances that ooze from certain trees and plants. Resins are used in products such as varnishes, lacquers, adhesives, plastics, and drugs. *See Note at* **amber. 2.** Any of various artificial substances, such as polyurethane, that have similar properties to natural resins and are used to make plastics.

re•sis•tance (rĭ-zĭs′təns) **1.** A force, such as friction, that prevents or slows down motion: *a car shaped to lessen wind resistance.* **2.** The ability of a material or object to slow down the free flow of electrons of an electric current. Good conductors, such as copper, have low resistance. Good insulators, such as rubber, have high resistance. Resistance results in a change of electric energy into heat. **3.** The degree to which an organism can defend itself against a disease or withstand the effects of a toxic substance, such as an environmental pollutant.

re•sis•tor (rĭ-zĭs′tər) A device used to control current in an electric circuit by providing resistance.

res•o•nance (rĕz′ə-nəns) The phenomenon whereby an oscillating system, such as a swing, will oscillate more strongly when it is exposed to a periodic force that is applied with the same frequency as that of the oscillating system. For example, a swing will swing to greater heights if each consecutive push on it is timed to be in rhythm with the initial swing. A radio is tuned by adjusting the frequency of the receiver so that it matches that of the incoming radio waves.

res•pi•ra•tion (rĕs′pə-rā′shən) **1.** The process by which organisms exchange gases, especially oxygen and carbon dioxide, with the environment. In air-breathing vertebrates, respiration takes place in the lungs. In fish and many invertebrates, respiration takes place through the gills. Respiration in green plants occurs during photosynthesis. **2.** *See* **cellular respiration.**

res•pi•ra•to•ry system (rĕs′pər-ə-tôr′ē) The system of organs and structures in which gas exchange takes place, consisting of the lungs and airways in air-breathing vertebrates, gills in fish and many invertebrates, the outer covering of the body in worms, and specialized air ducts in insects.

re•tic•u•late (rĭ-tĭk′yə-lĭt) Resembling or forming a net or network: *reticulate veins of a leaf.*

re•tic•u•lum (rĭ-tĭk′yə-ləm) The second division of the stomach in ruminant animals, which together with the rumen contains microorganisms that digest fiber. The reticulum's contents are regurgitated for further chewing as part of the cud. *See more at* **ruminant.**

ret•i•na (rĕt′n-ə) The light-sensitive membrane that lines the inside of the back of the eyeball, connected to the brain by the optic nerve. The retina of vertebrate animals contains specialized cells, called rods and cones, that absorb light.

ret•i•nol (rĕt′n-ôl′) *See* **vitamin A.**

re•tort (rĭ-tôrt′, rē′tôrt′) A glass laboratory vessel in the shape of a bulb with a long, downward-pointing outlet tube. It is used for distillation or decomposition by heat.

ret•ro•grade (rĕt′rə-grād′) Relating to the revolution in an orbit or rotation about an axis of a

USAGE

revolution/rotation

We use the words *revolution* and *rotation*—or the verbs *revolve* and *rotate*—to indicate cyclic patterns. We talk of *crop rotation* to refer to the successive planting of different crops on the same land, or of a *revolving door* to refer to a door turning about a central pivot. In everyday speech *revolution* and *rotation* are often used as synonyms, but in science they are not synonyms and have distinct meanings. The difference between the two terms lies in the location of the central axis that the object turns about. If the axis is outside the body itself—that is, if the object is orbiting about another object—then one complete orbit is called a *revolution.* But if the object is turning about an axis that passes through itself, then one complete cycle is called a *rotation.* This difference is often summed up in the statement: "Earth *rotates* on its axis and *revolves* around the sun."

WORD HISTORY

rhinoceros/hippopotamus

Two of the largest land mammals, the rhinoceros and hippopotamus, also have rather large names. These names, in fact, tell us something about the animals if we know how to figure it out. The rhinoceros's name comes from Greek and is formed from *rhino–,* meaning "nose," and *keros,* meaning "horn." A rhinoceros is thus a "nose-horn." *Hippopotamus* also comes from Greek and is made of the words *hippos,* "horse," and *potamos,* "river." A hippopotamus is therefore a "river horse." The name was invented because hippos spend most of their lives in rivers or other shallow bodies of water (although they are not horses).

celestial body that moves clockwise from east to west, in the direction opposite to the movement of most celestial bodies.

ret•ro•vi•rus (rĕt′rō-vī′rəs) Any of a group of viruses containing RNA in which the RNA can convert to DNA inside a cell. Some retroviruses cause cancer in humans. The virus that causes AIDS is a retrovirus.

re•verse fault (rĭ-vûrs′) A geologic fault in which the hanging wall has moved upward relative to the footwall. Reverse faults occur where two blocks of rock are forced together by compression. *See more at* **fault.**

rev•o•lu•tion (rĕv′ə-lo͞o′shən) **1.** The motion of an object around a point, especially around another object or a center of mass. **2.** A single complete cycle of such motion.

Rf The symbol for **rutherfordium.**

Rg The symbol for **roentgenium.**

Rh The symbol for **rhodium.**

rhe•ni•um (rē′nē-əm) A very rare, dense, silvery-white metallic element with a very high melting point. It is used to make catalysts and electrical contacts. *Symbol* **Re.** *Atomic number* 75. *See* **Periodic Table,** pages 262–263.

rhe•o•stat (rē′ə-stăt′) A resistor whose resistance can be continuously varied between two extremes so as to control the flow of current in an electric circuit.

rhe•sus monkey (rē′səs) A small, yellowish-brown monkey of India, widely used in biological and medical research. The Rh (Rhesus) factor was first discovered in rhesus monkeys.

rheu•mat•ic fever (ro͞o-măt′ĭk) A disorder that usually follows infection by certain bacteria and has as symptoms inflammation of the joints, skin, and heart. It occurs mainly in children and can cause permanent damage to the heart valves.

rheu•ma•toid arthritis (ro͞o′mə-toid′) A chronic disease in which the joints, especially of the hands and feet, become inflamed, leading to stiffness, weakness, and loss of movement.

Rh factor (är′āch′) An antigen present in red blood cells, used in the classification of human blood. The blood cells of most people contain an Rh factor. For a blood transfusion to be successful, the blood of the donor must match that of the recipient—both must have or must be missing the Rh factor.

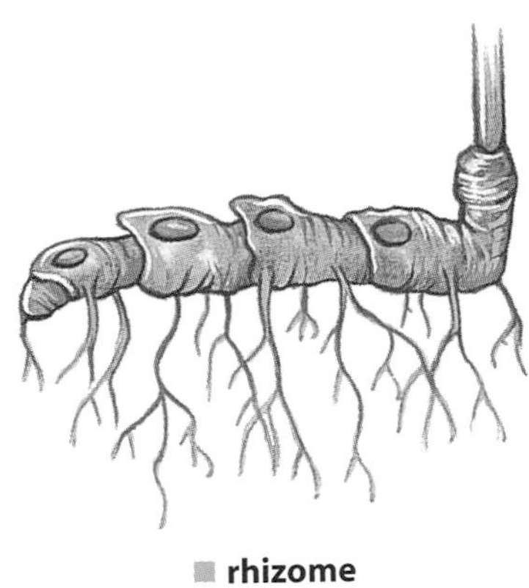

rhizome

Ellen Swallow Richards

rhi•noc•er•os (rī-nŏs′ər-əs) Any of several large African or Asian mammals having tough, mostly hairless skin, short legs with broad hooves, and one or two upright horns on the snout. Rhinoceroses are plant-eating animals.

rhi•zoid (rī′zoid′) A slender, root-like filament by which mosses, liverworts, fungi, and the reproductive generation of ferns attach themselves to the material in which they grow and absorb nourishment.

rhi•zome (rī′zōm′) A plant stem that grows horizontally under or along the ground and often sends out roots and shoots. New plants develop from the shoots. Ginger, iris, and violets have rhizomes. Also called *rootstock*. *Compare* **bulb, corm, runner, tuber.**

rho•di•um (rō′dē-əm) A rare, silvery-white metallic element that is hard, durable, and resistant to acids. It is used as a permanent plating for jewelry and is added to platinum to make hard alloys that can withstand high temperatures. *Symbol* **Rh.** *Atomic number* 45. *See* **Periodic Table,** pages 262–263.

rhom•bo•he•dral (rŏm′bō-hē′drəl) *See* **trigonal.**

rhom•bus (rŏm′bəs) A parallelogram having four equal sides. A square is a rhombus with 90-degree angles.

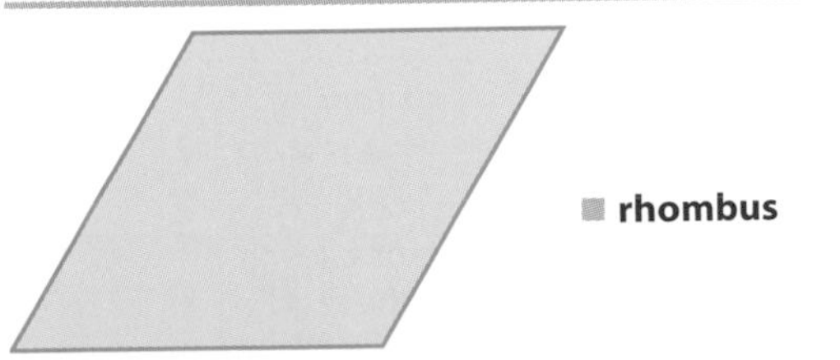

rhombus

rib (rĭb) **1.** Any of a series of long, curved bones extending from the spine and enclosing the chest cavity. In mammals, reptiles, and birds, the ribs curve toward the center of the chest and in most cases attach to the sternum (breastbone). There are 12 pairs of ribs in humans. *See more at* **skeleton. 2.** One of the main veins of a leaf.

rib cage The bony structure in the chest formed by the ribs and sternum (breastbone) that encloses and protects the heart and lungs.

ri•bo•fla•vin (rī′bō-flā′vĭn) A vitamin belonging to the vitamin B complex (B_2) that is important in carbohydrate metabolism and the maintenance of mucous membranes. It is found in milk, leafy vegetables, meat, and egg yolks.

ri•bo•nu•cle•ic acid (rī′bō-no͞o-klē′ĭk) *See* **RNA.**

ri•bo•some (rī′bə-sōm′) A sphere-shaped structure in a cell's cytoplasm that is composed of RNA and protein and is the site of synthesis. Ribosomes are often attached to the membrane of the endoplasmic reticulum. *See* **cell.**

Rich•ards (rĭch′ərdz), **Ellen Swallow** 1842–1911. American chemist and educator. Her survey of water quality led to the establishment of the first water quality standards in the US and the first modern sewage treatment plant.

Rich•ter scale (rĭk′tər) A scale used to rate the strength or total energy of earthquakes. The scale has no upper limit but usually ranges from 1 to 9. Each increase in whole number represents a tenfold increase in magnitude, so that an earthquake rated as 5 is ten times as powerful as one rated as 4. An earthquake with a magnitude of 1 is detectable only by instruments (seismographs); one with a magnitude of 7 is a major earthquake. *See Note at* **earthquake.**

WORD HISTORY

Rigel and star names

The history of astronomy owes much to Arabic scientists of the Middle Ages, who preserved the astronomical learning of ancient Greece and made improvements on it. The English names of many of the brightest stars in the heavens are Arabic in origin. The name of the supergiant star *Rigel,* for example, comes from the Arabic word for "foot" (the foot of the constellation Orion, that is). Some other important stars whose names are Arabic include *Aldebaran,* "the one following (the Pleiades)"; *Betelgeuse,* "hand of Orion"; *Deneb,* "tail" (of the constellation Cygnus, the swan); and *Altair,* "the flying eagle" (in the constellation Aquila, the eagle). The names of other stars are usually Greek or Latin, such as Antares or Sirius, as are the names of the constellations.

rick•ets (rĭk′ĭts) A bone disorder in children that is caused by lack of vitamin D, either in the diet or from lack of exposure to sunlight. In a child with rickets, the bones do not grow properly and become soft and misshapen.

rift (rĭft) **1.** A fault along the border of a rift valley. **2.** A narrow break, crack, or other opening in a rock, usually made by cracking or splitting.

rift valley 1. A long, narrow valley having normal geologic faults on either side. Rift valleys usually form where the Earth's outer layer (the lithosphere) has become thin because of plate-tectonic processes. *See more at* **tectonic boundary. 2.** The deep undersea valley located along the center of the mid-ocean ridge.

rift zone An area of the Earth's crust in which there are numerous rifts and rift valleys. *See more at* **tectonic boundary.**

Ri•gel (rī′jəl) A very bright, bluish-white star in the constellation Orion. It is a supergiant.

right angle An angle having a measure of 90°.

right ascension The position of a celestial object east of the vernal equinox along the celestial equator, measured as a horizontal angle and

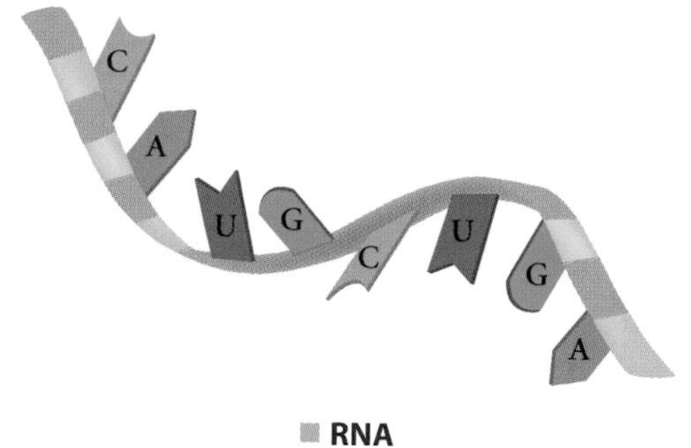

RNA

A: *adenine* U: *uracil*
C: *cytosine* G: *guanine*

expressed in degrees or hours. Right ascension and declination are the measurements used to map objects on the celestial sphere. *See more at* **celestial sphere.**

right triangle A triangle having a right angle.

rig•or mor•tis (rĭg′ər môr′tĭs) Stiffening of the muscles after death. It occurs because the energy needed to interrupt the contraction of muscle fibers is no longer being produced.

ring•worm (rĭng′wûrm′) Any of a number of contagious skin diseases caused by a fungus and resulting in ring-shaped, scaly, itching patches on the skin.

rip current (rĭp) A strong, narrow surface current that flows rapidly away from the shore. Rip currents form when water that has piled up along a shore due to wind and waves suddenly returns to deeper waters. Also called *rip tide.*

riv•er (rĭv′ər) A large, natural stream of fresh water that flows into an ocean, a lake, or another body of water, usually fed by smaller streams that flow into it.

Rn The symbol for **radon.**

RNA (är′ĕn-ā′) Short for *ribonucleic acid.* The nucleic acid that determines protein synthesis in all living cells and the genetic makeup of many viruses. RNA consists of a single strand of nucleotides in a variety of lengths and shapes and is mainly produced in the cell nucleus. v **Messenger RNA** is RNA that carries genetic information from the cell nucleus to the structures in the cytoplasm (known as ribosomes) where protein synthesis takes place. v **Transfer RNA** is RNA that delivers the amino acids necessary for protein synthesis to the ribosomes. *Compare* **DNA.**

ro•bot (rō′bŏt′) A machine that can perform a variety of tasks either on command or by being programmed in advance.

rock (rŏk) **1.** A relatively hard, naturally occurring mineral material. Rock can consist of a single mineral or of several minerals that are either tightly compacted or held together by a cement-like mineral matrix. The three main types of rock are igneous, sedimentary, and metamorphic. **2.** A fairly small piece of such material; a stone. *See Table* on page 298.

rock•et (rŏk′ĭt) A vehicle or device propelled by one or more rocket engines, especially such a vehicle designed to travel through space.

rocket engine An engine that contains all the substances necessary for its operation and is propelled by a jet of hot gases produced by burning fuel. Since they do not rely on the oxygen in the atmosphere, rocket engines can operate in space.

Rocky Mountain spotted fever A bacterial infection characterized by fever, extreme exhaustion, muscle pains, and skin rash. It is transmitted by the bite of infected ticks.

rod (rŏd) One of the rod-shaped cells in the retina of the eye of many vertebrate animals. Rods are responsible for the ability to see in dim light. *Compare* **cone.**

ro•dent (rōd′nt) Any of various very numerous, mostly small mammals having large front teeth used for gnawing. The teeth grow throughout the animal's life, and gnawing keeps them from getting too long. Rodents make up about half the living species of mammals, and include rats, mice, beavers, squirrels, shrews, and hamsters.

Wilhelm Roentgen

roe (rō) The eggs of a fish, often together with the membrane of the ovary they are held in.

Roent•gen (rĕnt′gən, rĕnt′jən), **Wilhelm Konrad** 1845–1923. German physicist who discovered x-rays and developed x-ray photography, revolutionizing medical diagnosis.

roent•gen•i•um (rĕnt-gĕn′ē-əm, rĕnt-jĕn′ē-əm) An artificially produced radioactive element that has only been produced in trace amounts. Its most stable isotope has a half-life of 3.6 seconds. *Symbol* **Rg.** *Atomic number* 111. *See* **Periodic Table,** pages 262-263.

ROM (rŏm) Short for *read-only memory.* Computer hardware that holds permanently stored data. After the data is installed in ROM, it cannot be added to, modified, or deleted. ROM usually contains instructions that enable the computer's operating system to communicate with other hardware.

rook•er•y (ro͝ok′ə-rē) A place where certain birds or animals, such as crows, penguins, and seals, gather to breed.

root (ro͞ot) **1.** A plant part that usually grows underground, secures the plant in place, absorbs minerals and water, and stores food manufactured by leaves and other plant parts. In certain plants, additional roots grow out from the stem above ground, bending down into the soil, to provide more support. **2.** Any of various other plant parts that grow underground, especially an underground stem such as a corm, rhizome, or tuber. **3.** The part of a tooth that is embedded in the jaw and not covered by enamel. **4.** *Mathematics.* **a.** A number that, when multiplied by itself a given number of times, produces a specified number. For example, since $2 \times 2 \times 2 \times 2 = 16$, 2 is a fourth root of 16. **b.** A solution to an equation. For example, a root of the equation $x^2 - 4 = 0$ is 2, since $2^2 - 4 = 0$.

root hair A hair-like outgrowth of a plant root that absorbs water and minerals from the soil.

root•stock (ro͞ot′stŏk′) *See* **rhizome.**

ro•ta•tion (rō-tā′shən) **1.** The motion of an object around its own axis: *the daily rotation of the Earth.* **2.** A single complete cycle of such motion. *See Note at* **revolution.**

ro•ta•tor cuff (rō′tā′tər) A group of muscles and tendons attaching the shoulder to the scapula (shoulder blade) that provide stability to the

ROCK TYPES

IGNEOUS ROCKS	METAMORPHIC ROCKS	SEDIMENTARY ROCKS

HOW THEY FORM

Igneous rocks: Igneous rocks form from cooling of magma (underground) or lava (at the Earth's surface). Many of the rocks that we see on the surface today actually formed deep down in the Earth and were later pushed to the surface by the processes of plate tectonics. Lava forms when magma from deep within the Earth comes up to the surface.

Metamorphic rocks: Metamorphic rocks form when igneous, sedimentary, or other metamorphic rocks are subjected to great pressure or high temperatures deep within the Earth. This can happen on a very small scale where only the rocks in direct contact with a source of heat or pressure become metamorphosed, or it can happen on a regional scale, as along a mountain chain.

Sedimentary rocks: Sedimentary rocks form at the surface of the Earth, through the transport and deposition of sediments by water, wind, or ice. The sediments can be fragments of fossils or sea shells, or small pieces of igneous, metamorphic, or other sedimentary rocks. Some sedimentary rocks form as precipitation of crystals, such as salt, during the evaporation of water.

EXAMPLES

IGNEOUS ROCKS	METAMORPHIC ROCKS	SEDIMENTARY ROCKS
granite, basalt, gabbro, pahoehoe	slate, schist, gneiss, marble	sandstone, limestone, shale, conglomerate

CHARACTERISTICS

Igneous rocks: The crystals of the minerals that make up igneous rocks are tightly locked together because they form close to each other when the magma or lava becomes solid. Individual crystals often have sharp edges and geometric forms reflecting crystal shapes. Because new magma can form underground and move through fractures in rock, igneous rocks often have fractures filled with different types of igneous rock; these magma-filled fractures are called veins or pegmatites.

Metamorphic rocks: The crystals of minerals in metamorphic rocks have been stretched, folded, or changed by the pressure or high temperature to which they have been exposed. Often the crystals have been reorganized into layers. Sometimes, if a mass of rock becomes very hot, partial melting of the original rock occurs, and new minerals form. These minerals are often of gem quality.

Sedimentary rocks: Sediment grains are often rounded because they have been eroded by water, wind, or ice. But they can also be sharp, especially in high mountainous areas, where rocks are mechanically broken down into sediments by the forces exerted by the formation and melting of ice. Sediment grains can be small, like sand, or they can consist of large cobbles and boulders. Often sedimentary rocks are layered, because their sediments were deposited over a long course of time. Sedimentary rocks often contain fossils.

A SLICE OF ROCK SEEN THROUGH A MICROSCOPE

IGNEOUS ROCKS	METAMORPHIC ROCKS	SEDIMENTARY ROCKS
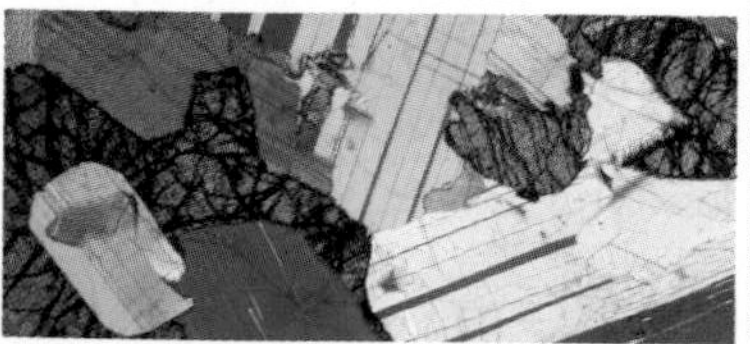	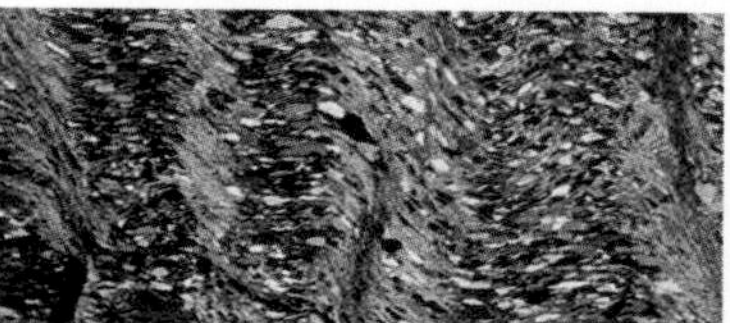	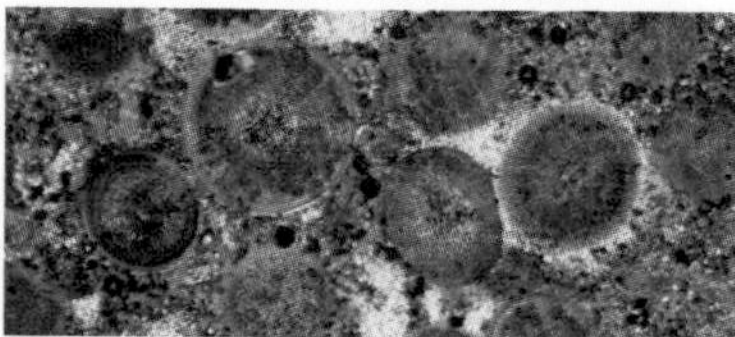

shoulder joint and act to rotate the arm. Injuries to the rotator cuff often happen when the arm is repeatedly moved over the head with great force, as when pitching a baseball.

ro•ti•fer (rō′tə-fər) Any of various tiny multicellular animals living in water and having a wheel-like ring of cilia at their front ends.

Roux (ro͞o), **Pierre Paul Émile** 1853–1933. French bacteriologist who assisted Louis Pasteur on most of his major discoveries. Roux carried out early work on the rabies vaccine and directed the first tests of the diphtheria antitoxin.

Ru The symbol for **ruthenium.**

rub•ber (rŭb′ər) **1.** An elastic material prepared from the milky sap of certain tropical plants, especially the rubber tree, and used after processing in a great variety of products, including electric insulation and tires. **2.** Any of various synthetic materials having properties that are similar to those of this substance.

ru•bel•la (ro͞o-bĕl′ə) *See* **German measles.**

ru•bid•i•um (ro͞o-bĭd′ē-əm) A soft, silvery-white element that is an alkali metal. It ignites spontaneously in air and reacts violently with water. Rubidium is used in photoelectric cells and in making vacuum tubes. *Symbol* **Rb.** *Atomic number* 37. *See* **Periodic Table,** pages 262–263.

ru•by (ro͞o′bē) A deep-red, translucent form of the mineral corundum that is valued as a precious stone.

ru•men (ro͞o′mən) The first and largest division of the stomach in ruminant animals, in which the food is fermented by microorganisms. *See more at* **ruminant.**

ru•mi•nant (ro͞o′mə-nənt) Any of various hoofed, usually horned mammals, such as cattle, sheep, and goats, that have an even number of toes. Ruminants have a stomach divided into four compartments (called the rumen, reticulum, omasum, and abomasum), and chew a cud consisting of regurgitated, partially digested food.

run•ner (rŭn′ər) A slender stem that grows horizontally and puts down roots to form new plants. Strawberries spread by runners. Also called *stolon. Compare* **bulb, corm, rhizome, tuber.**

rust

Rus•sell (rŭs′əl), **Henry** 1877–1957. American astronomer who studied binary stars and developed methods to calculate their mass and distances. He also demonstrated the relationship between types of stars and their brightness.

rust (rŭst) *Noun.* **1.** Any of the various reddish-brown oxides of iron that form on iron and many of its alloys when they are exposed to oxygen in the presence of moisture. *See Note at* **oxidation. 2.** Any of various plant diseases caused by parasitic fungi that produce reddish or brownish spots on leaves. —*Verb.* **3.** To become corroded or oxidized.

ru•the•ni•um (ro͞o-thē′nē-əm) A rare, silvery-gray metallic element that is hard, brittle, and very resistant to corrosion. It is used to harden alloys of platinum and palladium for jewelry and electrical contacts. *Symbol* **Ru.** *Atomic number* 44. *See* **Periodic Table,** pages 262–263.

Ruth•er•ford (rŭ*th*′ər-fərd), **Ernest.** First Baron Rutherford of Nelson. 1871–1937. New Zealand–born British physicist who was a pioneer of subatomic physics. He discovered the atomic nucleus and named the proton. Rutherford demonstrated that radioactive elements give off three types of rays, which he named alpha, beta, and gamma. He also invented the term *half-life* to measure the rate of radioactive decay.

ruth•er•ford•i•um (rŭ*th*′ər-fôr′dē-əm) A synthetic, radioactive element that is produced by bombarding plutonium with carbon or neon ions. Its most stable isotope has a half-life of 65 seconds. *Symbol* **Rf.** *Atomic number* 104. *See* **Periodic Table,** pages 262–263.

S

S The symbol for **sulfur.**

sa•ber-toothed tiger (sā′bər-to͞otht′) Any of various large extinct cats of the Oligocene to Pleistocene Epochs with long upper canine teeth.

Sa•bin (sā′bĭn), **Albert Bruce** 1906–1993. American microbiologist and physician who developed a live-virus vaccine against polio that contained an active form of the polio virus (1957). This replaced the vaccine, invented by Jonas Salk, that contained an inactivated (and less effective) form of the virus.

sac (săk) A bag-like part in an animal or plant, often containing liquids.

sac•cha•rin (săk′ər-ĭn) A white, crystalline powder used as a calorie-free sweetener. It tastes about 500 times sweeter than sugar.

sa•crum (sā′krəm, săk′rəm) A triangular bone at the base of the spine, above the coccyx (tailbone), that forms the rear section of the pelvis. In humans it is made up of five vertebrae that fuse together by adulthood. *See more at* **skeleton.**

Sag•it•tar•i•us (săj′ĭ-târ′ē-əs) A constellation in the Southern Hemisphere near Scorpius and Capricornus.

sal•a•man•der (săl′ə-măn′dər) Any of various lizard-like amphibians that have smooth skin and four usually short legs.

sal•i•cyl•ic acid (săl′ĭ-sĭl′ĭk) A white, crystalline acid used to make aspirin, to treat certain skin conditions, and to preserve and flavor foods.

sa•line (sā′lēn′) Relating to or containing salt; salty. —*Noun* **salinity** (sə-lĭn′ĭ-tē).

Albert Sabin

Jonas Salk

sa•li•va (sə-lī′və) The watery fluid that is secreted into the mouth by glands known as salivary glands. In many animals, including humans, it contains enzymes that help in the digestion of carbohydrates. Saliva also contains mucus, which lubricates food for swallowing.

sal•i•var•y gland (săl′ə-vĕr′ē) A gland that secretes saliva, especially any of three pairs of large glands that secrete saliva into the mouth.

Salk (sôlk), **Jonas Edward** 1914–1995. American microbiologist who developed the first effective vaccine against polio (1954).

salm•on (săm′ən) Any of various large food fish of northern waters, having pinkish flesh. Salmon swim from salt to fresh water to spawn, often climbing short waterfalls and swimming against the currents of rapids.

sal•mo•nel•la (săl′mə-nĕl′ə) A rod-shaped bacterium that causes food poisoning in humans.

salt (sôlt) **1.** A colorless or white crystalline solid, NaCl, found naturally in all animal fluids, seawater, and in underground deposits. It is used widely as a food seasoning and preservative. Also called *sodium chloride.* **2.** Any of a large class of chemical compounds formed when one or more hydrogen ions of an acid are replaced by metallic ions. Salts have an electric charge, conduct electricity, and dissolve completely in water.

salt•pe•ter (sôlt′pē′tər) *See* **potassium nitrate.**

salt•wa•ter (sôlt′wô′tər) Consisting of or living in salty water, especially seawater: *saltwater fish.*

sandbar
sandbars near Neil's Harbour, Nova Scotia

sa•mar•i•um (sə-mâr′ē-əm) A silvery-white metallic element of the lanthanide series that exists in several forms and has seven naturally occurring isotopes. It is used to make glass that absorbs infrared light and to absorb neutrons in nuclear reactors. *Symbol* **Sm.** *Atomic number* 62. *See* **Periodic Table,** pages 262–263.

sand (sănd) **1.** Small, often rounded grains or particles of disintegrated rock, larger than particles of silt. Although sand often consists of quartz, it can consist of any other mineral or rock fragment as well. Coral sand, for example, consists of limestone fragments. **2.** A loose collection or deposit of sand grains.

sand•bar (sănd′bär′) A long mass or low ridge of sand built up in the water along a shore or beach by the action of waves or currents.

sand•stone (sănd′stōn′) A sedimentary rock formed of fine to coarse sand-sized grains that have been either compacted or cemented together. Although sandstone usually consists primarily of quartz, it can also consist of other minerals. Sandstone varies in color from yellow or red to gray or brown. *See Table at* **rock.**

Sang•er (săng′ər), **Frederick** Born 1918. British biochemist. He determined the order of amino acids in the insulin molecule, thereby making it possible to manufacture synthetic insulin. Sanger also developed methods for mapping the structure and function of DNA.

san•i•tar•y landfill (săn′ĭ-tĕr′ē) *See* **landfill.**

sap (săp) The watery fluid that circulates through a plant that has vascular tissues. Sap moving up the xylem carries water and minerals, while sap moving down the phloem carries water and food.

sap•phire (săf′īr′) Any of several fairly pure forms of the mineral corundum, especially a blue form valued as a gem.

sap•ro•phyte (săp′rə-fīt′) An organism, especially a fungus or bacterium, that lives on and gets its nourishment from dead organisms or decaying organic material. *—Adjective* **saprophytic** (săp′rə-fĭt′ĭk).

sar•co•ma (sär-kō′mə) A usually malignant tumor arising in connective tissue.

sat•el•lite (săt′l-īt′) **1.** A celestial body that orbits a planet; a moon. *See Note at* **moon. 2.** An object launched to orbit Earth or another celestial body. Satellites are used for research, communications, weather information, and navigation.

sat•u•rat•ed (săch′ə-rā′tĭd) **1.** Relating to an organic compound in which all the carbon atoms are joined by single bonds and therefore cannot be combined with any additional atoms or radicals. Propane and saturated fatty acids are

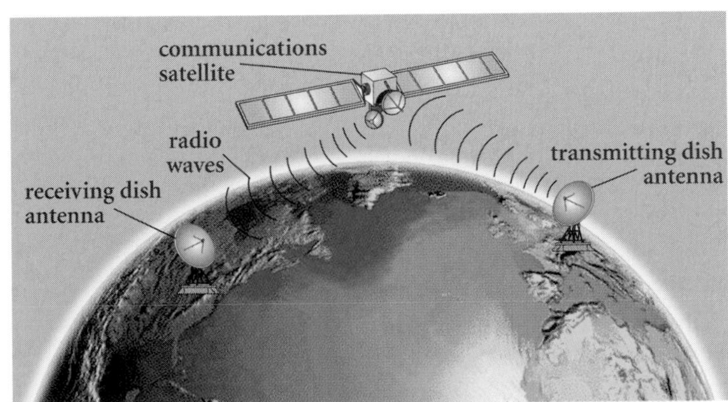

satellite
Communications satellites receive, amplify, and transmit radio signals between dish antennas that may be hundreds of miles apart.

examples of saturated hydrocarbons. *Compare* **unsaturated. 2.** Relating to a solution that is unable to dissolve more of a solute. **3.** Containing as much water vapor as is possible at a given temperature. Air that is saturated has a relative humidity of 100 percent.

saturated fat A fat whose triglyceride molecule contains three saturated fatty acids. Most fats derived from animal sources are saturated fats. Eating foods high in saturated fats can lead to cholesterol levels in the blood that are higher than normal. *Compare* **unsaturated fat.**

sat•u•ra•tion (săch′ə-rā′shən) The vividness of a color's hue. Saturation measures the degree to which a color differs from a gray of the same brightness or lightness. *See more at* **color.**

saturation point The point at which a substance can receive no more of another substance in solution under given conditions.

Sat•urn (săt′ərn) The sixth planet from the sun and the second largest, with a diameter about ten times that of Earth. Saturn is encircled by a large, flat system of rings that are made up mostly of tiny particles of ice. *See Table at* **solar system,** pages 316–317. *See Note at* **planet.**

sau•ri•an (sôr′ē-ən) A lizard or similar reptile.

saur•is•chi•an (sô-rĭs′kē-ən) One of the two main types of dinosaurs. Saurischians have a pelvis similar to that of modern reptiles, and include the meat-eating theropods and the plant-eating sauropods. *Compare* **ornithischian.**

sau•ro•pod (sôr′ə-pŏd′) One of the two types of saurischian dinosaurs, widespread during the Jurassic and Cretaceous Periods. Sauropods were plant-eaters and often grew to tremendous size, having a stout body with thick legs, long slender necks with a small head, and long tails. Sauropods included the apatosaurus (brontosaurus) and brachiosaurus. *Compare* **theropod.**

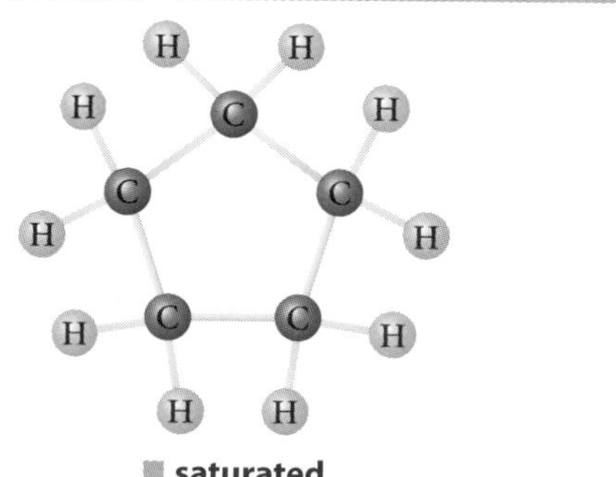

saturated

the ring chain of carbon atoms of a cyclopentane molecule

Saturn

sa•van•na *also* **sa•van•nah** (sə-văn′ə) A flat, treeless grassland of warm regions.

Sb The symbol for **antimony.**

Sc The symbol for **scandium.**

sca•lar (skā′lər) A quantity, such as mass, length, or speed, whose only property is magnitude; a number. *Compare* **vector.**

scale[1] (skāl) **1.** One of the small thin plates forming the outer covering of fish, reptiles, and certain other animals. **2.** A similar part, such as one of the minute structures overlapping to form the covering on the wings of butterflies and moths. **3.** A small, thin, usually dry plant part, such as one of the protective leaves that cover a tree bud or one of the flat structures that bear the reproductive organs on the cones of a conifer. **4.** A plant disease caused by scale insects.

scale[2] **1.** An ordered system of numbering or indexing that is used as a reference standard in measurement, in which each number corresponds to some physical quantity. Some scales, such as temperature scales, have equal intervals; other scales, such as the Richter scale, are arranged as a geometric progression. **2.** An instrument or a machine for weighing.

scale insect Any of various small insects related to the aphids. The young suck juices from plants, and the adult females live under waxy, scale-like shells that they secrete on plant tissue. Scale insects can be very destructive to plants.

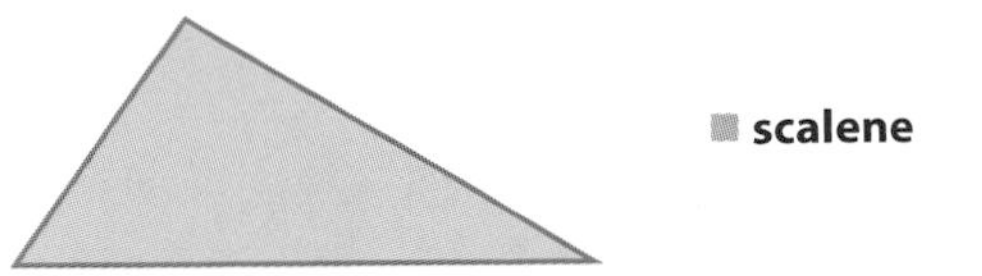

sca•lene (skā′lēn′) Having three unequal sides, as a triangle that is neither equilateral nor isosceles.

scan•di•um (skăn′dē-əm) A soft, silvery, very lightweight metallic element that is found in various rare minerals and is a byproduct in the processing of certain uranium ores. It has a high melting point and is used to make high-intensity lights. *Symbol* **Sc.** *Atomic number* 21. *See* **Periodic Table,** pages 262–263.

scan•ning electron microscope (skăn′ĭng) An electron microscope that moves a beam of electrons across an object and creates a three-dimensional image from both the electrons scattered by the object and the electrons knocked loose from the object.

scanning tunneling microscope A microscope used to make images of individual atoms on the surface of a material. The microscope has a probe ending in a tiny sharp tip that moves along the material's surface while emitting a stream of electrons. The flow of electrons is constant so long as the distance between the tip and the material's surface atoms is held constant. An image is formed based on the continual adjustments made to the height of the tip to keep the electron flow constant over the "bumps" that are the atoms.

scap•u•la (skăp′yə-lə) Either of two flat, triangular bones forming part of the shoulder. In humans and other primates, they lie on the upper part of the back on either side of the spine. Also called *shoulder blade. See more at* **skeleton.**

scar•ab (skăr′əb) Any of several often large beetles with broad black bodies that feed off of dung in which they also lay their eggs.

scar•let fever (skär′lĭt) A severe contagious bacterial disease that is characterized by a high fever and a scarlet rash on the skin. It mainly occurs in children.

scat•ter•ing (skăt′ər-ĭng) The spreading of a stream of particles or a beam of rays, as of light, over a range of directions as a result of collisions with other particles. Scattering is responsible for the color of the sky. On a clear day, the sky is blue, because blue light from the sun is scattered by the atmosphere's particles to a greater degree than other colors of light. At sunset and sunrise, the sky appears red and yellow, because the light from the sun has passed a longer distance through air and some of the blue light has been scattered away, leaving yellow and red light which are less easily scattered.

scav•en•ger (skăv′ən-jər) An animal that feeds on dead organisms, especially a meat-eating animal that eats dead animals rather than hunting live prey. Vultures, hyenas, and wolves are scavengers.

Schee•le (shā′lə), **Karl Wilhelm** 1742–1786. Swedish chemist who discovered a number of compounds and elements. He discovered oxygen around 1771, but because the results of his experiments were not published until 1777, Joseph Priestley is usually credited with the discovery. Scheele made extensive investigations of plant and animal materials, and his work was fundamental to the development of organic chemistry.

schist (shĭst) A metamorphic rock characterized by a very fine alignment of its minerals, which allows it to be easily split into flakes or slabs. Because schist often contains abundant mica, it usually has a shiny, gray appearance. *See Table at* **rock.**

schis•to•so•mi•a•sis (shĭs′tə-sə-mī′ə-sĭs) Any of a group of diseases caused by flatworm parasites that infest the blood of humans and other mammals. Symptoms of the disease include severe diarrhea and eventual damage to vital organs. Schistosomiasis is seen in rural areas of Africa, Latin America, and Asia and is transmitted through contact with contaminated water.

schiz•o•phre•ni•a (skĭt′sə-frē′nē-ə, skĭt′sə-frĕn′ē-ə) Any of a group of severe mental disorders in which a person loses touch with reality. People with schizophrenia also experience abnormal thinking that usually interferes with their ability to work and communicate with others. The biological causes of schizophrenia are not well understood. It is associated with an imbalance of chemical substances in the brain and often runs in families.

School•craft (sko͞ol′krăft′), **Henry Rowe** 1793–1864. American geologist and explorer who discovered the source of the Mississippi River (1832).

Schrö•ding•er (shrō′dĭng-ər, shrā′dĭng-ər), **Erwin** 1887–1961. Austrian physicist who was a founder of the study of wave mechanics. He developed a mathematical equation that describes the wave-like behavior of subatomic particles. Schrödinger's equation was fundamental to the development of quantum mechanics.

sci•at•ic nerve (sī-ăt′ĭk) A thick nerve that arises in the lower part of the spine and passes through the pelvis on its way to the back of the leg. It carries sensory information from the leg to the spine and controls the action of many muscles. The sciatic nerve is the largest nerve in the body.

sci•ence (sī′əns) The investigation of natural phenomena through observation, experimentation, and theoretical explanation. ❖ Science makes use of the **scientific method**, which includes the careful observation of natural phenomena, the formulation of a hypothesis, the conducting of one or more experiments to test the hypothesis, and the drawing of a conclusion that confirms or modifies the hypothesis. *See Note at* **hypothesis.**

sci•en•tif•ic name (sī′ən-tĭf′ĭk) A name used by scientists, especially the taxonomic name of an organism that consists of the genus and species. Scientific names usually come from Latin or Greek. An example is *Homo sapiens,* the scientific name for humans.

scientific notation A method of expressing numbers in terms of a decimal number between 1 and 10 multiplied by a power of 10. The scientific notation for 10,492, for example, is 1.0492×10^4.

scle•ra (sklîr′ə) The tough, white, fibrous tissue that covers all of the eyeball except the cornea.

sco•li•o•sis (skō′lē-ō′sĭs) Abnormal sideways curvature of the spine.

sco•ri•a (skôr′ē-ə) Rough, crusty, solidified lava containing numerous cavities that originated as gas bubbles in the lava while it was still molten.

Scor•pi•us (skôr′pē-əs) A constellation in the Southern Hemisphere near Libra and Sagittarius.

scro•tum (skrō′təm) The external sac of skin that encloses the testes in most mammals.

scur•vy (skûr′vē) A disease caused by lack of vitamin C in the diet. It is characterized by bleeding of the gums, rupture of capillaries under the skin, loose teeth, and weakness of the body.

sea anemone
white-spotted rose anemone

Se The symbol for **selenium.**

sea (sē) **1.** The continuous body of salt water that covers most of the Earth's surface. *See Note at* **ocean. 2.** A region of water within an ocean and partly enclosed by land, such as the North Sea. **3.** A large body of either fresh or salt water that is completely enclosed by land, such as the Caspian Sea. **4.** A mare of the moon.

sea anemone Any of numerous often brightly colored ocean-dwelling animals that resemble flowers and are related to the jellyfish and corals. Anemones are cnidarians and have a flexible cylindrical body with tentacles surrounding a central mouth.

Sea•borg (sē′bôrg′), **Glenn Theodore** 1912–1999. American chemist who led the team that discovered plutonium (1940). In 1944 they discovered americium and curium. By bombarding these two elements with alpha rays, Seaborg produced the elements berkelium and californium.

sea•bor•gi•um (sē-bôr′gē-əm) A synthetic, radioactive element that is produced by bombarding californium with oxygen ions or bombarding lead with chromium ions. Its most stable isotope has a half-life of about 20 seconds. *Symbol* **Sg.** *Atomic number* 106. *See* **Periodic Table,** pages 262–263.

sea cucumber Any of various invertebrate sea animals related to starfish and sea urchins, having a rough cucumber-shaped body and a mouth surrounded by tentacles. To distract an attacking predator, a sea cucumber can expel some of its internal organs, which later grow back.

sea horse Any of several small ocean fish having a head resembling that of a horse, a body covered with bony plates, and a tail that can be curled

■ sea horse

around a supporting object. The male stores eggs in a pouch on its belly until they hatch.

seal (sēl) Any of various meat-eating sea mammals having a streamlined body, thick fur or hair, and limbs in the form of flippers. Seals are related to but smaller than walruses.

sea level The level of the surface of the ocean, used as a standard in determining land elevation or sea depths.

sea lion Any of several large seals, mostly of Pacific waters, having a sleek body with visible ears and brownish fur.

seam (sēm) *Geology.* A thin layer or stratum, as of coal or rock.

sea slug Any of various colorful ocean mollusks that lack a shell and gills but have fringe-like projections that serve as respiratory organs. Also called *nudibranch.*

sea•son (sē′zən) **1.** One of four natural divisions of the year—spring, summer, autumn, and winter—in the North or South Temperate Zones. Each season begins as the sun passes through a solstice or an equinox. **2.** In some tropical climates, either of the two parts—rainy and dry—into which the year is divided.

sea squirt Any of various primitive sea animals having a transparent, sac-shaped body with two siphons. Sea squirts pump water through the siphons and filter it with gill-like structures to catch food particles. Sea squirts belong to the group known as tunicates.

sea urchin Any of various invertebrate sea animals having a round body covered by a shell with movable spines. Sea urchins are related to starfish.

sea•weed (sē′wēd′) Any of various algae or plants that live in ocean waters. Some species are free-floating, while others are attached to the ocean bottom. Seaweed range from the size of a pinhead to large fronds extending up to 100 feet (30.5 meters) in length.

se•ba•ceous gland (sĭ-bā′shəs) Any of the glands in the skin that secrete an oily material (called sebum) into the hair follicles.

se•bum (sē′bəm) The fatty substance secreted by the sebaceous glands in the skin of mammals. It protects and lubricates the skin and hair.

sec Abbreviation of **secant.**

se•cant (sē′kănt′) **1.** A straight line or ray that intersects a curve, especially a circle, at two or more points. **2.** The ratio of the length of the hypotenuse in a right triangle to the side adjacent to an acute angle; the inverse of the cosine.

sec•ond (sĕk′ənd) **1.** A unit of time equal to $\frac{1}{60}$ of a minute. **2.** A unit of angular measurement equal to $\frac{1}{60}$ of a minute of arc.

sec•ond•ar•y (sĕk′ən-dĕr′ē) **1.** Relating to a secondary color. **2.** *Botany.* Relating to the cambium layer of tissue in plants, whose cells divide to create new vascular tissue and cause the plant to become wider and thicker.

secondary color A color produced by mixing two primary colors in equal proportions. *See more at* **color.**

secondary sex characteristic Any of the physical traits in a sexually mature animal that are not directly involved in the act of reproducing. They include breast development in female primates, facial-hair growth in young men, the growth of antlers in antelopes, and colorful plumage in male birds. The appearance of secondary sex characteristics is determined by the sex hormones.

secondary wave An earthquake wave in which rock particles vibrate at right angles to the direction of wave travel. Secondary waves can travel through solids but not through liquids. Also called *S wave. See Note at* **earthquake.**

se•crete (sĭ-krēt′) To produce and discharge a substance, especially from the cells of specialized glands. For example, the endocrine glands secrete hormones.

sec•tor (sĕk′tər) The part of a circle bounded by two radii and the arc between them.

sed•a•tive (sĕd′ə-tĭv) A drug having a calming or quieting effect, often given to reduce anxiety.

sed•i•ment (sĕd′ə-mənt) **1.** *Geology.* Silt, sand, rocks, fossils, and other matter carried and deposited by water, wind, or ice. **2.** *Chemistry.* Particles of solid matter that settle out of a suspension to the bottom of the liquid.

sed•i•men•ta•ry (sĕd′ə-mĕn′tə-rē) Relating to rocks formed when sediment, such as sand or mud, is deposited and becomes tightly compacted. Sandstone, conglomerate, and limestone are examples of sedimentary rocks. *See Table at* **rock.**

seed (sēd) *Noun.* **1.** A part of a gymnosperm or flowering plant that contains an embryo and the food it will need to grow into a new plant. A seed is a mature fertilized ovule. —*Verb.* **2.** To plant seeds in soil. **3.** To attempt to produce rain by cloud seeding. *See more at* **cloud seeding.**

seed coat The outer protective covering of a seed. Also called *testa.*

seed leaf *See* **cotyledon.**

seed•ling (sēd′lĭng) A young plant that is grown from a seed, rather than from a cutting or bulb, for example.

seg•ment (sĕg′mənt) **1.** The portion of a line between any two of its points. **2.** The region bounded by an arc of a circle and the chord that connects the endpoints of the arc. **3.** The portion of a sphere included between a pair of parallel planes that intersect it or are tangent to it.

seis•mic (sīz′mĭk) Relating to an earthquake or to other tremors of the Earth, such as those caused by large explosions: *a seismic disturbance.*

seis•mo•graph (sīz′mə-grăf′) An instrument that detects and records vibrations and movements in the Earth, especially during an earthquake. By comparing the records produced by seismographs located in three or more locations across the Earth, geologists can determine the location and strength of an earthquake. ❖ The record produced by a seismograph is called a **seismogram.**

seismograph

seis•mol•o•gy (sīz-mŏl′ə-jē) The scientific study of earthquakes, including their origin, geographic distribution, effects, and possible prediction.

se•le•ni•um (sĭ-lē′nē-əm) A nonmetallic element that can exist as a gray crystal, a red powder, or a black glassy material. It can convert light directly into electricity, and its ability to conduct electricity increases as light striking it becomes more intense. Because of this, selenium is used in copy machines, photography, and solar cells. *Symbol* **Se.** *Atomic number* 34. *See* **Periodic Table,** pages 262–263.

se•men (sē′mən) A whitish fluid that is produced by the reproductive organs of male mammals and carries sperm cells.

semi– **1.** A prefix that means "half," as in *semicircle,* half a circle. **2.** A prefix that means "partly," "somewhat," or "less than fully," as in *semiconscious,* partly conscious.

sem•i•ar•id (sĕm′ē-ăr′ĭd) Having low rainfall but able to support grassland and scrubby vegetation; not completely arid.

sem•i•cir•cu•lar canal (sĕm′ĭ-sûr′kyə-lər) Any of the three looped tubes of the inner ear that together work to maintain the sense of balance of the body.

sem•i•con•duc•tor (sĕm′ē-kən-dŭk′tər) Any of various solid substances, such as silicon or germanium, that conduct electricity more easily than insulators but less easily than conductors. Semiconductors are able to do this because they have a small number of electrons that have escaped from the bonds between the atoms, leaving open spaces. Both the electrons and the open spaces can carry an electric current.

sem•i•pal•mate (sĕm′ē-păl′māt′, sĕm′ē-päl′-māt′) Having partially webbed feet or toes, as many wading and shore birds do.

Sem•mel•weis (zĕm′əl-vīs′), **Ignaz Phillipp** 1818–1865. Hungarian physician who was a pioneer of sterile surgical practices. He proved that

sessile
left: *tube sponges*
right: *leaflets of a palm frond*

infectious disease and death in the obstetric clinic where he worked were caused by medical students going directly from working on autopsies to treating patients. Semmelweis instituted strict rules governing hygiene that dramatically reduced the death rate.

sense organ (sĕns) In animals, an organ or part that is sensitive to a stimulus, as of sound, touch, or light. Examples of sense organs include the eye, ear, and nose, as well as the taste buds on the tongue.

sen•sor (sĕn′sər) A device that responds to a physical stimulus and converts the stimulus into a signal conveyed to another device. For example, a sensor in a printer detects that the paper tray is empty and sends a signal to the digital display that the tray is out of paper.

sen•so•ry (sĕn′sə-rē) Involving the sense organs or the nerves that relay messages from them: *sensory receptors; a sensory nerve. Compare* **motor.**

se•pal (sē′pəl) One of the separate, usually green parts extending from the base of a flower. Sepals look like small leaves, though in some plants they are colored like petals. As a group, they form the calyx, which surrounds and protects the flower bud. In some flowers, such as the poppies, the sepals fall off after the flower bud opens. *See more at* **flower.**

sep•sis (sĕp′sĭs) Infection of the blood by disease-causing microorganisms, especially bacteria. —*Adjective* **septic.**

sep•tum (sĕp′təm) *Plural* **septa.** A thin wall or membrane that separates two parts, structures, or individual organisms. The chambers of the heart are separated by septa.

se•quence (sē′kwəns) **1.** *Mathematics.* A set of quantities ordered in the same manner as the positive integers. A sequence can be finite, such as {1, 3, 5, 7, 9}, or it can be infinite, such as $\{1, \frac{1}{2}, \frac{1}{3}, \frac{1}{4}, \ldots \frac{1}{n}\}$. **2.** *Chemistry.* The order of molecules that make up the subunits of a chemical compound, especially the order of nucleotides in a nucleic acid or of the amino acids in a protein.

se•ries (sîr′ēz) *Mathematics.* The sum of a sequence of terms, for example $2 + 2^2 + 2^3 + 2^4 + 2^5 + \ldots$

series circuit *See under* **circuit.**

ser•ine (sĕr′ēn′) A nonessential amino acid. *See more at* **amino acid.**

se•rum (sîr′əm) *Plural* **serums** *or* **sera. 1.** *See* **blood serum. 2.** Blood serum extracted from an animal that has immunity to a particular disease. The serum contains antibodies to specific antigens and can transfer immunity to humans or other animals by means of injection.

serv•er (sûr′vər) A computer that controls a central storage area of data that can be downloaded or manipulated by another computer.

ses•sile (sĕs′īl′) **1.** *Zoology.* Permanently attached or fixed; not free-moving: *Corals and mussels are sessile animals.* **2.** *Botany.* Stalkless and attached directly at the base: *sessile leaves; sessile fruit.*

set (sĕt) A collection of distinct elements that have something in common. In mathematics, sets are commonly represented by enclosing the members of a set in curly braces, as {1, 2, 3, 4, 5}, the set of all positive integers from 1 to 5.

sex (sĕks) **1.** Either of two divisions, male and female, into which most organisms are grouped. Sex is usually determined by anatomy, the makeup of the chromosomes, and the type and amount of hormones produced. **2.** Sexual intercourse. —*Adjective* **sexual.**

sex cell *See* **reproductive cell.**

sex chromosome Either of a pair of chromosomes, usually called X and Y, that in combination determine the sex of an individual in many animals and in some plants, with XX resulting in a female and XY in a male. Sex chromosomes carry the genes that control the development of reproductive organs and secondary sex characteristics.

sex hormone A steroid hormone that regulates the sexual development of an organism and is needed for reproduction. Testosterone and estrogen are sex hormones.

sex-linked Carried on or transmitted by a sex chromosome. Sex-linked inheritance concerns the genes located on the sex chromosomes. Color blindness in humans is a sex-linked trait.

sex•u•al intercourse (sĕk**′**sho͞o-əl) The process by which sperm from the male is deposited in the female during sexual reproduction.

sex•u•al•ly transmitted disease (sĕk**′**sho͞o-ə-lē) Any of various diseases, such as chlamydia, gonorrhea, and syphilis, that are transmitted through sexual intercourse or other intimate sexual contact. Also called *venereal disease.*

sexual reproduction *See under* **reproduction.**

Sg The symbol for **seaborgium.**

shale (shāl) A fine-grained sedimentary rock consisting of compacted and hardened clay, silt, or mud. Shale forms in many distinct layers and splits easily into thin sheets or slabs. It varies in color from black or gray to brown or red. *See Table at* **rock.**

shelf (shĕlf) *See* **continental shelf.**

shell (shĕl) **1a.** The usually hard outer covering of certain animals, such as mollusks, insects, and turtles. **b.** The hard outer covering of a bird's egg. **c.** The hard outer covering of a seed, nut, or fruit. **2.** Any of the regions in which electrons are concentrated around the nucleus of an atom. Depending on the number of protons in the nucleus, atoms can have up to seven shells. Electrons in the outer shells have greater energy than those in shells closer to the nucleus. An electron in an inner shell can gain energy and move to an outer shell while, if there is space available, an electron can give off energy and drop from an outer shell to an inner shell. The energy is usually given off in the form of light. The innermost shell can hold two electrons while others can hold different amounts, with the greatest amount being 32 electrons. *See more at* **atom.** *See Note at* **metal.**

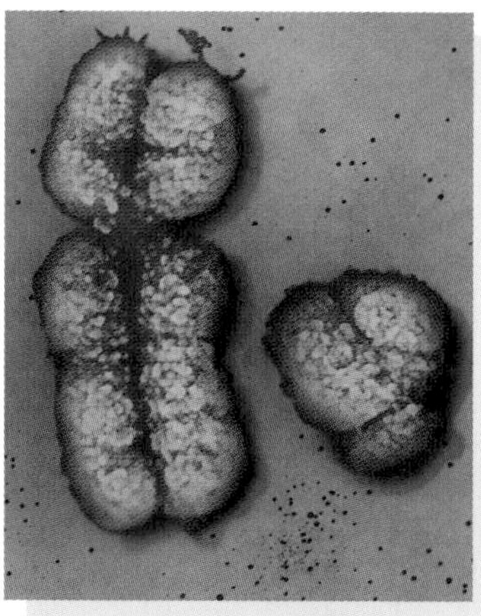

sex chromosome
photograph made through a scanning electron microscope of the human sex chromosomes X (larger) *and Y* (smaller)

shale

shin•bone (shĭn**′**bōn′) *See* **tibia.**

shoal (shōl) A sandy elevation of the bottom of a body of water; a sandbar.

shock (shŏk) **1.** A life-threatening condition marked by a severe drop in blood pressure, resulting from serious injury or illness. **2.** An instance of the passage of an electric current through the body. The amount of injury caused by electric shock depends on the type and strength of the current, the length of time the current is applied, and the route the current takes once it enters the body.

Shock•ley (shŏk**′**lē), **William Bradford** 1910–1989. American physicist who co-developed the transistor.

shock wave A large-amplitude wave formed by the sudden compression of the medium through which the wave moves. Shock waves can be caused by explosions or by objects moving through a fluid at a speed greater than the speed

Did You Know?
sickle cell anemia

Genetic mutations can be good or bad, and sometimes they can even be both. The mutation that causes *sickle cell anemia* is one example. It is harmful if a person inherits two copies of the mutated gene (one from each parent), but there is actually some benefit if only one copy of the gene is inherited. The defective gene causes red blood cells to be distorted into a sickle shape, which makes it hard for them to pass through the tiny blood vessels where they give oxygen to body tissues. If a person's chromosomes have two copies of the mutated gene, serious sickle cell anemia results, causing illness. With just one copy of the gene, though, only some mild sickling of the cells occurs. It so happens that this mild sickling is harmful to the parasite that causes malaria, and can protect a person from that disease. In a region like tropical Africa where malaria is common, people who have the mutation in one gene are more likely to ward off a malarial infection and to live long enough to have children, who then inherit the gene in turn. And because inheriting two copies of the gene is much less likely than inheriting just one, the benefits of the gene outweigh its risks for most people in these regions.

of sound. Because the waves generated in the fluid by the rapid movement cannot move at a speed greater than the speed of sound (thereby keeping pace with the object that caused them to form), they pile up and become compressed together.

shoot (sho͞ot) A new growth on a plant, such as a young branch or a sprout from a seed.

shoot•ing star (sho͞o**′**tĭng) *See* **meteor** (sense 1).

short circuit (shôrt) A path that allows most of the current in an electric circuit to flow around or away from the principal elements or devices in the circuit. Short circuits can cause too much current to flow through one part of the circuit, often causing the circuit to break.

short ton *See* **ton** (sense 1).

shoul•der blade (shōl**′**dər) *See* **scapula.**

shrub (shrŭb) A woody plant that is smaller than a tree, usually having several stems rather than a single trunk; a bush.

Si The symbol for **silicon.**

sick•le cell anemia (sĭk**′**əl) A hereditary disease characterized by red blood cells that are sickle-shaped instead of round because of an abnormality in the hemoglobin, the protein that carries oxygen in the blood. Because of their shape, the cells can cause blockage of small blood vessels in the organs and bones, reducing the amount of oxygen available to those tissues.

si•de•re•al (sī-dîr**′**ē-əl) **1.** Relating to the stars or constellations. **2.** Measured by means of the apparent daily motion of the stars: *sidereal time.*

si•er•ra (sē-ĕr**′**ə) A high, rugged range of mountains having an irregular outline somewhat like the teeth of a saw.

sie•vert (sē**′**vərt) A unit used to measure the amount of radiation necessary to produce the same effect on living tissue as one gray of high-penetration x-rays.

sig•nif•i•cant digits (sĭg-nĭf**′**ĭ-kənt) The digits in a decimal number that are warranted by the accuracy of the means of measurement. Significant digits are all the numbers beginning with the leftmost nonzero digit, or beginning with the first digit after the decimal point if there are no nonzero digits to the left of the decimal

sierra
the Eastern Sierra Nevada with Mount Whitney in the distance

point, and extending to the right. For example, 302, 3.20, and 0.023 all have three significant digits.

sil•i•ca (sĭl′ĭ-kə) Silicon dioxide, SiO_2, a compound that occurs widely in rocks and mineral forms, such as quartz, sand, and flint, and is used to make glass, concrete, and other materials. —*Adjective* **siliceous** (sĭ-lĭsh′əs).

sil•i•cate (sĭl′ĭ-kāt′) **1.** Any of a large class of chemical compounds composed of silicon, oxygen, and at least one metal. Most rocks and minerals are silicates. Silicates are also one of the main components of bricks. **2.** Any mineral containing the group SiO_4 in its crystal lattice. Micas and feldspars are silicate minerals.

sil•i•con (sĭl′ĭ-kŏn′) A nonmetallic element that occurs in both gray crystalline and brown noncrystalline forms. It is the second most abundant element in the Earth's crust and can be found only in silica and silicates. Silicon is used in glass, semiconductors, concrete, and ceramics. *Symbol* **Si.** *Atomic number* 14. *See* **Periodic Table,** pages 262–263.

sil•i•cone (sĭl′ĭ-kōn′) Any of a class of chemical compounds consisting of long chains of organic radicals that are each attached to silicon and oxygen atoms. Silicones are used to make adhesives, lubricants, and synthetic rubber.

silk (sĭlk) **1.** A fiber produced by silkworms to form cocoons. Silk is strong, flexible, and fibrous, and is essentially a long continuous strand of protein. It is widely used to make thread and fabric. **2.** A substance similar to the silk of the silkworm but produced by other insect larvae and by spiders to spin webs.

silk•worm (sĭlk′wûrm′) Any of various caterpillars that produce silk cocoons, especially the larva of a moth native to Asia. The fiber of silkworm cocoons is the source of commercial silk.

sill (sĭl) An approximately horizontal sheet of igneous rock located between layers of older rock.

silt (sĭlt) Small grains or particles of disintegrated rock, smaller than sand and larger than clay. Silt is often found at the bottom of bodies of water, such as lakes, where it accumulates slowly by settling through the water.

silt•stone (sĭlt′stōn′) A fine-grained sedimentary rock consisting primarily of compacted and hardened silt. It varies in color from black or gray to brown or red. *See Table at* **rock.**

Si•lu•ri•an (sĭ-lo͝or′ē-ən) The third period of the Paleozoic Era, from about 438 to 408 million years ago, characterized by the appearance of jawed fish and the rise of the first land plants and invertebrate land animals. *See Chart at* **geologic time,** pages 148–149.

sil•ver (sĭl′vər) A soft, shiny, white metallic element that is found in many ores, especially together with copper, lead, and zinc. It conducts heat and electricity better than any other metal. Silver is used in photography and in making electrical circuits and conductors. *Symbol* **Ag.** *Atomic number* 47. *See* **Periodic Table,** pages 262–263. *See Note at* **element.** ❖ An alloy of silver that contains up to 7.5 percent copper or another metal is called **sterling silver,** from which jewelry and silverware are made.

silver iodide A pale-yellow, odorless powder, AgI, that darkens when it is exposed to light. It is used in photography, as an antiseptic in medicine, and in cloud seeding.

silver nitrate A poisonous, clear, crystalline compound, $AgNO_3$, that darkens when exposed to light. It is used in photography and silver plating, and as an external antiseptic.

sim•i•an (sĭm′ē-ən) An ape or monkey.

sim•ple fraction (sĭm′pəl) A fraction in which both the numerator and denominator are whole numbers, such as $\frac{5}{7}$.

sin Abbreviation of **sine.**

sine (sīn) The ratio of the length of the side opposite an acute angle in a right triangle to the length of the hypotenuse.

si•nus (sī′nəs) **1.** A cavity or hollow space in a bone of the skull, especially one that connects with the nose. **2.** A channel for the passage of a body fluid, such as blood.

si•nu•soi•dal projection (sī′nə-soid′l) A method of making a flat map of the Earth so that the parallels and the prime meridian are straight lines and the other meridians are curved outward from the prime meridian. *Compare* **conic pro-**

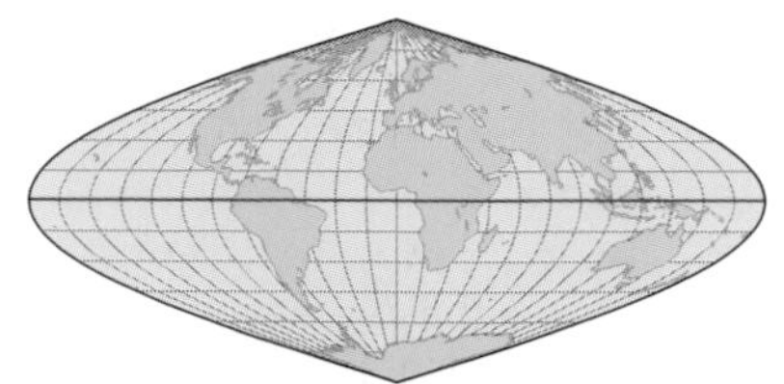

sinusoidal projection

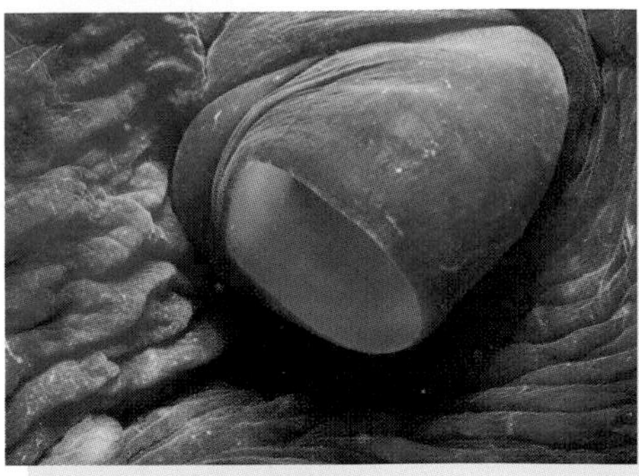

siphon
close-up of the siphon of a giant Pacific octopus

jection, homolosine projection, Mercator projection.

si•phon (sī′fən) **1.** A pipe or tube in the form of an upside-down U, filled with liquid and arranged so that the pressure of the atmosphere forces liquid to flow upward from a container through the tube, over a barrier, and into a lower container. **2.** A tubular animal part, as of a clam, through which water is taken in or expelled.

Sir•i•us (sĭr′ē-əs) The brightest star seen in the night sky. It is in the constellation Canis Major.

skel•e•ton (skĕl′ĭ-tn) **1.** The internal structure of vertebrate animals, composed of bone or cartilage, that supports the body, serves as a framework for the attachment of muscles, and protects the vital organs and associated structures. **2.** A hard protective covering or supporting structure of invertebrate animals. *See also* **endoskeleton, exoskeleton.** —*Adjective* **skeletal.** *See A Closer Look,* page 312.

skin (skĭn) The outer covering of a vertebrate animal, consisting of two layers of cells, a thick inner layer (called the dermis) and a thin outer layer (called the epidermis). Structures such as hair, scales, or feathers are contained in the skin, as are fat cells, sweat glands, and sense organs (called skin receptors). Skin provides a protective barrier against disease-causing microorganisms and against the sun's ultraviolet rays. In warm-blooded animals, it helps maintain stable body temperatures by providing insulation or by increasing blood flow to the surface, which rids the body of excess heat.

skull (skŭl) The part of the skeleton that forms the framework of the head, consisting of the bones that protect the brain and the bones of the face. *See more at* **skeleton.**

Did You Know?

sleep

Shakespeare had it right. He said that *sleep* was the "balm of hurt minds" and that sleep "knits up the ravel'd sleeve of care." In other words, sleep helps overcome the stress of everyday life. So the third of your life you spend asleep is not a waste of time. All warm-blooded animals have the need to sleep. Studies have shown that animals that are not allowed to sleep for a long enough time can actually die. Babies, human and animal, sleep even more than adults do. Researchers think that babies may sleep so much because it helps the young body continue to develop quickly. Not only are babies' bodies growing, but their brains are, too—and sleep is very important for the brain. During sleep, the brain sorts through experiences and stores important new information for later use. This processing of experiences, in fact, is thought to be a major source of dreams.

sky (skī) The atmosphere, as seen from a given point on the Earth's surface.

slate (slāt) A fine-grained metamorphic rock that forms when shale undergoes metamorphosis. Slate splits into thin layers with smooth surfaces. It ranges in color from gray to black or from red to green, depending on the minerals contained in the shale from which it formed. *See Table at* **rock.**

sleep (slēp) A natural state of rest, occurring at regular intervals, in which the eyes usually close, the muscles relax, and responsiveness to external events decreases. Growth and repair of the tissues of the body are thought to occur during sleep, and energy is conserved and stored. In humans and some other animals, scientists have identified one phase of sleep (called REM sleep) as the phase in which dreams occur.

sleep•ing sickness (slē′pĭng) An often fatal disease of humans and animals in tropical Africa, causing fever and extreme sluggishness. It is

A CLOSER LOOK

Skeleton

The human skeleton has 206 bones. It provides a stable framework for the attachment of hundreds of muscles, tendons, and ligaments. In addition, the bones of the skull and chest protect the brain and vital internal organs. The vertebral column, or spine, houses the delicate spinal cord, which transmits sensory and motor impulses between the limbs and the brain. Bones come together at flexible joints, which are acted on by a finely balanced system of muscles to produce coordinated movement.

Action of a muscle on a joint

The muscles of the skeleton often work in opposition to one another. For example, when the biceps—the muscle that bends the elbow—contracts, the triceps, which straightens it, must relax. (Similarly, for the triceps to straighten the elbow, the biceps must relax.)

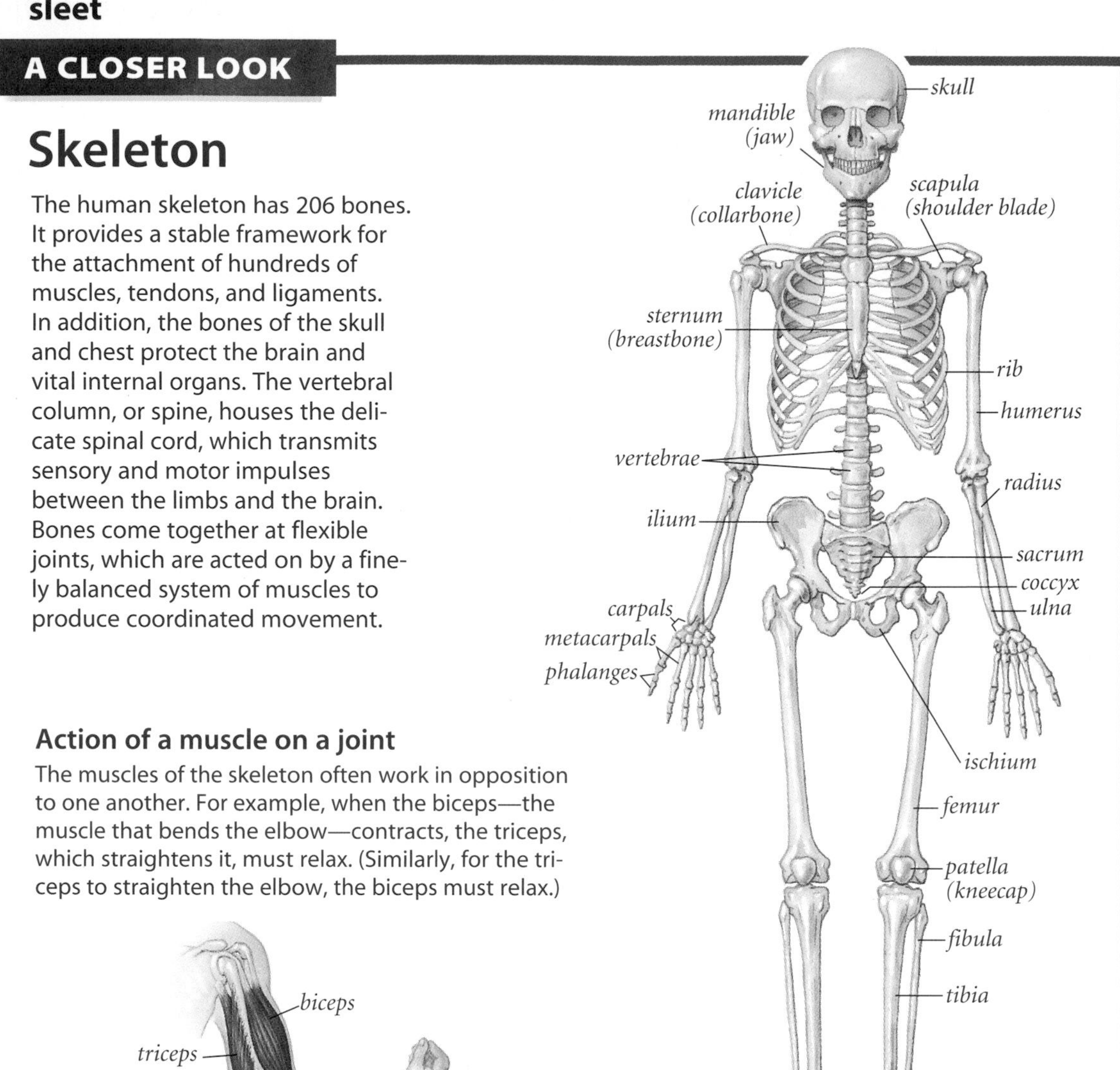

caused by infection with protozoans that are spread by the bite of the tsetse fly.

sleet (slēt) Water that falls to earth in the form of frozen or partially frozen raindrops.

slide (slīd) A thin, usually rectangular, glass plate on which something, such as a sample of rock or a microorganism, is placed for examination under a microscope.

slime (slīm) A slippery or sticky mucous substance secreted by certain animals, such as slugs or snails.

slime mold Any of various primitive organisms that exist in both unicellular and multicellular stages and are found on decaying plant matter. Slime molds are classified as protists. ❖ **Cellular slime molds** live as single, amoeba-like cells moving about feeding on bacteria. When food becomes scarce, they combine into large colonies that develop into multicellular, spore-producing structures. ❖ **Plasmodial slime molds** exist as a mass of amoeba-like protoplasm (called a plasmodium) that contains many nuclei within a single cell membrane. The slimy masses move along ingesting bacteria and yeast. When food grows scarce, they stop moving and grow multicellular, spore-producing stalks.

slough (slŭf) *Noun.* **1.** The dead outer skin shed by a reptile or an amphibian. —*Verb.* **2.** To shed an outer layer of skin.

Sm The symbol for **samarium.**

small calorie (smôl) *See* **calorie** (sense 1).

small intestine The long, narrow, coiled section of the intestine that extends from the stomach to the beginning of the large intestine and in mammals is made up of the duodenum, jejunum, and ileum. Nutrients are absorbed into the bloodstream from the small intestine.

small•pox (smôl′pŏks′) A highly infectious and often fatal disease caused by a virus and characterized by fever, headache, and severe pimples that result in extensive scarring. Smallpox was once a dreaded killer of children and caused the deaths of millions of Native Americans after the arrival of European settlers in the Americas. Following a worldwide vaccination campaign, smallpox was declared eradicated in 1980, although samples have been preserved in laboratories in the US and Russia. *See Note at* **Jenner.**

smelt (smĕlt) To melt ores in order to extract the metals they contain.

smog (smŏg) **1.** A form of air pollution produced when sunlight reacts with hydrocarbons and nitrogen compounds released into the atmosphere, especially from automobile exhaust. Smog is common in many large cities, especially during hot, sunny weather. It appears as a brownish haze and can irritate the eyes and lungs. **2.** Fog that has become polluted with smoke, especially smoke from burning coal.

smoke (smōk) A mixture of carbon dioxide, water vapor, and other gases, usually containing particles of soot or other solids, produced by the burning of carbon-containing materials such as wood or coal.

smut (smŭt) Any of various plant diseases caused by parasitic fungi that form black, powdery masses of spores on the affected parts. Smut chiefly affects cereal grasses like corn and wheat.

Sn The symbol for **tin.**

snake (snāk) Any of numerous meat-eating reptiles having a long narrow body with no legs, often just one lung, and a forked tongue. The jaws of a snake come apart and the body can expand to swallow prey that is much thicker than the snake itself. Some snakes have venom glands and sharp fangs that can give a poisonous bite.

snout (snout) The projecting nose, jaws, or front part of the head of an animal.

snow (snō) Crystals of ice that form from water vapor in the atmosphere and fall to earth.

snow line **1.** The boundary marking the lowest altitude at which a given area, such as the top of a mountain, is always covered with snow. **2.** The boundary marking the furthest extent around the polar regions at which there is snow cover. The polar snow lines vary with the seasons.

soap (sōp) A substance used for washing or cleaning, consisting of a mixture of sodium or potassium salts of naturally occurring fatty acids. Like detergents, soaps work by surrounding particles of grease or dirt with their molecules, thereby allowing them to be carried away. Unlike detergents, soap reacts with the minerals common in most water, forming an insoluble film that remains on fabrics. For this reason soap is not as efficient a cleaner as most detergents. The film is also what causes rings to form in bathtubs. *Compare* **detergent.**

soap•stone (sōp′stōn′) A soft metamorphic rock composed mostly of the mineral talc.

so•cial science (sō′shəl) **1.** The study of human society and of individual relationships in and to society. **2.** Any of various academic or scientific disciplines relating to such study, generally regarded as including sociology, psychology, anthropology, economics, political science, and history.

■ **smog**
over the city of Los Angeles

Did You Know?

solar cell

How can light make electricity? By exciting electrons to break free from their atoms. A *solar cell* has an upper layer of negatively charged silicon, with free-flowing electrons, and a lower layer of positively charged silicon, with atoms that are missing some electrons. The placing of these two charged layers next to each other creates a weak electric field. When light penetrates the solar cell and reaches the positively charged layer, its energy is absorbed by some of the electrons which, in their extra-excited state, break away from their atoms. The electric field along the surface where the two layers meet then pushes these electrons into the negative layer. Meanwhile, other electrons in the positive layer move upward into the space the first electrons left behind. In the negatively charged silicon layer, the electrons pile up, increasing the electric charge. When the two layers of a solar cell are connected to a circuit, the electrons flow out of the negative layer through the circuit and back to the positive layer, where they are attracted by the spaces left by the missing electrons. Along the way, the electrons power the inner workings of devices like calculators and spacecraft.

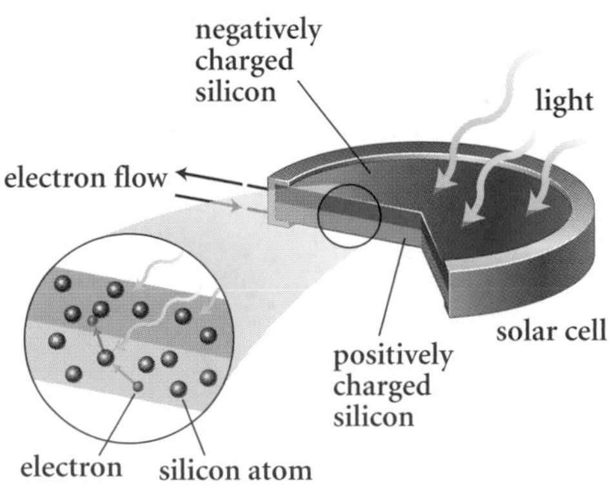

so•ci•ol•o•gy (sō′sē-ŏl′ə-jē) The scientific study of human social behavior and its origins, development, organizations, and institutions.

so•da (sō′də) *See* **sodium carbonate.**

Sod•dy (sŏd′ē), **Frederick** 1877–1956. British chemist who was a pioneer in the study of radioactivity. With Ernest Rutherford, he explained the atomic disintegration of radioactive elements. Soddy also coined the word *isotope* to describe elements that were chemically identical but had different atomic weights.

so•di•um (sō′dē-əm) A soft, lightweight, silvery-white metallic element that reacts explosively with water. It is the most abundant alkali metal on Earth, occurring especially in common salt. Sodium is very easily shaped, and its compounds have many important uses in industry. *Symbol* **Na.** *Atomic number* 11. *See* **Periodic Table,** pages 262–263.

sodium bicarbonate *See* **baking soda.**

sodium carbonate A white, powdery compound, Na_2CO_3, used in making baking soda, sodium nitrate, glass, ceramics, detergents, and soap. Also called *soda.*

sodium chloride *See* **salt** (sense 1).

sodium fluoride A colorless, crystalline salt, NaF, used to fluoridate water and treat tooth decay. It is also used as an insecticide and a disinfectant.

sodium hydroxide A strongly alkaline compound, NaOH, used in making chemicals and soaps, in refining petroleum, and as a cleansing agent. In solution, it forms lye.

sodium nitrate A poisonous, white, crystalline compound, $NaNO_3$, used in solid rocket propellants, as a fertilizer, and in curing meat.

soft palate (sôft) *See under* **palate.**

soft•ware (sôft′wâr′) The programs, programming languages, and data that direct the operations of a computer system. Word processing programs and Internet browsers are examples of software. *Compare* **hardware.**

soil (soil) The loose top layer of the Earth's surface, consisting of rock and mineral particles

Did You Know?
solar system

Usually, we think of the *solar system* as simply including the sun and the planets. We may even remember the moons that revolve around several planets. But actually, the solar system contains billions of other objects as well and extends far beyond the orbit of Neptune. Several hundred thousand asteroids have been discovered, and countless smaller asteroids, including the chunks of debris formed during the collision of larger bodies, are out there as well. Astronomers have recorded more than 800 comets passing through the inner part of the solar system. Billions more, however, lie in the area surrounding the solar system, in the far reaches of the swarm of comets known as the Oort cloud or in the disk of debris known as the Kuiper belt. All of these objects travel around the sun at high speeds in paths called orbits. Some of these orbits, like those of the planets near the sun, are almost circular. Other orbits, like those of comets that make their way in among the planets, are stretched out into long ellipses.

mixed with decayed organic matter (known as humus). Soil provides the support and nutrients that many plants need to grow.

so•lar (sō′lər) **1.** Relating to the sun: *solar radiation.* **2.** Using or operated by energy from the sun: *a solar heating system.* **3.** Measured in reference to the sun: *solar time.*

solar cell An electric cell that converts visible light into electrical energy. Solar cells are used as power supplies in calculators, satellites, and other devices, and as a prime source of electricity in remote locations. Also called *photovoltaic cell.*

solar eclipse *See under* **eclipse.**

solar energy 1. The energy produced or radiated by the sun. **2.** Energy derived from the sun's radiation. Solar energy is used on Earth in various ways. It is used as a passive source of energy, for example, in the form of sunlight that comes through a window and heats up a room, or as an active source, as in the conversion of sunlight to electrical energy in solar cells.

solar flare A sudden eruption of hydrogen gas on the surface of the sun, usually associated with sunspots.

solar system 1. *Often* **Solar System.** The sun together with the planets and all other bodies that orbit the sun, including moons, asteroids, and comets. *See more at* **nebular hypothesis.** *See Table, pages* 316–317. **2.** A system of planets or other bodies orbiting another star.

solar wind A stream of high-speed, charged atomic particles flowing outward from the sun's corona.

sol•dier (sōl′jər) A sexually undeveloped form of certain ants and termites, having a large head and powerful jaws that serve as fighting weapons.

so•le•noid (sō′lə-noid′) A coil of wire that acts as a magnet when an electric current passes through it.

sol•id (sŏl′ĭd) **1.** *Physics.* One of the three basic forms of matter, composed of molecules that have little or no ability to exchange places. Unlike gases and liquids, a solid has a fixed shape, and unlike gases, a solid also has a fixed volume. **2.** *Mathematics.* A geometric figure that has three dimensions.

solid solution A uniform mixture of substances in solid form. Solid solutions often consist of two or more types of atoms or molecules that share a crystal lattice, as in certain metal alloys. Much of

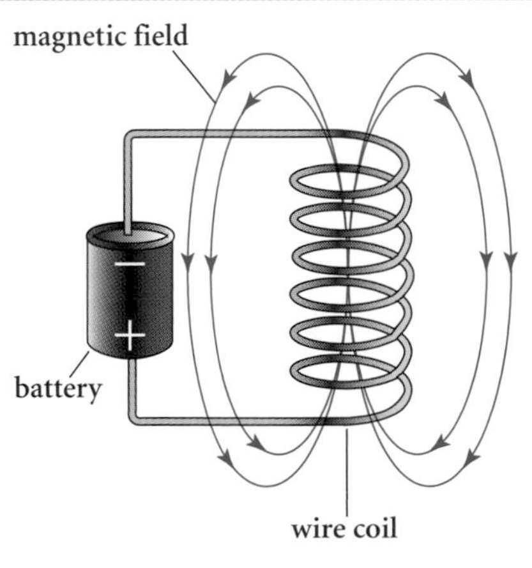

solenoid

THE SOLAR SYSTEM

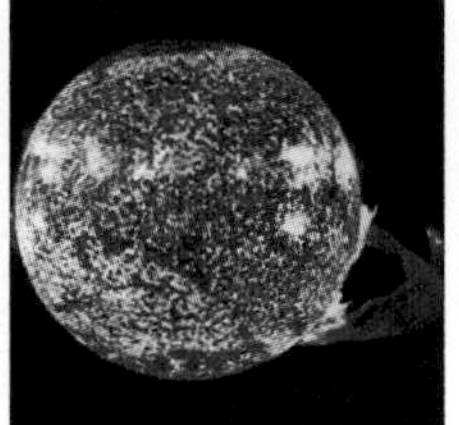
SUN

MERCURY

VENUS

EARTH

MARS

PHYSICAL PROPERTIES OF THE PLANETS

Listed below are the planets that have been identified in our solar system. The **sidereal period** is the amount of time it takes for a planet to make one complete revolution around the sun. This is measured in relation to the fixed stars, in order to observe the orbit from a place outside our solar system. The sidereal period of Earth is exactly one year long. The **rotational period** is the amount of time it takes for a body to make one

PLANET	EQUATORIAL DIAMETER		MASS	SIDEREAL PERIOD
	miles	*kilometers*	*× 10²⁴ kilograms*	*days*
Mercury	3,032	4,880	0.3302	87.97
Venus	7,521	12,104	4.8685	224.70
Earth	7,926	12,756	5.9736	365.2564
Mars	4,222	6,794	0.6419	686.98
Jupiter	88,846	142,984	1,898.6	4,332.59
Saturn	74,897	120,536	568.46	10,759.22
Uranus	31,763	51,118	86.832	30,685.40
Neptune	30,775	49,528	102.43	60,189.00
Pluto*	1,485	2,390	0.013	90,465.00

PHYSICAL PROPERTIES OF THE SUN

The **corona,** an irregular envelope of gas that surrounds the sun, extends about 8,000,000 miles (13,000,000 kilometers) past the sun's visible surface. The low-density gas in the corona ranges in temperature from 2 to 3.5 million degrees Fahrenheit (1 to 2 million degrees Celsius). In small, dark areas that appear on the surface, known as **sunspots,** the temperature drops by about 2,000 to 3,500 degrees Fahrenheit (1,000 to 2,000

DIAMETER		MASS
miles	*kilometers*	*× 10²⁴ kilograms*
865,000	1,392,000	1,989,100

*In 2006, the Interplanetary Astronomical Union demoted Pluto from the category of *planet* to the category of *dwarf planet*.

JUPITER

SATURN

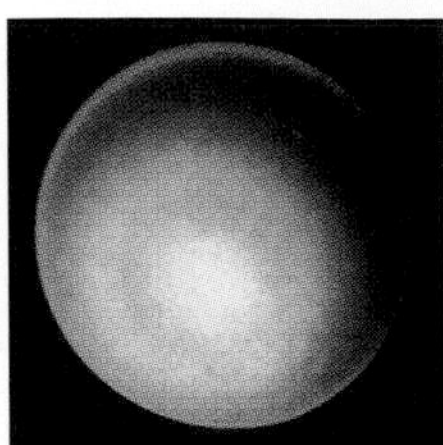

URANUS

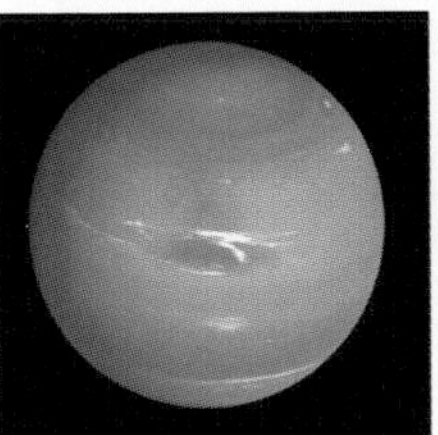

NEPTUNE

PLUTO*

complete rotation about its own axis. Earth rotates about its axis in slightly less than one sidereal day. Earth rotates from west to east, counterclockwise when seen from above the North Pole. If one of the other planets rotates on its axis clockwise from east to west (the manner opposite to that of Earth), the rotation is called **retrograde** and a minus sign (–) appears in front of the number of days in the planet's rotational period.

ROTATIONAL PERIOD	AVERAGE SURFACE TEMPERATURE		MEAN DISTANCE FROM SUN *(in millions)*	
days	*degrees Fahrenheit*	*degrees Celsius*	*miles*	*kilometers*
58.646	332	167	36.0	57.9
–243.02	867	464	67.2	108.2
0.99727	59	15	92.96	149.6
1.026	–81	–63	141.6	227.9
0.414	–162	–108	483.8	778.6
0.444	–218	–139	890.8	1,433.5
–0.718	–323	–197	1,784.9	2,872.4
0.671	–330	–201	2,793.1	4,495.1
–6.387	–369	–223	3,670.1	5,906.4

degrees Celsius). The sun is more than 330,000 times more massive than Earth and contains more than 99.8 percent of the mass of the entire solar system. Because the sun is not a solid body like Earth, its rotational period is not the same everywhere on its surface. Its outer layers rotate at different rates in different places, taking a longer time at the poles. The sun's core, on the other hand, does rotate as a solid body.

	TEMPERATURE		ROTATIONAL PERIOD (OUTER LAYERS)	
	degrees Fahrenheit	*degrees Celsius*	*days*	
Surface:	10,924	6,051	*Equator:*	25.4
Core:	28,278,500	15,710,000	*Poles:*	36

the steel used in construction, for example, is actually a solid solution of iron and carbon. The carbon atoms, which fit neatly within the iron's crystal lattice, add strength to its structure.

solid-state physics The branch of physics that specializes in the study of solids, especially in the electric and magnetic properties of solid crystalline materials, such as semiconductors.

sol•stice (sŏl′stĭs, sōl′stĭs) **1.** Either of the two moments of the year when the sun is farthest north or south of the celestial equator. In the Northern Hemisphere, the summer solstice occurs on June 20 or 21 and the winter solstice occurs on December 21 or 22. **2.** Either of the two points on the celestial sphere where the apparent path of the sun (known as the ecliptic) reaches its greatest distance from the celestial equator. *Compare* **equinox.**

sol•u•ble (sŏl′yə-bəl) Capable of being dissolved. Salt, for example, is soluble in water.

sol•ute (sŏl′yo͞ot) A substance that is dissolved in another substance, forming a solution.

so•lu•tion (sə-lo͞o′shən) **1.** *Chemistry.* A mixture in which particles of one or more substances are distributed uniformly throughout another substance, so that the mixture is homogeneous at the molecular or ionic level. The particles in a solution are smaller than those in either a colloid or a suspension. *Compare* **colloid, suspension. 2.** *Mathematics.* A value or values which, when substituted for a variable in an equation, make the equation true. For example, the solutions to the equation $x^2 = 4$ are 2 and –2.

sol•vent (sŏl′vənt) A substance that can dissolve another substance, or in which another substance is dissolved, forming a solution.

so•mat•ic (sō-măt′ĭk) Relating to the body. ❖ The cells of the body with the exception of the reproductive cells (gametes) are known as **somatic cells.** *See Note at* **mitosis.**

Som•er•ville (sŭm′ər-vĭl′), **Mary Fairfax Greig** 1780–1872. Scottish astronomer and mathematician whose writings, particularly on astronomy, helped make science understandable to the general public.

so•nar (sō′när′) **1.** A method of detecting and locating underwater objects, such as submarines or schools of fish, through the use of reflected sound waves. Because the speed of sound in water is constant (about 4,800 feet, or 1,463 meters, per second), the time it takes for a transmitted signal to reach an object and return can be used to calculate the object's distance. **2.** The equipment used in doing this.

Did You Know?
solution

A *solution* is a homogeneous mixture of two substances—that is, it has the same distribution of particles throughout. Technically speaking, a solution consists of a mixture of one or more *solutes* dissolved in a *solvent.* The particles of solute and solvent are molecules or ions, with one or more solvent molecules bound to each solute particle. Both the solvent and the solute can be solid, liquid, or gas, but the solvent is usually liquid. We use solutions every day without realizing it. The ammonia with which we clean windows and floors is a solution of ammonia gas in water. The vinegar we sometimes put on salads is a solution of acetic acid (a liquid) and water. And seawater is a solution of sodium chloride (a solid) and water. Other common solutions are gasoline and metal alloys, including the solution of copper and nickel that gets minted as dimes, nickels, and quarters.

son•ic barrier (sŏn′ĭk) *See* **sound barrier.**

sonic boom The shock wave of compressed air caused by an aircraft traveling faster than the speed of sound. It is often audible as a loud, explosive sound, and it sometimes causes damage to structures on the ground.

soot (so͝ot) A black, powdery compound consisting mainly of carbon. Soot forms through the incomplete combustion of wood, coal, oil, or other materials.

sorp•tion (sôrp′shən) The taking up and holding of one substance by another. Sorption is used especially as a general term for absorption and adsorption.

sound[1] (sound) **1.** A type of wave motion that originates as the vibration of a medium (such as a person's vocal cords or a guitar string) and

Mary Somerville

travels through gases, liquids, and elastic solids as variations of pressure and density. The loudness of a sound depends on the amplitude of the sound wave. The pitch depends on its frequency. **2.** The sensation produced in the organs of hearing by waves of this type. *See Note at* **ultrasound.**

sound[2] **1.** A long body of water, wider than a strait, that connects larger bodies of water. **2.** A long, wide inlet of the ocean, often parallel to the coast. Long Island Sound, between Long Island and the coast of New England, is an example.

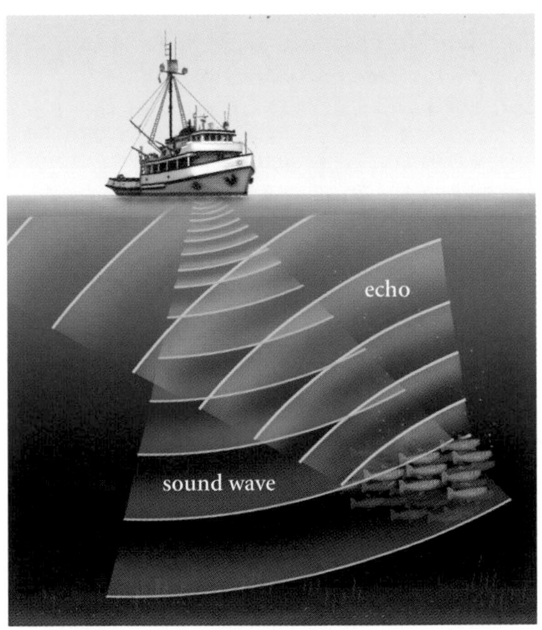

sonar

An electrical impulse is converted into sound waves that are transmitted underwater. The sound waves are reflected off objects in their paths, creating echoes that return to the vessel and are picked up by the sonar equipment.

Did You Know?

sound[1]

The form of energy called *sound* is produced when matter moves or vibrates. The vibrations are transferred to another medium, usually the air, and travel through it as sound waves. You hear a sound when its vibrations reach your eardrum, causing it to vibrate. The pitch of a sound is directly related to the frequency of the vibrations of its waves. People with excellent hearing can hear very low sounds, vibrating about 20 times per second, all the way up to high pitches with frequencies of 20,000 vibrations per second. Other animals can hear sounds at higher vibrations. Bats, for instance, can hear sounds with vibrations as high as 100,000 times a second. The loudness, or intensity, of sound is measured in decibels. For each increase of 10 decibels, the sound wave has 10 times as much energy. For example, a sound of 20 decibels is twice as loud as one of 10 decibels, but has 10 times the energy. The softest sound humans can hear, at the very threshold of hearing, has a loudness of 0 decibels. A moderate conversation has a loudness of about 60 decibels, and thunder at very close range has a loudness of about 140 decibels. Sound with intensity greater than 85 decibels can cause ear damage, and sound with intensity above 120 decibels causes pain.

sound barrier The sudden, sharp increase in drag experienced by aircraft approaching the speed of sound. Also called *sonic barrier.*

South•ern Cross (sŭ*th*′ərn) A constellation in the polar region of the Southern Hemisphere near Centaurus.

Southern Hemisphere 1. The half of the Earth south of the equator. **2.** *Astronomy.* The half of the celestial sphere south of the celestial equator.

southern lights *See* **aurora australis.**

South Pole (south) The southern end of the Earth's axis of rotation, a point in Antarctica.

space (spās) **1.** A set of points that satisfies some set of geometric rules: *a space of five dimensions.* **2.** The familiar three-dimensional region or field of everyday experience. **3a.** The expanse in which the solar system, stars, and galaxies exist; the universe. **b.** The part of this expanse beyond the Earth's atmosphere.

space-time The four dimensions in which all objects are located and all events occur, viewed as a single and continuous framework for existence. Space-time consists of length, width, and depth, plus the dimension of time. *See more at* **relativity.**

spa•dix (spā′dĭks) A fleshy spike of minute flowers, usually enclosed within a spathe, as in the jack-in-the-pulpit.

spathe (spā*th*) A leaf-like plant part that surrounds a spadix, as in the jack-in-the-pulpit.

spawn (spôn) *Noun.* **1.** The eggs of water animals such as fish, amphibians, and mollusks. **2.** Offspring produced in large numbers. —*Verb.* **3.** To lay eggs; produce spawn.

spe•ci•a•tion (spē′shē-ā′shən) The formation of new biological species by the development or branching of one species into two or more genetically distinct ones. According to the theory of evolution, all life on Earth has resulted from the speciation of earlier organisms.

spe•cies (spē′shēz, spē′sēz) A group of organisms having many characteristics in common and ranking below a genus. Organisms that reproduce sexually and belong to the same species interbreed and produce fertile offspring. *See Table at* **taxonomy.**

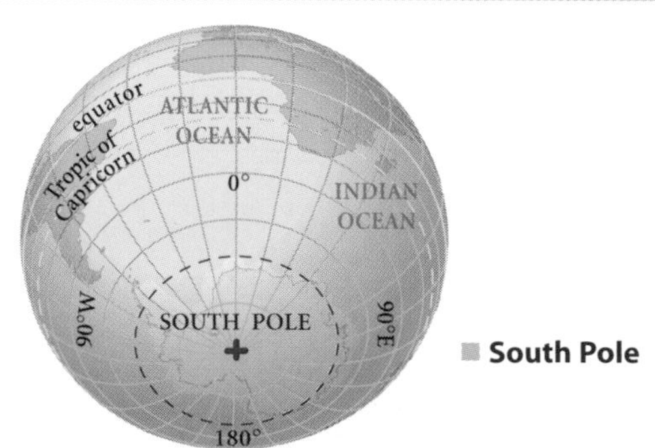

South Pole

Did You Know?

space-time

Before Albert Einstein's theory of relativity, people thought they lived in a three-dimensional world. Time was considered to be a completely separate entity. But Einstein realized that a more correct view put time and the three space dimensions on equal footing. Physicists call the four-dimensional construct within which they interpret nature *space-time.* In space-time two events that appear to happen at the exact same time to one person in one place can appear to happen at different times to someone else in a different place. In other words, whether or not the events occur at the same time depends on the position and movement of the observers. How is this possible? Think of thunder and lightning. Lightning reaches the eye at the speed of light, while thunder reaches the ear at the much slower speed of sound. To an observer right where lightning hits, the thunder seems to come at the same moment. Several miles away, however, the lightning appears well before the thunder is heard. Similarly, if one observer were moving faster than the other toward or away from the lightning strike, each observer would experience the events at different time intervals. As Einstein figured it, everything in space-time is relative.

spe•cif•ic gravity (spĭ-sĭf′ĭk) **1.** An amount equal to the density of a solid or liquid divided by the density of an equal volume of water that is at a temperature of 4°C (39°F). **2.** An amount equal to the density of a gas divided by the density of an equal volume of air or hydrogen that is at a specified temperature and pressure.

specific heat 1. The ratio of the amount of heat needed to raise the temperature of a certain amount of a substance by one degree to the amount of heat needed to raise the temperature of the same amount of a reference substance,

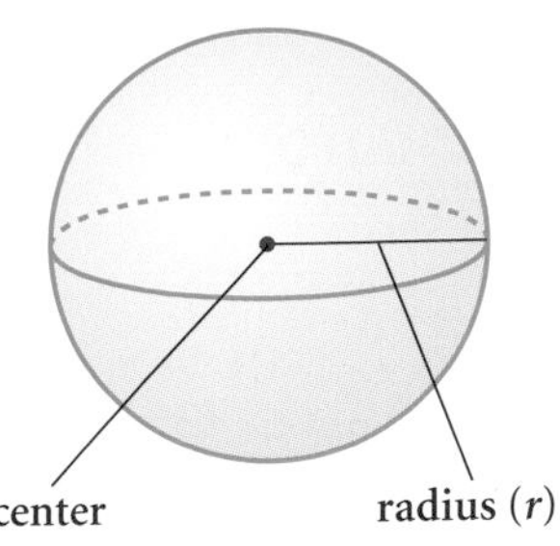

sphere

The volume (V) of a sphere can be calculated using the following equation: $V = \frac{4}{3}\pi r^3$.

usually water, by one degree. Because molecules of different materials have different weights and sizes, they require different amounts of energy to be heated to a given temperature. Knowing the specific heat of a material makes it possible to calculate how much energy is needed to raise the material's temperature by a given number of degrees. **2.** The amount of heat, measured in calories, needed to raise the temperature of one gram of a substance by one degree Celsius.

spec•tro•graph (spĕk′trə-grăf′) A spectroscope able to photograph or otherwise record spectra. ❖ The photograph of a spectrum produced by a spectrograph is called a **spectrogram.**

spec•trom•e•ter (spĕk-trŏm′ĭ-tər) A spectroscope equipped with devices for measuring the wavelengths of the radiation observed by it.

spec•tro•scope (spĕk′trə-skōp′) Any of various instruments used to measure the wavelengths and intensity of radiation by splitting the radiation up into a spectrum. In a light spectroscope, light enters a narrow slit, is focused into a thin beam of parallel rays by a lens, and passes through a prism that separates it into a spectrum. Other types of spectroscopes, such as the mass spectroscope, use magnetic fields to separate the incoming radiation.

spec•trum (spĕk′trəm) *Plural* **spectra** (spĕk′trə) *or* **spectrums. 1.** A range of possible wave frequencies, such as the electromagnetic spectrum. **2.** A distribution of the frequencies and intensities of a group of waves, usually arranged by frequency. The electromagnetic waves making up a beam of light are a spectrum of waves. Prisms and rainbows break sunlight into the component colors of its spectrum. **3.** A distribution of particles or molecules arranged according to their mass, especially when arranged by a mass spectroscope.

speed (spēd) The ratio of the distance traveled by an object (regardless of its direction) to the time required to travel that distance. *Compare* **velocity.**

spe•le•ol•o•gy (spē′lē-ŏl′ə-jē) The exploration and scientific study of caves.

sperm (spûrm) **1.** In male animals, the reproductive cell whose nucleus is capable of fusing with the nucleus of an egg cell to form a new organism; a spermatozoon. A sperm has half as many chromosomes as the other cells of the body and moves to unite with the egg. **2.** In plants, algae, and certain fungi, the reproductive cell whose nucleus is capable of fusing with the nucleus of a female reproductive cell to form a new organism. A sperm has half as many chromosomes as the other cells of the organism and moves to unite with the egg.

sper•ma•ce•ti (spûr′mə-sē′tē) A white, waxy substance obtained from the head of the sperm whale and sometimes other whales, porpoises, and dolphins, and used to make candles, ointments, and cosmetics.

sper•mat•o•phyte (spər-măt′ə-fīt′) A plant that produces seeds, such as a flowering plant.

sper•mat•o•zo•on (spər-măt′ə-zō′ŏn′) *Plural* **spermatozoa.** The mature reproductive cell of male animals. It is produced by the testis and is capable of fertilizing a female reproductive cell. A single spermatozoon carries only half as many chromosomes as the other cells of the body.

Sper•ry (spĕr′ē), **Roger Wolcott** 1913–1994. American neurobiologist who established that the right and left hemispheres of the brain each control specific functions.

sphag•num (sfăg′nəm) Any of various grayish mosses that grow in swamps and bogs and decompose to form peat.

sphere (sfîr) A three-dimensional geometric surface having all of its points the same distance from a given point.

sphe•roid (sfîr′oid′) A three-dimensional geometric surface generated by rotating an ellipse on or about one of its axes.

sphinc•ter (sfĭngk′tər) A ring-shaped muscle that encircles an opening or passage in the body. Contraction and relaxation of a sphincter closes and opens the passage.

spic•ule (spĭk′yo͞ol) A needle-like structure or part, such as one of the mineral structures supporting the soft tissue of certain invertebrates, especially sponges.

spike (spīk) **1.** An ear of grain, such as wheat. **2.** A long cluster of stalkless flowers, as in the gladiolus.

spi•na bif•i•da (spī′nə bĭf′ĭ-də) A congenital defect in which the vertebral column is not fully closed, causing part of the spinal cord to bulge out. Spina bifida often results in damage to the spinal cord.

spi•nal column (spī′nəl) *See* **vertebral column.**

spinal cord The long, cord-like part of the central nervous system that is enclosed within the vertebral column (the backbone) and descends from the base of the brain. It branches to form the nerves that convey impulses to and from the tissues of the body.

spin•dle (spĭn′dl) A network of cell fibers that forms in the nucleus during cell division. Duplicate strands of chromosomes attach along the center of the spindle before separating and moving to opposite ends of the cell. *See more at* **meiosis, mitosis.**

spine (spīn) **1.** *See* **vertebral column. 2.** A sharp-pointed projection on a plant, especially a hard, narrow modified leaf, as on a cactus. *See more at* **leaf.** *See Notes at* **cactus, thorn.**

spin•ner•et (spĭn′ə-rĕt′) One of the small openings in the back part of a spider or silk-producing insect larva, through which the sticky fluid that dries into silk is released.

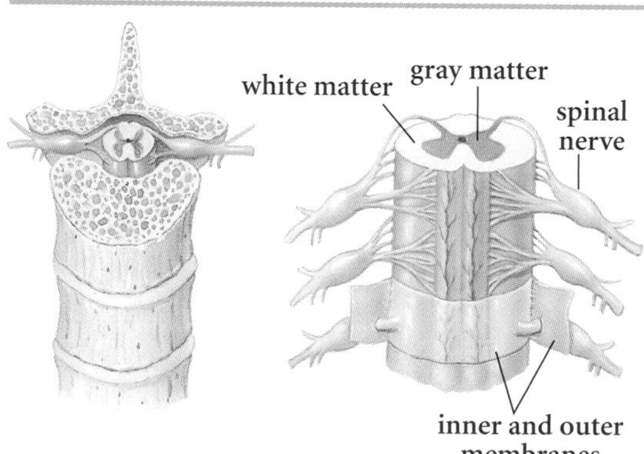

spinal cord

left: *section of vertebral column showing the spinal cord within the column*

right: *segment of spinal cord with nerve fibers arising from it*

spir•a•cle (spĭr′ə-kəl, spī′rə-kəl) An opening through which certain animals breathe, such as the blowhole of a whale or one of the openings in the exoskeleton of an insect.

spi•ril•lum (spī-rĭl′əm) *Plural* **spirilla.** Any of various bacteria that are shaped like a spiral.

spi•ro•chete (spī′rə-kēt′) Any of various bacteria that are shaped like a spiral, some of which can cause disease in humans.

spi•ro•gy•ra (spī′rə-jī′rə) Any of various freshwater green algae having spiral-shaped bands of chloroplasts.

spleen (splēn) An organ in vertebrate animals that in humans is located on the left side near the stomach. Mainly composed of lymph nodes and blood vessels, the spleen filters the blood, stores red blood cells, destroys old red blood cells, and produces white blood cells called lymphocytes.

splice (splīs) To join together genes or gene fragments or to insert them into a cell or other structure, such as a virus. In genetic engineering, scientists splice together genetic material to produce new genes or to alter a genetic structure.

sponge (spŭnj) **1.** Any of various primitive invertebrate animals that live in the ocean and are attached to rocks or other objects. Unlike other animals, sponges have bodies with only one type of tissue and no organs. The bodies have many passages and chambers that water flows through so that food can be filtered out. **2.** The soft, porous, absorbent skeleton of certain of these animals, used for bathing and cleaning.

spong•y parenchyma (spŭn′jē) A leaf tissue consisting of loosely arranged, irregularly shaped cells that have chloroplasts. The spongy parenchyma has many spaces between cells to facilitate the circulation of air and the exchange of gases. It lies just below the palisade layer. Also called *spongy mesophyll. See more at* **photosynthesis.**

spon•ta•ne•ous combustion (spŏn-tā′nē-əs) The bursting into flame of a mass of material as a result of chemical reactions within the substance, without the addition of heat from an external source. Oily rags and damp hay, for example, are subject to spontaneous combustion.

spo•ran•gi•um (spə-răn′jē-əm) *Plural* **sporangia.** A cell or structure in which reproductive spores are produced. Ferns, fungi, mosses, and

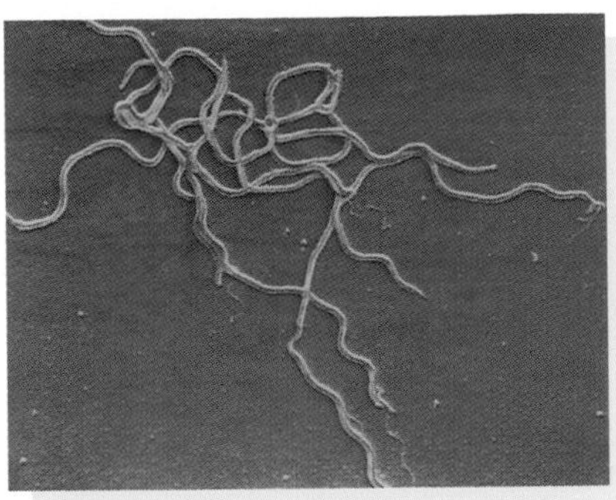

spirochete

photograph made through a scanning electron microscope of the spirochete that causes Lyme disease

algae release spores from sporangia.

spore (spôr) **1.** A usually one-celled reproductive body that can grow into a new organism without uniting with another cell. Spores have only a single set of chromosomes. Fungi, algae, plants that do not bear seeds, and certain protozoans reproduce asexually by spores. **2.** A similar one-celled body in seed-bearing plants that develops into either the embryo sac or a pollen grain. **3.** A rounded, inactive form that certain bacteria assume under conditions of extreme temperature, dryness, or lack of food. The bacterium develops a waterproof cell wall that protects it from being dried out or damaged.

spo•ro•phyte (spôr′ə-fīt′) In plants, algae, and certain other kinds of organisms, the individual organism or generation of organisms that produces spores. A sporophyte is formed from the union of the nuclei of male and female reproductive cells, and each of its cells has two sets of chromosomes. In nonvascular plants, such as the mosses and liverworts, the sporophyte is a small plant or a part that grows on top of the gametophyte. In vascular plants, such as the ferns, conifers, and flowering plants, the sporophyte is the main form of the plant. *Compare* **gametophyte.**

sponge

tube sponges

spread•ing zone (sprĕd′ĭng) *See* **divergent plate boundary.**

spring (sprĭng) **1.** A device, such as a coil of wire, that returns to its original shape after being compressed or stretched. Because of their ability to return to their original shape, springs are used to store energy, as in mechanical clocks, and to absorb or lessen energy, as in the suspension system of vehicles. **2.** A small stream of water flowing naturally from the earth. **3.** The season of the year between winter and summer, during which the weather becomes warmer and plants revive. In the Northern Hemisphere, it extends from the vernal equinox to the summer solstice.

spring tide A tide in which the difference between high and low tide is the greatest. Spring tides occur when the moon is either new or full, and the sun, the moon, and the Earth are aligned. When this is the case, their collective gravitational pull on the Earth's water is strengthened. *Compare* **neap tide.** *See more at* **tide.**

spruce (spro͞os) Any of various evergreen trees or shrubs that have short, four-sided needles and hanging or drooping cones. Spruces are found chiefly in cooler temperate regions in the Northern Hemisphere.

squall (skwôl) A brief, sudden, violent windstorm, often accompanied by rain or snow.

square (skwâr) *Noun.* **1.** A rectangle having four equal sides. **2.** The product that results when a number or quantity is multiplied by itself. The square of 8, for example, is 64. —*Adjective.* **3.** Of, being, or using units that express the measure of area: *square miles.* —*Verb.* **4.** To multiply a number, quantity, or expression by itself.

square root A number that, when squared, yields a given number. For example, since $5 \times 5 = 25$, the square root of 25 (written $\sqrt{25}$) is 5.

Sr The symbol for **strontium.**

sta•ble (stā′bəl) **1.** Not likely to change spontaneously into a nucleus or atomic particle with less mass. For example, the most common isotope of carbon, carbon 12, is stable. **2.** Relating to a chemical compound that does not easily decompose or change into other compounds or into elements. Water is an example of a stable compound. **3.** Relating to an atom or chemical element that is unlikely to share electrons with another atom or element; unreactive.

stain•less steel (stān′lĭs) Any of various steel alloys that are resistant to rusting and corrosion because they contain chromium and nickel.

sta•lac•tite (stə-lăk′tīt′) A cylindrical or conical mineral deposit projecting downward from the roof of a cave or cavern, formed by dripping water saturated with minerals. Stalactites form gradually as the minerals precipitate out of the saturated water. They usually consist of calcite, but can also consist of other minerals.

sta•lag•mite (stə-lăg′mīt′) A cylindrical or conical mineral deposit, similar to a stalactite, but built up from the floor of a cave or cavern.

stalk (stôk) **1.** *Botany.* **a.** The main stem of a plant. **b.** A slender structure that supports a plant part, such as a flower or leaf. **2.** A slender supporting or connecting part of an animal, such as the eyestalk of a lobster.

sta•men (stā′mən) The male reproductive organ of a flower, consisting of a filament and a pollen-bearing anther at its tip. *See more at* **flower.**

sta•mi•nate (stā′mə-nĭt) **1.** Having one or more stamens. **2.** Having stamens but no pistils. Male flowers are staminate.

stan•dard time (stăn′dərd) The time in any of the 24 time zones into which the Earth's surface is divided, usually the mean time at the central meridian of the given zone. In the continental United States, there are four standard time zones: Eastern, using the 75th meridian; Central, using the 90th meridian; Mountain, using the 105th meridian; and Pacific, using the 120th meridian. *See more at* **time zone.**

stand•ing wave (stăn′dĭng) A wave that does not appear to move. Standing waves occur when two similar waves travel in opposite directions between two fixed points, called nodes, at which there is no movement. Standing waves can be transverse waves, like ocean waves, or longitudinal waves, like sound waves. Also called *stationary wave.*

stan•nic (stăn′ĭk) Containing tin, especially tin with a valence of 4.

USAGE

stalactite/stalagmite

If you find it hard to remember the difference between stalagmites and stalactites, you are not alone. Both words refer to mineral deposits that form in caves. The source of each word is the Greek word *stalassein,* which means "to drip." This is appropriate, since each kind of deposit is formed by the dripping of mineral-rich water within caves. The difference is in position and orientation. A *stalactite* is an icicle-shaped deposit that hangs from the roof of a cavern, and a *stalagmite* is a conical mineral deposit that extends up from the floor of a cavern. And what do you call it when a stalagmite and stalactite meet and form a column? What else but a *stalacto-stalagmite!*

stan•nous (stăn′əs) Containing tin, especially tin with a valence of 2.

sta•pes (stā′pēz) The innermost of the three small bones, called ossicles, of the middle ear. The stapes is also called the stirrup.

staph•y•lo•coc•cus (stăf′ə-lō-kŏk′əs) *Plural* **staphylococci** (stăf′ə-lō-kŏk′sī, stăf′ə-lō-kŏk′ī) Any of various bacteria that are normally found on the skin and mucous membranes of warm-blooded animals. One kind of staphylococcus can cause infections in humans, especially in wounds.

star (stär) **1.** A celestial body that produces its own light and consists of a mass of gas held

stalactite/stalagmite

A CLOSER LOOK

Star

A star is a giant sphere of gas that produces its own light by making its own energy. It generates this energy through nuclear fusion in its core, using as fuel the elements that make it up. Fusion in a star combines atoms of lighter elements, such as hydrogen, into different, heavier elements, such as helium. A massive star can burn its fuel into elements as heavy as iron. Nuclear fusion begins when a star is fully formed out of a nebula and ends when a smaller star burns out and becomes a white dwarf or when a massive star's iron core collapses in a supernova. Because a star's composition changes as it burns its fuel, it goes through a series of stages during the course of its life, hundreds of millions or billions of years long.

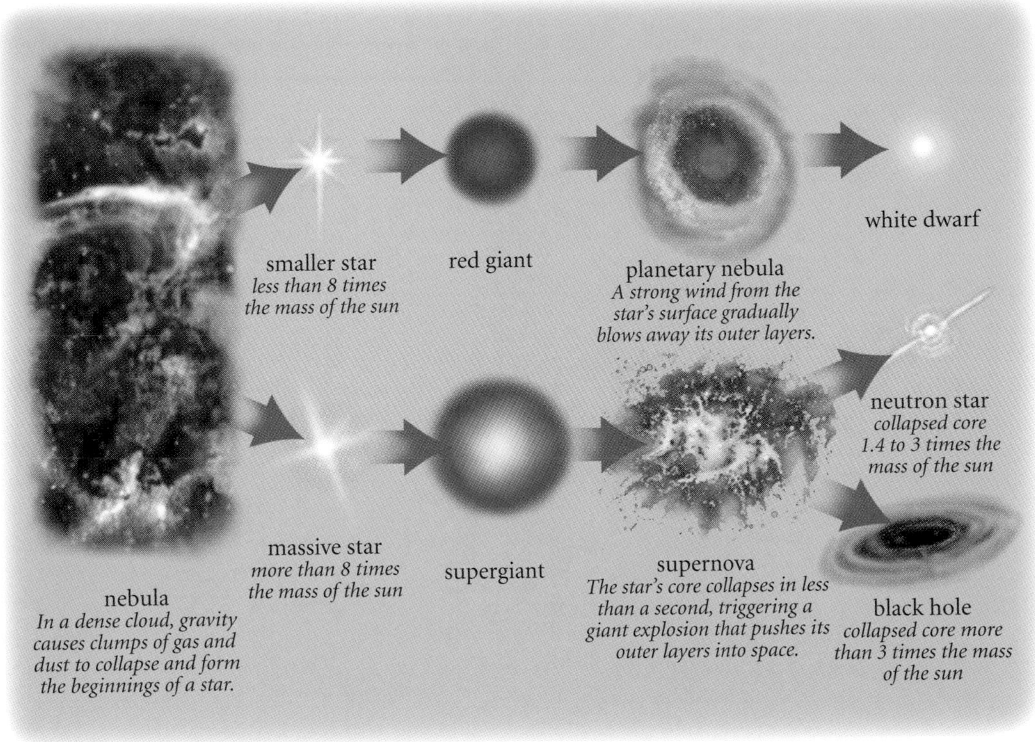
smaller star
less than 8 times the mass of the sun
red giant
planetary nebula
A strong wind from the star's surface gradually blows away its outer layers.
white dwarf
nebula
In a dense cloud, gravity causes clumps of gas and dust to collapse and form the beginnings of a star.
massive star
more than 8 times the mass of the sun
supergiant
supernova
The star's core collapses in less than a second, triggering a giant explosion that pushes its outer layers into space.
neutron star
collapsed core 1.4 to 3 times the mass of the sun
black hole
collapsed core more than 3 times the mass of the sun

together by its own gravity. Nuclear fusion in the core of a star is the source of its energy. **2.** Any of the celestial bodies visible at night from the Earth as relatively stationary, usually twinkling points of light, including binary and multiple stars.

starch (stärch) **1.** A carbohydrate that is the chief form of stored energy in plants, especially wheat, corn, rice, and potatoes. Starch is a kind of polysaccharide and forms a white, tasteless powder when purified. It is an important source of nutrition and is also used to make adhesives, paper, and textiles. **2.** Any of various substances, including natural starch, used to stiffen fabrics.

star•fish (stär′fĭsh′) Any of various invertebrate sea animals having a star-shaped body usually with five arms. The arms have rows of little suckers on the undersides, called tube feet, with which the animal moves around and grasps prey. Starfish are echinoderms, related to the sea urchins.

state of matter (stāt) One of the principal conditions in which matter exists. Matter is traditionally divided into three states—solid, liquid, and gas. Ice, liquid water, and steam, for example, are three states of matter of the same substance. The electrically neutral condition known as plasma is often considered a fourth state of matter.

stat•ic (stăt′ĭk) *Adjective.* **1.** Having no motion; being at rest. *Compare* **dynamic. 2.** Relating to or producing static electricity. —*Noun.* **3.** Distortion or interruption of a broadcast signal, such as crackling in a receiver or specks on a television screen, produced when static electricity or electricity in the atmosphere disturbs signal reception.

static electricity 1. Electric charge that accumulates on an object rather than flowing through it as a current. Static electricity forms especially when two objects that are not good electrical conductors are rubbed together, so that electrons from one of the objects rub off onto the other. This happens, for example, when combing one's hair or taking off a sweater. *See Note at* **charge. 2.** An electric discharge, such as lightning, resulting from the accumulation of such a charge.

stat•ics (stăt′ĭks) The branch of physics that deals with objects that are not in motion and with forces that are offset or counterbalanced by each other.

sta•tion•ar•y wave (stā′shə-nĕr′ē) *See* **standing wave.**

sta•tis•tics (stə-tĭs′tĭks) **1.** *Used with a singular verb.* The branch of mathematics that deals with the collection, organization, analysis, and interpretation of numerical data. Statistics is especially useful in drawing general conclusions about a set of data from a sample of it. **2.** *Used with a plural verb.* Numerical data used in drawing general conclusions from a sample of it.

stegosaurus
skeleton on display in Alberta, Canada

stat•ute mile (stăch′o͞ot) *See* **mile** (sense 1). *See Table at* **measurement.**

STD Abbreviation of **sexually transmitted disease.**

stead•y state (stĕd′ē) A stable condition that does not change over time or in which any one change is continually balanced by another.

steady state universe A model of the universe in which the ratio of the amount of matter to volume remains the same as the universe continually gets larger. This model requires the unending creation of matter to allow for the unending expansion of the universe. It is generally believed to be discredited by the discovery of radiation remaining from the big bang. *Compare* **big bang.**

steam (stēm) Water in its gaseous state, especially at a temperature above the boiling point of water (above 100°C, or 212°F, at sea level). *See Note at* **vapor.**

steam engine An engine in which the energy of hot steam is converted into mechanical power, especially an engine in which the steam expands in a closed cylinder and drives a piston.

steel (stēl) Any of various hard, strong, and flexible alloys of iron and carbon. Often, other metals are added to give the steel a particular property. Chromium and nickel, for example, are added to steel to make it stainless. Steel is widely used in many kinds of tools and as a structural material in building.

steg•o•sau•rus (stĕg′ə-sôr′əs) *or* **steg•o•saur** (stĕg′ə-sôr′) Any of several plant-eating dinosaurs of the Jurassic and Cretaceous Periods. Stegosaurus had a spiked tail and an arched back with a double row of large, triangular, upright, bony plates. Although stegosaurs grew to 20 feet (6.1 meters) in length, they had tiny heads with brains the size of a walnut.

stel•lar (stĕl′ər) Relating to or consisting of stars: *stellar life cycles.*

stem (stĕm) **1.** The main, often long or slender part of a plant that usually grows upward above the ground and supports other parts, such as branches and leaves. Some underground plant structures, such as rhizomes and corms, are stems rather than roots. **2.** A slender stalk sup-

■ Nettie Stevens

porting or connecting another plant part, such as a leaf or flower.

stem cell A cell that has the potential to develop into any of a number of different types of cells. Embryos have stem cells that can develop into almost any kind of body cell. Certain tissues in adults also produce stem cells, although the range of cells that they can develop into is limited.

steppe (stĕp) A vast, semiarid, grassy plain, as found in southeast Europe, Siberia, and central North America.

ster•e•o•chem•is•try (stĕr′ē-ō-kĕm′ĭ-strē) The branch of chemistry that is concerned with the spatial arrangements of atoms in molecules and with the chemical and physical effects of these arrangements.

ster•e•o•scope (stĕr′ē-ə-skōp′) An optical instrument through which two slightly different views of the same scene are presented, one to each eye, giving an illusion of three dimensions.

ster•ile (stĕr′əl, stĕr′īl′) **1.** Not able to produce offspring, seeds, or fruit; unable to reproduce. **2.** Producing little or no plant life; barren: *a desolate, sterile region.* **3.** Free from disease-causing microorganisms: *a sterile bandage.* —*Noun* **sterility** (stə-rĭl′ĭ-tē).

ster•ling silver (stûr′lĭng) *See under* **silver.**

ster•num (stûr′nəm) A long, flat bone located in the center of the chest, serving as a support for the collarbone and ribs. Also called *breastbone.* *See more at* **skeleton.**

ster•oid (stĕr′oid′) **1.** Any of a class of organic compounds having as a basis 17 carbon atoms arranged in four rings. Steroids include the sex hormones, such as testosterone, and hormones produced by the adrenal glands. They also include sterols, such as cholesterol, and certain forms of vitamins. **2.** Any of various hormones having the structure of a steroid that are made synthetically, especially for use in medicine.

ster•ol (stîr′ôl′) Any of various alcohols having the structure of a steroid, including cholesterol. Sterols are found in the tissues of animals, plants, fungi, and yeasts.

Ste•vens (stē′vənz), **Nettie Marie** 1861–1912. American biologist who identified the role of X and Y chromosomes in determining the sex of an organism. Stevens studied the chromosomes of mealworm beetles, first establishing that chromosomes are inherited in pairs. She later showed that eggs fertilized by X-carrying sperm produced female offspring, while Y-carrying sperm produced a male. She extended this work to studies of sex determination in various plants and insects.

stig•ma (stĭg′mə) The sticky tip of a flower pistil, on which pollen is deposited at the beginning of pollination. *See more at* **flower.**

stim•u•lant (stĭm′yə-lənt) A drug or other substance, such as caffeine, that speeds up or excites a body system, especially the nervous system.

stim•u•lus (stĭm′yə-ləs) *Plural* **stimuli** (stĭm′yə-lī′) Something that causes a response in a body part or organism. A stimulus may be internal or external. Sense organs, such as the ear, and sensory receptors, such as those in the skin, are sensitive to external stimuli such as sound and touch.

sting•er (stĭng′ər) A sharp stinging organ, such as that of a bee, scorpion, or stingray. Stingers usually inject venom.

stip•ule (stĭp′yo͞ol) One of the usually small, paired parts resembling leaves at the base of a leafstalk in certain plants, such as roses and beans.

sto•lon (stō′lŏn′) *See* **runner.**

sto•ma (stō′mə) *Plural* **stomata** (stō′mə-tə) **1.** *Botany.* One of the tiny openings in the outer

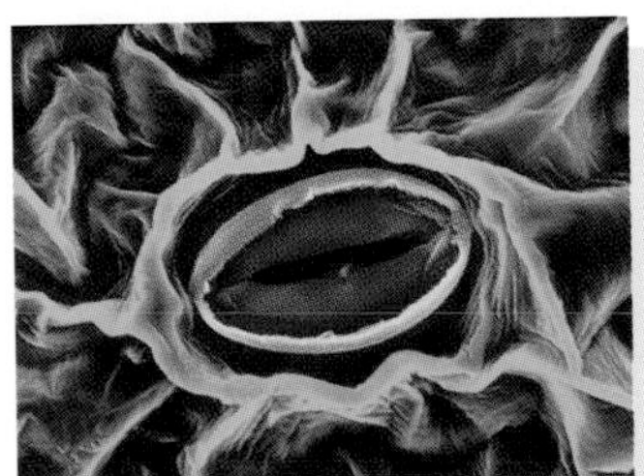

■ **stoma** *scanning electron micrograph of a pea leaf stoma*

surface of a plant leaf or stem, through which gases and water vapor pass. Most stomata are on the underside of leaves. **2.** *Zoology.* A mouth-like opening, such as the oral cavity of a nematode.

stom•ach (stŭm′ək) **1.** A sac-like, muscular organ in vertebrate animals that stores food and is a main organ of digestion. It is located between the esophagus and the small intestine. **2.** A similar digestive structure of many invertebrates. **3.** Any of the four compartments into which the stomach of a ruminant is divided; the rumen, reticulum, omasum, or abomasum.

stone (stōn) **1.** *Geology.* A general term for rock, especially as used in construction. **2.** *Botany.* The pit of certain fruits, such as the plum or cherry. **3.** *Medicine.* A hard mass of minerals or other substance, such as cholesterol, that forms in a body part or organ: *kidney stones.*

Stone Age The earliest known period of human culture, marked by the use of stone tools. *See* **Mesolithic, Neolithic, Paleolithic.**

straight angle (strāt) An angle having a measure of 180°.

strain (strān) **1.** A group of organisms of the same species, sharing certain characteristics not typical of the entire species but minor enough not to warrant classification as a separate breed or variety: *a drug-resistant strain of bacteria.* **2.** The extent to which a body is distorted when it is subjected to a deforming force, such as stress. The distortion can involve both a change in shape and in size. ❖ In **elastic strain** the distorted body returns to its original shape and size when the force is removed. ❖ In **plastic strain** the distorted body does not return to its original shape and size even after the force has been removed. *Compare* **stress.** *See more at* **Hooke's law.**

strait (strāt) A narrow waterway joining two larger bodies of water. The Strait of Gibraltar, for example, connects the Mediterranean Sea with the Atlantic Ocean.

strat•i•fi•ca•tion (străt′ə-fĭ-kā′shən) Formation or deposition of layers, as of rock or sediments.

strat•o•cu•mu•lus (străt′ō-kyōōm′yə-ləs) A low-lying, often patchy cloud formation occurring in extensive horizontal layers with distinct, rounded tops.

strat•o•sphere (străt′ə-sfîr′) The layer of the Earth's atmosphere lying above the troposphere and below the mesosphere, from the tropopause to about 31 miles (50 kilometers) above the Earth's surface. In the stratosphere, temperatures rise slightly with altitude.

stra•tum (strā′təm, străt′əm) *Plural* **strata** *or* **stratums. 1.** A layer of rock whose composition is more or less the same throughout. A particular rock stratum is visibly different from the rock strata above and below it. **2.** A layer of tissue, as of the skin or another organ.

strat•us (străt′əs) *Plural* **strati.** A low-lying, grayish cloud layer that sometimes produces drizzle. A stratus cloud that is close to the ground or water is called fog.

streak (strēk) The characteristic color of a mineral after it has been ground into a powder. Because the streak of a mineral is not always the same as its natural color, it is a useful tool in mineral identification.

stream•line (strēm′līn′) To design or construct something so that it offers the least resistance to the flow of a fluid, especially air or water.

strep throat (strĕp) Infection of the throat caused by streptococcus bacteria. Symptoms include fever, redness of the throat, and inflammation of the tonsils.

strep•to•coc•cus (strĕp′tə-kŏk′əs) *Plural* **streptococci** (strĕp′tə-kŏk′sī, strĕp′tə-kŏk′ī) Any of various bacteria that are normally found on the skin and mucous membranes and in the digestive

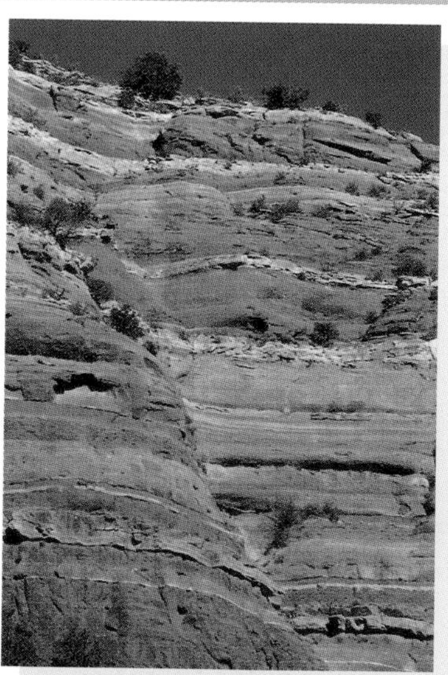

■ **stratification**
sandstone and limestone strata near Sedona, Arizona

tract of mammals. One kind of streptococcus causes especially severe infections in humans, including strep throat, scarlet fever, pneumonia, and blood infections.

stress (strĕs) **1.** A force that tends to distort or deform something by compressing or stretching it: *The stress of the books caused the wooden shelf to warp. Compare* **strain.** *See more at* **Hooke's law. 2.** A reaction by an organism to a disturbing or dangerous situation. In animals, the body's initial response to stress includes a rise in heart rate and blood pressure and a heightened state of alertness. A certain amount of stress may be necessary for an organism to survive, but too much stress can lead to ill health.

stri•a•tion (strī-ā′shən) One of a number of parallel lines or grooves on the surface of a rock. Striations form when pieces of rock frozen into the base of a glacier move across the rock and scratch it, or when two blocks of rock along opposite sides of a fault plane slide past each other, scratching the rocks' outer surfaces.

strike-slip fault (strīk′slĭp′) A geologic fault in which the blocks of rock on either side of the fault slide horizontally in opposite directions along the line of the fault plane. *See more at* **fault.**

string theory (strĭng) A theory in physics in which elementary particles are thought of as tiny, vibrating string-like objects, existing in a space-time that has more dimensions than the familiar three dimensions of space. Some of these extra dimensions are thought to be exceedingly small and string-like in shape.

strip mine (strĭp) An open mine, especially a coal mine, whose seams or outcrops run close to ground level and are exposed by the removal of overlying soil.

strobe light (strōb) A lamp that produces very short, intense flashes of light by means of an electric discharge in a gas. The ability of strobe lights to "freeze" the motion of rapidly moving objects makes them very useful in photography and in making measurements of vibration or other types of high-speed motion.

stroke (strōk) A sudden interruption in the normal functioning of the brain, often resulting in slurred speech and loss of muscle control and feeling on one side of the body. Strokes are usually caused by a reduction in blood flow to a part of the brain.

strip mine
lignite strip mine near Leipzig, Germany

strong nuclear force (strông) A force between elementary or subatomic particles that holds quarks together to form protons and neutrons, and also binds protons and neutrons together in the atomic nucleus. The strong nuclear force is one of the four basic forces in nature, along with gravity, the electromagnetic force, and the weak nuclear force. Also called *strong interaction.*

stron•ti•um (strŏn′chē-əm, strŏn′tē-əm) A soft, silvery metallic element that is an alkaline-earth metal and occurs naturally only as a sulfate or carbonate. One of its isotopes is used in the radiometric dating of rocks. Because strontium salts burn with a red flame, they are used to make fireworks and signal flares. *Symbol* **Sr.** *Atomic number* 38. *See* **Periodic Table,** pages 262–263.

strontium 90 A radioactive isotope of strontium having a mass number of 90 and a half-life of 28 years. Strontium 90 is the most dangerous component of the fallout from nuclear explosions because it can be absorbed by the body. It is also used in medicine to treat cancer.

struc•tur•al formula (strŭk′chər-əl) A chemical formula that shows how the atoms making up a compound are arranged within the molecule. For example, the structural formula of aspirin is $CH_3COOC_6H_4COOH$, indicating that it is an acetate (CH_3COO) of a phenyl (C_6H_4) organic acid (COOH). Since structural formulas can get quite long, formulas are usually given with all the atoms totaled up instead (in this case, $C_9H_8O_4$). *Compare* **molecular formula.**

strych•nine (strĭk′nīn′) An extremely poisonous, white crystalline compound derived from certain plants. It is used as a rat poison and was formerly used in medicine to stimulate the nervous system.

Did You Know?

subatomic particles

Until the 20th century, scientists thought that atoms were the smallest units of matter. This view started to change following some experiments in the late 1800s involving electrical discharges. By the early 1900s it was clear that these discharges were composed of a new kind of particle, one that was much lighter than an atom of the lightest chemical element, hydrogen. These particles were named *electrons*. It was further learned that atoms themselves contained electrons; the electron thus became the first known *subatomic particle*. Since electrons have negative electrical charge, but the atoms containing them are neutral in charge, researchers believed that atoms must also contain positively-charged particles that balanced the negatively-charged electrons. This idea, together with research into radioactivity, led Ernest Rutherford to the discovery of the atomic nucleus in 1911. Rutherford saw the nucleus as the home of these positively-charged particles (now called *protons*). Further experiments on radioactivity showed, by 1932, that the nucleus also contained a third kind of particle, the *neutron*. While electrons, protons, and neutrons are the most familiar subatomic particles, they are not the only ones: dozens more have since been identified. Scientists now think that many subatomic particles are themselves made up of smaller units called *elementary particles*, such as neutrinos and quarks.

stur•geon (stûr′jən) Any of various large, primitive freshwater or saltwater fish having bony plates rather than true scales on its body. It is widely used for food, and its roe is a source of caviar.

style (stīl) The slender part of a flower pistil, extending from the ovary to the stigma. *See more at* **flower.**

sub– A prefix that means: **1.** Underneath or lower, as in *subsoil.* **2.** A subordinate or secondary part of something else, as in *subphylum.* **3.** Less than completely, as in *subtropical.*

sub•a•tom•ic particle (sŭb′ə-tŏm′ĭk) One of the basic units of which atoms and all matter are made. Protons, neutrons and electrons are subatomic particles.

sub•class (sŭb′klăs′) A subdivision of a class of organisms. A subclass contains one or more orders.

sub•cu•ta•ne•ous (sŭb′kyo͞o-tā′nē-əs) Located or placed just beneath the skin.

sub•duc•tion zone (səb-dŭk′shən) A convergent plate boundary where one plate sinks (subducts) beneath the other, usually because it is denser. *See more at* **tectonic boundary.**

sub•king•dom (sŭb′kĭng′dəm) A subdivision of a kingdom of organisms. A subkingdom contains one or more phyla.

sub•li•ma•tion (sŭb′lə-mā′shən) The process of changing from a solid to a gas, or from a gas to a solid, without passing through an intermediate liquid phase.

sub•or•der (sŭb′ôr′dər) A subdivision of an order of organisms. A suborder contains one or more families.

sub•phy•lum (sŭb′fī′ləm) *Plural* **subphyla.** A subdivision of a phylum of organisms. A subphylum contains one or more classes.

sub•set (sŭb′sĕt′) A set whose members are all contained in another set. The set of positive integers, for example, is a subset of the set of integers.

sub•soil (sŭb′soil′) The layer of earth below the surface soil.

sub•spe•cies (sŭb′spē′shēz, sŭb′spē′sēz) A subdivision of a species of organisms, usually based on geographic distribution.

sub•strate (sŭb′strāt′) **1.** The material or substance on which an enzyme acts. *See Note at* **enzyme. 2.** The surface on which plants, algae, or certain animals, such as barnacles, live or grow. A substrate may serve as a source of food for an organism or simply provide support.

Did You Know?
sublimation

We've all seen a solid heated to a liquid and a liquid heated to a gas. Ice, for instance, melts to become liquid water, and liquid water can be boiled away as steam. However, under the right conditions of pressure and temperature something else can happen: the solid can turn directly into a gas. This strange process is called *sublimation.* The word also refers to the reverse situation, when a gas solidifies without becoming liquid first. The most familiar example of a solid turning into a gas is probably that of dry ice. Solid carbon dioxide, dry ice, seems to give off smoke at room temperature. This "smoke" is actually the solid carbon dioxide turning directly into a gas. Dry ice is useful for packing certain materials that need to stay cold, since it doesn't melt and get everything wet. A common example of a gas turning directly into a solid is the formation of frost from the extremely rapid cooling of water vapor.

sub•trac•tion (səb-trăk′shən) The act, process, or operation of subtracting one number or quantity from another to compute their difference.

sub•trac•tive (səb-trăk′tĭv) **1.** Being any of the primary colors cyan, magenta, or yellow, which can be combined using overlapping filters to produce all other colors. The filters absorb certain wavelengths and allow others to pass through. *See more at* **color. 2.** *Mathematics.* Marked by or involving subtraction.

sub•tra•hend (sŭb′trə-hĕnd′) A number subtracted from another. For example, in the expression 4 – 3, 3 is the subtrahend.

sub•trop•i•cal (sŭb-trŏp′ĭ-kəl) Relating to the regions of the Earth bordering on the tropics, just north of the Tropic of Cancer or just south of the Tropic of Capricorn. Subtropical regions are the warmest parts of the two Temperate Zones.

suc•ces•sion (sək-sĕsh′ən) The gradual replacement of one type of ecological community by another, involving a series of changes especially in the dominant vegetation. For example, if a meadow is left unmowed, its grasses might be replaced first by fast-growing bushes and conifers, which after some years might be replaced in turn by slower-growing hardwoods. *See more at* **climax community.**

suc•cu•lent (sŭk′yə-lənt) A plant having fleshy leaves or stems that store water. Cacti are succulents.

suck•er (sŭk′ər) **1.** *Zoology.* A part by which an animal sucks blood from or uses suction to cling to another animal. Leeches and remoras have suckers. **2.** *Botany.* A shoot growing from the base or root of a tree or shrub and giving rise to a new plant.

su•crose (so͞o′krōs′) A crystalline sugar having the formula $C_{12}H_{22}O_{11}$, found in many plants, especially sugar cane, sugar beets, and sugar maple. Sucrose is used widely as a sweetener.

suc•tion (sŭk′shən) An act or force that reduces the pressure in a space, causing a fluid or solid to flow into it from a region of greater pressure.

Suess (zo͞os), **Eduard** 1831–1914. Austrian geologist who was the first to propose the existence of the early supercontinent Gondwanaland. He also investigated the origin of the Alps.

sug•ar (sho͝og′ər) **1.** Any of a class of crystalline carbohydrates, such as sucrose, glucose, or lactose, that dissolve in water and have a characteristic sweet taste. **2.** Sucrose.

sul•fate (sŭl′fāt′) A chemical compound made from sulfuric acid and containing the group SO_4.

sul•fide (sŭl′fīd′) A chemical compound of sulfur and another element or radical, such as hydrogen sulfide.

sul•fur *also* **sul•phur** (sŭl′fər) A pale-yellow, brittle nonmetallic element that occurs widely in nature, especially in volcanic deposits, many common minerals, natural gas, and petroleum. It is used to make gunpowder and fertilizer, to vulcanize rubber, and to produce sulfuric acid. *Symbol* **S.** *Atomic number* 16. *See* **Periodic Table,** pages 262–263.

sulfur dioxide A colorless, poisonous gas or liquid, SO_2, that has a strong odor. It is formed naturally by volcanic activity, and is a waste gas produced by burning coal and oil and by many industrial processes, such as smelting. It is also a hazardous air pollutant and a major contributor to acid rain.

sul•fu•ric acid (sŭl-fyo͝or′ĭk) A strong corrosive acid, H_2SO_4. It combines very easily with water, making it a good drying agent, and is the most widely used acid in industry.

sum (sŭm) The result of adding numbers or quantities. The sum of 6 and 9, for example, is 15, and the sum of $4x$ and $5x$ is $9x$.

sum•mer (sŭm′ər) The usually warmest season of the year, occurring between spring and autumn. In the Northern Hemisphere, it extends from the summer solstice to the autumnal equinox.

summer solstice In the Northern Hemisphere, the solstice that occurs on June 20 or 21, marking the beginning of summer and the day of the year with the longest period of sunlight. *Compare* **winter solstice.**

sun (sŭn) **1.** Often **Sun.** The star that is orbited by all of the planets and other bodies of our solar system and that supplies the heat and light that sustain life on Earth. It has a diameter of about 864,000 miles (1,390,000 kilometers), an average distance from Earth of about 93 million miles (150 million kilometers), and a mass about 330,000 times that of Earth. *See Table at* **solar system,** pages 316–317. *See Note at* **dwarf star. 2.** A star that is the center of a system of planets.

sun•spot (sŭn′spŏt′) Any of the relatively cool dark spots that appear in groups on the surface of the sun. Sunspots are associated with strong magnetic fields.

su•per•con•duc•tor (so͞o′pər-kən-dŭk′tər) A metal or an alloy that at a very low temperature (close to absolute zero) conducts electric current with almost no resistance. Most superconductors work only at temperatures approaching –459.67°F (–273.15°C), but a few alloys become superconductors around –200°F (–128.88°C). Scientists hope to find materials that become superconductors closer to room temperature.

su•per•con•ti•nent (so͞o′pər-kŏn′tə-nənt) A large continent that, according to the theory of plate tectonics, is thought to have split into smaller continents in the geologic past. Pangaea and Gondwanaland are supercontinents. *See Note at* **Gondwanaland.**

su•per•gi•ant (so͞o′pər-jī′ənt) A star that is larger, brighter, and more massive than a giant star. Supergiants, such as Betelgeuse or Rigel, are thousands of times brighter than the sun. *See more at* **star.**

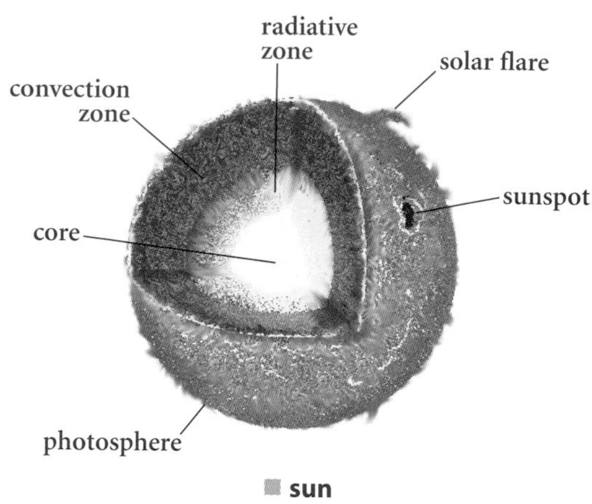

sun
cutaway diagram of the sun

su•per•grav•ity (so͞o′pər-grăv′ĭ-tē) A theory of supersymmetry that includes the theory of general relativity. In this theory, gravity, like other fundamental forces such as the electromagnetic force, is carried by a subatomic particle (in this case, the graviton); when matter undergoes the force of gravity, it is thought to interact with gravitons. No gravitons have been observed in the real world, however.

su•per•no•va (so͞o′pər-nō′və) *Plural* **supernovae** (so͞o′pər-nō′vē) *or* **supernovas.** A massive star that undergoes a sudden, extreme increase in brightness and releases an enormous burst of energy. This occurs as a result of the violent explosion of most of the material of the star, triggered by the collapse of its core. *See more at* **star.** *Compare* **nova.** *See Note at* **pulsar.**

su•per•son•ic (so͞o′pər-sŏn′ĭk) Relating to or traveling at a speed greater than the speed of sound in a given medium, especially air.

su•per•string theory (so͞o′pər-strĭng′) A type of string theory that assumes or is based on supersymmetry.

su•per•sym•me•try (so͞o′pər-sĭm′ĭ-trē) A theory of physics in which the subatomic particles that carry the fundamental forces (such as the photon, which carries the electromagnetic force) have corresponding particles with the same mass. The theory is an attempt to unify the fundamental forces—the electromagnetic force, the strong nuclear force, the weak nuclear force, and gravity—all under one theory. Supersymmetry has not been shown to hold in the real world, though some scientists suspect that evidence for it may be found only at extremely high energies.

sup•ple•men•ta•ry angles (sŭp′lə-mĕn′tə-rē) Two angles whose sum is 180°.

sur•face tension (sûr′fəs) A property of liquids whereby their surfaces behave as if they were covered by a thin, elastic film. Surface tension is caused by the uneven attraction that molecules at or near the surface of a liquid have for each other. Because of surface tension, small objects can be supported by the surface of a liquid without sinking. Insects, for example, can walk across the surface of a pond because of the surface tension of water. Surface tension also causes drops of a liquid to be shaped like spheres, since spheres have the least amount of surface area possible.

surface wave An earthquake wave in which rock particles vibrate at right angles to the direction of wave travel. Surface waves travel only on the Earth's surface, and not through it. Also called *L wave. See Note at* **earthquake.**

sur•fac•tant (sər-făk′tənt) **1.** A substance, such as detergent, that is added to a liquid to increase its ability to spread. **2.** A substance produced by the tiny air-filled sacs of the lung that reduces the surface tension of the fluids coating the lung. Surfactant helps keep the tiny air sacs from collapsing during normal breathing.

sus•pen•sion (sə-spĕn′shən) A mixture in which small particles of a substance are dispersed throughout a gas or liquid. If left undisturbed, the particles are likely to settle to the bottom. The particles in a suspension are larger than those in a colloid or a solution. Muddy water is an example of a suspension. *Compare* **colloid, solution.**

■ **supernova**
Supernova 1987a is the large, bright star at bottom right. The explosion appeared in 1987 in one of the Magellanic Clouds.

Did You Know?
symbiosis

Two organisms that live together in *symbiosis* may have one of three kinds of relationships: mutualism, commensalism, or parasitism. The *mutualism* shown by the rhinoceros and the tickbird benefits both. Riding on the rhino's back, the tickbird eats its fill of the ticks that bother the rhino while the rhino gets warning calls from the bird when it senses danger. In *commensalism,* one member benefits and the other is unaffected. Certain barnacles attach themselves to whales, gaining a safe home and transportation to food-rich waters. But the whales are generally unaffected by the barnacles' presence. In *parasitism,* though, one species generally gets hurt, as when fleas infest a dog's coat and feed on its blood.

swal•low (swŏl′ō) Any of various small, swift-flying birds that have narrow pointed wings, a forked or notched tail, and a large mouth for catching flying insects in the air. Swallows migrate over thousands of miles each year.

swamp (swŏmp) An area of low-lying wet or seasonally flooded land, often having trees and dense shrubs or thickets.

S wave *See* **secondary wave.** *See Note at* **earthquake.**

sweat (swĕt) The salty liquid given off by glands in the skin of mammals. As sweat evaporates, the skin cools, resulting in a reduction of body heat. ❖ The glands in the skin that secrete sweat are called **sweat glands.**

swim bladder (swĭm) *See* **air bladder** (sense 1).

sym•bi•o•sis (sĭm′bē-ō′sĭs) The close association between two or more different organisms of different species, often but not necessarily benefiting each member. —*Adjective* **symbiotic.**

sym•me•try (sĭm′ĭ-trē) An exact matching of form and arrangement of parts on opposite sides of a boundary, such as a plane or line, or around a central point or axis.

sym•pa•thet•ic nervous system (sĭm′pə-thĕt′ĭk) The part of the autonomic nervous system that tends to act in opposition to the parasympathetic nervous system, as by speeding up the heart and contracting the blood vessels. It also regulates the function of glands, particularly the sweat glands. The sympathetic nervous system is activated especially under conditions of stress.

symp•tom (sĭm′təm) A sign or an indication of a disorder or disease, usually a noticeable change in how a person feels or looks. Sore throat, headache, and higher than normal counts of white blood cells in the blood are symptoms of certain infections.

syn•apse (sĭn′ăps′) The gap across which a nerve impulse passes from one nerve cell to another nerve cell, a muscle cell, or a gland cell.

syn•chro•tron (sĭng′krə-trŏn′) A device that accelerates charged subatomic particles, such as protons and electrons, in a circular path, greatly increasing their energies. Unlike cyclotrons that consist of a continuous spiral through which particles are accelerated, synchrotrons consist of a single tube in the shape of a large ring. The particles rotate over and over again through this tube at increasing speeds. Synchrotrons are used to study subatomic structures. *See more at* **cyclotron.**

syn•cline (sĭn′klīn′) A fold of rock layers that slope upward on both sides of a common low point. Synclines form when rocks are compressed by plate-tectonic forces. They can be as small as the side of a cliff or as large as an entire valley. *Compare* **anticline.**

syn•drome (sĭn′drōm′) An abnormal condition or disease that is identified by a set group of physical signs and symptoms.

syn•the•sis (sĭn′thĭ-sĭs) The formation of a chemical compound by combining simpler compounds or elements. —*Verb* **synthesize.**

syn•thet•ic (sĭn-thĕt′ĭk) Produced by chemical synthesis, especially in a laboratory or other artificial environment.

syph•i•lis (sĭf′ə-lĭs) A sexually transmitted disease caused by a bacterial infection that is characterized in its early stages by sores on the genitals. If untreated, skin ulcers develop, followed by often fatal infection of major organs of the body.

sy•ringe (sə-rĭnj′) A medical instrument used to inject fluids into the body or draw them from it.

sys•tem (sĭs′təm) A group of elements or parts that function together to form a complex whole. For example, the bones, joints, and other structures making up the skeleton of an animal form its *skeletal system.* A *weather system* is made up of the different masses of warmer and cooler air that are present in a region, along with any winds, clouds, and rain or snow that they produce.

sys•to•le (sĭs′tə-lē) The period during the normal beating of the heart in which contraction of the ventricles occurs, forcing blood into the aorta and the arteries that lead to the lungs. *Compare* **diastole.**

Szi•lard (zĭl′ərd), **Leo** 1898–1964. Hungarian-born American physicist who introduced the concept of the nuclear chain reaction. With Enrico Fermi, he built the world's first nuclear reactor. Szilard was instrumental in the development of the atomic bomb.

T

Ta The symbol for **tantalum.**

tac•tile (tăk′təl, tăk′tīl′) Used for or sensitive to touch: *tactile organs.*

tactile hair A hair or hair-like structure that is highly sensitive to pressure or touch. Tactile hairs cover the bodies of most insects and are found in many mammals, especially as whiskers.

tad•pole (tăd′pōl′) The larval stage of a frog or toad. A tadpole lives in the water, has a tail and gills, and has no limbs. The tail and gills disappear as the legs and lungs develop on the way to the adult stage.

tai•ga (tī′gə) A forest located in the Earth's far northern regions, consisting mainly of cone-bearing evergreens, such as firs, pines, and spruces, and some deciduous trees, such as larches, birches, and aspens. The taiga is found just south of the tundra.

tail (tāl) **1.** The rear, elongated part of many animals, extending beyond the trunk or main part of the body. **2.** The long, bright stream of gas and dust forced from the head of a comet when it is close to the sun.

tail•bone (tāl′bōn′) *See* **coccyx.**

talc (tălk) A white, greenish, or gray mineral that is a silicate of magnesium, usually occurring as massive mica-like flakes. It has a soft, soapy texture, and is used in face powder and talcum powder, for coating paper, and as a filler in paints and plastics. Talc is the mineral used to represent a hardness of 1 on the Mohs scale.

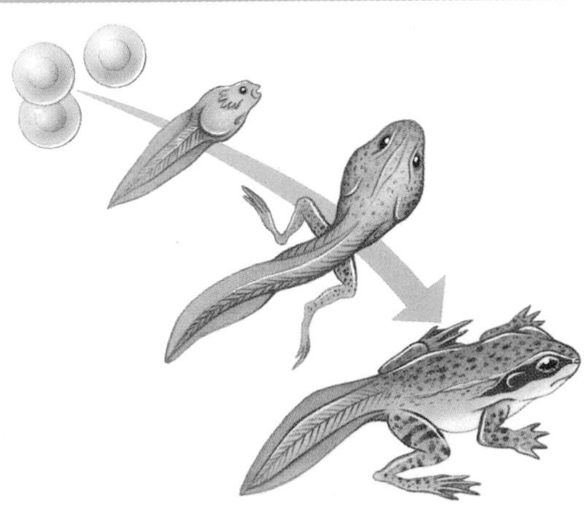

tadpole
development of a frog from a fertilized egg through several tadpole stages

Did You Know?

tails

The *tails* of cats and dogs are hard to miss. Sometimes they seem to be there only to be caught under chairs or get stepped on. But as a body feature, tails have many uses throughout the animal kingdom. Cheetahs use the tail for balance while running (as do cats and dogs), and the kangaroo balances with its tail while hopping. The Komodo dragon uses its heavy, powerful tail in combat with other dragons over food and mates. Birds in flight make quick course corrections by adjusting their tail positions. Wolves communicate to other wolves by how they position their tails. And as tadpoles change into frogs, they absorb their tails back into their bodies and make use of the nutrients stored in the tails. Monkeys sometimes hang from their tails, a talent apes gave up during evolution for reasons probably related to their more upright stance.

tal•on (tăl′ən) A sharp, curved claw on the foot of a bird or other animal such as a lizard, used for seizing and tearing prey.

ta•lus[1] (tā′ləs) The bone that forms a joint with the tibia and fibula, making up the main bone of the ankle. *See more at* **skeleton.**

talus[2] A sloping mass of rock fragments at the base of a cliff.

tan Abbreviation of **tangent.**

tan•gent (tăn′jənt) **1.** A line, curve, or surface touching but not intersecting another. **2.** The ratio of the length of the side opposite an acute angle in a right triangle to the side adjacent to the angle.

tan•ta•lum (tăn′tə-ləm) A hard, heavy, gray metallic element that is highly resistant to corrosion at lower temperatures. It is used to make light-bulb filaments, surgical instruments, and glass for camera lenses. *Symbol* **Ta.** *Atomic number* 73. *See* **Periodic Table,** pages 262–263.

tape•worm (tāp′wûrm′) Any of various long flatworms that live as parasites in the intestines of many animals, including humans.

tar (tär) **1.** A thick, oily, dark substance consisting mainly of hydrocarbons, made by heating wood, coal, or peat in the absence of air. **2.** *See* **coal tar. 3.** A solid, sticky substance that remains when tobacco is burned. It accumulates in the lungs of smokers and is considered to be a cause of cancer.

ta•ran•tu•la (tə-răn′chə-lə) Any of various large, hairy, mostly tropical spiders that have a painful but not dangerous bite. They do not spin webs, but live in burrows in the ground and hunt small frogs, toads, rodents, and birds.

tar pit An accumulation of natural tar or asphalt at the Earth's surface, especially one that traps animals and preserves their bones.

tar•sal (tär′səl) Any of the bones of the foot lying between the ankle and metatarsals. *See more at* **skeleton.**

taste bud (tāst) Any of numerous sense organs on the tongues of most vertebrate animals that are sensitive to four types of taste: sweet, sour, salty, or bitter.

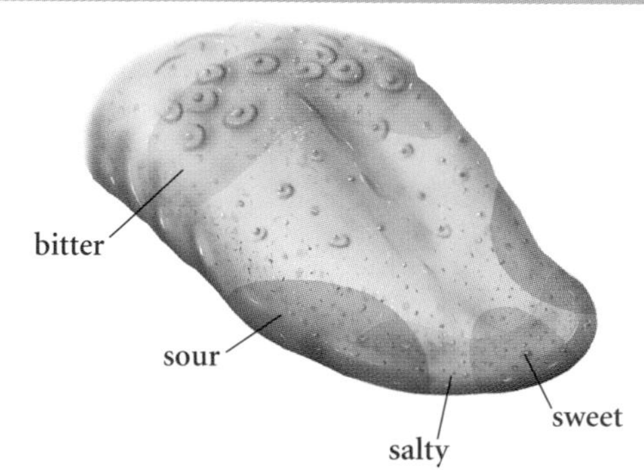

taste bud

There are four distinct tastes that the human tongue can detect. Each is identified by different taste buds, as shown in this illustration.

Tau•rus (tôr′əs) A constellation in the Northern Hemisphere near Orion and Aries.

tax•on•o•my (tăk-sŏn′ə-mē) The scientific classification of organisms into specially named groups based on shared characteristics and natural relationships.

Tay-Sachs disease (tā′săks′) A hereditary disease in which the products of fat metabolism accumulate in the nervous system, causing retardation, paralysis, and death by the age of 3 or 4. It mostly affects children of eastern European Jewish descent.

Tb The symbol for **terbium.**

TB Abbreviation of **tuberculosis.**

Tc The symbol for **technetium.**

T cell Any of the lymphocytes that act to defend the body against disease by binding foreign antigens to receptors on the surface of their cells. T cells also regulate the function of B cells.

Te The symbol for **tellurium.**

tear (tîr) A drop of the clear salty liquid secreted by glands (lacrimal glands) in the eyes. Tears wet the membrane covering the eye and help rid the eye of substances that cause irritation.

teat (tēt, tĭt) A projection near the center of the mammary gland of most female mammals that contains the outlets of the milk ducts.

tech•ne•ti•um (tĕk-nē′shē-əm) A silvery-gray, radioactive metallic element. It was the first element to be artificially made, and it is produced naturally in extremely small amounts during the radioactive decay of uranium. Technetium is used to remove corrosion from steel. *Symbol* **Tc.** *Atomic number* 43. *See* **Periodic Table,** pages 262–263.

tech•nol•o•gy (tĕk-nŏl′ə-jē) **1.** The use of scientific knowledge to solve practical problems, especially in industry and commerce. **2.** The specific methods, materials, and devices used to solve practical problems: *aerospace technology.*

tec•ton•ic boundary (tĕk-tŏn′ĭk) In the theory of plate tectonics, a boundary between two or more plates. The plates can be moving toward each other (at convergent plate boundaries), away from each other (at divergent plate boundaries), or past each other (at transform faults). Maps of seismic and volcanic activity across the Earth indicate that most earthquakes and volcanic eruptions occur along or near tectonic bound-

TAXONOMY

Taxonomy is the scientific classification of life. It was originally developed in the 18th century by the Swedish botanist Carolus Linnaeus, who divided all forms of life into two large groups—the animal and plant kingdoms. Modern biologists have expanded Linnaeus's system and now recognize five separate kingdoms, as shown in the following table:

KINGDOM	TYPE OF ORGANISMS
Prokaryota *or* Monera	bacteria and blue-green algae
Protista *or* Protoctista	single-celled organisms such as the amoeba, euglena, and paramecium; also dinoflagellates, slime molds, and most algae
Fungi	mushrooms, yeasts, molds, lichens
Plantae	plants
Animalia	multicellular animals

Kingdoms are the highest level of classification. Below the kingdom are six major lower levels arranged hierarchically. From highest to lowest these are: **phylum** (or **division,** in the plant kingdom), **class, order, family, genus,** and **species.** These can be further subdivided into subkingdom, subphylum, subclass, and so forth. These categories indicate how closely or distantly organisms are related to each other, based on structural and genetic similarities.

By convention, taxonomic categories are capitalized except for species and subspecies names. Genus and species names are written in italic, as in *Tyrannosaurus rex* or *Homo sapiens.* The chart below compares the taxonomy of three organisms—a human, a dog, and a goldfish. As the table shows, although the three species are different in many ways, they also share certain important taxonomic characteristics.

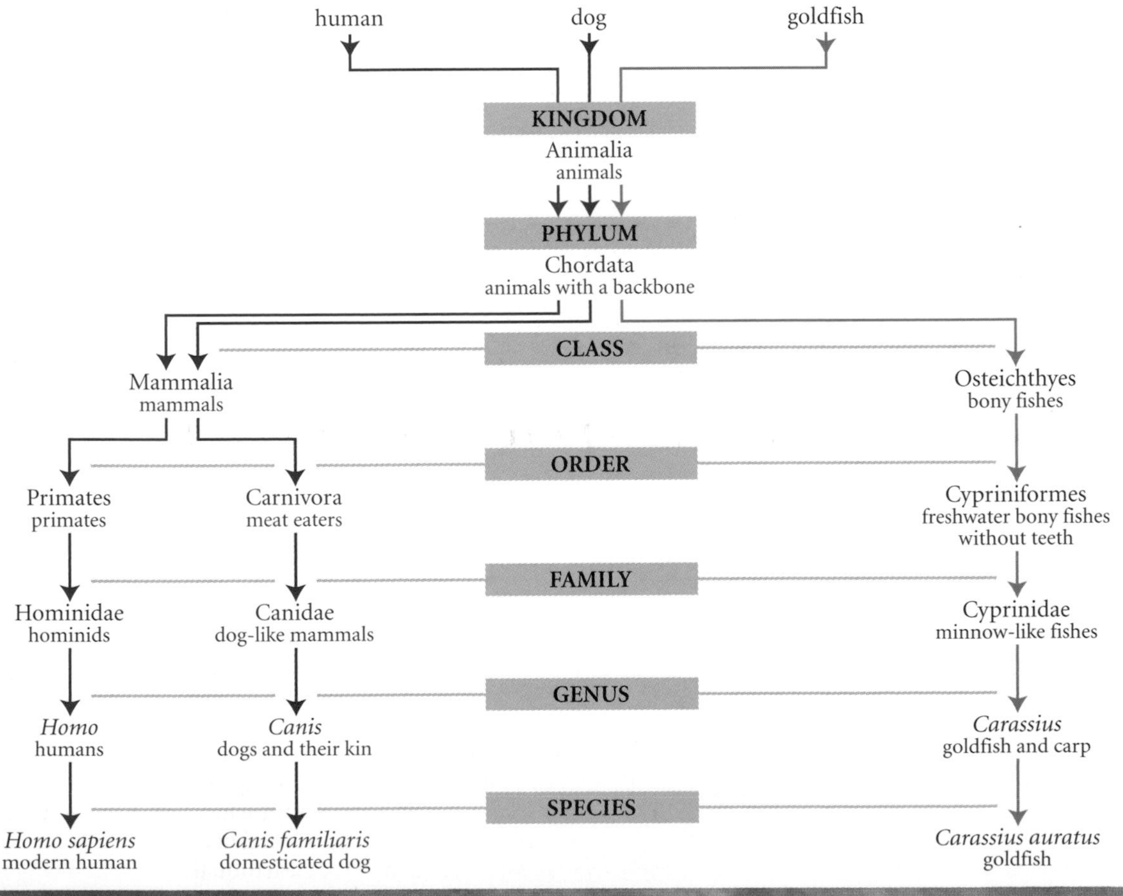

A CLOSER LOOK

Tectonic Boundaries

Subduction Zones

Two tectonic plates collide. The denser plate sinks below the other, and a deep trench forms where the two plates meet. The downgoing plate heats up with depth and begins to melt. A chain of volcanoes forms in the overriding plate, creating an island arc in the ocean or a mountain range along the edge of a continent. The Aleutian Islands and the Andes formed in this way.

Hot Spots

A volcano forms over a hot spot—an area within the Earth that gives off a lot of heat from radioactive decay. The Hawaiian Islands formed in this way.

Spreading Zones

As plates spread apart, new lava rises to the surface from deep within the Earth and cools to form new rock. The island of Iceland formed in this way. Before plates actually break apart, a rift valley forms. Sometimes sea water flows into it. This is how the Red Sea formed.

Collision Zones

Two equally dense plates collide. Neither plate sinks below the other, and as the two push against each other a mountain chain forms. The Himalayas formed in this way.

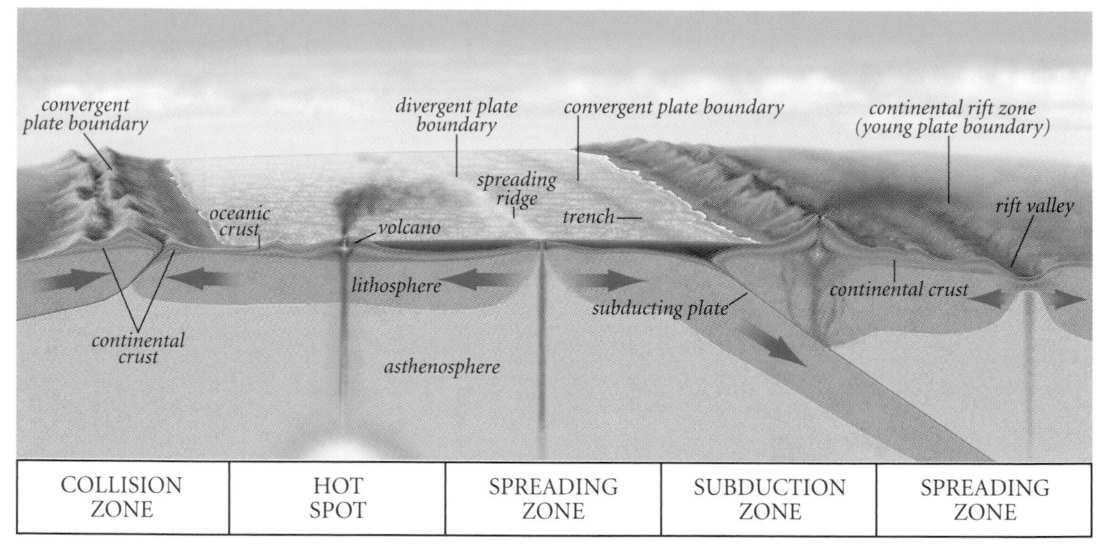

COLLISION ZONE	HOT SPOT	SPREADING ZONE	SUBDUCTION ZONE	SPREADING ZONE

aries. Scientists believe this is due to the scraping, pushing, pulling, and melting of the Earth's outer layer (the lithosphere) along these boundaries.

Teisse•renc de Bort (tĕs-rä′ də bôr′), **Léon Philippe** 1855–1913. French physicist and meteorologist. Using balloons outfitted with weather instruments, he discovered and named the stratosphere.

tek•tite (tĕk′tīt′) Any of numerous dark-brown to green glassy objects, usually small and round, composed of silica and various oxides and found in several parts of the world. They are thought to have come from the moon or to have resulted from impacts of large meteorites with the Earth's surface.

tele– A prefix that means "at a distance," as in *telemetry.*

tel•e•com•mu•ni•ca•tion (tĕl′ĭ-kə-myo͞o′nĭ-kā′shən) The science and technology of sending messages over long distances by electronic transmission of impulses, as by telegraph, telephone, radio, or television.

tel•e•graph (tĕl′ĭ-grăf′) A communications system in which a message in the form of electric impulses is sent, either by wire or radio, to a receiving station.

te•lem•e•try (tə-lĕm′ĭ-trē) The automatic measurement and transmission of data from a distant source to a receiving station. Telemetry is used, for example, to track the movements of wild animals that have had radio transmitters attached to them.

tel•e•scope (tĕl′ĭ-skōp′) **1.** An arrangement of lenses, mirrors, or both that collects visible light, allowing direct observation or photographic recording of distant objects. **2.** Any of various devices, such as a radio telescope, used to detect and observe distant objects by collecting radiation other than visible light.

tel•lu•ride (tĕl′yə-rīd′) A chemical compound of tellurium and another element.

tel•lu•ri•um (tĕ-lo͝or′ē-əm) A nonmetallic element that occurs as either a brittle, shiny, silvery-white crystal or a gray or brown powder. Small amounts of tellurium are used to improve the alloys of various metals. *Symbol* **Te.** *Atomic number* 52. *See* **Periodic Table,** pages 262–263.

tel•o•phase (tĕl′ə-fāz′) The final stage of cell division, in which membranes form around the two groups of chromosomes, each at opposite ends of the cell, to produce the two nuclei of the daughter cells. In mitosis, telophase is preceded by anaphase. *See more at* **meiosis, mitosis.**

tem•per•ate (tĕm′pər-ĭt) Marked by moderate temperatures, weather, or climate; neither hot nor cold.

USAGE

temperature/heat

The molecules of all substances are in motion, and the energy associated with this motion is called kinetic energy. Temperature and heat are both ways of measuring this energy, but they do not mean the same thing. A substance's *temperature* is the average kinetic energy of the substance's molecules. By contrast, a substance's *heat* is the total amount of energy contained in the substance. Thus, the water in two different pots, one four times as large as the other, might be at the same temperature, but the water in the larger pot would contain four times as much heat, since it requires four times as much energy to raise the temperature to the temperature of the water in the smaller pot.

Temperate Zone Either of two zones of the Earth of intermediate latitude, the **North Temperate Zone,** between the Arctic Circle and the Tropic of Cancer, or the **South Temperate Zone,** between the Antarctic Circle and the Tropic of Capricorn.

tem•per•a•ture (tĕm′pər-ə-cho͝or′) **1.** A measure of the average kinetic energy of atoms or molecules in a system. **2.** A numerical measure of hotness or coldness on a standard scale, such as the Kelvin scale. *See Note at* **Celsius. 3.** An abnormally high body temperature; a fever.

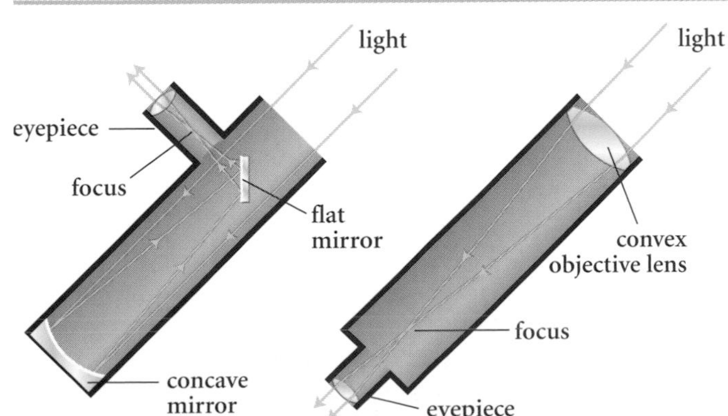

telescope
In a reflecting telescope (left), *light is gathered by reflecting off a concave mirror. It is then reflected off an angled flat mirror toward the eyepiece. In a refracting telescope* (right), *light is gathered by being refracted through a convex objective lens. It then exits in a direct line through the eyepiece.*

tem•po•ral lobe (tĕm′pər-əl) The portion of each cerebral hemisphere lying to the side and rear of the frontal lobe, containing the main speech and language centers of the brain.

ten•don (tĕn′dən) A band of tough fibrous tissue that connects a muscle to a bone.

ten•dril (tĕn′drəl) A slender, coiling plant part, often a modified leaf or leaf part, that helps support the stem of climbing plants by clinging to or winding around an object. Peas, squash, and grapes produce tendrils.

ten•sile strength (tĕn′səl, tĕn′sīl′) The ability of a material to resist a force that tends to pull it apart. It is usually expressed as the measure of the largest force that can be applied in this way before the material breaks apart.

ten•sion (tĕn′shən) **1.** *Physics.* A force that tends to stretch or elongate something. **2.** *Electricity.* A difference of electrical potential; voltage: *high-tension wires.*

ten•ta•cle (tĕn′tə-kəl) A narrow, flexible, unjointed part extending from the body of certain animals, such as an octopus, jellyfish, and sea anemone. Tentacles are used for feeling, grasping, or moving.

teph•ra (tĕf′rə) Solid matter, such as ash, dust, and cinders, that is ejected into the air by an erupting volcano.

tera– A prefix that means: **1.** One trillion (10^{12}), as in *terahertz,* one trillion hertz. **2.** 2^{40} (that is, 1,099,511,627,776), which is the power of two closest to a trillion, as in *terabyte.*

ter•a•byte (tĕr′ə-bīt′) **1.** A unit of computer memory or data storage capacity equal to 1,024 gigabytes (2^{40} bytes). **2.** One trillion bytes. *See Note at* **megabyte.**

ter•bi•um (tûr′bē-əm) A soft, easily shaped, silvery-gray metallic element of the lanthanide series. It is used in color television tubes, x-ray machines, and lasers. *Symbol* **Tb.** *Atomic number* 65. *See* **Periodic Table,** pages 262–263.

term (tûrm) *Mathematics.* **1.** Each of the quantities or expressions that form the parts of a ratio or the numerator and denominator of a fraction. **2.** Any of the quantities in an equation that are connected to other quantities by a plus sign or minus sign.

ter•mi•nal (tûr′mə-nəl) **1.** *Electricity.* A position in a circuit or device at which a connection can be made or broken. *See Note at* **battery. 2.** *Computer Science.* A device, often equipped with a keyboard and a video display, by which one can read, enter, or manipulate information in a computer system.

ter•mite (tûr′mīt′) Any of numerous pale-colored insects that live in large colonies and that feed on and destroy wood. Termites resemble ants in their appearance, manner of living, and social organization, but they belong to a different order of insects.

ter•res•tri•al (tə-rĕs′trē-əl) **1.** Relating to the Earth or its inhabitants. **2.** Relating to, consisting of, living on, or growing on land.

ter•ri•to•ry (tĕr′ĭ-tôr′ē) A geographic area occupied by a single animal, mating pair, or group. Animals usually defend their territory vigorously against intruders. Different animals mark off territory in different ways, as by leaving traces of their scent along the boundaries or, in the case of birds, modifying their calls to keep out intruders.

Ter•ti•ar•y (tûr′shē-ĕr′ē) The first period of the Cenozoic Era, from about 65 to 2 million years ago, characterized by the appearance of most modern classes of plants and mammals. *See Chart at* **geologic time,** pages 148–149.

Tes•la (tĕs′lə), **Nikola** 1856–1943. Serbian-born American electrical engineer and physicist. He discovered the principles of alternating current (1881) and invented numerous devices and procedures that were essential to the harnessing of electricity and the development of radio.

tes•ta (tĕs′tə) *See* **seed coat.**

tes•ti•cle (tĕs′tĭ-kəl) Either of the testes of a male mammal, usually contained within a scrotum.

tes•tis (tĕs′tĭs) *Plural* **testes** (tĕs′tēz) The reproductive organ of male animals, in which sperm and the sex hormones (androgens) are produced. Vertebrates have two testes, which in most animals are contained inside the body. In many mammals, they lie outside the body and are enclosed by the scrotum.

tes•tos•ter•one (tĕs-tŏs′tə-rōn′) A steroid hormone that regulates the development of the male reproductive system and male secondary sex characteristics. The main sources of testosterone in the body are the testes. Testosterone is the most important of the hormones known as androgens.

BIOGRAPHY

Nikola Tesla

In 1886, when Nikola Tesla went to work for George Westinghouse's electrical company, most commercially generated electricity was distributed over a direct current (DC) system. Such a system was very expensive to maintain, in part because much of the electricity was lost to resistance and wasted as heat in the wires. The alternating current (AC) system Tesla invented could be transmitted over very long distances through the use of transformers, and was cheaper and easier to maintain than the DC system. Tesla gave public demonstrations of electricity to ease peoples' fears about the safety of the system (even having currents passed through his body to ignite flames). Tesla's invention of motors and generators to use with the AC system helped ensure that it would rapidly replace direct current throughout the country.

test tube (tĕst) A cylindrical tube of clear glass, usually open at one end and rounded at the other, used as a container for small amounts of a substance in laboratory tests and experiments.

tet•a•nus (tĕt′n-əs) A serious disease caused by bacteria that usually enter the body through a wound. Tetanus is characterized by painful contractions of the muscles, especially of the jaw, and can be fatal if untreated.

te•trag•o•nal (tĕ-trăg′ə-nəl) Relating to a crystal having three axes, two of which are of the same length and are at right angles to each other. The third axis is perpendicular to these. The mineral zircon has tetragonal crystals. *See more at* **crystal.**

tet•ra•he•dron (tĕt′rə-hē′drən) A three-dimensional geometric figure with four triangular faces.

tex•ture (tĕks′chər) The spatial relationships between the mineral grains making up a rock.

Th The symbol for **thorium.**

thal•a•mus (thăl′ə-məs) The part of the brain in vertebrate animals that lies at the rear of the forebrain. It relays sensory information to the cerebral cortex and regulates the perception of touch, pain, and temperature.

Tha•les (thā′lēz) 624?–546? B.C. Greek philosopher who was a founder of geometry and abstract astronomy.

thal•li•um (thăl′ē-əm) A soft, easily shaped, very poisonous metallic element that has a low melting temperature. It is used in photography, in making low-melting and highly refractive glass, and in treating skin infections. *Symbol* **Tl.** *Atomic number* 81. *See* **Periodic Table,** pages 262–263.

thal•lus (thăl′əs) *Plural* **thalli** (thăl′ī) A part of certain plants and plant-like organisms that is a single cell or a mass of cells and cannot be distinguished as a leaf, stem, or root. Fungi, lichens, liverworts, and most algae have thalli.

Thé•nard (tā-när′), **Louis Jacques** 1777–1857. French chemist who discovered hydrogen peroxide in 1818. With Joseph Gay-Lussac, he also discovered boron (1808).

the•o•rem (thē′ər-əm, thîr′əm) A mathematical statement whose truth can be proved on the basis of a given set of axioms or assumptions.

the•o•ry (thē′ə-rē, thîr′ē) A set of statements or principles devised to explain a group of facts or phenomena. Most theories that are accepted by scientists have been repeatedly tested by experiments and can be used to make predictions about natural phenomena. *See Note at* **hypothesis.**

ther•mal (thûr′məl) *Adjective.* **1.** Relating to heat. —*Noun.* **2.** A current of warm air that rises because it is less dense than the air around it.

thermal vent An opening in the Earth, especially on the ocean floor, that emits hot water and dissolved minerals.

therm•i•on (thûr′mī′ən) An electrically charged particle or ion that is emitted by a conducting material when heated by an electric current.

thermo– *or* **therm–** A prefix that means "heat," as in *thermometer.*

ther•mo•cou•ple (thûr′mə-kŭp′əl) A thermoelectric device used to make accurate measurements of temperatures, especially high temperatures. It usually consists of a circuit having two wires of different metals welded together. When one of the metals is heated, and the other left cold, the difference in temperature causes an electric current to flow through the circuit. Because the amount of electromotive force generated depends on the temperature difference between the two metals, a measurement of the force can be used to calculate the temperature of the heated metal. Thermocouples are also used in the generation of electricity and in refrigeration devices.

ther•mo•dy•nam•ics (thûr′mō-dī-năm′ĭks) The branch of physics that deals with the relationships between heat and other forms of energy.

ther•mo•e•lec•tric (thûr′mō-ĭ-lĕk′trĭk) Relating to electric energy produced by heat or to heat produced by electric energy. The thermoelectric energy of a nuclear power plant is produced by the heat generated from nuclear fission. Thermoelectric energy in automobiles is generated by a thermocouple, which makes use of differences in temperature to generate electricity.

ther•mom•e•ter (thər-mŏm′ĭ-tər) An instrument used to measure temperature. There are many types of thermometers, each of which makes use of a physical effect of temperature to indicate the temperature of the medium being measured. The most common thermometer consists of a closed, graduated glass tube in which a liquid expands or contracts as the temperature increases or decreases. Other types of thermometers work by detecting changes in the volume of

thermal vent

Did You Know?
thermodynamics

It's not a bright picture. First, there is no free lunch. Second, you never get what you pay for, and third, you can't stop squirming in your seat, not until the universe freezes over. These are the three laws of *thermodynamics,* of how energy is transformed from one form to another. Energy can have any of five forms: physical, chemical, radiant, electrical, and thermal. The first law, often called the *law of conservation of energy,* states that energy cannot be created or destroyed; you can only convert one form of energy into another. For example, a car engine cannot create new energy, only transform the chemical energy available in its gasoline into a new form. The second law states that energy can only move from a state of higher activity to one of lower activity; it can never move from lower to higher without the addition of work. This means that heat, for example, will move from hotter areas to colder ones, but not the reverse. A consequence is that all machines are inefficient to some degree, since they must give off some waste heat. The third law states that nothing can ever be cooled to absolute zero. Since by the second law the heat from a warmer object flows into a cooler one, you could only cool something to absolute zero if there was nothing warmer around. And for that to happen, the whole universe would have to cool down to absolute zero at the same time. And what would do the cooling?

an enclosed gas or by registering changes in the electrical resistance of a conducting material at different temperatures.

ther•mo•nu•cle•ar (thûr′mō-no͞o**′**klē-ər) **1.** Derived from the fusion of atomic nuclei at high temperatures or the energy produced in this way. **2.** Relating to weapons based on nuclear fusion, especially as distinguished from those based on nuclear fission.

ther•mo•sphere (thûr**′**mə-sfîr′) The outermost layer of the Earth's atmosphere, lying above the mesosphere and extending hundreds of miles into outer space. In the thermosphere, which includes the exosphere and most of the ionosphere, temperatures increase steadily with altitude.

ther•mo•stat (thûr**′**mə-stăt′) A device that automatically controls heating or cooling equipment in such a way as to keep the temperature nearly constant.

the•ro•pod (thîr**′**ə-pŏd′) One of the two main types of saurischian dinosaurs, widespread during the Mesozoic Era. Theropods were meat eaters, walked on two legs, and had small forelimbs and a large skull with long jaws and sharp teeth. Most theropods were of small or medium size, but some grew very large, like the tyrannosaurus. *Compare* **sauropod.**

thi•a•mine (thī**′**ə-mĭn) A vitamin belonging to the vitamin B complex (B_1) that is important in carbohydrate metabolism and normal activity of the nervous system. It is found in bran, yeast, and meat.

Thomp•son (tŏmp**′**sən, tŏm**′**sən), **Benjamin.** Count Rumford. 1753–1814. American-born British physicist who conducted numerous experiments on heat and friction, which led him to discover that heat is produced by moving particles.

Thom•son (tŏm**′**sən), Sir **Joseph John** 1856–1940. British physicist who discovered the electron. While experimenting with cathode rays, he deduced that the particles he observed were smaller than an atom. Thomson went on to study the ability of gases to conduct electricity.

tho•rac•ic (thə-răs**′**ĭk) Relating to or located in or near the thorax: *thoracic vertebrae.*

tho•rax (thôr**′**ăks′) **1.** The upper part of the trunk in vertebrate animals. The thorax includes the rib cage, which encloses the heart and lungs. In humans and other mammals, the thorax lies above the abdomen. **2.** The middle division of the body of an insect, to which the wings and legs are attached. The thorax lies between the head and the abdomen.

USAGE

thorn/spine

It hardly makes a difference whether you get pricked by a thorn or a spine—it hurts just the same. But a person who studies plants might think there was a difference. Scientifically speaking, a *thorn* is a hard, pointed part of a stem or branch of a woody plant. While the word *spine* is used loosely to refer to any hard, pointed structure on a plant, it more properly refers to a leaf that has evolved into a narrow, sharp projection to conserve water and protect the stem, which stores water. Thus a cactus has spines but not thorns, and a rose bush and hawthorn have thorns but not spines.

tho•ri•um (thôr**′**ē-əm) A silvery-white, radioactive metallic element of the actinide series. It is used for fuel in some nuclear reactors and for improving the high-temperature strength of magnesium alloys. The only naturally occurring isotope of thorium is also its most stable, having a half-life of 14 billion years. *Symbol* **Th.** *Atomic number* 90. *See* **Periodic Table,** pages 262–263.

thorn (thôrn) **1.** A short, hard, pointed part of a stem or branch of a woody plant. **2.** Any of various plants bearing thorns.

thre•o•nine (thrē**′**ə-nēn′) An essential amino acid. *See more at* **amino acid.**

thrust (thrŭst) The force that causes an object to move forward. Thrust in a jet or rocket engine develops as a reaction to the ejection of exhaust gases from the rear of the engine. Thrust in a propeller results from the spinning of the propeller blades that pushes air or water in a certain direction.

thu•li•um (tho͞o**′**lē-əm) A soft, easily shaped, silver-gray metallic element of the lanthanide series. An artificial radioactive isotope of thuli-

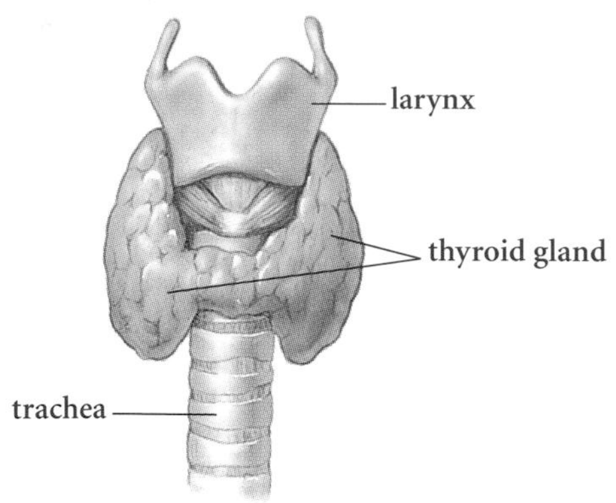

thyroid gland
front view of a human thyroid gland

um is used as a radiation source in small, portable x-ray machines. *Symbol* **Tm.** *Atomic number* 69. *See* **Periodic Table,** pages 262–263.

thun•der (thŭn′dər) The explosive noise that accompanies a stroke of lightning. Thunder is a series of sound waves produced by the rapid expansion of the air through which the lightning passes. *See Note at* **lightning.**

thun•der•storm (thŭn′dər-stôrm′) A storm of heavy rain accompanied by lightning and thunder and sometimes hail.

thy•mine (thī′mēn′) A base that is a component of DNA. It forms a base pair with adenine.

thy•mus (thī′məs) An organ in vertebrate animals located behind the top of the sternum (breastbone) where lymphocytes called T cells develop. In humans, the thymus stops growing in early childhood and gradually shrinks in size through adulthood.

USAGE

tidal wave/tsunami

In everyday speech, we use the word *tidal wave* to refer to a gigantic and enormously destructive wave caused by an underwater earthquake or volcanic eruption—what scientists would properly call a *tsunami.* When scientists use the word *tidal wave,* they normally are referring to an unusually large wave or bulge of water that sometimes occurs around a high tide. These tidal waves are certainly big and powerful, but they are tiny in comparison with tsunamis.

tide
high (top) *and low* (bottom) *tide at the Hopewell Rocks, New Brunswick, Canada*

thy•roid gland (thī′roid′) A two-lobed gland located at the base of the neck in vertebrate animals. It secretes many hormones that are important for cell metabolism and normal growth and development.

thyrse (thûrs) A dense flower cluster in which the side branches end in cymes, as in the lilac.

Ti The symbol for **titanium.**

tib•i•a (tĭb′ē-ə) The larger of the two bones of the lower leg or lower portion of the hind leg. Also called *shinbone. See more at* **skeleton.**

tick (tĭk) **1.** Any of numerous small animals related to spiders and mites. Ticks attach themselves to the skin of humans and animals, and suck their blood. They often carry microorganisms that cause disease. **2.** Any of various small blood-sucking insects resembling lice that are parasites on sheep, goats, and other animals.

tid•al pool (tīd′l) A pool of water remaining after a tide has retreated. Also called *tide pool.*

tidal wave 1. The swell or crest of surface ocean water created by the tides. **2.** An unusual rise in

■ timberline

the level of water along a seacoast, as from a storm or a combination of wind and tide. **3.** A tsunami.

tide (tīd) The regular rise and fall in the surface level of the Earth's oceans, seas, and bays caused by the gravitational attraction of the moon and to a lesser extent the sun. *See also* **ebb tide, flood tide, neap tide, spring tide.**

till (tĭl) A mass of boulders, pebbles, sand, and mud scraped up by a moving glacier and deposited either by the glacier's movement or by its melting.

tim•ber•line (tĭm′bər-līn′) A geographic boundary beyond which trees cannot grow. On the Earth as a whole, the timberline is the northernmost or southernmost latitude at which trees can survive; in a mountainous region, it is the highest elevation at which trees can survive. Also called *tree line.*

time (tīm) **1.** A continuous, measurable quantity in which events occur in a sequence proceeding from the past through the present to the future. *See Note at* **space-time. 2a.** An interval separating two points of this quantity; a duration. **b.** A system by which such intervals are measured or such numbers are calculated: *standard time; daylight-saving time.*

time zone Any of the 24 divisions of the Earth's surface used to determine the local time for any given locality. Each zone is roughly 15° of longitude in width, with local variations. Local time is one hour ahead for each time zone as one travels east, and one hour behind for each time zone as one travels west. So, for example, when it is noon in New York City, it is 11:00 A.M. in Chicago,

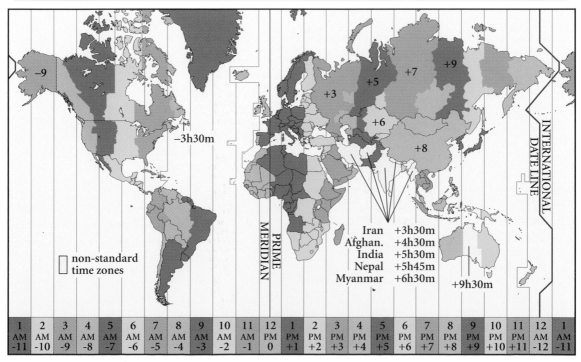

–9
+3
+5
+7
+9
+6
+8
–3h30m
PRIME MERIDIAN
INTERNATIONAL DATE LINE
non-standard time zones
Iran +3h30m
Afghan. +4h30m
India +5h30m
Nepal +5h45m
Myanmar +6h30m
+9h30m

1 AM -11	2 AM -10	3 AM -9	4 AM -8	5 AM -7	6 AM -6	7 AM -5	8 AM -4	9 AM -3	10 AM -2	11 AM -1	12 PM 0	1 PM +1	2 PM +2	3 PM +3	4 PM +4	5 PM +5	6 PM +6	7 PM +7	8 PM +8	9 PM +9	10 PM +10	11 PM +11	12 AM -12	1 AM -11

■ time zone

10:00 A.M. in Denver, and 9:00 A.M. in Los Angeles. *See more at* **International Date Line.**

tin (tĭn) An easily shaped, silvery metallic element that occurs in igneous rocks. It has a crystalline structure and crackles when it is bent and its crystals break. Tin is used to coat other metals to prevent corrosion and is a part of numerous alloys, including bronze. *Symbol* **Sn.** *Atomic number* 50. *See* **Periodic Table,** pages 262–263. *See Note at* **element.**

tis•sue (tĭsh**′**o͞o) A large collection of similar cells that together perform a specific function in an organism. The organs of the body and the parts of a plant are composed of many different kinds of tissues.

ti•ta•ni•um (tī-tā**′**nē-əm) A shiny, white metallic element that occurs widely in all kinds of rocks and soils. It is lightweight, strong, and highly resistant to corrosion. Titanium alloys are used especially to make parts for aircraft and ships. *Symbol* **Ti.** *Atomic number* 22. *See* **Periodic Table,** pages 262–263.

Tl The symbol for **thallium.**

Tm The symbol for **thulium.**

TNT (tē′ĕn-tē**′**) Short for *trinitrotoluene.* A yellow, crystalline compound used mainly as an explosive.

toad (tōd) Any of numerous amphibians related to the frogs. Toads usually have broader bodies and shorter legs than frogs, and their feet have only a little webbing. Their skin is thick, rough, and often bumpy, and sometimes secretes toxic substances. Toads usually do not live in water as adults but prefer cool, moist places on the ground. *Compare* **frog.**

tol•u•ene (tŏl**′**yo͞o-ēn′) A colorless liquid hydrocarbon, C_7H_8, that is poisonous and burns easily. It is used in fuels, explosives, dyes, medicines, and many industrial chemicals.

Tom•baugh (tŏm**′**bô′), **Clyde William** 1906–1997. American astronomer who discovered Pluto in 1930.

tom•bo•lo (tŏm**′**bə-lō′) A sandbar that connects an island to the mainland or to another island.

ton (tŭn) **1.** A unit of weight equal to 2,000 pounds. Also called *short ton.* **2.** A unit of weight equal to 2,240 pounds. Also called *long ton.* **3.** *See* **metric ton.**

tongue (tŭng) **1.** A muscular organ in most vertebrate animals that is usually attached to the bottom of the mouth. In some reptiles, such as snakes, the tongue is mainly used as a sense organ, while in some other animals, such as frogs, chameleons, and anteaters, it is used to capture prey. The tongue is the main organ of taste in mammals, and it is used to aid in chewing and swallowing. In humans, it is also used to produce speech sounds. **2.** A similar organ in certain invertebrate animals.

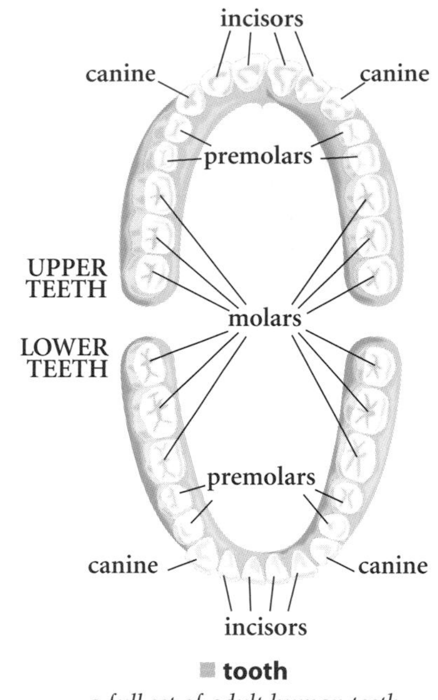

tooth
a full set of adult human teeth

ton•sils (tŏn**′**səlz) The two oval-shaped tissues at the back of the throat in mammals that lie between the mouth and the pharynx. The tonsils are thought to prevent infections of the breathing passages but often become infected themselves. ❖ Inflammation of the tonsils is called **tonsillitis** (tŏn′sə-lī**′**tĭs). ❖ Surgical removal of the tonsils is called a **tonsillectomy** (tŏn′sə-lĕk**′**tə-mē).

tooth (to͞oth) *Plural* **teeth** (tēth) Any of the hard bony structures in the mouth used to grasp and chew food and as weapons of attack and defense. In mammals and many other vertebrates, the teeth are set in sockets in the jaw. In fish and amphibians, they grow in and around the palate. *See also* **dentition.** A similar structure in certain invertebrate animals.

to•paz (tō**′**păz′) **1.** A colorless, blue, yellow, brown, or pink mineral consisting largely of aluminum silicate and valued as a gem. Topaz is often found in pegmatites and is the mineral used to represent a hardness of 8 on the Mohs scale. **2.** Any of various yellow gemstones, especially a yellow variety of sapphire or corundum.

to•pog•ra•phy (tə-pŏg′rə-fē) **1.** The shape, height, and depth of the land surface in a place or region. Physical features that make up the topography of an area include mountains, valleys, plains, and bodies of water. Man-made features such as roads, railroads, and landfills are also often considered part of a region's topography: *the mountainous topography of Switzerland.* **2.** The detailed description or drawing of the physical features of a place or region, especially in the form of contour maps. *See more at* **gradient.**

to•pol•o•gy (tə-pŏl′ə-jē) The mathematical study of the geometric properties that are not normally affected by changes in the size or shape of geometric figures. In topology, a donut and a coffee cup with a handle are equivalent shapes, because each has a single hole.

tor•na•do (tôr-nā′dō) A violently rotating column of air ranging in width from a few yards to more than a mile and whirling at speeds estimated at 300 miles (483 kilometers) an hour or higher. A tornado usually takes the form of a funnel-shaped cloud extending downward out of a cumulonimbus cloud. Where the funnel reaches the ground, it can cause enormous destruction.

torque (tôrk) The tendency of a force applied to an object to make it rotate about an axis. Torque is equal to the amount of the force acting on the object multiplied by the distance from its point of application to the axis around which the object rotates (or would rotate if it were not fixed in place).

Tor•ri•cel•li (tō′rə-chĕl′ē), **Evangelista** 1608–1647. Italian mathematician and physicist who discovered that the atmosphere exerts pressure. He demonstrated that this pressure affected the level of mercury in a tube, thereby inventing the mercury barometer.

Tor•rid Zone (tôr′ĭd) The zone of the Earth of central latitude, between the Tropic of Cancer and the Tropic of Capricorn.

tor•sion (tôr′shən) The stress that an object undergoes when one of its ends is twisted out of line with the other end.

tor•toise (tôr′tĭs) Any of various turtles that live on land.

Charles Townes

tour•ma•line (to͝or′mə-lĭn, to͝or′mə-lēn′) A silicate mineral consisting of aluminum, boron, and other elements. Tourmaline occurs in many different translucent colors, usually in crystals shaped like 3-, 6-, or 9-sided prisms. It is especially common in pegmatites.

Townes (tounz), **Charles Hard** Born 1915. American physicist who invented the maser, a device that amplifies and focuses short electromagnetic waves into intense beams. Townes's work laid the foundation for the development of laser technology.

tox•ic (tŏk′sĭk) Poisonous.

tox•i•col•o•gy (tŏk′sĭ-kŏl′ə-jē) The scientific study of poisons, of their effects and detection, and of the treatment of poisoning.

tox•in (tŏk′sĭn) A poisonous substance produced by a living organism. Toxins can be products of ordinary metabolism (such as lactic acid), can be produced to kill or immobilize prey (such as the toxins in snake venom), or can be produced for self-defense (such as the cyanide produced by several plants). Toxins produced by bacteria cause disease.

trace element (trās) An element present in an organism in only very small amounts but essential for normal metabolism. Iodine and cobalt, for example, are trace elements required by humans.

trac•er (trā′sər) An identifiable substance, such as a dye or radioactive isotope, that can be followed through the course of a mechanical, chemical, or biological process. Tracers are used to provide information about details of the process or about the distribution of the substances involved in it.

tra•che•a (trā′kē-ə) **1.** The tube-shaped structure in vertebrate animals that leads from the larynx to the bronchi and carries air to the lungs. In mammals, the trachea is strengthened by rings of cartilage. Also called *windpipe.* **2.** A similar structure in insects and other arthropods.

tract (trăkt) A system of connected body organs and parts that work together to perform a specialized function, such as digestion.

trade winds (trād) Winds that blow steadily from east to west and toward the equator over most of the Torrid Zone. The trade winds blow from the northeast in the Northern Hemisphere and from the southeast in the Southern Hemisphere, converging on the doldrums. *See more at* **wind.**

trait (trāt) A characteristic or condition that is determined by one's genes. The color of an animal's coat and the shape of a plant's leaves are physical traits. Nesting in birds and burrowing in rodents are examples of behavioral traits.

tra•jec•to•ry (trə-jĕk′tə-rē) **1.** *Physics.* The curve described by a projectile moving through space. **2.** *Geometry.* A curve or surface that passes through a given set of points or intersects a given series of curves or surfaces at a constant angle.

tran•scrip•tion (trăn-skrĭp′shən) The process in a cell by which genetic material is copied from a strand of DNA to a complementary strand of RNA (called messenger RNA). Transcription takes place in the nucleus before messenger RNA is transported to the ribosomes, the places in the cell where proteins are made.

trans•duc•er (trăns-do͞o′sər) A device that converts one type of energy into another. For example, the transducer in a microphone converts sound waves into electric impulses, while the transducer in a loudspeaker converts electrical impulses into sound waves.

trans•fer RNA (trăns′fər) *See under* **RNA.**

trans•form•er (trăns-fôr′mər) A device used to change the voltage of an alternating current in one circuit to a different voltage in a second circuit. Transformers consist of a frame-like iron core that has a wire wound around each end. As a current enters the transformer through one of the coils, the magnetic field it produces causes the other coil to pick up the current. ❖ If there are more turns on the second coil than on the first coil, the outgoing current will have a higher voltage than the incoming current. This is called a **step-up transformer.** ❖ If there are fewer turns on the second coil than on the first, the outgoing current will have a lower voltage. This is called a **step-down transformer.**

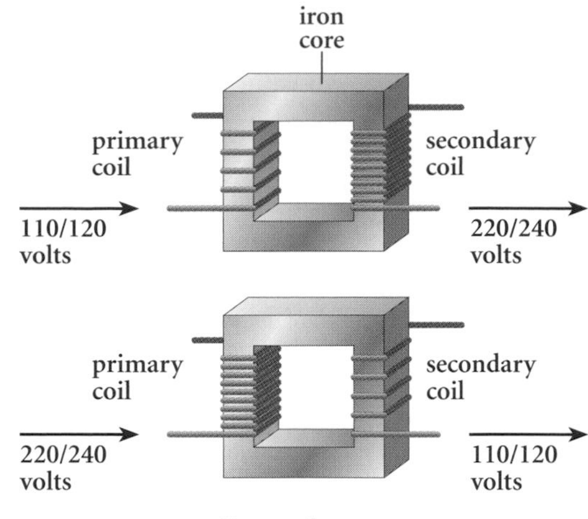

transformer

The increase or decrease in voltage is directly related to the number of turns of the wire. In the top transformer, the outgoing voltage is doubled because the secondary coil has twice as many turns as the first. In the bottom transformer, the voltage is halved.

trans•form fault (trăns′fôrm′) A type of strike-slip fault that is common along the edges of tectonic plates in mid-ocean ridge regions. *See more at* **fault.**

trans•fu•sion (trăns-fyo͞o′zhən) The transfer of blood from one person to another. *See more at* **Rh factor.** *See Note at* **blood type.**

tran•sis•tor (trăn-zĭs′tər) An electronic device that controls the flow of an electric current and is used as an amplifier or switch. Transistors consist of three layers of semiconductor material connected to an electric circuit. In some transistors, the outer layers have an excess of electrons; in others, the middle layer has more electrons. Transistors work like gates, allowing or closing off the flow of electrons when an electric current or voltage is applied to a particular layer. Because of their tiny size and increased efficiency, transistors have replaced electron tubes in most electronic devices.

tran•si•tion element (trăn-zĭsh′ən) Any of the metallic elements within Groups 3 through 12 in the Periodic Table. All the transition metals have two electrons in their outermost shell, and all but zinc, cadmium, and mercury have an incompletely filled inner electron orbital just beneath the outer orbital. Transition elements form alloys easily, have high melting points, and have more than one valence because of their incomplete inner shells. *See* **Periodic Table,** pages 262–263. *See Note at* **metal.**

trans•la•tion (trăns-lā′shən) The process in a cell by which a strand of messenger RNA directs the assembly of a sequence of amino acids to make a protein. Translation takes place in the ribosomes, the places in the cell where proteins are made.

trans•lu•cent (trăns-lo͞o′sənt) Transmitting light, but not clearly enough to be transparent. A translucent object causes enough diffusion of light that an object or image on the other side of it can only be seen indistinctly. Frosted glass is translucent. *Compare* **transparent.**

trans•mit•ter (trăns′mĭt-ər) A device that generates radio or microwave signals, changes their amplitude or frequency so that they can carry information (such as spoken words), and radiates the resulting wave by means of an antenna.

trans•mu•ta•tion (trăns′myo͞o-tā′shən) The changing of one chemical element into another. Transmutations occur naturally through radioactive decay, or artificially by bombarding the nucleus of a substance with subatomic particles.

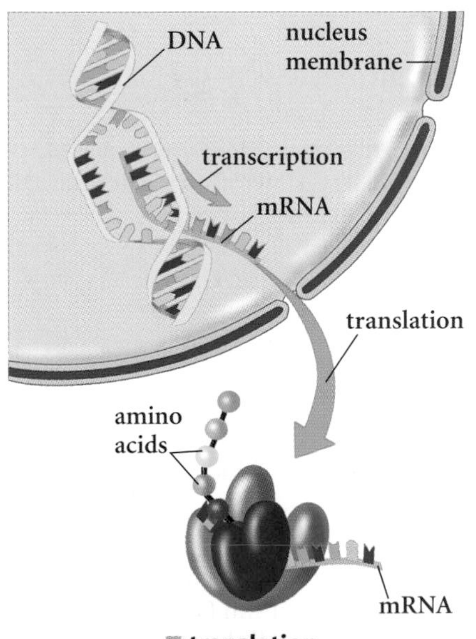

translation

Did You Know?
transpiration

Plants need much more water than animals do. But why? Plants use water not only to carry nutrients throughout their tissues, but also to exchange gases with the air in the process known as *transpiration.* Air, which contains the carbon dioxide that plant cells need for photosynthesis, enters the plant mainly through the stomata (tiny holes under its leaves). The air travels through tiny spaces in the leaf tissue to the cells that conduct photosynthesis. These cells are coated with a thin layer of water. The cell walls do not permit gases to pass through them, but the carbon dioxide can move across the cell walls by dissolving in the water on their surface. The cells remove the carbon dioxide from the water and use the same water to carry out oxygen, the main waste product of photosynthesis. All this mixing of water and air in transpiration, though, has one drawback: more than 90 percent of the water that a plant's roots suck up is lost by evaporation through the stomata. This is why a plant always needs water and why plants that live in dry climates, such as cacti, have reduced leaf surfaces from which less water can escape.

trans•par•ent (trăns-pâr′ənt) Transmitting light so as to be seen through clearly. The glass in windows is usually transparent. *Compare* **translucent.** *See Note at* **glass.**

tran•spi•ra•tion (trăn′spə-rā′shən) The process of giving off vapor containing water and waste products, especially through the stomata on leaves or the pores of the skin.

trans•plant (trăns′plănt′) *Noun.* **1.** A plant that has been uprooted and replanted. **2.** An organ or tissue of the body that has been transferred from one person or body part to another. —*Verb.* (trăns-plănt′) **3.** To uproot and replant a growing plant. **4.** To transfer tissue or an organ from one body or body part to another.

trans•pose (trăns-pōz′) To move a term or quantity from one side of an algebraic equation to the other by adding or subtracting that term to or from both sides. By subtracting 2 from both sides of the equation $2 + x = 4$, one can transpose the 2 to the other side, yielding $x = 4 - 2$, and thus determine that x equals 2.

trans•verse wave (trăns-vûrs′, trăns′vûrs′) A wave in which the particles of the wave's medium move at right angles to the direction of wave movement. For instance, in an ocean wave, the molecules of water move up and down as the wave passes on its way toward shore. *See more at* **wave.** *Compare* **longitudinal wave.**

tra•pe•zi•um (trə-pē′zē-əm) A four-sided figure having no parallel sides.

trap•e•zoid (trăp′ĭ-zoid′) A four-sided figure having two parallel sides.

tree (trē) A perennial plant typically having a single woody stem, and usually branches and leaves.

tree line *See* **timberline.**

trem•or (trĕm′ər) A shaking or vibrating movement, as from a small earthquake.

tri•an•gle (trī′ăng′gəl) A closed geometric figure consisting of three sides.

tri•an•gu•la•tion (trī-ăng′gyə-lā′shən) **1.** A method used to determine distances and directions of a region of land. The region is divided into a set of triangles based on a line of known length. The triangles are then measured using trigonometry. **2.** A method of determining the location of a boat or aircraft by means of trigonometry.

Tri•as•sic (trī-ăs′ĭk) The earliest period of the Mesozoic Era, from about 245 to 208 million years ago. During the Triassic Period, land life diversified, dinosaurs arose, and the earliest mammals appeared. *See Chart at* **geologic time,** pages 148–149.

trib•u•tar•y (trĭb′yə-tĕr′ē) A stream that flows into a river or larger stream.

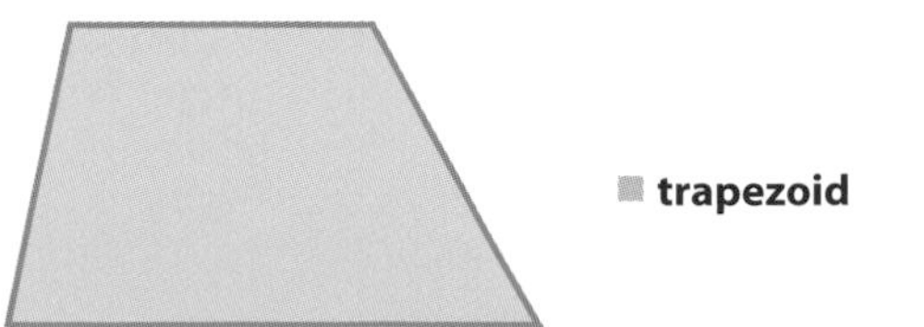

trapezoid

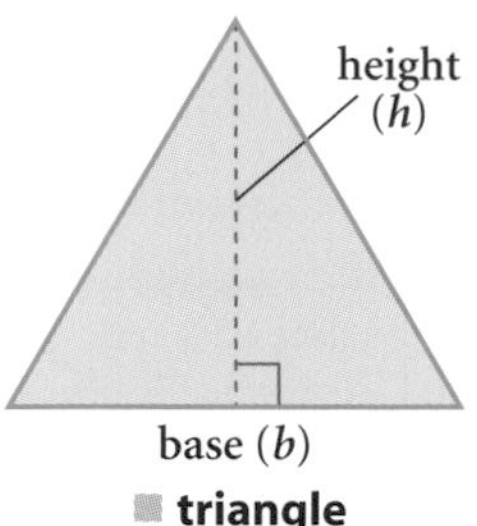

triangle

The area (A) of a triangle can be calculated using the following formula: $A = \frac{1}{2}bh$.

tri•ceps (trī′sĕps′) The muscle at the back of the upper arm that straightens the elbow. The triceps has three points of attachment to bone at one end.

tri•cer•a•tops (trī-sĕr′ə-tŏps′) A large, plant-eating dinosaur of the late Cretaceous Period, measuring up to 25 feet (7.6 meters) in length. The triceratops had a beak-like mouth with a short horn over it and a long horn over each eye. The back of its neck was covered with a wide, bony plate.

trich•i•no•sis (trĭk′ə-nō′sĭs) A disease caused by a parasitic worm and that is characterized by intestinal disorders, fever, and pain. Trichinosis is caught from eating pork that has not been thoroughly cooked.

tri•clin•ic (trī-klĭn′ĭk) Relating to a crystal having three axes of different lengths intersecting at oblique angles. The mineral microcline (a type of feldspar) has triclinic crystals. *See more at* **crystal.**

tri•cus•pid (trī-kŭs′pĭd) A tooth having three points or cusps, especially a molar.

tri•glyc•er•ide (trī-glĭs′ə-rīd′) A compound consisting of three fatty acids and glycerol that is the chief constituent of fats and oils.

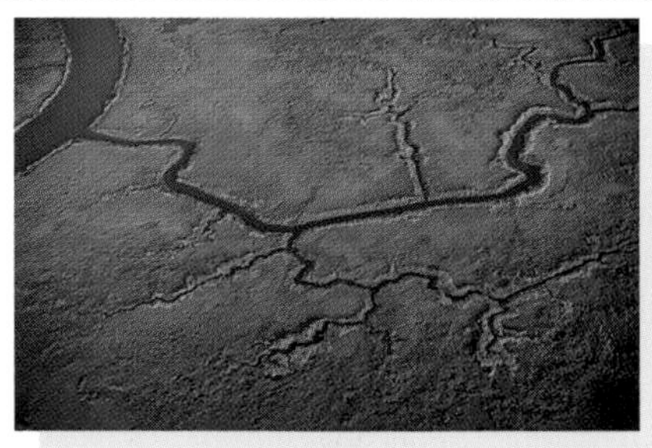

tributary

a system of tributaries flowing into the Mispillion River, Delaware

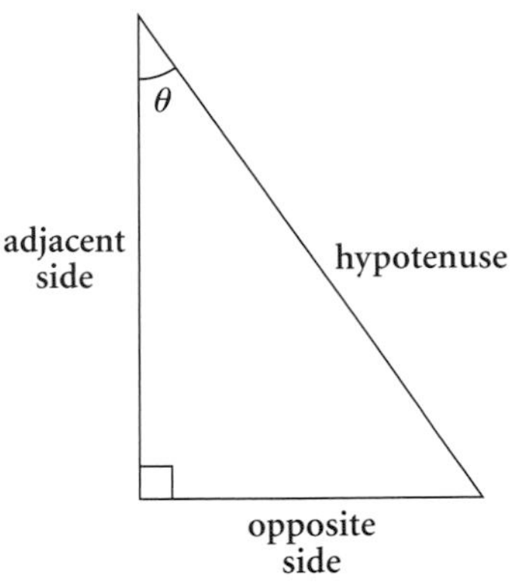

trigonometric function

In a right triangle, the trigonometric functions are:

$$sine\ \theta = \frac{opposite}{hypotenuse} \quad cosine\ \theta = \frac{adjacent}{hypotenuse}$$

$$tangent\ \theta = \frac{opposite}{adjacent}$$

tri•go•nal (trī-gō′nəl) Relating to a crystal having three axes of equal length intersecting at oblique angles. This crystal system is considered a subset of the hexagonal system. The mineral quartz has trigonal crystals. Also called *rhombohedral. See more at* **crystal.**

trig•o•no•met•ric function (trĭg′ə-nə-mĕt′rĭk) A function of an angle, as the sine, cosine, or tangent, whose value is expressed as a ratio of two of the sides of the right triangle that contains the angle.

trig•o•nom•e•try (trĭg′ə-nŏm′ĭ-trē) The study of the properties and uses of trigonometric functions.

tri•lo•bite (trī′lə-bīt′) Any of numerous extinct and mostly small arthropods that lived during the Paleozoic Era. Trilobites had a hard outer covering divided into three lengthwise and three widthwise sections. Horseshoe crabs are considered to be their closest living relatives.

tri•ni•tro•tol•u•ene (trī-nī′trō-tŏl′yo͞o-ēn′) *See* **TNT.**

trit•i•um (trĭt′ē-əm, trĭsh′ē-əm) A radioactive isotope of hydrogen whose nucleus has one proton and two neutrons and whose atomic mass is about 3. Tritium is rare in nature but can be made artificially in nuclear reactions. It is used in thermonuclear weapons and sometimes as a tracer. *See more at* **hydrogen.**

tri•va•lent (trī-vā′lənt) *Chemistry.* Having a valence of three.

troph•ic (trŏf′ĭk) Relating to the feeding habits of different organisms in a food chain or web: *the trophic interactions between insects and mammals.* ❖ A group of organisms occupying the same position in a food chain is called a **trophic level.**

trop•ic (trŏp′ĭk) **1.** Either of the two parallels of latitude representing the points farthest north and south at which the sun can shine directly overhead. The northern tropic is the Tropic of Cancer, and the southern one is the Tropic of Capricorn. **2. tropics.** The region of the Earth lying between these latitudes and corresponding to the Torrid Zone. The tropics are generally the warmest and most humid region of the Earth. —*Adjective* **tropical.**

Tropic of Cancer The parallel of latitude 23°27' north of the equator. It forms the boundary between the Torrid Zone and the North Temperate Zone.

Tropic of Capricorn The parallel of latitude 23°27' south of the equator. It forms the boundary between the Torrid Zone and the South Temperate Zone.

tro•pism (trō′pĭz′əm) Growth or movement of a plant or animal toward or away from an external stimulus, such as light, heat, or gravity. —*Adjective* **tropistic.**

tro•po•pause (trō′pə-pôz′, trŏp′ə-pôz′) The boundary between the upper troposphere and the lower stratosphere, varying in altitude from about 5 miles (8 kilometers) at the poles to 11 miles (17.7 kilometers) at the equator.

tro•po•sphere (trō′pə-sfîr′, trŏp′ə-sfîr′) The lowest region of the atmosphere, bounded by the Earth's surface and the tropopause and characterized by temperatures that decrease with increasing altitude. Weather and most cloud formations occur in the troposphere.

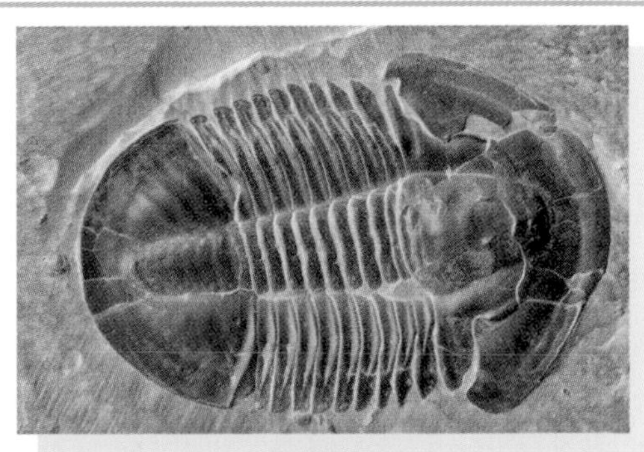

trilobite

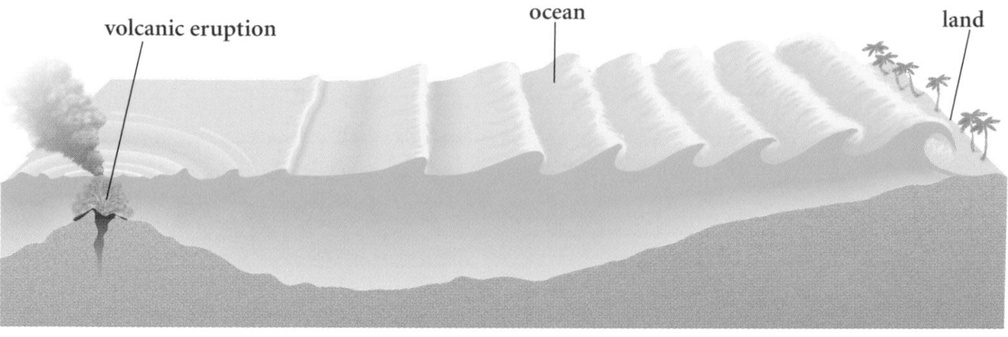

■ **tsunami**
Waves created by a powerful underwater disturbance lose speed as they reach shallower water, but they gain height and get closer together.

trough (trôf) The lowest part of a wave. *See more at* **wave.**

true bug (tro͞o) A wingless or four-winged insect having mouthparts adapted for piercing or sucking. Bedbugs and lice are examples of true bugs. *See Note at* **bug.**

true north *See* **geographic north.**

try•pan•o•some (trĭ-păn′ə-sōm′) Any of various parasitic protozoans that can cause serious diseases, such as sleeping sickness. They are transmitted by the bite of certain insects, such as tsetse flies.

tryp•sin (trĭp′sĭn) An enzyme that aids digestion by breaking down proteins. It is produced by the pancreas and secreted into the small intestine.

tryp•to•phan (trĭp′tə-făn′) An essential amino acid. *See more at* **amino acid.**

tse•tse fly (tsĕt′sē) Any of several bloodsucking African flies that often carry and transmit the protozoans that cause sleeping sickness.

tsu•na•mi (tso͞o-nä′mē) A very large ocean wave that is caused by an underwater earthquake or volcanic eruption and often causes extreme destruction when it strikes land. *See Note at* **tidal wave.**

tu•ber (to͞o′bər) The thickened part of an underground stem of a plant, such as the potato, bearing buds from which new plant shoots arise. *Compare* **bulb, corm, rhizome, runner.**

tu•ber•cle (to͞o′bər-kəl) A small rounded projection or swelling, as on the roots of legumes or on skin or a bone.

tu•ber•cu•lo•sis (to͞o-bûr′kyə-lō′sĭs) A contagious disease caused by a bacterium and characterized by abnormal growths in the lungs or other body tissues. It is most often transmitted by breathing contaminated air.

tu•fa (to͞o′fə) A rock formed of sediments deposited during the evaporation of lake water, spring water, or groundwater. Tufa is usually composed of calcium carbonate.

tuff (tŭf) A rock made up of particles of volcanic ash, varying in size from fine sand to coarse gravel.

tu•mor (to͞o′mər) An abnormal growth of tissue resulting from uncontrolled growth of cells and serving no function within the body; a cancerous growth. Tumors can be benign (unlikely to spread to other body parts) or malignant (likely to spread). *See Note at* **cancer.**

tun•dra (tŭn′drə) A cold, treeless, usually lowland area of far northern regions. The subsoil of tundras is permanently frozen, but in summer the top layer of soil thaws and can support low-growing mosses, lichens, grasses, and small shrubs.

■ **tundra**
Labrador, Newfoundland, Canada

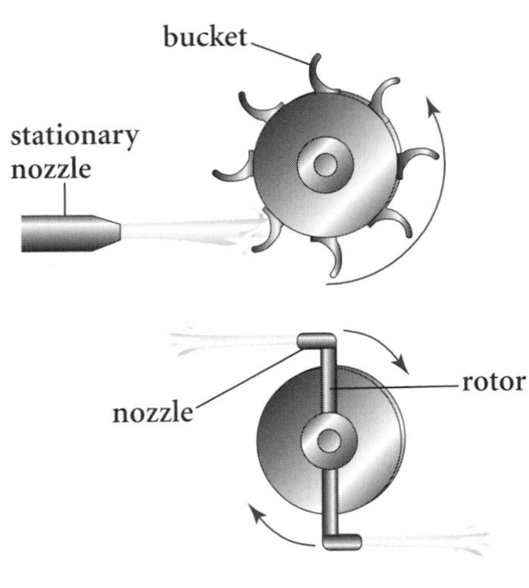

turbine

An impulse turbine (top) *rotates when the force of a stream of water hits cup-shaped buckets that are mounted around the perimeter of a rotor. In a reaction turbine* (bottom), *the pressure of the water being discharged from the nozzle forces the turbine to rotate in the direction opposite to the water's motion.*

tung•sten (tŭng′stən) A hard, gray to white metallic element that is very resistant to corrosion. It has the highest melting point of all elements. Tungsten remains very strong at high temperatures and is used to make light-bulb filaments and to increase the hardness and strength of steel. Also called *wolfram. Symbol* **W.** *Atomic number* 74. *See* **Periodic Table,** pages 262–263.

tu•ni•cate (to͞o′nĭ-kĭt) Any of various primitive marine chordate animals having a rounded or cylindrical body that is enclosed in a tough outer covering. Tunicates start out life as free-swimming tadpole-like animals with a notochord (a primitive backbone), but many, such as the sea squirts, lose the notochord and most of their nervous system as adults and become fixed to rocks or other objects.

tur•bine (tûr′bĭn, tûr′bīn′) Any of various machines in which the kinetic energy of a moving fluid, such as water, steam, or gas, is converted to rotary motion.

tur•bo•jet (tûr′bō-jĕt′) **1.** A jet engine in which the exhaust gas operates a turbine that in turn drives a compressor that forces air into the intake

Did You Know?

turbojet

Fully loaded, a jumbo-sized airliner weighs nearly 800,000 pounds. Yet its *turbojet engines* are so powerful that it hurtles down the runway fast enough to lift it into air and climb to 35,000 feet. Where does this power come from? From the movement of air itself. Every turbojet has a compressor, a series of small rotating fan blades. These blades draw in air and pressurize it, driving it back into a combustion chamber where a fuel (such as kerosene) is injected and ignited. The burning of the fuel causes the air to expand, adding to the already high pressure and causing the mixture of hot air and gas to rush over turbines with enormous speed. This causes the turbine blades to turn, and they spin a drive shaft that rotates the compressor fans. The hot pressurized air then blasts out the rear opening of the engine, forcing the plane forward. Most turbojet engines today are *turbofans* and have a large fan at the front that is turned by one of the turbines. Every second, the fan sucks in enough air to empty an average-sized house, adding to the volume and pressure of the air rotating the turbines and providing forward thrust.

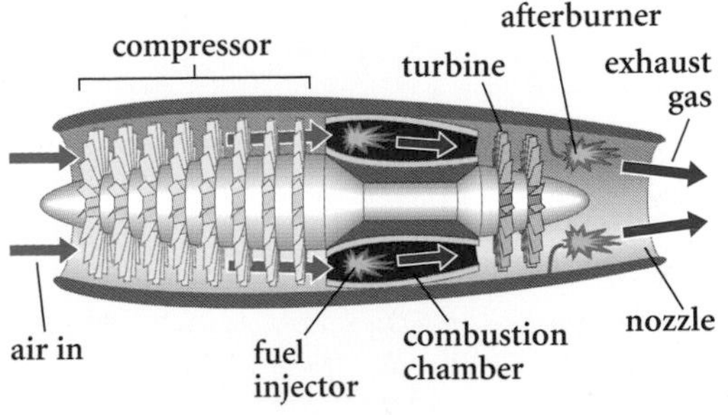

Alan Turing

of the engine. **2.** An aircraft powered by an engine or engines of this type.

tur•bu•lent flow (tûr′byə-lənt) Movement of a fluid in which the individual particles of fluid move in irregular patterns even though the overall flow is in one direction. Turbulent flow is common in nonviscous fluids moving at high velocities. *Compare* **laminar flow.**

turf (tûrf) A surface layer of earth containing a dense growth of grass and its matted roots.

Tur•ing (to͝or′ĭng), **Alan Mathison** 1912–1954. British mathematician. In 1937 he formulated a precise mathematical concept for a theoretical computing machine, a key step in the development of the first computer. During World War II Turing did important work on breaking German codes.

tur•pen•tine (tûr′pən-tīn′) **1.** A thin, easily vaporized oil, $C_{10}H_{16}$, that is distilled from the wood or resin of certain pine trees. It is used as a paint thinner and solvent. **2.** The sticky mixture of resin and oil from which this oil is distilled.

tur•tle (tûr′tl) Any of various reptiles living either in water or on land and having a bony or leathery shell into which the head, legs, and tail can be pulled for protection.

tusk (tŭsk) A long, pointed tooth, usually one of a pair, projecting from the mouth of certain animals, such as elephants, walruses, and wild pigs.

tym•pan•ic membrane (tĭm-păn′ĭk) *See* **eardrum.**

ty•phoid fever (tī′foid′) A life-threatening disease caused by bacteria and characterized by high fever, intestinal bleeding, and pink spots on the skin. It is transmitted through contaminated food and water.

ty•phoon (tī-fo͞on′) A hurricane occurring in the western Pacific Ocean. *See Note at* **cyclone.**

ty•phus (tī′fəs) Any of several diseases transmitted by lice, fleas, or mites and characterized by high fever and skin rash. Typhus carried by lice can cause epidemics of the disease, which may be fatal in people with weakened immune systems.

ty•ran•no•sau•rus (tĭ-răn′ə-sôr′əs) *also* **ty•ran•no•saur** (tĭ-răn′ə-sôr′) A very large meat-eating dinosaur of the Cretaceous Period. It had very small forelimbs and a large head with sharp teeth. It walked on two legs, probably bent forward with its long tail stretched out as a counterbalance. Tyrannosaurs grew to lengths of 47 feet (14.3 meters) or more.

ty•ro•sine (tī′rə-sēn′) A nonessential amino acid. *See more at* **amino acid.**

U The symbol for **uranium.**

ud•der (ŭd′ər) A bag-shaped part of a cow and the females of related mammals, in which milk is formed and stored and from which it is taken in suckling or milking.

ul•cer (ŭl′sər) An inflamed sore on the skin or on a mucous membrane, as of the mouth or stomach.

ul•na (ŭl′nə) The larger of the two bones of the forearm or lower portion of the foreleg. *See more at* **skeleton.**

ul•tra•sound (ŭl′trə-sound′) **1.** Sound whose wave frequency is too high (over 20,000 hertz) to be heard by humans. **2.** The medical use of ultrasound waves, especially to produce images of the inside of the body or to observe a developing fetus. —*Adjective* **ultrasonic** (ŭl′trə-sŏn′ĭk).

Did You Know?
ultrasound

Many people own and use simple ultrasound generators: dog whistles that produce tones that dogs can hear but are too high to be heard by humans. Any sound whose frequency is higher than the upper end of the normal range of human hearing (higher than 20,000 hertz—that is, 20,000 sound waves per second) is called *ultrasound.* (Sound at frequencies too low to be audible—about 20 hertz or lower—is called *infrasound.*) The familiar medical ultrasound images (of a fetus in the womb, for example) are made by directing ultrasonic waves into the body, where they bounce off internal organs and other objects and are reflected back to a detector. Ultrasonic waves have very short wavelengths, and so they can create images of very small objects. Ultrasound can also be used to focus large amounts of energy into very small spaces, making it possible, for example, to break up kidney stones without making any surgical incisions.

ul•tra•vi•o•let (ŭl′trə-vī′ə-lĭt) *Adjective.* **1.** Relating to electromagnetic radiation having wavelengths shorter than those of visible light but longer than those of x-rays. *See more at* **electromagnetic spectrum.** —*Noun.* **2.** Ultraviolet light or the ultraviolet part of the spectrum. *See Note at* **infrared.**

um•bel (ŭm′bəl) A flat or rounded flower cluster in which the individual flower stalks arise from about the same point on the stem. The geranium, milkweed, and onion have umbels.

um•bil•i•cal cord (ŭm-bĭl′ĭ-kəl) The flexible cord-like structure connecting a fetus at the abdomen to the placenta. It contains blood vessels that supply nourishment to the fetus and remove its wastes.

um•bra (ŭm′brə) **1.** The darkest part of a shadow, especially the completely dark portion of the shadow cast by Earth, the moon, or another body during an eclipse. **2.** The darkest region of a sunspot. *Compare* **penumbra.**

un•cer•tain•ty principle (ŭn-sûr′tn-tē) A principle in quantum mechanics stating that it is impossible to measure both the position and the momentum of very small particles (such as electrons) at the same time with accuracy. According to this principle, the more accurately the position of a small particle is known, the less accurately its mass and velocity can be known, and the more accurately its mass and velocity are known, the less accurately its position can be known. The uncertainty principle and the theory of relativity form the basis of modern physics.

un•der•growth (ŭn′dər-grōth′) Low-growing plants, shrubs, and young trees that grow alongside and beneath taller trees in a forest.

un•der•tow (ŭn′dər-tō′) An underwater current flowing strongly away from shore. Undertows are generally caused by the seaward return of water from waves that have broken against the shore.

un•gu•late (ŭng′gyə-lĭt) A hoofed mammal. There are two kinds of ungulates: those having an even number of toes (artiodactyls) and those having an odd number of toes (perissodactyls).

u•ni•cel•lu•lar (yo͞o′nĭ-sĕl′yə-lər) Having or consisting of a single cell; one-celled: *unicellular organisms. Compare* **multicellular.**

u•ni•fied field theory (yo͞o′nə-fīd′) A theory that combines the theories of the four basic forces of nature (electromagnetism, gravity, strong nuclear force, and weak nuclear force) by establishing basic principles that apply to all of them and by determining how they are related to one another. No unified field theory that has been proposed so far has gained broad acceptance. Also called *grand unified theory.*

un•ion (yo͞on′yən) A set whose members belong to at least one of a group of two or more given sets. The union of the sets {1,2,3} and {3,4,5} is the set {1,2,3,4,5}, and the union of the sets {6,7} and {11,12,13} is the set {6,7,11,12,13}.

U•nit•ed States Customary System (yo͞o-nī′tĭd) The main system of weights and measures used in the United States and a few other countries. The system is based on the yard as a unit of length, the pound as a unit of weight, the gallon as a unit of liquid volume, and the bushel as a unit of dry volume. *See Table at* **measurement.**

u•ni•va•lent (yo͞o′nĭ-vā′lənt) *Chemistry.* Having a valence of one.

u•ni•valve (yo͞o′nĭ-vălv′) A mollusk, such as a snail, having a single shell. All univalves are gastropods. *Compare* **bivalve.**

u•ni•ver•sal time (yo͞o′nə-vûr′səl) The mean time for the meridian at Greenwich, England (0° longitude), which runs through the former site of the Royal Observatory. It is used as a basis for calculating time throughout most of the world. Also called *Greenwich Mean Time.*

u•ni•verse (yo͞o′nə-vûrs′) All matter and energy, including Earth, the galaxies, and the contents of the space between the galaxies, regarded as a whole.

un•sat•u•rat•ed (ŭn-săch′ə-rā′tĭd) **1.** Relating to an organic compound in which two or more of the carbon atoms are joined by a double or triple bond and therefore can be combined with additional atoms or radicals. Benzene and unsaturated fatty acids are examples of unsaturated compounds. *Compare* **saturated.** *See also* **monounsaturated, polyunsaturated. 2.** Relating to a solution that is capable of dissolving more solute than it already contains.

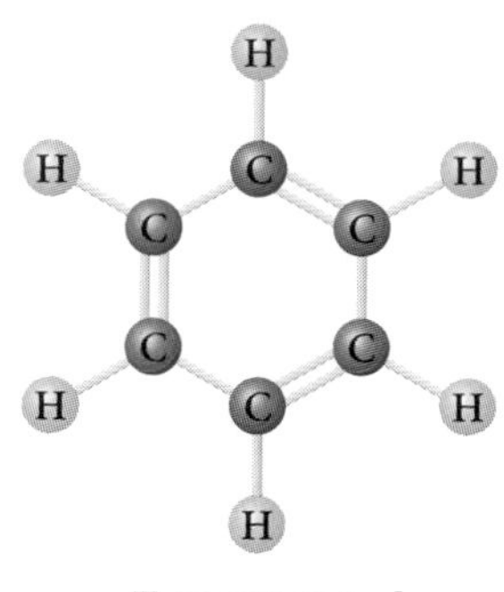

unsaturated

unsaturated fat A fat with a triglyceride molecule containing at least one unsaturated fatty acid. Fats derived from plants are often unsaturated fats. Eating foods high in unsaturated fats can reduce the amount of cholesterol in the blood. *Compare* **saturated fat.**

un•sta•ble (ŭn-stā′bəl) **1.** Liable to change spontaneously into a nucleus or atomic particle with less mass. For example, the nucleus of uranium 238 is unstable and changes by radioactive decay into the nucleus of thorium 234, a lighter element. **2.** Relating to a chemical compound that decomposes or changes into other compounds or into elements easily. Candle wax, for example, which is made of a mixture of hydrocarbons, decomposes into carbon dioxide and water when it reacts with oxygen during combustion. **3.** Relating to an atom or chemical element that is likely to share electrons; reactive.

u•ra•cil (yo͝or′ə-sĭl) A base that is a component of RNA, forming a base pair with adenine during transcription.

u•ra•ni•um (yo͞o-rā′nē-əm) A heavy, silvery-white, highly toxic, radioactive metallic element of the actinide series. It occurs in several minerals and ores, such as pitchblende. Uranium is used as a fuel for nuclear reactors to generate electricity. *Symbol* **U.** *Atomic number* 92. *See* **Periodic Table,** pages 262–263.

U•ra•nus (yo͝or′ə-nəs, yo͞o-rā′nəs) The seventh planet from the sun and the third largest, with a diameter about four times that of Earth. Uranus is composed mainly of hydrogen and helium gases and is encircled by a thin system of rings. *See Table at* **solar system,** pages 316–317. *See Note at* **planet.**

■ **Harold Urey**

u•re•a (yo͞o-rē′ə) The chief nitrogen-containing waste product excreted in the urine of mammals and some fish. It is produced by the breakdown of amino acids in the liver and is also made artificially for use in fertilizers and medicine.

u•re•ter (yo͞o-rē′tər, yo͝or′ĭ-tər) Either of two long, narrow ducts that carry urine from the kidney to the urinary bladder.

u•re•thra (yo͞o-rē′thrə) The duct through which urine passes from the bladder to the outside of the body in most mammals and some fish and birds. In most male mammals, the urethra also releases sperm during reproduction.

U•rey (yo͝or′ē), **Harold Clayton** 1893–1981. American chemist who discovered deuterium (1932). He also developed theories on the formation of the planets and on the synthesis of elements in the Earth's primitive atmosphere.

u•ric acid (yo͝or′ĭk) The chief nitrogen-containing waste product excreted in the urine of birds, insects, and most reptiles. It is produced by the breakdown of amino acids in the liver.

u•ri•nar•y tract (yo͝or′ə-nĕr′ē) The system of organs of the body involved in the formation and excretion of urine. In most vertebrate animals, the urinary tract consists mainly of the kidneys, ureters, and bladder. In most mammals, and some fish and birds, urine is discharged from the bladder through the urethra.

u•rine (yo͝or′ĭn) A liquid or semisolid substance containing waste products of metabolism that are filtered from the blood by the kidneys. In most mammals and some fish and birds, urine is stored in the urinary bladder and discharged from the body through the urethra.

Ur•sa Major (ûr′sə) A constellation in the polar region of the Northern Hemisphere near Draco and Leo. It contains the seven stars that form the Big Dipper.

Ursa Minor A ladle-shaped constellation very near the north celestial pole. It contains the seven stars that form the Little Dipper. Polaris, the North Star, is at the end of the dipper's handle.

u•ter•us (yo͞o′tər-əs) The hollow, muscular organ of female mammals to which a fertilized egg attaches before developing into an embryo. In most mammals the uterus is divided into two sac-like parts, whereas in humans it is a single structure. It lies between the bladder and rectum and is attached to the vagina and the fallopian tubes. Also called *womb. See more at* **menstrual cycle.**

UV index (yo͞o′vē′) A scale ranging from zero to ten, used to estimate the risk for sunburn in midday sunlight. The UV index takes into account conditions such as the amount of cloud cover and ozone in the atmosphere.

u•vu•la (yo͞o′vyə-lə) The small cone-shaped mass of fleshy tissue that hangs from the end of the soft palate above the tongue in the back of the mouth.

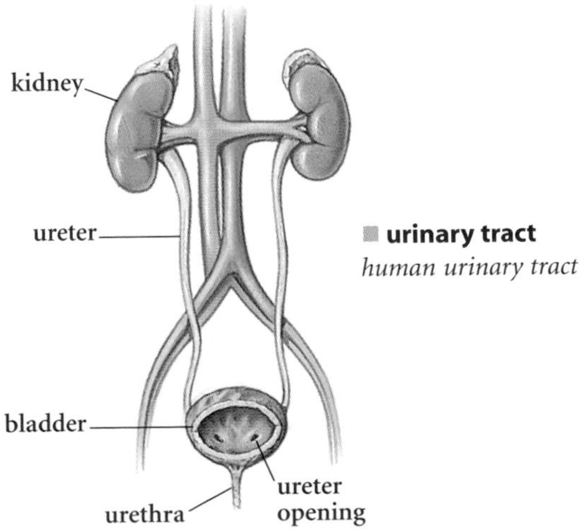

■ **urinary tract**
human urinary tract

V

V 1. The symbol for **vanadium. 2.** Abbreviation of **volume.**

vac•cine (văk-sēn′) A substance that stimulates cells in the immune system to recognize and attack disease-causing agents, especially through the production of antibodies. Most vaccines are given by injection or are swallowed as liquids. Vaccines may contain a weaker form of the disease-causing virus or bacterium or even a DNA fragment or some other component of the agent. *See Note at* **Jenner.**

Did You Know?
vaccine

In the 1950s, polio epidemics left thousands of children with permanent physical disabilities. Today, kids are given a polio vaccine to keep them from catching the virus. That *vaccine,* like most others, works by stimulating the body's immune system to produce antibodies—substances that defend the body against infection by recognizing and destroying disease-causing agents like viruses and bacteria. Scientists usually prepare vaccines by taking a sample of the disease-causing agent and weakening it with heat or chemicals. That way, the agent loses its ability to cause serious illness but is still able to stimulate the body to produce antibodies and provide immunity. But finding safe vaccines that are also effective is a challenge. Today, scientists are able to change the structure of viruses and bacteria at the level of their DNA. They remove the most harmful fragments of DNA and then use what is left in vaccines. New vaccines containing harmless bits of DNA from disease-causing germs have also been developed—all to make diseases like polio a thing of the past.

vac•u•ole (văk′yo͞o-ōl′) A space in a cell's cytoplasm that is surrounded by a membrane and filled with a watery fluid. The fluid stores food prior to digestion or waste products prior to excretion. *See more at* **cell.**

vac•uum (văk′yo͞om) **1.** A condition in which there is no matter or very little matter. **2.** An enclosed space, such as the space inside a container, in which there are far fewer gas molecules than in an equal volume of the air outside it. A vacuum has a much lower gas pressure than that of the atmosphere at sea level.

vacuum bottle A small container with a double wall and a partial vacuum in the space between the two walls. Vacuum bottles are used to minimize the transfer of heat between the inside and the outside and thus keep the contents at a desired temperature.

vacuum tube An electron tube from which all air has been removed so that the moving electrons don't collide with any gas particles and can move more efficiently from one electrode to the other. Cathode-ray tubes, which include television picture tubes and other video display tubes, are the most widely used vacuum tubes. *Compare* **electron tube.**

va•gi•na (və-jī′nə) The part of the reproductive tract in female mammals that is connected to the uterus at one end and opens to the outside of the body on the other end. Offspring pass through the vagina during birth.

va•gus nerve (vā′gəs) A long nerve that passes from the brain to the face, trunk, and abdomen. It controls the muscles of the larynx (voice box), stimulates digestion, and regulates the heartbeat. The vagus nerve is a cranial nerve.

va•lence (vā′ləns) A whole number that represents the ability of an atom or a group of atoms to combine with other atoms or groups of atoms. The valence is determined by the number of electrons that an atom can lose, add, or share. A carbon atom, for example, can share four electrons with other atoms and therefore has a valence of 4.

val•ine (văl′ēn′) An essential amino acid. *See more at* **amino acid.**

val•ley (văl′ē) A long, narrow region of low land between ranges of mountains, hills, or other high areas, often having a river or stream running along the bottom. Valleys are most commonly formed through the erosion of land by rivers or glaciers. They also form where large regions of land are lowered because of geological faults.

val•ue (văl′yo͞o) **1.** *Mathematics.* An assigned or calculated numerical quantity. **2.** The relative darkness or lightness of a color. *See more at* **color.**

valve (vălv) **1a.** Any of various mechanical devices that control the flow of liquids, gases, or loose material through pipes or channels by blocking and uncovering openings. **b.** The movable part or element of such a device. **2.** Any of various structures that prevent the backward flow of a body fluid. Examples include the valves between the chambers of the heart and the valves of the veins. **3.** One of the paired hinged shells of certain mollusks, such as clams and oysters.

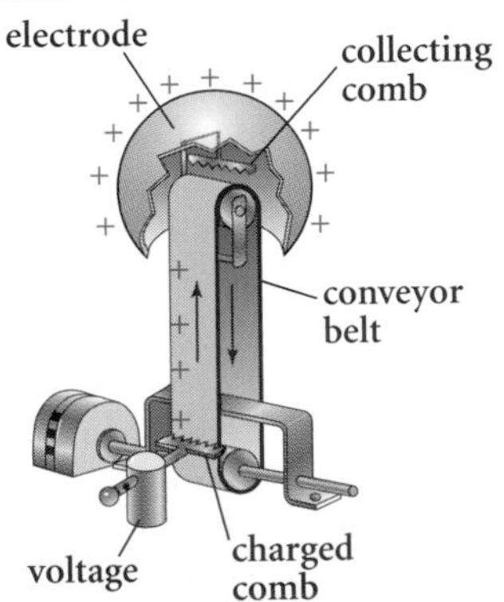

Van de Graaff generator

top: *An electric charge fed through the generator separates into positive and negative charges. The positive charge is carried up to the spherical electrode on a rubber conveyor belt.*
bottom: *Touching the electrode causes a person's hair to stand straight up as the positively charged particles race to the hair tips and then repel each other.*

va•na•di•um (və-nā′dē-əm) A soft, bright-white metallic element that occurs naturally in several minerals. It has good structural strength and is used especially to make strong varieties of steel. *Symbol* **V.** *Atomic number* 23. *See* **Periodic Table,** pages 262–263.

Van Al•len belt (văn ăl′ən) Either of two zones of high-intensity radiation surrounding the Earth. In these zones, a large number of atomic particles with high energies are trapped by the Earth's magnetic field.

Van de Graaff (văn′ də grăf′), **Robert Jemison** 1901–1967. American physicist. In 1929, he invented an electrical generator (later called the Van de Graaff generator) that was adapted for use as a particle accelerator and became an important research tool for atomic physicists. The generator was also used to produce a type of x-ray helpful in treating cancer.

Van de Graaff generator A device used to build up an electric charge by transferring charged particles from a high-voltage power supply to a spherical electrode. When an object, such as a person, touches the electrode, the generator transfers to the object the charge that has built up on the electrode.

van der Waals force (văn′ dər wôlz′) A weak force of attraction between electrically neutral molecules that collide with or pass very close to each other. The van der Waals force is caused by temporary attractions between electron-rich regions of one molecule and electron-poor regions of another. These attractions are very common but are much weaker than chemical bonds. The van der Waals force is what allows water vapor to condense into liquid water.

va•por (vā′pər) **1.** The gaseous state of a substance that is liquid at room temperature. Because the carbon dioxide gas associated with dry ice is often referred to as a vapor, some scientists classify the gaseous state of substances that are solids at room temperature as vapors as well. **2.** A faintly visible suspension of fine particles of matter in the air, as mist, fumes, or

USAGE

vapor/steam

When we use the words *vapor* and *steam,* we usually think of a fine mist or other visible suspension of particles in the air. We speak of the steam that clouds the bathroom after we take a shower or the vapor in the jet of water droplets that appears a short distance from the end of a boiling tea kettle. But to a scientist, this kind of talk is inaccurate. The word *vapor* refers to a gaseous state of a substance, and not to a mist of liquid droplets or fine solid particles. For instance, the fumes that arise when volatile substances such as alcohol and gasoline evaporate are (not surprisingly) a vapor. Similarly, the visible stream of water droplets that rush out of the spout of tea kettle is not steam. As the gaseous state of water heated past its boiling point, steam is invisible. Usually, there is a clear space of an inch or two between the spout and the beginning of the visible stream of droplets. This space contains steam. The steam loses its heat to the surrounding air, then falls below the boiling point and condenses in the air as water droplets. It is not, scientifically speaking, water vapor.

smoke. **3.** A mixture of fine droplets of a substance and air, as the fuel mixture of an internal-combustion engine. —*Verb* **vaporize.**

vapor pressure 1. The pressure exerted by water vapor in the atmosphere. **2.** The pressure exerted by a vapor on the solid or liquid phase with which it is in equilibrium. At pressures lower than the vapor pressure, atoms or molecules of the liquid or solid being vaporized can escape from the surface of the liquid or solid. At the vapor pressure, they cannot escape because the two phases are in equilibrium.

var•i•a•ble (vâr′ē-ə-bəl) **1.** A mathematical quantity capable of assuming any of a set of values, such as x in the expression $3x + 2$. **2.** A factor or condition that is subject to change, especially one that is allowed to change in a scientific experiment to test a hypothesis. *See more at* **control.**

variable star A star whose brightness changes periodically. The variation can occur because of internal changes in a single star or because a darker star periodically eclipses a brighter star in a binary star system.

var•i•cel•la (văr′ĭ-sĕl′ə) *See* **chickenpox.**

vas•cu•lar (văs′kyə-lər) **1.** *Zoology.* Relating to the vessels of the body, especially the arteries and veins, that carry blood and lymph: *the vascular system.* **2.** *Botany.* Relating to or having tissues that carry water and dissolved nutrients and food from one part of a plant to another. All seed-bearing plants and ferns have vascular tissues; bryophytes, such as mosses, do not. *See more at* **phloem, photosynthesis, xylem.**

vascular cambium The cambium that produces the vascular tissues xylem and phloem in woody plants. *See more at* **cambium.**

vas def•er•ens (văs′ dĕf′ə-rĕnz′) Either of two ducts through which sperm passes from a testis to the urethra.

vec•tor (vĕk′tər) **1.** A quantity, such as velocity or change of position, that has both magnitude and direction. *Compare* **scalar. 2.** An organism, such as a mosquito or tick, that spreads disease-causing microorganisms from one host to another without harm to itself.

Ve•ga (vē′gə, vā′gə) A star in the constellation Lyra. It is the fifth brightest star in the night sky.

veg•e•ta•ble (vĕj′tə-bəl) **1.** A plant that is cultivated for an edible part, such as the leaf of spinach. **2.** An edible part of one of these plants. *See Note at* **fruit.**

vegetable kingdom *See* **plant kingdom.**

vein (vān) **1.** Any of the blood vessels that carry blood toward the heart. Veins are thin-walled and contain valves that prevent the backflow of blood. All veins except the pulmonary vein (which returns to the heart from the lungs) carry blood having low levels of oxygen. **2.** One of the narrow, usually branching tubes or supporting parts forming the framework of a leaf or an insect's wing. *See more at* **leaf. 3.** A long, narrow deposit of mineral or rock found in another type of rock. Veins usually form when magma fills a fracture in a rock. —*Adjective* **venous** (vē′nəs).

veldt *also* **veld** (vĕlt, fĕlt) An extensive, treeless grassland of southern Africa.

USAGE

velocity/speed

We normally think of velocity as the speed at which an object is traveling. But in physics, *velocity* and *speed* are not the same. Like speed, velocity refers to the rate at which an object is moving—the distance per unit of time. But velocity in physics also includes the direction in which the object is moving, whereas direction has no bearing on an object's speed. For example, if two cars were driving at a rate of 50 miles per hour, and both headed due north, you could rightly say that they were both traveling at the same speed and at the same velocity. But if one of the cars were to turn west at a certain point, continuing at the same rate of 50 miles per hour, you could only say that they were traveling at the same speed, not at the same velocity. Similarly, traveling around a curve, a car may maintain the same speed throughout, but its velocity will be constantly changing. This change in velocity over time is called *acceleration*.

ve•loc•i•rap•tor (və-lŏs′ə-răp′tər) A small, fast, meat-eating dinosaur of the Cretaceous Period about 6 feet (2 meters) in length. It had long curved claws, walked on two legs that were adapted for leaping, and had a long stiff tail used as a counterweight. Velociraptors were a kind of raptor.

ve•loc•i•ty (və-lŏs′ĭ-tē) The rate at which an object moves in a specified direction.

ve•na ca•va (vē′nə kā′və) Either of two large veins that carry blood with low levels of oxygen to the right atrium of the heart. The lower one, called the inferior vena cava, is the largest vein in the body.

ve•na•tion (vē-nā′shən) **1.** The distribution or arrangement of a system of veins, as in a leaf blade. **2.** The veins of such a system considered as a group.

ve•ne•re•al disease (və-nîr′ē-əl) *See* **sexually transmitted disease.**

Venn diagram (vĕn) A diagram that uses circles to represent sets. Relations between the sets can be indicated by the arrangement of the circles, as for example by drawing one circle within another to indicate that the first set is a subset of a second set.

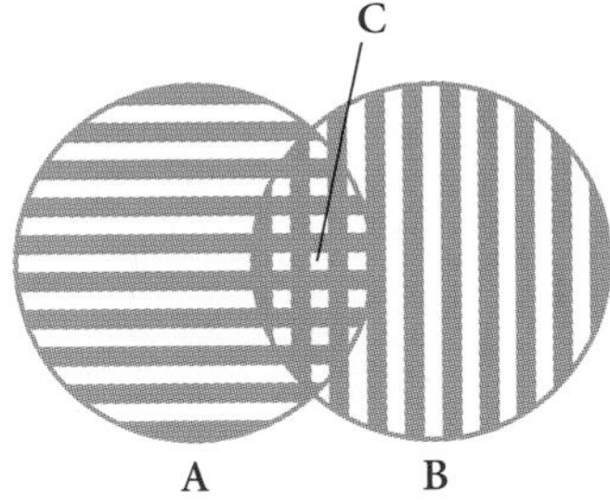

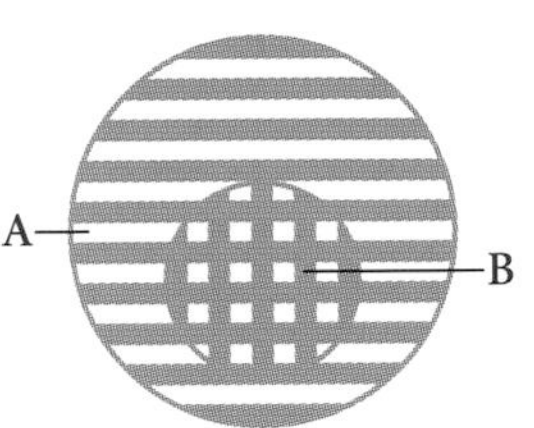

Venn diagram

top: *Sets A and B intersect to form set C. All members of C are common to A and B.*
bottom: *Set B is a subset of set A. All members of B are also members of A.*

ven•om (vĕn′əm) A poisonous substance that is secreted by certain snakes, spiders, scorpions, and insects. It can be transmitted to a victim by a bite or sting.

ven•tral (vĕn′trəl) Of or on the front or lower surface of an animal.

ven•tri•cle (vĕn′trĭ-kəl) **1.** A chamber of the heart that receives blood from one or more atria and pumps it into the arteries. Mammals, birds, and reptiles have two ventricles; amphibians and fish have one. **2.** Any of four fluid-filled cavities in the brain of vertebrate animals. —*Adjective* **ventricular** (vĕn-trĭk′yə-lər).

Ve•nus (vē′nəs) The second planet from the sun and the fourth smallest, with a diameter about 400 miles less than that of Earth. Venus comes nearer to Earth than any other planet and is the brightest object in the night sky aside from Earth's moon. It is the hottest planet in the solar system, with an average surface temperature of 867°F (464°C). *See Table at* **solar system,** pages 316–317. *See Note at* **planet.**

Venus flytrap A plant of North and South Carolina having leaf blades that are edged with

Venus flytrap

bristles and that can close and trap insects. The insects are then digested and absorbed by the plant.

ver•nal equinox (vûr′nəl) The moment of the year when the sun crosses the celestial equator while moving from south to north. It occurs on March 20 or 21, marking the beginning of spring in the Northern Hemisphere. *Compare* **autumnal equinox.**

Ver•nier (vĕr-nyā′), **Pierre** 1580–1637. French mathematician and maker of scientific instruments, known especially for his invention of a highly exact scale.

ver•te•bra (vûr′tə-brə) *Plural* **vertebrae** (vûr′tə-brā′, vûr′tə-brē′) *or* **vertebras.** Any of the bones that make up the vertebral column. Each vertebra contains a hollow section through which the spinal cord passes. *See more at* **skeleton.**

ver•te•bral column (vûr′tə-brəl) The series of vertebrae extending from the base of the skull to the coccyx (tailbone) that forms the supporting axis of the body in vertebrate animals. It encloses and protects the spinal cord and provides a stable attachment for the muscles of the trunk. Also called *backbone, spinal column, spine.*

ver•te•brate (vûr′tə-brĭt, vûr′tə-brāt′) Any of a large group of animals having a backbone, including fish, amphibians, reptiles, birds, and mammals. Vertebrates are bilaterally symmetrical and have an internal skeleton of bone or cartilage, a nervous system along the back that is divided into brain and spinal cord, and not more than two pairs of limbs.

BIOGRAPHY

Andreas Vesalius

Vesalius followed his family's tradition and studied medicine. Once he received his degree, he began teaching and overseeing demonstrations of anatomy to students. To improve his knowledge he also dissected cadavers—something that was unusual for a man in his position, who would properly have left such work to an assistant. After a few years, he became convinced that the anatomical theories put forward by Galen, a Greek physician whose ideas had been accepted as authoritative for over 1,000 years, were not based on the human body. Instead, Vesalius maintained that Galen's description of the human body was based on dissections of pigs, dogs, and other animals. Vesalius did what no one had done before: he critically evaluated Galen's anatomical texts, comparing them with the observations that he made himself during his dissections. Vesalius compiled his findings in a book on anatomy. He had artists make illustrations for it, and he supervised their work. His *On the Structure of the Human Body* was the most extensive and accurate description of the human body that had ever been compiled. By relying on careful observation instead of received wisdom, Vesalius revolutionized the field of anatomy, and of medicine and biology as well.

Did You Know?

vitamins

To help the cells in our bodies work properly, it is essential that we get a daily supply of *vitamins.* This link between vitamins and good health was made in the early 1900s by the Polish biochemist Casimir Funk. Funk was studying beriberi, a disease that damages nerves, when he discovered an organic compound that prevented this illness. He named the compound *vitamine,* or "life amine," a name that stuck even though most vitamins do not include the type of chemical called an amine. Today we know that vitamins help keep our bodies strong and healthy, in addition to preventing a variety of illnesses. But because our bodies cannot produce these compounds, we must get them in the foods we eat as part of a well-balanced diet.

ver•tex (vûr′tĕks′) *Plural* **vertices** (vûr′tĭ-sēz′) *or* **vertexes. 1.** The point at which the sides of an angle intersect. **2.** The point of a triangle, cone, or pyramid that is opposite to and farthest away from its base; the apex. **3.** A point of a polyhedron at which three or more of the edges intersect.

ver•ti•cal angles (vûr′tĭ-kəl) Two angles formed by two intersecting lines and lying on opposite sides of the point of intersection.

Ve•sa•li•us (vĭ-sā′lē-əs), **Andreas** 1514–1564. Flemish anatomist and surgeon who is considered the founder of modern anatomy. His major work, *On the Structure of the Human Body* (1543), was based on his own dissection of cadavers.

ves•i•cle (vĕs′ĭ-kəl) A small fluid-filled sac in the body.

ves•tig•i•al (vĕ-stĭj′ē-əl) Relating to a body part that has become small and lost its use because of evolutionary change. Whales, for example, have small bones located in the muscles of their body walls that are vestigial bones of hips and hind limbs.

vet•er•i•nar•y medicine (vĕt′ər-ə-nĕr′ē) The branch of medicine that deals with the diseases or injuries of animals and their treatment.

vi•bra•tion (vī-brā′shən) A rapid motion of a particle or an elastic solid back and forth in a straight line on both sides of a central position. Vibrations consist of many oscillations. *Compare* **oscillation.** *See Note at* **sound**[1]**.**

vil•lus (vĭl′əs) *Plural* **villi** (vĭl′ī) A small projection on the surface of a mucous membrane, especially that of the small intestine.

vi•nyl (vī′nəl) Any of various chemical compounds that contain the group C_2H_3 and are used to make plastics, fabrics, and paints.

Vir•go (vûr′gō) A constellation in the region of the celestial equator near Leo and Libra.

vi•rol•o•gy (vī-rŏl′ə-jē) The scientific study of viruses and viral diseases.

vi•rus (vī′rəs) **1.** Any of a large group of disease-causing agents consisting of a segment of RNA or DNA within a protein shell. All viruses are parasites because they can reproduce only inside the cells of plants, animals, and bacteria. Viruses are usually not considered living organisms. **2.** *Computer Science.* A computer program that is meant to disable or damage the computer's memory or to cause another program to malfunction. Computer viruses usually copy themselves over and over. —*Adjective* **viral.**

vis•cos•i•ty (vĭ-skŏs′ĭ-tē) The resistance of a substance to flow. A substance that can flow easily has a low viscosity. A substance that cannot flow easily has a high viscosity.

vis•cous (vĭs′kəs) Having relatively high resistance to flow. As the molecules of a viscous fluid, such as honey, slide past each other, the friction between them causes the fluid to flow slowly.

vi•ta•min (vī′tə-mĭn) Any of various complex organic compounds that are needed in small amounts for normal growth and activity of the body and are found naturally in foods obtained from plants and animals.

vitamin A A vitamin important for normal vision, tissue growth, and healthy skin. It is found in fish-liver oils, milk, green leafy vegetables, and yellow vegetables and fruits. Also called *retinol.*

vitamin B complex Any of a group of related vitamins important for normal cell growth and metabolism. The vitamins of the vitamin B com-

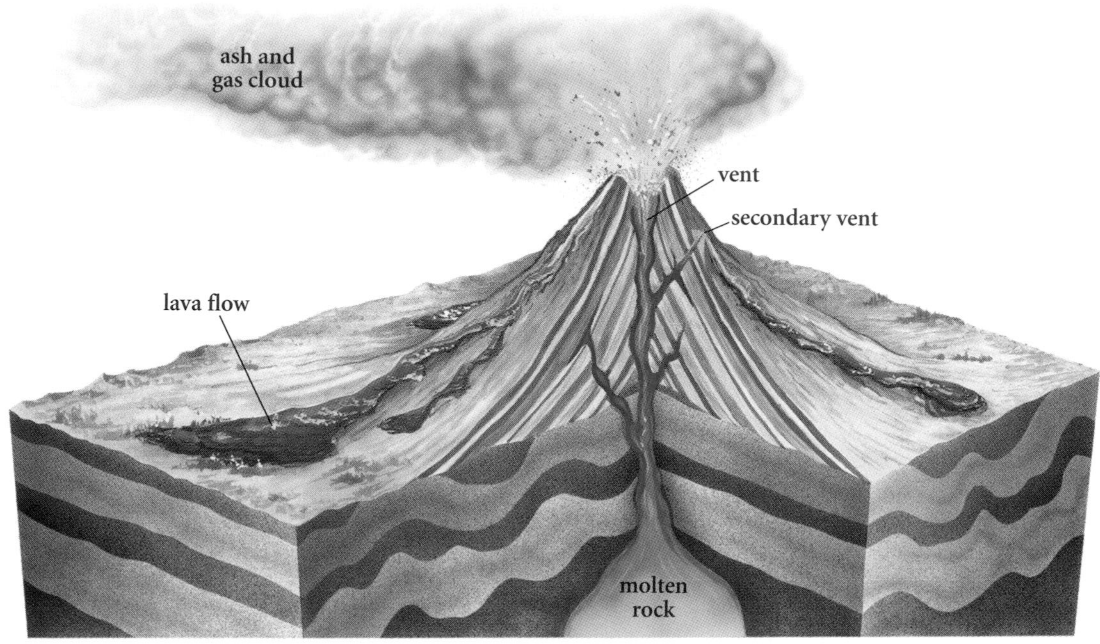

■ **volcano**

plex include thiamine (vitamin B_1), riboflavin (vitamin B_2), pantothenic acid, niacin, biotin, and folic acid. ❖ The complex also includes **vitamin B_6** (also called *pyridoxine*), which is important in protein and fat metabolism and in healthy nerve function. It is found in liver, whole-grain foods, fish, yeast, and many vegetables. ❖ Another vitamin in this complex, **vitamin B_{12}** (also called *cobalamin*), is important in maintaining the health of blood and nerves. It is found in meat, eggs, milk, and milk products.

vitamin C A vitamin important for healthy skin, teeth, bones, and blood vessels. It is found especially in citrus fruits, tomatoes, potatoes, and green leafy vegetables. Also called *ascorbic acid.*

vitamin D Any of a group of vitamins necessary for normal bone growth. Vitamin D is found in milk, fish, and eggs and can be produced in the skin on exposure to sunlight.

vitamin E A vitamin important for normal cell growth and function. It is found in vegetable oils, wheat germ, green leafy vegetables, and egg yolks.

vitamin K Any of a group of vitamins important for normal clotting of the blood. Vitamin K is found in green leafy vegetables, pork, liver, and vegetable oils.

vit•re•ous (vĭt′rē-əs) Relating to or resembling glass; glassy.

vitreous humor The jelly-like substance that fills the area of the eyeball between the retina and the lens.

vi•vip•a•rous (vī-vĭp′ər-əs) Giving birth to living young that develop within the mother's body rather than hatching from eggs. Most mammals are viviparous. *Compare* **oviparous, ovoviviparous.**

viv•i•sec•tion (vĭv′ĭ-sĕk′shən) The practice of examining internal organs and tissues by cutting into or dissecting a living animal.

vo•cal cords (vō′kəl) The two pairs of folded tissue in the larynx that people use to speak and sing. People make sounds when the lower folds are drawn together as air passes across them on its way out of the lungs. This causes the folds to vibrate.

voice box (vois) *See* **larynx.**

vol•a•tile (vŏl′ə-tl) Changing easily from liquid to vapor at normal temperatures and pressures.

vol•can•ic arc (vŏl-kăn′ĭk) A usually curved chain of volcanoes located on the margin of the overriding plate at a convergent plate boundary.

Alessandro Volta

vol•ca•no (vŏl-kā′nō) **1.** An opening in the Earth's crust from which lava, ash, and hot gases flow or are thrown out during an eruption. **2.** A usually cone-shaped mountain formed by the materials that flowed or were thrown out from such an opening. *See more at* **tectonic boundary.**

volt (vōlt) A unit used to measure electromotive force. One volt is equal to the force that carries one ampere of current through a conductor that has a resistance of one ohm.

Vol•ta (vōl′tə), Count **Alessandro** 1745–1827. Italian physicist who invented the electric battery (1800). Called the voltaic pile, it was the first device to produce a steady stream of electric current. The volt unit of electromotive force is named for him.

volt•age (vōl′tĭj) Electromotive force expressed in volts. A current of high voltage is used to transmit electric power over long distances.

vol•ta•ic cell (vŏl-tā′ĭk) An electric cell, especially one that uses a chemical reaction in which ions are formed and flow toward two electrodes, thereby creating a voltage between them. The electrodes are made of different metals and are immersed in a reactive solution of electrolytes. Car batteries are an example of voltaic cells. *Compare* **electrolytic cell.**

volt•me•ter (vōlt′mē′tər) An instrument used for measuring the difference in voltage between two points in an electric circuit.

vol•ume (vŏl′yo͞om) **1.** The amount of space occupied by a three-dimensional object or region of space. **2.** A measure of the loudness or intensity of a sound.

vol•u•met•ric (vŏl′yo͝o-mĕt′rĭk) Relating to measurement by volume or to a unit that is used to measure volume.

vol•un•tar•y (vŏl′ən-tĕr′ē) Under conscious control. The muscles attached to the skeleton are voluntary muscles because they can be moved at will.

vor•tex (vôr′tĕks′) *Plural* **vortexes** *or* **vortices** (vôr′tĭ-sēz′) A whirling current of fluid, such as water or air, that tends to draw the fluid toward its center. Eddies and whirlpools are examples of vortexes.

vul•ca•nize (vŭl′kə-nīz′) To harden rubber by heating it and combining it with sulfur. Vulcanization gives rubber more strength and elasticity.

vul•va (vŭl′və) The external genital organs of female mammals.

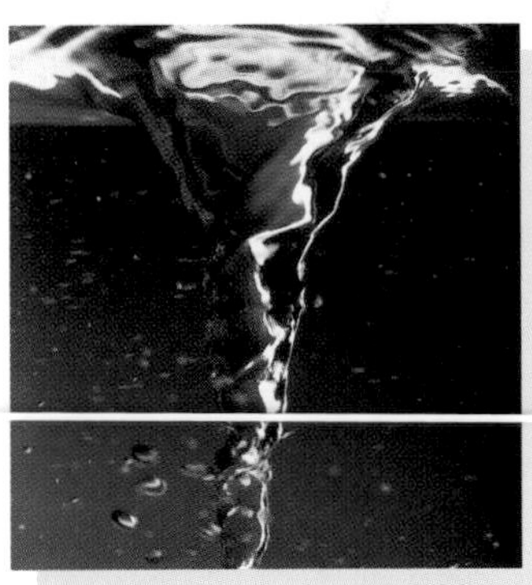

vortex

W

W The symbol for **tungsten.**

wa•di (wä′dē) A gully or streambed in northern Africa and southwest Asia that remains dry except during the rainy season.

Waks•man (wăks′mən), **Selman Abraham** 1888–1973. American microbiologist who pioneered the development of antibiotics. His discoveries included streptomycin (1944), the first drug effective against tuberculosis.

Wal•lace (wŏl′ĭs), **Alfred Russel** 1823–1913. British naturalist who formulated a theory of evolution by natural selection independently of Charles Darwin. Wallace spent eight years (1854–1862) traveling in Malaysia and assembling evidence for his theories, which he sent to Darwin in England. Their findings were presented to the public in 1858.

Wal•ton (wôl′tən), **Ernest Thomas Sinton** 1903–1995. Irish physicist who developed the particle accelerator with John Cockcroft. Their experiments with it led to the first successful splitting of an atom, in 1932.

warm-blood•ed (wôrm′blŭd′ĭd) Having a relatively warm body temperature that stays about the same regardless of changes in the temperature of the surroundings. Birds and mammals are warm-blooded.

warm front The forward edge of an advancing mass of warm air that rises over a mass of cold air. A warm front is often accompanied by a prolonged period of steady rain. *See more at* **front.**

war•ren (wôr′ən) An area where a colony of rabbits lives in burrows.

wart (wôrt) **1.** A small growth on the skin caused by a virus, occurring typically on the hands or feet. **2.** A similar growth, as on a plant.

wasp (wŏsp) Any of numerous insects having two pairs of wings, mouths adapted for biting or sucking, and in the females an egg-laying tube (called an ovipositor) that is often modified as a sting. Wasps are related to ants and bees and can be solitary or live in colonies.

wa•ter (wô′tər) A clear, liquid compound of hydrogen and oxygen, H_2O. Water covers about three-quarters of the Earth's surface and also occurs in solid form as ice and in gaseous form as vapor. It is an essential component of all organisms, and it is necessary for most biological processes. Water freezes at 32°F (0°C) and boils at 212°F (100°C).

water cycle The continuous process by which water is distributed throughout the Earth and its atmosphere. Energy from the sun causes water to evaporate from oceans and other bodies of water and from soil surfaces. Plants and animals also add water vapor to the air by transpiration. As it rises into the atmosphere, the water vapor condenses to form clouds. Rain and other forms of precipitation return water to the Earth, where it flows into bodies of water and into the ground, beginning the cycle over again. Also called *hydrologic cycle.*

water flea Any of various small aquatic crustaceans, mostly of microscopic size, having especially long antennae that are used for swimming. Water fleas are an important source of food for many fish.

wa•ter•shed (wô′tər-shĕd′) **1.** The entire region that is drained by a river system. **2.** A ridge forming a boundary between two different river systems.

water table The level at which the ground beneath the surface is saturated with water. The water table usually rises after heavy rainfall and

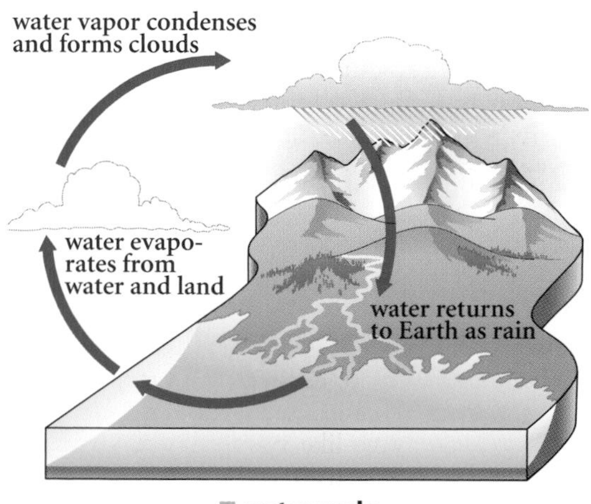
water vapor condenses
and forms clouds
water evaporates from
water and land
water returns
to Earth as rain

■ **water cycle**

the melting of snow and falls during drier periods.

water vapor Water in its gaseous state, especially in the atmosphere and at a temperature below the boiling point.

Wat•son (wŏt′sən), **James Dewey** Born 1928. American biologist who with Francis Crick identified the structure of DNA. By analyzing the patterns cast by x-rays striking DNA molecules, they discovered that DNA has the structure of a double helix, two spirals linked together by bases in ladder-like rungs. Their discovery formed the basis of molecular genetics.

Wat•son-Watt (wŏt′sən-wŏt′), **Robert Alexander** 1892–1973. British physicist who pioneered the development of radar. In 1919 he produced a system for locating thunderstorms by tracking their radio emissions. In the 1930s Watson-Watt led the team that developed radar into a practical system for locating aircraft.

watt (wŏt) A unit used to measure power, equal to one joule of work per second. In electricity, a watt is equal to the amount of current (in amperes) multiplied by the amount of potential (in volts).

Watt, James 1736–1819. British engineer, inventor, and scientist. He invented the steam engine (1769) and devised the unit of horsepower. The watt unit of power is named for him.

watt•age (wŏt′ĭj) An amount of power, especially electrical power, expressed in watts or kilowatts.

watt-hour A unit of power, especially electrical power, equal to the work done by one watt acting for one hour. It is equivalent to 3,600 joules.

wave (wāv) A disturbance or vibration that passes through a medium, such as air or water, transferring energy without causing a permanent change to the medium. *See also* **longitudinal wave, transverse wave.** *See Note at* **refraction.** *See A Closer Look, page 368.*

wave•length (wāv′lĕngkth′) The distance between one peak or crest of a wave and the next peak or crest.

wave mechanics A theory of the behavior of matter or energy understood in terms of waves. Quantum mechanics uses wave mechanics to describe the wave-like properties of all matter. The shape of electron orbits in an atom, for example, is described using wave mechanics.

wax (wăks) Any of various solid, usually yellow substances that melt or soften easily when heated. Waxes are produced in nature by various animals and plants, or are made artificially. They are similar to fats, but are less greasy and more brittle.

weak nuclear force (wēk) A force that causes subatomic particles within the nuclei of atoms to decay or break up into smaller particles and to give off energy as radiation. The weak nuclear force is one of the four basic forces in nature, being weaker than the strong nuclear force and the electromagnetic force but stronger than gravity. Also called *weak interaction.*

weath•er (wĕ*th*′ər) The state of the atmosphere at a particular time and place. Weather is described by variable conditions such as temperature, humidity, wind velocity, precipitation, and barometric pressure.

web (wĕb) **1.** A structure of fine silky strands woven by spiders or by certain insect larvae. The web of a spider is used to catch insect prey. **2.** A fold of skin or thin tissue connecting the toes of certain animals, especially ones that swim, such as water birds and otters. The web improves the ability of the foot to push against water. **3.** also **Web** The World Wide Web.

We•ge•ner (vā′gə-nər), **Alfred Lothar** 1880–1930. German physicist, meteorologist, and explorer who introduced the theory of continental drift in 1915. His hypothesis was controversial and remained so until the 1960s, when new scientific understanding of the structure of the ocean floors provided evidence that his theory was correct. *See more at* **plate tectonics.**

Alfred Wegener

A CLOSER LOOK

Waves

Sound, light, x-rays, and other types of energy spread outward in the form of waves. Waves travel through what is known as a medium: the medium of a sound wave consists of the atoms making up any form of matter, for example, and the medium of a wave in the ocean is the ocean water. Waves have a characteristic structure and fall into two basic types: longitudinal and transverse. They also have other properties that are illustrated below.

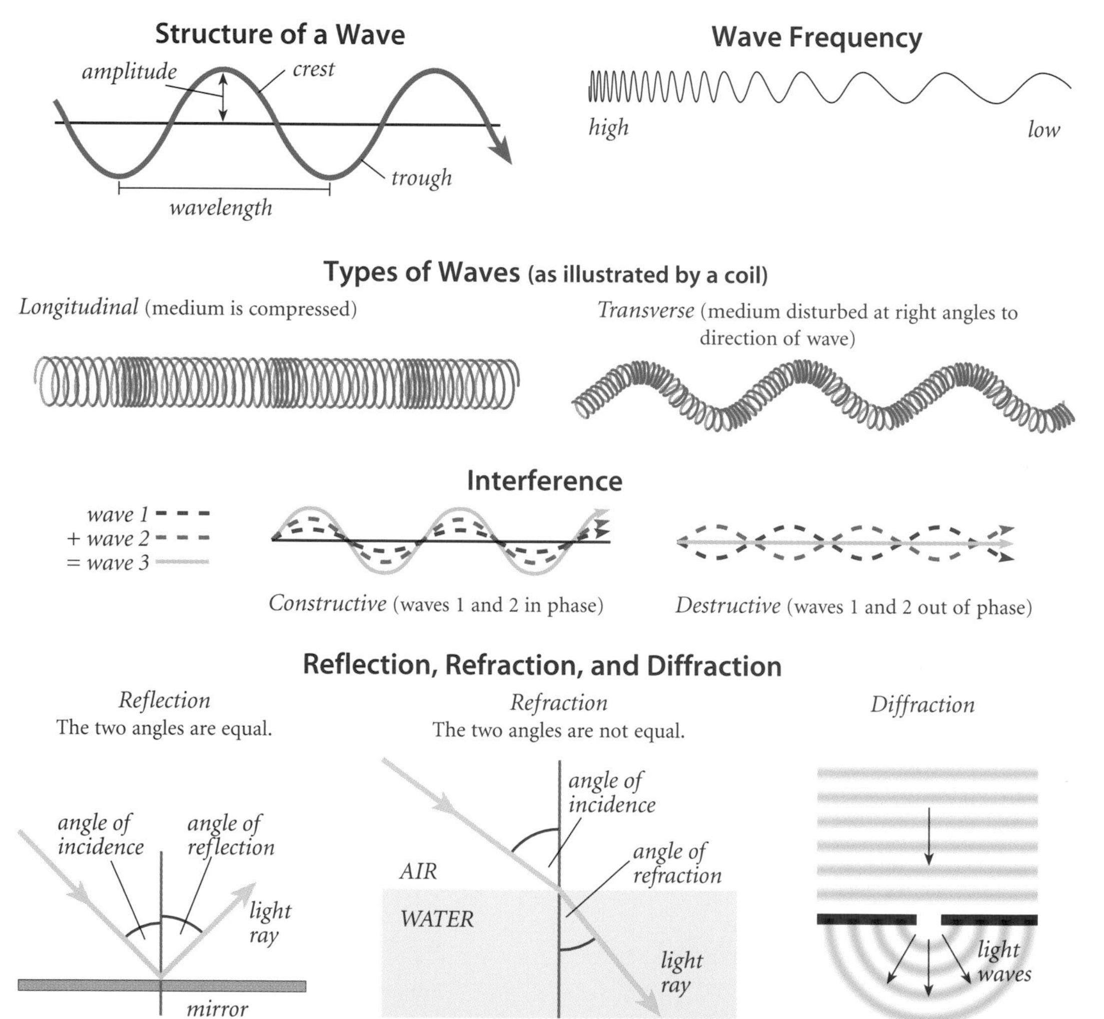

weight (wāt) **1.** The force with which an object near the Earth or another celestial body is attracted toward the center of the body by gravity. An object's weight depends on its mass (the amount of matter it consists of) and the strength of the gravitational pull. On Earth, for example, an object weighs less at the top of a very high mountain than it does at sea level, simply

USAGE

weight/mass

It's easy to convert pounds into kilograms: just multiply the number of pounds by .45 (or if you want greater precision, use .4536). But no matter how many times you do this conversion, you will always be making a mistake, because a pound is a unit of *force,* while a kilogram is a unit of *mass.* A pound is a measure of the force that a gravitational field exerts on an object. As such, a pound is a unit of *weight,* not of mass. An object's mass is its ability to resist changes in the speed or direction of its motion, and it is always the same regardless of what forces are acting upon it. If you were walking on the moon, for example, your mass would be the same as it is on the Earth, but your weight would be one sixth of what it is on the Earth because of the lower gravitational pull of the moon. If this is so, you might ask, how can my science teacher ask me to convert pounds into kilograms? When we make such conversions, we are assuming that the object in question is on the Earth, at sea level, where the conversion factor works for all practical purposes.

Did You Know?

wetland

The idea of a *wetland* may strike you as strange, because we usually think of the world as either wet (rivers, lakes, oceans) or dry (mountains, plains, coasts). But wetlands are both. They're soggy enough that you wouldn't want to go camping in them, but there's enough soil for plants like reeds, bushes, and even trees to take root and grow. In the past, many wetlands were filled in to make farmland or to develop the area for housing—more than half of the original wetlands in the continental United States are gone. Today, however, scientists have discovered that wetlands can act like huge filters, removing pollutants from the waters of an area before those substances can do harm. They can serve as reservoirs, and they may help in flood control by absorbing excess water. Wetlands are also home to many different plant and animal species that have evolved to live in the wetland's unique conditions.

because the gravitational pull at the top of the mountain is lower than it is at sea level. **2.** A unit used as a measure of gravitational force: *a table of weights and measures.* **3.** A system of such measures: *avoirdupois weight; troy weight.*

Wein•berg (wīn′bûrg′), **Steven** Born 1933. American nuclear physicist who helped develop important theories explaining the relationship between the electromagnetic force and the weak nuclear force, two of the four basic forces of nature.

West•ern Hemisphere (wĕs′tərn) The half of the Earth that includes North America, Central America, and South America.

West•ing•house (wĕs′tĭng-hous′), **George** 1846–1914. American engineer and manufacturer who introduced the high-voltage alternating current system for the transmission of electricity in the United States. A prolific inventor, Westinghouse received 361 patents in his lifetime, including the air brake, automated train-switching signals, and devices for the transmission of natural gas. His inventions made an important contribution to the growth of railroads.

wet cell (wĕt) An electric cell in which the chemicals producing the current are in the form of a liquid rather than in the form of a paste (as in a dry cell). Car batteries consist of a series of wet cells.

wet•land (wĕt′lănd′) A low-lying area of land that is saturated with moisture, especially when regarded as the natural habitat of wildlife. Marshes, swamps, and bogs are examples of wetlands.

whale (wāl) Any of various, often large sea mammals that have a streamlined body resembling that of a fish, forelimbs shaped like flippers, a tail

Did You Know?
whale

In a submarine, you can ride down thousands of feet underwater. But if you swam outside it, the water pressure would crush you like a soda can. Amazingly, there are many animals that happily exist in such conditions. The sperm whale, for instance, may dive as deep as two miles with no ill effects. A male sperm whale is like a living tractor-trailer truck, almost 60 feet long and weighing 45 tons. Many adaptations allow the huge creature, and other deep-sea organisms, to function normally at great depths. One important strength is actually a weakness: unlike our rigid ribs, the whale's flexible ribcage allows its chest cavity to collapse in a controlled way as the pressure increases. Other adaptations control the way gases are stored in the blood. Unlike people, whales do not have to return to the surface gradually to avoid getting the *bends*—the sometimes deadly formation of nitrogen bubbles caused by expanding gas in the blood. Because of this adaptation, whales can swim up and down as fast as they like, undergoing tremendous variation in pressure, with no ill effects. It's all just water to them.

with horizontal flukes, and one or two blowholes for breathing. The mouths of whales are toothed or contain baleen.

whale•bone (wāl′bōn′) *See* **baleen.**

whirl•pool (wûrl′po͞ol′) A rapidly rotating current of water or other liquid, such as one produced by the meeting of two tides.

white blood cell (wīt) Any of various white or colorless cells in the blood of vertebrate animals, many of which act to protect the body against infection and to repair tissues after injury. White blood cells have a nucleus, unlike red blood cells, and are formed mainly in the bone marrow. The major types of white blood cells are granulocytes, lymphocytes, and monocytes. Also called *leukocyte.*

white dwarf A whitish star that is very dense and very small, about the size of Earth. A white dwarf is what remains after the central star of a planetary nebula burns out and becomes cool and dim. *See more at* **star.** *See Note at* **dwarf star.**

white matter The whitish tissue of the brain and spinal cord in vertebrate animals, made up chiefly of nerve fibers covered in myelin sheaths. *Compare* **gray matter.**

Whit•tle (wĭt′l), Sir **Frank** 1907–1996. British aeronautical engineer and inventor who developed the first aircraft engine powered by jet propulsion (1937).

whole number (hōl) A positive integer or zero.

whoop•ing cough (ho͞o′pĭng, ho͝op′ĭng, wo͞o′pĭng, wo͝op′ĭng) A bacterial infection of the airways and lungs that causes spasms of coughing ending in loud gasps. It occurs mostly in children. Also called *pertussis.*

Wil•kins (wĭl′kĭnz), **Maurice Hugh Frederick** 1916–2004. British biophysicist who contributed to the discovery of the structure of DNA. He worked with Rosalind Franklin to produce x-ray studies of DNA that helped to establish its structure as a double helix.

Wil•son (wĭl′sən), **Charles Thomson Rees** 1869–1959. British physicist noted for his research on atmospheric electricity. He developed the Wilson cloud chamber, a device that makes it possible to study and photograph the movement and interaction of electrically charged particles. *See more at* **cloud chamber.**

Wilson, Edmund Beecher 1856–1939. American zoologist who was one of the founders of modern genetics. He researched the structure and organization of cells, emphasizing the importance of cells as the building blocks of life. Wilson demonstrated the function of the cell and the significance of chromosomes, especially sex chromosomes, in heredity.

Wims•hurst machine (wĭmz′hûrst′) A machine used to generate static electricity and consisting of mica or glass disks that rotate in opposite directions. The disks have metal carriers, often made of tinfoil, on which charges are produced by induction. Wimshurst machines are used to demonstrate how electric charge works.

wind (wĭnd) A current of air, especially a natural one that moves along or parallel to the ground.

wind-chill factor The temperature of motionless air that would make a person feel as cold as a particular combination of wind speed and air temperature. As the wind blows faster, heat is lost more quickly from exposed skin, making a person feel colder even though the air temperature remains the same.

wind•pipe (wĭnd′pīp′) *See* **trachea** (sense 1).

wind tunnel A chamber through which air can be forced at controlled speeds so its effect on an object, such as an aircraft, can be studied.

wing (wĭng) **1.** One of a pair of specialized parts used for flying, as in birds, bats, or insects. **2.** A thin projection on certain fruits that are dispersed by the wind, such as the fruits of ash, elm, and maple trees. **3.** A part extending from the side of an aircraft, such as an airplane, having a curved upper surface that causes the pressure of air rushing over it to decrease, thereby providing lift.

win•ter (wĭn′tər) The usually coldest season of the year, occurring between autumn and spring. In the Northern Hemisphere, it extends from the winter solstice to the vernal equinox.

winter solstice In the Northern Hemisphere, the solstice that occurs on December 21 or 22, marking the beginning of winter and the day of the year with the shortest period of sunlight. *Compare* **summer solstice.**

wis•dom tooth (wĭz′dəm) One of four molars, the last on each side of both jaws in humans, usually appearing in young adulthood.

wish•bone (wĭsh′bōn′) The forked bone in front of the breastbone in most birds, consisting of the two collarbones partly fused together. It serves as a spring, capturing some of the energy during the downward stroke of the wings for release on the upward stroke.

wolf•ram (wo͝ol′frəm) *See* **tungsten.**

Wol•las•ton (wo͝ol′ə-stən), **William Hyde** 1766–1828. British chemist and physicist who discovered the elements palladium (1803) and rhodium (1804).

womb (wo͞om) *See* **uterus.**

wood (wo͝od) The tough, fibrous substance lying beneath the bark of trees and shrubs, consisting of the vascular tissue known as xylem. The main components of wood are cellulose and lignin.

wood alcohol *See* **methanol.**

work (wûrk) The transfer of energy from one object to another, especially in order to make the second object move in a certain direction. Work is equal to the amount of force multiplied by the distance over which it is applied. If a force of 10 newtons, for example, is applied over a distance of 3 meters, the work is equal to 30 newtons per meter (or 30 joules). *Compare* **energy, power.**

work•er (wûr′kər) A member of a colony of social insects, such as ants or bees, that performs

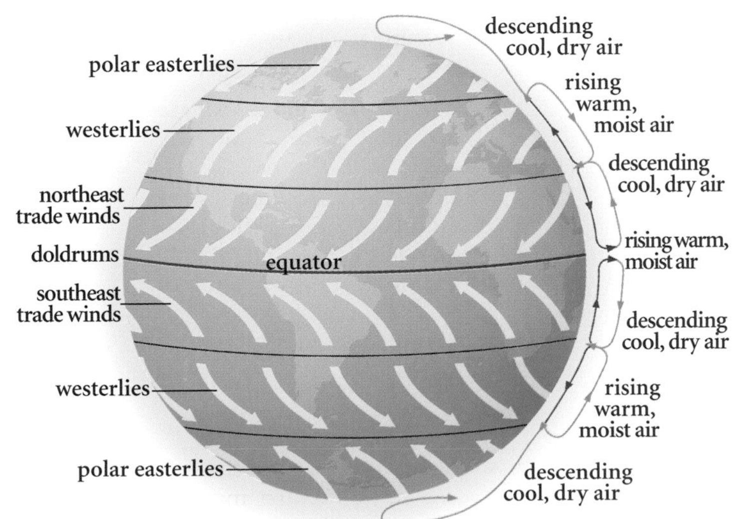

wind
Global wind patterns are determined by differences in atmospheric pressure resulting from the uneven heating of the Earth's surface by the sun. As warm, moist air rises along the equator, surface air moves in to take its place, creating the trade winds. Some of the air that descends at the two tropics moves away from the equator, creating the westerlies. The eastward and westward movement of these wind patterns is caused by the Earth's clockwise rotation.

Did You Know?

worms

Although there are many kinds of *worms,* both flat and round, we usually think of earthworms when someone mentions worms. Earthworms do not get a lot of respect these days, but Charles Darwin wrote an entire book explaining how important they are. "Long before [the plow] existed," he said, "the land was in fact regularly plowed and still continues to be thus plowed by earthworms. It may be doubted whether there are many other animals which have played so important a part in the history of the world." As they tunnel in the soil, earthworms open channels that allow in air and water. These channels improve drainage and make it easier for plants to send down roots. Earthworms eat and digest soil and the organic wastes it contains, and their own wastes provide nourishment for plants and other organisms. The tunneling of earthworms brings up nutrients from deep soils to the surface. It is estimated that each year, earthworms in one acre of land move 18 or more tons of soil. We enjoy the fruits of this labor in the form of rich soil and healthy vegetation.

specialized work such as building the nest. Workers are usually sterile females.

World Wide Web (wûrld) The complete set of electronic documents stored on computers that are connected over the Internet and are made available by the process known as HTTP (Hypertext Transfer Protocol). The World Wide Web makes up a large part of the Internet. *See more at* **Internet.**

worm (wûrm) **1.** Any of various invertebrate animals having a soft, long body that is round or flattened and usually lacks limbs. **2.** *Computer Science.* A destructive computer program that copies itself over and over until it fills all of the storage space on a computer's hard drive or on a network.

Wu (wo͞o), **Chien-Shiung** 1912–1997. Chinese-born American physicist. Her research on electron emission in the decay of radioactive elements led her to disprove a long-held law of physics, called the law of symmetry, which held that the laws of nature are always symmetrical.

XYZ

x-ax•is (ĕks′ăk′sĭs) **1.** The horizontal axis of a two-dimensional Cartesian coordinate system. **2.** One of the three axes of a three-dimensional Cartesian coordinate system.

X-chro•mo•some (ĕks′krō′mə-sōm′) The sex chromosome that in females is paired with another X-chromosome and in males is paired with a Y-chromosome.

Xe The symbol for **xenon.**

xe•non (zē′nŏn′) A colorless, odorless element that is a noble gas and occurs in extremely small amounts in the atmosphere. It was the first noble gas found to form compounds with other elements. Xenon is used to make lamps that make intense flashes, such as strobe lights and flashbulbs for photography. *Symbol* **Xe.** *Atomic number* 54. *See* **Periodic Table,** pages 262–263.

xer•o•morph (zîr′ə-môrf′) A plant adapted to saltwater marshes or highly alkaline soils.

xer•o•phyte (zîr′ə-fīt′) A plant that grows in an arid habitat; a desert plant. Cacti are xerophytes.

X-linked (ĕks′lĭngkt′) Relating to an inherited trait controlled by a gene on an X-chromosome.

x-ray *also* **X-ray** (ĕks′rā′) **1.** A high-energy stream of electromagnetic radiation having a wavelength shorter than that of ultraviolet light but longer than that of a gamma ray. X-rays are absorbed by many forms of matter, including body tissues, and are used in medicine and industry to produce images of internal structures. *See more at* **electromagnetic spectrum. 2.** An image of an internal structure, such as a body part, taken with x-rays. —*Verb* **x-ray.**

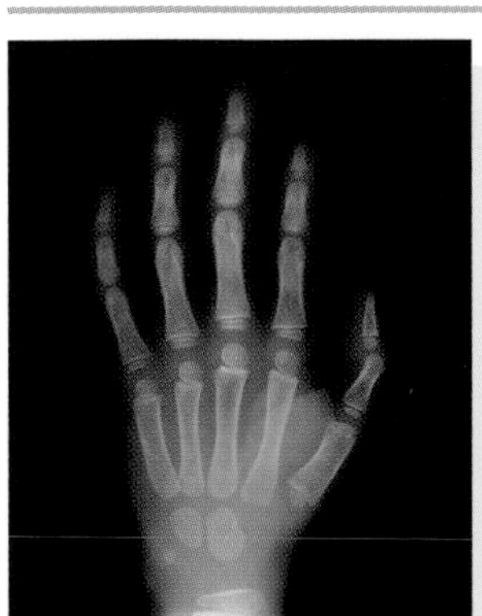

x-ray
x-ray of a human hand

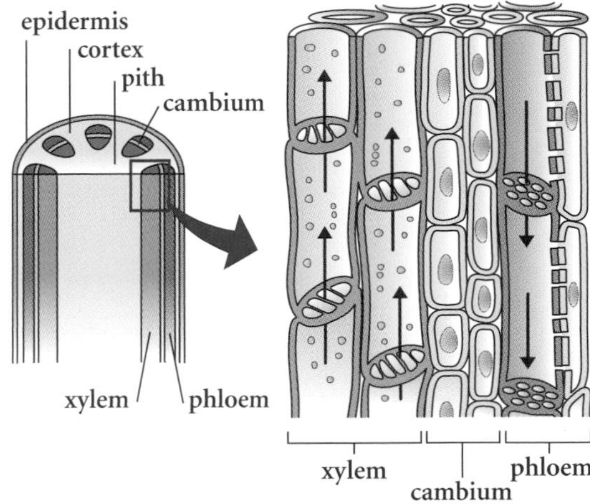

xylem
Xylem cells in the stem carry water from a plant's roots to its leaves. The phloem distributes food that is made in the plant's leaves to other parts of the plant. The cambium cells divide into either xylem or phloem cells. The cortex and pith, seen in the stem cross section, provide structural support.

x-ray astronomy The branch of astronomy dealing with the detection of objects in space by means of the x-rays they emit.

xy•lem (zī′ləm) A tissue in vascular plants that carries water and dissolved minerals up from the roots through the stem to the leaves and provides support for the softer tissues. Xylem consists of various elongated cells that function as tubes. In a tree trunk, the innermost part of the wood is dead but structurally strong xylem, while the outer part consists of living xylem, and beyond it, layers of cambium and phloem. *See more at* **cambium, photosynthesis.** *Compare* **phloem.**

Y The symbol for **yttrium.**

Yal•ow (yăl′ō), **Rosalyn Sussman** Born 1921. American physicist who developed the radioimmunoassay (RIA), an extremely sensitive technique for measuring very small quantities of

Rosalyn Yalow

substances such as hormones, enzymes, and drugs in the blood.

yard (yärd) A unit of length equal to 3 feet or 36 inches (0.91 meter). *See Table at* **measurement.**

y-ax•is (wī′ăk′sĭs) **1.** The vertical axis of a two-dimensional Cartesian coordinate system. **2.** One of the three axes of a three-dimensional Cartesian coordinate system.

Yb The symbol for **ytterbium.**

Y-chro•mo•some (wī′krō′mə-sōm′) The sex chromosome that is paired with an X-chromosome in males.

yd. Abbreviation of **yard.**

yeast (yēst) **1.** Any of various one-celled fungi that can cause the fermentation of carbohydrates, producing carbon dioxide and alcohol. **2.** A commercial preparation in either compressed or powdered form that contains yeast cells. It is used to make bread dough rise.

yel•low fever (yĕl′ō) A life-threatening disease caused by a virus and characterized by fever, jaundice, and internal bleeding. Yellow fever occurs mainly in tropical regions of Africa and Latin America and is transmitted by mosquitoes.

Yer•sin (yĕr-sä′), **Alexandre Émile John** 1863–1943. French bacteriologist. With Émile Roux, he isolated the toxin that causes the symptoms of diphtheria. Yersin later discovered the bacillus that causes bubonic plague and developed a serum to protect against it.

yew (yo͞o) Any of various evergreen trees or shrubs that have short, flat needles and solitary seeds contained in a red, berry-like covering instead of a cone. Yews are found chiefly in cooler temperate regions in the Northern Hemisphere.

-yl A suffix used to form the chemical names of organic compounds when they are radicals (parts of larger compounds), such as *ethyl* and *phenyl.*

yolk (yōk) The yellow internal part of the egg of a bird or reptile. The yolk is surrounded by the albumen and supplies food to the developing young.

yolk sac A sac attached to the gut of an embryo that encloses the yolk in bony fish, sharks, reptiles, mammals, and birds. In most mammals, the yolk sac functions as part of the embryo's circulatory system before the placenta develops.

yt•ter•bi•um (ĭ-tûr′bē-əm) A soft, silvery-white, easily shaped metallic element of the lanthanide series that occurs as seven stable isotopes. It is used as a radiation source for portable x-ray machines. *Symbol* **Yb.** *Atomic number* 70. *See* **Periodic Table,** pages 262–263.

yt•tri•um (ĭt′rē-əm) A silvery, easily shaped metallic element that is found in the same ores as elements of the lanthanide series. Yttrium is used to strengthen magnesium and aluminum alloys, to provide the red color in color televisions, and as a component of various optical and electronic devices. *Symbol* **Y.** *Atomic number* 39. *See* **Periodic Table,** pages 262–263.

z-ax•is (zē′ăk′sĭs) One of the three axes of a three-dimensional Cartesian coordinate system.

ze•bra mussel (zē′brə) A small freshwater mussel, usually having a striped shell, that is native to Europe and Asia but is now widely established in the Great Lakes and other North American waterways. Zebra mussels often clog water-supply pipes and reduce levels of plankton on which other water-dwelling life depend.

ze•nith (zē′nĭth) The point on the celestial sphere that is directly above the observer.

zebra mussel
a colony of zebra mussels

Did You Know?

zero

Zero is not nothing! It is a number that stands for nothing, and this is an important distinction. In many ways, zero is the most important of all numbers. When zero is added to or subtracted from a number, it leaves the number at its original value. Zero thus makes negative numbers possible. A negative number added to its positive counterpart always equals zero. Zero is also essential to representing many numbers, such as 203 and 1024. In these numbers zero serves as a placeholder in the system known as *positional notation*. Thus in 203, there are two hundreds, zero tens, and three ones. In other words, zero indicates that the value of the tens place is zero. In 1024, zero indicates that the value of the hundreds place is zero. When you think about it, if we didn't have zero, we wouldn't have hundreds, thousands, or millions in our number system.

ze•ro (zîr′ō) The numerical symbol 0, representing a number that when added to another number leaves the original number unchanged.

zero gravity The condition of real or apparent weightlessness occurring when the force of gravity acting on a body meets with no resistance, and the body is allowed to accelerate freely. Bodies in free fall toward the Earth, or in orbit around the Earth, are in a state of zero gravity; a body at rest on the Earth's surface is not, since it is subject to the counterforce of the surface supporting it.

zinc (zĭngk) A shiny, bluish-white metallic element that is brittle at room temperature but is easily shaped when heated. It is widely used in alloys such as brass and bronze, as a coating for iron and steel, and in various household objects. Zinc is essential to the growth of humans and animals. *Symbol* **Zn.** *Atomic number* 30. *See* **Periodic Table,** pages 262–263.

zinc•ate (zĭng′kāt′) A chemical compound containing zinc and oxygen in the group ZnO_2.

zinc oxide A white or yellowish powdery compound, ZnO, used in paints and in various medicines and skin cosmetics.

zir•con (zûr′kŏn′) A brown, reddish to bluish, gray, green, or colorless mineral that is a silicate of zirconium and occurs in igneous, metamorphic, and sedimentary rocks, and especially in sand. The colorless varieties are valued as gems.

zir•co•ni•um (zûr-kō′nē-əm) A shiny, grayish-white metallic element that occurs primarily in the mineral zircon. It is used to build nuclear reactors because it is not damaged from bombardment by neutrons and remains strong at high temperatures. Zirconium is also highly resistant to corrosion, making it a useful component of pumps, valves, and alloys. *Symbol* **Zr.** *Atomic number* 40. *See* **Periodic Table,** pages 262–263.

Zn The symbol for **zinc.**

zo•di•ac (zō′dē-ăk′) A band of the celestial sphere that extends about eight degrees both north and south of the ecliptic. It represents the path of the planets, the sun, and the moon.

zo•ol•o•gy (zō-ŏl′ə-jē, zo͞o-ŏl′ə-jē) The scientific study of animals, including their growth and structure.

zo•o•plank•ton (zō′ə-plăngk′tən) Plankton that consists of tiny animals, such as rotifers, copepods, and krill, and of microorganisms once classified as animals, such as dinoflagellates and other protozoans.

Zr The symbol for **zirconium.**

zy•gote (zī′gōt′) The cell formed by the union of the nuclei of two reproductive cells (called gametes), especially a fertilized egg cell.

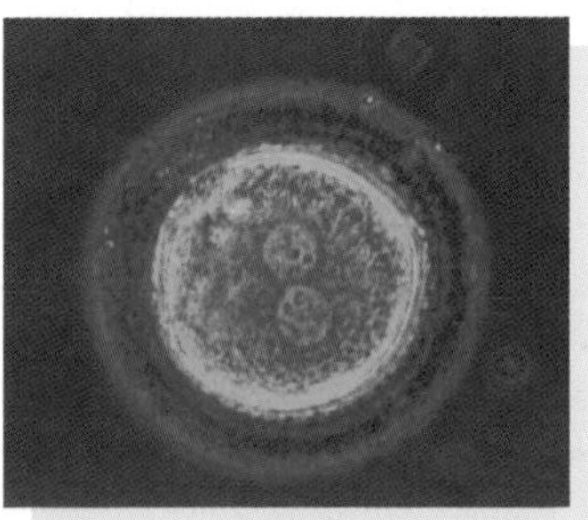

zygote
photograph through a microscope of a human zygote

PICTURE CREDITS

A-Z Text

Academy Artworks: **abscissa, acute angle, aerodynamic, aphelion, asymptote, atmosphere, atoll, complementary angles, conic projection, DNA, exterior angles, hypotenuse, interior angle, Klein bottle, nerve cell, perihelion, Pythagorean theorem, solenoid, sun, turbine, Van de Graaff generator**

AIP Emilio Segrè Visual Archives: **Perey, Townes**

Animals Animals: **landslide**/Jack Wilburn

Art Resource, NY: **Aristotle**/Scala

Carlyn Iverson: **adrenal gland, antibody, bone, brain, circulatory system, digestive tract, ear[1], eye, hair, heart, intestine, joint, kidney, meiosis, mitosis, nearsightedness, pancreas, respiratory system, RNA, spinal cord, taste bud, thyroid gland, translation, urinary tract**

Carnegie Institution of Washington: **Stevens**

© College Division, Houghton Mifflin Company: **conductivity**/Ken O'Donoghue, **effervescence**/Sean Brady, **polymorphism**/James Scherer **precipitate**/Richard Megna, **reaction**/Sean Brady

Corbis: **Agnesi**/Bettmann, **ammonite (right)**/Layne Kennedy, **badlands**/Pat O'Hara, **Blackwell**/Bettmann, **barnacle**/Ron Boardman/Frank Lane Picture Agency, **blowhole**/Brandon D. Cole, **camouflage**/Stephen Frink, **Carson**/Underwood & Underwood, **chrysalis**/Naturfoto Honal, **Copernicus**/Paul Almasy, **Curie**/Underwood & Underwood, **Darwin**/Bettmann, **drought**/Richard Hamilton Smith, **Einstein**/Bettmann, **Ehrlich**/Bettmann, **Fermi, galaxy (Whirlpool)**/Reuters NewMedia, Inc., **Galileo Galilei**/Bettmann, **geodesic dome**/Gunter Marx, **halite**/José Manuel Sanchis Calvete, **hive**/Michael Busselle, **lagoon**/Yann Arthus-Bertrand, **Leakey**/Bettmann, **Leonardo da Vinci**/Bettmann, **Lister**/Bettmann, **Marconi**/Bettmann, **McClintock**/Bettmann, **Mendel**/Bettmann, **molt**/Michael & Patricia Fogden, **mutualism**/Kennan Ward, **neon**/John Bartholomew, **oasis**/Sharna Balfour/Gallo Images, **octopus**/Stuart Westmorland, **oxbow**/Richard Hamilton Smith, **Pasteur**/Hulton-Deutsch Collection Limited, **pearl**/Jack Fields, **Planck**/Bettmann, **radial symmetry**/Raymond Gehman, **reservoir**/Craig Aurness, **rust**/Owen Franken, **sandbar**/Wolfgang Kaehler, **sessile (sponge)**/Lawson Wood, **sessile (palm)**/Lowell Georgia, **siphon**/Jeffrey L. Rotman, **trilobite**/Tom Bean, **tundra**/Wolfgang Kaehler, **Wegener**/Bettmann, **Yalow**/Bettmann

© Crown copyright: UK Government Art Collection: **Augusta Ada Byron**

Custom Medical Stock Photography: **CAT scan, Hippocrates**/SPL, **Roentgen, zygote**

David Mackay Ballard: **moon, pollution**

The Dian Fossey Gorilla Fund International, 800 Cherokee Avenue, SE, Atlanta, Georgia 30315, 1-800-851-0203, www.gorillafund.org: **Fossey**

Elizabeth Morales: **abdomen, artiodactyl, carbon cycle, coelacanth, constellation, elytron, enzyme, euglena, evaporation, Fahrenheit, fin, food chain, gill, inflorescence, metamorphosis, mitochondrion, nitrogen cycle, rhizome, tadpole, water cycle, xylem**

FPG International LLC/Getty Images: **coral reef (undersea)**/VCG, **desert**/Ron Thomas, **Franklin, prism**/Bald Headed Pictures

Fundamental Photographs: **acid rain**/Richard Megna, **corrosion**/Michael Dalton, **dispersion**/Richard Megna, **filtration**/Richard Megna, **gyroscope**/Richard Megna, **interference**/Robert Mathena, **meniscus**/Diane Hirsch, **stratification**/Kristen Brochmann, **Van de Graaff generator**/Richard Megna, **vortex**/Richard Megna

Grant Heilman Photography: **antenna (moth)**/Runk & Schoenberger, **ergot**/Runk & Schoenberger, **mimicry**/Runk & Schoenberger

Hulton Archive/Getty Images: **Bohr, Carver, Edison**/Museum of the City of New York/Byron Collection, **Mendeleev**/Hulton, **Mitchell**/Hulton, **Noether**/Pictorial Parade, **Pascal**/Kean Collection, **Pauling**/Nancy R. Schiff, **Salk**/APA, **Somerville**

Index Stock Imagery, Inc.: **peninsula**/Tina Buckman

Jerry Malone: **celestial sphere, equator, homolosine projection, International Date Line, longitude, Mercator projection, periscope, refraction, sinusoidal projection, tooth, tsunami**

Liaison Agency: **Hopper**/Carol Halebian

Library of Congress: **Bell, Morse**

Matthew Pippin: **piston**

MIT Museum: **Richards**

Courtesy of NASA/JPL/Caltech: **Mars**

National Geographic Society Image Collection: **bioluminescence**/George Grall, **Goodall**/Michael K. Nichols

Courtesy of The National Library of Medicine: **Linnaeus**

Courtesy of the National Portrait Gallery, London: **Banks**

© Naturalis, Leiden, The Netherlands: **Dubois**

Image provided by ORBIMAGE. © Orbital Imaging Corporation and processing by NASA Goddard Space Flight Center: **Gulf Stream**

Patrice Rossi Calkin: **hemlock, volcano**

Photo Researchers, Inc.: **Agassiz**/Tom McHugh, **alluvial fan**/Betty Derig, **Alvarez**/David Parker/SPL, **ammeter**/Charles D. Winters, **amoeba**/Biophoto Associates, **amphibian (frog)**/John Serrao, **amphibian (axolotl)**/Stephen Dalton, **anemometer**/Gary Retherford, **antenna (beetle)**/Gary Meszaros, **Archimedes**/SPL, **Babbage**/SPL, **bacterium (sphere)**/Hank Morgan/S.S., **bacterium (spiral)**/CNRI/SPL, **blood cell**/Andrew Syred/SPL, **burl**/Verna R. Johnston, **comet**/Jerry Schad, **commensalism**/François Gohier, **crater (moon)**/John Chumack, **crater (earth)**/Georg Gerster, **Crick**/A. Barrington Brown, **Dalton**/SPL, **diatom**/M. I. Walker, **epiphyte**/Kenneth Fink, **erosion**/William Bachman, **fold**/Martin Bond/SPL, **fossil**/Detlev Van Ravenswaay/SPL, **geothermal**/Simon Fraser/SPL, **Harvey**/SPL, **heliotropism**/John Kaprielian, **William and Caroline Herschel**/SPL, **iguana**/E. R. Degginger, **jellyfish**/Gilbert S. Grant, **Jenner**/SPL, **Joliot-Curie**/SPL, **Koch**/SPL, **Komodo dragon**/Tom McHugh, **Lavoisier**/Jean-Loup Charmet/SPL, **van Leeuwenhoek**/SPL, **lichen**/Michael P. Gadomski, **litmus**/Richard Hutchings, **lungfish**Tom McHugh, **magnetic field**/Grantpix, **mammoth**/François Gohier, **manatee**/Douglas Faulkner, **mesa**/Rod Planck, **nautilus**/Douglas Faulkner, **newt**/Gary Meszaros, **Newton**/Shiela Terry/SPL, **Oppenheimer**/LOC/Science Source, **ozone** /NOAA/SPL, **petri dish**/BSIP/Alexandre/Science Source, **plankton**/D. P. Wilson, **platypus**/Tom McHugh, **pollen**/Oliver Meckes, Eye of Science, **Priestley**/SPL, **pterodactyl** /Sinclair Stammers/SPL, **Ptolemy**/Wards Sci/Science Source, **pyrite**/Charles D. Winters, **quartz**/E. R. Degginger, **Ramsay**/SPL, **Sabin**/Will & Deni McIntyre, **sea anemone**/ Gregory Ochocki, **sea horse**/E. R. Degginger, **seismograph**/Tom McHugh, **sex chromosome**/ Biophoto Associates/Science Source, **shale**/James Steinberg, **sierra**/Dennis Flaherty Photography, **smog**/David Frazier, **stalactite/stalagmite** Millard H. Sharp, **stegosaurus**/François Gohier, **strip mine**/Georg Gerster, **supernova**/Royal Observatory, Edinburgh /SPL, **Tesla**/SPL, **thermal vent**/Ken MacDonald /SPL, **tide**/Andrew Martinez, **tributary**/Jeff Lepore, **Turing**/SPL, **Urey**/SPL, **Vesalius**/SPL, **Volta**/SPL, **zebra mussel**/Scott Camazine

© 2002 PhotoDisc, Inc./Getty Images: **ammonite (left), burette, dune, galaxy (Sombrero), Jupiter, mirage, nebula, Saturn, x-ray**

Phototake: **bacterium (rod)**/Dennis Kunkel, **colony**/CNRI, **compound eye**/Dennis Kunkel/CNRI, **corona**/Lee C. Coombs, **hydra**/Dennis Kunkel, **Milky Way**/Lee C. Coombs, **paramecium**/Eric Grave, **red blood cell**/ Dennis Kunkel, **spirochete**/Microworks Associates, **sponge**/David Mechlin, **stoma**/Dennis Kunkel, **Venus flytrap**/Ken Wagner

Precision Graphics: **aneroid barometer, anticline, atherosclerosis, bell curve, cathode-ray tube, centripetal force, circuit, cloud, cone (eye), convection, cyclotron, desalinization, diode, eclipse, electromagnetic spectrum, fluorescent lamp, fulcrum, fuse, incandescent lamp, induction, internal-combustion engine, laser, manometer, Möbius strip, nuclear reactor, oscillation, parallax, radiation, solar cell, sonar, telescope, turbojet, wind**

Robin Storesund: **aliphatic, aromatic, artesian well, benzene ring, bond, circle, cone (geometric), continental shelf, covalent bond, crystal, cylinder, earthquake, ellipse, equilateral, equinox, fault, hexagon, hyperbola, isosceles, octagon, osmosis, parabola, parallelogram, pentagon, Ptolemaic system, rectangle, rhombus, saturated, scalene, sphere, time zone, transformer, trapezoid, triangle, unsaturated, Venn diagram**

Rolin Graphics, Inc.: **germination**

The Schomburg Center for Research in Black Culture, The New York Public Library: **Banneker**

© School Division, Houghton Mifflin Company: **abacus, amber, geode**

Stone/Getty Images: **aurora borealis**/Tom Walker, **chalk**/Patrick Ingrand, **fractal**/Stephen Johnson, **glacier**/John Edwards, **parasite**/Tim Flach, **timberline**/George Hunter

The Image Bank/Getty Images: **coral reef (aerial)**/John William Banagan **iceberg**/Grant V. Faint

Thom Gillis: **axis, Earth, North Pole, South Pole**

UG/GGS Information Services: **acoustics, battery, biome, capacitor, Doppler effect, front, gear, graph, holography, hurricane, hydroelectric, inheritance, microwave, rain forest, satellite**

Courtesy of the U.S. Geological Survey: **fumarole, Hutton**

U.S. Geological Survey map: **gradient**

Wendy Smith: **fir**

A Closer Look features, Charts, and Tables

Corbis: **Leaf** (broad leaf/Frank Lane Picture Agency, needle/Frank Lane Picture Agency, spine/Eric & David Hosking), **Rock Types** (igneous rock/Elio Ciol, sedimentary rock/Galen Rowell, metamorphic rock/David Muench)

Cathy Hawkes: **Periodic Table of the Elements**

Carlyn Iverson: **Skeleton** (both)

Elizabeth Morales: **Flower** (all), **Leaf** (sorghum, sweetgum)

Courtesy NASA/JPL/Caltech: **Solar System** (Venus, Uranus)

Courtesy NASA/JSC: **Solar System** (Sun)

© 2002 PhotoDisc, Inc./Getty Images: **Leaf** (grass), **Rock Types** (igneous slice, sedimentary slice), **Solar System** (Saturn, Earth, Jupiter, Mars, Mercury, Neptune, Pluto)

Phototake: **Cell** (nerve cell, red blood cell, guard cell/Dennis Kunkel)

Precision Graphics: **Atom** (all), **Cell** (animal, plant), **Color** (all), **Fission** (both), **Geologic Time**, **Greenhouse Effect** (both), **Photosynthesis** (both), **Star, Taxonomy, Tectonic Boundaries**

Robin Storesund: **Organic Compounds** (all), **Wave** (all)

Univ. of North Carolina at Chapel Hill, Geology Department: **Rock Types** (metamorphic slice)

1 2 3 4 5 6 7 8 9 10 - QWT - 15 14 13 12 11 10 09